LA STORIA

LA STORIA

*Five
Centuries
of the
Italian American
Experience*

JERRE MANGIONE
& BEN MORREALE

HarperPerennial
A Division of HarperCollinsPublishers
Aaron Asher Books

HarperCollins books may be purchased for educational, business, or sales promotional use. For information please write: Special Markets Department, Harper-Collins Publishers, Inc., 10 East 53rd Street, New York, NY 10022.

First HarperPerennial edition published 1993.

Designed by Alma Orenstein

The Library of Congress has catalogued the hardcover edition as follows:

Mangione, Jerre Gerlando
  La storia : five centuries of the Italian American experience / Jerre Mangione and Ben Morreale.—1st ed.
    p. cm.
  Includes bibliographical references and index.
  ISBN 0-06-016778-5 (cloth)
  1. Italian Americans—History. I. Morreale, Ben. II. Title.
E184.I8M275 1992
973'.0451—dc20   92-52553

ISBN 0-06-092441-1 (pbk.)
    01 00   CC/RRD 10

To the memory of my immigrant parents, Gaspare and Giuseppina Mangione

For my father and mother, Marco and Teresa Morreale, who took part in the experience

Contents

Photographs follow pages 108 and 236.

Acknowledgments

S o ambitious a project as *La Storia,* which has been in the making
for more than a decade, could not have been initiated without the
sponsorship of the University of Pennsylvania during the tenure of
Provost Vartan Gregorian and the award of two consecutive grants
by the National Endowment for the Humanities. The grants enabled
the University to provide us with a team of research assistants and
the full-time services of Elaine Pascu, the chief researcher, to whom
we are grateful for her diligence and skills. Another N.E.H. grant
permitted us to take part in an Ethnic Studies seminar at the University of California at Santa Barbara directed by the noted anthropologist Paul Bohannan. Throughout the decade our research efforts
were greatly facilitated by the University's Van Pelt Library, especially in the person of its liaison officer, Hilda H. Pring.

We also wish to acknowledge our gratitude to the eminent scholars who from the inception of our project enthusiastically endorsed
its prospectus. Among the first to do so were Herbert J. Gans,
Rudolph J. Vecoli, Arthur Schlesinger, Jr., Virginia Yans McLaugh-
lin, Thomas C. Cochran, and Peter Sammartino. We are also indebted to four other scholars who are no longer living: Leonard
Covello, the educator, who was a pioneer in his investigations of the

Italian American experience; A. William Salomone, the noted historian of modern Italy; Edward P. Hutchinson, an internationally renowned authority on the subject of American immigration; and Leonard W. Moss, the anthropologist best known for his studies of southern Italy.

Among the many institutions that contributed to our search for material are several that specialize in documenting the history and culture of all the nation's ethnic groups, namely the Immigration History Center of the University of Minnesota, headed by Professor Vecoli; the Balch Institute for Ethnic Studies in Philadelphia and its librarian Joseph Anderson and his assistant, Pat Lusk; The Center for Migration Studies in New York, whose director is the priest-scholar Lydio F. Tomasi; and its counterpart in Rome, long operated with an international perspective by another priest-scholar, Gianfausto Roselli. We are also indebted to Richard Gambino, founder and director of the nation's first Italian American Studies Center at Queens College; Joseph V. Scelsa, who directs the John D. Calandra Italian-American Institute in New York City; Anne Paolucci of St. John's University, who as founder and head of the Columbus Countdown 1992 group has been promoting Italian American cultural events; Michael R. Cioffi and Angela Marrantino, chief officers of the American Italian Cultural Roundtable; Rosemarie Gallina, New York Governor Mario Cuomo's Assistant for Ethnic Relations; Alfred M. Rotondaro, Executive Director of the National Italian American Foundation in Washington, D.C.; and Joseph Maselli, one of the founders of the Italian Studies Center of the South, located in New Orleans's Piazza d'Italia.

We also benefited from research materials made available to us at the Library of Congress; the New York Public Library; the Weidman Library at Harvard; the Free Library of Philadelphia, especially its Print and Photo Department; the Rochester Museum and Science Center; the department of Urban Archives at Temple University; and the Collections of the Italians in Chicago Project assembled at the University of Illinois. Funded by the National Endowment for the Humanities in the late seventies, this project netted more than five thousand items, including some one hundred oral histories that span the lives of three generations of Chicago's Italian Americans. Our thanks to Dominic Candeloro, the director of the Chicago Project, for providing us easy access to its collections. We also received research assistance from members of his staff, among them Rose

Ann Rabiola, Christina Wells, and Mary Ellen Mancina-Batinich. Also deserving of our thanks is Anthony Sorrentino, another Chicagoan, for supplying us with research information we requested from time to time.

From the outset we were fortunate to have on hand a mine of scholarly information already developed by the researching members of the American Italian Historical Association, which since its founding in 1968 has been producing annually a series of volumes containing selections from the proceedings of the Association's annual conferences. Like the conferences, each volume addresses itself to some broad aspect of the Italian American experience. Its twentieth volume, dated 1990, is titled *Italian Americans in Transition*. We are beholden to the series for the scholarly information and fresh insights its contributors often provide. Among those to whom we owe special thanks, we salute: Carol Bonomo Ahearn, Emelise Aleandri, Valentino Belfiglio, Lucia Ciavoli Birnbaum, John M. Cammett, Philip Cannistraro, Rocco Caporale, Betty Boyd Caroli, Frank J. Cavaioli, Frank J. Coppa, Francesco Cordasco, the late Ernest Falbo, Fred L. Gardaphe, the late Robert Harney, Luciano J. Iorizzo, Richard N. Juliani, Jerome Krase, Salvatore J. La Gumina, Michael La Sorte, Joseph Lopreato, Salvatore Mondello, Gary Mormino, Humbert Nelli, Remigio U. Pane, Joe Papaleo, Jean Scarpaci, Joseph V. Scelsa, Joseph Tusiani, Regina Soria, Richard A. Varbero, Joseph Velikonja, Peter J. Venturelli, and Robert Viscusi.

Throughout the decade, from unexpected quarters quite removed from the academic world, we received, partly in response to brief announcements of our project in the press, an encouragingly large amount of material on the subject of Italian Americans. Much of it consisted of letters from immigrants and their offspring asking how they might be of assistance; there were also unpublished poems, memoirs, diaries, family histories, short stories, even a novel. There were also published histories of Italian Americans residing in widely scattered communities, publications that appear in no reference volume, as well as taped monologues and taped interviews conducted by volunteer interviewers who, like Irvin Rosenthal of Ellenville, New York, provided us with several interviews he had with his Italian American neighbors that were based on questions he had elicited from us. There were also all those extraordinary survivors we interviewed, from New York to Louisiana to various cities in California.

In more recent years we have enlisted and obtained the assistance of many acquaintances who, in one way or another, have added to our fund of information and understanding or helped us in the task of finding illustrative material for our book. Some who quickly come to mind are Annette Rizzo, Bernard Weisberger, Ramon Posel, Peter Rose, Werner Sollors, Carla Bianco, Laura Graham, Peter Dzwonkoski, George Grella, Rocco D'Erasmo, Charles Lee, Carlin Romano, Giuseppe Butta, Diana Cavallo, Anna Marie and Nino de Prophetis, John and Mary Costanza, Giancarlo Riccio, John Buffo, Robert Meltzi, Luigi Sera, Ilia Salomone-Smith, Victoria Donohoe, Rosabianca Tuzzo Lo Verso, and Joanna De Ritis.

We also thank Carol Ratelle Leach for her patient help in the final editing of *La Storia*.

Finally, we wish to express our gratitude to our wives, Patricia and Linda, whose faith in our project was strong enough to keep our lives on an even keel despite the inconveniences caused by so lengthy an undertaking. We also credit them with an uncommon supply of common sense, and with the knack to dispatch any demons that may have attempted to disrupt what has been for us from beginning to end the most felicitous of collaborations.

Prologue

Between 1880 and 1924, when there was a virtual hemorrhaging of people from Italy to America, small boys sang in the village streets of Italy:

> *Dami centu lire*
> *e mi ni vaiu a lamerica*
> *Maladitu lamerica*
> *e chi la spriminta.*

> Give me a hundred lire
> And I'm off to America
> Goddamn America
> And the man who thought it up.

That chant tells much of the story of Italians in America.

The story begins with the early Italian adventurers who, like Columbus, took part in the European expansion across the Atlantic, in the pay of other nations, since at the time there was no Italian nation. Their explorations helped open up the West for the Spaniards, and helped the French and the English lay claim to North

America. Italians fought in the American Revolution, and later as daredevils in the Civil War. In the nineteenth century they came as men of learning, as connoisseurs of art and founders of conservatories, as musicians, painters, and sculptors. They came from the land the French called *la mère des arts,* and some of them did their best work in America's new cities. Most of their names are now forgotten, although many of the monuments they built remain, from Columbus Circle in New York to the Capitol Rotunda in Washington. They came, also, as organ grinders, clowns, and ragpickers.

The heart of the story is the mass migration that took place between 1880 and 1924, when a whole culture left its ancient roots to settle in the cities and towns of America. There it was transformed and woven into the fabric of American life.

Demographers tell us that the great migration began internally. From villages perched on the mountaintops of Italy, people moved down to the plains, then to the cities by the sea where they first heard of the New World. It was those living by the sea who began the exodus of the late nineteenth and early twentieth centuries, not long after Italy became a nation. They were soon followed by that great mass of emigrants who lived in the impoverished towns of the interior.

The mayor of one such town was asked, as late as 1976, "Where can one find documents to help us understand why people left in such droves?" He shook his head, bunched his fingers together as if to present them to his audience, and said, "What documents? Documents. They left because they were *morti di fame*—dying of hunger."

Of course, he was right. Yet peasants had been hungry and despairing for centuries and there had not been an exodus until the late nineteenth century. Then came the great exodus, precipitated by an economic crisis in agriculture and mining.

There are many ironies in Italian history, but none greater perhaps than the phenomenon of Italians leaving Italy so soon after it became a united nation in 1871.

The *Risorgimento* (Uprising) originated in the North, and from the beginning it highlighted the differences between the North and the Bourbon-ruled South, the *Mezzogiorno.* Only through an awareness of these differences can there be an intelligent understanding of why the mass exodus of Italians began in the decade after Italy achieved unification, and why 80 percent of those who migrated were from the *Mezzogiorno.* The leaders of the *Risorgimento*—Cavour, Garibaldi, Mazzini—had different objectives in unifying Italy. When Cavour, the great manipulator, had the final word, the South was relegated to near-colonial status, worsening existing animosities.

The North's ignorance of the South, new tax structures that benefited the North, draft laws that took away young workers to armies that had little meaning to the southern peasant, all contributed to the massive exodus from the *Mezzogiorno*.

In effect, the South was brought into the Italian nation dragging its feet as the new government issued edict after edict that affected the southerners adversely. There was growing dissatisfaction throughout the *Mezzogiorno* with the new government's apparent indifference to their condition, prompting one politician to observe that Italy was a nation in name only.

The condition of the southern peasant was perhaps best documented by Booker T. Washington, who remarked after visiting Italy:

> The Negro is not the man farthest down. The condition of the coloured farmer in the most backward parts of the Southern States in America, even where he has the least education and the least encouragement, is incomparably better than the condition and opportunities of the agricultural population in Sicily.

A story fabricated by northerners is still told of guffawing northern soldiers who handed out soap to the southern population, only to see the recipients eat it.

In 1892–94, ambitious young southern Italians, less resigned than their fathers, rebelled in one of the first Socialist movements in Europe—the *Fasci Siciliani*. When they were put down by northern troops with the usual ferocity, they could not return to the old life of misery. Fortunately, there was somewhere to go. Nonetheless it was no easy matter to leave a place, a home, a culture as old as memory itself, deeply rooted in language, legends, and proverbs by which one regulated one's life. Those early emigrants had no concept of being Italians. They saw themselves first as Christians, then as men or women from a particular village or town. A man from Bari was a *Baresi*, from Palermo a *Palermitano*, from Naples a *Napolitano*. In America, confronted with other immigrants, he found his identity as an Italian. Certainly, if any American were to ask him what he was, there would be no point in saying that he was a *Baresi* or a

Napolitano; it was easier to say he was Italian, as the immigration officials did.

New York City was the principal port of entry for the Italians, lower Manhattan their beachhead. From Manhattan's Five Points area, notorious for its organized crime long before the arrival of Italians, the immigrants moved up the island to Harlem, then to Brooklyn, Staten Island, and Queens. Those who found jobs building the railroads settled in upstate New York or moved westward. New Orleans, though less important as a port than New York, provided a gateway to Texas and the Mississippi Valley. One Giovanni Martini even fought with Custer at the Battle of Little Bighorn and survived only because he belatedly was sent for reinforcements with the written message (probably because they mistrusted his English): "Come on. Big Village. Quick. Bring packs." Giovanni Martini lived out his life as John Martin in Brooklyn, where he died in 1922.

By 1910, Italians could be found in almost every nook and cranny of America—working in the textile mills of New England, sharecropping in Bryan, Texas, onion farming in Canastota, New York, mining and union organizing in Colorado, cow-poking in West Texas, and lumberjacking in Seattle, Washington.

Many, through marriage, blended in with the other immigrant peoples of Europe to become Irish Italian, Jewish Italian, Polish Italian, German Italian. Nonetheless, as Fernand Braudel, the French historian of the Mediterranean, said, "A civilization cannot simply transplant itself bag and baggage . . . there are cultural frontiers and cultural zones of amazing permanence: all the cross-fertilization in the world will not alter them." A memory of Italy remained in the voices of Frank Sinatra and Perry Como, in the accents of Phil Rizzuto and Robert De Niro, and in the athleticism of Joe DiMaggio on the playing fields of America.

The Italian family played a complex role in the lives of the immigrants. On the one hand, it gave a sense of security in a generally hostile land. But Italian traditions often kept the second generation set in the working-class ways of their parents, who had grown up with the proverb, "The little satisfies me, abundance overwhelms me." Yet the contributions of the children of Italian immigrants who came to America in the early part of the twentieth century have been varied and indelible. In music their influence has been pronounced, from the New Orleans spasm bands in the early period of jazz to Russ Columbo as the first modern crooner. Certainly Sinatra's style is a mixture of Columbo's lyricism and the Italian street singers. In Frankie Lane there are echoes of peasant coarseness. In film, of course, Frank Capra introduced a style of moviemaking so American it became known as "Capracorn."

In sports, Joe DiMaggio reflected the ideal of the dignity held by many of those immigrant mothers who wanted their sons above all to be *civili*, civilized. There is Italian peasant humor in Yogi Berra, who in his many comings and goings insisted that "It's déjà vu all over again," and waited patiently because "It ain't over till it's over." Vince Lombardi showed much of the peasant obstinacy so necessary in the game of football, where "Winning isn't everything; it's the only thing."

Certainly politics would have taken a different turn had it not been for John J. Sirica, Peter Rodino, John Volpe, Mario Cuomo, Fiorello LaGuardia, Vincent Impelliteri, Joseph Alioto, John Pastore, Ella Grasso, Geraldine Ferraro, Antonin Scalia, Jim Florio, and the hundreds of other Italian Americans who served in Congress and in state and city governments around the country. Italian politicians have been found on all points of the political spectrum, from the radicals Sacco and Vanzetti and Vito Marcantonio to the conservative John Marchi. In business, such men as Lee Iacocca and A. P. Giannini, founder of the Bank of America, have made their presence known.

Although Italian American critics and novelists have had difficulty finding an audience, many have contributed to the literature of immigration and assimilation. A number of the most successful, however, have been those who said little about the Italian American experience, such as Bernard De Voto, Frances Winwar (Francesca Vinciguerra), Hamilton Basso, and Don DeLillo, or those who gave American readers bestsellers, such as Mario Puzo's *The Godfather*.

The story of Italians and their American offspring must of course include the relatively few (nearly all of them American-born) whose criminality encouraged Hollywood, ambitious politicians, and the national media to exploit the dramatic nuances of the term "mafia," engendering a stereotype that slanders the great majority of Italian Americans. This, too, is a feature of Americanization.

It is the contributions of the great majority that are most difficult to record—those millions of anonymous immigrants who took part in building railroads, tunnels, and skyscrapers, who worked in factories and farms helping to clothe and feed the country, and who are old men and women today. Some live lonely lives in the worn streets of their old enclaves; others prospered and moved to the suburbs, or followed their memory of sunny Italy to Florida or California. As these men and women disappear, much of the life during the great migration disappears with them. We record their saga, as well as that of their American children, here, not only to show what it meant to be alive during the period of migration from Italy to America, but also to document the inner migration from *Abruzzese, Genovesi, Napolitane, Toscane,* or *Siciliane* to Italian, Italian American, and finally American.

The Song of the Emigrants*

Wolves have warmed themselves on our fleece and eaten our
   flesh.
We are the generation of sheep
Wolves have sheared us to the bone while we protested only to
   God.
In time of peace we sickened in hospitals or jails
In time of war we were cannon fodder
We harvested bales of grass, one blade for us, the rest for the
   wolves.
One day a rumor spread—there was a vast and distant land
   where we could live *meno male*.
Some sheep went and returned, transformed, no longer sheep
   but wolves and they associated with our wolves.
"We want to go to that vast and distant country," we sheep said.
   "We want to go."

"There is an ocean to cross," the wolves said.
"We will cross it."

*"The Song of the Emigrants" *(Il Canto Degli Emigranti)* was first published in New York
by Ferdinando Fontana in 1881. Fontana claimed to have found the *Canto* in a German
newspaper in 1880, and ascribed it to an anonymous author.

"And if you are shipwrecked and drowned?"

"It's better to die quickly than suffer a lifetime."

"There are diseases . . ."

"No disease can be more horrible than hunger from father
to son."

And the wolves said, "Sheep, there will be deceivers . . ."

"You've been deceiving us for centuries."

"Would you abandon the land of your fathers, your brothers?"

"You who fleece us are not our brothers. The land of our fathers
is a slaughterhouse."

In tatters, in great herds we in pain beyond belief journeyed to
the vast and distant land.

Some of us did drown.

Some of us did die of privation.

But for every ten that perished a thousand survived and endured.

Better to choke in the ocean than be strangled by misery.

Better to deceive ourselves than be deceived by the wolves.

Better to die in our way than to be lower than the beasts.

PART ONE

Italians Among the Colonizers

CHAPTER 1

The Colonial Period

Jesus cum Maria sit nobis in via.

—Columbus

THE ADVENTURERS

Nearly five centuries before modern Italy became a nation and Italians began migrating to the Americas in large numbers, Italians were adventuring under the sponsorship of French, English, Portuguese, and Spanish governments as explorers, warriors, sailors, soldiers, and missionaries. Starting with Christopher Columbus, who combined the characteristics of adventurer and missionary (he began many of his pronouncements with *Jesus cum Maria sit nobis in via*), the earliest members of the Italian vanguard were the explorers whose findings would reveal a new world.

Columbus was a religious man who defended the native population whenever he could against the cruelties of the times. In his diary, so Samuel Eliot Morison tells us, Columbus was struck by the beauty and gentleness of the people he found on his first trip—a people so kind and trusting that he had to protect them from the abuses of the sailors. He also found one tribe of natives who bred and raised their captured enemies for food. They particularly liked young children.

Besides Columbus, who after his first voyage became "Admiral of the Ocean Sea" by royal decree, the most prominent Italian explorers were Giovanni Caboto (John Cabot), Amerigo Vespucci, and Giovanni da Verrazzano. Collectively, their names and deeds generated enough excitement for four centuries to become a major subliminal force in precipitating the mass migration to the Americas in the final decades of the nineteenth century.

Ironically, none of them lived long enough to appreciate the true significance of their achievements: The first two, Columbus and Cabot, went to their graves still convinced that the lands they had reached were part of Asia.

Both men were born in the port town of Genoa; both became obsessed with the dream that the shortest route to the Orient could be attained by traveling westward. Fired by the triumph of Columbus's first voyage, Cabot, who was then living in England with his family, persuaded King Henry VII to grant him a patent for a modest expedition consisting of eighteen men and a small ship, the *Mathew*. Five years after Columbus had reached the New World, the thirty-six-year-old Italian with the Anglicized name set sail from the port of Bristol, confident that by following a westward course north of the lands discovered by Columbus, he would reach Cipango (Japan). Instead, the voyage brought the expedition to the northern areas of North America.

In London the report of the expedition evoked such enthusiasm that Cabot had no difficulty convincing the English monarch that, once provided with enough ships and men, he might well succeed in finding the route to Cipango. The second expedition left England in 1498, a year after Cabot's first voyage, and was never heard from again. Although there were no traces of either the ships or the men, there were many rumors. One of them alleged that the ships had been wrecked in a violent storm. The most bizarre was promoted by those who, believing the earth to be flat, were certain that on arriving at its rim, the expedition had tumbled into the abyss reserved for humans who dared defy the limits of God's creation. Cabot's career as a trans-Atlantic explorer was of short duration; yet his name would become indelibly fixed in the annals of New World history, if only because his first voyage foreshadowed the presence of the British Empire in North America.

Amerigo Vespucci belonged to a celebrated Florentine family that had come to Spain to represent the banking interests of the

House of Medici. He became part of the large Italian immigrant colony there. Unlike Columbus and Cabot, who were primarily seafaring men of action with little inclination, presumably, to do any more writing than necessary, Vespucci took advantage of his facility with the written word to record his experiences in detail. A self-promoter by instinct, he published (in Italian and Latin) two pamphlets about his experiences, *Mundus Novus* and *Quator Navitationes* (both in 1507), which were widely circulated throughout Europe. Their immediate effect was to make Vespucci better known than Columbus. Stimulating circulation was their sensational pronouncement that Vespucci had found a new continent—one which, according to the explorer, contained more people and animals than any other. To underline the significance of this claim, Vespucci added: "Our ancient forebears were of the opinion that there were no continents to the south of the equator, only the sea they called the Atlantic. . . . My voyage had made it plain that opinion is erroneous and entirely contrary to the truth."

Ironically, Vespucci, who had been so intent on fame, died with no inkling that the continent he had explored would soon bear his given name, and moreover that for several centuries his reputation as an explorer would shine more brightly than that of Columbus.

For the next three centuries the importance of Columbus went unnoticed except among a few sages, mainly because of lack of information. Although there were historians who had known Columbus personally and were aware of his achievement, their writings about him, like the first biography of Columbus by his son Fernando, were not read until long after their deaths. As for Columbus's own writings—his letters, travel diaries, and ship logs—they too went unread, mainly because for a long time after his death no one even knew that these documents existed. Not until the early decades of the nineteenth century was there a concerted effort to spotlight Columbus's rightful place in world history. Even then, his life story remained shrouded in mystery and his reputation limited to that of an adventurer. During the nineteenth century many people were still under the impression that Columbus had tried to rob Vespucci of his glory.

One of the angry voices was that of Ralph Waldo Emerson, who declared Amerigo Vespucci an unconscionable rogue, who had "managed in this lying world to supplant Columbus and baptize half the earth with his dishonest name." Another American writer, Washington Irving, contributed to the rehabilitation of Columbus's name and fame by publishing two books about him, one of them a biography (1828) based largely on the writings of the Spanish historian Navarette. Written while Irving served as a diplomatic attaché in France, its popular style attracted a large international audience. Mainly, however, it was the Catholic Church that was largely responsible for rescuing "God's Messenger"—Columbus's own image of himself—from more than three hundred years of oblivion. Anxious to counteract the black deeds of the Spanish Conquistadors and other Catholics engaged in acts of conquest and plunder in the New World, church members proposed the canonization of "God's Messenger." For those who favored the idea, Columbus was viewed as a martyr who, like Christ's apostles, had given his life to spread the Gospel.

His most powerful champion was Pope Pius IX, who, as a young papal delegate journeying throughout North and South America in 1845, had been appalled to find "not a single stone, from Labrador to Patagonia with Columbus's name on it." In 1866, the Pontiff instigated beatification proceedings in behalf of his hero, the first step in the canonization process. Turbulent political events in Italy intervened, and the procedure was not resumed until 1891, when Leo XIII occupied the papal throne. By then Columbus's fame had been authenticated through the numerous documents and letters scholars had unearthed and the publication of scores of books about him, though not all of them were favorably disposed. Some writers revealed information that belied the image of Columbus as a holy man.

The principal objections were threefold: For a number of years he had lived in an unmarried state with a woman who bore him a son; money which should have gone to the sailor who first sighted land on the initial voyage had been spent instead on Columbus's concubine; and on his return voyages from the New World he had brought back hundreds of enslaved Indians who were offered for sale, thereby "setting in motion the corrupt process of slavery."

The movement to beatification was dropped.

A Florentine residing in France, Giovanni da Verrazzano was engaged by Francis I, king of France, to find the water route to China. Following the imperialistic example set by other European nations, Francis I instructed Verrazzano to take possession, in the name of

France, of whatever lands the explorer discovered on his journey to the Orient.

While searching for the elusive water route, Verrazzano, on his first voyage, traversed the Atlantic coast of the United States from North Carolina to Maine. In the course of his journey he became the first European to enter New York Bay, where four centuries later a bridge spanning Brooklyn and Staten Island (two New York areas heavily populated by Italian Americans) would be named after him. His final voyage, in 1528, cost him his life. Visiting an island in the West Indies where he had expected to find the same kind of Indian hospitality he had experienced in New York and Rhode Island, he was beset by hostile Indians. After killing him, they butchered the corpse, roasted pieces of it over a beach fire, and ate them while his brother Girolomo and the rest of his crew watched helplessly from the deck of Verrazzano's flagship.

Except to motivate other Italians to engage in New World explorations, the achievements of the four great navigators were of no direct benefit to an Italy fragmented by Spanish rule, which exploited the resources of the South for its own imperial purposes, and by the bitter rivalries between city-states in the regions north of Rome. The immediate beneficiaries were the nations that had financed the trans-Atlantic expeditions—Spain, England, France, and Portugal. Their willingness to gamble on the success of the navigators paid off handsomely, with territorial acquisitions in one or both of the Americas bearing such grandiose names as the "New Spain," the "New France," the "New England."

The Italians north of Rome, as the only Italians who were permitted to travel to other countries, did their best to take advantage of the situation by initiating a migratory movement into neighboring European nations, where empire building and prosperity were expanding the job market.*

Italian émigrés represented a broad cross-section of sixteenth-century Italian society. Italy became the mother of the arts for France, where Italian architects built châteaux along the Loire. Others traveled as far as Russia to build churches in St. Petersburg and Moscow, where they also built the walls for the Kremlin. Experts in

*Those in the South under the tyrannical rule of the Bourbons were not permitted to travel.

cartography, mathematics, ship designing, and construction who easily became involved in the business of exploring the New World were joined by other more proletarian émigrés. Those with military experience enlisted in the service of their adopted country and accompanied commanding navigators on their overseas expeditions.

Many of the men who helped to conquer the New World for other European nations came from Italy. It is estimated that fully one third of the sailors and soldiers who sailed with Magellan under Portuguese auspices were Italian.

THE MISSIONARIES

There were many Catholic missionaries among the migrating Italians. With the blessings of the Church, the monarchs of the burgeoning empires encouraged priest missionaries of all nationalities to help pave the way toward colonizing newly discovered territories. Apart from the "pacifying influence" such missionaries might have on native Indian tribes, they were valued as scholars who could prepare maps of the new territories and also provide intelligence useful to the nations they served.

One of the earliest of these missionaries was Fra Marcos de Niza, an Italian priest from Savoy enlisted in the service of Spain. Within a decade after Verrazzano's explorations of the North American coast, Fra Marcos, from his station in northern Mexico, was exploring territories that would eventually become known as Arizona and New Mexico. In 1539, Fra Marcos erected a cross on a pile of stones and claimed possession of the region in the name of Spain.

Perhaps the most impressive priest missionary to help Spain gain a foothold in the American Southwest was an Italian-born Jesuit, Father Eusebio Francesco Chino, who arrived in the New World in 1681 as a well-known scholar and cosmographer. For a quarter of a century Chino combined missionary work with exploration, making some fifty journeys on foot and horseback mapping Spain's North American empire from the Colorado River to the Gulf of Mexico. He also founded many ranchos and mission settlements, helped to develop the Southwest's cattle industry, and introduced livestock, grains, fruits, and vegetables previously unknown to the Indians of the Southwest. Chino died in 1711 at the age of sixty-seven, in the mission village of Santa Magdalena, one of the twenty or more communities he had founded which survive to this day.

Chino's career, which was belatedly honored in 1965 with an unveiling of his statue in Washington, D.C., symbolized the aspirations of numerous Jesuits who ventured into the New World.

Among the Jesuits who became the precursors of Italian immigration in the West was Father Giovanni Nobili, who was also an extraordinarily gifted linguist. After arriving at Fort Vancouver in Oregon in 1844, Nobili spent five years working among nine thousand Indians of various tribes (all of whom spoke different languages), as well as the trappers of the Hudson Bay Company. Nobili baptized some fourteen hundred Indians, many of whom died during an epidemic of measles not long after their conversion. Hard work and scarcity of food impaired Nobili's health so seriously that after five years he was sent to a mission to recuperate and, on recovering, was assigned an educational post in California—for many Jesuits a way-station to heaven.

Perhaps the most peripatetic of the Jesuit missionary-adventurer-priests was Father Joseph Cataldo, a Sicilian who, along with ninety other Jesuits, had been exiled from his Palermo monastery during Garibaldi's occupation of Sicily in 1860. Cataldo spent sixty-three years among Indian tribes in Idaho, Washington, Wyoming, and Alaska, communicating with them in twenty of their languages. One of the missions he built still survives in Cataldo, Idaho.

But the Italian missionaries were most active in California. By 1879, there were 113 priests in California, including some who had been retired from active duty. Many worked to establish some of the state's first colleges, including Santa Clara, and St. Ignatius College in San Francisco. Some of the Jesuit missions also unexpectedly became pioneers in what was to develop into a leading industry: winemaking. A black muscat dessert wine, which was to become a standard staple in the wine market, was first produced from grapes grown in the vineyards of the Novitiate of the Sacred Heart of Los Gatos.

One of the great nonreligious adventurers of the time was Enrico de Tonti, a soldier of fortune, explorer, and fur trader who, in 1678, enlisted with the French military for duty in the New World. With the pioneering explorer Robert Cavelier de La Salle, Tonti explored extensive areas of the Mississippi Valley and took possession of much of the valley in the name of France. To the Indians, who feared him (probably with good reason), he was "the man with the Iron hand" because of the hooklike claw that replaced the hand Tonti lost while fighting for the French in Sicily. Yet they learned to trust him, and under his leadership formed an alliance that would protect them from other tribes.

The alliance not only protected the Indians but also made the territory more accessible and safer for white traders. In his twenty-five years on American territory, Tonti became known as an intrepid explorer and commander, who helped to open up Illinois, Arkansas, Wisconsin, and Louisiana. When La Salle failed to return from his quest to find the mouth of the Mississippi, Tonti was placed in command of Fort St. Louis. Eventually he settled in Mobile, Alabama, and married an Indian woman. He died of yellow fever on September 6, 1674.

The only memorial to Tonti is in Arkansas, where Italian immigrants, remembering that he was the first European to set foot in the state, named their community Tontitown.

Mingled in with these priest adventurers were Italians who came, like so many other European immigrants, to worship as they pleased. In 1657, less than forty years after the Pilgrims arrived in Massachusetts, a band of some 150 Italian Protestants—Waldensians—landed in the Dutch possession of New Amsterdam. Escaping from the religious persecution they experienced in Catholic Italy, some of them settled in Long Island in an area that was to become known as Stony Brook; the rest went to Delaware, another Dutch possession, where they occupied farmland purchased for them by Dutch Protestants and organized a community that eventually was named New Castle.

Three centuries later, another group of Waldensians (forty-eight families in all) escaped new harassment in Italy and founded a community in North Carolina they named Valdese. There they first raised grapes, then later turned to industry, constructing flour, cotton, and hosiery mills.

THE ARTISANS

More typical than the Waldensians, in the flow of Italian immigrants, were a group of artisans from Venice whose arrival in the New World coincided with that of the Pilgrims. They came in 1621, at the invitation of the British, to establish a project in Jamestown, Virginia, for manufacturing glass beads to be used as currency in trading with Indians. Little is known about these early settlers except that, according to at least one of the Jamestown colonists, "a more damned crew Hell never vomited." Nonetheless, other Italian artisans were invited to bring their skills to colonial America. Early in the eighteenth century, the newly established colony of Georgia imported a group of northern Italians, experts in the field of raw silk production, to initiate a silk industry.

Another favorite colonial destination of the earliest Italian settlers was Maryland, which early in its history served as a haven for Catholics of all nationalities. To encourage their migration to Maryland, the colony's first governor, in 1649, was empowered "from time to time to grant lands unto any persons of French, Dutch or Italian descent upon the same terms and provisos as those of British or Irish descent."

THE AMERICAN REVOLUTION

It was no doubt a bit of English subtlety that made Cornwallis give his sword not to General Washington at Yorktown but to the French commander. The gesture, too, was an acknowledgment that the American Revolution also was a European endeavor.

Francesco Vigo, the first Italian to become an American citizen, is generally neglected in American history. Vigo came to the New World as a member of the Spanish Army. On being discharged, he entered the fur trade and became one of the wealthiest traders on the western frontier. In the course of his business activities Vigo developed a close friendship with George Rogers Clark, the twenty-six-year-old Virginian who became commander of the western American forces that were battling the British during the early stages of the Revolution. Vigo adopted the American Revolutionary cause as his own, serving not only as colonel but also as an intelligence officer and financier, and supplied General Clark with information he had gleaned while being held prisoner by the British—information that was instrumental in driving the British out of Vincennes, Indiana, during a crucial battle.

Vigo spent his entire fortune advancing money for arms and supplies, and he died a pauper. Forty years after his death, in 1876, the American government awarded his heirs approximately $50,000 for the colonel's contribution to the success of the War of Independence.

Most Italians who took part in the Revolution were enlisted men. Regimental lists of the Continental Army include some fifty Italians, only two of whom were officers. There is no mention of the two regiments of volunteers who were recruited in Italy.

The Italian name most clearly identified with the Revolution, however, is not that of a warrior but of a political philosopher, Filippo Mazzei, a physician and agronomist of Tuscan origin. Mazzei had moved to England to establish an importing firm for Italian wines, cheeses, and olive oil. There he met Thomas Adams and Benjamin Franklin, who persuaded him to go to Virginia to conduct a series of agricultural experiments. Mazzei arrived in Virginia with several Italian peasants, a tailor, and an assortment of agricultural implements and cuttings from Italian vines, trees, and plants. While pursuing his agricultural experiments, Mazzei's longtime sympathy for the American colonies blossomed into passionate enthusiasm. Using his powers of persuasion to attack the British for their misrule of the colonies (especially the strategy of ruling by creating dissension between them), Mazzei urged the colonists to lose no time in seceding from England.

With Thomas Jefferson, his friend and translator, Mazzei published a series of polemics under the pseudonym "Furioso" in the *Virginia Gazette*. One of the articles, translated by Jefferson, included the words that were to reverberate for years to come: "All men are by nature equally free and independent . . . each equality is necessary in order to create a free government. All men must be equal to each other in natural law."

Mazzei's phrase was incorporated verbatim in the Bill of Rights issued by Virginia; but in drafting the 1776 Declaration of Independence for all thirteen colonies, Jefferson altered it to read, "all men are created equal." Scholars have argued that Mazzei's phrase is more valid than Jefferson's, if only because it is more precise. While Mazzei was aware that Jefferson's adaptation of his phrase did not jibe with his own meaning, he publicly acknowledged the Declaration to be "a true affirmation of the principles necessary to preserve American liberty."

As a patriot and citizen of his adopted country, Mazzei tried to enlist in its army at the outset of the Revolutionary War, but Jefferson, Patrick Henry, and others had different plans for him. It was decided that Mazzei could best serve the American cause by persuading the courts of Europe to donate army supplies and money.

He later became a prime mover in founding and organizing a constitutional society whose members included James Madison, James Monroe, and Edmund Randolph. The purpose of the society, Mazzei said, was to "communicate our thoughts to one another and to the people, on every subject which may either tend to amend our Government, or to preserve it from the innovations of ambition and the designs of the people." Mazzei and other members of the society were convinced that "the surest mode to secure Republican systems of Government from lapsing into Tyranny, is by giving free and frequent information to the mass of people."

A year after the establishment of the society in 1785, Mazzei decided to return to Europe to support the burgeoning democratic movements in France and Poland. In Paris, Mazzei wrote his *Historical and Political Enquiries,* a four-volume work which one historian described as "an accurate summary of the foundation of the thirteen colonies and a truthful exposition of the economic troubles which brought about the break between Great Britain and the Colonies. . . . He [Mazzei] showed how the example of the Americans, who translated their ideas of freedom from theory into practice, had helped and would help any European nation."

In 1941, President Franklin D. Roosevelt reminded Americans of Mazzei's contribution to Jefferson's draft of the Declaration of Independence and added this comment on Mazzei's strong ties with the United States:

When after many years of intimate relations with Jefferson and other great Americans of the time he had to return to Europe, Mazzei wrote to Madison in Italian: "I do not know what may happen when Sandy Hook disappears from my sight. But I know that wherever I go I shall always work for the well-being and progress of the country of my adoption."*

*Sforza, *Italy and Italians,* p. 146. In 1980 the U.S. Postal Service issued a 40-cent stamp commemorating the 250th anniversary of Mazzei's birth.

CHAPTER 2

Young America

The approximately twelve thousand Italians who came to America between the founding of the American Republic in 1783 and the establishment of modern Italy as a nation in 1871 were scattered throughout the nation, with large concentrations in the Northeast and in the Lower Mississippi Valley.* These early arrivals differed from the Italians who began arriving in massive numbers toward the close of the century in several respects. They were mainly tradesmen, artists, artisans, musicians, teachers, and political refugees, with a wide diversity of skills. Few came from an agricultural background. And unlike many of those who followed, the earlier immigrants arrived with the intention of staying.

Among the most successful of the early immigrants were the entrepreneurs, who were able to capitalize on the needs of a developing nation. Paul Busti, a nephew of Francesco Vigo, arrived in 1850 with a vision of transforming the virgin wilderness into a series of communities. As a representative of the Holland Lane Company, which owned 3 million acres in New York and Pennsylvania, Busti

---

*By comparison, between 1820 and 1860, 1.5 million Germans and 2 million Irish came to America.

succeeded in developing the vast area into sites for villages, towns, and cities, the largest of which became Buffalo.

Another entrepreneur was the financier Giovanni P. Morosoni, who arrived in New York as a penniless sailor and became an influential banker and partner of Jay Gould, the notorious railroad magnate. One legacy of Morosoni's wealth is the collection of European armor and arms that was willed to the Metropolitan Museum of Art. Two other Italians who were actively involved in the nation's developing economy were Giuseppe Taglialine, the inventor and manufacturer of instruments for navigators and meteorologists, and Luigi Tinelli, a political refugee who helped initiate the American silk industry by establishing a large silk-manufacturing complex in Weehawken, New Jersey (later a center for Italian workers involved in the Anarchist movement).

Except for the ubiquitous organ grinders, perhaps the most conspicuous Italians in the United States before the Civil War were the political refugees, who began arriving shortly after Mazzini's aborted attempt to establish a Roman Republic in 1848 and 1849. They made the United States their haven, while keeping an eye on the politics in Italy. Some of the younger refugees joined the "Italian Guard," a military training unit in New York, with the expectation of returning to Italy to fight for unification.

The arrival of refugees who were being deported to the United States because of their revolutionary activities generated resentment among Americans, who felt that their country was being used as a "dumping ground" for undesirables. Fueling this fear was the willingness of American authorities to accept groups of refugees who were said to have been given the choice in Italy of either going to jail or being deported to the United States.

In one similar instance, the American Minister to Rome, Lewis Cass, Jr., upon learning in 1851 that thirteen young Romans of "fine character and high standing" had been confined to dungeons along with hardened criminals for having participated in revolutionary activities against the papacy, managed to convince the Catholic authorities to release the men into American custody with the understanding that they would be sent to California at Cass's own expense. The American minister was widely praised for this "humanitarian" action. An Italian exile wrote from Paris: "If you have more of this breed [the American minister] send them, I pray you to Naples and Milan, to the dungeons in which the desolate champions of liberty . . .

are praying for death as a release." Official American Catholic opinion, however, sharply criticized Cass for extending American hospitality to anti-Catholic "propagandists."

The fact that many of the Italian refugees in the United States were, like Garibaldi and Mazzini, avowed enemies of the Catholic Church (a thousand-year-old obstacle to Italian unity, they claimed) contributed to the existing friction.

Particularly antagonistic was the American Catholic Church hierarchy, which openly pitted itself against the supporters of Mazzini and Garibaldi. One frequent target was Francesco Secchi de Casale, among the earliest Italian political activists to find refuge in the United States.

In 1849, Casale became the editor of a struggling periodical, *L'Europee-Americano,* which, in Italian and English, informed its readers of events in Europe while expressing enthusiastic support for the republican movements in Europe and attacking the papacy for its opposition to the democratic aspirations of the Italian people. The severity of his criticism provoked New York's first Catholic archbishop to denounce Casale as "a renegade both to creed and country." When *L'Europee-Americano* failed after nine issues, Casale pawned his gold watch and his wife's gold earrings and founded the first important Italian-language weekly published in the United States, *L'Eco d'Italia.* Despite its limited circulation, *L'Eco* survived for almost half a century, during which time Casale became the chief spokesman of the Italian immigrant population in the New York area.

A true idealist, whose humanitarian instincts transcended political considerations, he and his newspaper became deeply involved in promoting the welfare of his immigrant compatriots. Casale spearheaded a movement to establish an evening school in Little Italy of a notorious slum known as Five Points. There children were taught the three R's, as well as Italian and American history and geography. Casale was also among the first to come to the rescue of child street musicians brought from Italy by Faginlike *padrone.*

In yet another crusade, Casale failed to persuade Italian and American authorities to divert the increasing stream of Italian immigration to rural districts, where the majority of the Italians arriving after 1875 could have pursued the vocation they knew best: farming.

Casale's crusade was more successful in the private sector than it was with the American authorities. In New Jersey, his crusade attracted the attention of Charles Landis, an American landowner with Utopian views, who offered extensive tracts of his lands in and around Vineland for the development of Casale's colonization scheme. The success of the venture became apparent within three years after the Italian farmers began colonizing Vineland in 1881.

THE CIVIL WAR

Casale's concerns were by no means limited to the problems of his compatriots. As soon as the American Civil War broke out, his newspaper pressed for an Italian Legion to fight for the northern cause. One of the first to join was Luigi Tinelli, the silk industrialist and former American Consul to Portugal. As a member of the New York Militia who had acquired the rank of lieutenant colonel as early as 1843, Tinelli was chosen to head the Italian Legion. Later a second regiment of Italians known as the Garibaldi Guard merged with the Italian Legion. The Garibaldi Guard attracted not only Italians who had fought under Garibaldi but also other nationals who viewed the northern cause as an affirmation of the international aspects of Garibaldian ideology.

Many more Italians fought for the North than were represented in either the Garibaldi Guard or the Italian Legion. Approximately one hundred men, mainly from New York, served as officers, and three—Enrico Fardella, Eduardo Ferrero, and Francis B. Spinola—rose to the rank of brigadier general. Spinola succeeded in recruiting four regiments of troops in the New York City area which became known as the "Spinola Empire Brigade." For this achievement President Lincoln appointed him brigadier general of the brigade. Although he entered the Union Army at the age of forty-two without any previous military training or experience, Spinola won the respect of his fellow officers as a tactician and a courageous leader. In one of his fiercest engagements with the enemy, in which his men were outnumbered by six to one, Spinola headed a bayonet charge that drove the rebels back in disarray. He sustained two severe wounds during the battle but remained in the army until the war ended two years later.

There was a marked absence of glory in his postwar career. For all of Spinola's respect for his Italian roots, he showed little concern for the mounting problems Italian immigrants were experiencing in

New York City. Although appointed to a special House Committee on Immigration charged with investigating their situation, he refused to participate in the investigation on the grounds that he had more important responsibilities to attend to. At the time of his death, the American press noted the positive and negative aspects of Spinola's career. The most influential organ of the Italian American press, *Il Progresso Italo Americano,* ever reluctant to find fault with successful Italian Americans, praised him not only for his "distinguished career" in the army and in politics but also because "he did not repudiate nor deny the Italian heritage he admitted in public and private."

Typical of the haughty upper-class Italians who saw little point in involving themselves with the problems of their poor compatriots was Count Luigi Palma di Cesnola, perhaps the last of the Italian adventurers to come to the New World. He arrived in New York in 1858 as an impoverished aristocrat, with no prospects and no profession except that of a professional soldier who had fought in the Crimean War for the British. He was to achieve extraordinary distinction both as an officer in the Union Army and in the highest echelon of New York's cultural establishment as the first director of the Metropolitan Museum of Art.

Cesnola supported himself by teaching Italian and French until he married one of his students, an American heiress. To prove that he was capable of supporting his wife, Cesnola established a private military academy that offered New Yorkers a cram course in martial arts for a fee of $100, payable in advance. Across the facade of the building that housed his academy ran a huge sign: WAR SCHOOL OF ITALIAN ARMY CAPTAIN COUNT LUIGI PALMA DI CESNOLA. Within six months he had instilled the rudiments of infantry, artillery, and cavalry warfare into more than seven hundred graduates, many of whom went on to fight in the Union Army as officers. Cesnola then closed the academy and joined the Union Army himself. Despite his youth (he was only twenty-eight), his past army experience stood him in good stead, and he received the commission of lieutenant colonel with the 11th New York Cavalry Regiment.

Thereafter Cesnola's army career became a series of dramatic crises that occasionally overlapped. Nearly all demonstrated that although he was revered by the soldiers in his command, his superiors found his brashness and egocentric behavior intolerable.

Three weeks before the Battle of Gettysburg, while battling a

Confederate cavalry unit headed by General Jeb Stuart at Alduem, Virginia, Cesnola was relieved of his sword and placed under arrest for disputing the decision of a superior officer. When his men refused to return to the attack against the Confederates without him, Cesnola, disregarding his arrest and totally unarmed, leaped on his horse and led the men in two assaults which, though unsuccessful, so impressed his commanding officer that when the cavalry unit returned to camp, the officer handed him his own sword and released him from his arrest. The next assault, again led by Cesnola, almost proved to be his undoing. His horse was shot dead from under him. Many hours later, while the Confederate soldiers were collecting their dead and wounded, they found him pinned under his horse with a bullet wound in one arm and a saber cut on his head.

As a prisoner of the Confederate Army, Cesnola was no less intransigent than he had been as a Union Army officer. He complained vociferously about the prison in Richmond where he and some twelve hundred officers were jammed into six rooms. He demanded better treatment for the eighteen thousand enlisted Union soldiers held in nearby Belle Isle, where conditions were even worse. The Confederate prisoner-exchange commissioner became so incensed by Cesnola's incessant demands for improved conditions that he tried to delay Cesnola's release as long as possible. Other Confederate authorities, however, recognized and utilized Cesnola's leadership qualities by appointing him keeper of the commissary at Belle Isle, in charge of distributing food to his fellow prisoners. After ten months of imprisonment, Cesnola, thanks to his wife's efforts in Washington and a petition submitted by the men who served in his New York regiment, was released on May 21, 1864. Four months later, during a period of daredevil military action in which he resumed his old habit of winning the affection of his men while antagonizing his superiors, Cesnola's military career came to an end. He was then thirty-four years old.

His first action as a civilian was to seek a meeting with Abraham Lincoln. It took place at the White House in the spring of 1865, two days before Lincoln's assassination. At his meeting with the President, Cesnola asked that he be awarded the rank of brigadier general as an honor, without pay, and that he be assigned a consular post in Europe, preferably in Italy.

There is no record of Cesnola's elevation to the brevet rank of brigadier general, despite his contention that it was awarded in the presence of a New York senator, Ira Harris; but "General" became the title that Cesnola was to sport the rest of his life. Three weeks after his White House visit, Secretary of State Seward appointed Cesnola American Consul, not to Italy as he had fervently hoped, but to Cyprus. Before assuming the post, Cesnola went through the formalities, for the first time, of becoming a citizen of his adopted country.

In Cyprus, Cesnola's hobby of archaeology came to the fore with spectacular results. At his own expense he enlisted a small army of Cypriot workmen to unearth artifacts and jewelry that had been buried with the ancient dead, amassing a huge collection that he eventually sold to the Metropolitan Museum of Art. In addition, Cesnola persuaded the museum's board of trustees to plan an exhibition of his collection and appoint him its curator. Cesnola then returned to Cyprus to continue his archaeological explorations (again at his own expense) and within a few years hit upon the ancient city of Curium. Twenty feet underground he found the royal vault of an ancient temple. It contained 7,161 objects—including numerous solid gold bracelets, rings, and earrings—all of which Cesnola sold to the Metropolitan Museum in 1876. This discovery not only established Cesnola's reputation as a foremost amateur archaeologist but also led to his appointment as the first director of the Museum.

To some extent Cesnola's phenomenal rise in the art world can be attributed to the increasing perception among cultivated Americans that Italy was *la mère des arts,* a primary source of the arts and of its practitioners. Throughout the nineteenth century, American Italophiles made pilgrimages to Rome, Florence, and Venice. The world of Henry James was rooted in this discovery of Italy. Italian tutors were much in demand and provided many educated Italian refugees with a means of earning a livelihood.

As early as 1753, a course in the study of Italian was offered at the Philadelphia College, founded by Benjamin Franklin, which eventually became the University of Pennsylvania. In Virginia twenty-five years later, at the recommendation of Thomas Jefferson, Carlo Bellini, a friend of Mazzei, was appointed professor of Romance languages at the College of William & Mary, where he taught for more than two decades. But not until the arrival of Lorenzo Da Ponte, the celebrated librettist of Mozart, in 1802 did the teaching of Italian begin to flourish. Da Ponte launched a one-man educational campaign which, combined with tutorial teaching of Italian, culminated in his appointment as Columbia University's first professor of Italian literature. Harvard, Yale, and Princeton soon after added Italian studies to their curricula.

Thomas Jefferson, who not only visited Italy but could also read Italian, was among the most conspicuous of the early American Italophiles. He was especially impressed with Italian architecture, basing the design of his Virginia residence, Monticello, on prints by Palladio, the sixteenth-century Paduan architect. During his term as American Minister to France, confined to his office by the pressure of his duties, Jefferson had his secretary tour Italy to report in detail on architecture and art. Later, while planning the building of the United States Capitol in consultation with Charles Bulfinch, Jefferson sent Bulfinch to Italy for the specific purpose of familiarizing himself with its classical architecture. Bulfinch's observations in Rome of such buildings as the Pantheon and St. Peter's are credited with the style widely adopted for Federal architecture in Washington and other American cities.

The most aggressive promoter of Italian art and artists, however, was the government itself. As the nation's Capitol was being built, more and more Italian artists and artisans were invited to the United States and commissioned to help build and embellish the Capitol with sculptures and paintings.

One of the most celebrated Italian artists, the sculptor Giuseppe Ceracchi, came to America intent on using art to express his admiration for the ideology of the newborn democracy. Arriving in Washington in 1791, he brought with him an ambitious proposal for honoring his hero, George Washington. He proposed a monument made up of eleven famous figures sixty feet tall and six smaller statues, together with animals and varied ornaments—all to be executed in marble and all dominated by a bronze equestrian statue of Washington set on a large pedestal. While awaiting congressional approval of his project, several heroes of the American Revolution—including Washington—who were to be represented in the proposed monument posed for him. Those sittings have left us with busts of Washington, Jefferson, John Adams, James Madison, Benjamin Franklin, and Alexander Hamilton.*

*Alexander Hamilton's death in his duel with Aaron Burr, which occurred three years after Ceracchi's own death, created an unprecedented demand for the artist's bust of the nation's first Secretary of the Treasury. Subsequently, Ceracchi's portrait also served as a model for all of the Hamilton effigies produced, including his image on a 30-cent U.S. stamp

Thomas Jefferson, during his first years in the White House, asked the government's public architect, Benjamin Latrobe, to enlist the aid of his old friend Filippo Mazzei in finding Italian sculptors who might be persuaded to accept commissions for embellishing the Capitol, now nearing completion. The first two sculptors to accept the invitation were brothers-in-law, Giuseppe Franzoni and Giovanni Andrei, both from Carrara, the town famous for its marble.

Of all the Italian-born artists who left their mark on the Capitol, none was more significant than the painter Constantino Brumidi, who covered a large area of the Capitol's interior with monumental frescoes that led more than one writer to dub him "the Michelangelo of the United States Capitol."

A political refugee, Brumidi had been a well-known fresco painter in Italy. Upon his arrival in 1852, Brumidi was immediately engaged by the Capitol's architect and put to work decorating sections of the building, a task he was to pursue for the next quarter century.

The Italian artists who followed during the period of mass immigration received far more recognition; foremost among them was the Piccirilli family of sculptors and marble cutters. Soon after their arrival in 1888, they established a workshop in New York City which attracted the collaboration of such noted American artists as August Saint-Gaudens and Daniel Chester French, and quickly gained a reputation for knowing "more about the marble in the quarry and in the monument than anyone else in the nation."

After French had created his 8-foot model of Abraham Lincoln for the Lincoln Memorial in Washington, he turned it over to the Piccirilli workshop to convert into the 19-foot figure in the monument, to which French added his finishing touches. As sculptors working on their own, Attilio, the eldest, became the most renowned. He designed the memorial in New York's Columbus Circle to the soldiers and sailors who lost their lives on the *Maine* during the Spanish American War. The memorial was executed with the help of his brothers. Other commissions followed—the War Memorial in Albany, the Fireman's Monument in New York City, the Marconi Monument in Washington, D.C., and a number of sculptures in

---

in 1870. A portrait of Hamilton, based on John Trumbull's painting of Ceracchi's bust, is engraved on the U.S. ten-dollar bill.

New York's Rockefeller Center. One of his brothers, Furio, became best known for the groups he sculpted in the Court of the Seasons of the San Francisco Panama-Pacific Exposition. Another brother, Horace, achieved wide recognition for his decorations of such buildings as the Frick House, the Riverside Church, and the County Courthouse, all in New York City.

The Piccirilli family established the reputation of Italian artists and artisans that would later find echoes among the artisans who worked in stone in Vermont and northern New York, and who also left their mark with numerous decorations on apartment buildings on the West and East sides of Manhattan.

Recalling his first five years as an immigrant sculptor in America, Attilio Piccirilli made a comment to an interviewer in 1938 that stands as a verbal monument to all those who were assimilated into American society:

> I have been an American for so long—fifty years—that I often forget I was born in Italy. When anyone refers to me as a foreigner, or as an Italian, I pretend that I haven't heard and I don't usually answer. Of course, I am an American. . . . Once I went back to my native city and planned to stay there for a year or more. I locked the door of my studio in New York, said goodbye to all my friends and went to the homeland where I had been born. What did I find? I was a foreigner in Italy. I could speak the language of course, but I couldn't think Italian. . . . I had planned to be away for a year but in four months I was on my return trip to the Bronx.
>
> . . . I first *knew* that I was a real American when I brought my mother's body back from Italy where she had died on a visit. We buried her here and I made a statue of motherhood for her grave. I had worked here and succeeded a little, and taken an oath of allegiance. But it is when you bury one you love in a country's soil that you realize that you belong to that soil forever.

The Piccirilli brothers and other Italian artists in the United States prospered during an era when their Old World skills were much in demand. At a time when American artists had yet to establish an indigenous identity, the traditionalism of the Italian painters and sculptors provided a comforting connection with Western Europe, then considered the accepted purveyor of all the fine arts.

★ ★ ★

Although many of the early Italian immigrants were men of intellect and substance, it was the poorest of the early immigrants who became the nation's earliest purveyors of popular culture. The first artwork owned by thousands of American families was one of the small statues of historical and mythological figures sold by Italians who hawked their wares from street to street.

THE MUSICIANS

For most Americans, music was the art most closely associated with the Italians. The first public musical performances many had heard were those of strolling Italian musicians, guitarists, mandolinists, and, especially, organ grinders, who traveled from city to city cranking out favorite Italian arias. But more accomplished Italian musicians, who usually performed indoors for elite audiences, had long preceded them. It was not uncommon for affluent American families to avail themselves of the services of Italian piano and violin instructors. As might be expected, Thomas Jefferson and his wife were among them. Jefferson's appreciation for Italian musicians led him, during the early years of his presidency, to ask his representative in Rome to recruit enough Italian musicians to form the first American military band. The fourteen musicians who arrived aboard a U.S. frigate, the *Chesapeake,* in 1805 eventually became the nucleus of the United States Marine Band.

One of the earliest Italian composers to make his home in the United States was Filippo Traetta, who established the nation's first conservatory of music in Boston in 1803 and another in Philadelphia several decades later.

Italian opera was largely unknown in the United States until 1825, when a troupe presented Rossini's *Barber of Seville* in Italian before a New York audience. The enthusiastic response prompted the troupe to extend their engagement for three more months, during which they presented all ten of the other operas in their repertoire. By the 1850s, Italian opera companies were performing in several American cities. In San Francisco in 1854 alone, there were eleven opera productions. Many of the performers chose to remain in America and continue their careers as best they could, often teaching music or the Italian language.

Lorenzo Da Ponte, Mozart's former librettist, was an early champion of Italian opera in America. In 1825, he was already importing Italian opera companies to perform the first two operas Americans had ever attended, Rossini's *Barber of Seville* and Mozart's *Don Giovanni*. In 1833, he became one of the prime movers in the attempt to establish a permanent opera company, the Italian Opera House in downtown Manhattan. After twenty-eight performances the venture failed. Da Ponte died five years later at the age of eighty-nine, leaving behind memoirs in which he cited the establishment of Italian opera in New York as "the *desideratum* of my greatest zeal."

Not until the 1880s, when immigrants from Italy began arriving in massive numbers, did Italian opera become firmly established as a popular American entertainment appealing to all classes.

CHANGING IMAGES OF ITALIANS

The American perception of Italian immigrants before the era of mass migration was decidedly mixed. Among educated Americans, especially those familiar with Italian culture, the typical image was a collage of political refugees, artists, language and music teachers, fencing masters, opera singers—and a scattering of organ grinders. So ingrained in the American psyche was the stereotype of associating opera with Italians that when President Franklin Roosevelt, at the outbreak of war with Italy in 1941, was asked whether he planned to intern all Italian aliens, he responded, "I'm not worried about Italians. They're just a bunch of opera singers."

Nonetheless, up until the great migration, except for a few hardcore chauvinists who resented the presence of all foreigners, cultivated Americans generally regarded the Italians as a civilizing influence on a society that was largely dependent on Europe for cultural guidance.

The most negative aspect of the Italian image in America stemmed from sensational newspaper accounts, such as those about the *padrone,* who purchased or stole poor Italian children and brought them to the United States as enslaved street musicians, bootblacks, street acrobats, and beggars. Enforcing this lurid image was the press's fascination with *banditi* of the *Mezzogiorno* who robbed or kidnapped for ransom affluent foreign travelers. The tendency to blame the newcomer for all crimes was pervasive.

The adverse publicity about Italians caused little alarm in these early years, chiefly because their numbers were so small as to make them invisible to most Americans—only 3,500 in 1850, and 10,000 a decade later. Not until the close of the century, when Italians began arriving in large numbers, did the negative stereotyping affect the general population. Until then (particularly in the large cities where most immigrants lived), the adverse press was countered by the presence of Italian political refugees, often idealistic men of refinement and education. Many of these men were a constant reminder to Americans of the *Risorgimento*'s struggle to achieve a unified nation, free of foreign rulers, whose government would be based on democratic principles similar to those that led to the founding of the American Republic.

Not all Americans favored the cause of the *Risorgimento*. The American Catholic leadership realized that a unified, independent Italy would mean the end of the Vatican as a sovereign political power. Some also questioned the ability of Italians to establish and maintain a democratic form of government in a land they viewed as corrupt and intransigent. Still, the movement won enough sympathy and support from American intellectuals to convince leaders of the *Risorgimento* that the United States could be counted on to favor its cause.

American intellectuals had sympathized with the *Risorgimento* as early as 1848, when Garibaldi and Mazzini laid siege to the Vatican in a failed attempt to oust the papacy. Support increased throughout the 1850s, reaching its apex with Garibaldi's whirlwind 1860 campaign to wrest the *Mezzogiorno* from the Bourbon rulers. Even before Garibaldi and his One Thousand set out on their expedition to conquer Sicily, Americans raised approximately $100,000 worth of arms and supplies for the cause.

When unification was finally achieved, it was met with applause in America, despite disappointment that a king would head the new nation. In Manhattan, the event brought some three thousand men and women together at Cooper Union Institute to listen to paeans on Garibaldi's triumph, "one of the greatest achievements in military history," by "the George Washington of Italy."

Yet, for all such euphoric expressions of admiration and commonality, the American perception of Italians remained a multifaceted phenomenon: Italy was variously seen as friend of America, land of Garibaldi, martyr of popular liberty and freedom, birthplace of Dante, *la mère des arts,* Italy the brave, gallant, intelligent. Yet the image of Italian people as being fickle, immoral, and decadent persisted.

The worst early anti-Italian demonstration occurred in 1857, when mobs of New Yorkers attacked and harassed Italians indiscriminately upon learning that an Italian had killed a policeman. But the general attitude was one of benign tolerance. All that began to change in the closing decades of the century, with the sharp acceleration of Italian immigration. Open hostility became more pervasive than tolerance. The Italian immigrants were not the only foreigners arriving from Europe during the same era who were resented and despised, but because they outnumbered other nationalities they were more often targeted for attacks, particularly if they were from southern Italy. Their papers identified the latter as "Italians," but they were no longer the adventurers, singers, and artists; a large percentage of these new arrivals were lacking in education and skills. They were "foreign-looking," smelled of "garlic and harsh disinfectants."

Out of such observations developed the conclusion—seconded by immigrants from northern Italy who from birth had been conditioned to regard southerners as an inferior breed—that southern Italians, Sicilians especially, were an undesirable lot, who had neither the wish nor the capacity to assimilate into the American population. Most immigrants suffered such stigma with peasant patience.

Promoting those notions were the earlier European immigrants, mainly Irish and Germans, who regarded every shipload of arriving Italians as a threat to their economic welfare. Many Americans feared that before long the nation would be inundated by a population of immigrants who were neither Anglo-Saxon nor Protestant.

The unification of Italy was to exacerbate the conflict between North and South, and contribute to conditions that would soon provoke the "great hemorrhaging" of people from their ancestral lands.

PART TWO

The Land They Left

CHAPTER 3

Italy Before and After Unification

I'm a lost chicken
But no one calls.

—ITALIAN PROVERB

Modern Italy began in the early decades of the nineteenth century with the nationalistic longings of a few determined visionaries and revolutionaries. Obsessed with Italy's previous incarnation as the core nation of the ancient Roman Empire, these men instigated a movement whose name suggested both a promise and a battle cry—*"Risorgimento!"* It became the dramatic overture to the story of the Italian American experience.

At the time Italy was fragmented into eight separate states, all but one of them (Piedmont) ruled either by foreign governments or by the papacy. The *Risorgimento*'s goal was to oust the foreign rulers and establish a fully united Italian Republic.

After staging several failed insurrections, the movement reached its apex in 1860, when its most celebrated champion, Giuseppe Garibaldi, with a volunteer army and a whirlwind campaign, liberated from two hundred years of Bourbon tyranny all of the regions south of Rome—the area known as the *Mezzogiorno* that was to produce more than 80 percent of all the Italians who came to the United States. A few weeks later, in a gesture worthy of a Verdi opera, Garibaldi presented his conquest to Victor Emmanuel II, king of Piedmont, the only Italian state free of foreign or papal rule, which had become the spearhead of the *Risorgimento*. The southern regions were amalgamated into the recently formed northern Kingdom of Italy.

The Italian government promptly celebrated the event by restoring Rome to its ancient status as the nation's capital. But it was an uneasy celebration, for most of the previous decade had been fraught with destructive events that boded ill for the nation's future. They began in the South within weeks after Italy had first declared itself a nation, with fierce rebellions pitted against the new regime by the same peasantry that had permitted Garibaldi to free them from Bourbon rule. The rebellions were financed and directed by the deposed Bourbon king, Francesco II, in alliance with the papacy, whose role as a temporal power had been doomed by the establishment of the new regime. It took an army of 100,000 well-armed government troops five years to crush the rebellions. In effect, the struggles between the troops and the peasants were tantamount to civil war. This was followed by several revolts in Sicily, the only Italian region that had refused to fight for the restoration of the Bourbon regime. The desperate antagonism of the southerners against their new authorities inevitably gave rise to the speculation that Italy had become a nation in name only. Reflecting on the traumas and ironies attending its beginnings, an Italian statesman in 1870 cautioned that "although we have made Italy, we have yet to make Italians."

Less than a decade after Italy had been "unified," the emigration of Italians began accelerating at a phenomenal rate. During the next fifty years the exodus was to grow into one of the greatest migrations in world history, reducing Italy's population by one third. The basic impetus for the phenomenon was economic survival, but there were various other reasons, not the least of which was the inability of its impoverished population to feel any strong degree of allegiance toward the new nation. One was to hear from the emigrants, "Where I gain my crust of bread, there is my country"—or, from a woman whose brother was killed fighting for the U.S. Army in World War

I, "Instead of doing his military service over there, he did it over here."

Nor was this feeling different among the peasants of the North. A group of them in Lombardy, responding to an 1878 ministerial decree urging the population not to abandon the nation by emigrating, pointedly equated the definition of "nation" with its ability to provide a decent livelihood for its people:

> What do you mean by a nation, Mr. Minister? Is it the throng of the unhappy? Aye, then we are truly the nation. . . . We plant and we reap wheat but never do we eat white bread. We cultivate the grape but we drink no wine. We raise animals for food but we eat no meat. We are clothed in rags. . . . And in spite of all this, you counsel us, Mr. Minister, not to abandon our country. But is that land, where one cannot live by toil, one's country?

In their search for a land where they could "live by toil," the emigrants at first restricted their travel to European countries. But soon, lured by the belief that Latin Argentina and Brazil would be more congenial for Italians, they braved the Atlantic to migrate to those countries. When a yellow fever epidemic in Brazil killed nine thousand Italians, the emigrants changed their primary destination to North America, mainly the United States, where cheap labor was greatly in demand. The Italians from the northern regions were the first to leave in large numbers. The southerners, more conservative—though with less reason—did not succumb to the lure of America until the late 1880s, but once they began to leave, they migrated in droves.

By 1930, more than 4.5 million Italians had entered the United States. Their number would have doubled except for two restricting factors: the 1924 American immigration laws, which pointedly discriminated against would-be immigrants from Eastern and Southern European nations; and the recently established Fascist regime, which prohibited all but a few from leaving Italy for another country.

Northern Italy, center of the unification movement, implemented laws benefiting the areas north of Rome, leaving the South to stagnate while contributing taxes for northern economic expansion. The flow of northern emigrants diminished while those from the South increased. At least four fifths of the arriving immigrants hailed from the seven regions south of Rome: Abruzzo, Molise,

Campania, Basilicata (then known as Lucania), Apulia, Calabria, and the island of Sicily. Each region had its own dialect, folklore, traditions, and patron saints. Theirs was the residue of a culture communally affected by four hundred years of Spanish and Bourbon domination, which kept the *Mezzogiorno* outside the mainstream of history, affixed in a medieval world in which the vast majority of its inhabitants, the peasantry, lived in squalor and ignorance.

In 1860, only 2.5 percent of the population could speak Italian; the rest spoke the dialects of their regions. There was no unifying language. How can you speak of unity, one politician exclaimed, when in Italian the word for "cockroach" is *blatta,* and in Tuscan it is *piattola,* and in Rome they say *bagherozzo,* in Naples *scarafone,* and in Sicily *cacarocielu!*

If there was a sense of unity for those of the South, it came from Christianity. In Sicilian as well as in many other dialects of the South, the word for "person" was "Christian." Someone coming from Puglia or Sicily in 1890 still considered himself a Christian first, then a member of his community or region. He was hardly aware that he was Italian until he arrived in America.

Certainly the movement for Italian unity, led by the North, had a marked effect on conditions which precipitated the mass exodus in the South. Nonetheless, well into the twentieth century southerners still identified with their towns, villages, and regions more than they did with Italy. The northern men of power for their part had little knowledge of or interest in the circumstances of what it meant to be a Christian in southern Italy.

The world the mass of emigrants left was quite different from modern Italy; feudalism lingered, ancient legends taught morality, the Church ruled mind and body, life span was short (although if one survived childhood, one often lived to a ripe old age), and life ranged not much further than the horizon one could see with the naked eye.

LIFE IN THE MEZZOGIORNO

As late as the 1920s, when the great emigration from the South was coming to an end, townspeople and villagers still had the habit in summer of going out to their *aria,* an airy place in the countryside, usually a bare stone house surrounded by plum and peach trees, a cluster of almond or walnut trees, a patch of melon vines, and all around a sea of wheat fields in which, here and there, groups of olive trees rose like gray puffs of smoke in the blazing sun. Summers were ferociously hot and the earth so dry it would crack wide open, so that the fields became a danger to the horses, mules, and donkeys crossing them.

Almost everyone left the towns and villages in summer, whether as the owner of a small *aria,* as a field worker, a servant, a fruit grafter, or an invited friend. On those summer nights people sat in front of their stone houses watching the light fade and the world shrink.

Travel was slow then. Only aristocrats who had carriages could afford high-spirited, almost frail horses. These same horses that once won the Olympic crowns for the lords of Syracuse "enjoyed a renown which Athenian tragedians ventured to carry back to the mythic ages of Greece." In 1960 one could still see these auburn-colored horses with large open nostrils, half starved, their ribs showing, that stamped the wheat before winnowing. A man with a kerchief on his head gently led them round and round singing, "Wind, wind, St. Anthony, for today we'll be winnowing."

In spite of the fact that the railroad came to the areas of the South around 1880, the generation that started the migration was one brought up with animals. Mules were the great means of transportation, the trucks of the times.

The donkey is present in all the stories told in towns throughout the South. Some are wise, others are fools. One donkey who was wise beyond necessity was once loaded with salt. As he crossed a wide river, he noticed his load becoming lighter and lighter until it had completely disappeared. The not-so-clever donkey tried the same thing with a load of sponges—and drowned.

For the southern peasant, the donkey became the image of suffering and poverty—a poverty so dire it could not be faced directly and could be described only obliquely through animals. This might help explain why there is hardly an Italian writer of fiction who wrote of the emigrant experience in Italy. They were too preoccupied with the suffering at hand to be concerned with those who left.

For those who worked in the fields, it took an hour or two to reach one's plot of land. The trip, except in the summer months, was made every day. One left before the sun rose and returned after dark, in a countryside loud with the braying of the jackass, the barking of dogs, and a voice singing that chantlike Arabic song, "I'm a lost chicken / But no one calls."

Itinerant agricultural workers rode jackasses, or walked to and from cities and towns. Skilled agricultural workers such as the *nesturi* (the grafters), who traveled with little black bags containing their tools ("like doctors," one woman remembered), roamed even further.

Those small towns and villages of the South at the turn of the century consisted of clusters of cubelike houses that seemed to have spilled down from the high ground into the hollows below. Each town had its *chiazza* (as *piazza* is pronounced in dialect), usually with a church at one end and a winehouse at the other. The *chiazza* was the marketplace, the emotional and social center of the town. It was the place where men met and in their public relations gave character to one another. Here, too, they paid respect to the traditions and values of the century.

It was the climate, too, that gave character to the *chiazza*. The warm tropical climate of the South—the dry hot summers, the fall windy and rainy—was the sort of climate that permitted people, almost forced them, to live out of doors. Everything was out in the open, yet subtleties had to be found to hide feelings. People seemed to speak louder because of this outside living. One often felt on a stage, aware that one was being observed, watched. On those summer nights when the light lingered, the *chiazza* took on the dramatic air of a stage with many entrances.

Then men would stroll arm in arm, in groups of two or three, sometimes four or five, from one end of the square—stop, chat for a while; glance about at the others, then start out for the other end, to the café owned for generations by the same family. As they walked, they nodded to one another, greeting those of their own station. A passing woman was greeted only if she were accompanied by her husband. A woman walking alone was ignored, for a man could be made cuckold by a glance. At times some might walk the road to the cemetery, past a wayside chapel which in those days always had a candle burning inside the oven-shaped shrine.

Choosing a partner or partners for the evening stroll was determined by one's rank and status in the community. Truckers walked with truckers or miners, priests with priests or members of the bourgeoisie and a retinue of men seeking favors. It was here that a mother walked her marriageable daughters, dressed in color, to the church, to the shops, and home again. This was a way of defining class structure: the *borghesia,* the comfortable *contadino* (one who did not lack the absolute necessities of life) walked with his own kind.

There was, too, for lack of a better word, a lumpenproletariat: the agricultural worker from whom, we are told, "rose the phenomenon of mafia" in the time of the first immigrants.

The houses most people lived in at the time were simply single-story huts. The poor usually inhabited a loft above, a crude ladder leading to their beds. The ground level was left to the animals: a mule, chickens, and, for the more fortunate, a pig. The streets were narrow, cobblestoned, and in need of repair, the missing cobblestones usually filled with water and debris. In summer there was the fetid smell of clay, hot straw, and pungent herbs in the air, at times filled with clouds of flies disturbed by a passerby.

The aristocrats, the professional men, even the shipping agents who were prospering at the turn of the century, usually lived in an ocher-colored *palazzo* with a large porte-cochère, through which carriages could pass into the large courtyard flanked by walls with a simple, almost austere facade. Only the presence of the porte-cochère indicated the many splendid rooms within the *palazzo*.

For both rich and poor, plumbing did not exist until well into the twentieth century. Children defecated and urinated in the streets. At night, urinals and pots were emptied into those same streets. In some villages an area was set aside as a public toilet for children and men. Women or servants brought the accumulation of their masters' waste and dumped it there. In winter, one old miner remembered, the boys trapped canaries that flocked nearby, roasted them over straw and herb twigs, and ate them hungrily. "But that was the time we wiped our asses with a stone," he concluded.

The homes were lit with kerosene lamps, and in the poorer houses one could find lamps as ancient as those found in museums today. Most homes had an oven, though the very poor cooked outside on makeshift stone piles. Fuel was straw and twigs gathered in the fall and winter in bundles called *fasci,* stored in a corner of the floor-level cellar.

Food for the people of these towns and villages was simple, if not Spartan. The staples were lentils, split peas, or fava beans, called *macu,* which were often made into a soup with escarole or wild chicory gathered in the fields. On special occasions some form of pasta might be added. There was an abundance of fruit. Besides oranges, plums, apples, and lemons, there were the fruits that the immigrants would have a nostalgia for: the *ficud'inni* or figs of India (West Indies, that is), i.e., prickly pears. These grew like cactus weeds, cooling in the summer with their resplendent colors of magenta, purple, rose, and yellow hues. There were also *zorbi, zalori, scubali, nespoli,* and melons.

For most southern Italians their sturdy bread was the mainstay. When cutting a new loaf, one would make the sign of the cross on its level side and kiss the knife before cutting into it. One would never set the bread on its rounded side: bread was respected. A good man was said to be as good as "a piece of bread."

The family of modest means, not poor, ate meat twice a year: chicken or a capon for Christmas, a roasted kid for Easter. People were fearful of eating pork and it was avoided except in sausages, when it was carefully bought from the right person at the right time. Cheese, along with sardines and onions, was the staple for field workers and miners. Immigrant mothers in America often admonished their children: "Eat, or you'll have nothing but *pane e cipudda* (bread and onions) for a week." The father might say: "Eat, for one day you will be eaten."

The early immigrants brought simple and frugal eating habits with them. They came with a great hunger; the crowded Italian American stores made to look like an Ali Baba cavern of treasures, the very ceiling hung with cheeses and salami, reflected this memory of hunger. In time they would learn to cook less meager fare in America.

AMUSEMENTS AND ENTERTAINMENTS IN THE LAND THEY LEFT

Women found their entertainment in the narrow streets simply by talking with other women and at the church. Most entertainment for women took place at home: the simple visit *(la visita)*. It was largely the women who maintained, almost institutionalized, *la visita*. Visits ranged in importance. Heading the list was the death visit. When someone died, time was allowed for the immediate family, then the lesser family came, and finally the neighbors and friends arrived at the bereaved home with a black sash at the outer door.* Great friendships and enmities stemmed from this expected visit. Women remembered a friend with "He or she came all the way to the cemetery of Santa Maria when the good soul so-and-so died," or, adversely, "I won't even say hello—when I see them, I turn my face the other way."

There were visits when a child was born or confirmed. There were visits, too, when someone returned from a trip or was going abroad. The women maintained this web of visits. The men tolerated the visits, no doubt because they alleviated an otherwise tedious life. Then, too, this was one of the few occasions when men and women met socially.

The men had the *chiazza* as their entertainment: walking, strolling with friends and cliques. There was a favorite barber shop, a tailor shop with an open storefront where men might gather to chat, listen to stories, or tell stories. Storytelling was an old and cherished tradition. In the time of the great migration, storytellers still came to the village square and told stories of Normans and Saracens, of the Knight *Baiolardu* (Baylord).

Serenading was still practiced at the turn of the century. A group of friends would sing under the window of a woman or young girl. *Carnevale* was an important entertainment: masked men, followed by children, paraded through the streets throwing confetti and sugarcoated almonds to children and women. It was one of the few moments when men could approach women with a certain amount of frankness.

Christmas was celebrated as a communal feast. Musicians, paid by the wealthy, went from one wayside shrine to the next, serenading the newborn Christ. They also performed outside the homes of friends of the patrons. The airs were folk tunes, played on bagpipes, flutes, clarinets, sometimes a mandolin and tambourine.

The truly communal entertainment, however, was the festival dedicated to a town's patron saint or Madonna. This was Fourth of July, Bastille Day, and passion play all rolled into one.

None of the local legends make any mention of God the Father or the Son. To the village worshippers, these figures seemed far less accessible than their local Madonna or patron saint, who could

---

*To this day the black sash is allowed to remain on the door of a mourning household until it is destroyed by the elements.

be dealt with within the boundaries of their own village. To the pragmatic mind of the southerner, the old Sicilian phrase, "Above the king is the vice-roi," makes a great deal of sense: It is always better to deal directly with the one who has power, and local power is recognized as genuine power. Among many male southerners there was still another rationale for bypassing God in favor of the Madonna: the image of a male praying to another male struck them as distasteful.

CHAPTER 4

Saints and Legends to Live By

When Dame Fortune pales
Throw yourself upon the earth
And start collecting snails.

—ITALIAN PROVERB

A truly religious man, a good Neapolitan family man, when his prayers were not answered during a terrible drought, strangled the statue of the saint Gennaro, stamped it under his foot, spitting and cursing, raging. Then he stopped as if nothing had happened, and said, "Now let's see if that has taught you a lesson."

The saints were not always saintly. The following story of St. Paul shows an aspect of him that theologians have overlooked.

During the great persecution of the Christians, when suspected followers of Christ were torn to pieces, fed to lions, burned, and boiled alive, the *sbri,* police spies, were having trouble finding Christians. The head of Rome's spies went to the king of Rome and told him there was a way to recognize them: "They all have beards trimmed in this-and-that manner." A great massacre followed of Christians with beards.

St. Paul was in Rome at the time but knew nothing of all this until a number of bearded Christians came to him. Terrified, they pleaded with him, "You who have read all the books and know everything, you alone can save us. You must also know how to shave us. Shave us, for Christ's sake."

Paul took out his razor and began to hone it, then lathered the soap, sat down before a mirror, and began to shave himself.

The Christians were horrified. "Don't you know we were followed, they may be in the house right now! We'll be torn to pieces. Shave us, for Christ's sake!"

"Eeh," St. Paul said, "it's true that I am a friend of the King, but at times . . . who knows? It is better to be sure. If there is time and your throats are not cut, I'll shave you also. Eeh, true charity begins at home."

In the tradition of ancient Greece, St. Paul then is reduced to the level of a shrewd villager who looks out for himself first and, if there is time, helps his friends.

These stories were told over and over again in the tailor shops and pharmacies, wherever men worked together and children listened. In these almost Sufilike stories the listeners were taught how a truly good man must act. Here is another story they heard:

One day a holy friar had been witness to a murder. Now this friar was such a good and saintly man that even the wildest of animals licked his feet and he in turn, whenever he could, saved them from hunters' bullets. On this day he heard two voices arguing. Then there were shots, an agonizing shout, and he saw a young man of good family galloping away in a fury. He knew the young man. So he went to the victim, closed his eyes, and then resolutely started for the village to denounce the assassin.

On the way he met a rabbit who asked, "Where are you going, holy brother?"

"To town to denounce a murderer."

"Be careful," said the rabbit, "the assassin's family might be the benefactor of your monastery. You will be put on bread and water by the abbot."

"I don't care," the holy brother said and walked on.

"Well, go ahead, you rotten spy," the rabbit shouted after him.

Next he met an old dog for whom the friar had often cared.

"Where are you going in such head-down hurry?" the old dog

asked, all the while licking the holy man's hands and nuzzling up to him.

"To denounce a murderer."

"Oh, destroy the thought, holy brother. Don't you know that he has more gold pieces than you have hair on your head? He will corrupt justice, buy it, and imprison you for false testimony."

"I must do what I must," the brother said.

"Well, go ahead then, rotten spy. The woes will be all yours."

Next he met a lamb who also advised him, "Leave it to God. You can't interfere with His will." And when the brother trudged on, the lamb fled from him.

As he approached the city, he arrived before the gates, on top of which was a statue with a trumpet raised high. The statue guarded the city: whenever an enemy approached, it put the trumpet to its lips and sounded the alarm. As the holy brother approached, the statue moved to blow its trumpet.

"Am I an enemy, that you are about to blow your horn?" the brother asked.

"Oh, why have you come here?" the statue replied. "Why have you not taken the advice of the animals? Know this, you scoundrel, that the young man you want to denounce will in time become a great saint; he will leave all his riches to the poor of God and he will go into the desert to cry day and night for his sins."

The holy brother thought for a long time and in the dusk of the day returned to his convent, saying, "God does not wish me to denounce this man." And all along the way the rabbit, the old dog, and the lamb licked his feet and ran happily along with him.

The good friar in the story, before he was tempted to "denounce the murderer," was as one with nature. He spoke to animals, animals spoke to him. He protected the animals from hunters; they in turn would protect him. He was on nature's side, as one with it—a nature as old as earth itself—and against the unnatural ways of men. Human authority is the source of all evil. It was an old conflict in which St. Francis and the holy friar had chosen nature.

No doubt because of the desire for oneness with nature, death was ever present in the legends and myths of the South, beginning with the story of Persephone. But then there was a good reason for it. Beneath the broiling sun, the calcified, eroded soil, the shouting, strident voices, the bravura of manliness, lies a rock-hard banality:

the will to survive, tested here more often than elsewhere. Ever present Death is bound up with a love of life and a love for those close to one. Like ancient roots holding the soil together, these sentiments united southerners in the harmonious awareness of the realistic immigrant father who told his child, "Eat, for one day you will be eaten."

Oneness with the world did not mean passivity, however. In some villages, the patron saint was elected by plebiscite, and retained his position only as long as he complied with the needs of the villagers. If, as sometimes happened, the saint did not respond to their prayers or was sulky at performing miracles necessary to their survival, the villagers would hold an election and replace him or her with another. Southerners, in their own way, had experience of democracy.

During an eruption of Vesuvius, when its destructive lava stream seemed to be headed directly for Naples, the Neapolitans placed the statue of St. Gennaro, their patron saint, into the stream while they shouted, "You can die, or you can save us!" In response, the saint reputedly raised two more of his fingers (two by tradition were already raised) and performed the miracle which caused the hot lava to change its direction away from the city, toward the sea.

For the peasant, the conventions of religion, history, and even reason were beyond his ken. He responded to life as events presented themselves, with the instincts he had developed in the timeless battle against personal misfortune and society's aggravations. Writing of his life among peasants, Carlo Levi observed that "none of the pioneers of Western Civilization brought here his sense of the passage of time, his deification of the State. . . . No one has come to this land except as an enemy, a conqueror, or a visitor devoid of understanding . . . no message, human or divine, has reached this stubborn poverty." Even Christ, it was said, stopped at Eboli. While the peasant protected himself as best as he could, with the help of the saints, the Madonna, and the Church, he remained for the most part a fatalist, with a hopeless sense of inferiority ground into him by centuries of oppression. Only through nature could he feel a true oneness, an affinity that transcended life itself and made it possible for him to accept natural disasters with the same forbearance that a parent might have for its wayward child.

Norman Douglas, who lived among southern Italians for thirty years, saw the distrust between the gentry and the peasantry. He did not fault the peasants. "Ages of oppression and misrule have passed over their heads," he wrote in *Old Calabria* during the peak period of the southern Italian exodus. "Sun and rain with all their caprice have been kinder friends to them than their earthly masters."

THE POLITICS OF MISERIA

Several decades before the exodus began, while the southern Italians, as subjects of the Kingdom of the Two Sicilies, were still firmly in the grip of Bourbon rule, the dream of America was thriving as a quasi-religious vision of a paradise on earth—a comfort for the *miseria* (misery) of their lot. First inspired by the travels of Columbus, the dream grew into a myth fueled by other travelers: the occasional returning immigrant who gave it substance and shape through stories that became increasingly elaborate and vivid with each retelling. As more Italians returned from the United States, the myth became so Americanized as to incorporate the Statue of Liberty as the Madonna of Liberation, and the American dollar bill as a sacred object to be pinned to the garments of their most cherished religious statues. Adding to the weight of the myth were the legendary deeds of Garibaldi, the apotheosis of Italian heroes, who himself had been an immigrant both in South America and the United States.

As early as 1853, seven years before the North and South of Italy were to be joined into a single nation, the dream of America was poignantly reflected in a petition addressed to the Bourbon Minister of the Interior by the peasants in the Abruzzo village of Vasto. The petition requested that the deforestation then in progress in the area be stopped, since it was seriously interfering with their livelihood and robbing them of firewood. In deferential language the petitioners identified themselves as "His Majesty's faithful subjects," but the final sentence of the document warned that unless the request was granted, "the undersigned and all the other inhabitants of the Abruzzo region will be compelled to emigrate to California."

Travel was restricted to places within the kingdom, and even then required a passport. There was a chronic dearth of roads; of a total of 1,848 villages, 1,621 had no roads at all. The Bourbons attributed the lack to two centuries of Spanish rule, but made little effort to improve the situation. Like the Spanish viceroys, they found it to their advantage to keep communication between villages and provinces at a minimum. In every possible way the southern masses were insulated from developments outside the boundaries of their circumscribed world that might inspire them to disturb the status quo.

In keeping with the policy of enforced ignorance—the darkest legacy of the Spanish and Bourbon rulers—education was denied to most of the population. Schools were few and far between, and reserved for the children of the wealthy.

The Bourbons were not, of course, the first rulers to take advantage of a population accustomed to being exploited. The Romans were among the first to ravage the South. Their destruction of Apulia and Basilicata was so thorough as to wipe out all traces of any previous culture. In Sicily, where Greek civilization had flourished in all its glory for almost eight hundred years before the Roman conquest, the pillage of its magnificent art treasures and wealth by Gaius Verres, the Roman governor in 73 B.C., was so sweeping as to win him immortality as one of the greatest robbers in recorded history. The persistent exploitation of the South eventually produced the legendary rebellion of Spartacus.

Following the demise of the Roman Empire, Italy was overrun by a succession of foreign invaders, among them Lombards, Byzantine Greeks, Arabs, Normans, Catholic Germans, French, and Spaniards, all of whom established permanent settlements which, fusing with the rest of the population, turned Italy into the Western world's first great melting pot.

The Arabs contributed to the development of agriculture. The Normans brought respect for law and justice, which included the establishment of the first Sicilian parliament. Frederick II, the Norman-German who, until he was excommunicated by the Church, reigned as Emperor of the Holy Roman Empire and ruler of Italy, preferred to think of himself as a Sicilian and lived in Palermo. Though he ruled as a despot, he made Sicily the freest state in Europe. His court, an oasis of culture frequented by poets, scientists, and philosophers, reflected his own intellectual pursuits. When he died in 1250 at the age of fifty-six, there was great rejoicing by the papacy and all the other enemies who had come to regard him as "the Antichrist."

Frederick had made Sicily a center of economic and political power unto itself. But the reign of Charles I, which began sixteen years after that of Frederick, marked the beginning of six centuries of "unmitigated decay" throughout the *Mezzogiorno*. If Frederick had made Sicily a significant power center, those who followed him turned Sicily and the rest of the South into a colony to be exploited by rulers with imperial dreams.

The southern poor revolted during the so-called "Sicilian Vespers," a rebellion that broke out in Palermo on Easter Monday in 1282 and quickly spread through the island. The revolt was targeted against the abhorrent reign of the French monarch Charles I, who sixteen years before had been crowned king of Naples and Sicily by the Pope. In a rare manifestation of concerted popular action, the Sicilians massacred nearly every French person on the island.

The darkest period for the South began with the rule of the Spanish dynasty at the start of the sixteenth century. In the next two hundred years the *Mezzogiorno* was subjected to the tyranny of a long succession of notoriously predatory viceroys. There were sixty of them, with an average tenure of less than four years. With only a distant monarch in Madrid to answer to, each viceroy made the most of his short tenure, lining his pockets with *scudi* as rapidly as possible by a variety of iniquitous methods. Corruption became rampant. In exchange for bribes and personal favors, the most affluent members of southern society were exempted from paying taxes as well as from laws uncongenial to their interests. Favored landowners were granted the prerogative of acting as sole judge in any dispute between them and their employees. Heavy tax burdens were sometimes imposed on the poor for the purpose of appropriating their homes and possessions as soon as they fell behind in their payments.

The end of feudalism in 1806 legally freed the peasant from the tyranny of his feudal lord but did little to improve his general welfare. Within the feudal system, the peasant was able to rely on his lord to assume full responsibility for his well-being. Now that he was on his own, he was in worse economic straits than ever before. Lacking land, tools, and animals, he was obliged to revert to the role of hired hand. Poorly paid and in constant debt, working under the scrutiny of armed guards hired to prevent malingering, he became virtually the landowner's chattel.

The last Bourbon monarch to leave his stamp on the Kingdom of the Two Sicilies—as the *Mezzogiorno* was known during the time of his reign, from 1830 to 1859—was Ferdinand II, an epileptic despot with "an innate conviction of his divine right." Early in his career, possibly to show his European peers that his vision went beyond that of feudal overlord, he ordered the construction of a railroad extending between Naples (then the largest city in Italy) and the nearby town of Portici. The railroad was only 15 miles long, but in 1839 it had the distinction of being the first in Italy, at a time when railroads were commonplace in several other European nations.

In those early years of his reign, Ferdinand tried to win popular favor with his subjects through another program of land reform, only to find his effort sabotaged by his own supporters—either officials governing village life or members of the aristocracy with large landholdings who were determined to frustrate any laws and reforms that interfered with their personal interests. Ferdinand's aborted attempts at benign despotism came to a stop during the Sicilian revolt of 1848 when, fearing the loss of Sicily, he ordered the bombardment of Messina—a five-day assault of wholesale destruction that was to earn him the lifelong nickname of "King Bomba."

A few years later the repressive activities of his regime, particularly its infamous treatment of fifteen thousand political prisoners (one of them the father of Alexander Dumas) evoked such outrage in France and Great Britain that both nations, in protest, withdrew their envoys. It provoked William Gladstone, a prime minister not usually given to using extreme language, to denounce the reign of Ferdinand II as "the negation of God erected into a system of government." A more explicit condemnation of the Bourbon regime was expressed in a government report on the prevalence of brigandage throughout the South shortly after the end of Bourbon rule in 1860. The report charged the Bourbons with having corrupted the southern masses by undermining their faith in justice. Giuseppe Massara wrote that "The executioner's axe and the hangman's rope were neither the major nor the cruelest instruments of torture used by the Bourbons. With might and main they set about committing the most nefarious of parricides, namely, that of destroying in an entire people any notion of right and wrong." The Massara report concluded that "the greatest ill afflicting the southern populations is their lack of faith in legality and justice."

Long after Italy had become a nation, social disorder, rampant suspicions, and irreconcilable conflicts continued to plague the South.

Too demoralized to strike out against the upper classes, except with occasional spontaneous revolts that were easily crushed, the peasantry fell into the habit of turning against one another instead, thereby enacting a peasant caste system as rigid and heartless as the one imposed on them by the gentry. At the bottom of the social scale were the peasant servants in the employ of the gentry. Only slightly above them were the *giornalieri*, the day laborers, who constituted the bulk of the peasantry. Above them were the *contadini*, farmers who, unlike the *giornalieri*, owned a piece of land, however small, as well as a house and donkey.

Writing of the peasantry of his native village in the Abruzzo, Ignazio Silone classified both of them together in the lowest of social categories.

"God," he wrote, "is at the head of everything. He commands everything. Everybody knows that."

> Then comes Prince Torlonia, ruler of the earth.
> Then come his guards.
> Then come his guards' dogs
> Then nothing.
> Then more nothing.
> Then come the peasants.
> That's all.

Unlike the peasantry, the storekeepers and artisans—mason, blacksmith, shoemaker, tailor, barber, and others engaged in performing community services requiring skill—commanded the respect of all classes. The artisan with superior skills was the most respected and was usually addressed as *mastro*. Each trade had its *mastri*—artisans who received the most important commissions and presided over the apprenticeship of young boys fortunate enough to be selected by them. Notwithstanding occasional marriages between a member of an artisan family and a peasant one, there usually was little social interaction between them. The artisans were resented by the peasants for their alleged snobbery toward those who tilled the soil; and because artisans were generally less conservative than themselves, peasants tended to be wary of them as a matter of prudence.

This was particularly true during the early decades of the Italian nation, when the artisans were among the first to take advantage of the educational benefits offered by the new regime, and among the earliest of the emigrants to join the exodus to America.

Conditioned by centuries of feudalism to pay homage to the king, princes, dukes, and barons who, until recently, had the power of life and death over them, the peasantry for the most part remained staunch supporters of the monarchy, whether that of the Bourbons or, later, of the House of Savoy. From time immemorial they had clung to the belief that kings and divinity were virtually synonymous. "For God and the King" was the popular slogan they shouted even while rioting against gross injustices enacted against them with the approval of their king. Yet for all the superstition, ignorance, and ultraconservatism attributable to the peasant, he was by no means the simple and tractable individual so often depicted in romantic writing. His shrewdness and his insights into the human comedy have impressed many a sage. Despite his confusion and his awe about the superiority of the upper classes, the peasant never lost sight of two factors humankind would eternally have in common despite all other differences between classes: the smell of excrement, and death. But then, as Michelet tells us, "A person who knows how to live with poverty knows everything."

The ancestral proverbs and legends encapsulated the only kind of teaching a peasant would be likely to receive, and would incorporate all the wisdom presumably required to cope with the world outside the family. Underlying their education was the concept of being at one with all of nature, and with all the saints who might come to one's assistance when in need. In these stories animals speak and give advice, and saints are personified as members of the human race living in the actual world of the peasant.

EARTHLY MASTERS

Their earthly masters, known as *galantuomini* (the gentry), included nearly everyone who was not a peasant, fisherman, or artisan. Members of the gentry did no manual labor and could easily be identified since they customarily wore *cappeddi* or hats instead of caps, the headgear of lower-class males. To rebellious peasants, these *cappeddi* were a symbol of oppression.

The absence of a numerically significant middle class was caused by the general lack of medium-sized properties; there were either large estates *(latifundi)* or small landholdings, often not large enough to yield a livelihood for a single family. At times these parcels were so small they were said to be "pulverized."

The gentry, especially the large landowners and *padrone,* dealt with members of the lower class as they would with servants and, by custom, expected all the outward displays of subservience, including in some regions kissing the hand of the *padrone* by way of greeting. If he did not kiss the hand, he certainly had to pronounce the greeting, *"Vosia, sa benadica* (Bless me, your Honor)." The line of demarcation between classes was maintained as if time had passed by these towns and villages; the spirit and nature of feudal times lingered in the hollows and valleys of the countryside and in the minds of men and women.

By the time the Bourbon era came to a close, the number of aristocratic landlords who still presided over their estates had drastically declined, as had their prestige as men of culture. A typical nobleman during the early years of Italian unification, according to the British consul in Palermo, was "a half-educated person whose schooling, coming to an end at the age of sixteen, failed to prepare him for anything more than an idle life of enforced leisure. Prevented by class prejudice from entering the army or navy," the consul added, "he learns neither to command nor obey."

Absentee ownership further exacerbated the situation and had a profoundly damaging effect on agriculture productivity. By 1900, 65 percent of all the acreage in Italy was the property of land barons, whose estates varied in size from 3,000 to 18,000 acres. The largest of the estates were in the *Mezzogiorno.* The overseers were generally ignorant of farming techniques and either indifferent to the welfare of the soil or knew nothing of crop rotation and soil conservation. The main concern—one that was adopted by the peasants who tilled the fields for them—was to take as much from the soil as possible in the shortest length of time. In the absence of the lords, the overseers had but one purpose: "to enrich themselves as quickly as possible at the expense of the noble and the peasant both. All considerations of human regard, justice or charity were largely irrelevant."

More prevalent in Sicily, absentee landlordism spawned a class of notorious overseers known as *gabelloti.* Their rapid rise in society paralleled that of *mafiosi* (the word described a temperament—tough, fiery; a woman of a feisty nature would be called a *mafiosa*), whose services they frequently employed to collect unpaid rents or to intimidate sharecroppers into accepting unfair contracts.

Taking advantage of the absentee landlord's casual attitude toward his estate, the *gabelloto* would occasionally employ the *mafioso*'s powers of intimidation against the proprietor himself, in order to lease his estate on his own terms. It was not unusual for *gabelloti*, who had once been landless peasants, to become wealthier than the nobles they purportedly served.

The peasant's condition is well expressed in a Calabrian fable about a rabbit and a fox who agree to cultivate a farm together. When it was time to sow, the fox proposed to the rabbit: "Why don't you sow and when the time comes to I'll hoe." When it came time to hoe, the fox said, "If you will hoe, I'll reap." The rabbit hoed and later found himself gathering the harvest, at which point the fox said, "Now, partner, we are ready to divide the crop. You take the straw and I'll take the wheat." When the rabbit protested, the fox promptly ate him.

The most ruthless of the landowners were likely to be former overseers who were once landless peasants. Not content with the wealth and power that came with ownership of extensive acres, the more ambitious of them maneuvered to obtain public office in their village, which they could then staff with friends and relatives.

Silone left vivid descriptions of life in those villages he knew so well: "The life of the men, the beasts and the land seemed fixed in the inflexible circle, hemmed in by the position of the mountains and the passage of time, as if condemned by nature to life imprisonment." He describes the "prison" as

A hundred little huts almost on the same level—irregular, un-formed, blackened by time and worn down by wind, rain and fire, with their roofs poorly covered by all sorts of tiles and scrap lumber. Most of these hovels have only one opening which serves as a door, window and chimney. In the interiors, which seldom possess a floor, the men, women and children, and their goats, chickens, pigs and donkeys live, sleep, eat and reproduce, sometimes in the same corner.

Such conditions were to be responsible for peasant rebellions and the great rebellion of the *Fasci* in Sicily in 1890,* which after being crushed by the armies of the North triggered the great exodus at the turn of the century.

Until the fever of emigration virtually evacuated entire villages,

*This movement should not be confused with Mussolini's fascism, although an argument can be made that he did resurrect and distort the word *Fasci* from his own Socialist past.

the peasantry had only two routes of escape from the rigid, self-confined atmosphere prevalent in the rural districts of the *Mezzogiorno*. One was the priesthood, which offered a free education, social prestige, and the possibility of moving beyond the village. A second, more popular route was brigandage.

This was the land to which Garibaldi came with the intention of liberating and uniting it in the name of humanity and democracy.

CHAPTER 5

Italian Unity and the Southern Exodus

Without a country you are the the bastards of humanity.

—Mazzini

RISORGIMENTO

The Congress of Vienna in 1814–15 divided Italy into eight principalities under Austrian, Bourbon, and papal rule, with the intention of squelching whatever hopes of liberation and unification had been inspired among Italians by the French presence and liberal reforms. Only Piedmont and Sardinia, which the House of Savoy had lost temporarily to Napoleon, were permitted to survive as Italian regions independent of foreign rule.

Four men, all born in the northern region of Piedmont in the early years of the nineteenth century, were mainly responsible for Italy's unity: Giuseppe Mazzini, the philosopher and evangelical activist of the *Risorgimento;* King Victor Emmanuel II of the House of Savoy; Count Camillo Benso di Cavour, Piedmont's prime minister and administrator of the *Risorgimento;* and Giuseppe Garibaldi, the hero-adventurer and the only one of the four whose name remained vivid in the minds of many an emigrant long after he or she had settled in America.

Mazzini, the oldest of the four, was born in Genoa in 1805 but spent most of his adult life in exile, chiefly in London. As the pioneering leader of the *Risorgimento* his messianic voice attracted thousands of rebellious youths, mostly from middle-class families, to the cause of Italian unity. He convinced them that his cause—the unification of Italy—was nothing less than a religious mission ordained by God for which they must, if need be, give their lives. While appealing to their souls, he attacked the Catholic Church for its materialistic application of Christianity. He was a revolutionary, never a diplomat. "Without a country you are the bastards of humanity," he warned as he pursued his dream of Italian unity.

Mazzini's political aspirations for a genuine Republic of Italy—not one aligned to any monarchy—were interwoven with his vision of a United States of Europe, with Italy providing exemplary moral leadership. His gospel inspired disciples throughout Europe no less than his role as a revolutionary activist, causing Metternich to pronounce him "the most dangerous man in Europe." And he added: "I have united armies which fought bravely though made up of different races; I have reconciled kings and emperors and sultans; but nothing and no one has created greater difficulties for me than a devil of an Italian—thin, pale, poor, and as eloquent as a hurricane, as able as a thief, as indefatigable as a lover—in short Mazzini."

Yet it was Garibaldi, the idealistic hero-adventurer, who won the hearts of the future emigrants as none of the other *Risorgimento* leaders could. Pictures of him as the liberator of southern Italy hung in their American homes like icons.

Simplicity was one of Garibaldi's outstanding traits, but his was a complex personality, which baffled friends and enemies. He was beloved by millions of Europeans mainly because of his democratic attitude toward persons of all stations; yet he implicitly believed that a dictatorship—with benign motives—was the most effective means of imposing constructive social reforms on a people. "Sometimes," he was quoted as saying, "you have to force liberty on people for their own good." He was generally considered the most compassionate of men, one whose sensibilities could be "set in vibration by the slightest stimulus"; yet on the battlefield his favorite method of fighting was hand-to-hand bayonet combat. His talent as a general for improvising shrewd and successful tactics that defied all conventional rules of military strategy made him one of the most brilliant masters of guerrilla warfare. Yet there is ample evidence to indicate that he could be duped repeatedly by political leaders who exploited his idealistic nature for their unidealistic ends. This, too, endeared him to the poor of the South.

The "poet in action" was born in Nice, then part of Piedmont, on July 4, 1807. His father, like his grandfather, was a seaman engaged in the coastal shipping service. His mother was a devout Catholic who wanted Giuseppe to acquire an education, but at the age of fifteen he chose to leave school and work as a cabin boy on a Russian ship bound for Odessa. Ten years later he earned a master's certificate as a sea captain.

In his Mazzinian fervor young Garibaldi enlisted in the Piedmont Navy as a first-class sailor in order to participate in an insurrection against the navy planned by the National Society. The revolt proved to be a fiasco, and Garibaldi barely escaped being arrested and executed on a charge of high treason by running off to Brazil, to which entire villages along the Genovese coastline had been migrating.

At first Garibaldi tried to earn his living as a trader, plying a small boat up and down the Brazilian coast with stocks of sugar, brandy, and flour. Other Italian immigrants similarly occupied were becoming wealthy, but Garibaldi had too little business sense, too much faith in the honesty of his customers, and too little interest in money.

On learning that the southern Brazilian province of Rio Grande do Sud was waging a war for its independence, he quit his trade and became a member of its tiny navy. With a boat entitled *Mazzini*, he and a small crew of Italians operated as daredevils, high-minded pirates, disrupting Brazilian shipping, attacking and sometimes capturing enemy vessels. In the skirmishes, Garibaldi freed all the Negro slaves he encountered, one of whom was to become a comrade-in-arms until he was killed during the 1849 siege of the Roman Republic.

After fourteen years of wandering in the Latin American world as a warrior for freedom, Garibaldi returned to Italy in 1848, summoned by Mazzini, who had succeeded in setting up the Republic of Rome and needed Garibaldi's military assistance to fight off the armies that had come to regain Rome for the Pope. In the spring and summer of 1848 Garibaldi managed with a ragtag army to defend the republic, but the arrival of superior French forces spelled defeat.

After a valiant battle that could not be won, he calmly began a retreat in which most of his five thousand men were killed or captured. Barely managing to escape his pursuers, he was forced into exile once again, this time to Staten Island, where he led the life of an impoverished immigrant working as a candlemaker.

After nine lugubrious months Garibaldi left Staten Island for Peru, becoming skipper of a three-masted cargo ship that roamed the seas. He returned to the United States three years later, but only long enough to assume command of another cargo ship, the *Commonwealth,* property of a wealthy Italian American. A few voyages later he gave up the sea: Prime Minister Cavour had finally granted him permission to return to Piedmont, with the understanding that he was to abstain from political activities.

Within a few years, impatient with the military and diplomatic efforts of Cavour, Garibaldi mounted his invasion of southern Italy by way of Sicily. He resigned his commission as general in the Piedmont Army and called for "a million rifles and men." All he could muster, however, were a thousand who, lacking uniforms, wore simple red shirts and set sail for Sicily. In a surprisingly short time, with the help of three thousand native Sicilian recruits, they defeated the Bourbon forces.

Many in Sicily saw this as the beginning of a new era and an opportunity to seek revenge on their oppressors. In the town of Bronte, in the northeast corner of Sicily, insurgents took a terrible vengeance: men were massacred, their bodies torn apart and burned in public. In other towns, the gentry were hunted down and killed to the cries of *"Li cappeddi*—the hats. Kill them all!"

The violence and the slogans reflected the total misunderstanding and ignorance that existed between North and South. Clearly, neither Garibaldi nor Cavour—and certainly not the king—understood the deep hatred the peasantry had for their masters. In effect, the well-to-do northern leaders believed they were making a revolution for the poor of the South, when in reality they were making it for themselves.

Most of Garibaldi's volunteers, like Garibaldi himself, were northerners who knew little or nothing about the lives of the people they invaded. Nor did many southerners know anything about the North; some actually thought that *Italia* was the name of a northern king's daughter. Within these two perceptions lay seeds of ignorance and dissent that presaged the North's future exploitation of the

South, and the south's rebellion against the North—first in the form of violence, and later by simply leaving for America.

Garibaldi's response to the uprising was to inflict prompt and severe punishment as an example to Sicilians in other towns who might be tempted to take the law into their own hands. Nino Bixio, his notoriously hotheaded lieutenant, arrived in Bronte with a column of soldiers that imposed a series of harsh retributive measures, including the summary execution of half a dozen of the insurgent ringleaders, as well as the threat to shoot any villagers who failed to surrender their swords and muskets within three hours. The brutal repression prompted a newspaper in England to comment that "No savages in the most barbarous parts of Africa ever treated their prisoners with more summary violence than the Piedmontese troops have in Southern Italy."

Garibaldi could only follow the example of northern liberals, who endlessly analyzed the problems of the South, proposing solutions that resolved nothing and served their own interests. No wonder Marx took this occasion to write in the *New York Tribune* in May 1860: "In all human history no country or no people have suffered such terrible slavery, conquest and foreign oppression and no country and no people have struggled so strenuously for their emancipation as Sicily and the Sicilians."

As for the mass of Sicilians who had accepted Garibaldi as their liberator, they generally assumed that the end of Bourbon tyranny would improve their economic and social situation in some measure. About Piedmont they knew nothing. The only Piedmontese some of them had seen were the soldiers in Garibaldi's entourage who, like Garibaldi himself, spoke a language they could barely understand. The name of Cavour, who would have more to say about their future than anyone else, was unknown to them.

Between the layers of truth, half-truth, and fantasy glowed the single vision that Garibaldi and the little people had in common—liberation, the driving force in Garibaldi's own life, and the yearning that was to precipitate the mass migration of millions of Italians seeking to free themselves from the economic misery that continued to scourge the poor after unification. When, at the outset, their hopes were dashed by the new government in Turin, which struck them as worse than the Bourbon one, Garibaldi began to emerge in their thoughts as the hero who had fought valiantly to be their saviour but was crucified by the very same authorities who were now trying to crucify them.

Throughout Italy, but especially in the South, the legend of Garibaldi the liberator inevitably became woven into the myth of America—that paradisiacal land, rich enough to liberate impoverished Italians from their centuries-old *miseria*.

COUNTERREVOLUTION

In his autobiography, Garibaldi glumly acknowledged that his conquest of the Bourbon South received little support from the millions of Italians it was intended to benefit. Only in Sicily and Calabria had he encountered any marked enthusiasm for his cause; yet even there it had not developed into any substantial revolutionary action once he and his volunteers had come and gone. He observed that the same was true in the northern provinces; only for a brief period had their *popolino* regarded the armies of Piedmont as liberators. As a disappointed revolutionary, Garibaldi was inclined to blame the Church for the generally passive attitude of the poor during the campaign for unification. "This stalwart and laborious class," he wrote of the peasantry, "belongs to the priests, who make it their business to keep it in ignorance."

Garibaldi's propensity for simplistic conclusions failed to consider the more specific cause for the peasantry's passivity: their inability to feel any connection with the concept of Italy after so many centuries of foreign rule. Especially in the South, the general lack of a national consciousness was to impede the process of Italian unification for the greater part of the remaining century. History indicated that European peasantry in general would drag its heels in being forced into a new age. The southern peasantry of Italy was no exception.*

In 1861, the imposition of the 1848 Piedmont constitution on all regions of the nation without regard to their individual institutions and problems generated deep hostility throughout the *Mezzogiorno*. When the southerners had voted overwhelmingly in favor of annexa-

---

*In many ways it was the same problem that confronted the Parisian revolutionaries of 1792–93, who attempted to impose reforms and conscription upon the peasants of Brittany. There, too, counterrevolutionary rebellion broke out in La Vendée.

tion, they fully expected to be granted some form of regional government; but once the voting was over, it became apparent that the ministers and parliament in Turin had no intention of sharing their authority with any of the regions. No sooner had the Turin government begun to issue decrees imposing new taxes and military conscription than the southerners began transferring their old hatred of the Bourbons to the new rulers.

The troubles between North and South began almost as soon as unification became formalized in 1861. A few months earlier there had been intensive rebel activity in the Neapolitan sector. The Turin government, in its determination to demonstrate to foreign nations its ability to exert control, dispatched an army unit to the scene with orders to shoot down every person bearing a weapon. When rebellion broke out in Sicily, the general sent to put down the rebels reported that "soldiers had been crucified, policemen burnt alive, and the flesh of *carabiniere* was sold in the marketplace." This of course gave official endorsement to a series of allegations that the general himself "later admitted to be no more than gossip." Nonetheless, "Sicily was now branded as a region of cannibalism." The government troops moved by such "gossip" were no less vengeful. Whole villages were burned to the ground on the mere suspicion that they might be providing food and shelter for rebels; and any insult to the national flag or to a portrait of King Victor Emmanuel was considered reason enough to shoot the perpetrator. Over two thousand people, including some women, were arrested in Palermo alone, and summary executions took place in Alcamo, Racalmuto, and elsewhere. The military commander issued instructions that anyone of military age, or with the "face of an assassin," should be arrested.

From the widespread rebellions that began erupting throughout the South, it soon became clear that the *popolino* wanted no part of the Turin government. The extent and violence of the rebellions prompted Massimo D'Azeglio, a former prime minister of Piedmont, to write in August 1861: "At Naples we overthrew a sovereign in order to set up a government based on universal suffrage. And yet we still need today sixty battalions of our soldiers to hold the people down, or even more since these are not enough. One must therefore conclude that there was some mistake about the plebiscite." With an ingenuousness rare in a politician, D'Azeglio added: "We must ask the Neapolitans—the people of the *Mezzogiorno*—once again whether they want Piedmont or not." It seemed to him that "unification was a process of making Italians dislike one another . . . it was like going to bed with someone with smallpox."

The rebellions, which raged throughout the South for the next five years, requiring at one point the services of half the Italian Army, suggested that a second referendum might well have spelled the end of the Italian nation and the restoration of the Bourbon monarchy. It was disorganized civil and class warfare on a large scale, but fought in guerrilla style, an expression of blind and suicidal hatred led by the only heroes the peasantry traditionally admired—brigands, whose deeds of violence and defiance, financed by the Papacy and the deposed Bourbon monarchy, reflected their own feelings against a society that had long held them in bondage.

Many of the peasants were driven to join the brigand-led bands, at least on a part-time basis, to keep their families from starving; but *brigandaggio,* as it was euphemistically branded, also became a visceral response to forces that were pressing them beyond the limits of their patience. Wondering why so many of the southern poor were attracted to it, a parliamentary report of 1863 pointed out that the peasantry respected and emulated the brigand, "not as the thief, assassin, the man of sack and rapine, but as the person whose own powers sufficed to get for himself and for others the justice which the law fails to give."

Five years of political brigandage were the first major manifestation of southern protest against the new regime. There were to be others, including the final and most emphatic protest of all—the mass exodus of millions of Italians in forthcoming generations who were no longer able to tolerate the economic and political inequities decreed by the new government in the name of progress and social justice.

That there was no political brigandage in Sicily during the five years when it was so prevalent in the other southern regions was not surprising. Unlike the rest of the South, Sicily had repeatedly revolted against Bourbon rule during the nineteenth century in its effort to achieve independence, only to be frustrated by the military power of the Bourbons. The bombings of Palermo and Messina, for example, were so ruthless as to remain indelible in the memory of the people. The intense enthusiasm with which the Sicilians had cooperated with Garibaldi's invasion in 1860 was a measure of the animosity they had long harbored toward the Bourbon rulers; such virulent hostility ruled out the possibility of their fighting under the Bourbon banner for the restoration of its throne.

On the other hand, the great majority of Sicilians had no love for the Turin government, with its new set of rulers and unpopular edicts. Still smarting from the realization that the autonomy they had expected when voting for annexation had been denied them, the Sicilian reaction was to encourage widespread criticism and disregard for the edicts being imposed on them by the new regime. Crime and corruption flourished as they never had before. The same bandit bands and mafia groups that had supported Garibaldi's liberation campaign now became involved in a wide variety of criminal activity, often with the collaboration of corruptible administrative officials from the North.

According to Raleigh Trevelyan, "Smuggling was everywhere, often with the connivance of custom officials. Prisons were a scandal. The very way the tax system was administered bred graft, corruption and terrorism. Life became cheaper than ever; in two years there were 1500 murders in Palermo alone." During the reign of the Bourbons, the police had held a monopoly on crime. Under the "constitutional liberty" introduced by the Turin regime, crime became the monopoly of criminal groups, especially *mafiosi* from every segment of society. With mafia assistance, the Sicilian gentry were quick to adjust to the challenge of being governed by the *forestieri* from the North. They soon learned that these officials were easier to manipulate than their Bourbon predecessors and no less susceptible to corruption. For the first time in the island's history the gentry had to contend with elections, but they found that these presented no serious problem. The deputies representing them in the Turin parliament were quite willing to entrust management of local affairs to influential members of the gentry in exchange for their electoral support. That was easily provided. With only slightly more than 1 percent of the population eligible to vote, rigging elections to favor those already in power became a common practice.*

The landed gentry, in particular, emerged with far more authority than had been permitted when the Bourbons were in charge; and

---

*Norman Lewis in *The Honored Society* cites a famous case at the communal elections of Villalba in 1881: "The Marquis of Villalba, who was in league with the mafia, took his precautions ten days beforehand. Some 218 citizens were qualified to vote, so he locked them all into a granary, releasing eight at a time so that they could be conducted to the polls under armed escort. He was elected."

they made the most of it. Working closely with the police and the underworld, they frequently gained full control of local governments in a system not much different from the political boss system in the United States. They could practice nepotism on an unprecedented scale, punish their enemies, obtain exemptions from taxation as well as from military conscription for themselves and their supporters, and misdirect funds appropriated for charitable purposes. They could also ignore edicts from Turin which they judged to be contrary to their interests, most notably the new law that made elementary school education compulsory throughout Italy. Local authorities, who saw no point in educating the children of the poor, were known to circumvent the law by the simple expedient of not building the public schools needed for compliance. The funds appropriated for constructing the schools were used for their own unauthorized purposes.

Despite the best intentions of the new rulers to provide liberal reforms that would ameliorate the conditions of the poor, their situation became worse than it had been under the Bourbons. At least then, in the tradition of the feudal era, the ruling elite had treated them with a certain degree of paternalism. There was nothing paternalistic about the treatment the Sicilians received from the new authorities in the form of edicts that reduced rather than increased their ability to survive economically. Some of the peasantry who had been considered too poor to be taxed in Bourbon times were now having to pay taxes for the first time. Indeed, the new taxes pointedly discriminated against them. Mules, for example, which were essential to the lowly farm worker, were subject to taxation; but cows, nearly always the property of affluent landowners, were not.

Of all the edicts imposed by the Italian constitution, none antagonized the Sicilians and other southerners more than the conscription law, which mandated seven years of armed services duty.

Although of brief duration, the rebellion and the methods used to repress it left the southern masses and artisans with "a profound sense of disenchantment over the character of the 'new Italy.' " In Sicily the disenchantment deepened when the Turin government, alarmed by the population's continued disregard for legitimate authority, planted an army of occupation in its midst for the next ten years. For the islanders this served as a constant bitter reminder that they were expected to behave as subserviently as usual. The presence of the army prevented any further rebellions for the moment; but it did not stop the populace from disregarding and disobeying on a massive scale any government edicts they disliked. In this atmosphere of exacerbated tensions, the Sicilians' inclination to circumvent governmental authority when in need of assistance (and to rely instead on friends, relatives, and friends of friends) became, more than ever, an instilled habit.

Self-help and mutual aid *(mutuo-soccorso)* societies proliferated. Government agents, with their broad definition of crimes against the state as "any form of behavior that ultimately threatened or diminished the authority of the state," confused these societies with criminal agencies. In their paranoia, the agents began for the first time using the term "mafia" in reports to Turin to summarize any group activity that seemed to impinge on the state's monopoly of authority.

The imprecise use of the term had its amusing side. In 1874, when the government was preparing for "a war on the mafia," and prefects of each Sicilian province were requested to submit a list of *mafiosi* in their province, the prefect of the province of Girgenti responded that to comply with the request would mean listing all of Girgenti's male population between the ages of seventeen and seventy. Similar responses from the other precincts led to the government's decision to call off its "war."

The unpopularity of the regime during those turbulent early decades was expressed by a single phrase, which entered the everyday litany of Italian maledictions all the way from the Alps to Sicily: *ladro governo* (thief of a government). But it was in the *Mezzogiorno,* where poverty and misgovernment were most deeply experienced, that the government was most despised and defied. By the time the southerners began leaving their native provinces in great numbers, their distrust of all politicians had festered into a deep-seated conviction, which they carried with them wherever they settled.

In September 1870, Rome, suddenly and with only token resistance from a contingent of Papal guards, became part of the Kingdom of Italy, and the unification of the nation was finally completed.

In the *Mezzogiorno,* where the daily life of the people was inextricably bound with the rituals and strictures of the Church, the state's anticlerical policies were still another indication that its leadership had little regard for the feelings and needs of the poor, and therefore lacked true legitimacy. The state's apparent indifference to the spiritual welfare of the southern masses evolved into one more reason for seriously considering emigration.

PART THREE

Emigration Fever

CHAPTER 6

To Leave or Not to Leave

In the 1860s it was generally assumed that Italians by nature were "as attached to their soil as an oyster to its rock." Italians were not the only ones who clung to that belief. William Dean Howells, who became the first American consul to Venice in the 1860s, explained in *Venetian Life* (1866) that Italians were "a home-loving people," hardly the sort to abandon their native land for foreign shores. Throughout his travels in Italy he had not noted "any perceptible movement of group emigration." He was pleased to report that he had seen only one advertisement promoting emigration, a poster for a German steamship company in a small town bearing the unfortunate name of "Colica." After returning to America, Howell emerged as one of America's foremost novelists and social critics. By the time he died in 1920 at the age of eighty-three, more than 4.5 million Italians had entered the country.

Southern Italians, in particular, were believed to be irrevocably rooted to their native soil. The reports of northern government officials stationed throughout the *Mezzogiorno* confirmed the general impression of their superiors, notwithstanding the peasant revolts against the regime in the 1860s, that the southerners were an apathetic lot, hopelessly fatalistic, hardly the sort to stray from what they conceived as their preordained way of life. The Sicilians, who were to be the most numerous of the Italian American immigrants, were regarded as the least enterprising southerners of all by their masters. "Sleep, my dear Chevalley, sleep is what the Sicilians want," says the Prince in Lampedusa's novel *The Leopard* to an emissary from the North. "They will always hate anyone who tries to wake them, even in order to bring them the most wonderful gifts."

One of the "wonderful gifts" the new regime had bestowed on all Italians, except those due to be drafted for military service, was the constitutional right to travel whenever and wherever they pleased.

Yet for all the birth pangs the nation had experienced during most of the 1860s, there was little suggestion that Italians in general had any intention of leaving the country. In northern Italy seasonal migrants customarily supplemented their earnings by gaining temporary employment in the mines, building trades, and industries in France, Switzerland, and Germany. There were also some refugees from the law, as well as would-be Marco Polos who ventured as far as North and South America. But even including the internal migration of Italian farm workers during the planting and harvesting season, the total number of wanderers was too small to change the image of Italians as a people too deeply rooted in their native land to leave it for foreign parts.

The first indication that this stereotype might be inaccurate came on the eve of King Victor Emmanuel's announcement that Italian unification was complete. In the fall of 1870, a member of the Chamber of Deputies, Ercole Lualdi of Lombardy, sounded the alarm that Italians were beginning to leave the country in substantial numbers, "not only from the arid zone of the South but also from the fertile regions of Lombardy and Emilia in the North." An increasing number of Italians were gathering at the port of Genoa to embark for foreign destinations. "Do not delude yourselves into thinking that these people are leaving in search of riches," Lualdi warned his colleagues. Survival was their chief motivation. "They are leaving in tears, cursing the government and the *signori.*"

In his own district, Lualdi reported, several towns had already lost half their population through emigration, including many fourteen- and fifteen-year-old males who were shipping abroad in order to avoid military service. "If emigration continues at this rate, Italy will not have enough workers to develop its industries." Lualdi demanded an official inquiry into the root causes of emigration, arguing that "a nation which cannot provide its working classes with a liveli-hood seriously damages its reputation." His demand was ignored—the first of several to suffer the same fate. Too many other issues, seemingly more pressing and more likely to damage the nation, were worrying the Chamber.

Three years later a louder alarm, prompted by a sharp accelera-tion of emigration, was voiced by a southern deputy. Addressing himself directly to the prime minister, Gugliemo Tocci of Calabria characterized emigration as "our lifeblood, which is denying our people nutrition." He did not stop there. "I warn you that if the State doesn't deal with the situation, posterity will curse you." With the professional optimism common to heads of states, the prime minister responded that emigration was "a sign of vigor and energy that could enrich, not impoverish the nation"; he was confident that Italy's free enterprise system would produce the necessary prosperity to create sufficient employment for the working classes.

The decade of the 1870s was a portent of what was to follow. In the metaphorical view of Grazia Dore, it became increasingly clear that "the Italian rural world, formerly like a frozen immobile stream on which time had designed bizarre encrustations of archaic customs and magic rites, survivors of the death of the culture that had created them, was beginning to manifest deep breaks and to flow, slowly at first, then more impetuously, in unprecedented directions." This "flow" began from the mountaintop villages, an internal migration with a logic all its own. Statistics documented the metaphor. At the end of the 1870s, an annual average of 117,596 Italians, chiefly farm workers, emigrated to other nations. By the end of the century more than 5.3 million Italians of all ages had emigrated, nearly half a million more than Italy's population growth up to that point.

As emigration accelerated, parliamentary polemics became more heated, soon expanding into a national debate that questioned the state's economic policies. One of the sharpest critics was the disillu-sioned Garibaldi, who, a year before his death in 1882, lamented, "It is a different Italy than I had dreamed of all my life, not this misera-ble, poverty-stricken, humiliated Italy we see now, governed by the dregs of the nation." Characterizing emigration as a "significant evil," he deplored the disaffection of the peasants from their mother country and attributed it to the nation's failure to produce enough grain to feed its people.

Some of Garibaldi's worst enemies, among them the landowners, agreed with him. Speaking for the landed gentry, chambers of commerce in both the North and the South complained that the "emigration fever" had become so intense that in numerous areas the lands remained uncultivated for lack of available workers. They demanded that all emigration be halted. And they found other manifestations of the fever disquieting, not least the psychological effect on those workers who were not yet afflicted. The chambers reported that farm workers had become "unwilling to work, insubordinate, and more demanding." When authorities delayed their passports, a group of workers in Lombardy, one of the nation's most prosperous agricultural regions, set fire to dairy farms, all the while yelling, "To America! To America!"

"Oh sirs," declaimed a member of the Chamber of Deputies from Venetia who had called emigration "an immoral disease," "should we not make a law to prevent emigration to other countries? I believe we should." In response to the cries of "No, No" from colleagues who held that restricting emigration would be an infringement of constitutional rights, the deputy argued that emigration was not a spontaneous phenomenon, but was created artificially by agents of overseas nations, steamship and recruiting agents among them, luring Italians to foreign shores with false promises. This contention was repeatedly rebutted by others who maintained that it was too simplistic to blame emigration solely on the effective salesmanship of agents acting in behalf of foreign interests. The real causes of increasing emigration, they insisted, were the intolerable conditions governing the lives of agricultural workers and the failure of the state to intercede in their behalf.

When opponents of emigration failed to enact legislation that would place it under government control, they redoubled their attempts to frighten prospective emigrants from leaving the country. In the Chamber of Deputies, Pasquale Antinibon produced a sheaf of letters from emigrants in America who described the horrors of trying to survive away from home. "I am nailed to the cross," began one letter. "Of the 100 *paesani* who came here, only 40 of us have survived. And who is there to protect us? We have neither priests nor *carabinieri* to look after our safety. The *signori* in Italy treat us badly, but we were better off in Italy."

"Instead of finding a terrestrial paradise," Antinibon told his colleagues, "they found anguish, ill health and hunger." From another letter he read: "There isn't a single priest available to attend to the last rites of our dead. We are worse off than dogs attached to chains. You can tell our former *padrone* that we would be happier in Italy living in a pigpen than living here in America in some palace."

The *Rassegna Nazionale,* a conservative Catholic periodical, published a dramatic litany of the ordeals that befell the emigrants. Men, women, and children were commonly treated like baggage during their voyage, placed in hulls of ships where they sometimes died of suffocation. Others were assaulted and drowned by criminally minded sailors, or afflicted with incurable diseases. Nor were the survivors spared misfortune. Their most frequent fate was to be entrapped in forced labor camps, far from the protection of Italian consular authorities, and reduced to virtual slavery. Argentina and Brazil were most often cited as the settings for such servitude, but the United States was also considered guilty.

Labor recruiters and steamship agents were described as "merchants of human flesh." The unscrupulous agent could easily impress a poor peasant by telling him there was a way out of his backbreaking work, which left him hungry if not starving.

If the peasant said, "Unfortunately, there is no solution . . ." the agent would tell him, "Ah, but there is! I know exactly what you must do." Then he would tell the "credulous soul" of a far-off paradise that awaited him, of a friendly people who would welcome him into the land of his dreams.

The man selling the idea of America may have been an agent of a navigation company drumming up transoceanic ticket sales, or the recruiting agent of a *padrone* in the business of supplying unskilled laborers for American landowners or managers of mines, railroads, or factories. There were several types of *padrone*. Those who served as employment agents provided occasional work for individual emigrants who, in a foreign environment and unable to speak English, became totally dependent on them for jobs and guidance. Other *padrone* were interested only in supplying American employers with large groups of workers. In such instances, the *padrone* sometimes loaned the emigrant passage money at high interest rates, with the understanding that he would be repaid out of future earnings; the *padrone* also collected a fee from the American employer for each immigrant worker he was able to supply.

The promise of a financed voyage and a guaranteed job on arrival were strong enough incentives to overcome the worker's instinctive fear of leaving his native village for an unknown land. Occasionally the recruiting agent was not a total stranger but a *paesano*—a former villager who had migrated to the United States. Claiming to speak "Americano" as easily as his own dialect, the *paesano* could provide the kind of assurances the worker needed to hear before taking the drastic step of leaving his village and facing the uncertainties of a far-off and alien land.

The left-wing press explicitly linked emigration to social revolution, characterizing it as a viable substitute for the revolution that the *Risorgimento* had failed to achieve. It predicted that when the rich woke up to find their fields abandoned by the farm workers, they would finally be compelled to come to terms with the peasants, to grant them a fair share of their profits—unless they were willing to till the fields themselves. A popular song of the era was pointedly addressed to the sons of wealthy landowners accustomed to a life of leisure:

> Come on, you fine fellows,
> throw away your little umbrellas
> throw away your gloves
> and take our places in the fields.
> We are off to America.

The Italian political leadership found it expedient to adopt a *laissez-faire* stance toward the issue—which, after all, would neatly eliminate the most restless and potentially dangerous elements of the population. It concentrated instead on the formidable task of averting national bankruptcy, while trying to prove to other nations that the new state was not "merely the fragile creation of romantic nationalism and foreign patronage but could hold its own in a competitive, industrial world."

As part of its ambitious effort to attain the status of a first-class power, the national government began developing a huge peacetime army, as well as a navy which by 1890 was to "stitch the Italian boot together" with the addition of 13,000 kilometers of railroad to a paltry 2,200 kilometers throughout the entire kingdom in 1861.

To finance these expensive enterprises, unpopular economic measures followed, which acted as a spur to greater emigration. Church lands formerly available gratis to poor peasants for home gardening were expropriated and sold. And a program of direct and indirect taxation made the Italians the most taxed people in Europe.

The North of Italy, with 48 percent of the nation's aggregate wealth, assumed 40 percent of the public debt. Central Italy, with 25 percent of the wealth, was responsible for 28 percent of the debt. The South, which held 27 percent of the nation's resources, was made to pay 32 percent of the debt. The South therefore bore a disproportionate share of the burden.

Throughout the South, the gross inequities thrust on the farm workers resulted from absentee landlordism, which was far more prevalent in the *Mezzogiorno* than elsewhere in the nation. Patently unfair were the contracts between landowners, who usually dictated their terms, and sharecroppers and tenant farmers, who rarely were permitted to negotiate. The southerners, argued Sidney Sonnino in the Chamber of Deputies, needed to be freed from the "social serfdom" imposed on them by the ruling classes. He urged speedy legislation that would encourage the formation of cooperatives and peasant unions—already forming in the northern and central regions and in Sicily—as the most effective means of combating the unfair practices of landowners and their agents.

Sonnino's words fell on deaf ears. With only 2 percent of the Italian population qualified to vote during the early decades of the new regime, the rich and well-to-do remained firmly in command, wielding enough clout in parliament to defeat any attempt to enact legislation that might interfere with their interests. Viewed from this distance, there were other potent reasons for ignoring the social problems of the *Mezzogiorno,* reasons more affecting than those emanating from the dialectical situation of the "haves" as against the "have-nots." All were rooted in the failure of the new rulers to make allowances for the fact that Italy as a political entity had become a nation in which two sharply different civilizations existed simultaneously within a single national body. The leadership of the new regime tended to assume that since the southerners seemed either incapable or reluctant to accept the "more modern and enlightened" northerners as liberators who were willing to bring to them the benefits of democracy, they must be an inferior people, and should be dealt with accordingly. They could not be allowed to impede the rapid economic development of the rest of Italy.

It was in this period, too, that the image of the mafia was created in order to justify the government's policies in the South. Crime was attributed to the mafia and exaggerated. Later statistics would show that crime was not high in Sicily. British historian Christopher Duggan points out that "Increases in offences from 1863 to 1871 was less in Sicily than elsewhere in Italy and relative to its population the Island stood seventh in the national league table of crime in 1871." But then, as he goes on to say, "The image of mafia was created to suit the needs of Piedmont."

Irked by the resistance of the southerners to their legislation, successive government leaders denounced them as "barbarians" and "savages," and sometimes recommended that Italy cut itself off from the South, "a ball of lead at our feet" which no fledgling nation could afford to maintain. The continued backwardness of the southern regions, according to the rationale, was not the fault of the system of government, but of the prevalence of southern slackers, incompetents, and criminals. The South, often referred to as *Italia bassa* (low Italy), was declared to be stagnant, while the North, which became known as *alta Italia* (high Italy), was characterized as progressive. Ultimately, the conclusion evolved that the only useful function the South could serve was to provide cheap labor for the industrialization of the North and soldiers for the nation's military forces. Even more blunt was the conclusion of the northern political leader who held that "people are the only commodity the South can produce in abundance."

The politicians were not the only ones to disparage the South. In the first anthropological study of the "Southern Question," published when emigration from the *Mezzogiorno* was reaching flood proportions, an Italian academic, Alfredo Niceforo, achieved considerable notoriety by asserting that the moral and social structure of the South revealed an inferior civilization, one reminiscent of "the primitive and even quasi-barbarian times." Other northern academics, among them the noted criminologist Cesare Lombroso, joined Niceforo in attributing the stigma of "scientifically sanctioned" inferiority to the Southerners. One academic added to the hostility against southerners by stating that "One at first considers them naive until suddenly one perceives that they are accomplished rascals."*

---

*As late as 1958, Edward C. Banfield, an American academic who knew little of southern Italy's history and less of its language, visited a southern village. The visit was made possible by a grant. Out of the experience came a book, *The Moral Basis of a Backward Society*, in which he pronounced that "in a society of amoral familists no one will further the interests of the group or community except as it is to his private advantage . . ." Critics pointed out that "He [Banfield] arrived at an explanation when his mind 'came to rest.' Mind can find instant repose when unencumbered by knowledge of languages, the dialect, the history and the aesthetic structures of an Italian community" (Devos and Romanucci-Ross, *Ethnic Identity*, p. 223).

Contributing heavily to the tension was the increasing lack of economic equilibrium between the two areas: the northerners became the immediate beneficiaries of unification, a situation that was to remain onesided throughout the development of the new nation. Northern interests became the parliament's dominant concerns. Tariff systems enacted to promote the industrialization of the North virtually wiped out the southern industries that were functioning at the time of unification. Public works programs invariably favored central and northern regions. The first extensive railroad built after unification connected Turin with Paris, not Naples. While the rest of the nation was approaching the era of industrialization and, at the same time, improving the lot of its peasantry, the South was left to fend for itself.

Unlike the rest of Italy, which has broad and flowing rivers and deep natural lakes, the South suffers from an almost complete absence of waterways. Inevitably, the rains that fall in the winter and spring, combining with melted mountain snows, produce torrents which wash away precious topsoil and provoke devastating landslides before wasting themselves in the sea. Although the development of irrigation waters in the South would have improved its economy considerably, the new regime chose to create irrigation facilities mainly in the North. As late as 1921, only 8 percent of all artificially induced irrigation in Italy was developed in the South. Drinking water was a rare commodity. Many of the southern villages were completely without water, except for the rain they might capture from the sky.

During the hot dry season, peasants fortunate enough to have wells which yielded more water than they could consume strapped barrels of it to the backs of their donkeys and sold it in bottles to neighboring villages that had no water. An inferior grade of water was also peddled, which was not drinkable but was used for washing purposes. This was the water that became chiefly responsible for the spread of trachoma among the southern poor, the eye disease that was to prevent thousands of would-be immigrants from being admitted into the United States. Disease and famine added to the misery

---

Michael Parenti protested that Banfield "got a grant and he went to Italy. He found people there were poor. They kind of just oriented themselves to their families. He said these people were morally backward because, in fact, they don't act like middle class suburbanites" (*Power and Class*, AIHA). Still, Banfield's opinions found favor in some segments of academia.

of the impoverished masses during the early decades of unification. Cholera epidemics were not uncommon; the scourge of malaria was especially virulent in the South. Robert E. Foerster (who wrote so intelligently on Italian emigration) considered malaria "one of the prime forces" that impelled the southerners to abandon their homes and find refuge in some other country.

During the nineteenth century, Italy became notorious as the most malarial area in all of Europe. The disease increased markedly after unification, when deforestation was accelerated to attain additional land for farming and to provide lumber for Italy's expanding shipbuilding industry. Denuding hillsides once covered with thirsty forests prevented the earth from absorbing all of the winter rains and melting snows. The excess waters formed stagnant pools, which became natural breeding grounds for the malaria-bearing mosquitoes. Eventually, large tracts of fertile lands which had regularly yielded a cornucopia of crops declined into useless marshlands. The ravages inflicted on the peasantry by the disease are incalculable. Millions of workers became incapacitated; thousands of others died. As late as 1904 (when emigration was cresting), malaria killed at least twenty thousand persons annually. Wholesale casualties for nearly a half century sharply reduced agricultural productivity, and drove thousands of farming families, once again, away from mosquito-infested lowland settlements into villages perched on hilltops. Although the new settlements provided some protection for family members too old or too young to work in the fields, the workers in the family—who were now compelled to travel several miles a day to and from the lands they tilled—continued to run the risk of contracting malaria, especially during the predawn and twilight hours when they were traveling.

Entire villages became so notorious for their large numbers of malarial victims that other villages would have nothing to do with them. The notoriety was sometimes undeserved; but in the South, where there were few roads and little communication between villages, rumors rapidly assumed the aspect of unassailable truth.

The half measures adopted by the state toward the close of the nineteenth century to bring the *Mezzogiorno* into the orbit of modern society, such as the construction of highways and railroads, had little or no effect on improving the lot of the great mass of the poor. Nor did such efforts do anything to relieve the southerners' general sense of betrayal that the new regime, including the deputies who were supposed to represent them, was doing nothing to fulfill the promises made by Garibaldi. The greatest deception was the regime's failure to provide them with the opportunity of acquiring enough land to put food on their table, so as to free them to some extent from the rapacious demands of landowners. If anything, the new regime, from the peasant's point of view, had created an even greedier landlord.

The farm workers' sense of alienation was further stimulated by the presence of administrators sent from Rome—"a gang of French officials in Italian uniforms who hardly spoke Italian," who were seen as working hand in glove with the local gentry. Among the village collaborators of these "French officials" were members of the intelligentsia, who had been their protectors during the Bourbon regime and who now had become part of an administration handing down governmental edicts. The bureaucratic language of the edicts was beyond the ken of most southerners, but its thrust was all too clear: to saddle the lower classes with more taxes than they had ever paid before, and to require of them a greater degree of loyalty than could reasonably be expected from a people suffering from inadequate wages, increasing unemployment, rampant usury, and continued deforestation and soil erosion—all perilous factors of a dying economy which would soon impel a mass exodus from the *Mezzogiorno*.

Taking into account the situation of the average southern farm worker, Francesco Zannelli, an agricultural expert, applauded the "individualism and courage" of the departing peasants. "In America," he wrote, "they will be alone, fighting hunger and nature, fighting weather and disease, but at least they will be free of our irrational work contracts."

When, in 1876, the left finally came into power with the election of 414 deputies as against 94 of the right, there was much rejoicing among the nation's republicans, who hailed the event as the first step toward "a true republic" and the demise of the monarchy. But that expectation was thwarted by Victor Emmanuel's appointment of the latently promonarchist Agostino DePretis as prime minister.

As a practical politician, one of DePretis's first acts in office was to promote legislation that abolished the practice of arresting persons in debt. He also was largely responsible for the law that made education free and compulsory for children between the ages of six and nine—a law that, unfortunately, was sabotaged in many sections of the *Mezzogiorno* by local authorities, who saw no advantage in educating the children of the poor. But in the eight years of his premiership DePretis remained the arch compromiser, described by Pareto as "someone with a skeptical turn of mind, who never embarrassed himself with principles or convictions and never bothered much about the truth." Always ready to avoid the politically arduous, he became a champion of free emigration, regarding it as an invaluable "safety valve," and followed the example set by his predecessors in ignoring its causes. Confronted by social reformers who proposed urgent radical reforms to improve the life of the southern poor, he is said to have responded, like Lampedusa's Prince, "Sleeping misery is better not awakened."

DePretis's long premiership came to a close with his death in 1887, the same year in which Italy suffered its most severe economic depression since unification. Unable to compete with an enormous influx of American and Russian wheat, the price of Italian grain suddenly declined sharply. In 1890, a plant parasite, *Phylloxera,* destroyed most of the grapevines in the *Mezzogiorno,* relegating Italy to a second-place position (below France) in the export of wines.

The *Mezzogiorno* was also plagued by a series of cholera epidemics which, within a three-year period (1884–87), took the lives of 55,000 men and women; and there were volcanic eruptions of Vesuvius and Etna that demolished entire surrounding villages. In 1908 came the worst disaster of all: an earthquake and tidal wave that met in "calamitous coincidence" to destroy much of the Sicilian province of Messina and part of Calabria. "The earth opened and threw stones at us," one survivor remembered, adding that the smell of burning flesh was so pungent that "even now" (more than a decade after the disaster) "I can smell it." The dead numbered almost 100,000. The tidal wave reached a height of 40 feet, and for five days torrential rains totally flooded the province. Many of those who lived to tell the story interpreted the disaster as nothing less than a signal from Providence, and joined the migration of Sicilians and Calabrians to the United States already in progress when the holocaust struck.

For all their grievances against the new regime, the Sicilians were among the last of the southern Italians to migrate to America in large numbers. However, once they began leaving, their numbers swelled until they constituted more than one quarter of all the Italian American immigrants. Triggering the exodus was the Italian government's ruthless suppression of a popular cooperative movement known as the *Fasci Siciliani,* which became *La piccola favella che gran fuoco seconda* (the small spark that engenders great fires). The spark was to fall on a tinderbox. Ultimately it would drive more than 1.5 million Sicilians—40 percent of the island's population—to foreign lands.

THE FASCI SICILIANI—THE TINDERBOX

Asked in 1972 if there were any archives that might explain why Sicilians left for America at the turn of the century, the mayor of Racalmuto answered: "You want to know why people left? Hunger, that's why." If one insisted on archives, he answered again: "What archives? They fled here without regrets and most of them clandestinely. What records?" And he held up his fingers in a bunch as emphasis. "They were dying of hunger." Of course there was much truth in this. An old man who had left Sicily around 1898 recalled:

> It was unbearable. My brother Luigi was 6 then and I was 7. Every morning we'd get up before sunrise and start walking about 4 or 5 miles to the farm of the *patrunu*—the boss. Many times we went without breakfast. For lunch we ate a piece of bread and plenty of water. If we were lucky, sometimes we would have a small piece of cheese or an onion. We worked in the hot sun until the late afternoon, then we had to drag ourselves home. We got there exhausted, just before sunset, so tired we could barely eat and fell asleep with all our clothes on. If we complained that the work was too hard our mother—God rest her soul—would say, "And who is going to give you something to eat?" And life went on this way day in and day out, until *si vidiva surci virdi*—"we began to see green mice."

However, the explanation for the Sicilian migration was not simply hunger. It began with a revival of hope and ended with a mass exodus. The hope for a better life began shortly after the unification of Italy when, despite Sicilian antagonism toward the new regime for the broken promises of the *Risorgimento,* there had been a surge of economic and social progress that included a boom in agricultural production, more employment, and rising wages. The mining of sulfur, Sicily's chief export industry, which had doubled its production since 1860, continued to flourish. In the town of Racalmuto, the young and progressive took hold of the local government. In 1879 a theater was completed, and narrow streets were widened, with some of the townsmen donating land and houses for the renovation. A branch of the *Banco di Sicilia* opened in the town shortly after a branch of Sicily's first railroad arrived. All through the island, schools were being built and the rate of illiteracy was beginning to decline. All in all, there was good reason for optimism.

But then a rapid series of events took place that once again had a devastating effect on poor people in Sicily. The year 1890 saw a drop in agricultural prices that started a trade war, particularly with the French wine industry. A severe drought the following year caused grain and citrus fruit production to drop. Wine production was cut in half. The following year, 1892, saw more of the same. Everyone was hurt, but most of all the agricultural workers, the *braccianti*, who were left with a despairing hunger and a hatred of the land.

The most unexpected of the disasters was the discovery of sulfur in Texas and the American technique for producing it cheaply enough to eliminate Sicily as a major competitor in the world markets. A foreman in one of the few Sicilian mines still operating during the 1950s remembered: "The mines in America ruined us. They stick a tube in the ground and suck out the sulfur. We can't compete with our bare hands."

Ever since ancient times sulfur had permeated the island. According to mythology, the gates of Hell, through which Pluto spirited Persephone and made her his part-time queen, were located in the center of Sicily. The ancient Greeks of Sicily had Pluto sitting on a throne of sulfur, ruling his kingdom of sulfur and brimstone—both products of Sicily's mining areas. Mining the sulfur "with our bare hands" is only a slightly exaggerated metaphor. Well into the twentieth century, mine owners (many of whom represented British interests that had acquired ownership of the mines even before the unification of Italy) continued to rely on the most primitive methods for mining the sulfur. Elsewhere in the world it was being produced with modern tools, more efficiently and with far fewer accidents. In Sicily, safety measures for the workers as well as modern technology for extracting sulfur from the ground were disregarded. As late as the 1930s, sulfur workers went up and down the deepest mining shafts on foot at their own risk at a time when elevators were in general use. Although accidents were frequent, not until 1933 did the Italian government evince enough concern to require accident statistics from the mine owners. In general, working conditions were, as one observer put, "Hell in reality." In the province of Agrigento, miners chanted verses that expressed their feelings. One went: "In the infamous art of the sulfur miner/He works night and day in the dark."

The principal mine worker was the *picconiere,* the pickman, who, in addition to setting the explosives, splintered the exploded chunks of the sulfur with his pick. Each *picconiere* worked with a *caruso,* usually a young boy, who hauled out the sulfur from the depths of the mine in sacks that weighed about 75 pounds each. It was a long haul, sometimes as much as a half mile to the top of the shaft, an arduous task for children with backs not fully developed. Some of the survivors still remembered the songs they sang while carrying their loads to the top:

> Mother dear don't send me to the mines
> Day and night I'm frightened to death.
> As soon as I go down the walls cave in
> And the ceiling opens.
> It's the way of a rotten quarry
> That scares me to death.
> Now we're going to level one. OH.
> Praise the Lord and San Gaetano.
> Now we're up to the middle level. OH.
> Praise be to dear Santa Barbara.
> What a light my little lamp gives me. OH.
> It's a sign. It's a sign. It's time to quit. OH.
> I'll tell the *picconiere.* OH. This is the last.
> And he can come up. OH.

The *carusi* were contracted to the *picconiere* by their parents, who, in return for a son's services, would be paid in advance, not with money, but with foodstuffs such as flour and grain. The *carusi* were required to work off the advance by doing about fifty such trips up and down the shaft each day.

International events conspired to depress the Sicilian economy even further. Following the severance of trade relations with France in 1887, a long-term depression ensued. The *Fasci* movement became the catalyst for the rudely awakened aspirations of Sicilian workers.*

The Sicilian *Fasci* groups had their roots in the mutual benefit

Fasci is the plural of *Fasciu,* which in Sicilian means "bundle." Ironically, just thirty years before Mussolini's march on Rome, the *Fasci* meant the bringing together of workers and peasants in a Socialist-directed movement. It is understandable why the *Fasci* became the

societies and peasant associations, which began under the aegis of Socialist leadership in 1873 when *La Societa di Mutuo Soccorso* (the Society for Mutual Aid) was formed throughout the Sicilian provinces. Increasingly, the poor became radicalized—more aware, as one put it, "of the gentlemen who broke their asses watching their almond trees bloom." Out of such organizations emerged the movement that flourished during the period 1888–94, with a membership of more than 350,000 Sicilian farm and sulfur workers. The majority of them, despite the debates and proselytizing, were peasants, apolitical and uneducated, who naively believed the *Fasci* would bring about the independence of Sicily and, ultimately, social justice to all workers.

Fasci activity was spearheaded by local strikes of farm and sulfur workers, which gradually spread throughout the island until they achieved the impact of a general strike. The early success of the strikers not only served to make the workers aware of their collective strength for the first time in their history, but also proved to be their undoing. In the passion of their activity, they were unable to maintain the discipline necessary to deal with the opposition effectively. All too soon the momentum of their protests got out of hand. Despite the advice of their leaders, their strike demands proliferated, and when property owners refused to negotiate with them, they set fire to public buildings and cut telegraph wires. The frightened gentry, convinced that all of Sicily was on the verge of an anarchical revolution, appealed to federal authorities for military intervention, demanding that the *Fasci* be abolished.

In 1893, the prime minister, Giovanni Giolitti, responded by sending troops to Sicily to restore public order, but disallowed the use of firearms. When the troops confronted a group of demonstrators who were unarmed, the disallowance was ignored and twenty-two were killed. Yet Giolitti still refused to dissolve the *Fasci*, arguing that they had the constitutional right to engage in strikes and other activities of a peaceful nature.

Before the government could intercede, some members of the gentry began to take matters into their own hands. The king ordered

---

symbol of working-class unity in Sicily. Men, women, and children, even animals, were seen everywhere carrying on their shoulders the symbol of Sicilian poverty—*fasciu* of stacks of sticks collected in the fields and brought home. Mussolini was exploiting his Socialist past when he adopted the term.

steps to suppress the *Fasci;* police and military units were authorized to put a stop to all acts of arson and violence by whatever means they chose. In subsequent clashes with demonstrators in twenty-eight communities, the police and army units killed ninety-two workers and wounded many more. Not a single soldier or policeman lost his life. One of Prime Minister Francesco Crispi's favorite declarations was "I love the people; I too am a worker." But within weeks after he had assumed office he succumbed to a virulent attack of paranoia, induced by questionable reports from Sicily. Convinced that the disturbances were part and parcel of a conspiracy financed by France with the intention of separating Sicily from the rest of Italy, Crispi dispatched forty thousand soldiers—almost one soldier for every striker—to the island and imposed martial law.

The task of "restoring order" to Sicily was given to General Mara, who was granted full powers. The general proclaimed a state of siege on the island, declared the *Fasci* disbanded, and began a systematic arrest of all leaders, from the urban centers to the smallest villages, such as Milocca. There followed mass arrests and the deportation of one thousand Sicilians to penal islands, all without due process. Anyone suspected of *Fasci* activity was arrested. One man demanded to know on what evidence he was being arrested. Mara answered, "We will find some. If not, there is plenty of metaphysical evidence." Constitutional rights such as freedom of the press and public gatherings were suspended. All *Fasci* groups, cooperatives, and working-class organizations were declared illegal. The only demand made of Crispi by the Sicilian gentry, which the prime minister chose to ignore, was that all schools be shut down on the grounds that they contributed to the "restlessness" of the lower classes. Eleven of the *Fasci* leaders were court-martialed and received prison sentences of up to eighteen years. Crispi, with parliament's approval, also saw to it that some 100,000 "potentially subversive" voters were disenfranchised. Blaming the Socialists for the *Fasci* disturbances, the former Socialist declared socialism to be Italy's "most pernicious" enemy, one to be equated with anarchism, and ordered the dissolution of the Socialist Party. Outside of Sicily, many Italians spoke of him as "the saviour of Italy."

To justify their harsh repression, those in power declared that anyone involved in the *Fasci* was a criminal. Christopher Duggan tells us:

The landowners and government were terrified by the expression of peasant militancy, and as in 1866, they tried to criminalise it. The outbreak of social unrest in Sicily in 1892 was greeted with demands for the suppression of brigandage, even though there seems to have been only one bandit gang to speak of at the time. The authorities produced reports on the Fasci that tried to link them with mafia. . . . in September 1893, the Palermo Chief of Police said that local crime had assumed "alarming proportions": "I firmly believe that this situation stems directly from the evil influence of the Fasci. The mafia and the entire criminal class have enrolled in them. . . ."

The failure of the *Fasci* movement was attributed to many causes: to the northern Socialist leaders, many of whom did not understand Sicilian conditions and so "used" Sicily; to friction among the Socialists; to the backwardness of the Sicilian working class; and to an underestimation of the power of the bourgeoisie. From this distance, however, two factors stand out: the thoughtlessness and cruelty of the repression, and the exodus of the most militant in the great wave of migration to America that followed soon after.

"The emigration was a blight for this island," recalled a Sicilian in Racalmuto much later. "All the young left, all those who weren't afraid of taking on a policeman in broad daylight. If they had stayed, they would have brought about a change. But everybody was saying then, 'Why do anything, tomorrow we'll be in America.' The capitalists didn't care about this export of human meat. That's what we were exporting, human meat."

Some changes did take place, nonetheless. Workers began to dress in a more worldly fashion; they let their mustaches grow; they no longer took blows from their employers. This brought about the disillusion wearily expressed by Sicilian noblemen in the waning years of the nineteenth century:

What ugly times are upon us.
When a gentleman can no longer slap a peasant's face.

But anger remained, and from time to time exploded in minor shocks. In 1896, Napoleon Colajanni came through Racalmuto and caused the last of the *Fasci* shocks. Colajanni was from Castrogiovanni (or Enna, as it is known today). He had been one of the leaders of the *Fasci,* a moderating influence, a scholar in the nineteenth-century manner, a doctor, and an intellectual who had devoted his life to socialism. He was a hero to the *Fasci* of Racalmuto. In 1894 he had written, "I don't want the stupid cruelty of those in power but there must be changes so that revolutionary Sicilian cry of 'Death to the *Cappedda'* does not acquire that sad celebrity of *'Les aristocrates à la lanterne.'*"

Expecting his arrival, his followers mobbed the railroad station. They pressed in on the police sent to maintain order. The *carabinieri,* either frightened or arrogant, drew their swords. One of the *Fasci* leaders picked up a stone and, with a cry of "Brothers; workers!" led an attack against the police. Overwhelmed, the police were forced to strip naked. When Colajanni arrived, he could not prevent the crowd from parading the naked policemen through town. The baron-mayor was appalled that Sicilian policemen would allow themselves to be stripped naked "without at least killing someone." He responded by writing poetry to the glory of Crispi and to the great and glorious war fought in Abyssinia.

Decades later, Italian historian Francesco Renda came to the conclusion that

The masses, disillusioned by the failure of the *Fasci Siciliani* and crushed by the ferocious repression of Mara, looked to new horizons, the lands beyond the sea, America, Tunisia. The great hemorrhaging of our people was about to begin. The year 1900 rung in by the bells of Racalmuto was a cold night. The cynical Baron was at the height of his power. The people were anguished by a hunger for bread and work, and by the fear of turning to a new world for a life that was denied them in their own world.

Three *Fasci* leaders in Sicily—Rosario Garibaldi Bosco, Nicolo Barbato, and Bernadino Verro—fleeing their homes, were caught on board the *Bagnara* on their way to America. They were the harbingers of the great surge in emigration to follow.

CHAPTER 7

Parting

My love, my love, how far you are
Who's making your bed tonight?
Who does, is not doing it well.
How sickly comes the morning.

—ITALIAN LOVE SONG

THOSE WHO LEFT

An American consul in Catania, who was visited in 1888 by
several men between the ages of fifty and sixty, was struck by the
disparities between their expectations of America and reality. The
spokesman of the group explained that they were on their way to
Palermo, where they would board a steamer headed for *LaMerica*.
There, they had been told, high wages were being paid to laborers to
dig for gold. Their informant, who was from their own village, had
also assured them that they would not need passports; but the group
had decided that in order to avoid "any trouble with the *Americani*,"
they would consult with him. The following scene ensued:

"In what part of America do you intend to go?" the consul
asked.

"We don't know sir," answered the spokesman. "Wherever they dig the gold. Although we are a little old, we can dig well since we have worked in sulphur mines."

"Have you any relatives, friends, or acquaintances who would take care of you on your arrival, or feed you until you find something to do?"

"No sir. But we have plenty of money to live on for two full years. All we earn during that time we'll save, and come back very rich."

"How much money have you got with you?"

"Well, sir, we have about 169 lire each ($32). We sold everything we had to make it."

"That amount will just do you to pay for your passage ticket."

"No sir. The man told us at Palermo they gave us the passage money for nothing."

"The man is wrong," the consul told them. "Let him give you the ticket before you leave the country. He wants your money and would leave you in misery. You are too old to emigrate to a very far country where the people don't speak your language. Take my advice and go home to live happy and be with your families."

The consul, concluding his report to his Washington office, noted that "the elderly peasants became bewildered and left."

For those who did emigrate, parting was very painful. One old immigrant vividly remembered the night he left:

My father, *bon arma,* put my valises on the old mule, Old Titi, and we went up to the railroad station. It was pitch dark, early in the morning. From the cracks in the shutters over here and over there I could see the yellow light of the oil lamps. The streets were empty. I could smell the air like when the hay is damp. I could hear behind the doors the stamping of a mule, a horse breathing. At another door, somebody snoring. My father did not speak all the way to the train. I don't know when he said it to me, my father, he said, "Make yourself courage." And that was the last time I saw my father.

The same scene was to be reenacted many times.

★ ★ ★

By the start of the twentieth century, most of the southern émigrés were being lured to the United States not so much by exploiting agents as by close relatives and friends already there. Lonely for those they left behind, the new immigrants usually wrote glowing accounts of life in America and urged the recipients of the letters to join them, promising to help find them employment and, often as not, offering to loan them money for the passage. Along with enthusiastic letters from the new land came a steady flow of remittances, and the wondrous testimonials of those who had returned to their native villages with enough savings to buy land or establish a small business. They, together with the émigrés who had simply returned for a visit (usually to select a bride), reinforced the image of America as a land where Italians could prosper, and where, regardless of lack of property or artisan skills, one would be treated with respect and even kindness.

Whether the returning emigrant planned to stay or just to visit, he henceforth became known as the *Americano*. "The minute you see him you can spot him," wrote an Italian American explaining why he was persuaded to come to the United States. "He smokes an American pipe, he wears American shoes, a cap, American clothes. He has new ideas. But the great change is that he has money—more money than ever before, more money than his old neighbors have. He is an advertisement that there is prosperity for the stranger in America." But for those who returned to their villages with unhappy memories of their American experience, becoming known as an *Americano* had a derisive implication. They were the most silent of the returning emigrants. Some of them had saved American money, but not enough to compensate for the harsh industrial atmosphere of urban America and the loneliness of living without their families. There were also those who had been defeated by poor health. Frequently tubercular and facing death, they were unwilling to be buried in a foreign land. The casualties included, too, men suffering or disabled by injuries incurred while working in American factories, mines, and construction projects. Their complaints of inadequate or total lack of compensation were easily muted by the chorus of praise voiced by the more fortunate *Americani* who had returned with money and in good health.

At the height of the emigration fever, Italians found it difficult to believe that many of their compatriots in America were not faring well. Traveling through the *Mezzogiorno* in 1907 to study the effects of emigration on the area, Anthony Mangano, an Italian-born American writer, invariably met with skepticism when he explained that hundreds of Italian immigrants in New York and Brooklyn were dependent on charity for survival. The southerners also found it difficult to believe that emigrants had to do heavy or hazardous work, which immigrants of other nationalities preferred to avoid. And they often lived on poor and insufficient food in crowded quarters, where one diseased person could easily contaminate many others.

It was not unusual for the Italian immigrants to make more than one journey to America. Some traveled there periodically, unable to decide where they and their families would spend the rest of their lives. Known as "birds of passage," most intended to rejoin their families after two or three years of working in America. Because statistics made no distinction between those who undertook a single voyage to America and those who went more than once, there is no way of determining exactly how many finally chose to remain in their native country. But statisticians are agreed in their estimate that at least 50 percent of them reached that decision.

As trans-Atlantic travel became cheaper, the "birds of passage" traveled back to their villages more frequently; some returned to their families annually, in the winter months, when American jobs were harder to find. Some spent the greater part of the year in the United States, but revisited Italy long enough to become acquainted with a son or daughter born during their absence. One such immigrant, Giovanni Palumbo, who worked as a coal miner, made a dozen round-trip journeys before deciding that he, his wife, and their nine children would fare best in Scranton, Pennsylvania.

Although poverty was the multipronged incentive that drove most of them from their native land, only a minority were from the lowest economic strata. Basilicata, the most impoverished of all the regions of the *Mezzogiorno,* produced the fewest emigrants. Psychologically, the fear of descending to the level of poverty beyond redemption became a powerful stimulus for leaving. An immigrant blacksmith who arrived in America in 1906 explained why he left his native village: "When I found that the only way I could prevent my family from starving was to turn to stealing, I decided it was time to leave." Those who had already descended to the lowest poverty levels were often either too apathetic or had no relatives in America to provide moral and financial encouragement.

By far the largest group of Italian emigrants were from rural districts—a mixture of cultivators who owned some land but not enough to provide a family with a livelihood, tenant farmers, field workers, and shepherds. Another 20 percent were fishermen and artisans such as masons, carpenters, stonecutters, bakers, blacksmiths, cooks, shoemakers, barbers, tailors, and miners. The rest were a miscellany of tradesmen, entrepreneurs, and members of the gentry—among them doctors, lawyers, teachers, accountants, and pharmacists, as well as ambitious young men who aspired to one of those professions but saw no likelihood of achieving their goal in Italy.

Although Italy's tardy entry into the industrial age in the final years of the nineteenth century generated enough prosperity in the nation's northern and central regions to sharply inhibit the flow of emigration in those areas, it had the opposite effect in the *Mezzogiorno,* where there was virtually no industry nor any prospect of development. The spillover benefits from the prospering North were insufficient to convince southerners that it would be worthwhile for them to resist the temptation of seeking their fortunes elsewhere.

The chief concern among Italians who had been separated was how to keep the family together under one roof. Seldom did an entire family migrate together. Almost invariably a father or a son, or both, left for America with the assumption that they would either return or send for the other members of the family as soon as there was enough money to pay for their fares. Often, however, there were unexpected developments resulting in separations that either weakened or destroyed the family union.

Pascal D'Angelo's experience, described in his autobiographical odyssey *Son of Italy* (1924), was fairly typical. D'Angelo was fifteen when he learned that his father was about to leave for America and work there for a few years; just long enough, he hoped, to escape the clutches of usurious moneylenders and become more independent of exploiting landowners. At first, the boy was angry that "America was stealing my father from me"; but as he listened to his mother trying to comfort him with visions of "the wonderful new life" they would lead when his father returned "laden with riches," he became obsessed with the idea of accompanying him to a land that could confer such blessings. He began arguing with his parents that, despite his youth, he was as strong as any adult and therefore able to earn as much; together, he and his father could double their American savings and reduce by half the time they would be away. The father was easily convinced; but the mother, afraid she might never see her son again, was less sure. Yet she finally consented.

The Abruzzo region, where the D'Angelo family farmed, is the northernmost section of the *Mezzogiorno;* a small portion of it actually extends north of Rome. Yet the *contadini* of the Abruzzo were no better off during the emigration era than those in the southernmost regions. For the D'Angelos, America offered the hope of escaping "the spectre of starvation" and returning "with thousands of liras—riches unheard of before among peasants."

But emigration brought no riches either to the father or the son. After both had worked as manual laborers for four years, barely able to support themselves and unable to save any money, the father decided to return to Abruzzo, convinced the situation would not improve. He urged his son to return with him; but Pascal, despite all the hardships he had endured going from one work gang to another, uncertain at times that he and his father could have food and shelter without borrowing money, decided to stay. "Something had grown in me during my stay in America. Something was keeping me in this wonderful perilous land where I suffered so much and where I had so much more to suffer." He was unable to make his father understand. "He went away from me, a broken-hearted man."

D'Angelo could not have known that he would never set eyes on either of his parents again, nor that he would eventually blossom into an American poet. For the moment he was driven to the following expression of his brooding uneasiness:

The factory smoke is unfolding in protesting curves
Like phantoms of black unappeased desires, yearning and
    struggling and pointing upward;
While through its dark streets pass people, tired, useless,
Trampling the vague black illusions
That pave their paths like broad leaves of water-lilies
On twilight streams;
And there are smiles at times on their lips.
Only the great soul, denuded to the blasts of reality,
Shivers and groans.
And like two wild ideas lost in a forest of thoughts,
Blind hatred and blinder love run amuck through the city.

THOSE WHO STAYED BEHIND

Women were especially affected by family separations. When their men left for America, mothers and wives wept bitterly. Some went into mourning. America, they said, was like a *mala femmina*—a bad woman—who lures men away from their families.

For the women left behind, America was perceived as a *terra maledetta* (cursed land) where their husbands, sons, and fiancés were at the mercy of an infected atmosphere that made them forget their Italian past. "There must be something in the American air they breathe that shortens their memory," was the lament of many a wife. Especially disturbing was the departure of the father, who always promised to return in a few years. Those "few years" would often stretch into five and ten; for months at a time there would be neither letters nor remittances—only silence. Writing of his boyhood in Avigliano, Leonard Covello evokes the gnawing anxiety that permeated a household when there was no word from its faraway father. "You must watch for the butterfly," his mother would say in an effort to comfort her son. "As soon as a butterfly enters the window, then we will have news of your father, and it will be news that he is sending for us." Covello recalled how he caught butterflies and turned them loose in the house. "My mother smiled and tried to pretend and play the game with me, but it was an empty smile which fooled no one. My father had troubles of his own in America. He sent what money he could but he did not write very often. It was difficult for him to put words to paper, as it was with all our people in those days."

The years dragged on. A son or daughter might write the letters his mother regularly sent. The opening paragraph was the standard one usually found in correspondence between southern Italians: "My dear Husband: I am writing these few lines to let you know that we are all well . . ." after which would follow a few village news items, births and deaths. Finally would come the message of the letter. Covello's mother would instruct her son to say that "we are anxiously waiting to hear from you." The boy would ask her hopefully: "What about *l'embarco*?" Always tactful, ever aware of her husband's own anxieties, her answer was always, "No, mention nothing about money. Just write as I said it."

For women with husbands in America, the trauma of separation was exacerbated by the problem of how to maintain themselves and their children. The remittances from America were often insufficient to support the family. Unless there were children strong enough to work and contribute, the wife had no choice but to do farm labor that was formerly considered too hard for women.

An early Italian feminist, Irene DeBonis, described the "sad odyssey" of the women she interviewed who, when a husband, father, or brother left, remained alone, obliged to assume not only the hard field work of the men but also the debts incurred by the emigrants before they left. The typical woman left behind was "young, strong, healthy, married only a few years and often only a few months at the time of her husband's departure. Frequently, she was pregnant or with small children, and invariably prey to the malice of village gossips."

If the wife received a letter from her husband asking her to join him, the summons was interpreted as a sign of love, an assurance that no other woman had come between them. But it created a host of problems she was usually unprepared to cope with. Within a short time she was expected to obtain the documents and belongings she and her children needed for the voyage, sell whatever possessions there were, borrow money for the train fare, and do whatever else was necessary to make the journey possible. In many instances, the wife had never gone beyond the boundaries of her village, nor had she ever dealt with bureaucrats and moneylenders. Unless there was a friend or relative in the village who could help with the arrangements, her only resort was to turn to the services of a subagent.

An agent's threat that he could delay her departure from Italy, coupled with the woman's fear that her husband might renounce her if she did not arrive when expected, induced some wives to submit to a demand for sexual favors the night before the ship's departure. The victim would be taken to a hotel by the agent and represented as his wife. "He told me he could ruin me forever if I didn't do what he wanted," was the explanation DeBonis often heard in her interviews with emigrant wives.

Not all women summoned to America by their husbands were willing to go. Their reluctance usually derived from the realization that they might never see their parents again. A common tactic was to repeatedly invent excuses that would postpone the departure to some future unnamed date. In many such instances the husband would eventually lose patience and threaten to stop sending maintenance money for his wife and children unless they joined him by a given date. When there were no children, the husband, feeling abandoned himself, threatened to discard the wife altogether.

Abandonment is one of the darkest aspects of the emigrant story; it usually befell young married women whose husbands left for America shortly after their first child was born and were never heard from again.

The wives were not the only women who suffered the effects of the massive male emigration. In a culture where a dowry was mandatory if a daughter was ever to marry, the protracted absence of a father or older brother virtually doomed her to spinsterhood. Many of the few eligible bachelors left in the village took advantage of the situation by raising their demands for dowries to levels that only families of the wealthy could afford. A young laundress, washing hotel sheets in a mountain stream, explained to an American journalist that in her village she was one of twenty young women of marriageable age, but that their chances of being married were virtually nil. "The few men who remain in the village ask forty, even eighty dollars before they will marry. Eighty dollars? How can a girl earning twenty cents a day save such a fortune? 'Pray to the Madonna of the Rock' says my mother. Talking is easy. Of what use are prayers when you have not a penny to spare for a candle?"

LEAVING FOR PERSONAL REASONS

In addition to the larger issues such as hunger, tyranny, and the failure of the *Fasci Siciliani,* those who emigrated often had personal reasons for leaving. Many of the departing bachelors from *Mezzogiorno* villages were the younger sons of large families who, as soon as they were of legal age, free of their father's dominance, embraced emigration as a pathway to personal liberty and independence. The eldest sons, who enjoyed a position of prestige in the family hierarchy, were less likely to leave. It was the eldest who took charge of the family in the event of the father's death and who became the chief beneficiary of whatever properties the family had. The younger male siblings had little to gain by staying. Even the choice of a wife was often denied them by parents who followed the tradition of selecting "suitable" mates. Parents had their own reasons for favoring the emigration of their younger sons. One, which was seldom admitted, was that there would be one less mouth to feed. There was also the expectation that if the son was able to save money in the New World, he would send some of it to his family.

Often a young man succumbed to emigration fever for reasons that were more psychological than economic. An overly strict father who made too many demands on a son encouraged the notion of escape. Young men also left after being jilted by girls they had expected to marry.

Eventually, many of the sons who emigrated returned to their villages—some only long enough to visit their families, others to select a wife, unwilling to be wed to one whose dialect and past was unknown to them. Some never returned.

Until the emigrant felt at ease in his alien environment, the trauma of separation was likely to affect him even more deeply than it affected the family he left behind, particularly if he expected to rejoin his family. His sense of guilt for having left was often compounded by an inability to send home enough money to justify having left, however temporarily. Attuned to the mythology of America, with its promise of easy access to affluence, the émigrés' families would sometimes sharpen their anxieties by letting them know of their disappointment.

One son, in exasperation, responded to such a letter by writing that "it is not as you believe that here in America money is found on the ground." Insisting he had been a dutiful son, he informed his father that he had "labored day and night" and reduced his standard of living to an absolute minimum so as to have "a penny more" to send home. Although money was mentioned in nearly all the correspondence between the emigrants and their family members, it was seldom the main subject.

As a rule, the emigrants' letters revealed close involvement with the lives of the families they had left behind. Fathers were often insistent on asserting their role as head of the family. One letter from America ordered the writer's wife to invite her father-in-law to a meal now and then "out of respect," but not to extend the invitation to the woman he had married. In another letter a husband scolded his wife on learning that she had loaned one of their tablecloths to a neighbor. He warned her never to give anything away without his permission, and threatened to beat her on his return if he ever found out that she had. Some husbands sent detailed instructions as to what vegetables to grow in their absence. A recurring concern of emigrant fathers and sons was that a daughter might take liberties that would dishonor the family name. One father demanded of his wife that he be kept informed of anything in the behavior of their daughter that struck her as suspicious, such as weeping during the night, and commanded his wife never to submit to their daughter's "caprices." A son became so worried about the potential misbehavior of a sister that he wrote to each member of his family—except the sister—begging each of them to keep a watchful eye on her.*

Political opponents of emigration frequently charged that it caused "immorality" in the southern villages. The extent of the dislocation in the South is reflected in the fact that throughout all Italy the percentage of families without a male head (for reasons either of emigration or death) was 9.10 percent, whereas for the southern region of Basilicata it was 22.7 percent and for Calabria 29.1 percent. That nearly all those emigrating were in their prime years (aged between twenty-one and fifty) added weight, for some, to the argument that emigration was endangering the moral health of the southern population.

"Years ago we had family order here," the prefect of Cosenza, capital of Calabria, told an Italian American reporter shortly after the turn of the century. "Children were brought up to obey their parents. Now, without close surveillance, they do as they please. Worse still, we are confronted with prostitution among a class of people who, despite their poverty, had remained respectable until now. The number of illegitimate children is steadily increasing. And infanticide, an evil entirely unknown here a few years ago, is rapidly making itself felt."

The prefect attributed the decline of morality directly to the absence of male heads of families, as well as of adult sons, whose

*The information on these letters is based on a sheaf of letters by Italian immigrants from the region of Abruzzo who, at the turn of the century, were living in the Philadelphia-Wilmington area. The letters were addressed to the families that the immigrants had left behind, usually to parents. Since most of the immigrants were illiterate, letters were composed for them by compatriots who could at least write the Abruzzese dialect. The Italian volume in which the letters appear is *Lettere di Illetterati: Note di Psicologia Sociala,* published in 1913 by Nicola Zanichelli Editore.

In his Introduction, the author, Filippo Lussana, writes, "There may be those who will object to the fact that among the lower classes, especially among the peasants, the letters are not written by the person who signs them. The objection is of minimal value since everyone who knows the habits of the *contadini* is aware that if it is at all possible, they will try to write the letters themselves, and when they are unable to write, they dictate word by word, often insisting that the words be read back to them to make certain that nothing had been added, nothing deleted, and nothing changed."

traditional duty it was to serve as protectors of their unmarried sister—making certain, for example, that they remained virgins and gave no cause for gossip until they were wed—and after. In a land where most men possessed nothing but their wives, to take that from them was to leave them morally and psychologically destitute.

The continuing dislocation of families and other negative aspects of mass emigration had little effect on Italy's lawmakers, who generally assumed that most of the men leaving for foreign shores would eventually return. A surprisingly large number did—as many as 1.5 million between 1900 and 1914. However, many others continued to migrate: during the same period, some 9 million Italians (chiefly from the South) looked for and found work in foreign countries.

The American writer William Weyl, investigating emigration in the *Mezzogiorno,* found that the mass exodus had added another serious component to the "Southern Problem": the moral and physical decay of communities in the aftermath of depopulation. "The village is dead," wrote Weyl in his commentary on ghost towns.

> Nowhere is there the vibrant toil of young men; nowhere the cheerful sound of intense, hopeful activity. Its people aimlessly filling a weird, fatal silence, seem like denizens of an accursed land. Their only thought is America. Periodically some new group receives prepaid tickets. A house is given up, and sold for nothing; a few listless farewells are made. For a moment the incurious village is galvanized into a vague sporadic interest. Then it lapses into its wonted lethargic state.

One of these ghost towns was San Demetrio, in Calabria, whose history dated back to the fifteenth century. By the turn of the century the town had been so depopulated that no one was left to light its street lamps. The original inhabitants had been Albanians who fled the vengeance of Turkish oppressors. When Anthony (Antonio) Mangano, a Calabrian-born American journalist, visited San Demetrio in 1907, he found that the natives were still speaking their original Greek-studded dialect, once the language of several distinguished poets and scholars born in San Demetrio. But one could not have guessed it from the omnipresent squalor Mangano observed along medievally putrescent streets.

A majority of the population, approximately two thousand San Demetrians, had left for the United States with no intention of returning. Remittances from abroad were few and far between. None of the American money was being spent to build new or repair old houses, and no steps were taken to lessen the squalor. Yet the San Demetrians in America had sent an annual collective contribution for the operation of a high school, and from the more religiously inclined emigrants, money arrived to finance the village's annual *festa* of music, fireworks, and cannonfire staged for its patron saint.

A few of the southern towns, though depopulated, prospered after the emigration of their able-bodied men. Toretto, in the region of Apulia, lost 4,000 of its 7,000 residents within a single decade, but the emigrants maintained strong ties with those they left behind. Not only did nearly all of them plan to return for permanent residence, but there were also frequent visits during the winter months and a steady flow of remittances averaging more than $1 million annually. That money was used to build an entirely new town adjacent to the old one, consisting mainly of comfortable dwellings that became known as *case Americani*. Although most of the remaining inhabitants were elderly or decrepit, there was no "fatal silence" and no beggars in sight.

The father figure of the community, who had inspired the wholesale emigration to *LaMerica*, was a crippled cobbler nicknamed "Cristoforo Colombo" for being the first in Toretto to have migrated to the New World. When Colombo first heard, by chance, that a worker in *LaMerica* could earn in a single day what it would take a week to earn in the village, he sailed from Naples with no other information to guide him. On board ship he learned from fellow émigrés, who were returning to New York after having visited their families, how to establish himself in Manhattan at his trade. That advice proved invaluable. Within a year, the cobbler had saved enough money to send for two of his brothers, thereby instigating a chain of migration that eventually brought more than half of Toretto's population to the new land and resulted in the incarnation of a new Toretto.

Ironically, during one of Cristoforo Colombo's extended visits to Toretto, the American Congress enacted legislation that excluded immigrants for reasons of advanced age and physical infirmity. Not until Colombo had crossed the ocean again and reached Ellis Island did he learn that he was no longer eligible for admission.

By 1908, some two hundred *case Americani* had been erected in the new Toretto and more were under construction. Unlike the dark and airless hovels most of the villagers had occupied in the old Toretto, the new houses had separate rooms for adults and children. They were also equipped with good-sized windows, a novelty in southern Italy. Even more surprising was the increasing number of children who, at the urging of their relatives in America, were attending school and receiving far more education than their elders ever had.

What distinguished Toretto from other towns Mangano surveyed was a strong communal concern, which remained intact both in Toretto and wherever in America its natives were working. While it was not uncommon for emigrants to prosper from their American sojourn, their prosperity was usually limited to the emigrant and his immediate family; seldom did it benefit the entire community, as happened in Toretto. The town may also have benefited from being in the region of Apulia, where workers tended to be more tightly organized and better able to contend with the demands of large landowners. Significantly, there was less emigration from Apulia to the United States than there was from any other southern region.

Elsewhere in the *Mezzogiorno* the dire consequences of mass emigration were all too evident. The barren hillsides and abandoned fields where emigration had taken its heaviest toll of able-bodied workers—Sicily, Calabria, Campania—bore silent testimony to the price the southern economy paid for the remittances that came from America. Farming had often stopped, and terrace walls were falling in decay. The orange and lemon groves within those crumbled walls were themselves decimated by heavy spring rains.

Big landowners were not disturbed when emigration first increased, since there remained a glut of farm workers willing to work long hours for as little as 16 cents a day. But twenty years later emigration had eliminated the glut, and landowners were unable to find workers at two or three times the pay. Wheat and grape production fell to new lows, and prices for bread and wine increased accordingly. "We poor landholders are at the mercy of the few able-bodied men who remain," said one. "But we cannot expect anything from Rome [i.e., legislation stopping free emigration]. They do not think of us; they are engrossed too much in the interests of northern Italy."

The southern labor shortage became so serious that the larger employers tried to colonize the *Mezzogiorno* regions hardest hit with workers from regions north of Rome. All such efforts failed. Workers in the central and northern regions refused to put up with the primitive conditions of living and working prevalent in the South.

For the small landowners, the loss of tenants sometimes meant the loss of lands. Unable to find farmhands to do the work previously done by tenants, they sometimes tried to cultivate their own lands, but lacking experience, went bankrupt and had to sell their properties at auction to pay overdue taxes. Some resorted to emigration themselves.

Although the labor shortage eliminated some of the most blatant exploitation, farm workers returning from America had problems as well. The victims were usually those who had saved enough money during their American sojourn to buy land and establish themselves as independent cultivators, free at last of greedy landowners and their farm managers. But for many such émigrés, that dream was doomed from the start. The land they purchased was frequently of the poorest quality and priced exorbitantly. Taking advantage of the *contadini*'s eagerness to acquire farmland as quickly as possible, the landowners had no difficulty disposing of their least desirable holdings at high prices set in collusion with neighboring landowners.

The land acquired by a would-be independent farmer frequently produced an inconsequential harvest, too small to justify the effort of continuing cultivation. After two or three such harvests, the state would start pressuring the owner for unpaid taxes and he would be left with no alternative but to sell back the property to its original owner at a price far below what he had paid. With what money remained or could be borrowed, the ex-farmer, out of embarrassment or economic necessity, would often return to the United States, this time taking his family with him, with no expectation of returning.

Social critics urged legislation to prohibit this type of abuse, but after much discussion nothing came of it except a general agreement that southerners who could not improve their lot were entitled to seek a better life across the ocean.

The returning emigrants, whether successful or unsuccessful, often came back with a new degree of self-confidence and an appreciation of human rights. In towns where educational facilities were not adequate, they demanded that schools be built. In 1907 Mangano found that "a spirit of hope and progress" was finally stirring. What socialism had been unable to achieve, emigration was doing in a most natural manner.

Spurring Italian emigration to the United States was the fear that the U.S. Congress would enact a literacy test similar to those in Australia and South America, barring immigrants unable to read forty words in any language. Before the turn of the century, nearly half of all Italian immigrants were illiterate.

The first attempt to enact a literacy test law passed both houses of Congress in 1890, but was defeated by a presidential veto. Repeated attempts to pass the law were made in 1898, 1902, 1913, 1915, and 1917, when Congress finally overrode President Wilson's veto.

Other factors boosting immigration were the impending world war and steamship fares that had fallen as low as $10. Naples became the busiest passenger port in all Italy, with approximately ten thousand people employed in handling the numerous facets of emigration.

THE VIA DOLOROSA

The emigrants' problems began with reaching the port of embarkation. Unless they lived near a railroad stop or were accompanied by returning émigrés, the journey to the port was lined with potential hazards. If the distance was not too great, they traveled on foot, some over distances of 40 and 50 miles. For longer distances they used donkeys or horse-drawn carts piled high with their belongings, sleeping wherever they could find any kind of shelter.

One emigrant who left Italy in 1900 with five other members of his family described the first phase of their journey to Naples via Palermo.

We left in a two-wheeled cart that carried a big home-made trunk, my mother, two of my brothers, my sister and also a cousin. . . . On our way to Palermo, which was forty miles away, we had a horse and a driver. We stayed overnight in a small town where we slept in a stable; the horse slept on the hay. After we got to Palermo I remember that we hopped onto a small launch—there was no such thing as a dock.
The Mediterranean was very rough and we had to travel some distance to get to the ship. It took all night. And I remember so well that there was really a lot of crying going on because of the frightfulness of the Mediterranean. The boat was not a boat to come across the ocean. You had to go to Naples—and there you took the ship.

In the early days, emigrants avoided Italian ships, the "vagabond ships" that went from port to port looking for cargo. One never knew when they would reach New York. German ships were preferred. Only later did Palermo become a port of embarkation. In the meantime, emigrants had to travel to Naples or Genoa.

Many of the emigrants travelled from remote villages and had never before seen a city. Wherever people were leaving for America there was the cacophony of families separating, crying, entreating, promising, and the din of children shouting and laughing, too young to comprehend the poignancy of the farewells.

At the Neapolitan port area many pitfalls awaited the emigrant. Cunning peddlers sold "American" clothes: "You don't want to look like a greenhorn, do you?" Con men sold false certificates for smallpox vaccinations and cures for trachoma, the eye disease. Others, dressed as Franciscan monks, peddled saints' pictures and cards assuring a safe passage to the New World. One "dentist" warned that the voyage would bring on severe toothaches and for a small price offered to extract potentially troublesome teeth. And there were the porters who promised to take all suitcases "right to your cabin," and disappeared with them forever. Agents sometimes sent emigrants to port several days before sailing time, obliging them to pay for extra meals and overnight accommodations.

Similar hazards awaited those in Genoa and Palermo. The port of Genoa was especially notorious before laws to protect and assist passengers were enacted in 1901, in part through the intercession of the bishop of Pazienza, who trained missionaries for work with emigrants.

Authorities now were required to provide prospective emigrants with reliable advice for every aspect of their journey, including information on approved boardinghouses, hotels, and restaurants. Emigration officials published a bulletin for distribution, warning emigrants not to believe everything they had heard about life in the United States.

In addition, in response to U.S. concerns, emigrants now would receive a preliminary medical examination to determine whether they could meet the health requirements established by American immigration authorities.

Entire shiploads of Italian immigrants were rejected after reaching New York with passengers infected with cholera or some other contagious disease. The preliminary medical examination at the port of embarkation became the most dreaded station of the *via dolorosa*. The most frequent reason for disqualification was the examiner's detection of trachoma. Many argued in vain that they had no eye problem, that their condition was nothing more than the residual effect of overly tearful farewells or caused by sleepless nights spent on a train where the air was polluted by the engine's use of cheap coal.

Sometimes one person failed to pass the examination and the rest of the family was suddenly confronted with the dilemma of whether to leave him or her behind. In at least one instance a mother who was disqualified because she was blind in one eye insisted that her family leave without her.

The same government regulations formulated to protect the emigrants before their departure also prescribed conditions affecting their comfort and health at sea, including sleeping arrangements, food, and sanitation.

Despite such assurances, few of the regulations, particularly those applying to shipboard life, were ever enforced. Ships were overcrowded, more like cattle ships, and smelled of human waste. Steerage—the only class most emigrants could afford—was quite literally next to the ship's steering equipment, below the waterline. The term "steerage" became synonymous with the travails of trans-Atlantic emigration. Passengers were packed in to a dangerous degree, each ship compartment holding at least three hundred people. Women traveled without husbands, men traveled alone, and families were installed in small cubicles, each passenger allotted a berth that served both as bed and storage place.

The only open deck space available to steerage passengers was usually small and situated in an area most directly affected by dirt from the stacks. Because of limited deck space, passengers had to take turns on deck. An emigrant who had embarked at Naples with his sister recalled that he never saw her the entire voyage. On some ships, steerage passengers were made to share their meager deck space with crew members butchering livestock for the meals to be served to cabin- and first-class passengers.

The regulation requiring separate washrooms for men and women was frequently ignored, and often only saltwater was provided for cleaning purposes.

U.S. Immigration investigators were alarmed by the indecent attitude and conduct of the men (crew as well as passengers) toward women in steerage. Some of the more graphic impressions of what life was like among steerage passengers bound for America were recorded in 1904 by an American investigative journalist, Broughton Brandenburg, who traveled with his wife. Posing as Italian emigrants, they booked passage on a German ship, the *Prinzessin Irin,* because of its reputation for treating steerage passengers more humanely than most other trans-Atlantic carriers. Throughout the crossing the Brandenburgs saw little evidence to warrant that claim. They soon became aware that crew members generally treated the emigrants as "inferior beings, to be knocked and pushed about."

For many, the steerage passage across the Atlantic was remembered as a kind of purgatory, a period of punishment imposed on them by Providence for having abandoned their motherland.

In an effort to prevent overcrowding in steerage, the U.S. Congress in 1902 enacted the Passenger Act, which required that chairs and tables be provided for passengers in every class. Acting for the Italian Immigration Office in 1904, Adolfo Russo charged that many of the ships bringing immigrants to New York were ignoring the regulation. An investigation by American authorities showed that 90 percent of the ships were indeed in violation of the Passenger Act; moreover, not a single mention of the violations was found in the annual reports of the U.S. Immigration Bureau. Six years later, a more comprehensive investigation by a U.S. Immigration Commission reported little or no improvement in steerage conditions.

The persistence of such violations may well have been encouraged by the mounting prejudice developing among Americans against the massive immigration of peoples from both Eastern and Southern Europe—a prejudice which the navigation companies found useful. The Immigration Commission pointed out that the ships bringing Northern European immigrants to America had more acceptable steerage sections.

Forewarned by friends who had already been to America, some of the emigrants brought their own bread, salami, cheese, and pickled vegetables, along with bottles of wine.

ARRIVAL IN THE PROMISED LAND

Except for the misery of seasickness, the physical discomfort suffered en route was not nearly as disturbing as the foreboding emigrants shared about their impending debarkation at Ellis Island. Foremost was the worry that the American authorities might yet find a reason to bar their entrance. This fear was aggravated by the knowledge that they would also be confronted by questions which, if not answered correctly, would doom them to deportation.

Most of the questions were simple and had already been asked by the crew preparing the ship's manifest, required by American law, which included each passenger's sex, occupation, literacy, last residence, "zone" of destination, type of immigration (temporary or permanent), and ports of embarkation and debarkation. The two additional questions they would be asked at Ellis Island caused the most concern, since in many instances they could not be answered truthfully with a yes. First, had the émigré paid for his own passage, or had it been paid by another person or by "any corporation, society, municipality or government"? And if so, by whom? Although many émigrés had passages prepaid by an American relative, steamship agents and officials instructed them to answer in the negative. Second, had he (or she) "by reason of any offer, solicitation, promise or agreement, expressed or implied, agreed to perform labor in the United States?" In many instances the émigré had already been assured by some solicitous American relative that a job would be awaiting him. Yet, again, he was told to answer no. "Remember," warned the ships' agents, "you have no job waiting for you, and you have paid your own way." Some emigrants failed to grasp the logic of lying when there seemed to be no reason to do so; in their confusion, a surprising number answered one or both questions truthfully, and were promptly deported, at the expense of the navigation company.

These two questions stemmed from American efforts to eradicate the evils of the *padrone* system* with legislation which, as of

---

*A House Investigating Committee, reporting on violations of the contract labor law, described in 1889 the conditions which that law was designed to prevent:

A practice had prevailed among certain foreigners residing in this country of importing men for the purpose of contracting them to perform services chiefly in the construction of railroads. The principal is connected with numerous agents in Europe, who scour the country, picking up laborers. The agent pays the expense of bringing them to the United States, but takes an agreement from each one to repay the principal, within a certain time, a sum usually twice as large as the actual cost of the transportation.

Upon their arrival, the laborers are entirely under the control of the principal, and are subject to many impositions and frauds, and in some instances are kept in al-

1885, forbade the importation of foreign workers under any type of contract. The complexity of the law, which did not precisely answer the question of what constituted a contract, made its enforcement extremely difficult.

For all of their good intentions, the contract labor laws failed to eliminate the *padrone* system. The *padrone* or his agents could easily circumvent them simply by substituting oral agreements for written ones. Few of the *padrone* agents were ever prosecuted successfully. The decline of the system came about not through law enforcement but through the increasing number of Italian immigrants in the United States upon whom the prospective arrival could count for whatever assistance he might need to find a job and a place to live. Yet the *padrone* system, by circumventing the law, continued to operate through the peak years of Italian immigration. *Padrone* agents went so far as to book passage on American-bound immigrant ships in order to spot steerage passengers who might be susceptible to their sales pitch. Once an émigré had agreed to the agent's offer, he would be carefully instructed on what to say and how to conduct himself at Ellis Island.

The general mood in steerage was one of high anxiety. Stories of ship disasters seemed to be the preferred topic. One such story concerned a ship full of émigrés that left Palermo in the early years of the new century. It was bound for New York but never arrived. Somewhere in the Atlantic the ship's rudder broke, and for several weeks the vessel drifted helplessly at the mercy of frightful storms. Despite careful rationing, food and supplies were soon exhausted. Tables, benches, chairs, and even the wooden doors of the ship were chopped as fuel for the engines. More and more passengers became ill and hopes of survival dimmed. After several months, a heavy wind blew the rudderless vessel close enough to a Portuguese fishing village to permit some of the crew to swim ashore and enlist assistance. The families in the village sheltered and ministered to the stricken families, until a second ship arrived to complete the journey

---

most a state of slavery. They come here with no intention of becoming citizens, but merely for the purpose of accumulating a small sum of money, with which to return to their homes. If sickness or distress overtake them in this country they become public charges. Many thousands have been brought here in this manner.

Report of the Select Committee of the House of Representatives to inquire into alleged violations of the laws prohibiting contract labor.

to New York. But long before news of their rescue reached Palermo, the ship had been reported lost and all its passengers dead. Masses were said; the city was draped in black, and the mayor ordered all flags to fly at half-mast since most of the passengers were from the Palermo province. The eventual safe landing was not reassuring to listeners.

Rumors were repeated until they took on the aspect of reality. The most persistent concerned imminent changes in the American laws that would exclude them from the promised land.

Yet not all was gloom and doom. Between bouts of seasickness and depression the younger steerage passengers sang to the accompaniment of mouth organs, tambourines, accordions, mandolins, and guitars. When the ocean was peaceful, there was dancing. In almost any kind of weather there were games of *lotto* and *mora;* but most frequently *briscola* and *scopa,* the card games traditional to southern Italians. On ships with passengers who had been to the United States before, the American dice game of craps was introduced.

Except for men who had served in the Italian Army with others from the various regions, the journey marked the first time southern Italians had a chance to commune with compatriots not from their own native area. While southerners managed to converse with one another, communication with Italians from north of Rome was another matter. Apart from the linguistic barriers, which few northerners and southerners could surmount, there was an additional problem: northerners had been conditioned to see southerners as an inferior people; southerners, in turn, regarded northerners as *superbi* (snobs). Nonetheless, as the ship neared the new land, common concerns helped to reduce the barriers between them.

The passage provided the Italians with contacts from other countries as well. In 1905, an American traveling in steerage witnessed a *festa* in which passengers of three different nationalities participated. A Russian Jewish woman who had fled her native village when her father was beaten to death during a pogrom entranced the audience with the vibrancy of her singing. A group of Slavs won applause with what the American observer described as "guttural tunes and clumsy dances." The Italians, the most numerous of the performers, presented a sleight-of-hand magician, a Punch and Judy marionette show, and operatic tunes from a hurdy-gurdy operated by a passenger named Pietro, who expected to earn his livelihood this way on the streets of New York. *"Signore e Signorini,"* announced Pietro after he had exhausted his repertoire, "I have the great honor of presenting to you the national anthem of the great American country to which we are traveling." He began turning the crank of the hurdy-gurdy, and out came the ragtime notes of "Ta-ra-ra boom-de-lay."

Another distraction during one crossing was the news that stowaways had been discovered trying to conceal themselves on board. They were ordered deported as soon as the ship reached Ellis Island.

Cristoforo Colombo, the Discoverer, born in Genoa, Italy, in 1454. He made four voyages to the New World and died in 1506, still believing he had discovered the coast of Asia.

Amerigo Vespucci, the fifteenth-century Italian explorer who declared America to be the New World. Both North and South America were named after him.

Giovanni da Verrazzano, the Florentine navigator who, while exploring the coast of North America in 1524, discovered New York and Narragansett Bays.

Giuseppe Garibaldi, the charismatic general whose leadership led to the establishment of Italy as a modern unified nation in 1871.

Once a day immigrant passengers were permitted on deck for a bit of sea air, weather permitting. *(Courtesy of Centro Studi Emigrazione, Rome.)*

Italian immigrant family en route to Ellis Island on a small ferryboat operated by the Immigration Service for steerage passengers. *(Photo by Lewis W. Hine, courtesy of New York Public Library.)*

Immigrants moving into an all-Italian enclave in lower Manhattan, 1905. *(From* Gli Italiani negli Stati Uniti d'America, *New York, 1906.)*

Mulberry Street in 1906, the heart of lower Manhattan's Little Italy. *(Courtesy of Library of Congress.)*

Bedroom of an Italian family in a rear tenement on New York's East Side, 1910. *(Photo by Lewis W. Hine, courtesy of New York Public Library.)*

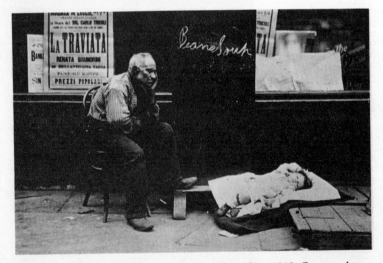

Fresh air for the baby, Italian quarter, New York City, 1910. Congested tenement living led to high rates of tuberculosis. *(Photo by Lewis W. Hine, courtesy of New York Public Library.)*

The first strawberry harvest in Tontitown, Arkansas, circa 1890, one of several agricultural communities of Italian immigrants escaping urban congestion. In the East, an outstanding one was Vineland, New Jersey, founded by an American real estate developer with a Utopian vision. *(Courtesy of Centro Studi Emigrazione, Rome.)*

Organizing a lynch mob in New Orleans at a citizens' mass meeting following the shooting of the city's police superintendent. On March 14, 1891, the mob lynched eleven Sicilian immigrants, although a court had found them not guilty. *(From* Harper's Weekly, *March 28, 1891.)*

New York public school children (predominantly Italian) pledging allegiance to the American flag. *(Photo by Jacob Riis, 1892, courtesy of Library of Congress.)*

Antonio Simonelli played the role of Christ in the passion play staged by a cast of working-class immigrants in an effort to reduce anti-Italian bigotry in Rochester, New York. *(From the 1909 scrapbook of social worker Florence Kitchelt Cross.)*

Italian weeklies in the United States, 1906. *(From Gli Italiani negli Stati Uniti d'America.)*

Children and families in their Sunday best were often the subject of photographs sent to relatives in Italy. *(Courtesy Di Marco Family Photographs, the Balch Institute for Ethnic Studies Library.)*

Those left behind. Once a family of twelve in Racalmuto, Sicily, emigration reduced it to the parents and two daughters.

A former coal miner, John Ricci escaped the hazards of such employment by becoming self-employed, 1907. *(Courtesy Ricci Family Photographs, the Balch Institute for Ethnic Studies Library.)*

Drying out pasta. Producing pasta became an early business enterprise of the immigrants. *(Courtesy of Library of Congress.)*

Italian crew working in the virgin timberlands of Washington State, ca. 1917. *(Courtesy of Achille Forgione.)*

A group of Italian street laborers during the construction of the Sixth Avenue Elevated in New York City, 1910. *(Photo by Lewis W. Hine, courtesy of New York Public Library.)*

Housewife bringing home unfinished garments for homework, ca. 1915. *(Courtesy of Library of Congress.)*

Bootblacks, ca. 1910. Children of poor immigrant families often dropped out of school to supplement the family income. *(Courtesy of Library of Congress.)*

"The Great Strike—Lawrence, Mass. 1912," from a painting by Ralph Fasanella commemorating one of the most dramatic strikes in American history, in which **Italian** workers and labor leaders played key roles. *(Courtesy of the artist.)*

An Italian immigrant expressing his opinion of strikebreakers in a Labor Day Parade in Rochester, New York, ca. 1915. *(From the Stone Negative Collection, Rochester Museum & Science Center, Rochester, New York.)*

Berardo Scarpone, of Bryn Mawr, Pennsylvania, was a private first-class in the American army during World War I. He was wounded on Armistice Day, but survived. *(Courtesy of Mary Costanza.)*

Typical Chicago street scene in an Italian district during the twenties.
(Italian/American Collection, University of Illinois at Chicago, The University Library, Department of Special Collections.)

Enrico Caruso, the legendary tenor, in the lead role of
Puccini's *Girl of the Golden West*. In his seventeen-
year association with the Metropolitan Opera, Caruso
sang in more than six hundred performances. *(New
York Public Library, Music Division.)*

Rudolph Valentino, born Rodolpho d'Antonguolla, the most popular romantic idol of the silent movies in the twenties. (*New York Public Library, Theater Collection.*)

Edoardo Migliaccio—better known by his stage name, Farfariello ("Little Butterfly")—was the favorite comic of the Italian immigrants, ca. 1932. (*Center for Migration Studies of New York.*)

Frank Capra in 1931 while directing *Ladies of Leisure,* in which Barbara Stanwyck emerged as a star. By the end of the decade the Sicilian-born Capra had become famous for movies that reflected the American Dream. *(New York Public Library, Theater Collection.)*

CHAPTER 8

Arrival

Until yesterday I was among folks who understood me. This
morning I seemed to have awakened in a land where my
language meant little more to the native (as far as meaning
was concerned) than the pitiful noises of a dumb animal.
Where was I to go? What was I to do? Here was the
promised land. The elevated rattled by and did not answer.
The automobiles and trolley sped by, heedless of me.

—BARTOLOMEO VANZETTI

The émigrés' earliest sighting of the Manhattan skyline incited a
fever of excitement that would be remembered along with the
discomfort and anxieties of the journey. Among the young Italians,
shouts of *Viva LaMerica!* could be heard above the battle of cheers
and cries in diverse languages as passengers pressed forward to the
railings for a clearer view. For the older passengers, there was more
relief than joy; the weariness of the journey had taken its toll by that
time. The paramount emotion was anxiety as to what would happen
to them before they were permitted to enter the new land.

Those sailing into New York Harbor after 1885 were likely to
notice Bartholdi's colossal figure of a woman with an uplifted arm
bearing a torch. Yet few of them could have been aware of its
significance until it was explained by passengers who had already

been to the United States. Dedicated in 1886, the Statue of Liberty was originally known as "Liberty Enlightening the World." Some of the immigrants missed it altogether, so intent were they upon identifying Ellis Island, which was only half a mile away.

Not until the mass immigration from Southern and Eastern Europe was well under way did Ellis Island begin functioning as the nation's chief receiving station. Under the auspices of the federal government, which had only recently assumed responsibility for the processing of immigrants, Ellis Island opened on January 1, 1892, nearly four centuries after Columbus's discovery of America. At this time the number of Italian immigrants was beginning to surpass that of all other foreigners entering the country. Five years after its formal opening, the flimsily constructed complex of buildings on the island caught fire and burned to the ground.

During the rebuilding of Ellis Island in the next two and a half years, processing was returned to the Barge Office on Manhattan's Battery near Castle Garden, the nation's first major immigrant receiving station. Originally built as a fortress in 1807 to protect Manhattan from foreign invasions, Castle Garden was later converted into an amusement hall and opera house, where P. T. Barnum introduced Jenny Lind, the famed Swedish songbird, and where Americans first attended performances of Italian opera. In 1855 it began functioning as an immigrant receiving station under the jurisdiction of New York State. As the numbers of immigrants increased, Castle Garden developed a scandalous reputation among its personnel for stealing and extorting money from arriving foreigners. The station's unsavory reputation was heightened by the sensational revelation that corpses of immigrants who had been detained in the Castle Garden hospital on Ward Island for reasons of ill health were being used for dissection.

Such skulduggery finally persuaded Congress to enact legislation to assume federal control of immigration processing. The legislature also called for the building of a larger receiving facility away from the corrupting influence of the mainland. Possibly because of its proximity to the Statue of Liberty, Ellis Island was chosen as the site of the new facility. During the rebuilding that followed the disastrous fire of 1887, the island's original 3.5 acres (known to the Indians as Gull Island) were enlarged to 10; eventually the receiving station was to encompass 27 acres and thirty-five fireproof buildings, among them a multi-winged hospital once rated the best in the nation.

Because Ellis Island could not accommodate large vessels, the first stop of the immigrant ships was the Lower Bay of New York Harbor, where they were placed in quarantine. It was at this point that the steerage passengers were made to understand that, despite the vaunted egalitarianism of America, first- and second-class passengers, along with American citizens, would receive preferential treatment. Steerage passengers received their medical examinations on Ellis Island, while non-steerage passengers were given cursory examinations on board.

Following the inspection of first- and second-class passengers, the ship moved toward the tip of Manhattan, to a pier where passengers who had already been inspected would disembark to be greeted by demonstrative friends and relatives. The spectacle did nothing to bolster the spirits of the steerage passengers, who were given green identification numbers and herded aboard barges for the trip to Ellis Island.

When there was no overcrowding, the medical inspection took no more than three or four hours and sometimes as little as forty-five minutes. Unless the inspector found reason for detaining an immigrant for further investigation, he or she was let into the promised land. If a problem arose, the inspector could imprison the immigrant on the island for several days or longer.

The medical examination took place in an enormous high-ceilinged area known as the "Registry Room," which reminded one observer of the Chicago Stock Yards. There were often as many as twenty lines of immigrants herded into compartments awaiting their turn for inspection.

The physical examinations were conducted in a spacious area dubbed "Judgement Hall" by a team of Marine physicians attired in braided blue uniforms. Even more intimidating than the uniform was anticipation of the moment when the examiner would snap back the immigrant's eyelid with a buttonhook to look for signs of trachoma. Aside from the physical discomfort was the awareness that, if detected, "sickness of the eye" would mean detention and possibly deportation.

Immigrants who were to be detained were identified by a chalk mark on their clothing. A simple "X" meant that the immigrant was suspected of mental deficiency; if a specific symptom was detected, there would be a circle around the "X." "B" signified back problems;

"C" conjunctivitis, "CT" trachoma, "E" eyes, "F" face, "FT" foot, "G" goiter, "H" heart, "K" hernia, "L" lameness, "N" neck, "P" lungs, "PG" pregnancy, and "S" senility. Those with chalk marks, about 50 percent of the people examined, were directed to a room set aside for further examinations, where a doctor would determine whether the condition was serious enough to warrant deportation. If an ailment was considered easily curable, the immigrant would be treated in the Ellis Island hospital before being certified for admission into the country.

During the peak years of immigration, as many as five thousand people were processed in a single day, leaving many of the immigrants in a state of bewilderment. This gave birth to an anecdote told by Ellis Island staff members about a visit Theodore Roosevelt had made to "Judgement Hall." As he watched the immigrants line up to be examined, President Roosevelt was particularly struck by their apathy. Wondering what effect an unexpected gift of money might have on one immigrant woman in line, he summoned an aide and instructed him to present a five-dollar gold piece to the first woman on line with a child in her arms. Spotting a mother who fitted that description, the aide handed her the gold piece. The woman accepted the coin without comment, slipped it into her dress, and moved on, "without even raising her eyes or giving any indication that the incident had made any different impression on her than any of the regular steps in the inspection."

Adult immigrants with families in tow suffered the constant fear that the family might become separated. These fears were so deepseated that Ellis Island became known to the Italian immigrants as *L'Isola dell lagrime*—the Island of Tears.

For unmarried women and young widows unaccompanied by family members, Ellis Island was liable to be traumatic. Inspectors subjected them to the closest scrutiny in order to prevent the admission of women who might become public charges or prostitutes. A woman whose hands had not been callused by hard labor came under immediate suspicion and was detained on the island until the authorities could be convinced that her sponsors had acceptable credentials. A case in point was that of a young Sicilian widow, Rita Alfano, who arrived at Ellis Island in 1905 with her five-year-old daughter under the sponsorship of a sister-in-law and her husband. After both had passed all the Ellis Island examinations, she expected to be released into the custody of her sister-in-law. But the sister-in-law failed to present herself with her husband. The suspicions of the authorities were aroused, and Rita Alfano and her daughter were ordered detained on the island. The young widow feared deportation to her native village, where her late husband's aged parents had made it clear that they were no longer able to harbor the widow and the child. Sicilian mores of that era strictly precluded the possibility of finding employment, except as a servant, which would make her a social outcast, becoming a prostitute or entering a convent, which would mean giving up her child to an orphange.

On the third day of her detention, the widow sent her Rochester relatives a cry for help. "I have spent every day and night crying," she wrote, "racking my brain hopelessly trying to find a way of escaping this hell. . . . What if they send me back to Italy? Oh God, what should I do? I am here desperate with poor Fortunata who keeps on crying and asking when we can leave this place." In a postscript she added: "My dearest sister-in-law, I beg you in the name of God to send your husband as soon as possible because I can't stay here any longer. Please do not forget your unfortunate sister-in-law who has had so many troubles in her life and is now in trouble again." The letter had the desired effect. Her sister-in-law and husband left for Ellis Island as soon as the letter arrived. The husband's credentials, which included a bankbook showing substantial savings, satisfied the authorities. Rita Alfano and her daughter were finally released into his custody.

Not all women traveling alone had authentic sponsors. There were times when "brothers" and "uncles" at Ellis Island were, upon investigation, found to be frauds. The women they had come to claim were ordered deported.

Many men engaged to marry newly arrived immigrant women but had never seen their prospective brides until they met at Ellis Island, except perhaps in a photograph sent from Italy by a friend or relative acting as a marriage agent. Matchmaking was a traditionally approved practice in most of the *Mezzogiorno,* especially when the prospective bride and groom hailed from the same town. There were some instances where the man considered his prospective bride too homely and refused to accept her. In other instances the prospective bride would take a dislike to the man who had expected to marry her and ask to be deported. Less resolute women married their unappealing fiancés anyway, feeling obliged to do so because the men had already paid for their journey.

No one was better qualified to understand the variegated drama that daily unfolded at Ellis Island than Fiorello La Guardia in his role as interpreter. The son of an Italian immigrant, he spoke not only Italian but also German, Croatian, Yiddish, Spanish, and French. Many of the scenes he witnessed disturbed him. "I never managed during the three years I worked there [1907–10] to become calloused to the disappointment and despair I witnessed almost daily," he wrote in his memoirs some thirty years later. La Guardia was particularly distressed when he was assigned to interpret for physicians examining so-called "mental cases." He felt certain that "many of those classified as mental cases were so classified because of ignorance on the part of the immigrants or the inability of the doctors to understand the particular immigrant's 'norm or standard.' " One such case, involving a teenage girl from the mountains of northern Italy, "haunted" La Guardia for many years.

On the whole, he found the Ellis Island personnel "kindly and considerate," considering especially the brief time an inspector was permitted for each immigrant. Still, he was highly critical of inspectors who seemed to enjoy trapping people into giving the wrong answers to the questions they asked.

La Guardia approved of the intent of the laws to prevent the exploitation of immigrant labor through the *padrone* system, which he characterized as "one of the most sordid and blackest pictures in our entire history." Yet he was bemused by a basic contradiction in the law: any immigrant without a job was excluded since he was likely to become a public charge; at the same time the immigrant could also be excluded if he was certain of employment. It rankled La Guardia that too many of the men who had been deported for such violations may well have been borderline cases whose only assurance of employment came from relatives or *paesani* already in the United States.

Suicides among those ordered deported were not uncommon. According to estimates, at least three thousand émigrés of various nationalities took their lives in the course of Ellis Island's forty-year history. The frustration of having crossed the ocean only to be rejected was too much to bear. One of the few suicides recorded in some detail was that of Lorenzo di Renzo, who, on arriving in 1914 with no funds and no expectation of finding a job, was ordered deported on the grounds that he might become a public charge.

Feeling unable to go home again after having vowed to his *paesani* that he would become a successful American, he shot himself just as the French liner transporting him back to Italy was pulling out of New York Harbor. Had he arrived at Ellis Island only a month later, when World War I had broken out and jobs in the United States were easily available, he would have been admitted.

In addition to the deaths by suicide were the drownings of immigrants slated for deportation who, under cover of darkness, tried to swim to the New Jersey shore, only to be inundated by rising tides. In a corner of Ellis Island the government built a small crematorium for immigrants who had died in their attempts to enter the land of hope. "This," wrote Willard A. Heaps, "was the only gesture the government could make for these tragic people who had no hope and rarely any next of kin who could trouble about them in a strange land and situation."

One last question asked of those slated to be released from Ellis Island was how much money each immigrant was bringing into the country, although the immigration laws did not require a specified minimum amount. Occasionally the inspectors were willing to stretch the law if they could be persuaded that, despite the immigrant's lack of funds, he was not likely to become a public charge.

For many of those detained, Ellis Island became an extension of the ordeal they had known in steerage. On an average night in 1907, some seventeen hundred women and children would be crowded into a room with a normal capacity of six hundred. "The clean ones were pressed against those infected with vermin, and it wasn't long before everyone was contaminated, including inspectors," according to Frank Martucci, an immigration inspector during the floodtide years of immigration.

The food served to those immigrants was even worse than what they had known in steerage. For nine years, until a newly appointed Commissioner of Immigration ordered a more varied and conventional fare at no charge in 1910, the immigrants were fed nothing but rye bread and prunes, morning, noon, and night.

The harsh treatment sometimes extended to taking unlawful advantage. Staff members were found guilty of accepting bribes and tips. Occasionally an immigrant was cheated when he converted his Italian money into American currency. There were also instances where some inspector, attracted to a young and pretty immigrant, would promise her admission if she would agree to a rendezvous.

Misconduct and corruption took place among the island's employees as well, but unlike those infractions that occurred at Castle Garden, they were almost always investigated and punished.

The history of Ellis Island is replete with stories of such incidents. Yet it did not lack defenders. Henry Pratt Fairchild, a prominent sociologist of the era, conceded in 1912 that with some six hundred staff members dealing daily with an average of five thousand immigrants, there were bound to be some who were careless, irritated, or vicious; but he contended that the degree of maltreatment inflicted on the immigrants at any given period was largely dependent on the competency and character of the Immigration Commissioner in charge. One Ellis Island inspector, speaking in behalf of his colleagues, said: "It is all right to talk of kindness and consideration but there comes a time, usually of overwork and the pressure of thousands of the waiting, when good intentions are discarded, self-control reaches a breaking point, and the immigrants become victims. Unfortunately, they frequently try our patience beyond endurance. The only solution at such times is a vacation, which is exactly what we cannot take during the rush periods."

Most of the immigrants, particularly those who had not suffered the trauma of detention, had little or no complaint. Broughton Brandenburg, still retaining his disguise as an Italian immigrant while at Ellis Island, was impressed by the "diligence and kindliness" of the examiners. Yet for all the good marks it received, the image of Ellis Island as a hellhole where immigrants were treated cruelly persisted throughout its history.

For the average immigrant, the experience was no better and no worse than what they were to undergo during their early years in the United States. In retrospect, Ellis Island simply became another station along the *via dolorosa* that would fade in time from memory. A surprising number of immigrants, however, would leave the island bearing one memento that remained with them for the rest of their lives and was passed on to their descendants. An inspector who found an immigrant's actual name too difficult to spell or pronounce would either abbreviate the name or substitute an entirely different one.

Some of the changes were made by inspectors with a perverse sense of humor. A prime example is that of the Irish American inspector who, while questioning a young Italian immigrant, decided his name was unpronounceable and changed it to O'Neill. The immigrant, who eventually became a Philadelphia judge (possibly because of his presumed Irish ancestry?), had difficulty explaining the name to his Italian relatives and friends. More often, inspectors would simply shorten the names. "Buonomo" became "Buono," "Randazzese" was reduced to "Randa," "Ragnoni" lost out to "Ragno," "Benedetto" to "Bennett," and so on.

Except for those immigrants who were being detained for further examinations, the final action of the inspectors was to divide released immigrants into two groups: the one third headed for New York City, and those destined for areas beyond New York and its environs. The New York-bound immigrants boarded the ferry to Battery Park in Manhattan. The scene became wildly emotional as soon as the entrance gate to the ferry opened and visitors and immigrants could embrace, weeping and laughing.

Impressed by the large numbers of Italian Americans on hand to greet the immigrants as they stepped off the Ellis Island ferry, *The New York Times* estimated that for every arriving immigrant there were at least five Italian Americans at the dock to welcome him. The enthusiastic crowds often got out of hand, and "Riot of Italians at the Battery" became a familiar headline in the New York newspapers. For many, the impression of *LaMerica* was that of a violent country with a police force that had no love for them.

The least fortunate of new arrivals were those who had no relatives or friends to greet them. Traveling alone, they often became the immediate prey of con artists as clever as their counterparts in Naples. Their favorite ploy was to act as friendly compatriots eager to be of assistance, often convincing the wariest immigrant that they were sincere in their determination to prevent a *paesano* from being cheated by criminal *Americani*. The victims would be taken to a boardinghouse where they were charged exorbitant prices for accommodations obtainable elsewhere at a fraction of the cost. The most blatant predators were the cab drivers, who would offer to take the new arrival to his destination for a reasonable fee, then stop the cab several times on the way, each time demanding additional money before going any further. Laden with baggage and alone in a large city, the immigrant would comply out of fear that he might be ejected from the cab with all of his bags. "New York was worse than Naples," recalled one Italian American who was swindled in both cities during his 1906 migration to the United States.

There were also fraudulent schemes to exploit people whose

relatives were being detained on Ellis Island. Italians already living in the United States, in collusion with American lawyers, would encourage their worried compatriots to acquire legal aid in order to "facilitate" their relatives' entry into the country, knowing full well that in most instances the lawyers could do nothing to influence the immigration authorities. The fees that resulted would be divided between the lawyers and the Italians who had brought them clients.

The vulnerability of newly arrived immigrants led to the formation in 1901 of the Society for the Protection of Italian Immigrants, consisting of a coalition of American social workers and concerned Italian Americans. Spearheaded by Gino Speranza, an Italian-born but American-educated attorney, the society lived up to its name. Besides offering advice and assistance to the immigrants, it identified and brought to justice swindlers, and found employment that could save the newly arrived immigrant from the clutches of a *padrone* or from the demoralizing ignominy of becoming a public charge. Although limited by the number of its personnel, the society undertook the task of "investigating and remedying, if possible, all abuses to which the Italian immigrants are exposed, and familiarizing the immigrants with the constitutional rights to which they are entitled."

The society's services also extended to the problems of immigrants returning to Italy, particularly in 1908, a year of severe economic depression when far more Italians were leaving the country than entering it (57,095 arrivals as against 171,370 departures). In their fierce scramble for passage back to Italy, the Italians became the target for unscrupulous steamship agents selling tickets for specific vessels in numbers that far exceeded their capacity. In one instance, when the agents had sold 1,800 tickets for a passenger ship that could only accommodate 1,500, the society arranged for the passage of 300 Italians on the next scheduled ship and provided them with free food and lodgings until they could embark.

Impressed by the society's efficiency, Italian authorities joined with a group of American philanthropists to help the society establish a base in New York City. Here for a modest fee as many as 182 immigrants at a time would receive temporary shelter and three meals a day, in an atmosphere conducive to New World optimism.

The helplessness of those Italian Americans who had no relatives to guide their entrance into the New World prompted the founding of several other organizations—notably an American branch of the San Raffaele Society, founded in Italy by Bishop John Baptist Scalabrini. This society operated missions, schools, hospitals, and hostels in fourteen states and in New York City, where its chief function was to assist immigrants from the time they disembarked until they were capable of being on their own. Women and children received special attention, being sheltered and fed free of charge until they could be turned over to the custody of relatives or, in some instances, until the society could find employment for those who had to fend for themselves.

Two years before the founding of the San Raffaele Society, Pope Leo XIII, dissatisfied with the slowness of the American Catholic Church in recognizing its responsibility toward the predominantly Catholic Italian immigrants, dispatched Sister Frances Xavier Cabrini, a disciple of Bishop Scalabrini, to New York City to provide leadership for establishing hospitals, schools, orphanages, and nurseries in the United States and in Latin America. Arriving as a representative of the Missionary Sisters of the Sacred Heart, founded in Italy in 1880, she made New York and Chicago the main base of her operations. In 1892, to celebrate the four hundredth anniversary of the discovery of America, she established her first hospital, the Columbus Hospital of New York. It was a small beginning: two private houses that served as a field hospital for the Italian workers who were employed in the most dangerous occupations in the New World, in a time when there were no social services available to the sick or injured. Later she opened branch hospitals, known as Columbus Extension Hospitals, in Chicago, Denver, and New Orleans (during the time of the cholera there). When she died in 1917, a series of hospitals, orphanages, and social agencies had been established all over the world to care for immigrants in need. In this work she attracted followers from all ethnic groups. It was the memory of her work and devotion that brought about her canonization in 1946. As a naturalized citizen, Mother Cabrini, as she became known, was the first American to achieve sainthood.

Unlike the Catholic organizations, which were generally operated by Italians, the Society for the Protection of Italian Immigrants had a strong American constituency. Its first president was Eliot Norton, the son of Harvard President Charles Eliot Norton. Like his father (who was quoted as saying that "The Italians are the sweetest people on earth; if I ever come back, may I be born an Italian"), he too was an Italophile. But while the father was captivated by cultured and educated Italians (like many upper-class Americans), the son's enthusiasm also encompassed the impoverished and uneducated immigrants arriving from the *Mezzogiorno* during a period when they were generally despised and maligned. As far as Eliot Norton was concerned, "the more Italian immigrants come to the United States the better."

As a secular organization with a board of directors that included prominent Americans, the society, though partially financed by the Italian government, was able to perform services in behalf of the immigrants that no Catholic-oriented organization was in a position to provide. One was to expose some of the abuses suffered by Italian immigrant workers in various parts of the nation.

The society's investigation of how Italian immigrant workers were being treated in four counties in West Virginia revealed that, after being lured there by false representations, workers were held in a state of virtual slavery. Gino Speranza, who personally headed the probe, found the Italians installed in isolated labor camps shut off from the outside world by mountains and surrounded by armed guards. One worker who tried to escape was locked up, presumably for the night, and never seen again. As a warning to anyone who had escape in mind during the hours when the guards were not on duty, a Gatling gun set on a hill pointed toward the largest of the labor camps. In all the camps, the contractors and their foremen carried guns.

Speranza, as the society's chief spokesman, headed an educational program to prevent the maltreatment of Italian workers and to urge legislation that would protect immigrant workers from false promises and blatant exploitation. In one of his published reports, Speranza describes how easily an immigrant could be victimized by an exploitative process that often began the day the immigrant set foot on American soil—or earlier.

The few dollars which the immigrant possesses on landing are skillfully taken out of his pocket by the hotel keeper before the hotel keeper gives him a chance to work. When he is reduced to absolute indigence, the lowest kind of work is offered to him and he has to accept it. He walks through Mulberry Street and sees a crowd around a bar in a basement. He enters the basement and finds a man employing men for a company. He adds his name to the list without knowing anything about the work he will be called upon to do, or about the place to which he is to be transported, or the terms of his engagement.

In those instances where the worker was given details about the work, the contractors almost invariably acted in bad faith, departing from the terms of the agreement "either as to wages, or hours of labor, or the very nature of the work." Contractors were known to pocket the fees paid to them by workers, and then lead the men to lonely places and abandon them.

On the assumption that "public opinion would not tolerate such abuses if they knew of them," the society entreated the American and Italian American press to give "fearless publicity" to the maltreatment of newly arrived Italian workers. It recommended that the wrongs perpetrated by exploiting "bankers" and other hiring agents toward their countrymen be described in specific detail, "not relying on generalities but giving names and addresses of the guilty." Unfortunately for the immigrants, the Italian American newspapers with the largest circulations seldom risked offending their more affluent readers (and advertisers), among whom were the very "bankers" and agents under attack by the society.

Nevertheless, Speranza was encouraged by the number of responses the society received to its exposure of the abuses in West Virginia. He declared that he had never before appreciated "the full importance and beneficial influence of a society like ours . . . standing as a bulwark for fair play [which was] not only a forceful lesson for the people there, in Italy, but an inspiring example of the American civil sense."

However, these efforts and the contributions of American philanthropists and subsidies from the Italian government were not enough to assist all of the Italians during the difficult early days of their American experience. Those who had already visited the United States often advised prospective immigrants to memorize the presumably American word "Ghiraraier" (the phonetic rendition of "Get out of here") and to shout it at any *Americano* who offered to help or tried to sell him something. Seldom were they told that the predators might include their own *paesani*.

Perhaps the most common advice the immigrant received was to conceal his Italian identity, at least to the extent of substituting American clothes for Italian ones. One immigrant from Avelino arrived in an expensive Italian suit he had bought to celebrate his entrance into the United States. On meeting him at the dock in Manhattan, his brother screamed, "Take it off, you greenhorn!" He went on to explain how important it was to look like an *Americano,* since Italians were generally regarded and treated as "a very low people." In an interview many years later, the former "greenhorn" said that his brother had been right; he had learned that "if you look like everybody else in this country, you've got a chance."

Thanks to the agencies formed for the protection of arriving immigrants, and also to the warnings spread by Italians returning to their native villages, the defrauding of immigrants gradually declined. But one form of exploitation continued throughout the peak years of immigration, despite federal attempts to prevent it. Federal investigators found that immigrants traveling by train got the poorest cars in the service; that the cars were overcrowded (some to the point where there were no seats available on long journeys); that immigrants were denied the use of dining and sleeping cars; and that no porters or brakemen were provided to assist women with their children and baggage. More seriously, the investigators reported that "little care is taken to have the immigrants get off at the right stations, or otherwise safeguard them en route." The Society for the Protection of Italian Immigrants, which joined in the investigation, complained that immigrants, though obliged to pay the same fare for railway travel as American citizens, invariably received inferior treatment.

Even after agencies were created to protect the immigrants, railroads still engaged in the cruelest practice of all: separating families by placing members on different trains arriving at different times. The purpose was to allot each of the railroads in the corsortium its share of the immigrant patronage. Sometimes this meant sending family members to their destinations by the most roundabout and expensive routes. The historian Rudolph Vecoli noted that "a large part of the immigrant traffic bound for Chicago was forwarded by boat from New York to Norfolk, Virginia, and from there it was carried by the Chesapeake and Ohio and connecting lines to Chicago. Since the immigrant trains were sidetracked for all other kinds of traffic, the journey seemed interminable. Their scanty resources by now depleted, many of the immigrants were literally starving when they finally arrived in Chicago."

In response to protests by the social agencies, the major railroads formed a Trunk Line Association, which purported to provide the immigrant passenger with the most direct route to his destination. Nevertheless, federal investigators in 1907 revealed that the practice of indirect routing continued. In a confidential report on the situation, Gino Speranza, in behalf of the Society for the Protection of Italian Immigrants, wrote: "To use our future citizens, tired from a long journey, homesick in a new country, penned up in cars often without food or money, to balance up the traffic by adding even one more hour to their hardship, is an injustice. The most direct route and the best trains for the fares paid, is the least that the American citizen, fond of fair play, can ask for the immigrant who cannot ask it himself."

Apart from the ruthless treatment imposed on them, the immigrant travelers also had to contend with their own ignorance of American geography. For a people whose past traveling experience had been chiefly limited to the next village, American railroad travel could easily become a nightmare. When Angelo Pellegrini landed in New York in 1913 with his mother and siblings, they had no idea of the distance to the state of Washington, nor could the immigration authorities find the town of McCleary, where his father would be waiting for them, on any map or train schedule. The father had arrived the year before, with the intention of working for three years and then returning to Italy with what he had saved; but before the year was up he became convinced that the Northwest was a good place to rear his family, and sent for his wife and five young children. Unable to locate McCleary, the authorities finally put the family on a train headed for a city in Washington, hoping that someone there could direct them to McCleary. The family (who may have confused Washington, D.C., with the state of Washington) expected to be joining the father within a few hours. Instead, they traveled for seven days, with not enough to eat because they could not make themselves understood.

When they finally reached the place indicated on their tickets, they were alarmed to find that nobody was there to meet them. Their alarm turned to horror when the Americans in the railroad station insisted there was no such town as McCleary. "Tired, hungry, desperate, convinced that the whole journey had been a malignant hoax," Pellegrini wrote in his memoir, "we children burst into tears." Then suddenly, "a little man" appeared in the station and spoke to them in Italian, a language they had not heard since leaving New York. "Why are you crying?" were his first words. Miraculously, he turned out to be a friend of their father's who knew exactly where the tiny community of McCleary was located (200 miles farther west) and he took them there himself. At last, after a journey of 7,000 miles that had taken almost a month, the family found its father.

For people who had been steeped in the myth of America all their lives, the first encounters with the promised land were bound to clash with preconceived expectations. "Noise is everywhere," exclaimed one in his diary. "The din is constant and it completely fills my head." Others were shocked by the dirt and ugliness. "New York was awful," remembered another. "The streets were full of horse manure. My town in Italy, Avelino, was much more beautiful. I said to myself; 'How come, America'? On hot days when the manure dried, the wind lifted it into the air like confetti and breathing became difficult."

Edward Corsi, arriving at the age of ten with his parents and siblings, was delighted with the hustle and bustle of Manhattan's "hurrying crowds," but depressed by the sight of the four "sordid tenement rooms" in East Harlem that were to be their home. His mother, unable to help contrasting the squalor of their neighborhood with the serenity and beauty of the Abruzzo countryside, never left the tenement unless it was absolutely necessary. Most of her time was spent sitting at the only outside window in the apartment, staring up at a small patch of sky.

The new arrivals were awed by the tall skyscrapers, elevated trains, and enormous bridges, but some of these dark first impressions frightened and dismayed many—especially the women, most of whom were confined to squalid railroad flats. Only the expense of a return journey and the prospect of undergoing the ordeal of steerage a second time prevented them from leaving immediately.

The stories of cultural shock sometimes involved hostile policemen. Julian Miranda learned from his immigrant grandfather that shortly after he had landed in lower Manhattan and managed to get through the gauntlet of "thieves, crooks, *padroni* and labor contractors," he was walking down lower Broadway, "dressed rather well [despite his lack of money] carrying a cane—a real *signore*," when a policeman, spotting him from across the street, shouted, "Where did you get that suit, dago?" Nervous after a rough ocean trip, Miranda's grandfather walked across the street and belted him with the cane. "Grandpa always said he did not understand the word, but he recognized the tone. That is why he left Italy and he did not wish to put up with the same here. He was arrested and a family member was contacted who raised enough money to bribe him out."

Others, however, were invigorated by New York. Arriving in the city at the age of fifteen, Pascal D'Angelo was startled, then entranced, by the spectacle of an elevated train dashing around a curve. "To my surprise not even one car fell. Nor did the people walking beneath scurry away as it approached." Minutes later, while riding a trolley, he was distracted by the sight of a father and son moving their mouths in continuous motion "like cows chewing on cud." Never having known of chewing gum, he assumed, "with compassion, that father and son were both afflicted with some nervous disease." Later, just before he and his immigrant companions reached their destination, he was surprised to note signs at streets with "Ave., Ave., Ave." printed on them. "How religious a place this must be that expressed its devotion at every crossing," he mused, though he could not understand why the word was not followed by "Maria."

Another immigrant, also able to laugh at his naivete years later, recalls that minutes after his arrival in Chicago he was thrilled to note a group of men who looked like Italians digging away on a street. He assumed this must be one of the American streets where gold could be had for the digging, and looked forward to the prospect of trying his own luck. "In the old country," he explained to an interviewer, "they used to say that America was a rich and wonderful place—so rich you could pick gold up in the street. And I believed it!"

After parting with loved ones in the old country, after a journey filled with anxiety and discomfort, the new arrivals now had to contend with understanding and accommodating to a whole new way of life.

PART FOUR

The Land They Came To

CHAPTER 9

Security in Tight Little Islands—The Early Days

Sam Tornatore came to Louisiana as a boy of ten to work in the cotton fields around Monroe. As a young man he had witnessed a lynching of three Italians in neighboring Mississippi. Now eighty-nine, and living in a nursing home, he explained how he fought against prejudice: "With my fists."

From the beginning, every group coming to the New World felt a sense of dislocation, of loneliness and insecurity that at times threatened violence—sometimes chronic violence. This environment, says Ray A. Billington in *America's Frontier Heritage,* created a "rivalry and with it a hostile tension which breeds distrust (and fear) of others."

The great Italian migration began at a time when America was beset by bank failures, stock market crashes, panic, and mass unemployment—a time without unions or any of the securities provided by a welfare state.

After leaving a closed, known, and structured place, the immigrant must have felt bewildered upon landing in this open, diffuse, and chaotic new land.

The ancient ceremony of strolling in the *piazza* was now transformed into a turbulent Saturday night out on the grand avenues of the cities of America; mountain villagers massed together on the beaches of Coney Island. Bartolomeo Vanzetti wrote upon his arrival in 1908:

> Until yesterday I was among folks who understood me. This morning I seemed to have awakened in a land where my language meant little more to the native (as far as meaning was concerned) than the pitiful noises of a dumb animal. Where was I to go? What was I to do? Here was the promised land. The elevated rattled by and did not answer. The automobiles and trolley sped by, heedless of me.

So the early immigrants tended to form tight islands in the urban centers of America that became their frontier.

The flow of Italians, once it reached the shores of America, clustered along the eastern shore, then slowly spread out into the vast expanse of North America. Rumors of jobs brought them to every corner of the Union. And work on the railroads scattered men all over the country to the tune of:

> Where de you worka John?
> On the Deleware Lackawan.

In New York City, the starting point for most, enclaves were formed of people who had come from the same region or village, sometimes even the same part of a village that had been home for centuries. They clustered together for comfort, for security from the animosity of those who had come from other countries before them, and for the sociability of being with those who spoke their language, ate their foods, and understood their humor and insecurities. The early arrivals settled on the the lower tip of Manhattan; a few moved north to Mulberry, the Bowery, then up to Second Avenue, until, with the Jews, they were the principal settlers of lower Manhattan. Some moved further north, to East Harlem. Others, lured by rumors of jobs, left New York City altogether and moved upstate to Glens Falls; Utica; Rochester; Buffalo; Barre, Vermont; Providence, Rhode Island; to Boston, Philadelphia, and on to the Midwest and the West. Relatively few moved south, except for those who settled in New

Orleans, where an Italian community prospered early on. A histori-
cally agricultural people became urban industrial workers.

In one decade (1900–10) more than 2 million Italian men,
women, and children entered the country. The flood did not abate
until restrictive immigration laws were enacted in the twenties. By
1930 another 2.5 million Italians had arrived, despite the absence of
sea traffic created by World War I. There were now more than 5
million Italians in America, a total exceeded only by the number of
immigrants from Germany, most of whom arrived during the nineteenth century.

Because the Italians came "too many and too late" to take advantage of the distribution of free lands to immigrants with farming
experience (government policy had benefited earlier immigrant
groups such as the Germans and Scandinavians), most Italians,
though from rural districts, gravitated toward urban centers where
jobs were more quickly available. Their mass arrival coincided with
the spectacular growth of American industries and cities, when
cheap and unskilled laborers were in great demand. As early as 1910
there were Italian urban enclaves throughout the country, some three
thousand of them, with as many as seventy in the New York metropolitan area alone. Nearly three quarters of all the arriving Italians
wound up in the nation's most industrialized northeastern states.

The most sizable concentration was not far from the port of entry
at Battery Park, within a few blocks of City Hall. The Mulberry
District, as it became known, was the first and largest of the nation's
Italian enclaves.

When the Italians first arrived, the district still had a terrible
reputation. In 1845, the once well-to-do area had become a center of
organized crime. The narrow cobblestoned streets were lined with
dives, sheltering the members of such celebrated river gangs as the
Daybreak Boys, Buckoos, Hookers, Swamp Angels, Slaughter Hous-
ers, Short Tails, Patsy Conroys, and the Border Gang. If the wealthy
wandered into the Mulberry District, they were often murdered or
robbed, or both, before they had gone a block. A common trick,
according to Herbert Asbury in *The Gangs of New York,* was for a
woman to dump a bucket of ashes from her window on the head of
a well-dressed man. As he gasped for breath, he was grabbed by her
accomplices and taken down to the cellar, where he was murdered
and stripped of his clothes and money. His naked body was then

tossed out onto the street. The police patrolled the district only in platoons of six or more.

The Brewery, a complex of "apartments" in the heart of Mulberry, was the most notorious area, housing more than one thousand men, women, and children almost equally divided between Irish and blacks. "The house swarmed with thieves, murderers, pickpockets, beggars, harlots, and degenerates of every type. It has been estimated that for almost fifteen years the Old Brewery averaged a murder a night. Few of the killers were ever punished, for unless the police came in great force they could not hope to leave the Old Brewery alive, and the inhabitants were very close-mouthed."

In 1853, when the Brewery was torn down, "laborers carried out several sacks filled with human bones which they had found between the walls and in the cellars."

By the time the Italians arrived in great numbers, however, conditions had improved in the district, thanks to the efforts of church groups.

The Italians were brought into the district by contract labor agents who paid for their passage. The agent would take the new arrivals in hand as soon as they landed, leading them to the heart of the district, where he and his compatriots would then fleece them— overcharging for rent and food. This aroused the indignation of Jacob Riis, an immigrant from Denmark who became famous for his graphic exposés of abuses imposed on immigrants in need of housing. Riis was particularly outraged by a section of Mulberry Street known as "the Bend," which "by day was a purgatory of unrelieved squalor," and at night "an inferno tenanted by the very dregs of humanity where the new arrivals lived in damp basements, leaky garrets, clammy cellars and out houses and stables converted into dwellings." He found as many as forty families packed into five small houses. "The Italian comes in at the bottom and . . . he stays there. In the slums he is welcomed as a tenant who makes less 'trouble' than the contentious Irishman or the order-loving German; that is to say, he is content to live in a pigsty and submit to robbery at the hands of the rent collector without a murmur."

Gradually, the Italians left the Mulberry District, fanning out in all directions of the city and across into New Jersey. Within the metropolitan area they settled in Greenwich Village south of Washington Square, in Hell's Kitchen on the West Side, and in a large area of Harlem that became known as Italian Harlem. They also moved into the Bronx, Queens, and Staten Island. The completion in 1883 of the Brooklyn Bridge, built with Italian immigrant labor, paved the way for the invasion of Brooklyn; by 1935, two thirds of the residents of South Brooklyn were Italians. They also established enclaves in fourteen Brooklyn neighborhoods, from Highland Park to Coney Island. Even before Garibaldi came to work as a candlemaker on Staten Island, Italians had chosen it as their home. By 1935, Italians made up almost 30 percent of the foreign white population on Staten Island.

Even while Italians were still arriving in large numbers, it was claimed that "There are more Italians in New York City alone than in Rome, Milan, or Naples." The statement became one of the alarms sounded by proponents of restrictive immigration laws.

Many Italian immigrants worked in the factories of lower Manhattan that became notorious as "sweatshops," where employees worked for long hours and scandalously little pay. Most of these workers were women, who were paid lower wages than men. As one sweatshop operator admitted, ". . . these green horns . . . cannot speak English and don't know where to go and they just come from the old country and I let them work hard, like the devil, for less wages."

Women who could not leave home were exploited. Finishing garments for nearby clothing factories was usually their main work. Others worked with artificial flowers and notions, pins, and cheap jewelry. All of this was piecework. The son of a Sicilian immigrant family had vivid recollections of life in their Brooklyn tenement when his parents and brother set to work assembling lapel pins in the shape of crucifixes, studded with tiny rhinestones of various colors:

What you had to do was to glue tiny artificial diamonds in the holes on the lapel pin.

After supper my mother would clear the table, take the glass protectors off the wheels of the furniture, and pour some glue in each glass coaster. It smelled like nail polish remover and gasoline. My kid brother was put to bed, then my father brought the lapel pins and spilled them on the table. They made a huge pile . . . we'd work until after midnight but never after one. At least I wouldn't for I had to go to school in the morning. Yet sometimes I would hear my mother get up because she couldn't sleep with that "thought" in her head. And then my father would holler at her, *"Rimbabita,* you will kill yourself"; and my mother would answer, "Sh-hhh. The children are sleeping."

The Mulberry enclave continued to be a popular destination. By the time one Adolfo Rossi arrived in 1880, the Italians had become the dominant population of a multi-ethnic area in the Mulberry District. At the age of twenty and of middle-class background, Rossi was repelled by his compatriots' living conditions. They occupied dirty tenements, often with rooms no larger than the hovels they had left behind in Italy, but with many families living in the same room, eating and sleeping together "in the same hole without air and light." Their situation improved a little in the summer, when the men could find outdoor work away from New York. In the winter, however, "they return to fill the streets where the boys are bootblacks and the men are employed at the more repulsive tasks scorned by workmen of other nationalities—carrying offal to the ships and dumping it into the sea, cleaning the sewers—or going about with sacks on their shoulders rummaging the garbage cans, gleaning paper, rags, bones, broken glass."

An investigating association founded "for improving the conditions of the poor" echoed Rossi's sense of horror as it examined the so-called "Mulberry Bend." In 1884, New York's first Tenement House Commission recommended that the Bend be eliminated. Not until eight years later did the city take possession of "these disgraceful barracks of the disinherited" and order them destroyed. The wrecking took place, but a clutter of ruins remained for another three years. Only after the municipality was arraigned before the Board of Health on charges of maintaining a nuisance was the wreckage taken away. The former Bend was converted into Mulberry Park and opened to the public in June 1901.

Still, the district continued to draw harsh criticism from strangers who saw it for the first time. Giuseppe Giacosa, the Italian playwright, who visited the East Side in 1898, wrote that "It is impossible to depict the degradation, the squalor, the stinking muck, the rubble, and the disorder of the neighborhood."

LIFE WITHIN THE ENCLAVES

Despite these negative conditions, the Mulberry District quickly achieved a social structure which, though hidden from outsiders, was sound and stable. In May 1896, a decade before Italian immigration crested, *The New York Times* reported that the district offered all the business activities and professional pursuits "present in a big city." While acknowledging that its residents included the lowest caste of workers, ragpickers, and junkmen, it pointed out that all grades of manual work were represented, as well as bankers, doctors, apothecaries, undertakers, lawyers, and notaries. "There is a monster colony of Italians who might be termed the commercial and shopkeeping community of the Latins, with all sorts of stores, boarding houses, grocery and fruit emporiums, tailors, shoemakers, wine merchants, musical stores, toy and clay molders."

As a way station for thousands of Italian immigrants, the Mulberry District surpassed all other Italian enclaves in population and business enterprises. Aside from the banks, lodging houses, barber shops, bars, and restaurants, there was a galaxy of specialized trades and services that catered to the diverse needs of the inhabitants. Many of the services were initiated by men who had come with the intention of returning to Italy but who remained to capitalize on the self-contained community. Entire tenement floors were devoted to raising, selling, and renting monkeys to the organ grinders who plied their trade in the streets of Manhattan. Undertakers specialized in shipping bodies back to the homeland; photographers featured stylized formal portraits to be sent to relatives and friends left behind; marriage brokers and matchmakers acted as intermediaries between bachelor immigrants and young women in their native villages. There were even bakeries that collected discarded old bread and sold it to immigrant women, who in turn retailed it for a few cents a loaf.

Jacob Riis could not resist noting that "When the sun shines, the entire population seeks the street, carrying on its household work, its bargaining, its lovemaking. . . ." The streets seethed with vitality. Hacks, delivery trucks, and pushcarts competed for right of way. Above the streets, the fire escapes of the tenements were festooned with lines of drying laundry, while housewives exchanged news and gossip with any neighbor within shouting distance.

The roofs became the remembered fields of Italy where residents could visit one another on summer Sundays while the young played cowboys-and-Indians in the tar-filled air. The roofs were a place for a storyteller with stories and legends of the old country. Children listened with one impressionable ear while they imagined themselves out west cooking spaghetti over a campfire. On the roofs, too, women made their *astrato* (tomato paste) just as they did in Italy, spreading masses of crushed tomatoes on bedsheets stretched over wooden frames. It took days for the sun to turn the mass into a thick paste, which was then canned and put aside for the winter.

Eating habits did change, however. In most southern Italian towns and villages, bread had been a staple, along with a variety of vegetables. Pasta was a luxury. Minestrones were made with spinach; escarole was cooked along with a variety of greens found in the wild—fennel, dandelion greens, with lentils or fava beans. Fava beans were crushed to make a *macu* (literally, a mashed soup). And there was the sturdy bread, often eaten hot with olive oil and pepper and salt, that may have been the original pizza. A peasant or miner would take a chunk of bread, a small onion, and perhaps a sardine for lunch. In America, the hearty peasant bread of Italy changed to the fluffy white bread of the rich. Some Italians preferred to spend more money for food than for rent; wages now could buy, from the local grocer, a variety of pastas—*bucattini, perciatelli, ditelli, acini di pepi, capelli d'angelo*—wonders many had not seen in the old country. Meat, seldom affordable in Italy, became popular: "la bif steka," meatballs, lamb chops, "Lu turkie," and "la chicken." The Sunday and holiday meal became a cooking festival, which only those who had known hunger could appreciate. The Italian grocer stocked his store from ceiling to floor, reflecting the emotion of a people accustomed to austerity who had come to a land of plenty. Within a generation many a lean immigrant was to turn into a heavyweight.

Almost anything the immigrant families wanted could be purchased within the boundaries of their enclave. Despite the allegations of the southern Italian's mental inferiority, there were plenty of bookstalls and bookstores that provided a great variety of reading matter in Italian, ranging from Neapolitan and Sicilian songs and literary classics to cartoons and popular fiction.

The district abounded with theaters, puppet shows, and music halls, some of which operated in the rear of coffeehouses. Nearby Second Avenue became Broadway for the young immigrant men. To hear it remembered in the old age of those who participated evokes an image as ceremonious as any Sunday mass.

We came home from work Saturday afternoon and the rest of the day we got ready. My brother Angelo worked in a laundry, but his heart was in dancing. Tony, my other brother, was the tallest, 6′ 1″, well built, a little flat footed. He had the ambition to be a movie actor. He was a plasterer with *compare* Toto. But Saturday afternoon we got ready; the suits were inspected, the shirts with detachable collars and cuffs were laid out, shoes well-heeled and soled. Then we dressed in the dark bedroom where we all slept. We put on these elegant clothes: first the garters to hold up our black silk socks; suspenders, more comfortable for dancing; over the shoes, spats; a tie pin and handkerchief in the breast pocket. I was the youngest and I'd go get the whiskey flask and the hand warmer, a small tin container covered with red felt with chunks of burning charcoal in it.

The flask and hand warmers in their back pockets, the three brothers were ready to enjoy Saturday night on Second Avenue. One would meet friends strolling up Second Avenue to 14th Street. There were bars and saloons, restaurants and dance halls, theaters with thirteen acts of vaudeville, ice cream parlors and cabarets, and movie houses, all of which catered to the various ethnic groups. There were Russian and Polish cabarets, Hungarian and Ukrainian restaurants serving goulash and borscht, steaks and chops—restaurants too foreign and too expensive for most Italians.

There were also crap games in the alleys. And if Saturday night led to debauchery, there were always the bathhouses catering to those who lived in bathless tenements. For many of the immigrants and their children, Second Avenue was the *piazza* of the New World; but within the boundaries of Little Italy the Italians did their best to live as they had in their native villages.

In the early days, since there was a scarcity of women, men danced with one another at the boardinghouses where they lived.* Before the phonograph, music was provided by one or two of the boarders with an accordion, flute, or violin, echoes of the musicians who serenaded the wayside shrines in the old country. "Clomping away to the rhythm of mazurkas, polkas, or waltzes," recalls the

---

*As late as the 1950s, dance halls for men were not uncommon in the rural areas of Sicily. Men purchased a ticket good for one dance that began when the owner started up an old phonograph playing the tango. The men danced elegantly, their eyes closed, apparently imagining the day when they would have a woman as partner.

daughter of an immigrant couple that housed twenty-six boarders, "they talked as they danced, laughed, sweated profusely and seemed to enjoy the dances as endurance challenges. They only stopped when musicians quit or when my father chased them all to bed, saying, *'Basta, domani si travaglia. A dormire tutti'* ['Enough, tomorrow is a working day. To bed, everyone']."

Wherever they congregated, Italians were both admired and despised for their frugality, as well as for their need to earn money. Parents often yanked their children out of school as soon as they were old enough to work. Earnings were considerably higher than in Italy, yet Italians earned less than other ethnic groups and the cost of living was high. A 1910 study of southern Italian families conducted by the U.S. Immigration Commission revealed that their average earnings for that year amounted to $688, $112 below the $800 deemed necessary to maintain a man, woman, and three children too young to qualify for employment. The Italians were second only to blacks in low income. And yet there was a passion for savings. For the families who intended to stay in America, the money was used to pay off debts incurred in Italy or put aside to purchase a home. Some of the money was sent to family members in Italy. Almost invariably such a show of "affluence" represented "the most humiliating deprivation of the bare necessities of life," since each remittance meant a lower standard of living for the sender.

The more than $7 million sent from the United States in 1902 accelerated to $66 million in 1914, preventing the economic collapse of many *Mezzogiorno* villages that had been depleted by emigration fever.

The great majority of the lives of the Italians were not success stories. They lived in poverty while working at whatever jobs were available, even when working conditions were dangerous or unhealthy. Their determination to work whatever the salary created a wide demand for their services, particularly in the larger cities. Ninety percent of the labor force employed by New York's Department of Public Works in 1890 was Italian. "We can't get along without the Italians," observed a city official. "We want someone to do the dirty work: the Irish aren't doing it any longer."

The "dirty work" entailed a variety of unskilled jobs such as sewer laying, tunneling, subway construction, street grading, general construction, and street cleaning. The most desirable of these jobs placed the worker on the city payroll, providing a steady job and a minimum of danger. The twelve hundred Italians sweeping the streets of New York in 1904 were the envy of their compatriots. Since American citizenship was required of every street cleaner, many immigrants filed naturalization papers as soon as possible, assisted by politicians eager to have their vote. Most of the unskilled jobs were in construction, where the Italians were drawn into union activity.

The American historian who wrote, "The greatest metropolis in the world rose from the sweat and misery of Italian labor," may well have had in mind, among others, the four thousand southern Italians who burrowed their way through Manhattan's rock and soil to build the Lexington Avenue subway. Yet it was on such a project that Italian unskilled workers, defending themselves against deplorable working conditions, formed one of the immigrants' largest American unions. Led by a twenty-one-year-old Sicilian, Salvatore Ninfo, who had picked up enough English to articulate the workers' demands, they struck for safer working conditions, higher wages, and shorter hours—and won.

To some degree, the success of the Lexington Avenue subway strike could be attributed to the fact that most of the strikers hailed from the same region—Sicily. Unlike most other South Italian workers, they had some experience with the concept of unions. The *Fasci* cooperative movement that had been crushed by the Italian Army was still fresh in their memory. Then, too, Italians were beginning to adjust to the communal needs of their new environment.

The adjustment became instinctive. Whereas in the *Mezzogiorno* the southern family had been large enough to look after its own, in the new land the immigrant family was relatively small, and not nearly as extended as it was in its native setting. Now it was obliged to reach out to mutual aid societies, which paid sick benefits or funeral expenses; these societies provided a sense of community as well as nostalgia, since each was made up of members from the same village or province. The groups proliferated during the peak years of immigration, numbering between two and three thousand by 1915. While some were offshoots of societies that had existed in the home village, most originated in the Little Italies of America. There were attempts to bring these local societies together.

Inspired by the hope of uniting the Italians into a national fraternal organization that would enable its members to become "the authors of their own destinies and progress," an Italian physician, Dr. Vincenzo Sellaro, founded the Order of the Sons of Italy, an umbrella organization that would meet the social as well as the insurance needs of its members. It aimed also to promote "their moral, intellectual and material betterment" and to emancipate "the masses from every prejudice." For his cabinet members, Dr. Sellaro chose two barbers, a pharmacist, a sculptor, and a lawyer. Dr. Sellaro assumed the title of "Supreme Venerable." Lodges and Grand Lodges were named after such distinguished Italians as Columbus, Garibaldi, Benvenuto Cellini, and Dante Aleghieri. After a shaky start there was an aggressive campaign to establish lodges wherever there were enough Italians who might welcome the order's insurance benefits and the opportunities it offered the lowliest of immigrants for socializing with others more successful than themselves. By 1922, the order included thirteen hundred lodges across the nation. They did not, however, supplant the local social and mutual aid societies made up of members from the same villages. Only there could the immigrant feel completely at ease.

For reasons that combined patriotism with individual opportunism, the Order of the Sons of Italy had no difficulty attracting the most prominent members of the Italian community. One of the best known of these opportunists was the travel agent Louis V. Fugazy, usually addressed as *Commendatore,* a knighthood title bestowed on him by the Italian government for having served under Garibaldi and with Victor Emmanuel as chief of Italy's secret police. In 1896, *The New York Times* reported that Fugazy was president of at least fifty Italian societies in the New York area and "the leading spirit if not actual President of 132 mutual benefit associations," adding that "he is without a doubt the one man to whom all Italians—that is to say, the majority of the simple, everyday Italians of New York City—look for advice and aid in personal affairs." Known affectionately as "Papa Fugazy," he was described by the *Times* as the political boss for the Little Italies of New York.

In various Little Italies around the country there were *prominenti* who, though profiting from their dealings with Italian immigrants, were men of conscience who contributed to their general welfare.

Among the most impressive was a Neapolitan who became a father figure for thousands of Italians in Syracuse, New York. Gaetano Marinelli first came to Syracuse as part of a gang of railroad workers. More educated than most immigrants, he served as a court interpreter as well as a notary public, and before long became proprietor of a steamship agency. Marinelli, who anglicized his name to Thomas Marnell, also worked as a labor contractor for the railroads. Marnell became highly respected as "the supreme arbiter of the affairs of the Italian colony," an all-ar und benefactor, writing letters for the illiterate, finding jobs for the unemployed, helping immigrants bring their families to Syracuse, and extending loans to the needy. As a one-man assimilation force, he developed enough political clout to deliver the Italian vote in Syracuse. President Theodore Roosevelt invited Marnell to the White House for consultation shortly before he ran for reelection.

Marnell was killed on Memorial Day, 1906, when the horse of his carriage bolted and he was thrown to the ground. An unprecedented ten thousand spectators turned out for the funeral and to witness a procession of one thousand marchers and a cortège of sixty-five carriages. Marnell had mastered the art of combining politics and commerce during an era when immigrants needed guidance from Italian Americans they could trust.

For the mass of immigrants, men like Marnell provided advice and services that were otherwise unavailable. But unfortunately, too many of the Little Italy *prominenti* were motivated by self-interest rather than altruism. Among them were ex-lawyers trained in Italy who, unable to qualify for legal practice in the United States, established themselves as "notaries"—a title that commanded respect in Italy, since it could only be achieved by men of character who underwent a lengthy period of training. Hundreds of saloon keepers, boardinghouse owners, steamship agents, and bankers also became "notaries," many exploiting the immigrant's faith in that title. The swindling ranged from fees for unnecessary seals and stamps to collusion with undertakers who charged exorbitant fees. The most victimized immigrants were those who entrusted notaries with money to be transmitted to Italy. The "leeches of the Italian immigrants," as one observer described them, formed a closely knit network of many entrepreneurs within the enclave.

Luigi Villari, a noted Italian journalist who made a study of these *prominenti* in 1904, found that they existed wherever Italians had settled. The typical *prominente* was a middle-class southern Italian male, with enough education to set him apart from the illiterate compatriots on whom he preyed.

He may have first worked as a laborer himself and somehow been able to save enough money to establish himself and his family in the United States. He boasts of friendship with many important Americans, though they are probably lower level Irish or Jewish politicians and professionals. While not necessarily dishonest, he takes advantage of his clients' ignorance. He is president or treasurer of various Italian societies, is invariably an American citizen and is usually politically active, directing his clients' votes toward the party from whom he can expect the greatest favors. He goes from Republican to Democrat, offering a block of 20,000 votes, which are usually no more than 1,000. After determining the source of his greatest gain, he persuades those eligible to vote to follow his example.

Villari reserved his harshest criticism for those in the banking business. The *banchista* (banker) without capital or resources used his clients' money for personal investments, many of which were of high risk. No interest was paid; it was enough for the average depositor to know that a *persona d'onore* (a person of honor) was safeguarding his money. It took the recession of 1907 to reveal to more than twelve thousand immigrant depositors that their faith in *banchiste* had been misplaced when twenty-five declared bankruptcy. Of the nearly $1.5 million deposited with these men, only $500 was paid back.

The *banchiste* and other *prominenti* conspired to retard the immigrants' understanding of the American world by keeping them tightly entrenched within their Little Italies. These *prominenti* had become the gentry of the New World and exploited the immigrant just as the gentry of the Old World had exploited the lower classes in Italy. The New World *padrone, banchiste,* and *notaie* continued to be treated as men of respect. The artisan too was respected, though to a lesser degree, and was addressed with the ancient title of "Don." The laborer continued to regard himself and his family as socially inferior to everyone. The old ways were difficult to eradicate. Only when the children of the laborers began to absorb some sense of democratic equality in the public schools was there any rebellion against the undemocratic systems that governed the lives of their parents.

HEALTH AND HOUSING IN THE LITTLE ITALIES

The vibrant character of the immigrants was belied by the miserable housing conditions endured by thousands who lived in the congested Italian enclaves of Manhattan long after the tenements they occupied had been declared health hazards.

Immigrants made up 63 percent of the densely packed slum population. Only thin air spaces gave light to some flats. The first room of the string of rooms, arranged like railroad cars, had some light from the air shaft. Beyond the kitchen were small dark rooms, without windows. Tenement entrance halls were made of stone or ceramic tiles much like the toilet rooms in the subway; the ceiling was of embossed sheet metal. There were no windows. At night the housekeeper (janitors were to appear later) lit the gas jets in the halls. One could hear their soft hissing once the "issaskeeper" lit them. It was one of the first words the immigrants learned. He was the man who took care of the tenement.

Investigators found the tenements adjoined so closely together as to prevent sufficient air and light from entering outside rooms; except for those on the top floors, none of the inside rooms had access to air or light. During the summer, the occupants had to sleep on fire escapes to escape the heat. Children were encouraged to play in the streets until a late hour, when the air cooled. Addressing a Tuberculosis Congress in Washington, D.C., one investigator said: "If we had invented machines to create tuberculosis, we could not have succeeded better in increasing it."

Alarmed by such reports, a committee acting in behalf of the Italian government conducted its own investigation and found that 18 percent of the families (usually large) examined lived in a single room.*

The American investigators found that congestion and lack of air

*The housing situation of the newly arrived immigrant was a main element in the cultural shock he experienced. While it is true that the hovel in his native village often consisted of a single room with no sanitary facilities, it was used primarily as a sleeping place. His working day was spent in the fresh air, working on the land; his outdoor life under the sun contributed to his good health and longevity. His one room in Italy often was not large enough for him and his family; but his tenement flat in New York was likely to be even more congested. In addition to family, there were often lodgers—newly arrived *paesani* who could not be turned away. Also, in order to meet expenses, it sometimes became necessary to take in paying boarders. For many of the immigrants, their congested housing situation continued even after the heavy influx of immigration had come to an end.

were not the only health hazards. The tenements were cold, dirty, and dark. In one sample block there was only one family with a hot-water range, and none had bathtubs. The water supply was so poor that residents on the upper floors could not get water for hours at a time. One of every nine children died before the age of five.

The Italians in Italy were less likely to contract tuberculosis than any other European people, but the same could not be said of those in the United States. "And how could it have been otherwise?" asked Dr. Antonio Stella, a physician member of the Italian Committee on the Prevention of Tuberculosis. Dr. Stella cited the infectious character of the disease, the overcrowded and filthy conditions of tenements inhabited by a people "made up chiefly of agriculturalists, fresh from the sunny hills and green valleys of Tuscany and Sicily, abruptly thrown into unnatural abodes and dark sweatshops, a population overworked, underfed, poorly clad, curbed with all the worries and anxieties of the morrow and only free, thank God! from the worst ally of consumption—alcoholism. . . ."

Stella disputed statistics which claimed that Italians in the United States were among the least afflicted of the foreign-born groups, pointing out that many cases went unreported, either because the Italians were often scattered in the search for jobs or because victims were likely to return to their native villages, preferring to die there*

Contrary to general impressions that the large percentage of the Italians stricken were the children of immigrants, Stella found that it was usually the parents themselves, especially if they came from the rural areas of Italy and were unaccustomed as yet to "the poisoned atmosphere" of city life. "Six months of life in the tenements are sufficient to turn a sturdy youth from Calabria, the brawny fisherman of Sicily, the robust women from Abruzzo and Basilicata, into the pale, flabby undersized creatures we see dragging along the streets of New York and Chicago." Apart from the unsanitary housing conditions, which were considered mainly responsible for the spread of the disease, Stella's committee found that certain occupations were particularly hazardous to the lungs—among them bootblacks, barbers, tailors, plasterers, marble and stonecutters, and cigarmakers.†

---

*The number of Italian immigrant men and women who became tubercular was so large that the Sicilian town of Sciacca built a small sanitarium on its outskirts to receive the stricken who came home to die.

†An 1894 Commission of Labor stated that all but one of New York City's foreign

But it was in the large cities that the great majority of immigrants gathered. Mono Cino, a retired construction worker, remembered having left his native village in 1910, "when the kids ran through streets shouting *li stiddi cu la cuda*—the stars with tails" as Halley's Comet streaked across the Italian sky.

> The comet wasn't a good sign, everybody thought. And my mother rubbed vinegar on my mouth and told me not to sleep as long as the comet was in the sky. We had a cholera that summer, so I was glad to leave. I was a kid. We came to New York. I don't know how we found it but we lived in a small short alley, it's still there, called Extra Place, near the Bowery on First Street. I remember the cobblestones, and you could smell what everybody was cooking. The halls were lit by gas jets. The toilets were made of cast iron and were in the halls.

More important to the immigrants than housing conditions was the need to be in the big cities where the great majority lived and where jobs were more easily available. An immigrant who first lived in New York recalled that

> Everybody went to work upon arrival, women, children, old men. If school was obligatory there were ways of avoiding it. A boy would tell the principal of his school that his family was moving to another school district. The principal would fill out the transfer papers, telling the boy, "You must present these papers to your new school." Of course the boy never did and he was free to get a job as wagon driver, delivery boy, boot black, anything that would contribute to the family income.

One woman remembered that as a girl she worked as a C.P.A.— Coats, Pants, and Alterations. "In the summer the streets were filled with horses. The horse manure was piled up in the gutter and it dried into powder and the wind blew it in the air and it covered your clothes, your hair, your face, and you could hardly breathe. Opposite our place there was a barn with small elephants in it. Nobody knew what they were doing there. Late at night I could hear them crying. It was so sad."

---

bootblacks were Italian. The same agency reported that by 1910 more than half of New York's barbers were Italian.

★ ★ ★

Although later there would be mixing between the various Italian regions, in the early days each region sought out its own. In New York City the immigrants from the Sicilian village of Cinisi eschewed the larger Italian enclaves, living exclusively among themselves on East 69th Street. There, two hundred families were bound together by the instinct for self-preservation and by the urge to abide by the customs and traditions of Cinisi. Any deviations from the group's moral standards would not only tarnish the reputation of the miscreant in New York but also in Cinisi, with which there was constant communication, and where, more often than not, the immigrants expected to return. That expectation tied them to the traditions of their homeland.

Similar considerations motivated the immigrants who in these early days moved into larger Italian enclaves. Each became a hodgepodge collection of small village clusters that kept largely to themselves. Not only did the immigrants from Abruzzo, Campania, Apulia, Calabria, and Sicily live on different streets, but in many instances they would subdivide according to the village or province from which they hailed. As in the case of the immigrants from Cinisi, each cluster tried to conform to the main features of the life it had left behind. By habit and tradition, everyone else was suspect. This attitude was not unique to Italians. Like most immigrants who came from isolated, near-feudal villages in Russia, Romania, or Bessarabia, their suspicion of "others" was affirmed by provincial beliefs that held that the people of a particular town, however near to one's own, were largely criminals or that the town was cursed with a disproportionate number of women of easy virtue.

Stereotypes of this kind were of such ancient vintage as to be accepted as indisputable truths which, in the early period of the immigrants' life in America, continued to be taken seriously. While there was no open hostility between those of different villages, there were barbed or sardonic comments, or a display of intolerance so obvious as to verge on contempt. Although most of the negative attitudes would eventually wither into amicability, each of the self-segregated groups continued to operate on its own, with its own leadership, its own religious holidays, and its own mutual aid societies.

The northern Italians, as the first Italians to settle in the United States in significant numbers, were the founders of the nation's larger

Little Italies. At first they easily outnumbered their compatriots from the *Mezzogiorno*, but by the turn of the century they were a minority. (San Francisco was one of the few cities where northern Italians continued to outnumber those from the South.) Regardless of the region the northerner hailed from, to the southerner he seemed like the member of *un altra razza* (a different race), readily associated with the northern officials the new Italian regime had sent to the *Mezzogiorno* to rule and to collect taxes.

The resentments, prejudices, and accusations that separated northerners and southerners in Italy continued to prevail in the New World. To a northerner, southerners were a distinctly inferior lot, who were largely illiterate, incapable of speaking proper Italian, and generally peasantlike (which in fact many of them were). Their presence was an embarrassment that might prejudice the American establishment against all Italians. In turn, the southern immigrants disparaged the northerners' aloofness, but among themselves envied their ease in communicating with Americans, earning their livelihood with jobs that did not require manual labor, and, in many instances, being able to keep their children in school for a longer time. Seldom did the two groups meet on a social basis. While occasionally there were marriages within the enclave between couples whose roots were from different villages, rarely did they occur between southerners and northerners.

Some of the northerners resolved their displeasure by leaving the enclave and clustering to be free of Italians from the South. This first happened when northerners left the heavily populated Mulberry District to establish a community a short distance to the north in the area New Yorkers know as Greenwich Village. The Village had once been the genteel home of Jamesian characters, although the rebel and the radical found a place there also. (An impoverished Tom Paine died not far from Bleecker Street.) But the arrival of the Irish and blacks had caused property values to plummet, encouraging northern Italians to move up from the Mulberry District. Soon the area became predominantly Italian. Only the poorer Irish remained.

The largest and perhaps the drabbest of the Italian enclaves was the Little Italy that developed uptown during the 1880s and by 1900 had become the largest of all the Italian enclaves in the nation. Italian Harlem, as it became known, bordered the East River with its shoreline of massive, ugly gas tanks that shadowed the squalor of five-story tenement dwellings clustered nearby. Accentuating the dreariness of the environment was the thunder of two elevated train lines that crisscrossed the area every few minutes. In the streets below, the Italians carried on as though they had never left their native towns and villages. Despite the presence of a score of other nationalities living in adjoining streets, it was the Italians who by sheer numbers left their imprint on the entire area. They dominated the marketplace that displayed everything from freshly baked loaves of bread, shaped and marked to ward off the evil eye, to children's underwear and men's work shoes. The voices of Italian housewives haggled for food for which Americans had yet to develop a taste: squid, eels, dandelion greens, zucchini, finocchio, and pomegranates. Crowding the same area were small restaurants serving the same dishes offered in the *trattorie* of Naples, Palermo, or Rome. The coffeehouses were popular meeting places, with their varied and gaudy pastries and *caffè espresso* served amid loud conversation and pungent clouds of smoke from Italian stogies.

None of the early Little Italies pleased the Italian consular officers stationed in the United States. For them the term "Little Italy" was an offensive misnomer, a caricature of the image they were trying to promote. With their preponderance of poor and uneducated southern Italian immigrants largely from rural areas, each new "Little Italy" struck them as a gross misrepresentation, a denial, of Italian civilization. The consular officers, who were mainly from the North of Italy, preferred to refer to the enclaves as "the Italian colonies," a less inclusive term than "Little Italy," which had the further advantage of suggesting that its inhabitants—especially those from the *Mezzogiorno*—would be returning to their native villages in the not-too-distant future.

CHAPTER 10

Beyond the Biggest City

There was great mobility among the immigrants, especially those living on Manhattan's Lower East Side. Newark attracted many immigrants during the early years with its quiet atmosphere and green yards, as did Connecticut. Others in search of better living conditions went to Philadelphia, Baltimore, Boston, Chicago, and nearly every other city in America.

PHILADELPHIA

Italians were living in Philadelphia before the Revolutionary War. In the early nineteenth century, small colonies of settlers from northern Italy established themselves in South Philadelphia. But not until the 1850s, when political refuges from the *Risorgimento* turmoil began arriving, could one speak of an Italian community in the city. Most of these early immigrants—artists, musicians, teachers, organ grinders—had lived near Genoa.

Although the first settlements were in South Philadelphia, there were at least four other Italian neighborhoods: in Frankford, Germantown, Chestnut Hill, and Nicetown. As early as 1853, an Italian community established the Church of St. Mary Magdalen de Pazzi, the first Italian national parish anywhere in the United States.

By 1900, Italians were the largest foreign-born group in Philadelphia, with 45,000 immigrants. This was now the third-largest community after New York and Brooklyn, in spite of the fact that the major steamship lines offered no direct service to Philadelphia.

Much of the early history of the Italian communities in Philadelphia revolves around six families: Baldi, DiBerardino, Cuneo, Raggio, Sbarbaro, and Lagomarsino. These men would be the merchants, bankers, and labor contractors who both exploited and helped the early immigrants.

The career of Frank DiBerardino in many ways documents the history of the Italian immigrants in Philadelphia.

DiBerardino came from Torricella Peligna, in the region of Abruzzo. By 1887 he established the DiBerardino Bank, a title and trust company, as well as a steamship ticket agency. All this proved useful when he contracted to furnish the Pennsylvania Railroad Company with laborers. DiBerardino advertised for workers in his home region of Abruzzo. In an interview, his son remembered his father's methods of operation:

> Agents travelled through the countryside of Abruzzo encouraging and channelizing emigration to Philadelphia with promises of immediate employment. They came as couriers of good fortune. Villagers and country dwellers alike passed on the good tidings that in Philadelphia, some place in America, there were "paesans" who not only had good jobs to give, but who also lent emigrants assistance in obtaining passage across the ocean and in becoming settled among other "paesans" and friends in a strange country. The branch office of the Philadelphia contractors, located in strategic places throughout Abruzzo, became the direct link between the hintermost hamlet in Abruzzo and adjacent regions and the Italian colony in Philadelphia.

DiBerardino provided passage money at no interest; he even acted as matchmaker whenever a shipload of Italian women arrived. The new arrivals sent letters home which were read and passed from house to house until "the most rustic villager who had probably never ventured beyond the limits of his own town became so familiar with Philadelphia as to be able to mention its streets with a specious familiarity. . . . Some labor contractors, realizing the effect of such letters upon emigration, contrived to gain the permission of their immigrant friends to write their letters for them, and in these letters they wrote every description calculated to hasten expatriation and thus to swell the reservoir of common laborers in America."

From 1900 to 1940, 37,000 immigrants received services from the DiBerardino firm. Although nearly half were from his own native region of Abruzzo, DiBerardino helped bring thousands of others from Campania, Sicily, Calabria, and almost every part of Italy (including Sardinia and Venezia).

Despite contract labor laws, DiBerardino enticed workers by paying for their passage through his agents in Abruzzo. He would meet the ships himself and help his clients pass through customs. Officials recognized him as an accredited representative of the immigrants. He even helped immigrants write letters home, often adding his own descriptive passages of the wonders of the New World. Many a marriage was traced to an introduction made by DiBerardino. A family man, he understood, was more likely to be a reliable worker.

DiBerardino eventually became the largest labor contractor in Philadelphia, establishing work camps from Pennsylvania to North Carolina. Interviews in the WPA records of the Pennsylvania Historical Society describe the DiBerardino camps, which were rated as better than most camps of that type:

> The shacks housed groups numbering from 20 to 60 men. They slept in cots in constant use by first one shift of laborers and then another. . . . There were no shelves or lockers in these shanties. Clothes were hung on nails pegged over the cots. There were no arrangements for bathing or washing or for other sanitary needs. The men washed from metal or wooden buckets they bought from the company store. The water had to be carried from the nearest spring. . . . The most undesirable days . . . were the rainy ones, when both shifts were in the small shanties at the same time.

DiBerardino was one of the more caring and philanthropic of those men known as *padroni*. While building a commercial empire for himself, he helped found new Italian communities as he sent new arrivals to work on the railroads and in the mines of America.

* * *

Long before Di Berardino began bringing southern Italian immigrants to Philadelphia, the local entrepreneurs were mostly from Genoa. Gradually the merchants from northern Italy were replaced by immigrants from Calabria and Sicily. Turned away by the established merchants who sold their wares in stores, the Sicilians built wooden carts ("pushcarts," as they became known) and began to sell their wares in streets that were then outside the Italian shopping district. From the first they evoked the hostility of residents, not only because of the impression from the media that most Sicilians were a cold-blooded, homicidal lot who should never have been admitted into the country, but also because the Sicilians shouted out their wares, as they had in their native land. Resenting their noisy presence, the Irish began moving to districts where there were no Italians. The Sicilian pushcart operators held firm and eventually won favor with an increasing number of compatriots who were moving into the area and could now purchase their vegetables in the shadow of their homes, more cheaply than at the stores.

By 1910, the pushcart district had become the dominant shopping area of South Philadelphia. Restaurants followed, and soon a new Italian community, the largest in Philadelphia, came into being, extending its boundaries before long to the Delaware River. As more Italians moved into the area, more Irish abandoned it. By the time World War I was over and the last wave of immigrants was arriving, South Philadelphia had become the home of thousands of workers employed in tailoring factories and construction. They also helped build the city's transportation system and suburban railroads. As early as 1902, work and thrift permitted some Italians to purchase their own homes.

For the most part, the early years were far from idyllic. Richard Varbero, a first-generation American who became a historian, remembers: "Children skirmished in the narrow spaces allotted for play while parents gazed out in an attitude of almost helpless dejection upon the ugly, depressing surroundings, which placed a heavy handicap on the health and well-being of their children."

Housing conditions for many were deplorable, due in part to the indifference of Italian community leaders like C. A. Baldi, a noted slumlord. The conditions were like those in other cities: high rents resulted in overcrowding in small, poorly ventilated rooms; toilets were in yards or hallways and often did not function; fire escapes were constructed of wood. Some families kept goats. Only surface drainage was available to carry off sewage and other debris. In hot weather, the streets became incubators for disease; in cold weather, filth froze where it was thrown. These conditions produced epidemics of tuberculosis that became known as the "white plague," made worse by the release of infected workers from the hospitals.

Yet South Philadelphia had to be captured from the Irish, block by block. Brawls broke out and neither group wandered freely in the other's territory. In some neighborhoods, Italians were confined to sit in segregated sections of movie houses. Children were marched to school with a guard of parents.

As the Italian community began to prosper, so did arts and entertainment. It was Ferruchio Giannini who founded Verdi Hall, then known as the "Metropolitan" of South Philadelphia. Audiences were large and made up of ordinary people who went to hear the songs of their old country. Because of fire laws, however, the Hall was closed in 1917; it was later converted to an Italian movie house.

For the wealthy, of course, there were the visits of Enrico Caruso. He first appeared in 1903 in Philadelphia as the Duke in *Rigoletto*. Every opera that boasted his name was sold out.

For the more humble there was the marionette theater, crowded every night with men and boys who hung in breathless attention upon the continued stories acted there from evening to evening. There were church festivals, too, even though the Irish Church hierarchy looked down on such activities as pagan shenanigans.

Out of the ragpickers, laborers, and organ grinders came merchants, pushcart owners, bankers, labor contractors, and slumlords. By 1910, an Italian American community was firmly established in South Philadelphia.

BALTIMORE

In the spring of 1874 there were some forty Italian ships in Baltimore Harbor, most of which took part in the profitable triangular trade that brought Italian marble and luxury items, picked up grain for England, and there loaded coal for the furnaces of northern Italy. The first immigrants to settle in Baltimore were from Genoa, home port of this trade. Although the city's Italian community never rivaled those of New York, Boston, or New Orleans, it did develop an Italian Colony, as it became known there.

When Italians first arrived in Baltimore, they found a city that was both southern and German. In fact, the German population was so large that laws had to be published in German. Some of the city's districts established schools that taught in German.

Early in the nineteenth century, Italian immigrant sculptors built several monuments out of Carrara marble, including one commemorating the defense of the city during the War of 1812. The Neapolitan painter Nicolino Calyo made paintings of the harbor as early as 1836. But in those days, most of the jobs were taken by slave labor, freed blacks, or the large German population. Apart from a few merchants and artisans, the Italian community remained sparse for most of the nineteenth century. Sicilians, mostly from around Cefalu, began arriving in 1890 to found fruit-importing companies, as other Sicilians were doing in New Orleans. These companies nurtured the many vendors who sold their wares from stalls and pushcarts. By 1903, common laborers began to arrive, finding work at $1.00 to $1.50 a day. These new arrivals lived in the low-rent areas near the port and factories which became the Little Italies where one could walk to work and live cheaply.

In 1902, there were eight mutual aid societies in Baltimore, with a membership of about one thousand, all reflecting the origins of their members—the Abruzzo-Molise Society, the Caltanisetta (Sicily) Society, the Rome-Lazio Society. Later they organized along trade lines.

These aid societies and newly founded loan associations were held together by personal and regional loyalty. Money was lent to home buyers and others "out of pocket," with no credit backing other than a good reputation required. The scheming *padrone* banker was absent in Baltimore.

Records show that not one of these borrowers defaulted on a home loan, even during the Depression. Individuals who were unable to make payments were "carried" until they could continue.

The community became tightly knit, eventually making its political power felt by electing to Congress the first Italian representative, Vincent Palmisano, who was born in Termini, Sicily.

BOSTON

Although Boston had a busy international harbor, it was not a principal port of entry for immigrants until the Irish potato famine in 1847 brought a flood of Irish immigrants. By 1850, the Irish made up 75 percent of the foreign-born and 25 percent of the general population of Boston; by 1875, Boston was second only to New York as a port of entry. At the turn of the century, as Irish immigration diminished, the Italians became the largest immigrant group.

The first small enclave of Italians was made up of Genovesi who settled in Boston in the 1860s. Most of these were merchants dealing in fruits, wine, olive oil, and cheeses. The 1890s saw an influx of Sicilians, Abruzzese, and Neapolitans, who increased the Italian population of the North End to well over seven thousand and pushed the Genovesi to the outlying districts of Roxbury.

By the turn of the new century, tenement blocks were primarily occupied by individuals from Campania, Sicily, and Genoa, with an especially large contingent from Avellino of the Campania region. At first the North End had been settled by a variety of ethnic groups, but the increasing number of Italian enclaves and the departure of prosperous immigrants to more desirable neighborhoods left the North End almost exclusively Italian by World War I.

The Sicilians, as the most recent arrivals, monopolized the entire length of North Street, with the heaviest concentration near the fishing piers. Many of these settlers had come from fishing villages on the Sicilian coast and, either for a livelihood or for shopping, made greater use of the city's fishing facilities. Some who had been fishermen in the past eventually owned their own fishing fleets in America. To escape the heavy competition around Boston, some moved to smaller coastal cities, such as Gloucester and Rockport, where they shared fishing waters with the Portuguese.

When the great mass of Italians arrived in 1880, they found the once proud North End sadly deteriorated. Successive waves of German and Irish poor had settled there, living six to ten in a room where the Hutchinsons, the Mathers, and Paul Revere once lived. By 1840, the North End was Boston's first slum, and at the turn of the century it was said to rival Calcutta in density of population.

Although most of the new arrivals lived in squalor on a dollar or so for a day's work, food was cheap: you could get two ears of corn for 2 cents, two dozen pears and bananas for 5 cents, a barrel of

bread (although a bit stale) for 50 cents, and (from the Jewish peddlers) a coat for 50 cents. The diet was mainly vegetarian.

Again, there was great conflict with the established Irish. Since
the Irish were Democrats, the Italians eventually turned toward the
Republican Party. As one immigrant from Avalino said, "No like the
Democrats," which might have meant, "No like the Irishman."

It was from this foothold in Boston that thousands went to work
in the textile mills of Lawrence, Massachusetts, where difficult labor
struggles were to take place early in the twentieth century.

CHICAGO

Italians began arriving in Chicago in great numbers soon after the
Civil War. When the economic panic of 1873 created widespread
unemployment, there was an influx of immigrants from New York.
Most failed to find jobs and became scavengers, roaming the streets
of Chicago and plucking rags and bones from the trash. Despite early
denigration, these ragpickers were finally viewed by the papers as
"frugal, industrious and peaceable men who by the strictest economy
and labor saved enough to repay the money they had borrowed for
their passage."

Between 1890 and 1910, Chicago grew to 200 square miles, with
a population of 2,185,283, a gain of 1 million people in two decades.
It became the second-largest city in the country.

The great influx of Italians coincided with Chicago's expansion.
By 1900 there were 45,000—25 percent from the North of Italy and
75 percent from the South (of which 24% were from Sicily, 15%
from Basilicata, 14% from Campania, 13% from Calabria, and 6%
from Abruzzo).

As the population of Chicago swelled (at the rate of half a million
persons per decade), housing became a serious problem. As in New
York and Philadelphia, the newly arrived huddled into tenements
with no plumbing or ventilation.

The southerners settled for the most part in an industrial-belt
neighborhood known as "Little Hell," which had been primarily
inhabited by Irish and Swedish workers. The presence of the Italians
aroused considerable friction, much of it among the children. But as
the city expanded the demand for cheap labor grew, and more
immigrants came to Chicago, among them large groups of Sicilians.

The Irish and Swedes moved to other neighborhoods, and "Little Hell" became "Little Sicily."

By the late twenties Little Sicily had become solidly Sicilian, with immigrants from nearly all of the Sicilian provinces. Until 1914, Little Sicily remained a tight little island augmented by Italian workers from Louisiana dissatisfied with their situation on the large sugar cane plantations. In part because the district was isolated by poor transportation, it remained an almost completely foreign enclave, a replica of Sicilian village life hemmed in by the noise and speed of a booming American city.

Except for tailors, barbers, and shoemakers, most men worked at unskilled jobs, on the railroad tracks or construction projects. Even those who came with skills (cabinmakers, blacksmiths, and harness-makers) became laborers or merchants.

In Chicago, as in most American industrial centers, World War I proved a blessing in some ways for Italian immigrants. Workers who until then had to be content with low-paying jobs now found themselves beneficiaries of what the historian Rudolph Vecoli described as "an acute labor famine," caused in part by the sudden decrease in immigration and the drafting of Americans for military service. For the first time, industry's needs overrode ethnic prejudices and factory gates that formerly had been closed to the *braccianti* now swung open to receive them. War jobs released them from railroad work, which was generally available only six to eight months a year with wages that averaged $1.50 per day, out of which the worker paid a commission to the *"bosso"* who hired him. These new opportunities to work beside other ethnic groups also furthered integration. For housewives, it was the garment industry that helped to ease the transition.

Most of the immigrants worked at one time or another in a gang (*ghenga,* as they said) on the *tracca* (track), furnishing the pick and shovel labor needed to maintain 2,000 miles of track within the city limits.

In the early days there was a strong sense of regionalism among the Italians in Chicago. The Calabrese clustered around the Near West Side, while those from Potenza settled in Armour Square. If the Venetian bricklayers went on strike, the Sicilians and Calabrese opposed it. Each church had to have an altar dedicated to the patron saint of a particular region: St. Alessandro for the Calabrese, the Virgin of the Rosary for the Sicilians. The anticlerical Piedmontese wanted none at all. And there was a great deal of friction between the wealthy Genovese (who had been the first to come) and those from the Italian South.

The Chicago newspapers furthered southern Italian stereotypes by depicting the southerner—and Sicilians in particular—as a knife-wielding hothead. Then, too, there were the child musician beggars who crowded the streets of Chicago at the turn of the century. These enslaved children of Faginlike masters were brought to Chicago after a police crackdown in the East. When gangs of little strolling musicians were found on the South Side, the *padroni* were arrested and convicted for cruel treatment. Young boys were discovered wandering the streets lugging harps, fearful of returning to their *padrone* because they had not earned enough. One such *padrone* had twenty children on the street gathering alms for him. Some of the surviving "slave children" who had been brought to Chicago during the 1870s by their *padrone* grew up to become *padrone* themselves, or labor agents. When Amy Bernardy visited Chicago in 1910 and spoke with the ex- "slave children," she found a number of them to be well-to-do members of the Italian community, among them professional musicians, as well as a banker and a lawyer.

Most of the Italian settlements were in the city's vice district, where poverty and disorder had preceded the Sicilians by several decades. During the Civil War, Chicago had become known as "the wickedest city in the United States," especially the Cicero section, which later became Al Capone's territory. Soon after the Civil War, the area bound by Polk, State, and Taylor Streets was known first as "Hell's Half-Acre," then as "Little Hell." It was crowded with gin mills, whorehouses, saloons, gambling joints, and streetwalkers' cribs. The police never entered this area—where the grog shops of Tim Reagan were noted for "the desperate character" of both proprietor and patrons—save in pairs, and seldom even then.

The red-light district, known as the Levee, was part of "Satan's Mile," where women were kept for the pleasure of black men and the tough saloons were the resort of the most desperate burglars, thieves, and sure-thing gamblers. Even the children here were taught to steal. Barefooted boys would jump on the footbars of the streetcars as if to steal rides and then snatch pocketbooks from the women passengers.

Between 1871 and 1890 one Michael Cassius McDonald was the mastermind behind much of the crime in Chicago. He established a foundation for criminal organization from which all ethnic groups would learn. McDonald was a bounty broker, saloon and gambling-house keeper, eminent politician, and dispenser of political privileges; anyone who wanted to operate inside the red-light district had to "see Mike" and arrange to pay over a large proportion of his profits to the police, city officials, and members of McDonald's syndicate. McDonald never held office, but he ruled the city with an iron hand. He named the men who were to be candidates for election; he elected them; and after they were in office, they were merely his puppets.

By the turn of the century, the Abruzzesi and Marchegiani living in Chicago Heights had organized a Socialist Party from which came a number of union organizers, among them Emilio Grandinetti and Giuseppe Bertelli. Grandinetti was born to a well-off family in Calabria and studied engineering at the University of Messina, where he became an ardent Socialist. When his political activities made him unwelcome in Italy, Grandinetti migrated to the United States, where he worked with immigrant laborers. In Chicago he founded his own paper, *Il Corriere Di Chicago,* which became the guiding light for other Socialists, such as Arturo Caroti and Aldo Cursi, and for many of the strikers in the garment industry between 1910 and 1915.

The strikes were often long and costly, but by 1919 over 25,000 had been enrolled in the clothing workers union, and negotiation with the owners had finally produced livable conditions and wages. These strikes also forced many of the immigrants to work with Poles, Jews, and other ethnic groups. Grandinetti, one of the Italian union leaders, broke with the International Workers of the World (IWW) because its leaders would not work with Jews in the garment industry.

In Chicago, as in many eastern cities, the Italians who once had been criticized for accepting substandard wages now took part in the labor struggles of the nation.

THOSE WHO RETURNED

Official Italian statistics of 1905–06 indicate that "it was the general desire of virtually all Italians to go back to Italy"; but, as frequently happens, statistics can be misleading even when accurate. Still, of the 4.5 million Italians who arrived in the United States between 1880 and 1924, fewer than half remained.

Many of the families who did return to their native villages had difficulty readjusting. Their language, dress, and diet had changed; having grown accustomed to eating meat, "la bif steka," almost every day, the diet of the villagers now seemed simple. The world was more exciting in America. The American-born children found it especially hard to become acclimatized to the hordes of flies, and open fields used for toilets. All the loving affection of their grandparents could not compensate for the alienation these children experienced in the homeland of their parents, where they felt more American than ever. Others who wanted to return were stopped by World War I, and later by *La parentesi Fascista* (as Mussolini's rise to power was known).

LANGUAGE AND SECURITY

Unless the immigrants attended night school (which rarely happened) or learned English from their children, their grasp of the language seldom developed beyond an amalgam of fractured English and a native dialect. "All that my father ever learned of the language, he picked up during his first six months in America," said one first-generation American who was not allowed to speak English at home. His father's first factory *"bosso,"* a noisy Irishman whom he disliked, provided the incentive. "My father wanted to learn enough English so that he could talk back to him. He was quite successful; the boss fired him the first time he understood what he was saying."

It was not uncommon for immigrants to spend their entire lives in the United States without any knowledge of English. This was particularly true of the women, who, self-imprisoned by Old World customs, seldom ventured beyond the boundaries of their enclave. "One of the great surprises of my life," wrote an Italian American minister, himself an immigrant, "is to hear from time to time, especially from Italian women who have lived in America for years, 'I have been down to America today,' meaning they had gone a few blocks outside the district of the Italian colony."*

New words crept into the language of the immigrants, creating a patois that reflected the first contacts with America. These were mainly practical words that did not exist in the dialects: "ticket" became *ticchetto,* "job" *na gioba,* "factory" *fatoria.* Later there would

---

*Sartorio, *Social and Religious Life of Italian Americans* (Clifton, N.J.: Kelly, 1918, 1974).

be *la investigat* (the investigator) and *lu omme reliev* (home relief). Whenever possible, the Italian word was still used. A man who went to work in a factory, or as a "bricklaya," still said he went to *zapare* (to hoe the fields). As the boundaries of their life expanded, so did their language. Women went to the *marchetta*—the market—*fari la spisa*, to shop. They were soon using *lu strittu* for street; "backhouse" became *bacausu*. Bringing strange words into the security of the mother tongue was a way of reducing those anxieties.*

Italian enclaves were separated from the larger American communities by physical boundaries—a railroad track, hill, or stream—but more often by invisible boundaries that were no less effective in marking the Italian territory. Store signs and official announcements were printed in Italian as well as in English.

Most of the men and some of the women left the enclave each weekday morning to work in the American world, but often their colleagues were compatriots. Only when the Little Italies began attracting outsiders, lured there by the European ambiance, was there significant interaction with the American world. Even then the Italians (though generally cordial) kept their distance.

Within the confines of these areas, the immigrants felt able to criticize the outside American world. "What they learned of this strange country often repelled them," observes Vecoli, the historian son of Italian immigrants. "From their perspective the *'Mericani* appeared a foolish people, without a sense of humor, respect, or proper behavior. Ideas of youthful freedom, women's rights, conspicuous consumption, they dismissed as *Americanannate*. Efforts on the part of teachers and social workers to Americanize them and their children were resented as intrusions on the sovereignty of the family."

The most disadvantaged were those who upon arrival were solely dependent on the boss who had contracted for their labor and who were deprived of the sanctuary provided by a Little Italy. Ignorant of American geography and lacking guidance, the immigrant had to go wherever he was sent. Shrewd bosses understood that a work gang made up of men from one village was likely to be more manageable and productive than one of workers from different regions. The first

---

*"Among the motives that might have provoked these and other linguistic interferences, the desire for security for oneself in the New World was probably one of the principal. . . ." Ciacci, M. *Note sul comportamento linguistico,* in *Gli Italiani Negli Stati Uniti.*

consideration, however, was the commission received for each immigrant recruited. This sometimes meant separating workers from their townsmen and dispatching them to some other workplace. The unhappiest Italian recruits were those who found themselves among strangers. Immigrants would often quit their jobs and try to find another with a work gang that included *paesani*. Failing to find such a group, they would return to Italy as soon as they had saved enough for their fare.

At the heart of the need to band together was the fear of not surviving in a hostile environment. The first Italians in German and Irish districts of New York were not welcomed. One son of a mixed marriage had curious memories of those early days. His Italian mother told him the story of her brother who, while running home from work (he always had to run), was caught by an Irish gang. "Your uncle was saved because he was very good-looking, and an Irish girl stopped the men from beating him." His Irish father said of the Italians, "They have violent tempers, they use knives, they don't fight with their fists." His father recalled his marriage: "The Italian family accepted me, because, and I don't mean this in a bad way, but they thought they were moving up a little. Not that we were any better but we had a big advantage. I mean, to get a job with the city, in the transit, you had to pass a written exam in English. The Italians couldn't read or write English. So they were out. And these were steady jobs."

Some Italian immigrants reacted to the hostility by forming gangs. One man who worked on the docks all his life, and who at eighty still drove down to his old produce firm, put it this way: "Look, if you didn't organize your friends for your own protection you were dead. Or you'd spend the rest of your life a loser. Sure we had gangs. There was the Elizabeth Street gang, the Mulberry Street gang. That's all there was, gangs."

Beyond New York, the immigrant's life was still more precarious.

In Rochester, New York, where newspapers featured accounts of (real and imagined) stiletto-carrying Italians, the townspeople did everything possible to encourage Italians to leave. Storekeepers refused to serve them; landlords would not rent to them. When the weather was mild, these early immigrants lived in boxes and makeshift tents, subsisting largely on dandelion greens. After some became ill, their compatriots armed themselves with pickaxes (the tool they used in their work) and marched into the town's grocery. Using vigorous body language, the Italians threatened to tear down the store unless they were permitted to buy the food they needed. The proprietor complied. Shortly thereafter, when the weather turned cold, the workers paid a second visit to the store, again with pickaxes, to demand housing. The police informed the mayor, who, after consulting with the town's political leaders, ordered the discriminating landlords to accept the Italians as their tenants.

Railroad work brought many Italian immigrants to the northern reaches of New York State. They came to cities and towns such as Albany, Syracuse, Utica, Messina, Buffalo, and Rochester.

> Where do you worka John?
> On the Deleware Lackawan,
> And whatta you do-a John
> I poosh, I poosh, I poosh.

In Rochester, as elsewhere, many stayed on and sent for their families after work on the railroad was completed. The Italian enclave in Rochester grew into one of the largest in upstate New York, with its own church (with an Italian-speaking priest) and shopping centers. Not all its inhabitants remained within the enclave. Some, inspired by the prospect of owning a home with a "yarda" in which to grow vegetables and flowers, moved into neighborhoods where real estate values had begun plummeting as soon as the first Jewish, Italian, and Polish immigrant families moved in. One neighborhood, formerly known as "Little Dublin," later as "Mount Allegro," experienced a drastic change when immigrants from Eastern and Southern Europe replaced the Irish and the Germans. The Irish had wanted no such neighbors: the Jews were abhorrent to them because they were regarded as "Christ Killers." The Italians were equally repugnant, not only because the Italian government had divested the Pope of his temporal power but also because of their heathenish beliefs. The Italians in turn had a curious image of Irish Catholicism. One old man remembered: "In Italy I always saw Jesus coming on a jackass you know. In America Jesus came to me out of the Irish churches riding in the back seat of a Ford, his legs crossed and smoking a Camel cigarette."

Moving into a mixed neighborhood was a significant step toward

mainstream America—especially for the children, who were exposed
to far more than those who remained in the self-contained world of
Little Italy.

"We were ethnics in every sense of the word," wrote a former
inhabitant of Mount Allegro,

> yet our neighborhood could hardly be called a ghetto. There
> were Austrian, Russian and German Jews, Poles, Italians and a
> few Anglo-Saxon families that had chosen not to escape the
> neighborhood. Although the Jews outnumbered everyone else, no
> single group dominated the neighborhood. There were street
> gangs but their membership was based on territorial considera-
> tions rather than nationality. On the street and at school we were
> Americans, though not sure what that meant; inside the home,
> my siblings and I were Sicilians, and there was never any mistak-
> ing what that meant.

Moving into a mixed neighborhood usually made little difference
to immigrant parents since relatives would inevitably join them, usually within no more than five or six blocks. That was about as far
apart as they could get without feeling that America was a lonely and
desolate land.

The neighborhoods often had little visual appeal, especially in
the larger cities, where Italians usually lived in slum areas abandoned
by more established immigrant groups. Nearly always the enclaves
were in or near an industrial district that spewed factory fumes and
smoke, the blackest smoke coming from locomotives in the nearby
railroad yards.

For the southern Italian, the least appealing aspect of life in
America was the long winters, particularly in the northeastern states
where most of the factories were located. Although the neighborhoods were grim, rents were cheap and the slums were near the
workplace. For the more entrepreneurial, these enclaves would provide a satisfactory base.

CHAPTER 11

Mixing the Old and the New

CRIME

In an effort to stop the flow of immigration, some in the American press alleged that hundreds of Italian criminals had entered the United States as a result of Italy's careless system for issuing passports, suggesting that the criminals were leading *mafiosi* and members of the *camorra*. It is doubtful, however, that these immigrants were anything more than petty criminals (abandoned-farm burglars, goat stealers), or former *banditi* whose "unorganized" crime in Italy had been a form of rebellion against an oppressive authority, part of which was made up of *mafiosi* and *cammoriste*.

In the inbred enclaves of America some of these former petty criminals turned their rebellious activity against their own. The immigrants, when speaking of criminals in their midst, used the word *cammorista*—a term also used to identify anything or anybody that was a burden to be endured. An outrageous, aggressive, egotistical, selfish person was a *cammorista*. So was a greedy landlord. A splitting headache was often described as having a *"cammoria* in my head."

Virtually forgotten by the Italian government, which was pleased with the financial and political advantages derived from its policy of exporting labor, and scorned by the aristocrats in the diplomatic service, the immigrants found themselves at the mercy of criminals—just as they had been in Italy. And the American police focused mainly on trying to confine the criminal activity to the Italian ghetto. William McAdoo, police commissioner of New York in 1906, and later Secretary of the Treasury in the Woodrow Wilson administration, wrote in an official police report:

> In view of the frightening crowding of the population, the large number of families that every tenement contains, the conditions of the neighborhoods and the narrowness of the streets, the Lower East Side, where the Italians live, represents an insoluble problem for the police. The density of population in some areas verges on the unbelievable. It is simply impossible to pack human beings into these honeycombs towering over the narrow canyons of streets and then propose to turn them into citizens who respect and obey the laws.

The attitude of the authorities seemed to be one of resignation: Let the Italians straighten things out for themselves. Of the 30,000-man police force, only eleven could understand any Italian.

Criminal activity—breaking and entering, extortion, blackmail, pickpocketing—was rampant, prompting this observation from the historian James Truslow Adams in 1908:

> It is impossible to blame the situation on the "foreigners." The overwhelming mass of them were law abiding in their own lands. If they became lawless here it must be largely due to the American atmosphere and conditions. There seems to me to be plenty of evidence to prove that the immigrants are made lawless by America rather than that America is made lawless by them. If the general attitude towards law, if the laws themselves and their administration, were all as sound here as in the native lands of the immigrants, those newcomers would give no more trouble here than they did at home.

Certainly kidnapping, blackmail, and extortion were committed against the early Italian immigrants. But what made it different from that of native criminals was the use of the foreign words—*mano nera,* which translated into the "Black Hand." In Europe, the word was first used in Spain in the nineteenth century by Spanish anarchists, and later by Serbian nationals responsible for Archduke Ferdinand's assassination in 1914.

Mano nera in New York consisted of individuals and small groups of criminals who used the imprint of a coal-blackened hand to spread the fear that facilitated their criminal activity. The black hand pressed against the door of a house was enough to frighten its occupants into leaving town. The chief targets were prospering immigrants.

The Black Handers gained such notoriety, through extortion letters and violence, as to create the exaggerated impression that the criminals constituted a large and powerful secret society, responsible for all of the crimes committed in the Little Italies and elsewhere. H. W. Zorbaugh in a study of crime in Chicago (1928) found, however, that "Black Hand is not an organization. Its outrages are the work of lawless individuals or of criminal gangs."*

The Black Handers had a clear pattern of operation. When a would-be victim turned to the police, the Black Hand was quick to retaliate. Salvatore Spinelli, who defied the extortionists, explained what happened in a letter to *The New York Times:*

My name is Salvatore Spinelli. My parents in Italy came from a decent family. I came here [to New York] eight years ago and went to work as a house painter, like my father. I started a family and I have been a citizen for thirteen years. My children all went to school as soon as they were old enough. I went into business. I began to think I was doing well. Everybody in my family was happy. I had a house at 314 East 11th Street and another one at 316, which I rented out. At this point the "Black Hand" came into my life and asked me for seven thousand dollars. I told them to go to hell and the bandits tried to blow up my house. Then I asked the police for help and refused more demands, but the Black Hand set off one, two, three, four, five bombs in my houses. Things went to pieces. From 32 tenants I am down to six. I owe a thousand dollars interest that is due next month and I cannot pay. I am a ruined man. My family lives in fear. There is a policeman on guard in front of my house, but what can he do? My brother Francesco and I do guard duty at the windows

*Zorbaugh, *The Gold Coast and the Slum.*

with guns night and day. My wife and children have not left the house for weeks. How long is all this going on?

The techniques of the Black Hand, so successful in New York City, were quickly adopted by Italian criminals in other Little Italies throughout the country. According to a study of 141 criminal cases involving the Black Hand during 1908 in settlements in ten major cities, ranging from New York to San Francisco, every one of the crimes was perpetrated inside the immigrant enclave. In *The Business of Crime,* Humbert Nelli explains:

> The Black Handers themselves remained in the immigrant community, where there was an almost limitless supply of compliant, hard working victims; the territory was familiar, and the Black Hander blended in with other residents. In the non-ethnic neighborhood he would be a conspicuous alien if he delivered a note at the home of the intended victim. Some of the letters were crude and threatening:
>> This is the second time I have warned you. Sunday, at ten o'clock in the morning, at the corner of Second Street and Third Avenue, bring three hundred dollars without fail. Otherwise we will set fire to you and blow you up with a bomb. Consider this matter well, for this is the last warning I will give you.
>> I sign the Black Hand
> Some were civil:
>> Various men of my society as you know well will demand some money because we need it in our urgent business and you finally have never consented to satisfy us to fulfill your duty. Therefore today finishes your case. . . . I have decided that you must do your duty otherwise death will take you and you must not worry over it because these are our rules. . . . etc. etc. . . .

Among the Black Handers were Italian immigrants who worked on railroad or construction projects during the summer and returned to Italy for the winter. The economic situation of these men was precarious; often the money that had been put aside for the winter months was spent by December. At that point, many borrowed more, usually at usurious rates, but there were some who chose to prey on fellow immigrants with extortion letters.

The publicity accorded the Black Hand led to many non-Italian imitators. On January 17, 1910, the Cohen family was notified "that it was next on the list of the Black Hand, that $2,000 was wanted immediately, and that failure to meet the demands of the band was always followed by death, kidnapping and ruin of their daughters." The note was signed "Esperanto Chief of the Black Hand," who turned out to be a male called Bennett C. Silver, who was Jewish. J. C. Cropsey, the New York police commissioner, received threatening letters demanding $50,000 signed by the "Jewish Black Hand," which turned out to be A. C. Schwartz.*

Others who were caught included members of the police force, angry tenants, and native extortionists. Young boys wrote letters as pranks. The publicity also led to cooperative efforts to combat the Black Hand. In Chicago, the White Hand Society was organized—with the support of the city's Italian-language press, the Italian ambassador in Washington, and the Italian Minister of Foreign Affairs in Rome. But apart from generating more publicity, the society proved ineffectual. More effective was the special police unit headed by Joseph Petrosino (see Chapter XV). At the same time, the federal government enacted laws prohibiting mail fraud. To deliver extortion notes by hand, rather than by mail (to avoid mail-fraud charges), now became risky. Also, by 1915 the tide of immigrants was waning, reducing the number of potential victims. But what really put an end to the Black Handers was the advent of the Prohibition era, during which criminals of all national origins were to find a new source of easy money.

FESTIVITIES

Writing of the "turn of the century years," the Italian historian Arrigo Petacco described the Lower East Side Italian settlement as "a kind of human antheap in which suffering, crime, ignorance and filth were dominant elements . . . an ant hill in constant movement where pedestrians had always to be on the alert to the showers of slops that poured down from the windows. In that settlement 5,000 pushcarts clogged the streets, selling everything from shoelaces to sausages." Yet Petacco also says that every day was a feast day to some patron saint, during which the streets rang with shouts in every Italian dialect.

The feast day that surpassed all others in attendance and inten-

*New York Times, 1910 notes.

sity was the annual religious festival honoring some favorite patron saint or Madonna, not only in the Little Italies of New York but in nearly every Italian enclave in the nation of any size. Each feast day, according to Rudolph Vecoli in *The People of New Jersey,* became an assertion of the southern Italian peasants' Old World belief that "magic rather than the sacraments was their way of dealing with the supernatural, and sorcerers rather than priests were sought out by those afflicted in mind and body."

The annual religious festival was an occasion when animosities between Italians from different villages and regions were temporarily put aside as a mark of respect for the holy personage being celebrated.

Few immigrants could resist the music, dancing, eating, drinking, and fireworks that invariably served as the festival's coda. Those who organized the festivals, despite Irish and German Catholic accusations of paganism, replicated in detail the festivals as they had been staged for centuries throughout the *Mezzogiorno.* As in Italy, the church that housed the honored saint or Madonna was the focal point of the celebration. Yet the clergy's role was minimal (a fact that may well have contributed to the popularity of the festival). Hundreds and sometimes thousands of worshippers followed the holy statue through the streets of the Italian community to the accompaniment of marching bands. Now and then the procession would come to a halt as spectators pinned money on the statue while saying a prayer in behalf of a sick or suffering relative in need of divine intervention.

A favorite *festa* in the Mulberry District honored St. Rocco, who though born in France and canonized for miracles in northern Italy was widely revered among southern Italians for his cures of the diseased and maimed. Paraders reminded spectators of San Rocco's miracles by carrying wax arms, legs, hands, and, so one newspaper reported, "other portions of the body not normally exposed to view."

The saint with the largest constituency was San Gennaro, the patron saint of Naples, who was martyred by Romans at Pozzuli during the pre-Christian era. Richard Gambino, a first-generation American who attended the *festa* of San Gennaro as a child, still recalls his fascination with the festivals:

Their aromas of food, the sight of burly men swaying from side to side and lurching forward under the weight of enormous statues of exotic Madonnas and saints laden with money and gifts, the music of the Italian bands in uniforms with dark-peaked caps, white shirts, and black ties and the bright arches of colored lights spanning the city streets are essential memories of my childhood, as they are of many second-generation Italian Americans. True to the spirit of *campanalismo,* each group of *paesani* in New York had its own *festa.* People from Catania celebrated Sant'Agata, who according to legend saved the ancient city from destruction by lava during one of Mount Etna's more violent outbursts. The people from Palermo honored their saint, Santa Rosalia, who saved Palermo from pestilence.

Two other large festivals were held in the New York area each year. San Gandolfo, patron saint of Polizzi Generoso, in the Sicilian province of Palermo, was honored in September on the Lower East Side. The three-day event began on Saturday with concerts by bands and vocalists and culminated Monday with a parade followed by a grand procession for "compatriots and the faithful." The event climaxed in the evening with a "flight of angels"—a spectacle achieved by suspending two young girls dressed as angels on ropes stretched across a street between two fire escapes, and then, by means of pulleys, lowering the "angels" over the saint's statue as it passed. The procession would stop for ten minutes while the girls recited verses praising San Gandolfo. The celebration ended with more music and fireworks.

The annual celebration of the Madonna of Mount Carmel attracted many worshippers who came on a pilgrimage from other cities and states. The festival became so significant in the religious life of New York's Catholics that Pope Leo XIII elevated the Mount Carmel church to the status of a sanctuary. Few other holy figures revered by the Italian immigrants incited as much fervor as "the Queen of Heaven," as the Madonna was known. Her devotees often brought gold and silver plaques in gratitude for favors received; in recognition of the Madonna's powers, they also brought wax offerings in the shape of human limbs and other parts of the body (purchased from stalls near the church), which they laid on the church's altar after each mass.

But it was outdoors, during this annual procession honoring the Madonna, that the fervor reached its peak. The float, bearing a large statue of the Madonna surrounded by an entourage of schoolgirls and young women dressed in white, was pulled through the streets of Italian East Harlem by a team of devotees who had competed for that privilege. Often, as the float first entered a new street with thousands of marchers behind it, the sight of the Madonna was enough to set off an explosion of fireworks and shouts from the spectators. There were also occasional periods of stillness prompted by members of the procession chanting haunting religious songs of the *Mezzogiorno*. Some, unable to contain their religious zeal, kicked off their shoes (as a sign of poverty and suffering) and joined the procession.

The women tended to be more aggressive than the men. All along the route, mothers pushed their children toward the Madonna to pin dollar bills to her robes. Usually at least one woman, fiercely determined to inform the Madonna of some dreadful event that could only be righted by divine intervention, succeeded in bringing the procession to a halt to describe the problem, beg for assistance, and promise some act of penance or reward. At the rear of the procession were the penitents, men and women who had made similar vows to the Madonna in previous years and were now marching barefoot over a pavement burning with the heat of the July sun. Some, even more penitent, crawled along the pavement on hands and knees.

There were some difficulties when a celebration honored the patron saint of a village who was not held in high esteem by immigrants from another village. The tensions that existed in Italy were no less intense in the urban Little Italies of America. At times, insults were exchanged and traffic was blocked as a quarrel gained momentum and police were summoned to restore order.

Outsiders criticized the festivals. A common complaint was that the elaboration of the festivals sometimes overshadowed the religious figures they were honoring. Others, annoyed by the noise, called them "a public nuisance." Some social workers objected to the processions on the grounds that they lacked "the sober restraining influence of the Italian village, particularly of the village priest." And educated Italians feared that the festivals' "excesses" reflected badly on all Italians.

In some communities, officials tried to ban the use of fireworks at the festivals but were thwarted by political pressure. The immigrants were beginning to learn about American politics.

For the immigrants, an American journalist noted, the religious parades were "what a returned hero's parade is to us—a bond, a reminder, and the thrill of the uncommonplace." To some extent, the popularity of the processions also rested on the fact that entire families participated, even the many anticlerical Italian males who were usually reluctant to attend any church-oriented affair (Sunday mass particularly). As one cynic put it, for the average Italian male, church attendance was compulsory only on three occasions: when he was "hatched, hitched and dispatched."

Next in popularity to the *feste* was the wedding ritual, which in the New World was even more elaborate than in the Old. This was often something of a mini-spectacle, beginning with the bridal party traveling in open carriages from the tenement to the church—the bride's finery well in evidence—with relatives and friends following on foot or in carriages. After the ceremony, the bride was pelted with confetti and sugar-coated almonds (symbols of fertility) by the cheering throng. The success of the event (the cost of which usually went well beyond the means of the couple and their families) was judged by the number of carriages, the size of the crowd, and the repasts served.

An invitation to the wedding invariably included the entire family, even infants. A clarinet-led trio played waltzes, mazurkas, and polkas, accompanied by the screams of young children as guests recalled the wedding festivals of the *Mezzogiorno,* often forgetting that they had seldom seen any as lavish as the ones of their new world.

Festivals and weddings were not the only amusements for the young. In preparation for election day celebrations in New York, young boys stole straw hats off the heads of well-dressed men and strung them on a line between fire escapes. This went on all summer; hats were added to the line until a giant necklace of straw hats hung high across the street.

A few weeks before the election, the boys collected old furniture (some found, some stolen) and hid it away. When it grew dark, the boys "from 16 to 70," as one old man remembered, brought out the stored furniture, piled it up below the hats, and ignited it with the object of setting the hats on fire. Some cheered from the windows, others shrieked as they saw their own furniture go up in flames. If police came and put out the fire, a new one was started at another section of the block.

No one knew how the tradition began, but it was done in many streets around the Bowery. Many years later some people, no doubt after seeing Fellini's *Amarcord,* said that it was an Italian tradition celebrating spring. That was, of course, pure nostalgia.

BREAKING WITH THE PAST

Although the majority of the immigrants were from the farmlands of their native country, few continued farming in the United States.

The immigrants desperately needed to earn money, not only to pay debts incurred in their homeland but also to help the families left behind. For those who would have preferred to farm there were formidable obstacles, a major one being a lack of capital for land and equipment. In 1910, the average male immigrant declared only $17 as he entered the country at Ellis Island. Unless he signed on as a contract laborer, there was little chance of working as a farmhand. The money he had would only take him to the nearest Italian enclave, almost always in a city. Not surprisingly, a third of all arriving Italians got no further than New York City.

American and Italian authorities bemoaned the fact that most of the immigrants wound up in congested urban areas rather than on the land, where they could make use of their farming skills. But a government report issued in 1901 explained that most Italians

> had no hint at all of Homestead law by which, after a few easy formalities, he [the immigrant] would obtain 160 acres of land at once. There is not an Italian *cafone* doing unskilled work on a railroad grading who, at the sight of an American farm with a white-fenced and red-roofed house, with extensive fields where crops are growing . . . does not feel the nostalgia of the old calling and a strong attraction to the soil, which he would like to till again in the diversified and intensive way for which he is so famous.

In its fervor, this report suffered from several misconceptions. The immigrant *cafone* was hardly a farmer in the American sense. He was limited by his ignorance of modern farming techniques and tools, and unlike the *contadino* (who usually owned some land and operated as a part-time farmer), the *cafone* lacked the entrepreneurial experience needed to succeed as an independent farmer. Then, too, many of the *cafone* who had left the land in anger were happy never to see a hoe again.

As for the "easy formalities" (i.e., red tape), they often seemed insurmountable to a new immigrant. Also the American farmer's isolated way of life had little appeal for a gregarious people accustomed to working their fields and returning to village life in the evening. The loneliness of this life was seen as an invitation to illness.

Northern Italians and American bureaucrats nonetheless still believed that peasant immigrants were superior farmers yearning for a plot of land. Some recommended that poorly cultivated farmlands be sold to Italians at prices they could afford. Others described immigrant southern Italians as "untamed" and urged that they be sent to southern states to grow fruit, instead of congesting the cities as a "mob." An Italian American editor in Chicago, who tried unsuccessfully to promote Italian agricultural colonies, concluded that the plow provided the only means "to rebuild the reputation of the Italian American in general." After centuries of abuse, he maintained, these peasants tended to distrust the soil "as a cruel and ungrateful stepmother" and discarded their former occupation "with the same pleasure that Hercules had in tearing from his body the shirt of Nessus."

Yet, however unwilling the immigrants might feel about farming in the New World, some could not contain their love for cultivating the soil on a modest scale. Wherever there were backyards, the immigrants gardened, producing for their own use the same vegetables they had grown in Italy. The tiny backyards often included a fig tree which, nurtured by warm summers, flourished. To protect his fig tree from winter's harshness, the immigrant wrapped it in rags, or linoleum, as soon as cold weather set in.

Where there were no backyards, as in Manhattan, the Italians looked for cheap idle land such as they found in the Bay 50th area, near Coney Island. Many of these small plots fed into the burgeoning truck-farming industry whose produce was sold in the street by peddlers.

Truck gardening offered the immigrant several advantages. He could pursue it in his spare time without endangering the family's livelihood. It did not require farm implements, and labor could be extracted from family and friends. Perhaps the most irresistible lure of truck gardening was that it permitted the immigrant and his family to continue living in the secure environment of their relatives and *paesani*. "Their social instincts are strong," reported a team of government investigators in 1910. "It may be asserted confidently that the primary reason for the Italians' choice of trucking and vegetable gardening is a social one; they can have both land and neighbors. . . . In almost every instance they seem to succeed best when they live close together, cultivating small farms and raising crops that require hand labor."

By the 1920s, the Italians were recognized as the nation's chief suppliers of fruits and vegetables. Ex-President Taft echoed the sentiments of other political leaders when he complimented the Italian community on recognizing the potentialities of the vast stretches of land surrounding cities and, in effect, creating a new source of wealth.

The success in truck gardening encouraged other Italians to abandon the city, except as a place to market produce, and to become small-scale farmers in nearby rural communities.

For many, the first step toward small-scale farming was a job as section hand for the railroad or canal that took them into small towns near fertile lands. In New York State there were Italians in every town lining the route of the Erie Canal, which extended from Albany to Buffalo.

A typical community was Canastota, between Utica and Syracuse, an industrial center with four railroads serving factories producing glassware, furniture, and wagons. Extensive tracts of remarkably fertile mucklands surrounded Canastota, much of them undeveloped until an industrial collapse set in during the early decades of the century.

The Italians cleared and developed the swamplands into cultivatable acres. This was hard work: ditches had to be dug for drainage; trees, roots, and lumber had to be removed. Not everyone had the necessary endurance and patience. An immigrant farmer had to produce one or two successful crops before he could obtain any financing. The initial lack of confidence in the immigrant's farming skills also meant that he was generally required to pay cash for land. Often his family had to work the land while he earned their livelihood on a neighbor's farm or in a factory.

Despite these obstacles, the immigrants became the dominant onion growers of Canastota and were credited with putting it on the map as "Onion Town."

Unlike the American owners of muckland, whose holdings generally consisted of 60 acres or more, those of the Italians seldom exceeded 10. The sociologist Joseph T. D'Amico, himself the son of a Sicilian onion grower, cites three reasons for the smallness of the Italian farms: the vast amount of hand labor required for the cultivation of onions and celery (the two most lucrative crops), the increasing costs of cultivatable muckland, and the reluctance of the Italian farmer to hire help. In some cases the numbers of acres they purchased was determined by the number of children in a family.

Italian families began settling Vineland, New Jersey, in 1880. Within 30 years some 950 families had made it the most successful Italian farming colony in the nation. The roots of the colony were established earlier by Charles K. Landis, a wealthy American, who in the 1860s planned and founded the town of Vineland on 57,000 acres of wilderness. He had a vision of "happy, prosperous and beautiful homes," surrounded by farms, gardens, and vineyards. By offering uncleared land at 25 cents an acre, he had succeeded in attracting nine thousand farmers within five years. Vineland prospered until the years following the Civil War, when the community overextended itself and many of the original farmers, unable to continue mortgage payments, forfeited their properties.

At this point one of the few Italian farmers involved at the time persuaded Landis to bring Italian immigrants to his project. To attract the Italians, Landis joined forces with Francesco Secchi de Casale, editor of *L'Eco d'Italia* and a disciple of Garibaldi and Mazzini. Together, Landis and de Casale launched a campaign to lure immigrants away from their urban enclaves. At first the Italians were slow in responding to the advertising in *L'Eco,* but as the word spread that land was available at low prices, the number of applicants increased substantially. By 1880, there were some one hundred Italian families settled in and around Vineland. Five years later, Landis purchased an additional tract of 3,500 acres, which when settled became known as "New Italy," with streets named after the northern Italian provinces of the earliest settlers—Venezia, Trento, Piacenza. After 1890, following the surge of immigration from the *Mezzogiorno,* the northerners were joined by groups of Calabrians, Sicilians, and immigrants from the area of Naples.

Usually a family could earn its livelihood from the produce of a farm within two years of purchase. Yet family members continued to work for others, in order to save enough to pay off the mortgage and purchase a few more acres. As the confidence and profits of the Italians increased, they introduced little-known vegetables into the marketplace such as peppers, zucchini, eggplant, fennel, and broccoli.

Shortly before Landis died, in 1900, he revealed that in all of his dealings with the Italians not once had it been necessary for him to institute foreclosure proceedings.

Other prominent Italian agricultural colonies were located in Fredonia, New York; Genoa, Wisconsin: Sunnyside, Arkansas; and Tontitown, Arkansas.

The anti-Italian prejudice developing and intensifying in various parts of the nation was less pronounced in these areas. The Italians gradually won the respect, if not total acceptance, of their American neighbors. They were, however, criticized, on two counts: for failing to become Americanized, and for allowing their children to drop out of school as soon as they qualified for work permits. A less serious complaint was their unwillingness to sacrifice vegetable garden space for the requisite shade trees and grassy lawns—a luxury unknown to them in their native towns and villages.

PART FIVE

New Roots Across the Nation

CHAPTER 12

Life in the South and West

THE SOUTH

Soon after the Civil War, when the migration of ex-slaves to the North created a labor shortage, Louisiana became one of the first southern states to encourage Italian immigration, with advertisements throughout southern Italy describing Louisiana as a land that had a Mediterranean climate and plenty of jobs. By 1870, only about a thousand had answered the call. The Louisiana government persuaded German shipping companies to establish routes from Palermo and Naples directly to New Orleans; but not until the early 1890s, after the *Fasci Siciliani*, did the Italians begin to arrive in sizable numbers—more than 2,500 of them in the first year of the decade, nearly all from Sicily.

While some found jobs right in the port of New Orleans, a large number were recruited to work in the sugarcane fields. This work, supervised by armed guards, was arduous, and living conditions were poor even by South Italian peasant standards. The more enterprising moved westward to work as section hands on the Texas railroads under construction. When those jobs ended, they settled in small plains towns such as Hearne, Caldwell, and Dilly Shaw to work as sharecroppers until they could save enough to own land. Other ex-railroad workers went to Dickenson, where the cultivation of strawberries was flourishing, or to Galveston to work in the oil fields.

The Texas farming town that drew the largest number of Sicilians (some 2,400 from Poggioreale, Corleone, and Salaparuta) was Bryan, in Brazos County. By pooling their money, they purchased a large tract of bottomland on the banks of the flood-prone Brazos River. The state allowed the immigrants free access to additional land for a two-year period, with the option to buy later on the understanding that the settlers were to clear the land of its timber.

The resourceful immigrants prepared the fallen timber and sold it for their own profit. On the cleared land they planted cotton and corn for the marketplace and vegetables for their own consumption. They also hired out as sharecroppers to other farmers and, when self-sufficient, sent for their wives and children. By 1905, Bryan's population numbered 5,000, 3,000 of whom were Sicilian.

It was not an easy life. "They made just enough to eat and sleep and buy a few clothes," recalled the grandson of one of the first settlers. "There were no herbicides or pesticides; insects were controlled by sprinkling calcium arsenate from the back of a mule." Mules and donkeys transported children to the nearest school, 10 miles away. The most difficult times came in 1899 and 1900, when the Brazos River area experienced the worst flood ever recorded in the area. Thirty-five people lost their lives, and property damage was estimated at $9 million.

In this alien land the ancient Sicilian proverb, "The man who plays alone never loses," was put aside; mutual trust became their chief defense against failure. "We became like a family," recalled a former resident of Bryan. "If a man who had started a crop became ill, we would all pitch in to harvest his corn and cotton—free of charge. When a man lost his mule, he had another one on his lot the next morning."

Yet, while immigrants from the same village quickly learned to help one another, this spirit of cooperation rarely extended to outsiders. Those from the village of Corleone settled on the east side of the Brazos River while those from Poggioreale chose the west side. They spoke differently, worshipped different patron saints, and accepted the mutual animosity of their ancestors.

Intermarriage was rare, and when it occurred, the couple was seen as breaking the proverbial law, "Who exchanges the old way for the new is headed for trouble." Not for another half century did the groups begin to admit to compatibility with one another.

The Italian government, eager to have its nationals branch out from urban enclaves, praised Texas as "the state best suited for Italians." This enthusiasm was echoed in the American press, which predicted that Texas would become "the California of the future." However, Texas never became a favorite destination for the Italians. One explanation was that Texas's motto, "the Imperial State," may have been a source of apprehension for the average Italian. Or, more likely, the Italians may have been responding to the rumors that Texas real estate promoters were conducting an undue amount of land speculation at the expense of the Italians.

The rumor was confirmed by an Italian journalist, Giuseppe Prezioso, who investigated immigrant settlements in the American South in 1908. Throughout that region, he reported, immigrants paid exorbitant prices for land and were subjected to conditions approaching those of slavery. "They live in badly built wooden houses without the most elementary precautions against weather conditions. The dwellings are really barracks where the colonists sleep piled up against one another without regard to age and sex. Hygiene is disregarded."

As Prezioso continued his travels, he was especially appalled by conditions in northern Louisiana and Mississippi, where laborers worked for the lowest wages in the nation. The living quarters were as bad, if not worse, as those of their compatriots in urban areas. Like other observers, Prezioso held the *padroni* mainly responsible for the plight of the farm workers. These labor agents routinely sent workers to the employer who paid the highest fee, regardless of unhealthy and unfair conditions.

Determined to be free of the *padroni,* some immigrants who had been working in Louisiana on railroad construction pooled their savings. "Fighting with their fists and heads" in the face of prejudice, they bought a tract of land near the town of Independence that had been abandoned by American farmers. They succeeded in organizing it into a model agricultural community, achieving proper moisture control through ditches and drainable canals, and cultivating a single crop—strawberries. They marketed the strawberries jointly and purchased supplies in bulk at wholesale prices. When this gamble paid off, the immigrants sent for their families in Palermo, triggering a process of migration that continued steadily for generations.

Within 20 years, the settlement had grown to 250 families, and Independence became "the blue ribbon strawberry shipper of Louisiana."

Few of the southern colonies matched the success of Bryan and Independence. In some instances, would-be colonists fell prey to the false promises of harebrained schemes of compatriots. Adolfo Rossi, who was an official of the Italian Emigration Office, investigated one such scheme in 1905, that had left one hundred men, women, and children stranded in Alabama. The victims had been lured from New York City to an Alabama settlement named "New Palermo" by newspaper advertisements, followed by personal solicitations promising a place in a community that urgently needed "barbers, tailors, or any type of worker." The immigrants were assured that the streets of the community were already laid out, and that each of them, in exchange for a sum of money, would be given land and a house. When the Italians arrived, however, they found that only a few houses had been built and no more would be constructed until they, the immigrants, cleared a large tract of land.

The men, artisans or factory workers unaccustomed to heavy labor, were told that the sooner they cleared the land, the more quickly it would be divided among them. The immigrants, furious, went in search of the promoter of "New Palermo," Salvatore Pampinella, who had disappeared, leaving behind a wife, five children, and a large debt. The immigrants took the wife and children hostage, then appealed to Italian and American authorities. With the assistance of a detective, Adolfo Rossi ferreted out Pampinella in nearby Mobile, telling him, "You have behaved in such a way that were you brought to trial, the judge would not know whether to send you to jail or to a sanitarium."

Rossi faulted both Pampinella and the immigrants who failed to check Pampinella's credentials before leaving New York. In his official report, Rossi pointed out that "neither the Italian authorities nor the Italians in Mobile can be called upon to remedy Pampinella's mistakes and the settlers' irresponsible behavior. All we can do is bring the women and children back to New York. The men should try to find a job in Mobile or in New Orleans." On October 24, 1904, Salvatore Pampinella was shot to death by one of the colonists stranded in New Palermo.

The movement to bring European immigrants to the American South originally was led by plantation owners and industrialists, who hoped to put an end to the black monopoly on unskilled labor. Louisiana was the most aggressive state, even going so far as to advertise its employment opportunities at Ellis Island. In 1907, when Congress was debating a bill that would require a literacy test for future immigrants, Louisiana plantation owners used their influence to block its passage.

Owners had come to rely heavily on Italians to work their cotton and sugarcane fields. While much of the labor was done by men and women who worked the fields all year round, the plantations also supported large numbers of migratory workers, often construction workers from other states. As many as eighty thousand arrived each fall for the harvesting and returned home in the spring. The work was hard and the pay small, but for them it was a way to survive the winter months when construction work was scarce.

Unskilled sugarcane workers worked from sunup to sundown, often for no more than a dollar a day. When it rained, they earned nothing. Old men, women, and young boys were paid as little as 25 or 50 cents a day. To earn extra money, some of the immigrants worked at night by kerosene flares—cooking, grinding, and refining the cane.

Despite primitive living conditions, workers were encouraged to send for their wives, partly because owners needed more help but also to keep the workers rooted. Some plantation owners provided married couples with plots where they could grow vegetables for their own use.

Sicilian wives and daughters now joined their men in the fields for the first time. In Sicily, the sight of a woman working in the fields was rare. But in the United States, women were often seen working side by side with men. The Sicilians were not only aware that they could break with tradition in the New World without censure, but also that by employing every member of the family, they could move more quickly beyond the barriers of subsistence living. A Louisiana cotton planter marveled at a number of them who, "with single-minded concentration," were able to purchase their own farms within four years or so.

In 1898, the sugarcane districts of Louisiana were contaminated with yellow fever. New Orleans, where the epidemic was said to have started in a district of the city known as Little Palermo, was hardest hit. The epidemic was blamed on the Sicilians, who were accused of having brought the disease from Sicily. In fact, contaminated water had caused the outbreak. The baseless charge was one more expression of the anti-Italian bigotry mounting through the South.

THE WEST

Italians generally fared better in the West, where the population consisted largely of newcomers who tended to be more accepting of foreigners. "More important than nationality," writes the historian Andrew Rolle, "were more tangible matters such as how well a man integrated into frontier life; how quickly he could put up a house or clear a field; how well he could break the sod. These qualities frequently determined acceptance." A glaring exception was the treatment of Italian immigrants in Colorado, to which they came (along with Slovaks, Poles, and Russians) to work in the mining camps. The presence of thousands of foreign-speaking immigrants who had been imported as cheap labor from the northeastern states antagonized the English-speaking workers, who feared a reduction in their wages. In time, however, the Italians and other immigrants found that the real adversaries were their employers. The workers came to believe that only by forming a union could they defend themselves against the abuses of the mine owners. For most of the Italians it was their first experience with organized labor.

One of the chief grievances was the failure to provide adequate ventilation and safety devices. After recurring complaints, the owner-controlled press published bigoted pieces stigmatizing the immigrant workers as anarchists, Communists, and nihilists who were "infecting" the nation with radicalism.

When the complaints were ignored, the Italians, who by then comprised about 40 percent of the union membership, went on strike—along with the other foreign-speaking members. The refusal of the English-speaking members to join them prompted the strikers to arm themselves and force their colleagues out of the mines. The mine owners retaliated by persuading the governor of Colorado that six companies of the state militia were needed to prevent any further violence. Workers and owners reached an agreement a week after the strike had begun, but it was at the expense of the Italians. The agreement stipulated that the Italians could no longer remain in the employ of the company and were required to leave the area as quickly as possible.

Five years later, in another confrontation between owners and union members, the governor of Colorado declared martial law during the union's strike at Cripple Creek, a major gold-producing area. He also issued instructions to banish all "troublesome" strikers, along with the Italian publisher of a local pro-labor newspaper. The evicted strikers, who included eighty Italian workers and the publisher, were herded together by a troop of mounted soldiers and forced to march 18 miles on a hot day over mountain roads without stopping for food or water. At the end of the journey the men were released, but not before being photographed and warned not to return.

In the tough and drunken ambiance of Colorado's mining towns, where shootings and lynchings were common occurrences, vigilantism cost the lives of seven Italians. Their lynchings received little attention in the press, not enough to deter Italians from migrating into a state where the economy was booming and jobs were plentiful. By 1910, some 40,000 Italian Americans were living in Colorado, 15,000 of whom were of Italian birth. Except for a few individual mine owners who openly discriminated against employing Italians, Colorado state authorities put out the welcome mat for the immigrants—particularly for Italians looking for farming opportunities—and many Italian laborers and truck farmers responded by settling in the Denver area.

As the bitter memories of the labor strife began to fade, the Italians in Colorado ventured beyond their initial enclaves in Denver and into the Pueblo state's mainstream. Within a single generation they were providing an increasing number of professional men, especially in law and medicine.

With the exception of California, the Italians remained a minority in the states west of the Mississippi. By 1884, four railways connecting the Mississippi Valley with all the western states had increased the general foreign-born population considerably, but Italians were numerous only in California, Washington, and Colorado.

In Arizona, they worked in the mines and on the extension of the Southern Pacific and Santa Fe railroads, but the Wild West atmosphere of Arizona mining centers was not conducive to Italian family life. The number of Italians in Arizona peaked at 1,500 in 1910, but declined thereafter.

The Italians who worked on the railroads or in mining and lumber camps usually came west as itinerant laborers, recruited by hiring agents who dispatched them to states they had never heard of. Most remained only as long as the work lasted.*

Arizona became indelibly imprinted in the memory of one young boy of six who arrived there with his Italian immigrant parents in the 1880s and spent most of his boyhood as an Army brat in the city of Prescott. That boy was Fiorello H. La Guardia, who, after his job on Ellis Island and several terms as a U.S. congressman, served as mayor of New York City for three consecutive terms, from 1934 to 1944.

In his autobiography, in a chapter entitled "Arizona Influences," La Guardia wrote that

> Many of the things on which I have such strong feelings were first impressed on my mind during those early days. Though I have been in politics for well over 40 years, I loathe the professional politicians. . . . This attitude had its origin in the loudly dressed, slick and sly Indian agents, political appointees, I saw come into Arizona. . . . They got their jobs because they were small-fry wardheelers. I saw hungry Indians and the little Indian kids watch us while we munched a Kansas apple or ate a cookie mother baked. I knew, even as a child, that the government in Washington provided food for all those Indians, but that the "politicians" sold the rations to miners and even to general stores, robbing the Indians of the food the government provided for them.

What disturbed La Guardia, even as a child, was that if a worker was injured, he lost his job. "If he was killed, no one was notified, because there was no record of his name, address or family. He just had a number. As construction moved on, it left in its wake the injured, the jobless, the stranded victims. This struck me as all wrong, and I thought about it a great deal."

Years later, while studying law, La Guardia learned that all the laws applying to injuries and deaths incurred by workers on the job were for the benefit of the employer. As a congressman, he joined

---

*During its colonization period, New Mexico's most famous Italian resident was Giacomo Puccini, who, while living in Albuquerque, wrote sections of *La Fanciulla del West*, based on David Belasco's play *The Girl of the Golden West*. Puccini's opera premiered in New York City in 1910. Despite its popularity, it is doubtful that the work inspired Italian Americans who saw it to seek their fortunes in the West.

other legislators in having "these antiquated rules of law" replaced by employers' liability and workmen's compensation laws for injury.

The most poignant of La Guardia's boyhood memories of Arizona centered on an episode that made him the butt of jokes by his non-Italian playmates. He was ten years old when an organ grinder with a monkey came to town and his playmates began to tease him. "I can still hear the cries of the kids," he wrote fifty-six years later. "Dago with a monkey! Hey, Fiorello, you're a Dago, too. Where's the monkey?" To make matters worse, his father came along, began chatting with the organ grinder, and wound up by inviting him home for some macaroni. "The kids taunted me for a long time after that."

The episode rankled long after he had become an adult. When first elected mayor of New York, one of La Guardia's earliest edicts was to ban all organ grinders from the streets of New York.

La Guardia's Arcadian years in Prescott came to an abrupt end when his bandmaster father, who had been mobilized with his regiment at the outbreak of the Spanish American War, contracted a serious illness from eating beef sold to the armed forces by "crooked contractors." The illness, which was to prove fatal within a few years, triggered the family's return to New York City. The cause of his father's death also made an impression on La Guardia. Elected to Congress during World War I, the first measure he introduced in the House was a bill providing the death penalty for contractors who supplied the armed forces with defective goods or other supplies and equipment in times of war. The measure was allowed to die in committee.

In Wyoming, the most sparsely settled of all the western states, the Italians again came as miners and railroad workers. Some settled there and engaged in truck farming or sheep ranching, a novel occupation for Italians.

Utah began attracting Italians as early as 1855 when, as converts to the Mormon faith, former Waldensians settled in Salt Lake City. Not everyone understood the full implications of Mormon rules; some found themselves excommunicated for "rebellion" or "general immorality." Polygamy had an appeal for some converts. One Italian Mormon wrote to the editor of *L'Eco d'Italia* in 1874, "What would your readers say if I were to boast of an offspring of 62 children?" He went on to remind the editor that since he was only fifty years old and had twenty-two wives, he could expect "a still greater number of children . . . all of them healthy and able to procreate."*

Mormon mine owners, recognizing that their immigrant employees were likely to work better in the company of their own kind, encouraged their segregation by nationality as early as 1870. Each group was headed by an English-speaking foreman. In the mining area of Bingham Cannon, each group was allotted its own territory, with boardinghouses, restaurants, and stores that catered to its ethnic tastes. These arrangements pleased the immigrants but did little to promote harmony between the groups or within the community at large.

The idea was adopted on a larger scale in several Nevada company towns, where mine owners favored it as a way to maintain a stable work force. They were particularly anxious to prevent infiltration by union organizers. Their expectations were thwarted on both counts.

This segregation stimulated prejudice against the new immigrants. In Nevada the sudden influx in the 1900s alarmed native workers. Capitalizing on these fears, Nevada's *Ely Mining Record* charged that the "mission" of the immigrant was to reduce the wages of Americans to the point where they could not subsist, adding that "No community can prosper on this cheap class of labor."

The same angry refrain was heard everywhere Italians and other new immigrants were employed. This hostility led to the passage of highly restrictive immigration legislation in the early twenties. Among the strongest supporters of the legislation were the nation's most powerful unions, despite the fact that by then their membership included a considerable number of the new immigrants.

Except for the missionaries and occasional surges of immigration sparked by rumors of fortunes to be made with gold and lumber, there was no great influx of immigrants to the state of Washington until its first intercontinental railroad was built in 1883. Only a few Italians came at first, but the numbers increased rapidly with the construction of two more railway systems in the 1890s—the Great Northern and the Northern Pacific. With the discovery of gold in the Klondike, Seattle became a boomtown as the "Gateway to Alaska." The state's Italian population had doubled by the turn of the century; within the next decade it exceeded thirteen thousand as more and more of the Italians sent for their wives and children.

*The Mormon Church withdrew its sanction of polygamy in 1890.

For the Italians as well as for the larger immigrant groups that had preceded them—Scandinavians, Germans, and Japanese—Washington offered more attractions than most other western states. The chief magnet was Seattle, which at the turn of the century was burgeoning into a metropolis that required strong arms and backs. From Chicago, where his job on a street construction gang had come to an end, Leonardo Patricelli in 1910 wrote his young wife in Foggia: "They say that it [Seattle] is a seaport on the Pacific Ocean close to a country called Alaska, and about 2,000 miles west of Chicago. There are Indians there and huge forests. We are told there will be steady work for at least fifty years."

There was good reason to hope. Within the single decade 1900–10, Seattle's population tripled, increasing from 80,000 to 240,000, and its prosperity spilled over into other areas of the state. Yet, for all the advantages Washington could offer—an abundance of unskilled jobs, plenty of easily available fertile land for truck farming or gardening—the Italian population remained relatively small. La California, with its Italian-sounding name, had long been seen by Italians as the El Dorado of the New World. Washington's failure to attract more Italian settlers may also have been the result of occasional anti-Italian sentiment.

Next to the Japanese, who were associated with the "yellow peril" and forbidden to own property, the Italians were considered the least desirable local foreign group. Italians were seen as the "Dark People," and the press in Spokane published unverified accounts of "Black Hand" criminality that left the impression of universal criminality among Italian immigrants.

The most outspoken anti-Italians were the city's union leaders, who spearheaded an ultimately unsuccessful movement to bar Italians and other aliens from municipal employment. Their primary target was Italians hired by city contractors for road work: "wandering laborers, for the most part single men, who are working for barely enough to exist," and who sent "the bulk of their savings back to the old country."

For the most part, though, the prejudice against Italians throughout the Pacific Coast seldom took the serious turn it did in other parts of the country.

The hardships of those early workers made it possible for their children to prosper and in time to remember the efforts of their parents.

Angelo Pellegrini, the son of Tuscan parents, who became an English professor at the University of Washington, remembered his childhood in the village of McCleary, Washington. "Many of the natives were kind and generous; but others spared no effort to let us know that we were intruders and undesirables." Willy, the school bully, targeted Pellegrini for abuse, calling him "a goddamn wop" who did not "belong to the white race." Pellegrini eventually rebelled and plowed into Willy with a maniacal rage that left his tormenter stunned and bleeding on the ground.

Pellegrini attributes that rage to the feelings of inferiority common among foreign-speaking immigrants. "In our attempt to gain status, to be accepted, to be respected as equals, we always had that handicap to overcome," he says. "And in order to escape that dreaded isolation and feeling of inferiority, some of us submitted to humiliating relationships with unscrupulous natives and vied with one another for their favors."

Pellegrini was one of the first to point out that among poor and uneducated Italians, regardless of origin, there were more similarities than differences. Despite varied cultural legacies, southerners and northerners were imbued with the fatalistic medieval notion that the individual was powerless to change his or her station in life. Pellegrini recalled that in his home town of Casabianca, near Florence, the doctor, priest, schoolmaster, and mayor all "expected and received from us obsequious acknowledgment of their superiority. They entered our world for favors; we entered theirs in service."

Pellegrini's mother, whom he called "La Bimbina," noticed the injustice long before he did. After a few years in America, she decided that there was no reason to be obsequious to anyone. When her husband was killed in an industrial accident, she was left with five children to support. Her lawyer told her that she could not claim a state pension since the physician who treated her husband wrote an unacceptable report. La Bimbina set out to the state capital and presented her case directly to the state's Commissioner of Industrial Insurances, who reversed the decision, and became Bimbina's friend and adviser.

Living in a community consisting almost entirely of non-Italians with a frontiersman mentality, La Bimbina learned that she could speak her mind with impunity; excessive deference didn't figure into the American style of communication. This was seldom true for

Italians confined to the nation's Little Italies, where Old World habits died hard.

SAN FRANCISCO

"If California had not been so far away from Italy, all of the Italian immigrants would have gone there in search of heaven. In Italy I got the idea that California would be like the best parts of Italy—but without the poverty."

—BROOKLYN INTERVIEW, 1983

The image of American streets paved with gold may have struck Italians for the first time in 1848, when gold was discovered at Sutters Sawmill near San Francisco, a city named by Spaniards to honor one of Italy's favorite saints.

Among those hit with gold fever were several hundred Italians from northern Italy. Some came after wandering through South America and the southwestern states. Italian sailors on board ships bringing Carrara marble to San Francisco jumped ship to join the gold seekers. The pioneers also included Italian farm laborers and fishermen who came directly from Italy, after hearing from unscrupulous steamship agents that in California they could pluck gold rocks from the nooks and crevices "with their bare hands and a knife."

Most arrived too late to stake out claims in the most desirable sites and had to travel far beyond Sutters Sawmill to find unclaimed areas. Wherever they went, the Italians encountered American prospectors guarding their claims. Suspicion and greed resulted in shootings, knifings, and fistfights. Also discouraging to the Italians was the reality that, though they worked steadily from early morning until dark, they gained little more than sore muscles for their efforts. Many soon shelved their dreams of quick riches and looked elsewhere, abandoning mining for more stable and familiar occupations such as farming.

Many of the Italians settled in the fertile Sacramento-San Joaquin Valley. Others drifted north, as far as Oregon and Washington, to work in lumber camps, coal mines, and vineyards. Still others returned to San Francisco, where they worked for other Italians who, unmoved by gold fever, catered to the city's growing foreign population with restaurants, boardinghouses, groceries, and clothing stores. The California economy, especially in San Francisco, flourished in the Gold Rush era. By 1870, San Francisco's population numbered 149,000, half of whom were foreign-born. Of these, only 1,600 were Italians; 50 years later the Italians were the leading immigrant group, comprising 20 percent of all foreign-born residents.

The Italians in San Francisco settled first around Telegraph Hill, a rocky bluff 300 feet high stretching down to the waterfront and reminiscent of a Mediterranean seaside village. The Irish, first to arrive, lived at the top of the hill; the Germans were in the middle; and at the base, where the rents were cheapest and access to the fishing boats quickest, were the Italians. A ditty of the time put it this way:

The Irish they lived on the top av it,
And the Dagos they lived at the bas av it,
And the goats and the chicks and the brickbats
And Shticks
Is joombled all over th' face of it . . .

The Italian settlement grew, displacing the Germans and the Irish. As more Italians arrived, they moved into the North Beach district adjacent to the Hill. The combined section became known as the Latin Quarter, and later as the Italian Quarter, where not a sign was printed or written in English. At first the Italian settlers were mostly fishermen and farmers, but as the immigration from Italy increased in the early twentieth century, their ranks included laborers, artisans, mechanics, shopkeepers, and restaurant owners. Those intent on farming (mainly Neapolitans, Ligurians, and Tuscans) gravitated to the Outer Mission district, where they worked together to turn sandy dunes into productive acres, specializing in lettuce and artichokes.

The Italians in the Telegraph Hill enclave maintained many of their native customs, one of which may have saved the quarter from complete disaster during the 1906 earthquake. When quake fires began to creep up the Hill, the residents rolled barrels of wine from their cellars and, forming a bucket brigade, succeeded in protecting their houses from the flames with blankets soaked in the wine.

Although it was assumed that most Italians in San Francisco came from northern Italy, the anthropologist Paul Radin in a 1930 government-sponsored study revealed that 36 percent came from southern Italy, 10 percent from central Italy, and 54 percent from northern Italy.

As in many other states, the early San Francisco immigrants were mostly Genovesi and Tuscans; later arrivals hailed from Calabria, Campania, and Sicily. Most came directly from Italy, via New York, where they had boarded the transcontinental train to San Francisco. Railroad agents promised good wages and cheap land in California, and the immigrants paid from $110 to $120 for their fares to a place where they were assured they could recoup that investment within a few weeks. Many arrived during a period of national economic crisis and high unemployment which provoked gangs of unemployed men, such as Coxey's Army in 1894, to march on Washington demanding relief. The new immigrants were not welcomed by their Italian compatriots, who disparaged them for their lack of skills and feared that the discrimination often practiced by American employers against southern Italians, especially after the New Orleans lynchings*, might be extended to them. Eventually, the newcomers found jobs as fishermen, farmhands, garbage collectors, and in canning factories, usually among the *paesani* from their home villages who had preceded them.

There was intense competition between southerners and northerners in agriculture and fishing, which extended over a period of years, with the Sicilians finally winning control of the fishing industry by the first decade of the century.

In 1930, the preponderance of Italians in the fishing industry was explained by Paul Radin:

> first by the fact that many of those engaged in the fleet were employed in the commercial fishing before coming to America . . . second, several of the large buyers and distributors of California fish are Italian-born or of Italian extraction; third, the nature of the work does not appeal to the average American, and can be endured only by those of the most rugged constitution; fourth, Italians are good sailors, and the small boats in which they operate in rough waters require seamanship.

By 1920, Italians made up 20 percent of all foreign-born residents in San Francisco. Only in New York City was the percentage higher.

*See next chapter.

In the Bay area the fishermen were especially conspicuous. On Sundays, as they and their families gathered in the morning to repair nets and boats as was the custom in the small fishing villages around Palermo, they sang folk songs and operatic arias while they worked. In good weather they would board their boats and picnic on the shores of Marin County. For all of the immigrant families, their two-hour Sunday meal was the highlight of the day. After dinner, the women would chat and sew while the men sat in Washington Square or went to the social club of *paesani* to which they belonged and played cards. Sunday afternoons were also reserved for *bocce* teams, which competed at Fisherman's Wharf. The Tuscans had their own favorite sport, *pallone,* which was played on empty lots with wheels of Tuscan cheese. A leather strap was placed around a wheel of *Pecorino* and sent rolling. The winner was the player who could send it the farthest along a straight line. The audience, as well as the players themselves, bet with one another, and the player who won got the cheese and whatever bets he had made. One of the few annual events that attracted San Franciscans of all nationalities was Discover's Day—one of the first events in the nation dedicated to Christopher Columbus. Following church services there was a lengthy parade to the Municipal Pier, the site of the explorer's statue.

North Beach grew into San Francisco's dominant Italian enclave after 1900, as more men sent for their families. In North Beach and Washington Square in particular, the immigrants could recapture the memory of their native village with its *piazza,* the outdoor social center of the community. Another gathering spot was Fisherman's Wharf, which on Sundays became picnic grounds for fishermen and their families. The most popular of the festivals were staged annually by the fishermen, Sicilians paying homage to the Madonna of Porticello (an area near Palermo noted for its swordfish) during "the blessing of the fleet," whose boats were painted blue and white for the occasion.

Fisherman's Wharf served as the harbor for 700 fishing vessels, which averaged a daily catch of 11,500 tons. The Genovesi were the first Italians to dominate the industry, which they did by driving away the Greeks and Slovaks. The Italians introduced two pieces of fishing equipment they had known in Europe which gave them a distinct advantage over their competitors: the *paranzella,* a trawling net that was dragged over the fishing grounds; and the *felucca,* a small, shallow vessel specially built to withstand high winds and rough water. The *felucca* permitted as many as a half dozen men to spend two or three days at a time fishing. The vessel was easily identifiable by its colorful triangular sail, denoting the native region of its fishermen.

As a result of the fierce competition with the Genovesi, groups of Sicilian fishermen left San Francisco to join compatriots who were already established in such fishing centers as Monterey and Black Diamond (later renamed Pittsburg), near the confluence of California's two largest rivers, the Sacramento and the St. Joaquin. The first of the Sicilian fishermen along the Black Diamond waterfront were two brothers, Pietro and Russel Aiello, who arrived in 1870 and fished for four years before returning to their native town of Isola delle Femmine to bring back their families. Their arduous trip precipitated a chain migration which eventually increased the Sicilian population of Black Diamond to three thousand, all of them from Isola delle Femmine (an island in name only, on the Sicilian coast about 10 miles from Palermo).

Fishing was their main occupation, but there were also craftsmen able to build sailing boats sturdy enough to warrant annual trips to Alaska for salmon, the most lucrative of the catches. These trips were mean and hazardous. Tony Aiello, who first came to Pittsburg in 1888 when he was eleven years old, remembered:

> In those days it was common to spend on a voyage, 50 to 60 days on a trip. This was only one way. In a wooden ship, a sailing ship. I remember one called the "Diane." Those ships carried sometimes 50 other times 100 men. In those days we ate a lot of salted meats, anyway we ate what there was to be had, and sometimes nothing! If it was rough weather or if time was delayed we ran out of provisions. If the cook was able to make meals in rough weather, we had to be extra careful not to fall or spill and the like because we had no tables. We ate anywhere and we didn't want to slip on deck because that was bad. Pigs . . . were for the ships officers, the Captain. They also brought a cow, for them not us . . . when in Alaska, for us it was potatoes, fish fry, and Salmon, no other kind of fish. . . . When going through Unimak Pass, which opens up into Bristol Bay, we got caught in the icebergs . . . and sometimes we couldn't get into the cannery because the barges couldn't be maneuvered in this weather, so we may stand by for an additional 15 days.

The first time Pittsburg fishermen went to Alaska was in 1886, and the trip took about six months. These were usually the poorest of all Italian fishermen, who in order to supplement their meager earnings from local fishing began to go to Alaska.

One of the most enterprising Genovesi in the area was Andrea Sbarbaro, who founded the first building and loan association in San Francisco. He also established a night school for fishermen and their children in the North Beach area. An idealist who had been influenced by Tolstoy and Mazzini, Sbarbaro organized a cooperative in the Sonoma Valley known as the Italian-Swiss Agricultural Colony (so named because there was a Swiss on its board of directors), which hired peasants who had worked in the Italian vineyards. Sbarbaro paid them fair wages, provided them with all the wine they could drink, and offered them shares in the cooperative. The shares, originally worth $135,000, were valued at $3 million by 1910. Italian Swiss Colony became one of the earliest American wineries able to market its wine products nationally.

If Sbarbaro saved the Colony, it was Pietro Carlo Rossi who made it prosper. Rossi, a winemaster from Asti, Piedmont, improved the quality of the wine and attracted world attention by winning the Grand Prix for his wines at an international congress held in Turin. He also provided seasonal employment for area families.

If the gold-lined streets of California turned out to be a myth, Amadeo Pietro Giannini did his best to make it a reality in San Francisco.

Giannini—future founder and chairman of the Bank of America—was born of immigrant parents from Genoa in 1870 and began his career as a fruit peddler. Giannini opened the Bank of Italy in 1904 with capital from his stepfather and a few friends. He solicited deposits and loans door to door for farmers, laborers, and small merchants.

During the great San Francisco earthquake of 1906, Giannini harnessed two horses to a wagon and rushed to his bank, through burning streets filled with looters and drunks, to rescue $2 million in gold and securities. His was the only bank open for business (housed temporarily in a waterfront shed) when the fires burned out. From then on, Giannini's rise in the banking world was spectacular. In 1919, he innovated the branch banking system. In 1928, he formed Transamerica Corporation, a holding company for all his financial enterprises; by 1930, it had become the Bank of America. By 1945 the Bank of America was the world's largest private bank, with more than 3 million depositors, $6 million in resources, and 495 branches.

Giannini never lost his (in the eyes of other bankers) eccentric concern for the small man, lending money to fruit growers, small merchants, and laborers on their signatures alone. He was the first to finance filmmakers, Charles Chaplin, Mack Sennett, and Darryl Zanuck among them. At seventy-five Giannini, a *faitature* (fighter), as the immigrants might have called him, retired to live with his daughter, "to swim, to listen to music," until his death in 1949.

CHAPTER 13

New Orleans—Wops, Crime, and Lynchings

> Mafia is a good word with which to conjure up prejudice
> and hide unpleasant truths. It had been, and is, so used by
> the press all over this country; but I think, if ever the real
> facts come out (and they may) it will be seen that the late
> Chief of Police was murdered at the instigation of
> individuals, out of fear that he would be instrumental in
> letting their enemies loose upon them, and not by any
> organized Society.
>
> —BRITISH CONSUL'S REPORT, NEW ORLEANS,
> MARCH 26, 1891*

When Edward A. Freeman, Regius Professor of Modern History at Trinity College, Oxford, and author of a much-admired history of ancient Sicily, arrived in New Haven in 1881, he was asked what he thought of America. "This would be grand land," he answered, "if only every Irishman would kill a Negro and be hanged for it." This was the attitude of a supposedly intelligent, well-educated historian. Among the less sophisticated, the attitudes toward those

---

*Duggan, *Fascism and the Mafia*, p. 46.

who differed from themselves, though not as dramatic, were no less hostile.

The mass arrival of foreigners provoked a growth of racism in America, from the visiting Oxford don to the ordinary person who decried the "Mick," the "Kike," and the "Dago."

Of course, the American view of Italians varied, especially among the educated. Some admired Italy as the mother of the arts. The *Case Italiane* established in some American cities employed Italian scholars to teach the children of the rich about the culture of the Grand Tour. Yet, in speaking of Dante, Da Vinci, and Michelangelo, the greater reality of Italy and Italians was ignored. Even the most astute historian of the Italian immigration, Robert E. Foerster, wrote in 1919 of the brutalizing effects of the labor in which the Italians engaged. He saw their spirits calloused by work, but attributed it to a lack of mental ability. Their endurance he explained by their Helot sense of timelessness; they spoke of events which had taken place weeks ago as if they had happened the day before or hours before (psychiatrists now tell us this is a form of repression). Foerster also wrote of the Italians as being miserly, sober, tricky, lazy, docile, passionate, tireless workers, having short-lived enthusiasm, suspicious, secretive; as time servers, utility was their guide.

This bigotry was an affront and humiliation to the immigrant, and abstract negative views often translated into physical violence.

If there had been widespread admiration for the cultural achievements of Italians during the 1880s, these sentiments began to change. The changes were most obvious in New Orleans, where Italians, encouraged by the state of Louisiana, came to find work. As more and more arrived, caricatures of the immigrants began to appear in the New Orleans newspapers. In *The Mascot*, the Italian immigrant was drawn as a dirty, bearded, hook-nosed man carrying a battered basket filled with bananas. Italian fruit peddlers were pictured with broad thick mouths and hooked noses, cluttering up the walks with their fruit stands. They slept ten to a room in the midst of filth and were seen killing one another with knives. The best way of disposing of them, the next series of drawings suggested, was to drown them in batches, or at least beat them and jail them. In a series of cartoons of October 1890 entitled "The Italian Population," one panel shows a group of immigrants in a cage being lowered into the river. The caption reads: "The Way to Dispose of Them."

In these caricatures, Jews did not fare better. Images of Solomon, the money grubber, with his hooked nose and fat lips, are not far from the images to be found in Germany forty years later. Such bigotry helped create the notion that organized crime was brought to New Orleans by Italian immigrants.

New Orleans in the 1880s was corrupt, violent—and growing. The Crescent City, as it was called, was a port where rivermen coming down the Mississippi sold their wares alongside their boats. The city prospered by catering to these men, who, away from home, reveled in its vices: whoring, gambling, and drugs. There were great fortunes to be made in these "victimless" crimes, and politicians and police fought to take part.

David Hennessy, the key figure in the lynchings of Italians, was one of many such men who fought his way to the post of chief of police. Hennessy was a northerner whose father had come to New Orleans soon after the Civil War to help rebuild the South. David Hennessy became involved in the city's vice, first as a private detective working for the city. When the job of chief of police became open, Hennessy's chief rival for the job was Thomas Devereaux. One Robert Harris also had his supporters for the job.

On October 13, 1881, David Hennessy and his cousin Mike Hennessy went looking for Devereaux. They found him in the offices of the *City Item,* a local newspaper, where Mike drew a pistol and fired at Devereaux through a plate-glass window. Devereaux fired back. David Hennessy drew his gun and returned the fire; then, running to a side door, he burst into the offices and at close range put a bullet in Devereaux's head as the chief of detectives was trying to escape. Both Hennessys were arrested and tried for murder. A jury decided it was a matter of self-defense, and both men were acquitted. The whole affair prompted the publisher of the *Daily States* to comment:

> The fact is patent that neither of the two murderers nor their victim were proper men to hold any position on the police force much less the responsible positions they did hold. . . . The Hennessys are desperate men and no one can read the story of yesterday's terrible tragedy, conflicting as the reports are, without a conviction that Dave Hennessy is a murderer. We are astounded that a jury in a Christian and enlightened country would return

such a verdict as "not guilty" in this case. All the facts prove that this was a deliberate and bloody assassination.

Nevertheless, soon afterward Hennessy was appointed chief of police. As such he bought into whorehouses and joined and supported the Red Lights Social Club, whose main activity was procuring and selling women. The Red Lights, as it was generally known, was "under the arm of the Chief of Police Hennessy."*

Mike Hennessy moved to Galveston, then to Houston, where on September 29, 1886, he was found dead with bullets in his head. It was common knowledge but never proven (for no one bothered to investigate) that his killer had been sent from New Orleans.

On October 15, 1890—two days after the anniversary of the day David Hennessy killed his rival—Hennessy himself was shot dead while returning from an evening of carousing with his friend Bill O'Connor.

Most of the Italian community in New Orleans (20,000 to 25,000) at the time was made up of Sicilians, farmers from Corleone and the Palermo area, and fishermen from Trapani who lived in the "Little Palermo" enclave of the French Quarter. Some who had found work as stevedores fought with the Irish and blacks who had until then controlled the waterfront jobs. The "dagos" did not fare well in the local papers, which called them "dirty, lazy, ignorant and prone to violence."

By the 1880s, in this wave of anti-Italian bigotry, the police were unfairly attributing most murders to Sicilians, going so far in a few instances as to Italianize the names of the killers, as in 1883 when Pedro Echave was murdered by Jose Bilboa, and the *Picayune* changed "Eschave" to "Escaro" and "Jose" to "Joseph." On June 14, 1885, "Juan Martini" 's murder was reported as having the "appearance of a mafia killing," despite a coroner's report stating that the victim was John Martin, born in Germany. On January 18, 1887, the coroner's report recorded that two French citizens, Dominique and Jean Tribique, had been murdered. But the names reported to the mayor were changed to "Domenica Tribega" and "Jean Tamora." If a murder went unsolved, it was attributed to "unknown Sicilians."

---

*Despite the nature of the crime, as late as 1959 Frederic Sondern, Jr., in *The Brotherhood of Evil*, was repeating the story (as did the lynchers to excuse their actions) that Chief Hennessy was "an honest, intelligent, imaginative policeman of a kind most unusual in his day."

* * *

Among those who prospered in the corrupt and violent environment of the New Orleans waterfront were two Italians, Joseph Provenzano and Charles Matranga.

For many years, Joseph Provenzano had the exclusive business of unloading ships bringing fruit from Latin America. Provenzano flourished until 1886, when Charles Matranga and one Locascio started a second stevedore company. There began a competition for the rights of unloading ships which ended when the city's merchants gave Matranga/Locascio exclusive rights to the work. Matranga exacerbated the situation by persuading most of the Provenzano workers to work for him instead.

Provenzano then threatened Matranga, informing him that if he would not join forces, "there would be bloodshed." Matranga notified the police while the Italian business community tried to mediate between the two. The affair seemed settled after both parties "came to an agreement and gave their word to the police [in this case Chief Hennessy] that there would be no further trouble."

One evening after unloading a load of bananas from the *Foxall*, a group of Matranga workers were ambushed on their way home. Two stevedores were wounded, and Anthony Matranga, brother of Charles, was hit in the left leg, which soon after had to be amputated. No one was killed.

On the testimony of many of the Italians who went to the police, the brothers Joseph and Peter Provenzano, along with some of their workers, were arrested by Police Chief Hennessy. At their trial the Matranga forces testified against the Provenzano brothers, pointing them out as the would-be murderers. A jury found them both guilty and sentenced the brothers to life imprisonment.

It seemed like a clear-cut case of attempted murder, quickly solved by the willingness of the victims to testify openly in court. However, the convoluted politics of New Orleans intervened. A large number of police officers had testified during the trial that the Provenzano brothers and the other accused were not at the scene of the crime, that they had seen them elsewhere.* The question then arose: Were the Matranga witnesses lying, or the police officers?

A committee appointed to determine whether the police had perjured themselves returned with a verdict that the police had told

---

*The courts records were later lost; only the newspaper accounts are available.

the truth. As a result, the Provenzanos' lawyers won a new trial for their clients. The leading politicians, and a group known as "the custom house gang," all testified in favor of the Provenzanos. This time they were found not guilty. Hennessy was listed as a witness for the Provenzanos, but apparently did not testify. At this second trial it was the police's word against the word of members of the Italian community who had come to testify against Provenzano.

Hennessy himself had many enemies, not least Kevin O'Mally, a longtime rival, with whom he had come to blows when O'Mally called him a scoundrel in the summer of 1890. Provoked, Hennessy was quoted as seeking "satisfaction at pistol's point."

It was in this tense and violent atmosphere on October 19, 1890, on "a dark, dreary, rainy night" at the corner of Girod and Basin Street, at 11:30 P.M., that a volley of shots rang out and Chief Hennessy fell to the ground with several bullets in his body. Still alive, he was taken to Charity Hospital, where he lived for 9 hours, chatting with attendants and doctors. The *Times-Democrat* reported that "When he was asked if he knew who shot him he shook his head from side to side in a negative way."

Yet his dying words, as reported by his friend William O'Connor, were, "The Dagos did it."

Mayor Shakespeare called out the entire police force, almost to a man Irish, and ordered them to "Arrest every Italian you come across." Over a hundred Italians were arrested and the jail filled, as the papers reported, with "Sicilians, whose low, receding foreheads, repulsive countenances and slovenly attire, proclaimed their brutal natures."

Three days later, Mayor Shakespeare roused the City Council with a public statement that found the Sicilians guilty before the trial:

The circumstances of the cowardly deed, the arrests made
and the evidence collected by the police department, show
beyond doubt that he [Hennessy] was the victim of Sicilian vengeance, wreaked upon him as the chief representative of law and
order . . . because he was seeking by the power of our American
law to break up the fierce vendettas that have so often stained
our streets with blood.

We owe it to ourselves and to everything that we hold sacred
in this life to see to it that this blow is the last. We must teach
these people a lesson they will not forget for all time. What the

means are to reach this end, I leave to the wisdom of the council to devise.*

The mayor's conclusion that the Sicilians were guilty before they were tried and his call for measures beyond the law were the natural culmination of a long period of bigotry directed at the newcomers. Newspapers called for speedy justice in order to preserve the American way of life. In such a climate of opinion, a grand jury indicted nineteen Italians for the murder, of whom only nine men, with no reason given, were put on trial (among them, Charles Matranga, Antonio Scaffidi, Asperi Marchesi, Joseph Macheca, Antonio Bagnetto, and Manuel Polizzi).

Nor did the prejudice abate. The *Daily Picayune* chose this time to run a long piece on Sicilian bandits, mafia, and mysterious crimes committed in the Italian community. Tom Duffy, a newspaper distributor and friend of Hennessy, went to the parish prison where he often visited imprisoned friends. He told the guard he could identify Antonio Scaffidi as Hennessy's killer. When he reached Scaffidi's cell, he promptly pulled out a revolver and shot him. Scaffidi survived—only to die later in a more brutal fashion.

That same day, *The Mascot* reported:

STARTLING REVELATIONS
Some Prominent People Associated with This
Horrible Affair

The police today are very mysterious in their movements and manner of treating the subject in conversation and the fact is due, so it was given out pretty extensively this morning, that a startling tip had been received, which if true would cause the city to shake from end to end. There are many who never did believe that the dagoes murdered Chief Hennessy for their own account, or for their satisfaction if really he was murdered by dagoes, and so generally was this theory shared that after the arrest of the above listed men, the question arose as to whether or not others

---

*Mayor Shakespeare's city had seen many a policeman involved in murder before the killing of Hennessy. Not only had Hennessy killed Devereaux in 1881, but in 1883 there had been a gun battle in the streets between Sheriff Brewster and rival politicians and James Houston, in which three people were killed and wounded. Two years later Houston, then a tax collector, was killed. That same year, Thomas Ford hired two policemen, John Murphy and Patrick Ford, to find Captain A. H. Murphy, whom they promptly shot dead. Thomas Ford soon after was chosen by the city machine as the next mayor.

than dagoes might have been associated with the murder. Some attention to this important suggestion has resulted in connecting several prominent men with the plot to assassinate the police superintendent. No disclosures will be made public. If the information herein referred to should prove true, then New Orleans has indeed struck a horrible era.

In reasoning it was held that the Chief had never arrested or disturbed the dagoes in any way. The only dagoes ever arrested and brought to the bar of justice were his friends and companions—the Provenzanos. The Matranga gang could certainly bear no grudge against him for having arrested their assailants . . . there is nothing in the records to show that he had at anytime during occupancy of the office ever made any war on the Italians. And besides this is just as sure as fate that none of the three men identified by Mr. Peeler [chief witness for prosecution] ever saw the Chief. . . .

No attempt was made to follow up on this lead. On February 28, 1891, a twelve-man jury was chosen, none of whom could be considered a peer of the accused. In this racially charged affair, none was of Italian origin. The trial itself began in March. When a number of Italian communities around the country raised money for the defense of the nine men, the action was denounced as a "mafia" conspiracy.

At the trial M. L. Peeler testified that the oilcloth coat found in Scaffidi's house resembled the one he saw the killer wearing the night of the murder. The fact that Scaffidi was not at his job in the Poydras Market at the time of the shooting was also presented as evidence. Yet Peeler could not identify Scaffidi. A black witness, Z. Foster, testified that he saw Scaffidi and three other men firing at Hennessy. Upon cross-examination, he was not sure.

The prosecution, sensing its weak case, resorted to putting Pinkerton agents in the prisoners' cells in an attempt to extract information from the accused. Frank Dimaio, a Pinkerton agent, had himself arrested as a counterfeiter and was sent to the parish prison. He later admitted that in the time he spent with the prisoners, they all told him they were innocent.

The defense for their part called witnesses who testified that the accused were elsewhere at the time of the murder.

The piece of evidence that swayed the jury more than any other was evidence not presented: no one bothered to call O'Connor, who had reported Hennessy's last words, "The Dagos did it." Nor had anyone bothered to question Hennessy himself, who lived nine hours after the shooting and talked lucidly with people in the hospital.

On March 12, 1891, a banner headline on the front page of the *Picayune* read:

NONE GUILTY!

The Jury in the Hennessy Case Deliver Their Verdict A Mistrial as to Three, and All the Others Acquitted.

Instead of being released, the acquitted men were returned to the parish prison to await further charges.

The next day newspapers carried an advertisement:

MASS MEETING

All good citizens are invited to attend a mass meeting on Saturday, March 14, at 10 o'clock A.M., at Clay Statue, to take steps to remedy the failure of justice in the Hennessy case.
Come prepared for action.

The meeting was called by a Committee of Fifty formed by Mayor Shakespeare, "a rabid, pro-papal Irish Catholic," and was made up of the leading politicians and professional men of the city. Among them was James Houston, head of a syndicate of politicians known as "the Ring." (This was the same Houston who in 1883 led his Ring politicians in a shootout with a rival group that left three dead and eight wounded.)

The call for a mass meeting was answered by ten thousand. On the morning of March 14, William S. Parkerson, confidant and aide to Mayor Shakespeare, stood on the pedestal of Henry Clay's statue and roared out to the crowd:

People of New Orleans! When courts fail, the people must act! The time has come for the people of New Orleans to say whether they are going to stand for these outrages by organized bands of assassins, for the people to say whether they shall permit them to continue. I ask you to consider this fairly. Are you going to let it continue? Will every man here follow me, and see the murder of D. C. Hennessy vindicated? Are there men enough here to set aside the verdict to that infamous jury, every one of whom is a perjurer and scoundrel? Men and citizens of New Orleans follow me, I will be your leader!

The crowd then surged toward the prison, where the warden opened the cell doors and told the prisoners to hide as best they could.

Outside, the mob battered down the prison gates and spread out into the prison. They hunted through the corridors and corners and found six of the acquitted men in a small courtyard used for exercise. There, men dressed in frock coats and derby hats from close range of 20 feet pumped over a hundred rifle shots and gunshot blasts into the six men, tearing their bodies apart while others cheered.

Macheca, Scaffidi, and the old man Asperi Marchesi were found hiding in the women's section and their heads were blown off.

When the demented Polizzi was found, half alive from bullet wounds, he was dragged out to the crowd. There the half-dead body was tossed overhead from hand to hand the length of several blocks to come to rest below a street lamp. *The Mascot* seemed to revel in these details:

> . . . a youth had climbed to the top of a lamppost and had ad-
> justed a small cord over the crossbar, just below the dismantled
> lampframe. A noose was quickly thrown over the head of the
> doomed man and the other end of the cord was pulled by men
> in the crowd. The small cord cut deeply into the prisoner's neck,
> but before his toes left the ground the cord broke and Plitiezz
> [sic] fell to the banquette.
>
> A strong rope (a new clothesline) was at hand, and again the
> wretch was dragged above the heads of the crowd. Slowly with
> his head thrown back and his pallid upturned face contrasting
> weirdly with his great shock of jet black hair, Politez's [*sic*] head
> and shoulders were above the heads of those around him. His
> unpinioned hands waved wildly above his head till one of them
> touched the rope; then, quick as thought his fingers clutched the
> cord, and in an instant he had pulled himself up hand over hand
> to the crosspiece where he hung by his hands. The man who had
> before climbed the lamp-post to adjust the rope struck him in the
> face and forced him to relax his hold upon the crosspiece. . . .

As Polizzi insanely climbed with the rope around his neck, men with rifles began to fire as the crowd roared out, "Kill the fuckin'

Dago, kill him!" Bullets slammed into his body, now twitching and swaying, round after round until he swayed limply in the air.

The mob was distracted by a dozen men dragging another body along the ground by a stout rope.

> At the end of the rope was the writhing form of Antonio Bag-netto and the rope was fastened by a running noose around his neck. . . . Bagnetto's journey to the gallows tree was a short and swift but terrible one. As he was hauled through that narrow lane in the crowd those nearest him jabbed him with their canes, beat him with sticks and kicked him as he was dragged past them, so that by the time he had reached the foot of the tree he appeared to be more dead than alive. An active man climbed the tree and threw the end of the rope over a limb, but before the weight of the prisoner was more than half off the ground the rotten limb broke and Bagnetto fell to the ground once more. . . .

The body was raised, and finally death came to Bagnetto as many used the swaying figure for target practice.

In all, eleven men (including 2 who were not on trial) were killed. Charles Matranga escaped the lynching and was later released from prison to marry a New Orleans woman. He lived to over eighty, working as a simple stevedore—not so fitting an end for a man who supposedly was a "mafia chieftain."*

However, there was a secret society in New Orleans, entrenched within the city's top establishment. One of its members eventually confessed that a conspiracy existed within the Committee of Fifty, which secretly selected an execution squad the night before the lynchings with instructions "to enter the prison under cover of mob action." Many of those who took part in the lynching or railed against "mafia" profited by the killings. George W. Vandervoort, among the first to blame the killing of Hennessy on the "mafia," along with his friends in the City Council, soon after the lynchings passed an ordinance giving control of *all* business on the docks to a syndicate known as the Louisiana Construction and Improvement

---

*There are many distorted versions of the New Orleans affair. One of the oddest is Richard Hammer's *Playboy's Illustrated History of Organized Crime* (Chicago, 1975), which echoes the racism of the nineteenth century. Hennessy is portrayed as an innocent Gary Cooper.

Company. The victims of the execution squad were individuals who had established themselves as rising businessmen along the docks. John D. Houston,* who was part of the squad that killed Joseph Macheca, rose to power along the docks. E. T. Leache, who signed the advertisement in the *Picayune* calling for the lynching, also made his fortune on the same docks. Maurice Hart, another lyncher, was part of the syndicate that took over the docks in the name of the Louisiana Construction and Improvement Company

In fact, the men who cried "mafia" became wealthy by replacing the Italian American businesses in the port city of New Orleans. This "lynch squad" was made up of top members of the city's press, political, and business establishment.

Their actions were generally condoned and even applauded throughout the country, encouraging slander and violence else- where. The day after the lynchings, the *Times-Democrat* devoted its front page to the action under the one-word headline, "AVENGED," justifying its support of the lynching with the statement that "Des- perate diseases required desperate remedies."

The next day, the *New York Times* indicated its approval with a headline that read:

CHIEF HENNESSY AVENGED
11 OF HIS ITALIAN ASSASSINS LYNCHED BY MOB

The *Times* published the first of two editorials which justified the lynchings on the grounds that the Sicilians were "sneaking and cow- ardly . . . the descendents of bandits and assassins, who have trans- ported to this country the lawless passions, the cut-throat practices and oath-bound societies of their native country, [who] are to us a pest without mitigation."

In West Virginia, a group of miners demanded that their em- ployer discharge their Italian colleagues; when the employer refused, they went on strike. In Congress and throughout the country the movement to curtail immigration from Italy and from other "non- Aryan" nations gathered fresh impetus, with Senator Henry Cabot Lodge expounding that the southern Italians were an undesirable breed.

---

*John Houston also took part in the clan battles that saw James Houston killed six years before (see above).

Only *L'Italo-Americano,* which proclaimed itself to be "A journal dedicated to interests of Italian colonies in the Southern States," ran the banner headline:

SATURDAY'S OUTRAGE
MAJESTY OF JUSTICE TRAMPLED
ELEVEN INNOCENT MASSACRED

When President Harrison, trying to ease the rupture of relations between Italy and the United States created by the lynchings, allocated a cash indemnity of $2,500 for the families of three victims who were Italian nationals, Congress protested. Harrison was accused of "unconstitutional usurpation of congressional powers," of spending money from an emergency fund when there was no emergency. No indemnity was paid to the families of the victims who were American citizens. When the President denounced the lynchings as "an offense against law and humanity," there was talk of impeaching him.

In the aftermath of the lynchings and the kind of press they received, with repeated emphasis on "mafia," the five-letter word so easily fitted into headlines and so instantly evocative of crime and horror became an indelible stigma, which to this day continues to plague the Italian American population.

Lynching of Italians in the South occurred sporadically for the next twenty years. On August 9, 1896, the "respectable citizens" of Hahnville, Louisiana, emulating the New Orleans episode, hanged three Italians accused of murdering white natives, despite lack of evidence to support the charge. "If they were to be punished at all," explained the Hahnville *Times-Democrat,* "they had to be punished extra-judicially, as their trial would surely prove a slip in the courts." The lynchers received further justification for their action when the press reported that a large number of blacks, sympathizing with the Italian community, were present at the burial of the victims.

Five more lynchings took place in 1899 in Tallulah, Louisiana, a state where Italian children were not permitted to attend white schools. The victims were Italian storekeepers who, unaware of racial prejudice, had aroused the resentment of the local white community by their friendly attitude toward blacks.*

*Some blacks, however, took part in the lynchings.

The lynchings were a manifestation of growing anti-immigrant feelings generally. In their early years of recruiting white immigrant workers, southern employers had expected to hire foreigners they considered "desirable," such as Germans, Scandinavians, Britons, and Irish; but what they got mostly were Mediterranean and Slavic peoples. In South Carolina, there was such strong opposition toward the latter groups that in 1904 its state legislature restricted immigration to "white citizens of the United States, and citizens of Ireland, Scotland, Switzerland and France together with all other foreigners of Saxon origin." Alabama and North Carolina followed suit with similar legislation.

These laws helped keep the numbers of Italians in the South much lower than they were in the Northeast; by 1910, new immigrants constituted only 2 percent of the entire southern population. And few of those had any significant contact with the native population, especially in agricultural areas.

In Georgia, the Federation of Labor objected to "flooding the South and Georgia with a population composed of the scum of Europe, a people in no ways in sympathy with our institutions and our form of government, whose presence in our midst will foment race troubles and tend to destroy the cherished ideals of every loyal Southerner, putting us on a place with the Northeast, with its tenements crowded with unassimilative pauper labor."

Anger erupted once again in New Orleans six years after the lynchings, when the Italians of that city staged a parade to protest a proposed state constitutional amendment that was chiefly aimed at taking the vote away from blacks in Louisiana, but would also disenfranchise "landless and illiterate" Italians. The newspapers denounced the protest as "Italian interference."

CHAPTER 14

Identity—Character and Assimilation

> I did not know why they called me those names. I became
> aware of the people called *paesanos (sic)* who I saw in our
> flat, in church and in the food markets. It grew on me that I
> belonged to them, a people of Father's and Mother's own, a
> kind distinct from the cold American. And I felt the
> possessive, clinging love of my *paesanos (sic)*.
>
> —PIETRO DI DONATO, *THREE CIRCLES OF LIGHT* (1960)

> The reality is that the stereotypical Italian American pond
> has been overfished while the ocean of Italian American
> experience is yet uncharted.
>
> —JERRY KRAUSE IN *MULTIPLE SOCIAL RELATIONS* (1979)

From the very beginning, Europeans in America became aware of
their changing identity and character through their relationships
and experiences in the new environment, especially their relationship
to the Native American, who became known as the "savage Indian."
The early European settler felt his very identity threatened by the
new way of life he encountered. He became aware of his own great
anxiety at being assimilated into the "savage Indian's" way of life.

This conflict and anxiety set the pattern for future generations of immigrants.

In 1919, while the nation was still admitting thousands of immigrants daily from Southern and Eastern Europe, the American historian Robert E. Foerster warned the arriving Italians that whether or not they planned to remain in the country, "a mysterious process of unmaking and remaking" would take place within them; that as rural dwellers who had been "dropped into the unaccustomed brutal part of the city," many of them would suffer enduring loneliness, disappointment, and demoralization. Foerster regarded "Americanization" as "a two-edged sword" that would complicate adjustment to the new land, since America "exacts for all she gives" and would be "imperious" in what she expected of them. "She applies tests, imposes conventions, demands compromises, stipulates concessions to her very practical ways, with the result that the nature of the Italian would, of necessity, either atrophy or metamorphose."

To sharpen his warning, Foerster quoted an Italian visitor, A. A. Bernardy, "a perspicacious observer," to the effect that in order to be happy in America one must have, among other things, "A practical and opportunist spirit, a nature that is sharp in business but in other things narrow and matter-of-fact," and apparently above all, "a great interest in whatever is American and a high disdain for all that is Latin or that glorifies the Latin life."

However well intended, Foerster's warnings would have better been directed to the American-born children of the immigrants. For except for the small percentage of those with "a practical and opportunist spirit," the Italian immigrants had little difficulty resisting the "two-edged sword" of Americanization, and remained unwilling to turn their backs on their chief source of strength: the well-defined values and traditions passed down to them by a millennium of ancestors. The few accommodations they made to the American way of life were generally relatively minor ones in the interest of maintaining family harmony. It was their children who were more interested in Americanization.

The children who had the hardest time adapting were those who were born in Italy and who resented being taken to live among strangers, many of whom were hostile.

Their speech and mannerisms were an amalgam of what they picked up in the streets and what they had brought from Italy, and except for those who immigrated as infants, their limited English usually precluded non-Italian friendships. Their experience with American schools was usually quite brief. (The school experience of those who became the superstars of crime bears witness to this.) As soon as the law permitted, they were put to work to supplement the family income, often at the same unskilled labor as their fathers and *paesani*. And they were more likely than their secluded parents to become the targets of anti-Italian bigotry. They heard the words "greenhorn," "Dago," and "Wop" whenever they wandered out of their enclaves, and were made uneasy by what they read in the faces of those who said nothing. In every way they were reminded that America "demanded the complete renunciation of the immigrant's ancestral culture in favor of the behavior and values of the Anglo-Saxon Group."

In 1909, Ellwood P. Cubberly, a New York educator, expressed the prevailing view of immigrants and assimilation explicitly:

> These Southern and Eastern Europeans are of a very different type from the Northern Europeans who precede them. Illiterate, docile, lacking in self-reliance and initiative, and not possessing the Anglo-Teutonic conceptions of law, order and government, their coming has corrupted our civic life. . . . Our task is to break up these groups of settlements, to assimilate and amalgamate these people as part of our American race, and to implant in their children as far as can be done, the Anglo-Saxon conception of righteousness, law and order, and popular government, and to awaken in them a reverence for our democratic institutions and/ or those things in our national life which we as a people hold to be of abiding worth.

The enormous increase in immigrants with little or no grounding in Anglo-Saxon culture intensified the general fear that, unless the newcomers were quickly Americanized, the national culture would be endangered. A crusade was begun to impress upon the immigrants that to be acceptable members of American society, they and their children must become Americanized as quickly as possible.

During the crusade, a play by the English-born Zionist Israel Zangwill entitled *The Melting Pot* (1908) became a hit. Americanizers seized upon its title for their cause. While the play was new, the metaphor was not. Some of the nation's founding fathers had argued that everyone entering the country should abandon their native ways and replace them with those of their adopted land. John Adams was especially firm on this point, maintaining that "If the immigrants cannot accommodate themselves to the moral, political and physical character of the country, the Atlantic is always open to them to return to the land of their nativity. . . . They must cast off their European skin . . . never to resume it."

This crusade was paralleled by an effort, both in the media and in Congress, to restrict immigration from Eastern and Southern Europe, mainly on the grounds that the nation was in danger of being outnumbered and influenced by "the inferior races" of Europe. (Nathan S. Shaler, a Harvard geology professor who preceded Hitler, argued that it would be "impossible to Americanize immigrants from southern and eastern Europe since they were non-Aryan.") Senator Henry Cabot Lodge (despite his middle name, which derived from the northern Italian Giovanni Caboto, an explorer of America) warned his colleagues that the flow of heavy non-Aryan immigration would jeopardize the nation's character. His warning was echoed by a noisy chorus of others convinced that the survival of American democracy depended on preserving the English racial heritage. Woodrow Wilson wrote in his *History of the American People* (in 1902, before he became an admirer of Italian immigrants as President):

> Now there came multitudes of men of the lowest class from the South of Italy and the man of the meaner sort out of Hungary and Poland, men out of ranks where there was neither skill nor energy nor any initiative of quick intelligence; and they came in numbers which increased from year to year, as if the countries south of Europe were disburdening themselves of the more sordid and helpless elements of the population.

With a few notable exceptions (among them Jacob Riis, William Dean Howells, Frank Norris, and Upton Sinclair), American writers of that era showed little sympathy toward the new immigrants. Henry James saw little future for them; he said he was appalled to find on Manhattan's East Side "a great swarming of Italians and Jews." Only the "picturesque ways" of the immigrants drew any notice (however patronizing) from such writers.

Others accused the Italians of creating ghettos by their unwillingness to mix; of tolerating filth, vice, and crime; and of refusing to spread out over the nation's far-flung farmlands where they could pursue the occupation most of them knew best.

There were defenders of Italians, but not enough of them to reduce the hostility of their accusers. One son of Italian immigrants was moved to ask: "Is it in the chemistry of human nature or in the interest of the national welfare for my relatives to become Anglo-Saxonized? I find it hard to swallow the arrogant assumption of some politicians and sociologists that American civilization, though still in its infancy, should presume to take cultural precedence over the older civilizations of the immigrants from southern and eastern European nations."

For the offspring of the immigrants—the second-generation Italian Americans—the contrasts between the cultural attitudes of their parents and those they encountered in the "American Worlds" were bound to be confusing and often unsettling. Their parents' ambivalent opinions about Americans added to their confusion. On the one hand, they were highly critical of what they considered to be a lack of moral standards and the liberties Americans permitted their children. On the other hand, though they criticized Americans for their willingness to exploit immigrants, they admired their energy, enterprise, and ability to make money.

The wide gulf between the Old World and the New went beyond custom and moral values. At the center was a basic difference in philosophy. Ingrained in the southern Italian's peasant soul by centuries of poverty and oppression were strong elements of fatalism, which some of them referred to as *Destinu*. This fatalism contradicted the philosophy that their children brought home from school, where repeatedly their teachers talked of freedom, free enterprise, and free will, constantly stressing the individual's capacity to change and improve his or her situation. For the second generation that grew up in the 1920s and 1930s, the message of freedom was further accentuated by images of flappers, Rudolph Valentino, the gospel of free love, and the sermons of Emma Goldman and Margaret Sanger—images that conflicted with the old ways of their parents. Inevitably, these sons and daughters became aware of the basic differences between their parents and other Americans, which heightened their dissatisfaction at being obliged to lead a double life, a state of mind that often generated serious identity problems as they approached adulthood. An erosion of self-esteem was not uncommon for those who ventured into the American mainstream.

Studies dealing with the condition found that Italian Americans were vulnerable to lower self-esteem as they began to interact with the larger culture. Ethnotherapists also indicated that as second- and third-generation Italian Americans became assimilated into American society, the WASP ethic became their cultural ideal.

The erosion of self-esteem was further affected by the negative stereotypes exploited by the media. A study of prime-time television programs as recently as 1981 revealed that denigrating presentations of Italian Americans outnumbered positive ones by a margin of nearly two to one. Those portrayed as professional criminals far exceeded the educated professionals and business executive types. Most Italian American characters held low-status jobs, only one in seven being shown working as an executive, manager, or professional, and the majority spoke improper English, which made them the butt of jokes.

Out of the numerous conflicts that immigrants and their children experienced came, inevitably, psychological disorders. Whereas in Italy the suicide rate was 6.2 per 100,000, in the United States the rate for Italian Americans tripled, to 18.2 per 100,000. (All of the new immigrant groups had a higher suicide rate than native-born Americans.) Psychiatrists attributed the increase to the Italians' proclivity for depression and anxiety, but could not determine to what degree those symptoms related to the family problems of Italian Americans. They could, however, point out how each generation regarded their psychiatric problems, and so suggest some clues as to the substance of their problems. The first generation attributed their difficulties either to physical illness or to unfriendly actions directed against them outside the family. In accordance with their habit of protecting the family, they seldom ascribed their problems to any of its members. The offspring of the immigrants, the second generation, complained of "more typical neurotic or psychotic systems," and harbored a sense of guilt toward their parents, whether dead or alive. The third generation tended to be more extrovert, to engage in "acting out behavior, often of a psychopathic type." There was anger in their complaints, directed not only toward their family but also toward American society. While the mental disorders of the three generations are extreme cases representing a tiny percentage of the Italian American population, they suggest the fear, anger, hurt, and inferiority which all generations experienced to some degree, though generally secretly among the first and second generations.

With the aging of the first generation and with increased assimilation, native-born Italian Americans became more willing to speak of family relations in negative terms without experiencing a sense of betrayal, as well as more inclined to speak of the family's positive qualities without sentimentality. One of the most common complaints was that of being "smothered" with family devotion to such a degree as to negate any individuality not directly related to family unity. Yet even among the most objective of the native Italian Americans, the image of family was often nurtured by a nostalgia for a time when love was given and received unquestioningly.

Despite the prevalence of tensions within the Italian family in America, Old World concepts of family unity and loyalty generally survived, though at a price. The family structure held firm even though the offspring retained only some of the parents' culture. The unspoken motto of the Old World Italian family, "One for all and all for one," continued to permeate the psyches of second-generation children. Maintaining this strong sense of family, according to psychologists, was the gregarious nature of the Italian immigrants, which amounted to a clannishness. "Only the family clannishness of my Jewish playmates approached that of my relatives," recalls Gerry Amoroso, who was reared in a mixed ethnic neighborhood. But "Whereas they were content to see one another occasionally, my relatives were constantly seeking out one another's company. If it could have been managed they probably would have all lived under the same roof."

The same Amoroso, on visiting close relatives in Sicily for the first time, was surprised to find how far less gregarious they were in their family relationships than his relatives in America, where "in addition to parties for birthdays, weddings, anniversaries and saint days there were also parties when a child was baptized, confirmed, or received a diploma. The arrival of another relative from the old country or the opening of a new barrel of wine was still another pretext for another gathering of the clan." It was as if, having left their native home, they had a visceral need to confirm the presence and support of one another as often as possible.

One immigrant did not have to understand English to perceive the hostility of the host society. If an Italian family attempted to move into an Irish neighborhood, it was not welcome and its children might be beaten. The artist Claudia Demonte remembered:

> In our neighborhood the Irish and the Italians did not speak to one another. They did not get along. The Irish considered us almost black and would call us niggers. Sometimes they called us wops. I was made aware of prejudice, but I always thought it was a result of their ignorance, I never took it seriously. I thought of the Irish as stupid rather than ignorant. One time, in the sixth grade, we had a teacher who was Irish and gave the Italian kids extra homework. Then the next year we had an Italian teacher who gave the Irish kids extra homework. The Irish Italian thing could be pretty bad. And yet eventually there was a lot of intermarriage. . . . I myself married an Irishman, Ed McGowin.

In those early years it was safer for Italians to remain in their own enclaves or mixed neighborhoods inhabited by other new immigrants who generally respected one another. The *Americani*, on the other hand (nearly everyone fluent in English was considered an *Americano*), usually came under suspicion among the Italian immigrants. The collective attitude toward Americans and America in general was expressed in the expletive *Mannagia L'America* (Damn America), which was used almost synonymously with *Mannagia La miseria* (Damn poverty). These curses were applied indiscriminately to a variety of annoyances and disappointments that had no connection with America or *Americani*.

Many of the immigrants of that era, now dead or grown old, were inarticulate about their feelings, which as a result rarely found their way into print. Those who remain say that "The Italians were *disprezzati* in those times," meaning they were held in contempt or not appreciated. When asked to name some of the ways in which they were *disprezzati,* they are likely to shrug their shoulders, as if to say that the past is past. One of the better-educated immigrants was able to articulate his feelings: "We came to America in search of bread and felt the inferiority of beggars. Everything about us—our behavior, our diet, our groping, uncertain speech—was interpreted in terms of that inferiority," he said.

The schools were largely responsible for emphasizing the differences between the immigrants and their new country. Thousands of children received their American names at school. Calogero became

Charlie; Baldassaro, Ben; Salvatore, Sam or Sal; Luigi, Louie; Gaetano, Guy; Concetta, Connie; Antonio, Tony; Giuseppina, Josephine or Josie. These new names quickly became imbedded in the
public records (report cards and later, job applications and marriage
licenses), as well as in the minds of the children, many of whom
answered to an Italian name at home and to an American one elsewhere.

The teacher felt a duty, often carried out with affection, to
Americanize the immigrant child as quickly as possible. This was
school policy. There were daily patriotic flag drills, something that
was absent in European schools, and English was learned in such
gulp-down phrases as "My cuntree tis o di" and "O Say kin you
see." Assemblies on Fridays and special holidays were usually dedicated to patriotic themes. On Washington's Birthday, speeches by
principals reminded children of the legendary father of America,
reinforced in some schools by cherry-flavored lollipops in the shape
of axes. English was learned along with the myths and legends of
America.

Outside school, most children learned quickly which identity felt
more comfortable. Many Italian men and women have at least one
childhood memory of an incident on public transportation with a
parent speaking in the native tongue. An American passenger looks
at them angrily and storms off the car, declaring, "Can't you speak
English!" and "Goddamn Wops!" A child could feel it even in a
glance. There is much truth in Leonard Covello's memory of his
schooldays: "We were becoming American by learning to be
ashamed of our parents."

Italian Americans accepted the prevalent image of Italians in the
schools and in the streets. Most immigrant parents knew little of the
Italian culture admired by genteel America. Those who went on to
discover this culture felt deceived and cheated for having been taught
little of it in the American schools.

Some social critics were aware of the consequences of sudden
assimilation. Mary McDowell, a social worker, wrote: "The contempt for the experiences and languages of their parents which foreign children sometimes exhibit . . . is doubtless due in part to the
overestimation which the school places upon speaking English. This
cutting into his family loyalty takes away one of the most conspicuous and valuable traits of the Italian child." She attributed the lawlessness of some of the immigrant children to their disrespect for

their parents and therefore for all authority. Frank Costello and Charlie "Lucky" Luciano were not the only children from poor working-class families terrified of ending up, as Luciano said, like their "crumb bum" fathers.

It is common now, in memoirs, novels, and other remembrances, to read of the child who always answered his parents in English. To this day there are many old men and women who can understand but not speak or write the dialect of their parents.

In 1904, Mary McDowell pleaded for an educational program which would tell the immigrant child of the heroes, the beauties, the legends and stories of his or her parents' country. "Will it not place the parents in an atmosphere of poetry of idealization and make them an important factor to the children? Admiration is a strong factor in education. Win back the parental authority by admiring all that is admirable in their past. Create a historic perspective that will give self-respect to the new citizenship and will lead to respect for authority in the home and the state." Her advice was not—perhaps could not be—followed in the face of overwhelming demand to assimilate the mass of new immigrants as soon as possible.

Assimilation took place largely in the streets, where the image of Italians was more often that of bootblacks, barbers, ragpickers, and other common laborers. The young wanted to disassociate themselves from these images projected onto their parents. To the inevitable conflict of any father and son was added the explosive conflict of cultures between the Italian immigrant father and son, often as the son stormed out of the house with, "I'm not taking orders from no dumb Guinea!" In many cases, the choice of America over the father's world produced great tension, which contributed to stress, mental illness, and criminality. Certainly the rage created by the son's rejection of his father's culture, along with the son's experience of feeling like a foreigner in the land of his birth, contributed to the criminality in all ethnic groups during their assimilation. For some, it seemed that self-esteem could be recovered only through a life of crime that might bring enough wealth and power to show Americans how important the immigrant's offspring had become.

One successful immigrant commented presciently on the ethnic violence in America in 1924:

Changing a man's language, upsetting his moral and social conventions, altering his inherited tradition of conduct, unsettling his ancestral faith, these are the very best means possible for making him a disbeliever in all established institutions including those of the United States. Yet this is precisely what Americanization aims to do with the best intentions, when unduly accelerated or made compulsory.

Ironically, few within the early immigrant group were thoroughly assimilated; many lived out their lives as if they were still in the villages of Italy. Nonetheless, they were changed by their confrontation with America.

The parents in their late forties or fifties usually withdrew to a narrow circle of compatriots after a few attempts to make their way in America. They rarely learned more than a few words of English, but language was only one of the major hurdles that would prevent their assimilation. In comparison with most other immigrant groups, there was hardly an aspect of the southern Italian tradition that did not contrast with existing American patterns.

There were exceptions. Some Italians were eager to become Americanized. They anglicized their names, became Protestant, moved into non-ethnic neighborhoods, and forbade their children to learn Italian. These families were apt to send at least one child to college to become a doctor, lawyer, dentist, or professor. But such families were relatively few in number and, not surprisingly, a good many were from central or northern Italy, where the advantages of education were better understood. The great majority of the immigrants instinctively clung to their old customs, maintaining them (with minor New World modifications) throughout their American lives.

While the social worker may have been concerned with the child's problem of confused identity, for the mother, trying to communicate with her children in a foreign language deprived her of full motherhood.

Unless English was spoken in the household, there was little chance of an immigrant mother becoming Americanized. It was not unusual for such a person to spend most of her life in the new land without knowing any English. Unlike her husband, whose job might take him among Americans from whom he picked up enough English to be understood, his wife seldom had any occasion to hear the language. Nearly always she was in the company of relatives or other Italians. Whatever shopping she did was likely to be in stores operated by Italians. Her doctor and her dentist were Italian. Even if employed in a factory, more often than not she found herself among other Italian women who spoke dialects similar to her own.

Undoubtedly, the American-born children who grew up in a home where the parents' dialect was spoken were able to absorb their ancestral culture. While this made for closer family ties, the situation had its drawbacks for both parents and children. It denied the parents an easy line of communication and understanding of their children's American world. At the same time, the children—Italian at home and American elsewhere—often suffered a conflicting sense of identity, which in some instances led to schizophrenia and agoraphobia.

The poet John Ciardi recalled his problems:

In my childhood it was always two worlds. I have always felt that when you have a second language, you have three things: the first language, the second language, and the difference between them. . . . I had to use a double standard: one thing out-of-doors and another thing indoors. It did not always work that way, that peaceably. Sometimes, in this generation gap, Italian boys especially, realizing that their parents were dead wrong, became nastily indignant. That led to shouting matches in which the kids and the father, sometimes the mother, said terrible things to one another. Two or three of the boys I grew up with ran away and were never heard again.

Often a tug-of-war ensued between teacher and parent for the minds, if not the hearts, of the children. The parents tried to insist that their children conduct themselves according to the code of behavior and value system that had kept the Italian family intact for centuries. The teachers, on the other hand, often presented sharply different ideas. Since most children then did not stay in school long, the influence of the parents usually prevailed. The offspring remained fixed in their environment, with an underdeveloped sensibility that was neither Italian nor American.

There were those who escaped this fate, mainly because their fathers, ignoring the Italian proverb that cautions fathers against making their sons "better" than themselves, permitted them to finish high school and occasionally even (in the case of a son) to go on to college. Although these children usually paid their own way through college with part-time and summer jobs, the family would regard the loss of full-time wages as a financial "sacrifice."

If a child, against the parents' wishes, insisted on continuing his education, this kind of disobedience would be blamed on the *terra maladitta* (cursed land) which caused the son to become *mal educato,* an epitaph which southern Italians frequently equated with American education. *Mal educati,* often hurled by parents at their American-born children, means literally "badly educated." For the immigrant parents from the *Mezzogiorno,* one of the primary purposes of any school system was to teach their children good manners, especially respect for their elders.

One son of immigrant parents who defied tradition by continuing his education at an out-of-town university explained:

> As much as I loved my father and the rest of my family, I had to follow my own bent, even though it meant leaving home and going to another city. In those days it was considered something of a sacrilege for an unmarried son to be leaving his family for any reason. Most of my relatives were shocked, but I had to leave. Apart from wanting a college education, I knew that unless I lived in the American world for a while—that is, the world outside that of my Italian relatives—I might well go through life not really knowing which world I belonged to, feeling like an imposter.

A college education was likely to generate a sense of alienation between the educated offspring and the rest of the family. One young woman who earned a college degree remembered, "I belonged nowhere. That is the price you pay for growing up in one culture and entering another."

The bitterness Americanization could engender is illustrated by the story of an immigrant named Bentolinardo who had worked hard and lived the life of a miser to finance his son's medical education, only to have his son change his name from Bentolinardo to Bentley. When the old man saw his son's gold-lettered shingle for the first time with the name "Dr. Bentley" on it, he went to pieces. "He could not read English, but that betrayal he could read."

But then, as the son of another immigrant recalled, "Like most children we were mindless conformists. More than anything else, we wanted to be regarded as Americans, though we couldn't be sure what they were like. We were constantly worried about making a bad impression on the Americans around us. The most excruciating times were those when the Italian mother during family picnics in a public park, not caring how many Americans might be watching, bared their breast to feed their infants." Only after he had become an adult did he remember the telling remark made during childhood by one of his sisters: "When I grow up I want to be an American."

Survival, rather than upward mobility, was uppermost in most parents' minds. The ideal job, from their point of view, was one that provided the security of a steady "joba." Mario Puzo, the son of Neapolitan parents, writes that as a youth he was "contemptuous" of the adults around him and felt a "condescending pity" for them—for their illiteracy, for their lack of economic security, and for their willingness to settle for very little in life. He resented the fact that his widowed mother's highest ambition for him was to become a railroad clerk. As a youth, Puzo—who wanted to become rich, famous, and happy either as an artist or, in more sophisticated moments, as a great criminal—would hear his mother say to him: "Never mind about being happy. Be glad you're alive."

While they came with an inkling that America afforded some opportunity for improving their lot, for the vast majority of immigrants their expectations seldom went beyond the ambition of steady employment, or of establishing a small business and perhaps owning a house with some ground for a vegetable garden.

Responding to the concern of a Boston audience that not enough progress was being made to "assimilate" the Italian immigrants, William Dean Howells surprised his audience by saying that "it is not up to us to assimilate them but for them to assimilate us."

Unlike their children, the earlier immigrants continued to spurn assimilation. Most were by nature deeply suspicious of foreigners and their motives, an attitude rooted in the *Mezzogiorno*'s long history of exploitative invaders and rulers. Adding to this were the articles published by the Italian American press in which Italian-educated physicians and lawyers described America as "a ruthless, rapacious, hypocritical, puritanical country." American men were characterized as "superficial, weak, ridiculous," while American women were "vain and prefer to have a good time rather than to be good wives and mothers." Churches in America were "places of business . . . to furnish fat salaries to innumerable office-holders; the political life is incurably corrupt."

Reverend Sartario, an Italian American Protestant minister, reserved his sharpest criticism for those social workers who were insensitive to the psychology of the immigrant families they expected to help. He attributed their lack of understanding to the American propensity for standardization. "The strongest argument in this country is: 'This is not the way we do it' or 'I have never seen it done that way.' " The result of this attitude was that Italian families often complained about "the aggressively blunt way in which some social workers burst into their homes and upset the usual routine of their lives, opening windows, undressing the children, giving orders not to eat this and that, not to wrap up babies in swaddling clothes, etc. Social workers are well-intentioned but they forget that they are dealing with human beings and not with cattle."

An even more serious error of the social workers was disregard of the Italian concept of family life as a single unified unit. Instead of dealing with an Italian family as a whole, the social worker usually concentrated on individual members—an error based on the common assumption that the immigrants were "socially disorganized and without traditions." To a large degree, this spurious view was shared by other would-be Americanizers.

In fact, the efforts to accelerate assimilation had the opposite effect. Among the older immigrants there was some degree of superficial assimilation, but it usually amounted to nothing beyond the acquisition of American citizenship. Unbeknown to the more avid Americanizers, who tended to mistake the metaphor of the "melting pot" for a pressure cooker, the assimilation process would necessarily be a gradual one.

One subtle form of resistance to Americanization was the conscious and unconscious manipulation of the new and old language. American words were brought into the dialects of the immigrants until a new language began to appear, which in itself spoke eloquently of the immigrants' condition.

It was astonishing how much could be communicated in this new language, and not without some humor. One immigrant merchant could order new stock by

shouting at the top of his voice into a wall phone: "Alo! Alo! Me, Martino Turano. Senti me wan hindi quort biff (send me one hind quarter of beef), tenne ponti linki sossiggi (ten pounds of link sausage), to hemme (two hams), fiffity ponti liffi lardo (fifty pounds of leaf lard)". . . . After many repetitions he brought his conversation to a close with "gooddi byee." But when a new clerk happened to be at the other end and he was not understood, the merchant turned away in disgust muttering, "Arriti, me come messelfa," then crying out in Italian, "Some of these clerks are turnips. They can't even understand their own language."

The new words that were neither English nor Italian created tragicomic situations, and as they became part of the immigrant folklore, reflected intimate anxieties that could not be spoken of openly. The tale of *ezzolle* speaks to this.

An immigrant sent his wife in Italy a money order for 100 lire, with a note saying, *Ezzolle,"* intending to let her know that for now "That's all" (*ezzolle*) he could send her. The wife found the money order, but could not find the *ezzolle*. At the post office the clerk cashed the money order and handed her 100 lire, but she refused to leave until he had also given her the *ezzolle* her husband mentioned in his note. The clerk shrugged his shoulders and stuck out his chin. "I know nothing of this *ezzolle."* But the wife, suspicious now, upbraided him for not giving her what was hers and again demanded the *"ezzolle."* The exasperated clerk told her: "All right, I'll give you *ezzolle*. Come into my office and you will have your *ezzolle*. If that's what you want that's what you're going to get." In his office he made love to her, then told her that was the *ezzolle* she demanded. After nine months the wife had a baby. She was in a rage; she already had nine children and didn't need any more. So she had her *compare* write to her husband in America: "Dear husband, send me another 100 lire but don't send me the *ezzolle* anymore."

Because of increased stress, the incidence of mental disorders was significantly higher among immigrants. Although the Italians were the most mentally stable of the immigrant groups in America, their suicide rate (as we have seen) almost tripled. The Italian immigrants were less prone than Americans to schizophrenia; alcoholism and drug addiction were virtually unknown among them. American statistics indicated that Italians rated among the lowest in admissions to both general and mental hospitals; but those particular statistics can be attributed to the great distrust that Italians (both in Italy and the United States) had for hospitals, which were seen as institutions of authority where bodies, especially of the poor, were used for experimental purposes. Hospitals and death were closely associated in the Italian mind, and many preferred to die at home. In Italy it was common for the family to care for the mentally ill at home, except in truly violent cases.

A few literally submerged their anxieties in telling activities. One such was Baldassare Forestiere, who became known as the "Human Mole." He had been a subway worker in Boston, came to Fresno, California, and began digging underground tunnels in a 20-acre area. Over a period of thirty-two years, beginning in 1904, he dug sixty or so galleries, which included a kitchen, bedrooms, and a spacious dance hall. It was rather obvious, as Andrew Rolle commented, "that Forestiere liked living away from the world he saw above ground. Outside of Julesberg, Colorado, Umberto Gabello lived as a hermit, after making a fortune in gold fields at Cripple Creek, in house-caves he tunnelled and decorated. The underground home became known as 'The Italian Cave.' "

Recent studies of the first and second generations show that those who fell ill had a "higher level of affective disorder"—"a rejection attitude towards authority, fixity in delusions systems and hypochondriacal complaints . . . and generally higher levels of depression and anxiety."

The disorders differed by generation. The first generation suffered from somatic complaints, physical ailments which the immigrants sometimes attributed to *malocchio*—the evil eye. Their offspring tended to develop "typical neurotic or psychotic symptoms"—guilt toward the parents whose culture they had broken with. The third generation's mental disorders were often of a "psychopathic type."*

Assimilation, however limited, had other negative effects. Poor living conditions made the immigrants susceptible to anemia, catarrh, poor appetite, bad teeth, curved spines, pneumonia, meningitis, diphtheria, and tuberculosis. And they died quickly. Industrial accidents also took a large toll. Some of the men were literally buried

---

*Psychological reality is not, of course, so patly observed. If, for example, the community was a large one, mental abnormalities were likely to be fewer in number among all generations. Also beyond the scope of statistical studies were the unrecorded "minor" effects of assimilation on the immigrant psyche, such as insomnia and the more incapacitating psychosomatic ailments, including paranoia and panic.

in cement; the tunnels around New York and the coal mines of Pennsylvania became the graveyards of others. Even more disturbing to the immigrants than the hostility of the Americans was the emergence of health problems they had seldom encountered in Italy.

Visiting Italian scholars who observed the physical and emotional difficulties of the immigrants blamed the ordeal of trying to cope in a land to which they had come with high expectations.

"What has the immigrant really learned in America?" Luigi Villari asked. "Justice here encourages lawlessness and corrupts the sons of honest peasants who are now accused of being blackhanders by courts and juries which convict Italians haphazardly without evidence because, 'If they haven't committed this crime, they must have committed another' and so are declared guilty." Villari concluded that although the immigrants retained their Italian characteristics which were "their best element," they learn little that is good from American life. "Many *contadini* who in Italy led a temperate and honest life, in America become immoral and vice-ridden." More critical of their progeny, Villari asserted that they became "a hybrid type" who had not become better, describing them as "spendthrifts who frequent bars and are often drunk. They have the air of braggarts; in short, they become all that is worse and odious. They are seldom in touch with good Americans, only the worse." [Luigi Villari, *Gli Stati Uniti D'America e L'Emigrazione Italiana*]

The social worker Mary McDowell, agreed, and went even further in criticizing the immigrants' offspring. ". . . the criminals of the cities," she wrote in 1904, "come from the ranks of the children of the immigrants, not from the immigrants themselves. Those who live near these transplanted people tell us of the struggle in the family life between the standards of the old country upheld by the father and mother and those of the children who have learned the language and caught the spirit of the new country."

Most knowledgeable observers recognized that crime, disorganized or organized, was not imported from Sicily or Naples, but learned in the streets of urban America, where the children did indeed catch "the spirit of the new country."

LA FAMIGLIA

Among the many changes life in the New World brought, changes in the family affected the immigrant most deeply.

During the lives of the first generation, the welfare of the family was considered the primary responsibility of each of its members. Children were expected to contribute to the family's support as soon as they were strong enough to do manual labor. In the southern regions of Italy boys began earning money at the age of twelve, while girls began sharing household tasks at ten. A popular Sicilian adage says: "When hair begins to grow between the legs, one is fit to work."

The ideal family in both countries represented two structures. There was the family of procreation (the nuclear family), and the extended family, which included kin to the third and fourth degrees. The extended family was often augmented by the custom of *compareggio,* which permitted a couple to go outside the circle of blood relatives when choosing godparents for children about to be baptized or confirmed, and also in the selection of a maid of honor and "best man" for a couple about to be married. The couples who made the selections and those who were selected thereafter addressed one another as *comare* (co-mother) and *compare* (co-father), and they often forged ties that were as strong as those of blood relatives. These usually proved quite useful to all parties involved, especially in the United States, where the circle of family in which the immigrants could find support was considerably enlarged.

Though closely allied, the extended family seldom functioned collectively. The nuclear family, on the other hand, almost invariably operated as a single unit on the principle of all for one and one for all. Nominally, the family was patriarchal. The father ruled the family as long as he remained in good health and was the chief breadwinner. In old age the eldest son superseded him, but even then the father retained much of his prestige. In some areas of the *Mezzogiorno* where traditions were more likely to be observed, the father's authority was considered absolute; no new dresses were purchased, no doctor consulted, no gifts made, no employment accepted without his approval.

Outwardly, at least, the father's decisions were accepted as law, even among his married children. To criticize one's father was considered sacrilege. Nonetheless, the typical Italian father frequently demonstrated affection for his children (though less frequently in public for his wife). He played with the youngest ones at home and took the older children on picnics in the country. But his insistence that they comply with his rules of conduct, which were sometimes enforced with corporal punishment, made the children regard their father with mixed feelings of fear and love.

If the husband lacked the qualities that made for benevolent despotism, it was often the wife who assumed command of the family while publicly wearing the mask of submissiveness. Under this guise she was able to take actions and make decisions which traditionally were husbandly prerogatives. Such a wife would rarely contradict her husband in the presence of strangers, but once left alone with her eldest children, she would drop the mask of docile wife and "speak her own mind openly and eloquently." As the sociologist Constance Cronin notes, she becomes, in effect, the family manager, relying on her wits as well as on her ability to outtalk her husband. "She usually does not yell or scream for that provokes a violent physical reaction from him. Instead she wears him down by an ever-flowing stream of words which, like the Chinese water torture, finally produces the desired answer." If that strategy is unsuccessful, she uses "the ultimate weapon; she becomes cool in bed. The husband may well be aware that he is being manipulated but if he has been married to her long enough to realize that her primary concern is the welfare of the family, he will find a way of submitting to her point of view without losing face."

The rules governing family membership were simple and explicit, according to *la via vecchia* (the old way):

1. Fear God and respect the saints or else you will really repent it.
2. The father is the father and he is experienced. The son will never fail if he imitates him.
3. The elders are prudent and experienced; do as they do and you will learn and prosper.
4. Always honor and obey your parents; then even the stones will love you.
5. If you don't listen to your helpful mother, everything will turn to shit right in your pants.
6. Father is the master.
7. Experience gives power.
8. Work hard, work always, and you will never know hunger.

9. Work honestly, and don't think of the rest.
10. Whoever doesn't want to work, dies like a dog.

Some of these rules were at the core of the conflicts that developed in immigrant families as the children became old enough to perceive the duality of their lives.

The Italian family gradually began to change: women found freedom to play a larger role in and out of the family; sons refused to follow the work of the fathers, which brought about tensions and uncovered the not-so-loving Italian family so often seen in the stereotypes in such films as *The Godfather* and *Moonstruck*.

The concept of family with which immigrants came to America was as old as Italy itself. Sexuality was not mentioned, in spite of the fact that it was sex that attracted the man to the young girl who was walked in the *piazza* and to the church by her mother for this very purpose. The woman came to marriage worshipped as a virgin and yet feared for her sexual powers. Sexuality became the complaint in the literature of the country for centuries. Dante condemned Francesca and Paolo to being *insiemi* ("joined") for eternity, Paolo wearily moaning and Francesca with a slight smile on her face. The complaint persisted to Lampedusa, whose Prince in *The Leopard* lamented: ". . . how can I find satisfaction with a woman who makes the sign of the Cross in bed before every embrace and then at the crucial moment just cries 'Gesumaria!' When we married and she was sixteen I found that rather exciting; but now . . . seven children I've had with her, seven; and never once have I seen her navel. Is that right?"

If this was the mentality of a prince in the nineteenth century, Corrado Niscemi could speak of it from another angle in 1968: "Sex is without love in this country; it is an act of rage and bitterness, not tenderness. The man pins the woman to the bed with the attitude: 'I work hard to support you; the least you can do is to give me a male child.' "

Although marriage produced relationships which created a public image of unity and warmth, privately they often seethed with tensions. In the New World such tensions were intensified. The husband came with the tradition of *gallismo* (roosterism) on his side, the wife with the Church as an ally and the confessional a center of conspiracy. Men, in turn, regarded the Church as an enemy and secretly looked upon Christ as a prime *cornutu* (cuckold) for letting himself be killed in the manner of a common criminal. The men's curse words are evidence to that effect.

Many Italian proverbs demonstrate male attitudes toward women:

Like a good weapon, she should be cared for properly.

Like a hat, she should be kept straight.

Like a mule, she should be given plenty of work and occasional beatings.

Above all, a woman should be kept in her place as subordinate.

Life for those peasant women was not easy. In Italy they had been governed by the Napoleonic Code, which gave women few rights and many responsibilities. Certainly they had the concern of the family. They had to fetch water from the well, wash the family clothes in a public water trough, bake bread, prepare food, shop and bargain, and, weather and time permitting, roam the open fields with their children for dandelions or wild fennel. In the fall they gathered *ristucia* (twigs and dried wheat stalks) and returned with a giant bundle on their heads, children beside them. They helped harvest olives, almonds, and walnuts, and hired themselves out to gather grapes for the making of wine. Women were also *levatrici*—midwives (doctor, pharmacist all in one), who did cupping, set leeches, brought infants into the world, and helped bury the dead. A California bookstore owner as a boy witnessed his grandfather's death in Italy:

I remember the women waiting silently at my grandfather's bed. As soon as the *Levatrici* gave the signal, the women almost pounced on my grandfather's dead body and stripped him naked. They washed his body, including his genitals, then dressed him in the suit he was married in, they did this hurriedly silently before his body would stiffen. Only when the work was done did the women begin to cry and wail.

Women's services brought them close to the clergy and made them the mainstay of the Church. They helped clean and decorate the local church, they taught catechism. Those who did not marry lovingly served the children and the old. Some entered nunneries to care for the sick and the aged. And if need be, they castigated the wayward priests. Many men resented this attachment to the Church.

Women's roles, since they were so intimately involved with the social life of their communities, in times of trouble become more evident. During the *Fasci Siciliani,* in many Sicilian towns it was the women who stormed the police barracks or city halls to release prisoners or help throw out bureaucratic files that were burned in the streets. Often, when the men were in need of help, the cry was heard: "Go get the women."

There were women Socialists and feminists such as Anna Maria Mozzoni, who in the 1890s protested the popular stereotype of the woman as a Madonna, "imposed by those who dominated the energies of the dominated." In the upheavals of the late nineteenth century and the early twentieth, women throughout Italy were in the streets along with men demanding *Pane e Pace*—Bread and Peace.

There were Italian women writers, now mostly forgotten, such as Maria Messina, who portrayed the life of peasant women, and Grazia Deledda of Sardinia, who began publishing in 1885 when she was twenty and went on to write thirty books. She won the Nobel Prize for Literature in 1926. But these women of independence were the exceptions.

As women's roles in America changed, the force and power they showed in the old country in times of stress reasserted themselves, creating new conflicts and tensions.

Men's attitudes within the family still produced stifling and angry incidents that their children resented. The daughter of an Italian immigrant recalled that even after she had been married several years, her father, as protective of her virtue as he had been before her marriage, would drop by her home unexpectedly while her husband was at work and peer under her bed to make sure she was not harboring a lover. Another woman told of "feeble protests of my husband" while her father beat her for lack of obedience toward her husband. While such incidents were not typical of family relationships, there were enough to indicate that the Old World rule—of the father as "the master" of the family—was being challenged.

An Italian American psychiatric social worker, the daughter of immigrant parents, observed that not all immigrant women accepted the dictatorship of the husband.

Nicola Sacco and Bartolomeo Vanzetti shortly before their execution on August 22, 1927. From a 1958 serigraph by Ben Shahn in *Ben Shahn: The Passion of Sacco and Vanzetti* by Martin Bush. *(Courtesy of the author.)*

IF IT HAD NOT BEEN FOR THESE THING, I MIGHT HAVE LIVE OUT MY LIFE TALKING AT STREET CORNERS TO SCORNING MEN. I MIGHT HAVE DIE, UNMARKED, UNKNOWN A FAILURE. NOW WE ARE NOT A FAILURE. THIS IS OUR CAREER AND OUR TRIUMPH. NEVER IN OUR FULL LIFE COULD WE HOPE TO DO SUCH WORK FOR TOLERANCE, FOR JOOSTICE, FOR MAN'S ONDERSTANDING OF MAN AS NOW WE DO BY ACCIDENT. OUR WORDS—OUR LIVES—OUR PAINS NOTHING! THE TAKING OF OUR LIVES—LIVES OF A GOOD SHOEMAKER AND A POOR FISH PEDDLER—ALL! THAT LAST MOMENT BELONGS TO US—THAT AGONY IS OUR TRIUMPH.

Italian fondness for drinking wine with meals greatly increased the demand for wine presses during the Prohibition era. *(Italian/American Collection, University of Illinois at Chicago, The University Library, Department of Special Collections.)*

Vito Marcantonio in an East Harlem Italian American social club at the start of his political career, ca. 1930. *(Center for Migration Studies of New York.)*

Luigi Antonini, organizer of the Italian-speaking Local 89 of the ILGWU in New York, 1931. *(Center for Migration Studies of New York.)*

Mending nets on Fisherman's Wharf in San Francisco, 1948. *(Courtesy of Alberto Spadaro and sons.)*

Mayor Fiorello La Guardia of New York trying to pet a young tiger named Winston Churchill at the Bronx Zoo, 1941. *(Courtesy of Free Library of Philadelphia.)*

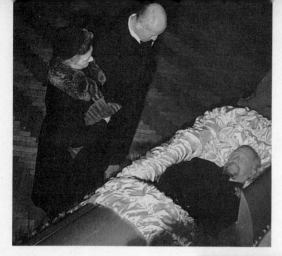

Carlo Tresca in his coffin. Labor leader, anti-fascist activist, he was assassinated by an unknown gunman in January 1943. *(Courtesy of Library of Congress.)*

Arturo Toscanini, ca. 1943. Still the preeminent orchestral conductor of the twentieth century. In the last sixteen years of his career his NBC Symphony concerts on national radio were enjoyed by millions of listeners. *(Adrian Siegel Collection, Philadelphia Orchestra Archives.)*

Daughters of Italian immigrants performing at a Columbus Day celebration in 1941. *(Temple University Libraries Urban Archives.)*

Italian American leaders from fifteen states pledging their loyalty to the United States following declaration of war with Fascist Italy, 1941. *(Temple University Libraries Urban Archives.)*

A wartime rally of Italian Americans in East Harlem, 1944. (At left, front row, with flowered hat, is Congressman Marcantonio's grandmother.) *(Courtesy of the Balch Institute for Ethnic Studies Library.)*

Jimmy ("Shnozzola") Durante entertained the nation for a half century in nightclubs, radio, television, and films. *(Courtesy of Library of Congress.)*

"Memories of the Feast of Santa Lucia in Manhattan's Lower East Side," 1937. From an oil painting by John Costanza. *(Courtesy of the artist.)*

Paying homage to St. Joseph on his day with offerings of bread to all who wished to partake, 1948. *(Courtesy of the D'Erasmo family.)*

On religious feast days in Chicago, revered figures like that of Santa Maria Incoronata would be paraded in Italian neighborhoods, 1945. *(Italian/American Collection, University of Illinois at Chicago, The University Library, Department of Special Collections.)*

Our Lady of Mount Carmel Church in the Bronx, 1950. In 1904 its figure of the Virgin Mary became a shrine by Papal decree. *(Courtesy of Rocky D'Erasmo.)*

Feast of the Lilies (*Festa dei Gigli*). Parishioners carrying favorite religious figures in Astoria, Queens, New York, while the band plays on, 1973. *(Center for Migration Studies of New York.)*

Saint Frances Xavier Cabrini, born in Italy. For her work in behalf of Italian immigrants, she became the first United States citizen to be canonized by the Catholic Church. *(Courtesy of Cabrini College.)*

The DiMaggio brothers—Vince, Joe, and Dom—in the early fifties, shortly after Joseph Paul DiMaggio had completed his career with the New York Yankees. *(Courtesy of Rocky D'Erasmo.)*

Seventeen-year-old Anne Italiano of the Bronx eventually became Anne Bancroft, film and stage star. *(Courtesy of Mrs. Mildred Italiano.)*

John Fante, one of the first Italian Americans to win critical acclaim with novels and short stories about Italian immigrant life, in Naples during his first trip to Italy in 1957. *(Courtesy of Black Sparrow Press.)*

John Ciardi, Prix de Rome–winning poet, author of some forty books of poetry and criticism, and translator of Dante's *Inferno*, 1962. *(Courtesy of Mrs. John Ciardi.)*

Lawrence Ferlinghetti, a Beat generation poet who operates San Francisco's City Lights Bookstore, a favorite hangout for writers. His best known work, published in 1958, is *A Coney Island of the Mind. (Photo by Paul Glines, courtesy of New Directions.)*

Judge John Sirica (left) and Congressman Peter W. Rodino, Jr., key figures in bringing justice to bear on the Watergate scandals of the Nixon Administration, in a 1977 photo. *(Courtesy of the National Italian American Foundation.)*

Frank Sinatra, the only performer in American history to win fame both as a pop singer and Hollywood actor, with New Jersey congressman Peter Rodino. *(Courtesy of the National Italian American Foundation.)*

Honorees at the 1982 awards dinner of the National Italian American Foundation, from left to right: A. Bartlett Giamatti, president of Yale; Sophia Loren, Italian screen star; and Lee Iacocca, chief executive of Chrysler Corporation. *(Photo by Michele Iannacci, courtesy of Alfred M. Rotondaro.)*

A future governor at home while writing *The Diaries of Mario M. Cuomo* during his first campaign for the governorship of New York State, 1983. *(Photo by Don Pollard, courtesy of Random House.)*

Geraldine Ferraro, the first woman to run for the office of Vice President of the United States, right after her debate with George Bush, the then Vice President, 1984. *(Photo by Michael Mercanti/*Philadelphia Daily News.*)*

Antonin Scalia with President Ronald Reagan following his appointment to the United States Supreme Court, 1986. *(Courtesy of the National Italian American Foundation.)*

Madonna, whose full name at birth was Madonna Louise Veronica Ciccone, performing at the Philadelphia Spectrum in 1990. *(Photo by Michael Mercanti/Philadelphia Daily News.)*

Robert Venturi, Pritzker Architecture Prize laureate in 1991 with Denise Scott-Brown, his long-time spouse and collaborator. *(Photo by J. T. Miller.)*

Anne Paolucci, author, playwright, scholar, and president of the "Columbus Countdown 1992" Foundation, with Edward Albee, 1991.

Inaugurating the Italian Academy for Advanced Studies in America,
funded with a $17.5 million gift from the Italian government, 1991. On
stage at the Casa Italiana of Columbia University are, from left to right:
Jonathan Cole, Provost of the University; Italian Prime Minister Giulio
Andreotti; Francesco Cossiga, President of Italy; Michael Sovern,
President of Columbia; and Maristella de P. Lorch, Director of the new
Academy. *(Courtesy of Casa Italiana.)*

Philadelphia Orchestra Conductor Riccardo Muti and tenor Luciano Pavarotti
preparing for the singer's performance in *I Pagliacci,* 1992. *(Photo by Michael
Mercanti/*Philadelphia Daily News.*)*

> The concept that the Italian family was a patriarchal one is part a myth. The women came from family origins in which they had no real closeness with a father. So, her husband remained a stranger who usually failed to meet her infantile dependency needs. She turned to the sons, overdoing for them in order to bind these spoiled males to her forever by infantalizing them. [Rolle, *The Italian Americans—Troubled Roots*]

Consciously or not, some women aligned the children against their fathers while presenting themselves as martyrs. When such strategy was in play, the mother usually selected her oldest daughter as a confidante to whom she related her complaints, even those relating to the father's unsatisfactory performance in bed. "In a distorted way," adds the historian Andrew Rolle, "daughters became substitute husbands, acting out the unexpressed anger of the passive-aggressive mother," and enabling the mother to remain "the idealized Madonna in the eyes of the sons." These were often the same daughters who were trapped into spinsterhood to become the guardians of their aging parents.

The second generation of Italian women in America, particularly those who had families of their own, felt burdened by the traditional caretaker role.

"I almost hit my mother yesterday," revealed one harried daughter. Her mother, now eighty-four, and one of the few survivors of the generation that had taken part in the mass migration early in the century, had been living alone in a small Brooklyn apartment since the death of her father ten years earlier. She had arrived in New York at the age of sixteen, married soon afterwards, and spent the rest of her life raising four children while working as a seamstress in Brooklyn sweatshops. She knew little or nothing about American life; hers revolved entirely around her family and relatives. Now she suffered from what she called *la solitudine*.

Once the Italian immigrants were committed to the American race, it was inevitable, if regrettable, that the second and third generations looked at the reality of the Italian family and caught the spirit of the new land.

PART SIX

Crime and Prejudice

CHAPTER 15

Crime Remembered

"Sicilians have gone all over the world, Argentina, Brazil, Australia, all over and the only place where this mafia developed was here in America. Can you tell me why?"

—BROOKLYN INTERVIEWS

"The foreign element excuse is one of the hypocritical lies that save us from the clear sight of ourselves."

—LINCOLN STEFFENS

A woman remembered the violence she witnessed as a young immigrant in the streets of New York:

I came from Italy in 1920 and my sister and brother lived in a house on Crist [Chrystie] St. called the street of the *camorriste*. One day I was seated at home in a small apartment of two rooms I lived in with my brother Salvatore. All at once I heard 3 revolver shots. I didn't know where it came from. I looked out and saw a man on the ground in great fear. I closed the window. In 10 minutes the police came knocking at my door. I was afraid to open the door but I was forced to because they said they were the law. I didn't understand not even one word of American. They looked all over the house then they looked in the room where I slept where there was a large barrel of wine that my brother made for himself. They took a long stick and they saw if there was someone in the barrel, but they didn't find anything. Out of fear I went to my sister Giovannina who lived on the second floor and I cursed the day I came to America. I lived always with fear.

The early immigrant used the word *camorriste* to describe the criminal element: men who intimidated, lived at the edge of the law, and victimized their own people. There was no implication of an organization. The word "Don," now associated with mafia, meant not a criminal, but a man of accomplishment—a fine artisan, a priest, or a successful businessman, who had achieved a certain demeanor and therefore deserved the respect bestowed by the old aristocratic title. The early immigrants did not even know such terms as *consigliere* or *capo di tutti i capi* (Italian words not of their southern dialects).

Statistics show that the Italian immigrants involved in American racketeering were few compared to the sons of immigrants who were assimilated into American criminal life. Just as the cartel-like criminal organizations that evolved soon after World War I reflect a development in American corporate structure, the changes in Italian American criminal activity reflect the American environment.

Crime of all sorts existed in America long before the great waves of immigrants from Eastern Europe or southern Italy. There was no common mafia image in the 1920s or 1930s; there were "gangsters" like Al Capone. The mafia image of the 1890s was resurrected by the politicians after World War II.* This image served the interests of those who revived it; just as Americans drove out their Italian and American-born Italian competitors on the New Orleans docks in 1891, so Attorney General Edwin Meese, in 1988, found a Sicilian drug ring to capture while himself under suspicion of corruption.

---

*The supposed "families" headed by Joe Columbo or John Gotti had little to do with families. If Nick Scarfo had relatives in the business, they were the exception, not the rule. Giancana in Chicago, or criminal elements in other cities who have captured the imagination of the public, had a variety of people in their organizations, ranging from Jews to Irish and native-born Americans.

ORGANIZED CRIME IN THE LAND THEY CAME TO

From the beginning, Italian immigrants had been active in the labor movement, a few in the anarchist movement. The radical Italians, with their *circoli di studi sociali,* attempted to convert new arrivals to socialism, if not anarchism. Their antiwar stance in 1914–18, so Rudolph Vecoli tells us,

> brought down upon the *sovversivi* the full wrath of the American government. After the war, their leaders were imprisoned or deported during the "Red Scare." The culmination of this repression, the execution of Sacco and Vanzetti, rang the death knell for the Italian radical movement and sent a shudder of terror through the "Little Italies." Clearly a radical identity was not a viable option in the land of triumphant capitalism.

The young, the poor, and the ambitious, in this atmosphere, certainly were not going to be attracted to radical politics; for some, crime was a sure and quick road to success.

At the turn of the century, non-Italian criminal syndicates in New York City's Five Points area controlled the card game of poker, bull baiting, and dogfights. Around Grand Street, leaders of gambling rings tied bulls to poles in sandpits and dogs were let loose upon them, while bets were taken as to how many dogs would be gored to death before the bull succumbed. In one pit, the surrounding area could hold two thousand spectators. Here, too, terriers that had been starved for days were let loose on packs of rats, for the benefit of gambling bosses and the pleasure of the spectators. In the nearby dance halls, men were served drinks and drugs and serviced by "hot corn" girls. As entertainment, there were bareknuckle fights in which one George (a.k.a. Snatchem) Leese sucked the blood of bleeding fighters. Between fights one could throw dimes to Jack the Rat and see him bite the head off a mouse. For a quarter he would bite the head off a rat. The whorehouses had bouncers such as Gallus Mag, a giant Englishwoman well over six feet tall who, if needed, clubbed disorderly men and dragged them out with one ear firmly in her teeth.

Prostitution by 1880 was so organized that pimps belonging to various gangs auctioned off women at regular meetings. The activity was permitted by a police department so corrupt that promotions to inspector could cost up to $15,000. But it was worth the money. One chief inspector (Max Schmittberger) admitted to payoffs from gamblers, pimps, and whiskey merchants.

A woman who owned a chain of whorehouses testified in one of those perennial investigations on organized crime that

> she paid thirty thousand dollars annually for protection, and others said that when they opened their establishments they were called upon for an initiation fee of five hundred dollars and that hereafter a monthly charge ranging from twenty five dollars to fifty dollars was placed upon each house according to the number of inmates. Street walkers told investigators that they paid patrolmen for the privilege of soliciting, and gangsters, sneak thieves, burglars, pickpockets, footpads, and lush workers, all testified that they gave the police or politicians a percentage of their stealings. More than six hundred policy shops paid an average of fifteen dollars a month each, while three hundred dollars was collected from pool rooms, and even larger sums from the luxurious gambling houses. [Asbury, *The Gangs of New York*]

The sources of these illicit incomes were fought over by criminal organizations such as the Roach Guards, the Bowery Boys, the Whyos, the Hudson Dusters, and the Dead Rabbits. These organizations became so powerful that their battles, engaging hundreds of private "soldiers," could only be stopped when the 27th Infantry was sent in.

Soon after the Civil War, crime, like commerce, became more corporate in nature.

> Fences converted stolen goods into cash. . . . [They] could handle fifty thousand worth of needles and thread . . . they had better political and police connections . . . one of the notorious places of the city was the Thieves' exchange in the 8th Ward, near Broadway and Houston St., where fences and criminals met each night and dickered openly over their beer and whiskey for jewelry and other loot. Annual retainers were paid to criminal lawyers and politicians and policemen received stated fees, and occasionally commission on gross business.

Marm Mandelbaum, one of the great fences, organized a burglary ring which handled $5 to $10 million worth of stolen goods a
year. She had regular salaried employees and the best and most
expensive lawyers, Hummell & Howe, on retainers. No friend of a
friend could go to jail.

Piker Ryan, a member of the crime organization known as the
Whyos, was one of the early hit men for hire—a forerunner of the
1930s Murder Inc. When he was arrested, this price list of "Jobs"
was found on him:

Punching	$2
Both eyes blacked	4
Nose and jaw broke	10
Jacked out (knocked out with a black jack)	15
Ear chawed off	15
Leg or arm broke	19
Shot in leg	25
Stab	25
Doing the big job	100 and up

Along with the list was a notebook showing half a dozen names
with check marks beside them—hits which this hit man had carried out.

When Italian immigration peaked, according to Herbert Asbury
in *The Gangs of New York,* Manhattan south of Times Square "was
divided by the gangs into clearly defined kingdoms, and the boundaries were garrisoned and as carefully guarded as are the frontiers of
civilized nations. The Five Pointers, successors to the Dead Rabbits,
the Plug Uglies and the Whyos, mustered 1500 members and were
lords of the area between Broadway and the Bowery, and Fourteenth
Street and City Hall Park."

All this could not have been possible without political protection—a tradition that had already flourished in New York under the
aegis of William Marcy (Boss) Tweed.

ASPECTS OF ORGANIZED CRIME

William Marcy Tweed was a big man; big-fisted, broad-shouldered, his presence was imposing and intimidating. He came from a good Scottish Protestant family, and was brought up in the then fashionable Cherry Hill section of New York, which would be home to many Italian immigrants fifty years later. He was a devoted family man, a dutiful husband, a loving father, and a man who provided jobs for all of his family and relatives. He contributed generously to his church as he did to the poor and the sick. As a young man he frequented the rough-and-tumble firehouses which became the power base for his political career. Out of the in-fighting with Tammany Hall he emerged as Grand Sachem and chairman of the General Committee. As chairman, he became the power behind the elected officials. Corruption and extortion within the city were divided into seven rings, headed by the powerful Tweed Ring.

There were thirty thousand professional thieves and two thousand gambling joints in New York during Tweed's reign. In one year, 1870, seventeen thousand sailors were robbed. Around City Hall itself there were four hundred brothels. Ropers, as pimps and procurers were called, openly advertised for "stylish girls." There was more crime in New York City, "with a population of just over a million than in London with a population of three million."* And there were many "soldiers," or "braves," as they were called within Tammany, to see that all voted correctly and often. One such soldier was Patrick Duffy, who served as a link between organized criminals and the politicians who protected them. They served each other. No criminal who befriended a politician went to jail, no matter how violent or terrible the crime.

Those early immigrants were aware of the ties between criminals and politicians. It seemed to them that such ties were not much different from those in the old country. Alex Callow reminds us that

petty and important criminals, involved in vice, gambling, confidence games and the like, were tributaries of the Ring. . . . To be sure, crime was not so highly organized nor so intimate with politics in the Tweed Ring era as it was from the 1890's on; nevertheless *the basic pattern existed.* The criminal depended upon the

*Callow, *The Tweed Ring.*

political protection for his crimes. The control and protection of crime was, in fact, one of the Ring's sources of power, not only as a means of building and modernizing the machine, but also as a source for exacting tribute.*

By the turn of the century, most American cities were similarly corrupt. Lincoln Steffens, the investigative reporter, could go from city to city and almost predict the criminal organization he would find there. In Minneapolis,† he found "a New England town on the upper Mississippi . . . the metropolis also of Norway and Sweden in America. Indeed it is the second largest Scandinavian city in the world. But Yankees, straight from Down East, settled the town and their New England spirit predominates." Steffens found the city in the hands of Albert Alonzo Ames, a doctor turned political boss who organized the vices of the city along the lines of Tweed's ring; whorehouses, gambling rings, and graft were distributed among friends and relatives and those willing to pay.

The pattern that emerged and defined the "quality of life" was one of crime with direct links to politicians. There was a network of relatives and friendships held together by understandings and a code of silence. Organized crime was so endemic to the urban society that most men despaired of ever correcting it. Exposure taught these criminal cartels to improve their methods of extortion until the most honest of men in their frustration looked every which way except to the heart of the matter to explain it. One New Yorker told Steffens, "The Irish, the Irish Catholics were at the bottom of it all," prompting Steffens to reply, "The foreign element excuse is one of the hypocritical lies that save us from the clear sight of ourselves."

Such was the urban condition as the great wave of Italian emigrants came to America.

A MAFIA OF THE MIND

The concept of "mafia" as it developed in America was closely tied to the fear of anarchism the early immigrants provoked in the minds of many Americans. The lumping together of anarchists and crimi-

*Ibid., p. 144.

†When Steffens arrived in Minneapolis in 1901, there may have been 350 Italian immigrants, mostly poor miners or railroad workers, in all of Minnesota.

nals in the United States was not much different from the Italian government's tactic of dismissing rebellion in southern Italy as banditry and mafia.

In Monza, Italy, on July 29, 1900, Gaetano Bresci, who had been nurtured in the anarchist community of Paterson, New Jersey, assassinated King Umberto I. This set in motion a series of events that set another stone upon the mafia monument.

Paterson then was a mill town where many Italian workers, fleeing the repressive measures of the Crispi government, had come to find work. They were skilled textile workers from Como, Biella, Vercelli, and Prato. The town developed as a center of American anarchism, fueled by thousands of immigrants from Spain, Germany, and the Jewish ghettos of Russia and Poland. Of the ten thousand Italians in the area, two thousand called themselves anarchists. Paterson became a highly politicized city. Meetings were held night after night and debates went on well into the morning. These debates developed into violent arguments between the followers of Errico Malatesta, who proposed organizing workers in America into one big union, and the followers of Giuseppe Ciancabilla, an advocate of direct action who opposed all organization that would lead workers to "the firing squads of the capitalists."

News that the Crispi government in Italy had suppressed the *Fasci* in Sicily, and that bloody clashes in Milan had killed hundreds of workers, enraged the anarchists of Paterson. In a spirit of vengeance, Bresci returned to Italy to fire the shot that killed King Umberto I.

That the assassin had come from America caused great consternation in Italy. There was an outcry against American influence. *La Tribuna* wrote angrily, "Our peasants go to America carrying pruning knives and return with six shooters." Many poor textile workers who had returned from America were picked up and imprisoned as suspected anarchist killers. Paterson, New Jersey, was depicted in the *Corriere della Sera* as *"il grande focolare dell' anarchia italiana.—*The hearth of Italian anarchy."

In Paterson, two Italian anarchists, Benjamin Mazzotta and Filippo Moreni, denied any conspiracy and accused the newsmen of "being obliged to invent sensational stories to make a living." In New York City, where anarchist accomplices reportedly gathered, authorities moved to form a special task force to combat anarchists and criminals—which many saw as one and the same. Joseph Petrosino, an Italian American detective, was given a top job on the task force.

A square-shouldered, thick-necked man, Petrosino had been a shoeshine boy, a tailor, a clerk, and a street cleaner until he joined the police force, where he found his niche as a hard-nosed cop. He rose to the rank of lieutenant, and when the furor against the Black Hand broke out in the city he was put in charge of the Italian Squad. Publicly he pushed for deportation of all anarchists and criminals. In one case, he arrested the Pelletieri brothers at pistol point after "relieving them of murderous knives." Giuseppe Pelletieri was deported, and Petrosino became the darling of the authorities—so much so that he was commissioned to investigate anarchism and criminality in Italy. Shortly after his arrival in Sicily, on March 12, 1909, while walking alone from a restaurant to his hotel near the Palermo waterfront, he was shot dead.

The immediate reaction to his death was "the mafia kills Petrosino." No one pursued the idea that it might have been anarchists who killed him. Or that the Italian police, who resented his intrusion in their affairs, might have been responsible.

Years later, Don Vito Cascio Fero, with great bravura and little proof, claimed to have been the killer, thus adding to the image of the all-powerful Mafia.* This image of indestructible power meant money in the bank for such criminals. As an astute old anarchist remarked in an interview, "It is not enough to ask who is doing the shooting. But you should ask who profits from the shooting."

The Petrosino murder was barely ten years old when a robbery took place in April 1920 in South Braintree, Massachusetts. The paymaster and the guard of the Slater & Morrell Shoe Company were shot dead and the thieves got away with $15,000. Within a few days Nicola Sacco, a shoemaker, and Bartolomeo Vanzetti, a fishmonger, both anarchists, were arrested and indicted for robbery and murder.

During the trial, the Reverend Billy Sunday shouted from his Boston pulpit: "Give them the juice. Burn them, if they're guilty. That's the way to handle it. I'm tired of hearing these foreigners, these radicals, coming over here and telling us what to do."

The old bricklayer who had asked why mafia developed only in

*In 1982, Leonard Sciascia could write that this act, though not proven legally, gave prestige to Don Vito and permitted him to assume direction of the Mafia "for all of the territory of the province of Palermo." *Futura Memoria*, p. 38.

the United States, when questioned about Sacco and Vanzetti, simply said, "I remember," and looked away. In his silence one could sense the fear that the execution of the two anarchists had instilled in Italian radicals of their time. Vecoli's observation that "a radical identity was not a viable option in the land of triumphant Capitalism" became more understandable. (A fuller account of the Sacco and Vanzetti case appears in Chapter 17.)

A ROAD TO ASSIMILATION

The violence in American life to which young immigrants were introduced in the early decades of the twentieth century began with ethnic gang violence. As one survivor of those gangs remarked in 1976, "What mafia, mafia, we had gangs, gangs. There was the Elizabeth Street gang, the Stanton Street gang, the Delancey Street gang. Without a gang you were *niente,* nothing, a loser."

The parents of those who became gang members were distraught as they lost their sons to America. These were poor people, hardworking to the point of exhaustion, parents who tried to instill in their sons the values of work, patience, and resignation. Some of these sons turned instead to values they learned on the streets. And some of the gangs became criminal organizations.

In the late 1890s, the Neapolitan Paolo Antonio Vaccarelli, leader of the Five Points gang, changed his name to Paul Kelly. As Kelly, he led a gang (they were not called organizations yet) of fifteen hundred Italian, Jewish, and Irish men who controlled the area between the Bowery and Chrystie Street. Kelly carried his power lightly; he learned to dress smartly, and he never raised his voice. A former bantamweight boxer, Kelly looked like a bank clerk. He spoke French, Spanish, and Italian, although his new name implied a desire to be considered American. His chief rival was Monk Eastman, the son of a Jewish restaurateur who had changed his name from Osterman.

Kelly eventually moved into labor relations, organizing ragpickers working on the dumps along the East River. As a vice president and agent of the Longshoremen's Association, he battled with other gangsters hired by the owners for control of the waterfront. He lived out his life as a real estate developer, forcing the owners of the old mansions north of Yorkville to sell their homes, which he remodeled into cheap tenements, renting them to newly arrived Italian immigrants.

Eastman was shot on East 14th Street in a typical "organized crime" killing. The field was left to a new generation of young and ambitious men.

The 1920s saw the growth period for older crime organizations such as Five Points and the Eastman gang. For the young ethnics caught between the first and second generations, it was a time of difficult assimilation. Such men as Lucky Luciano, Arnold Rothstein, and Al Capone found criminal activity not only a quick way up the economic ladder, but also a quick way of becoming American.

The Italians who gained notoriety in crime were either born in the United States or brought by their immigrant parents as small children.

Frank Costello, born Francesco Castiglia in Lurapoli, Italy, in the province of Calabria, came to America as a boy of nine. His family was poor, and young Castiglia roamed the streets of East Harlem with Irish and Jewish toughs. Like most of those of his generation who became leaders of criminal business organizations, Castiglia grew up "uncontrolled and determined to avoid his parents' life time struggle for money." In partnership with Henry Horowitz, he manufactured punchboards and slot machines, which became the cornerstone of their gambling empire in 1919. But it was Rothstein, according to Wolfe and Dimona in *Frank Costello,* who "financed Frank and showed him how to organize and how to cut your rivals' throats."

With the advent of Prohibition, Frank Castiglia dominated the illegal liquor business in the Northeast. Helped by such gunmen as Bugsy Siegel (with whom he had grown up), Castiglia organized distribution along business and military lines. He set up guards and way stations to protect his convoys of liquor coming in from abroad. He took the Coast Guard into his confidence by paying them handsomely to look the other way. At times, "coast guard ships themselves were used to carry the liquor ashore." Frank Castiglia carried on in the great tradition of Boss Tweed, courting and buying politicians. He even had General Lincoln C. Andrews, Assistant Secretary of the U.S. Treasury, in his pay. Fleets of ships brought in fine Scotch whiskey from overseas. In all this Castiglia did not belong to any "family." His associates were Jews, Irish, Italians, and Americans of many generations. There was less ethnic prejudice among criminals than among many employers at the time. His family life revolved around a young Jewish woman, Geigerman, whom he married in 1914 when for the first time he changed the spelling of his name to Costello.

No less notorious than Costello was "Lucky" Luciano, born Salvatore Lucania in 1897 in Licardi Freddi, a treeless, stony sulphur-mining town in Sicily. Lucania was brought to America when he was not quite ten. He, too, was educated in the streets of New York. He developed into a thin young man with a full head of black hair and a pockmarked face, scarred by street battles with toughs and by police beatings. His mentor was Arnold Rothstein, and his cohorts included Bugsy Siegel and Meyer Lansky, who, it was said, was as close to him as a lover, "although there was nothing sexual in the relationship."

Lucania grew up around 14th Street and Second Avenue, where he ran small crap games and other schemes with Meyer Lansky, Bugsy Siegel, Louis Lepke, and George Uffner. In such company his entrepreneurship flourished as he grew older.

His father, he explained, was a laborer in Sicily, and

> he really believed all those fairy tales about the streets paved with gold in America. He never did admit it was bullshit. Christ, we were starving. I was hustlin' in the streets when I was twelve, stealing and runnin' penny-ante crap games. . . . You're a kid in the slums, and you see your old man bustin' his hump for peanuts. At the same time you see the local sharpies—the bookies and the torpedoes—all makin' dough and driven limousines. . . . So what's the kid to do? He gotta decide whether he's going to be a crumb, or make dough. Me, I made up my mind pretty young. I'd rather shoot myself than be a crumb.

It was the beginning of Lucania's assimilation and the conflict with his father, who, upon hearing of Lucania's hustling, beat him. At one point his father was so angered by the son "who brought disgrace to the family" that he aimed a gun at the boy and swore he would kill him if he continued his criminal ways. Nor were the schools he attended around Second and Third Avenues near 14th Street any more useful to him. "The teachers," Lucania told a probation officer, "treated Italians like they were dirt, just stupid people who would never learn. . . . I hated the teachers and hated school. So I dropped out and started to hustle."

It has been repeated over and over again by journalists and some academics that Lucky Luciano rebelled against the older generation of Italian criminals. This rebellion became known as the Castellamare War, and Luciano stands convicted—by nearly everyone who writes on the subject, on evidence that would not call for an indictment, let alone a verdict of guilty, in court—of ordering the killing of Salvatore Maranzano.

The Italian American underworld in the late 1920s was dominated by two men: Salvatore Maranzano and Joe "the Boss" Masseria. Because they both belonged to an older generation, both were known as "Moustache Petes." Luciano, as a young American hood, first joined forces with Masseria, the weaker of the two, and on April 5, 1931, had him killed while they were eating in a Coney Island restaurant. On September 10 of the same year, Maranzano was killed in his Park Avenue office. The rise of Luciano became known as the "Americanization of the Mobs." Soon after the killings, journalists asserted that "There was about ninety guineas knocked off all over the country." The story was made all the more believable when, during the McCellan Committee's congressional hearings, La Verne Duffy presented a chart he entitled "Masseria-Maranzano War and Evolution of Gang Control, 1930 to the Present." It was Duffy who constantly interrupted the hearings to interject remarks and then speak for witnesses. Such procedure would not have been permitted in a court of law or by a working historian. When Sergeant Ralph Salerno was asked if the police were "ever able to get any lead on who committed the crime?" he answered that there was not enough evidence 'that could be presented to a grand jury'." (Moquin, *A Documentary History of the Italian Americans*).

This version became entrenched in academic circles when the sociologist Donald Cressy, in *Theft of a Nation,* concluded that "some forty Italian Sicilian gang leaders across the country lost their lives in battle. Most, if not all of those killed on the infamous day occupied positions we would now characterize as 'boss.' . . . ," etc.

However, when the historian Humbert Nelli looked into this purge, which supposedly "Americanized the Mob," he found that

A careful examination of newspapers issued during September, October, and November of 1931 in twelve large cities . . . turned up evidence of only one killing that occurred at about the time

Maranzano died and might have been linked to the death of the "Boss of Bosses." Denver, where this killing occurred, contained gangs that routinely used violence to settle disputes, so that the timing of the murder to coincide with events in New York might not have been intentional. Moreover, the leaders of the two rival factions were Calabrians, not Sicilians.

Overlooked in these self-serving distortions is the Americanization of Charles "Lucky" Luciano. By 1936, he was well established (with offices in the Waldorf-Towers) as an American criminal boss, so much so that Thomas Dewey built his career on Luciano's prosecution. (If Luciano had known labor history, he would have realized that Dewey employed the same tactics that were once used by the Pinkerton agent McPartland and others against Wobblies and radicals in the West.)

Dewey's career, which almost led to the White House, began when he captured the public's attention as a "gangbuster." The year 1936 was a propitious one to be a criminal prosecutor in New York if one wanted attention in the political arena. American gangsters with Italian names were already the image and symbol of organized crime. Edward G. Robinson had played the role of Rico Bandello in the enormously popular film *Little Caesar* (1930), and Paul Muni had enacted the role of Tony Camonte in the even more popular *Scarface* (1932). Both films contributed to the public's vision of crime syndicates that were dominated by men with marked, no matter how stilted, Italian accents. In such films the Italian was well on his way to replacing the Irishman as the symbol of the hood.

Luciano was arrested on April 1, 1936, in Hot Springs, Arkansas. Indicted with him were Thomas Pennochio, David Betillo, James Frederico (who Americanized his name to Fredericks), Abraham Wahrman, Peter Baletzer, Al Wiener, David Marcus, and Jack Ellenstein. All of these men were involved one way or another in the business of prostitution. Luciano's indictment (along with that of the other men) was part of Dewey's overall strategy. He had lobbied and succeeded in having the state legislature pass a law that made it legal "to try a man against whom there was little evidence, and convict him by joining his trial with the trial of his associates against whom there was much evidence." This became known as the Dewey Law.

Dewey arrested a string of prostitutes, madams, and pimps who swore that Luciano was the ringmaster of prostitution in New York.

That many of them had criminal records was understandable; but it was Dewey's methods that were questionable. To Dave Miller, a corrupt cop who pimped for his wife and his girlfriend, Dewey promised leniency. To Danny Brooks, imprisoned for seven and a half years, he promised freedom; to Joe Bendix, serving fifteen years to life as a fourth offender, he promised he would put in a good word with the governor. Still, Dewey needed direct evidence. For this he turned to the prostitutes, applying psychological techniques. He worked on two prostitutes, "Cokey" Flo Brown and Nancy Presser, cajoling and pleading with them, even promising leniency. When that didn't work, he concentrated on "Cokey" Flo, who was suffering cocaine withdrawal pains in prison. For weeks she was so ill she could eat no more than a few spoonfuls of milk and cereal each day. Finally she broke. Cokey Flo "manufactured" the story that Dewey wanted to hear, giving testimony so that "maybe," she was quoted as saying, "I can get a break from the judge when I'm sentenced." Dewey also permitted *Liberty* magazine to buy her story for $2,000 while she was in prison.

Only much later, in 1955, did Polly Adler, the famed brothel keeper, tell Sciacca: ". . . every one of those girls later said, quite specifically, that Dewey and his staff put words into their mouths and gave them all the information they needed to tell a convincing story. Those girls lied because they'd been threatened by Dewey, they admitted that quite freely."

Luciano was convicted, given the extraordinary sentence of thirty to fifty years in prison, and sent to the state prison at Dannemora, the Alcatraz of the East. Dewey sent the prostitutes, who were key witnesses, to France, all expenses paid.

Dewey was determined not to have his methods exposed at a time when he was thinking of running for the presidency, a position he had said was "written in the stars." With the help of Frank Costello, a deal was struck. Luciano would be freed if he consented to leave the country. With Luciano out of the country, the case would be closed. But an excuse was needed to keep it closed securely. This was done by turning Luciano into a war hero. In exchange for his supposed services in aligning the criminal elements in Sicily on the side of the invading American troops, Luciano was given his freedom—on one condition, which Dewey insisted on: that after the war he be deported and never be permitted to return.

Luciano explained the deal in his own words:

Dewey and all those politicians claim I got out because of my efforts to help the Navy. That wasn't it at all.

Sure I did everything I could when those Navy guys got suckered into coming to me. But I was looking out for numero uno first. The Navy was gonna get me out.

See I been around in politics for a long time and I know politicians. I been in court in my life, I know how things work. Dewey was gonna free me, I knew that. But he needed an excuse, something for the record they call it, so the papers wouldn't jump on him and say he sold out to me. The stuff about the Navy was the excuse, to make it all legit for the papers.

But I didn't trust Dewey. He wanted to be president so bad he would have framed me on a murder charge if he figured it could help. No way could I trust the bastard. So, I told some of my friends to get together a big, fat book on Dewey. Startin' with the money my friends gave him to run for Governor. Stuff on how he let some of my friends run wide open gambling joints in Saratoga while he was governor. Stuff on the money he got to run against Roosevelt durin' the war. . . . Why do you think Meyer [Lansky] and Frank [Costello] came up to see me so much? To play cards. No, to get the stuff together for the book, to get me out.

Luciano's "help" in the invasion of Sicily was at best questionable and at worst pure fraud. Senator Estes Kefauver, who headed one of the perennial investigating committees into organized crime, wrote: "During World War II there was a lot of hocus-pocus about allegedly valuable services that Luciano . . . was supposed to have furnished the military. . . . We dug into this and obtained a number of conflicting stories. This is one of the points about which the committee would have questioned Governor Dewey . . . the governor declined our invitation. . . ."

What help could Luciano have given? He had been in prison since 1936, he had been brought up in New York and could not speak Sicilian, and everyone had been out of touch with Sicily because of the Fascist regime. Finally, Max Corvo, a Sicilian American who took part in the planning and invasion of Sicily as a member of the OSS, made the comment that "There was no truth whatsoever in the story that Luciano helped us, none whatsoever."

The official stories on Luciano's alignment of Sicilian *mafiosi* were apparently intended as a coverup of the Dewey deal. What was also covered up was the fact that Dewey had been elected governor of New York with the help of Lansky and Costello, who contributed $250,000 to his campaign. They also delivered the Italian and the rackets-controlled unions' votes. Elaborate rumors were circulated to the effect that Luciano was in Sicily helping in war operations.* The reality was that Luciano was incarcerated in Dannemora state prison and never set foot in Sicily during the war. It was Charles Poletti, a former lieutenant governor of New York, who, as military governor of liberated Sicily, knowingly or carelessly released many imprisoned *mafiosi* who could then pose as anti-Fascists and easily assume positions of power. Vito Genovese, who had returned to Italy in 1937 to avoid murder and racketeering charges, became a liaison official to an American unit, until he was spotted by an American sergeant and returned to the United States to stand trial.†

The effect of Poletti's action on Sicily, as Dennis Mack Smith concluded, was that "the Americans in 1943 had deliberately reintroduced the Sicilian mafia as a *ruse de guerre* and given it effective power over large areas of Sicilian society."

In February 1946, Luciano prepared for deportation aboard the *Laura Keane,* docked at Bush Terminal in Brooklyn. An honor guard of longshoremen, each armed with a bailing hook, prevented reporters and photographers from going on board, where a farewell party was being given. Those friends and colleagues allowed onto the ship were a cross-section of the Irish, Jews, and Italians who made up the political-criminal elite Luciano had grown up with and those he had learned to trust: Meyer Lansky, Joe Adonis, Willie Moretti, Bugsy Siegel, Longy Zwillman, Moses Polakoff, Joe Bonanno, Tommy Lucchese, and Owney Madden. They all came bearing gifts and good wishes.

In a final irony, when Luciano arrived in Palermo, he was so ignorant of Sicilian criminal activity that he was swindled out of 15

---

*In a recent biography of Dewey, no mention is made of the release of Luciano by Dewey.

†"An important factor in the re-emergence of men such as Vizzini and Genco Russo [as *mafiosi*] was that with the collapse of fascism a power vacuum opened up which they were well suited to fill. Not only were they respected local figures, but as victims of Mori's [Mussolini's appointed destroyer of mafia in Sicily] operation against the mafia, they were also in a good position to pose as anti-fascists."—Finley, Smith, and Duggan, *History of Sicily* (New York: Viking Press, 1986).

million lire by the very *mafiosi* he supposedly controlled. He was talked into investing in a candy factory, *na caramela,* which was set up in such a way that the more money it made, the more Luciano lost.

As the Italian journalist Luigi Barzini, who had lived and worked in the United States, wrote:

> There are Americans who believe that criminal groups in their country belong to the Sicilian Mafia, are in effect overseas branches of the main organizations, and that they are all directed by orders from Palermo. This myth is shared even by some naive American criminals of Italian descent, who learned it by reading the newspapers. They sometimes land in Sicily believing not only that they belong to the *societa* but that they have a high rank in it. At the most they are *uomini rispettati* like all moneyed foreigners. Soon enough most of them discover to their dismay that they are considered merely strangers by the real *amici.*

Salvatore Lucania spent the rest of his life in Italy, where he was known as *L'Americanu.*

It was in the streets of Brooklyn that another superstar of crime, Alphonse Capone, acquired his education.

Capone was born in Brooklyn on January 17, 1899, the son of a barber from Naples. He grew up in the Red Hook section among Irish and Italian families. With little time or inclination for school, he became a dropout at an early age.

Al Capone's volcanic temper threatened his very survival as a youth in Brooklyn, where each block was dominated by an ethnic gang. Near the Navy Yard, where Irish gangs felt their monopoly on dock jobs threatened by the Italians, he was attacked by men carrying brickbats and onion sacks filled with stones. In the Williamsburg section, Jewish gangs stoned any stranger who entered.

Capone, 5 feet 11 inches tall and 255 pounds, was a brawler who "ran with" the ethnic gangs of Brooklyn's Red Hook district, where he made himself a reputation as a bouncer in the Irish-operated brothels. He, too, was driven by a desire to be seen as an American. "I'm no Italian," he said scornfully. "I was born in Brooklyn."

Capone belonged to no "family," nor was the term "mafia" ever applied to him or his cohorts. His criminal organization included seven hundred to one thousand men from every ethnic group in New York and Chicago.

All of Capone's activity had but one objective—to become prosperous within the American system of free enterprise. "This system of ours," he said, "gives to each and every one of us a great opportunity if we only seize it with our hands and make the most of it." These were not thoughts rooted in Naples or Sicily, but in the American frontier mythology.

Capone brutally ruled the corridors of corruption in Chicago until he roused the ire of the federal government by flaunting his power and wealth. He was finally convicted on tax evasion charges, given an extraordinarily long sentence, and sent to Alcatraz. There it was said he refused injections to counteract the syphilis he had contracted, "because he was afraid of needles." Kenneth Rexroth, the poet, who was then a reporter in San Francisco, said it was rumored that treatment for his disease was withheld on the orders of Franklin D. Roosevelt as punishment. Capone was left to deteriorate slowly in body and mind until his death in 1947 at the age of forty-eight.

Joseph Bonanno, regarded by the media as a superstar *mafioso,* was the only "head of a family" who came to America from Sicily as an adult. Yet even he had first come to America as a child of three with his parents to settle in the Williamsburg section of Brooklyn, when "Sicily had not yet entered my young consciousness." He went to school in Brooklyn at least to the second grade, when the family returned to Sicily, where young Bonanno, more American than Sicilian, had difficulty speaking Sicilian. During the early days of the Mussolini regime, Bonanno was expelled from the Merchant Marine Academy for refusing to wear a black shirt as a mark of support for the Fascist Party. He then returned to America in 1924 at the age of nineteen, just in time to join the competitive scramble among bootleggers.

For Bonanno, extortion was a method already used by large corporations to control prices through monopolies. In this he echoed Walter Lippmann's view that no society can live by truly free-market principals. Organized crime profited by cutting down on the competition in an otherwise wildly competitive society.

Bonanno wrote in his memoirs:

No matter how deeply I treasured memories of Sicily, I was Joseph Bonanno of America. I was from Sicily, but not of that world anymore. . . . Tradition has died in America. The way of life that I and my Sicilian ancestors pursued is dead. What Americans refer to as "the Mafia" is a degenerate outgrowth of that life-style. Sicilian immigrants who came to America tried to conduct their affairs as they had in Sicily, but we eventually discovered this was impossible . . . what Americans call "mafia" never was an institution, an organization, a corporate body. As best as I can figure out, this fallacy continues to receive its strongest acceptance not in the minds of ordinary people but in the minds of law-enforcement agents.

Those singled out by the Drug Enforcement Administration and investigating committees for the most part do not fit the common image of *mafiosi;* many were not born in Sicily, a number were born in other parts of Italy, and all, in any case, came to America as children or teenagers. Vito Genovese was born in Naples. Carlos Marcello was born in Guatemala. Al Polizzi was born in Sicily, but came to America as a small boy. Joe Roselli was born Filippo Sacco in Esteria, Italy, and brought to America when he was six. Joseph Gallo was born in Brooklyn. Paul Ricca was born in Naples, Joe Valachi and Anthony Strollo in New York.

Most of these men were born at the turn of the century, and were part of the generation of the great migration. All came from poor, working-class families. (The established *mafiosi* had no reason to leave their position of power and comfort in Sicily.) They were the children who were assimilated into American life.

CAPITALIZING ON THE MAFIA IMAGE

The image of Italian mafia crime families, *capo regime, capo di tutti capi,* was repopularized by the U.S. Senate investigations on organized crime led by Senator Estes Kefauver in 1950–51. For a long time J. Edgar Hoover had insisted that the mafia did not exist, but he changed his mind when it became apparent that the FBI and other law enforcement agencies could with little or no explanation receive large appropriations for investigating a criminal organization whose secrecy had yet to be unlocked.

Once politicians became aware that the mafia was a politically lucrative issue, it gained public attention; all crime could now be blamed on a foreign conspiracy, and investigating organized crime opened up routes to the highest offices. (In 1876, Samuel Tilden almost made it to the White House after investigating and breaking up the Tweed Ring, forerunner of modern-day organized crime.)

The Kefauver investigation produced the first charts of names constituting a web of "mafia." This committee had investigative powers and could accept hearsay evidence that would not be permitted in a court of law. The concept of "mafia" as defined by the committee was established in the public mind: ". . . there is a sinister criminal organization known as the Mafia operating throughout the country with ties in other nations in the opinion of the committee. The Mafia is the direct descendant of a criminal organization of the same name originating in the Island of Sicily."

Although twenty-four Italian American witnesses denied the existence of a criminal organization known as the Mafia,* the Kefauver Committee report disregarded the testimony, attributing it to *omerta,* the ancient Sicilian code of silence which, during an era of rampant corrupt government in Sicily, discouraged cooperation with the police. The committee's failure to produce clear evidence that there was an organization called "the Mafia" led Rufus King, a lawyer formerly associated with the California Crime Study Commission, to fault its report in the *Stanford Law Review.* King pointed out that "The cumulative denials and professed ignorance . . . suggest that it is either a *very* elusive, shadowy sinister organization—or else, equally credibly, a romantic myth."†

Nonetheless, Kefauver held the attention of the television cameras, and a little later, wearing a coonskin cap, made a galloping but futile run for the White House. Baron Turkus, one of the prosecuting attorneys in the Murder Inc. trial, concluded of the Kefauver Report:

> Perhaps the most pertinent evidence against the existence of Mafia in modern-day crime is found in the committee's own confession that after an investigation which lasted one year, travelled to fourteen cities from coast to coast, heard more than six

*Later, during the Nixon administration, Attorney General John Mitchell issued a Department of Justice edict instructing employees to use the term "organized crime" instead of "Mafia."

†Quoted in Smith, *The Mafia Mystique,* p. 144.

hundred witnesses and cost $250,000, it was unable to uncover one single member of Mafia, or anyone, for that matter, who even admitted he knew a member.

Ten years later, the McClennan investigation created more charts based on secondhand information of dubious quality about the alleged five New York "crime families." Unable to prove the existence of an international organization calling itself the Mafia, the committee seized upon the phrase the gangster Joseph Valachi had used in his testimony—"*cosa nostra*" (commonly used in Italian households to mean "our thing") and ballyhooed it to the press as another name for "mafia." The press was delighted with the foreign-sounding phrase and the implication of secrecy. In spite of the fact that at no time in history had there been a documented criminal organization by that name, the term became synonymous with "mafia."

Valachi, a confessed murderer, was born in the Bronx of Neapolitan parents. He could not speak Sicilian, and his experience was that of a small-time gangster whom the authorities made good use of for their own purposes. Certainly his testimony was considered "amateur-night material": his "cosa nostra, button men, families" were ridiculed by another gangster, Vincent Teresa, who had known Valachi as a "nothing." In a court of law, the word of a plea-bargaining confessed murderer (who obviously was being told what to say by the committee) would have been discounted. The British historian Christopher Duggan concludes that

> Valachi's statements make puzzling reading, not least because his grasp of English was rudimentary. It is often hard to see how the idea of a formal structure could have been extrapolated from his incoherent and often contradictory remarks. Indeed, there seems to have been some uncertainty as to whether the organization he referred to was called "Cosa Nostra," "Causa Nostra," or "Casa Nostra." Yet it was largely on his evidence that the Godfather image of mafia became imbedded in the mind of bureaucrats within the law enforcement establishment.*

This image was swiftly to be reinforced by an avalanche of novels and films.

*Duggan, *Fascism and the Mafia*.

Precipitating the avalanche was the publication in 1969 of Mario Puzo's *The Godfather*. Although Puzo, the son of poor immigrant parents from Naples, admitted that all he knew about the Mafia derived from what he read in the newspapers, the novel was praised by several reviewers as an authentic portrayal of the Mafia in America. The book brought fame and fortune to its author and went on to become the source of three *Godfather* films, which further impressed the Mafia image on the psyche of the American public. In the next five years its enormous success triggered what became known as "the Godfather industry," the publication of more than 150 books of fiction and nonfiction. "Sons of the Godfather," one scholar dubbed them, many of which boasted of their lineage to the Puzo novel. "It is virtually impossible now to find a book about gangsters that does not identify them as members of the Mafia or Cosa Nostra," wrote the crime historian Dwight C. Smith in 1976.

Three years after the publication of *The Godfather*, in a collection of essays entitled *The Godfather Papers and Other Confessions*, Puzo explained that as the debt-ridden father of a family of five children, he deliberately set out to write a bestseller. "I'm ashamed to say that I wrote *The Godfather* entirely out of research. I never met a real honest-to-goodness gangster." In another published statement, Puzo added that he wrote the novel with no intention of denigrating Italian Americans.* "I was looking to present a myth . . . a legend. . . . To me *The Godfather* isn't an expose; it's a romantic novel."

Some Italian Americans failed to see the romance in a novel where murder, terrorism, and betrayal are the dominant themes and, with one or two minor exceptions, the protagonists are devoid of virtue. *The Godfather* and the copycat books and films that followed conveyed the impression that the great majority of Italian Americans must somehow have underworld connections. How readily this impression lends itself to further generalization is documented in a tape that surfaced during the Watergate affair. After agreeing with his aides that it would be politically wise to appoint some Italian American to a top-level federal post, Richard Nixon asks, "Yes, but where would we find an honest Italian American?"

*In his 1985 novel *The Sicilian*, Puzo presents the Sicilian people as a thoroughly villainous lot. As one reviewer of the novel wrote: "Puzo, a New York native whose parents had grown up near Naples, repeatedly portrays Sicilians as little more than blood-thirsty, murdering, odious, criminal savages. In short the book involves alarming racist diatribes about Sicilians, all Sicilians." (Review of *The Sicilian* by John Buffo in *Il Caffe*, April 1985.)

The damage done to the Italian American image may have disturbed the children of the immigrants, but the older generation, accustomed to the prejudice they had lived with over a long period, remained focused on the struggle to earn a living free of the exploitation they had been subject to before the advent of labor unions.

PART SEVEN

Work, Politics, and Divertimenti

CHAPTER 16

Before the Unions, 1900–1920

Where de you worka John?
On the Delaware Lackawan
And whatta you do-a John?
I poosh, I poosh, I poosh.

—WORK SONG

S oon after the Civil War, when Italian immigration was still below five thousand a year, towns and villages in America were growing and great masses of laborers were needed by the entrepreneurs who sought to build empires. Conditions, of course, were miserable.

Mining, an industry essential to the industrialization of America, had the most deplorable working conditions. The mines were usually set in isolated and distant territories—in Minnesota, Utah, Idaho, and Colorado, "where the town was two streets wide, the rear street occupied by prostitutes, black, white and Chinese," and where there were "17 saloons" to each street. The mining towns were run by managers, who operated them for absentee owners living in New York or San Francisco.

The work was dangerous and paid barely enough to keep a family together; many miners worked two jobs or homesteaded to put food on the table. Company stores, known euphemistically as

"Pluck me stores" (which in its time was no doubt a more earthy expression), took a good portion of the men's salaries, as the prices were 100 percent higher than elsewhere. Equipment, shovels, carts, and pickaxes had to be rented. If there was an outcry against conditions, a militia could be called out. And if the militia refused to fire upon the miners, who sometimes included their friends and relatives, armies of strong men led by the Pinkerton agents would be brought in. Men were deputized at $5 a day, twice the wage of miners. The conflicts often led to tragedy.

In 1890, Frederick W. Taylor, one of the early efficiency experts, introduced "Scientific Management," which led to "incentive wages." This new language for the workers simply meant piecework. When workers called these innovations "speed up," the owners answered that the industrial worker on piecework "was essentially in business for himself, an entrepreneur in overalls."* Such talk led to actions which created abominable conditions for workingmen. Understandably, they protested. In the words of the labor leader Daniel De Leon: "As sure as a man will raise his hand by some instinct, to shield himself against a blow, so surely will workingmen, instinctively, periodically, gather into unions. The Union is the arm that labor instinctively throws up to screen its head."

The infamous Ludlow Massacre (as it became known), the most brutal of all confrontations between workers and mine owners, took place on April 20, 1914. The tragedy stemmed from a strike called by the United Mine Workers against John D. Rockefeller, Jr.'s, Colorado Fuel & Iron Company Works. The strikers, chiefly English and Italian immigrants along with a smaller number of Greeks, Slavs, Austrians, and Mexicans, were demanding union recognition, higher wages, an eight-hour day, and the right to trade in other than company-owned stores. During the strike, its participants and their families were living in a tent colony near Ludlow's coal mines—approximately one thousand inhabitants, most of them wives and children.

The massacre was instigated by a detachment of troops, armed with machine guns, who directed their fire toward the canvas tents, causing them to ignite. Two Italian women and ten children were among those who died in the blaze. A military commission investigating the disaster blamed the troops for spreading the fire with the

*Rodgers, *Work Ethic.*

assistance of strikebreakers. The commission was convinced that the fire had been deliberately started with the intention of destroying the entire colony.

On April 21, 1914, the *New York Times* report read:

45 DEAD 20 HURT
SCORE MISSING IN STRIKE WAR
WOMEN AND CHILDREN ROASTED
MEN FROM OTHER CAMPS
JOIN FIGHTERS IN HILLS

Trinidad. Col. April 21.—Forty-five dead, more than two-thirds of them women and children, a score missing, and more than a score wounded, is the result known to-night of the fourteen hour battle which raged with uninterrupted fury yesterday between State troops and striking coal miners in the Ludlow district on the property of the Colorado Fuel and Iron Company, the Rockefeller holdings.

The Ludlow camp is a mass of charred debris and buried beneath it is a story of horror unparalleled in the history of industrial warfare. In the holes which had been dug for their protection against the rifle fire the women and children died like trapped rats when the flames swept over them. One pit uncovered this afternoon, disclosed the bodies of ten children and two women. Further exploration was forbidden by the position of the camp which lies directly between the militia and the strikers' positions.

. . . Italian, Greek and Austrian miners have appealed to their consular representatives for protection.

Open warfare throughout the state followed. Battalions of workers captured mines, killed guards, strikebreakers, and policemen, and dynamited and set fire to company properties. The war continued for eight days with the army of workers commanding large areas of the state, at which point Colorado Governor Elias M. Ammons asked President Woodrow Wilson for federal troops to stop "an open insurrection against the State." Wilson sent several regiments that put an end to the conflict. The battle, however, continued in Congress and in the minds of Americans.

More than any other American episode during the peak years of European immigration, the Ludlow Massacre and its aftermath were stark reminders for the new immigrants that not all of their worst oppressors had been in Europe.

Many other confrontations took place, incidents which soon faded from the memory of the public. Over one hundred were wounded at Coeur d'Alene, Idaho, as striking miners battled militia and strikebreakers. Here the strikers captured the mine only to be turned back by federal troops sent in by President Harrison. Similar violence broke out in Telluride and Cripple Creek. Violence in the mining districts of eastern Pennsylvania around 1875 became so endemic that Irish miners organized secret paramilitary groups known as "the Molly Maguires." During their confrontations with owners and years of guerrilla warfare, they were infiltrated by Pinkerton agents. On evidence gathered by such agents, twenty-four miners were arrested and ten hanged. In Pittsburgh in 1877, pitched battles killed twenty-seven.

If violence in the miners' warfare took its toll, death through accidents was even greater. In 1910, in Colorado alone, 323 miners were killed in mines.

The great mass of Italian immigration came just when the confrontation between capitalist America and American labor reached warlike proportions. In 1893–94, when 72,000 Italians arrived in the United States, armies of unemployed men led by populist "Generals" marched on Washington to demand relief. News of this kind quickly spread to Italy and may well explain why in the next year Italian immigration dropped to 35,000. However, it picked up again in 1896, to 68,000, and continued to rise until the peak year of 1907, when 286,000 arrived.

THE EARLY PERIOD, 1900–20

In 1885, in an effort to protect foreign workers from unscrupulous hiring agents, Congress enacted the contract labor laws that made it illegal to recruit immigrants before they reached the United States. But the laws could easily be circumvented, and the practice of recruiting workers abroad continued well into the next century. Agents representing American industries regularly went to Italy to entice workers with false promises of steady jobs, good pay, and good housing.

Some men after long journeys found themselves dumped in a

lonely valley, abandoned, minus the money they had paid for supposed jobs. Employment agencies worked in collusion with the employers, who after a few weeks would fire the workers in order to hire
a new crew and so share in the agencies' new "fees." Those who
were abandoned and fleeced may have been the fortunate ones.
Many men who were taken to real jobs never forgot the experience.
Recalled one:

> We started from New York on November 3, 1891, under the
> guidance of two bosses. We had been told we should go to Con-
> necticut to work on a railroad and earn one dollar and seventy-
> five cents per day. We were taken instead to South Carolina, first
> to a place called Lambs and then after a month or so to the "tom
> tom" sulfate mines. The railroad fare was eight dollars and
> eighty-five cents; this sum, as well as the price of our tools,
> nearly three dollars, we owed the bosses. We were received by an
> armed guard, which kept constant watch over us. . . . At sunset
> the work ceases and the men retire to a shanty, very much like
> the steerage of a third-class emigrant ship, the men being packed
> together in unclean and narrow berths. . . . Our daily fare was
> coffee and bread for breakfast, rice with lard or soup at dinner-
> time, and cheese or sausage for supper. Yet we were not able to
> pay off our debt; so after a while we were given only bread. . . .

Camille Tornatore remembered his early days in Louisiana as
"the slaving times." He recalled seeing "a man harnessed to a plough
like a mule, working for 85 cents a day." There were a variety of such
dark remembrances by those who had fallen into the hands of contractors of labor. One social worker wrote, for instance:

> In foul Mulberry Street a half-dozen carts were being loaded
> with bundles of the poorest clothes and rags. One man after an-
> other brought his things; women and children lounged about,
> and the men gathered together in small groups, chattering about
> the work, their hopes and their fears. For these men there was
> *fear*. They have heard of the deceit practised upon those who
> have preceded them and their sufferings. Each man carried a tin
> box containing stale bread and pieces of loathsome cheese and
> sausage, his provision for the journey . . . the sausage, for in-
> stance which, rotten as it was, cost them four cents a pound in

New York was sold for twenty cents a pound at the place of their work. Of course, the destination and the wages and the nature of the work have been agreed upon in some informal way. But the contract is a sham. I do not believe there is a single instance in which a contract was honestly fulfilled by the contractor.

Although such instances of peonage were not uncommon, they are rarely found in American history books. The press seldom reported them, but in May 1906 a tragic incident in North Carolina triggered by immigrant peonage focused national attention on the phenomenon. Its exposé began when Giovanni Sottile, an Italian consulate officer in Charleston, South Carolina, complained to the U.S. Attorney in Winston-Salem, North Carolina, that some fifteen hundred Italian workers were being held in a state of peonage by their employer, the South & Western Railroad Company. Precipitating the complaint was the jailing of nine workers on charges of engaging in a conspiracy to murder the superintendent of the company's work force. A prompt and diligent investigation of the situation by A. E. Holton, the U.S. Attorney, revealed a different story. The jailed Italians, it developed, had formed a committee to meet with the superintendent to ask that the workers be paid back wages in order to feed themselves properly.

Unable to speak English, the committee spokesman resorted to sign language to spell out his message. First he pointed a finger to his mouth, then to his stomach; finally with his foot he scratched out the form of a box on the ground, meaning that unless the workers were paid so that they could purchase food, they would wind up being buried. The superintendent misinterpreted the signs to mean that unless the Italians were paid, the superintendent would be buried. Convinced that a mutiny was about to take place, he and a deputy sheriff quickly organized a posse and invaded the tents occupied by the workers. In the fracas that ensued, two of the Italians were killed. In August 1906, due largely to Italian diplomatic pressures, the railroad company settled out of court for $7,500 in damages to the families of the murdered men.

Of the 286,814 Italians who arrived in America in 1906, 4,692 were listed as professional and "miscellaneous"; 37,561 were skilled workers; 59,729 (mostly women and children) had no occupation; and 184,832 were unskilled. In the eyes of urban America, however, they appeared a docile and ignorant lot, unaware of the ways of the world—a stereotype encouraged by vaudeville comics, writers of doggerel, and cartoonists. The stereotype was due in part to the hostility directed at all newcomers during the period of heavy immigration, as well as to widespread ignorance about the native background of the Italian immigrants. In fact, most of the immigrants came from densely populated villages where, after a day's work in the fields outside the villages, the men congregated in the *piazzas* to exchange news, ideas, and gossip, and to debate one another on issues that were of common concern. By ancient habit and temperament they were individualists who, despite their lack of formal education, represented a variety of opinions and attitudes reflecting a cultural history older than that of most Europeans.

Regardless of how they earned their livelihood in Italy, all had to adjust and work at the jobs that were available in America. Teachers became miners; lawyers, grocery store owners; and many peasants, though often skilled in the arts of tree surgery, soil irrigation, and animal breeding, became bootblacks, miners and factory workers, fieldhands and common laborers.

Some came, too, with a tradition and experience in fighting for their well-being. Giocchino Artoni, son of a *contadino* from Emilia, started as a miner in Pennsylvania, but eventually rose to become general organizer in the Clothing Workers of America. Girolamo Valenti also became a labor organizer.

Most Italian workers, however, unable to speak English, were isolated and often abused by their own people and cheap lawyers. Adolfo Rossi wrote that "Until a short time ago American workers were jealous, hostile, diffident toward Italians; they in turn felt rejected, ridiculed and refused them jobs that were controlled by unions. So it was that when given the opportunity, they acted as scabs while the other workers were striking." Yet once the Italians found their own leaders, most of whom had Socialist or union experience in Italy, the former scabs fought to better their conditions.

In 1896, Ciceri Ercole organized the Socialist Union of Italian Workers in Houston, with twenty active members and eighty or so dues-paying members. The group held three meetings a month in which they discussed the principles of socialism and tactics to spread their ideas, particularly in Galveston and in Baton Rouge, Louisiana. The Union published *L'Unione Operaia—Organo delle classi Operaie Dello Stato del Texas (Organ of the Working Class of Texas).* In the minutes of one meeting, *L'Unione* reported that a Texan joined the

Socialist Party after hearing "a beautiful and elevated speech in English" by an Italian comrade, who pointed out the "most salient points of Socialism and the causes which push us deeper and deeper into misery," to which the Texan added, "not only have you Italians always been masters of science, art, music and exploration, but you will also be the chief agitators for the evolution and emancipation of humanity."

The meeting was closed with all crying out: *"Viva il Socialismo!"**

These were chiefly the men and women who had fled the oppression of Crispi's army that crushed the Sicilian revolutionary movement of the *Fasci* just a few years before. No doubt they remembered the words of one woman who had taken part in the *Fasci* uprising, who when asked what the demonstrators wanted, replied:

> We want everybody to work, as we work. There should no longer be either rich or poor. All should have bread for themselves and for their children. We should all be equal. I have five small children and only one little room where we have to eat and sleep and do everything, while so many lords have ten or twelve rooms, entire palaces . . . there ought to be fraternity, and if anyone failed to be brotherly, there would be punishment.
>
> Jesus was a true Socialist and he wanted precisely what the Fasci are asking for, but the priests do not represent him well, especially when they are usurers. . . . Our president has said that the object of the Fascio is to give men all the conditions for no longer committing crimes. Among us the few criminals feel that they still belong to the human family, they are thankful that we have accepted them as brothers in spite of their guilt and they will do anything not to commit crimes again. If the people were also to chase them away, they would commit more crimes. Society should thank us for taking them into the Fascio. We are for mercy, as Christ was.

Immigrants arriving at the turn of the century found a divided labor movement. Some were followers of Marxist socialism, others were Anarchist/Communists inspired by the European Revolutionary Friedrich Sorge. Still others formed the Socialist Labor Party. There were LaSalleian Socialists as well. All were echoes of European

*Vecoli, *Gli Italiani negli Stati Uniti* (Florence: Institute for American Studies, 1969), p. 383.

Revolutionary labor movements attracting mostly unskilled workers. In addition to Italians, members included Germans, Russians, Jews, Poles, and Irish—all immigrants fleeing from European repression. The skilled workers turned to unions led by such men as Samuel Gompers and T. V. Powderly, leaving the unskilled to the more radical elements of the Western Federation of Miners and eventually to the Industrial Workers of the World (better known as IWW or the Wobblies).

Among the immigrants were many men of ideas who took up the cause of the worker, including Pietro Gori, Francesco Merlino, Errico Malatesta, Giacinto Serrati, Giuseppe Ciancabilla, Luigi Galeani, Arturo Giovannitti, and Carlo Tresca. Most came from southern Italy: Abruzzo, Molise, Campania, Calabria, and Sicily.

In the early days, fighting the demands of harsh owners was limited to individual rebellion against a manager or foreman. In charge of some railroad workers, one Fulvio, a man of around forty, of medium height, with broad, Herculean shoulders, was typical of such foremen. His whole appearance was calculated to inspire more dread than respect. "His large apish head, resting upon a solid, bull-like neck, gleamed from a pair of eyes that recalled those of the screech-owl." This formidable presence pushed the men laying track, while they "sweated like sponges and melted like candles under the blazing sun-heat." Ordinarily, six or eight men with tongs were employed to carry rails. Fulvio insisted that four were sufficient. It was strenuous work and not without danger. One day as a huge rail was being moved, one man was borne down by the weight and the rail fell on his partner, cutting his foot badly.

"Come, come, that is nothing," the boss said.

"Are we slaves, beasts or men, sir?" inquired a man, his eyes flashing with anger.

"Whatever you like," replied Fulvio. "If you don't like the job you may quit."

The man muttered, "God, if I did not have wife and children in Italy!"*

The men returned to their barrack, which housed 150 men. It resembled a huge box turned upside down, with tiny holes for win-

*The account that follows is taken from "When the Boss Went Too Far," in Moquin, *A Documentary History of Italian Americans.*

dows. Cots nearly touched one another, some suspended from the ceiling. There was no floor but the hardened soil, which became a mudhole on rainy days. The air at night, poisoned by the fetid smell of garlic and strong tobacco smoke, "became as thick as Spartan broth." To one man the work seemed as child's play compared with "the torture of sleeping in this infernal box—sleepers snoring, the legions of bed bugs, men swearing by all the saints in the calendar, flies, gnats, mosquitoes, moths, a pestilent kerosene lamp, bats fluttering above one's head and on top of it all the suffocating heat."

Fulvio and his brother contractors bought bread that was often moldy, and cheap beans and bologna which they sold to the workers at high prices. Finally, the men's patience reached its limits: "Secret meetings were held under the leadership of a young Sicilian and measures were taken to dethrone Fulvio and his associates."

One Friday afternoon, a shabby-looking Italian came trudging along the uncompleted tracks with a hand organ on his back. The men shouted, "Eh, countryman, play us a tune." As it grew dark the organ grinder began to play the "Anvil Chorus." The men stopped working, picks and shovels were laid aside, and they all sat on the grass listening as intently as if they were hearing mass. The Chorus was followed by "L'Inno di Garibaldi." They all broke out singing.

Just then an Irishman, Fulvio's chief aide, came along, followed by Fulvio himself. With the arrogant tone of the despot, Fulvio shouted aloud to the organ grinder:

"They have had enough. Get away from here."

"No. More. More. More."

As the shouts subsided, a young Sicilian stepped forward, pale and trembling. Standing between Fulvio and the organ grinder, he said in a low, choked voice:

"You keep on playing, sir. We do as we please in this place. Let anyone dare send you away."

"You little shrimp, have you the nerve to gainsay my word?" retorted Fulvio. "You shall never do it again. I'll show you who is boss here." And he dealt the young Sicilian a powerful blow on the face.

It was the signal for a general attack. The outraged gang surged forward in a sold phalanx. Fulvio and those of his henchmen who had failed to take to their heels were dragged left and right, punched, and kicked until the cries for mercy died out.

As the evening sun sank slowly behind a thick mass of flaming clouds, the tumult gradually quieted down. When the moon rose, a company of men could be seen wending their way along the valley. Like dark, hushed phantoms they moved, leaving behind a trackless silence.

This kind of ruthless behavior on the part of labor agents and employers drew most workers to unionization; but, because the established unions would not admit unskilled workers, the mass of Italians gravitated toward the radical unions. Moreover, the rebellious, even revolutionary experience of some of the rank and file, and particularly their leaders, steered them toward unions of "advanced ideologies." The role of Italians in the cigar industry around Tampa, Florida, provides a good example of their involvement with unionization.

In 1908, the Italians made up almost 20 percent of the cigar industry's work force. Among them was Alfonso Coniglio, who credited his "formal education in radicalism" to the readers who read for the cigar workers at their workplace. He first heard the readers at a factory called Rosa Espanol. "It was a small factory but we had our reader. Oh, I cannot tell you how important they were, how much they taught us. Especially an illiterate like me. To them we owe particularly our sense of the class struggle."

The reader—known as *El lector*—was appointed by the workers to read to them while they worked. In four shifts he read the national news, international politics, news from the proletarian press, and finally extracts from a novel. While they rolled cigars, the workers listened to Emile Zola's *Germinal,* Victor Hugo's *Les Misérables,* and Cervantes's *Don Quixote,* as well as the works of Marx, Errico Malatesta, Kropotkin, and Bakunin. Yet it was not the lector who radicalized the workers but rather the workers who influenced the lector. One lector remembered: "They [the owners] say we became too radical, reading the news from labor organizations and political groups. We read those things, it is true, but we read only what the cigarmakers wanted us to read."

Much of the Italian militancy during the labor strife from 1910 to 1920 could be attributed to their leaders—Giovanni Vaccaro, Carmelo Rocca, and Alfonso Coniglio—all of whom brought with them the memory and experience of the *Fasci Siciliani.* Vaccaro was not quite thirty when he became an ardent Socialist and a militant leader of workers in Tampa. Rocca, as a leader of the 1910 strike, had witnessed the lynchings of two strikers.

The three leaders, however, were pulled in two different directions. Rocca worked with black Cubans "with ease" until, as he put it, "We became civilized," which was his way of saying that he had come to accept the prevailing prejudices of the South. Although Coniglio also shifted to a more conservative position, he worked frantically to keep disparate groups—Catholics, Protestants, Socialists, anarchists, and Communists—together in the strikes. But Tampa's business elites, city government, the courts, and even the Immigration Office, which began deporting active union leaders, proved too strong for the strikers.

The Red Scare of the 1920s finally wiped out the union community. The Justice Department, investigating Ybor City, concluded that Vaccaro "has very bad ideas, he is very revolutionary; he is one of those communists that cover themselves under the Socialist Party shadow to be free. Here in Tampa he is known by everybody to be one of the most active radicals . . . he went to work always with his gun in his pocket."

When arrest warrants were issued for Vaccaro, Coniglio, and Rocca, they fled. Vaccaro moved with his wife and family to New York City, never to return to Ybor City. Rocca soon followed, to Brooklyn, where he made a living operating a small cigar shop. Deportations and arrests weakened the union still further.

The rebellious spirit among the cigar workers in Tampa remained, however. In November 1921, after "twelve months of hunger," Italian women walked out, only to be quickly arrested by deputized men. Between an aisle of the men, the leaders were walked to a spot where strikers had been lynched in 1908 and shown a rope. The strike collapsed; none of the Italians returned to the factories. By the 1930s, the lector was replaced in all shops by a radio—and those who once listened to the words of Victor Hugo and Cervantes now listened to Arthur Godfrey.

THE MINERS

Philip Foner tells us in his *History of the Labor Movement in the United States* that the American Federation of Labor made it "exceedingly difficult, if not impossible, for these immigrants to become members of the A.F. of L." Special requirements were imposed, the most difficult being the initiation fee, which often ran as high as $500, a year's wages for most immigrants. "Little wonder that the foreign worker was attracted to the more radical unions and, in the absence of such unions, resorted to taking the place of those striking workers who felt no class bond with them."

If belonging to an established union like the American Federation of Labor was so difficult, belonging to unions with a less conservative leadership could mean running the risk of being shot, lynched, or deported. This was the painful lesson learned by the early Italian workers who had been brought to the mines of Colorado and Utah by labor contractors who recruited them in northern and southern Italy. By 1900, there were 6,818 such Italians in Colorado, enough to support a community newspaper, *Il Lavoratore Italiano,* edited by Charles Demolli, who had come from Cuomo in 1895, and Adolfo Bartoli, a Florentine who had migrated to the United States in 1893.

Both men came to America with a belief in "Labor's struggle to achieve the good life through Socialism." Bartoli had even praised Bresci, the assassin of King Umberto—a remark that made him suspect as an anarchist in the eyes of the establishment.

In nearby mines in Utah there were 1,062 Italians by 1900, mostly northern Italians. In both areas there were fraternal societies which in many ways were auxiliaries of the unions. Most of the members were from Trentino, Milan, and Turin, a few from the Tirol and Austria. In 1903, the United Mine Workers of America began a campaign for the eight-hour day, the abolition of company stores, a fair load of 2,000 pounds instead of 2,400, better ventilation systems, and a weightman representative of the union. When the owners countered by setting up a paternalistic "Sociological Department" to "aid" the workers, a strike was authorized. Of the 8,503 strikers, almost 3,000 were Italians.

As an excuse that violence was about to break out between various ethnic groups in the rough-and-tumble atmosphere of the mining towns along the border of Colorado and Utah, Governor M. Wells of Utah called out the militia. Tensions mounted. It was Charles Demolli who tried to defuse the situation. "We do not intend to fight the company with violence," he wrote in *Il Lavoratore Italiano.* "We have 303 who have gone out. Every Italian and 100 Finns are out. I am glad the militia has come because it will stop the violence on both sides, especially by the guards."

Demolli spoke to strikers, held parades with flags and music, and encouraged the women to take part. One newspaper gave an admiring description of Demolli:

> [he] is in appearance far from being the wild-eyed anarchist he is pictured by his enemies. . . . He has a handsome face, typically Italian. . . . His voice is soft and his manner suave . . . he can talk in their native tongues with Finlanders, Slavs, French or representatives of other nationalities . . . he is regarded as one of the strongest men and he is idolized by his followers.

The Salt Lake *Desert Evening News,* however, saw Demolli as an agitator, who was "no better than the average Italian fruit peddler; and this newspaper talk about his fine presence . . . is all rot."

As was usual when strikes broke out in the West, management in Colorado evicted the miners from the company houses. The union set up a tent city with soup kitchens for the miners and their families. Early in 1904, a striker was killed and workers began to arm themselves. As tensions mounted, Colorado's Governor Peabody ordered out the National Guard, which was determined to crush the strike. Pinkerton Agency spies sent the name of union leaders to the Italian counsel, with the request that they be investigated. If any criminal record could be found, workers would be deported.

Some fifty-two men were taken to the state line and told never to return. There had been no charges or trial. Others were arrested as vagrants while they ate at soup kitchens and were forced to work off fines imposed by court judges.

By June 1904, John Mitchell, one of the national leaders of the AF of L, called for an end to the strike at a national convention. Despite the opposition of delegates, the national union cut off funds, dooming the strike to failure. The strikers, predominately Italians, endured until October, in some mines until well into 1905.

There were similar struggles in the Iron Range of Minnesota, in West Virginia, and in Cherry, Illinois, where the burden and hardships of mining continued.

One Saturday in November 1909 while five hundred men worked below in the St. Paul Mine Company in Cherry, Illinois, a wagonload of hay coming down to feed the working mules caught fire. Timbers quickly began to burn, unnoticed by those who had put out the hay fire. The timbers continued to burn until someone spotted the blaze and ordered the ventilating system shut down to cut off oxygen. The miners below began to suffocate. The ventilating fans were turned on again and the blaze roared up. According to Philip Foner in *History of the Labor Movement in the United States*, "Miners, who were told of the fire nearly two hours after it had started, sought familiar escape routes only to learn that they had been changed. In the end 250 men died, making this one of the worst mine disasters in American history. The largest number—seventy-three—were Italians."

THE STONECUTTERS OF BARRE, VERMONT

With the expansion of the granite industry in Vermont in the 1880s, the workers—mostly of Scottish origin at that time—organized into the Granite Cutters International. Toward the end of the century, Italian granite workers from Carrara began to join them, following a long battle in their native town with Italian police that resulted in martial law. In the suppression that ensued, many left Italy. Those who came to Vermont swelled the ranks of the unions there, and by 1907 nearly eighteen hundred stonecutters belonged to the union.

When conflict arose in 1908 over the owners' introduction of new pneumatic tools, Moe Cerasoli and his cousin Joe became heavily engaged in union activity. The new tools, the union said, amounted to a speed-up; then, too, they were dangerous: the quartz particles produced lung diseases. Moe Cerasoli, whose brother and father both died of silicosis, described what happened next.

A meeting was called to take a vote on whether they'd accept the latest offer by the granite manufacturers, or whether they'd reject it. They voted to return to work, to accept the conditions. It seemed to be the Anglo-Saxon section that voted to go back under their terms. . . . It seemed a clean split. The Italians, in the vast majority, refused to accept that decision—called it a sell out. It wasn't exactly money, it was a lot of things besides that. So finally, they were going to take another vote, on whether to go back to work or not.

[On the day of the vote] the Italians organized down Granite Street. That's where the parade started, with red flags. The vote box hadn't been counted yet. Then the battle started. Mostly

Scottish. They defended themselves on the stairs by pullin' off the rails, wrenched them off. The Italians, driving up the stairs, grabbed the ballot box, then they came up through the streets singin'. There was music, a band, and the red flags. The most active crowd was anarchist. Anarchists were good people . . . most of 'em were blacklisted or driven out of the city.

The union survived and won its strike. Eventually, some owners refused to work without union men.

Understandably, when the Lawrence textile worker strikes broke out in 1912 and again in 1919, the strikers sent their children to live with the Barre workers—and they were welcomed.

THE TEXTILE INDUSTRY

Boston was the port of entry for many of the Italians who settled in New England. They first moved into the North Street area, where Cotton Mather once preached his sermons on the dangers of Popism and where Paul Revere once lived. North Street, like its counterpart, Cherry Street in New York, once had been a fashionable district. When the Italians arrived, they found the Irish already firmly established there. Gradually the new immigrants replaced them, not only in the North End but also in the most menial jobs.

In the years 1855 to 1880 the Italian population in Boston gradually grew to 1,277. By 1900, just twelve years before the tumultuous strike at Lawrence, there were about 18,000. Many were transient, "single men, who move from city to city with little inconvenience," we are told. No doubt these single men were in part responsible for bringing back word of jobs in Lawrence. But on a larger scale the owners of the town's textile mills made great efforts to attract labor.

The textile industry, woolens in particular, grew with the industrialization of America. The rivers of New England were harnessed to power the mills that sprouted in Manchester and Nashua, New Hampshire, and in Lowell and Lawrence, Massachusetts, all of which furnished cloth for the needle trades of New York. Lawrence quickly became a major center where the American Woolen Company employed 30,000 workers—a mosaic of European immigrants: 7,000 Italians, 6,000 Germans, 5,000 French Canadians, 2,500 Poles, 2,000 Lithuanians, 1,100 Franco-Belgians, 1,000 Syrians, and a sprinkling of Greeks, Jews, Russians, and Turks.

The American Woolen Company had launched recruiting campaigns around the turn of the century in the towns and villages of Europe, circulating posters depicting images of happy workers in picket-fenced houses, men and women reading books while holding bags of gold.

The conditions the immigrants found instead promoted a sense of deception. They entered a Dickensian world of treeless stone tenements, crowded four-story houses squeezed in one upon the other, rents so high families had to live in primitive communelike fashion. Salaries were so low the entire family—husband, wife, and children—were obliged to work a fifty-six-hour week in order to survive. Wages were $9 a week for men, less for women and children doing the same work. Understandably, the radical Industrial Workers of the World (IWW) had a large following among immigrant workers.

For many in America in 1911, socialism was looked upon as one road to social justice. There were over one thousand Socialists in political office in America in 1911. Leading Socialist intellectuals included Eugene V. Debs, a presidential candidate five times, who had garnered almost a million votes in 1912; the feminist anarchist Emma Goldman; Lincoln Steffens, who exposed the ties between organized crime, business, and politics; muckraking reporter, Ida Tarbell; and all the other widely read muckrakers who would reflect the conscience of America. Among the Italian immigrants were a large number of Socialists (fleeing the repressive measures of Crispi) who had some influence with their compatriots. This certainly was true in Lawrence in 1912, when Italians played no small part in the first major strike to be organized and carried out by the immigrant textile workers themselves.

The strike was precipitated by the action of the Massachusetts legislature which, presented with statistics depicting deplorable working conditions in the mills, passed a law reducing the work week for women and for children under eighteen from fifty-six hours to fifty-four. The owners, who had opposed even this modest improvement in working conditions responded by cutting the salaries of the women and children by 32 cents at a time when bread was 10 cents a loaf. When the women opened their pay envelopes, they were enraged; they began shouting, "Short Pay! Short Pay!" and ran out of the mills. All the festering grievances exploded: the firing of children if they were late three times; the tyranny of foremen who insisted that women sleep with them if they wanted to hold on to their jobs; the name calling of workers as "ignorant Dagoes" and "Hunkies." The next day, Italian workers smashed machinery, blew fuses, and walked out into the streets shouting, "Better to starve fighting than to starve working."

Within days of the first walkout twenty thousand workers were out in the streets. The looms in the mills came to a halt.

The strike was spontaneous, a case of the strikers leading the unions for the moment. The unions could only claim three thousand members and the IWW had little more than three hundred. Faced with the enormity of leading a strike made up of workers speaking fifty different languages, the local IWW leaders wired to the national office in New York for help. Within a week, the fiery Elizabeth Gurley Flynn, in the prime of her youth and her radicalism, along with Joe Ettor and the Socialist poet Arturo Giovannitti, converged on Lawrence. Both Ettor and Giovannitti were young—twenty-six and twenty-seven, respectively—and both could speak eloquently in English and Italian.

Giovannitti's immigrant experience in some ways paralleled the lives of those peasants of his native Molise. He was born in 1884 in Ripabottoni, a town that "continued to live in misery." His father was a doctor who existed by bartering his services for food. Giovannitti attended the Mario Pagano school in Campobasso. From his teachers, Giovannitti quickly absorbed their anticlericalism, their republicanism, and their love of poetry. In 1884, when Giovannitti was born, his home town of Ripabottoni had nearly five thousand inhabitants. By the time Giovannitti left for America in 1900, it had three thousand. He became part of that exodus which was emptying the towns and villages of Italy. He went first to Canada, where for a short while he studied for the Protestant ministry. There was a quality of the missionary about the man—one who watched his fellow immigrants' illusions about America evaporate in the misery of the work they had to endure. Unlike them, however, he turned away from religion and toward socialism, with all the fury of an angry poet.

Giovannitti, then editor of *Il Proletario,* arrived in Lawrence wearing the flowing black bow tie sported by poets and radicals.

Joseph Ettor's gentle disposition and calm air told little of the hardships he had suffered. He was born in Brooklyn soon after his family's arrival from Italy. As a boy he was taken to Chicago in time to see his father, a radical militant, severely wounded when the bomb exploded in Haymarket Square. At the age of fifteen, in San Francisco soon after the earthquake of 1906, he organized the debris workers, fought with Pinkerton agents, was often beaten, and spent time in jail. Nonetheless, Ettor's capacity for leadership, his physical vitality and easy smile, gave him the nickname of "Smilin' Joe." In the photographs left to us, he is a sturdy man with a thick head of hair, a large head, and striking eyes that quietly peer out at the world.

When he came to Lawrence, Ettor already had experience as a Wobbly (the radical wing of the IWW) organizer, having directed the stormy lumber mill strike in Portland, Oregon, in 1907 which ultimately affected the entire Pacific Northwest. In Lawrence, he quickly saw to it that interpreters were found for the various ethnic groups. He also organized elections of delegates into strike committees representing men and women from each mill.

The owners were determined to keep the mills running, since this was their busiest season. The strikers were equally determined to shut the mills down. Nearly a thousand militia and police were in the city, armed with artillery and Gatling guns. Mayor Scanlon in his meeting with a strike leader shouted, "I want you to understand that a crowd of bandits is not going to run this city. I will keep order here if I have to call on the whole Federal Army and believe me if today's riots are repeated tomorrow there will be a terrible slaughter. Why don't you go out there and tell those strikers to go home?" Governor Foss, a mill owner himself, complied, sending the militia to Lawrence. The Massachusetts authorities were so intent upon ending the strike that Harvard University gave credit on mid-term exams to those students who served in the militia. One officer leading the Harvard boys later wrote: "Most of them had to leave Harvard for it, but they rather enjoyed going down there and having a fling at those people."

The presence of troops angered the strikers, and many clashes followed. Scores of strikers were arrested; three were sentenced to two years in prison by a judge who believed that "the only way to teach them is to deal out the severest sentences." Yet the strikers seemed to become more and more resolute in spite of the hardships. Philip Bonacorsi remembered that: "1912 was the worst. It hit a lot of people. Things were really tough. See, I was ten years old. I remember I had to read the paper for my father. I remember the bread lines. On Common Street they set up a place for the strikers. They used to give 'em a loaf of bread and some salt pork. That's what you had to eat. Things were pretty damn bad."

It was Giovannitti, the poet, who organized soup kitchens and distributed food, as strikers formed larger and larger picket lines around the mills. Thousands of them tried to prevent managers and scabs from entering the mills. Many strikers were hurt in these daily confrontations.

On January 16, 1912, the *New York Times* reported:

BAYONET CHARGE ON LAWRENCE STRIKERS

Half a thousand militiamen, 300 policemen and a company of artillery were sufficient to overawe the strikers to-day. One of their number lies dying of a bayonet thrust, scores are nursing broken heads from policemen's clubs, and the long ash sticks of Battery C. Twenty-eight of the leaders arrested to-day have been sentenced to jail, several for two years, the others for one year, yet to-night the most enthusiastic mass meeting the strikers have had jammed City Hall full, overflowing into the square and the commons.

The three local militia organizations, Companies F of the Ninth and L of the Eighth, both infantry companies and Battery C, light artillery, were called out early when it was seen the police could not cope with the situation. Until awed by the show of arms at the Pacific Mills the strikers pressed forward when Capt Radlett of Company L ordered his men to fix bayonets and charge. In the charge several persons were injured, a Sicilian boy, Dominic Raprasa, being so badly hurt that he will probably die.

Tensions mounted still further when dynamite was found near Ettor's headquarters, causing the police to ban all picketing. Fearing arrest, Joe Ettor announced: "I may be arrested . . . but others will be here to conduct the strike, men more able than I."

January 21, the day Bill Haywood arrived, was a festival. Big Bill—all 240 pounds of him in boots and cowboy hat—had come to help immigrants who were scorned, and it made them feel in a curious way part of America. Emotions ran high; thousands met him at the station, some carrying roses.

Haywood spoke to them: "You are men and women who clothe the world. You are more important to society than any judge. . . ." In his words they heard echoes of their experience. "You all came to

America with the expectation of improving your condition. You expected to find the land of the free. But you found that we of America were but economic slaves as you were in your homeland. I come to extend to you the hand of brotherhood with no thought of nationality."

Then the crowd lifted Big Bill and carried him over their heads while a band played the *Marseillaise,* each singing in the language he or she knew best: *"Aux armes les citoyens."*

Haywood found energy in Lawrence, and also exerted it. Those who could not understand English too well, he spoke to in small groups, with gestures. He held out his powerful hand, he gripped one finger after the other. "Do you see that, do you see that, every finger by itself has no force." Then, closing his hand into a fist which lifted in the air, "See that? That's IWW." The crowd went wild, and Ettor and Giovannitti had difficulty preventing the more militant workers from storming the mills. As long as Smilin' Joe Ettor was present, violence was somehow avoided.

One evening, however, in the absence of Ettor, push came to shove between the police and the pickets. A policeman was stabbed; the police drew their guns and fired. Young Anna Lo Pizzo lay on the ground, dead. The next day martial law was declared. A few days later, Joe Ettor and Giovannitti were arrested and charged with causing the death of Anna Lo Pizzo. They, like the Haymarket anarchists, were charged with murder, a charge that could lead to the gallows. A cold determination took hold of the strikers. Even the skilled workers who had continued working in the mills now came out in the streets bearing posters which read: "We want bread and roses too." The air echoed with Joe Hill's songs:

Long-haired preachers come out every night,
Try to tell you what's wrong and what's right;
But when asked about something to eat,
They will answer with voices so sweet—

"You will eat, bye and bye
In that glorious land above the sky
Work and pray, live on hay,
You'll get pie in sky when you die."

The striking families began to feel the pangs of hunger as the strike dragged on. The Italian Socialists, borrowing from their European experience, devised a plan to send the children to workers' families around the country. Families in New York, Barre, Vermont, and New Jersey offered to take the children, and thousands of youngsters left, relieving the already strained food supplies of the strikers. The sight of the haggard, half-starved children appearing on the front pages of newspapers touched the hearts of many Americans. The owners, aware of the bad publicity, persuaded the mayor to stop the children from leaving. This brought a confrontation at the railroad station, where the police beat mothers senseless and clubbed children as well as the women who had come to take them away. Newspaper reporters watched mothers and children being tossed into trucks like so much meat. The sight so disturbed people that Congress called for an investigation of the events. A congressional committee invited Samuel Gompers, John Golden (head of the AFL United Textile Workers union), and Bill Haywood to testify. Gompers and Golden consented. But Haywood, having learned much about the value of publicity, sent sixteen teenage workers in his stead.

When the teenagers had their turn to bear witness, Carmella Teoli told of having her scalp ripped off when her hair caught in a loom. Others spoke of being forced to buy false birth certificates in order to work because they were not yet fourteen. They had to pay 10 cents a week for drinking water. They were docked an hour's wages if they came two minutes late. They worked overtime without pay.

The hearings swayed public opinion in favor of the strikers, and the mill owners, behind in orders for the coming season, now made an offer of a 5 percent increase. After a negotiating session, a settlement was announced: an average 15 percent increase, time and a quarter for overtime, no reprisals for any of the strikers.

In the Commons, almost twenty thousand workers gathered to ratify the agreement; bands played, and a group of strikers presented Haywood with a bouquet of roses. In taking them he said, "I want a member from families of all who have been sent to jail . . . to take a flower from it."

The crowd roared, many wept, and the band struck up the *Internationale*. Ettor and Giovannitti were still in jail, where Giovannitti wrote one of his first poems in English:

The Walker

I hear footsteps over my head all night.

They come and they go. Again they come and again they go all
    night.

They come one eternity in four paces and they go one
    eternity in four paces, and between the coming and
    the going there is Silence and the Night and the
    infinite.

For infinite are the nine feet of a prison cell, and
endless is the march of him who walks between the yellow
brick wall and the red iron gate, thinking things
that cannot be chained and cannot be locked, but
that wander far away in the sunlit world, in their
wild pilgrimage after destined goals.

CHAPTER 17

The Road to Sacco and Vanzetti

Quante vote a culumbo jastemmammo
che scoperchio sta terra 'e liberta!
La liberta, se ntenne,
ca i' no vengo li frutte!
vene lu pulizzimmo
e se li piglia tutte!
Si parle si' arrestato,
e . . . zitto . . . Ca pe niente
ti mannano a la seggia!

How often we cursed Columbus
who discovered this land of liberty!
But he took Liberty
because I don't see its fruit!
Comes the policeman
and he take everything
If you speak you're arrested
Keep your mouth shut . . . Because for nothing
they send you to the chair.

—CARLO FERRAZZANO, *LA MERICA SANEMAGOGNA*
(AMERICA SON-OF-GUN)

In Italy, socialism had come to mean social justice even for those who were not Socialists. As the historian Dennis Mack Smith tells us,

> Many diverse strands had come together in Italian socialism: the simple enthusiasm for social justice of Garibaldi, the republicanism of Mazzini, the anarchism of Bakunin, the Marxism of Antonio Labriola. . . . The peasants were potentially the most rebellious element in Italian society. Republicanism and anarchism were strongest in Emilia, and Italian Marxism was to center in Milan. But the most revolutionary part of the kingdom was Sicily. Socialism was already something to be feared and suppressed.

In the United States, the immigrants, including Socialists and even anarchists, eventually learned to work with mainstream unions. But in the early days they turned to the more radical unions almost by default.

Industry's leaders collaborated with government authorities to discourage unions by holding labor leaders legally responsible for any violence committed during strikes and demonstrations, regardless of whether those leaders were present at the events. As in the Lawrence strike, the cases ensuing from this tactic involved a dangerous precedent for labor unions—the question of indirect responsibility of strike leaders; that is, whether their words and ideas were sufficient to bring charges of criminal violence against them.

The first and most dramatic application of that tactic occurred in connection with Chicago's Haymarket Square riot in 1886, in which four German immigrants were hanged and three imprisoned after a bomb exploded, killing seven policemen, at a demonstration for better working conditions. None of the immigrants, anarchist leaders of the Knights of Labor, were present at the demonstration.

But more than martyrs were created in the Haymarket affair. A principle was fashioned there that led to the electrocution of Sacco and Vanzetti, and in many ways changed the course of Italian American history.

A few years after the Haymarket affair, in 1899, this same principle was again used to crush union activity—this time that of miners in Coeur d'Alene, Idaho. Although Paul Corcoran was not at the scene of the crime, he was tried for murder in the death of two men who were killed when a company plant was dynamited. Convicted for being "a participant in the conspiracy," Corcoran was sentenced to a seventeen-year jail term at hard labor.

In October 1910, during a strike of metalworkers, the *Los Angeles Times* Building was blown apart by a bomb, killing twenty persons and injuring seventeen. Two months later, John J. McNamara and his brother, James, two leaders of the AFL Structural Iron Workers Union, were indicted for the bombing.

On March 25, 1911, a fire broke out at the Triangle Shirtwaist Company in downtown Manhattan that galvanized the labor movement in its effort to convince workers that women as well as men must belong to unions that would look after their rights and safety. One hundred forty-five workers, seventy-five of whom were young Italian women, lost their lives in the fire. The Triangle work force of five hundred employees, mostly young girls and women, had been trapped in the factory unable to escape because (as was discovered during the investigation of the tragedy) its doors had been locked to prevent late arrivals from coming to work. None of the owners was accused of murder.

The Triangle fire was hardly extinguished when Ettor and Giovannitti found themselves in a Lawrence prison accused of murder in the death of Anna Lo Pizzo.

The charge, as in the Haywood and Haymarket cases, was "accessory" to murder. As usual, the prisoners insisted and had proof that they were elsewhere at the time of the shooting. Joseph Caruso, a striker, was also arrested and charged with the actual murder, and Ettor and Giovannitti were now accused of provoking Caruso to murder. In this case, all three pleaded not guilty. Again, labor rallied around the accused. The sum of $60,000 was raised by a defense committee. Demonstrations took place throughout the world: Australia, Argentina, Sweden, Cuba, and France. The Socialists in Italy nominated Giovannitti to parliament. Mass meetings were held in Pittsburgh, collections taken up all over the country, especially in Barre, Vermont, where many of the children had been sent during the strike. Helen Keller spoke in their defense. Referring to Giovannitti, she said: "The crime with which he was charged was, of course, a legal fiction devised by the mill owners and their agents."

In defending himself in Salem, where once men and women were tried as witches, Giovannitti told the court:

I learned at my mother's knee to revere the name of a republic. . . .
I ask the District Attorney, who speaks about the New England
tradition, what he means by that—If he means the New England
traditions of this same town where they used to burn the witches
at the stake, or if he means the New England traditions of those
men who refused to be any longer under the iron heel of the
British authority and dumped the tea into Boston Harbor. . . .
And if it be that these hearts of ours must be stilled on the same
death chair and by the same current of fire that has destroyed the
life of the wife murderer and the patricide and parricide, then I
say that tomorrow we shall pass into a greater judgement, that
tomorrow we shall go from your presence into a presence where
history shall give its last word to us.

All three were acquitted.

The publicity given such cases created a fear of anarchism and
revolution in many people and, of course, fear in many union leaders. When the crescendo of voices demanding the crushing of radicals rose higher still in the 1920s, and Sacco and Vanzetti were on the
road to the electric chair, Bill Haywood fled. From the S.S. *Oscar II*
he saluted "the old hag with her uplifted torch," and said: "Good-
bye, you've had your back turned on me too long. I am now going
to the land of freedom." He sailed for Revolutionary Russia, where
he died in 1928.

It was in this atmosphere that many Italian immigrants emerged
from that "docile and ignorant mass that was interested only in
making money" to enter American life. Before World War I, the
radicals predominated. Those who would work within the systems
and institutions would emerge later.

RADICALS, SOCIALISTS, AND ANARCHISTS

Italians who were attracted to anarchy were part of the European and
American reaction to the uncontrolled capitalism of the turn of the
century.

Italian anarchists found their inspiration in Carlo Pisacane, an
Italian noble who was killed fighting against the Bourbons in Ca-
labria in 1857. Like most men who read much into the French
Revolution, he concluded that political revolution was not enough—

total social revolution was needed. From Pierre-Joseph Proudhon, the French anarchist philosopher, he learned that "Ideas result from deeds . . . and the people will not be free when they are educated but will be educated when they are free." Such aphorisms gained many followers among the streetwise workers with little formal education. Anarchism had its strongholds in the urban centers: Boston, New York, Philadelphia, Hoboken and Paterson, New Jersey. The latter two cities were centers of the silk industry, which had attracted many weavers from northern and southern Italy.

Paterson's taverns were centers of education and information for many immigrant workers where two itinerant Italian anarchists, Giuseppe Ciancabilla and Errico Malatesta, often debated. Malatesta quietly called for the creation of an anarchist organization. He urged workers to "Organize. Organize." The young Ciancabilla, elegant, with an almost gaunt beauty that gave a hint of the tuberculosis from which he was already dying, spoke ardently, at times in a rage: "We are the enemies of every form of organization; we reject every form of authority. . . . Anarchists must obey only their own impulses."

The supporters of each often came to blows, and more often the meeting broke up with shouts of "We are united above all by our faith in anarchism!" Some meetings were held in Paterson, others in West Hoboken in the "Tivola and Zucca's Saloon," with huge crowds, in a back hall lined with red and black banners, listening to a few musicians play arias from Verdi's operas. La Signora Zucca, better known as "Mamma Berta" to the steady customers, tended bar, offering great pitchers of beer to the men and women who came to hear the speeches. Anarchism was an education for the workers, as well as a coming together for lonely immigrants. The saloons were crowded with anarchists of all nationalities—Germans, Spaniards, Poles, and Jews—who had come to hear the refugees from Italy.

There were, moreover, as many currents of anarchist thought as there were personalities. In addition to the luminaries Emma Goldman and Alexander Berkman, there was the the Italian immigrant Luigi Galleani, whose home in Boston was often visited by Nicola Sacco, and who became his devoted friend. Both Sacco and Vanzetti read Galleani's newspaper *La Cronaca Sovversiva (The Subversive Chronicle)* faithfully.

But Carlo Tresca perhaps epitomized the anarchist free spirit. From the day he arrived in America in 1904 (four years before Sacco and Vanzetti), he was a whirlwind of activity. Tresca was born in

Abruzzo to a wealthy family "in decline." At twenty-two he became editor of a Socialist paper, *Il Germe (The Seed)*, in which he wrote so violently against the clergy and authorities that he was about to be imprisoned for defamation when he fled, first to Switzerland, then on to America.*

In Philadelphia, he assumed the editorship of the Italian Socialist Federation of America's *Il Proletario*. His restless spirit made him break with the Socialist Party, and took him to the minefields of western Pennsylvania, where a razor-wielding assailant tried to cut his throat; whether the assailant was a hired thug or a jealous husband is part of the Tresca legend. Tresca in any case survived and covered his scars with a beard.

Tresca was a moving speaker. In Tampa with Elizabeth Gurley Flynn, with whom he now lived, he sustained the strike of the cigarmakers. He recruited miners for the IWW on the Mesabi Iron Range in Minnesota, where he was arrested as an accessory to murder following a funeral for a striker killed by local hired thugs at which Tresca declared: "Fellow workers swear with me: I solemnly swear that if any Olover [one of the mine owners] gunman shoots or wounds any miner, we will take an eye for an eye, a tooth for a tooth, blood for blood."

Soon after he spoke these words, a deputy sheriff and bystanders were killed in a confrontation with strikers in a nearby town. Tresca and the other organizers were arrested as "accessories to murder."

Tresca became a *cause célèbre*. There were worldwide demonstrations and protests; funds were raised for his and the others' defense. The prosecution, for lack of coherent evidence, plea-bargained a resolution that dropped all charges against Tresca and the IWW organizers.

The strikers who pleaded guilty were offered three years in prison with release after one year. Such confrontations created a tension within the country that was exacerbated with America's entry into World War I in 1917, when American nationalism was reaching a peak that stigmatized pacifists and radicals as traitors.

In the West the IWW was known as the "Imperial Wilhelm's Warriors" (referring to the German Kaiser). In Bisbee, Arizona, two

---

*In Switzerland, Tresca roomed for a while with Benito Mussolini, then an ardent Socialist, who had come to Lausanne to escape military service in the Italian Army. There, while secretary of a workers' association, Mussolini developed his talent for oratory.

thousand vigilantes put twelve thousand miners in cattle cars and dumped them out on the desert without food or water. A Tulsa *Daily World* editorial urged readers "to strangle the IWW, kill them, just as you would kill . . . a snake . . . don't waste money on a trial . . . all that is necessary is the evidence and a firing squad."

Tresca was under constant surveillance. IWW offices around the country were raided, and in October 1917, Tresca, Flynn, Giovannitti, and Ettor were indicted, along with Bill Haywood (among others), under the Espionage Act.

Both Sacco and Vanzetti would have read in the newspapers that in 1918, 101 IWWs were found guilty and sentenced to terms varying from 2 to 20 years. They would know, too, of the numerous deportations, and of Bill Haywood's flight to Moscow, of the vigilante raids, of homes broken into by wartime "patriots." Many of their own comrades had been arrested, among them Luigi Galleani in Barre, Vermont, Sacco's mentor and editor of the *Cronaca Sovversiva*. Not surprisingly, both men walked the streets at night armed with revolvers.

The Bolshevik Revolution in 1917, together with America's entry into World War I, unnerved many Americans. It seemed like a good time to crack down on the left, the Wobblies, and the Reds, many of whom were immigrants. Attorney General A. Mitchell Palmer began proceedings against thousands of "suspected" radicals and the movement he defined as "a distinctly criminal and dishonest movement in the desire to obtain possession of other people's property by violence and robbery."

The "Reds" were Socialists, Communists, anarchists, and anyone who opposed the war. Some labor unions supported Palmer's effort against immigrant radicals, many of whom they believed provided cheap labor that deprived Americans of jobs.

Nicola Sacco came to the United States at age seventeen in 1908, from Torremaggiore, an impoverished agricultural town between the regions of Molise and Puglia.

Sacco went to work at fourteen, but he did not "like most agriculture" and thus accompanied a brother to America. He came, too, as he said, because "I was crazy to come to this country." His early days in Boston were typical of any immigrant. He worked as a water boy, and as a laborer hauling paving stones. Later he paid a man to teach him the trade of edge trimmer in the shoe industry. He married at twenty-one and, with the birth of a son, had to work hard to support his family. He was a quiet man, with few interests apart from his family and anarchism and freedom.

Anarchism for Sacco and his friends was a core belief that gave life meaning. Countryless, tradeless, if they were asked who they were, they could answer, "Anarchists"—men who believed in human dignity, freedom, and justice. Anarchism made the Italians feel superior to the materialists who scorned them as ignorant and docile. It was essential to their mental and spiritual survival. It encouraged Sacco, both before and during his prison years, to become self-educated. He devoured all the books he could obtain, from Dostoevsky's *Crime and Punishment* to Max Stirner's *The Ego and His Own.*

Bartolomeo Vanzetti was born in Vallefalletto in Piedmont, where he went to school until grade six or seven, when he was apprenticed to a baker and pastrymaker. At age twenty-one, after the death of his mother, he too left Italy. His mother's death grieved him as though "I was burying part of myself," he wrote, ". . . and the void left has never been filled." Upon his arrival in New York, Vanzetti worked as a kitchen helper in several restaurants. Later, in New England, he worked in quarries, in brickyards, and on street construction, and helped build railroads around Springfield. He carried stones for two years for the building of water reservoirs in Worcester. By April 1920, on the eve of his arrest for robbery and murder, Vanzetti was peddling fish in the streets of Plymouth. Without family, his only entertainment seemed to be socializing with anarchist friends. Seven years on Death Row, for a murder and robbery he did not commit, gave him the opportunity to read Proudhon, Kropotkin, Malatesta, Emerson's *Essays,* and Thoreau's *On Nature.* Also like Sacco, Vanzetti learned his anarchism in America. The Brini house where he boarded was a center for anarchists. Mrs. Brini, who ran the house, worked in the woolen mills around Boston. Sacco was a friend and both were members of the Italian Naturalization Club. Their testimony during the trial tells us that Vanzetti often spent the day at Sacco's, helping to split wood and "speaking about many things."

Andrea Salsedo was a Brooklyn printer who, like Sacco and Vanzetti, was an admirer of the anarchist Luigi Galleani. It was through Salsedo's underground newsletter that Vanzetti received the not-so-reassuring news that Eugenio Vico Ravarini, an agent-provocateur, was posing as an anarchist, and that fellow anarchists were being arrested in the middle of the night without due process of law. When news of Salsedo's disappearance reached the Italian Naturalization Club, Vanzetti went to New York to investigate. He could do little for Salsedo, who was being held incommunicado in the private offices of the Department of Justice. Vanzetti returned to Boston, advising his friends to prepare for raids.

Sacco and Vanzetti learned that Salsedo had been provided with a lawyer who was a Department of Justice agent and that he had been tortured.

On May 3, 1920, Salsedo either jumped or was pushed to his death from the fourteenth-floor window of the Justice Department's offices. His body cracked the concrete walk when it hit the ground. His printer friend Roberto Elia, who had been arrested with him, was hurriedly deported, but not before he issued a statement attesting to the torture of Salsedo.

Two days later, on May 5, 1920, Sacco and Vanzetti were arrested at gunpoint while attempting to disburse and hide their anarchist literature. Found in Vanzetti's pocket was a call to a meeting which read:

Fellow Workers, you have fought all the wars. You have worked for all the capitalists. You have wandered over all the countries. Have you harvested the fruits of your labors, the price of your victories? Does the past comfort you? Does the present smile on you? Does the future promise you anything? Have you found a piece of land where you can live like a human being and die like a human being? On these questions, on this argument, and on this theme, the struggle for existence, Bartolomeo Vanzetti will speak. Admission free. Freedom of discussion to all. Take the ladies with you.

Both men were taken to the jail in Brockton. According to Vanzetti,

When he [an officer] reach my face he spit. Then he go back and took a revolver from his pocket, put out the bullet of the revolver and show me the bullet and then put the revolver—put the bullet in the revolver again and put the revolver like that (indicating) on the top of the gate and point the revolver toward my cell near where I stand. He maybe want to look if I go away, if I get scared and go away from the door. And I don't go away. I don't move. That is all, and he don't shoot, anyhow.

Sacco and Vanzetti were charged with the murder of Frederick A. Parmenter, a shoe factory paymaster, and Alessandro Berardelli, a guard, during a robbery in South Braintree in April 1920. They were tried, found guilty, and sentenced to death in July 1921. After almost seven years on Death Row, both were executed on June 1, 1927.

What is significant for the history of Italian Americans is not so much whether the men were guilty, but what the case tells us of the relationship that existed between those early immigrants and the rest of America. The Sacco and Vanzetti case was a crossroads for the Italian immigrants and their children. Significantly, it was during this period that some of the young and ambitious turned their energies to crime rather than politics or honest work as a way out of the ghetto.

The trial pitted two immigrant workers against all those of power and authority who felt threatened by the labor violence of the preceding years, which seemed to them to come together in a world conspiracy headed by the Russian revolutionaries. That these two foreigners were as intellectually and socially aware as the most educated American was another source of fear and resentment. In court before the sentencing, Sacco said:

I never know, never heard, even read in history anything so cruel as this court. After seven years prosecuting they still consider us guilty.

I know the sentence will be between two class, the oppressed class and the rich class, there will be always collision between one and the other. We fraternize the people with books, with the literature. You persecute the people, tyrannize over them, and kill them. We try the education of people always. You try to put a path between us and some other nationality that hates each other. This is why I am here today on this bench, for having been the oppressed class. Well, you are the oppressor.

Vanzetti was even more specific:

Not only am I innocent of these two crimes, not only in all my life I have never stole, never killed, never spilled blood, but I have struggled all my life, since I began to reason, to eliminate crime from the earth.

Everybody that knows these two arms knows very well that I did not need to go in between the street and kill a man to take the money. I can live with my two arms and live well. But besides that, I can live even without work with my arm for other people. I have had plenty of chance to live independently and to live what the world conceives to be a higher life than not to gain our bread with the sweat of our brow.

We have proved that there could not have been another judge on the face of the earth more prejudiced and more cruel than you have been against us. We have proven that. Still they refuse the new trial. We know, and you know in your heart, that you have been against us from the very beginning, before you see us. Before you see us you already know that we were radicals.

That is what I say: I would not wish to a dog or to a snake, to the most low and misfortunate creature of the earth—I would not wish to any of them what I have had to suffer for things that I am not guilty of. But my conviction is that I have suffered for things that I am guilty of. I am suffering because I am a radical and indeed I am a radical; I have suffered because I was an Italian, and indeed I am an Italian; I have suffered more for my family and for my beloved than for myself; but I am so convinced to be right that if you could execute me two times, and if I could be reborn two other times, I would live again to do what I have done already.

I have finished. Thank you.

There was more than simple anxious eloquence in Sacco's last words and more than angry poetry in Vanzetti's. Both men believed that they were being executed because they were radicals and Italian.

Judge Webster Thayer, a graduate of Dartmouth, Class of 1879, came from that class who felt most threatened by foreigners and "Reds." He said so, often and bluntly.

The judge's prejudices and character were attested to and summed up by testimony presented in the appeal to Governor Alvan T. Fuller by William Thompson, who made a motion for a new trial:

. . . he is a narrow minded man, he is a half educated man, he is an unintelligent man, he is full of prejudice, he is carried away with his fear of reds, which captured about 90 percent of the American people. Unfortunately all the half educated, uncultivated class joined in that propaganda. His categories of thought are few and simple—reds and conservatives and "soldier boys." No margin between them. No intermediate ground where people cannot be placed in the one class or the other. He knows only a few simple things; the country, the war, the reds. That is the way I size him. Not that he intended to be wicked, or that he intended to be bad. I think he thought that he was rendering a great public service. As he said . . . "I will protect the citizens against the reds. . . ." That is the type of man you are to think about, violent, vain, and egotistical.

Katzmann, the prosecutor, insisted on emphasizing the question of love of America, and with the help of Judge Thayer, the badgering of Sacco continued for several days.

Demonstrations of sympathy took place in America and throughout Europe, demanding freedom and justice for Sacco and Vanzetti.

The case was tried before a prejudiced judge, with an aggressive prosecutor who played to all the prevailing antipathies of the time, and before a jury chosen from a population that largely shared the judge's viewpoint. When Sacco and Vanzetti were executed, on August 22, 1927, there was good reason to believe that the case was just as much a lynching as that of the more than thirty Italians lynched elsewhere in the nation.*

ITALIAN LABOR MOVES TO THE RIGHT

Attorney General Palmer's raids against radical elements, along with the Sacco and Vanzetti Case, captured the attention of the American public and the Italian Americans who by the 1920s were assimilating into American life. In that process, many of them gravitated, like other immigrant workers, toward more conservative unions.

Most union workers belonged to the UTWA (the United Textile Workers of America), affiliated with the American Federation of Labor. In the fall of 1918, the union began negotiating for an eight-

*On August 23, 1977, Governor Michael Dukakis of Massachusetts declared the anniversary of their execution as Sacco and Vanzetti Memorial Day.

hour day; the owners consented but cut wages accordingly. The workers again balked and 32,000 mill hands walked out, shouting, "48-54" (that is, a 48-hour week with 54-hour pay). Most of the Irish and French Canadians continued to work, however, leaving the Italians—who were the majority—along with Poles, Russians, Syrians, Germans, and Jews, to carry on the strike.

On one side were the non-striking workers, supported by the authorities and the Catholic Church, whose leaders looked upon the strikers as part of the worldwide Bolshevik Revolution; on the other side were the great mass of non-English-speaking strikers. The laborers settled in for a long strike: soup kitchens were set up, a relief committee organized, medical services made available. Under pressure, the Clothing Workers of America Union sent two organizers to help, A. J. Rubenstein and Anthony (Nino) Capraro.

Capraro came originally from Sciacca, the town in southern Sicily where once the ancient Greeks had discovered an entrance to Hell. Capraro served as an apprentice in a Sicilian tailor shop, the intellectual center of the town, where he heard his first talk of socialism and anarchism. In 1904, more out of a sense of adventure than necessity, Capraro joined his older brothers in the United States. In 1908, after four years in America, an agent-provocateur framed Capraro on charges of carrying a concealed weapon. He was convicted and sentenced to three to four years in Sing Sing.

Capraro continued his education in prison and became, in his words, a "mature revolutionary." He was then twenty years old. Through a fellow townsman, August Bellanca, he became an organizer for the Clothing Workers of America (CWA). In Lawrence, Capraro organized relief, mounted picket lines, spoke to gatherings of thousands, visited the families of strikers, wrote, educated the young, and helped send children to less dangerous settings. He also begged for money, receiving $100,000 from other unions when the 1919 strike faltered.

But there were signs of the Italian community moving to a more conservative position. Angelo G. Rocco, for example, who in 1912 had been a young strike leader, was now a lawyer who tried to mediate the strike. Capraro denounced him, along with the clergy, as "the most bitter enemies of the striking mill workers." It was a Father Mariano Milanese who advised the workers to return to work. Yet Capraro was not part of his union's most radical element. That faction now was led by La Signora Cacici, of whom it was said, "She could arouse an audience to murder with her violent rhetoric."

But even Capraro's relatively moderate position was not moderate enough for some. On May 6, 1919, a gang of hired thugs caught him in his hotel room and took him for a ride outside the city, where they beat him senseless and threatened to lynch him. Capraro escaped by promising to leave town. Instead, he had his battered face and body photographed and returned to Lawrence to a hero's welcome, determined, as he said, to erase the humiliation.

The attack on Capraro unified the strikers, bringing aid from other unions as the strike dragged on into its fourth month. Later in May, when the owners tried to reopen the mills and only a few workers showed up, the strike was over; the owners conceded a 15 percent increase and a promise of no discrimination against the strikers.

Capraro's dream had been to unite the textile workers with the ACWA so that the whole industry, from weaving to the finished garment, would be organized in "one big industrial union"—the dream of the radical IWW of 1912. But it was not to be. The textile workers considered the ACWA too conservative and went their own way, only to collapse in a 1922 strike. The remnants of the textile workers were picked up by David Dubinsky's International Ladies Garment Workers (ILGWU).

The 1919 strike led by Capraro may have been the last truly radical strike among immigrants. The 1922 strike in New York and the Passaic strike of 1926 marked the end of a viable—or what the immigrants imagined to be a viable—radical movement. Thereafter they turned more and more to the conservative leadership of Sidney Hillman, Dubinsky, and Luigi Antonini, who proved to be more successful in dealing with employers.

Antonini, secretary-general of Local 89 and vice-president of the ILGWU, once complained that the Italians were either strikebreakers or militant radicals. But then, with his broad-brimmed Borsolino, flowing cravat, and silver-headed cane, he seemed quite removed from the mothers and daughters who worked at the thundering machines of the needle trades.

THE NEEDLE TRADES

In most southern Italian villages, young girls were taught the arts of dressmaking, crocheting, and weaving as part of their training for adulthood. When they came to America, they made up a good part of the labor force in the immigrant-dominated garment industry.

Before World War I, most of this work was done in the home. It was difficult to organize these widely dispersed workers, who spoke many different dialects.

The tailor shops in Italy where men learned to design, cut, and make whole garments also provided many skilled workers in America. A few, such as Garibaldi Cupaiulo and Jerome Giuseppe, became leading designers. Most of the men and women, however, became piecework operators.

Eighty-four percent were women, of whom half were teenagers. Three fifths were Jewish. At the turn of the century, nearly 70 percent of the nation's women's apparel and 39 percent of men's clothing was manufactured in New York City. It was there that the first needle trades union was organized; by 1909, the ILGWU had twenty thousand members and felt strong enough to strike for better wages and working conditions.

Together, the ILGWU and the Amalgamated Clothing Workers of America (ACWA) dominated the garment industry, which was centered in Chicago, Philadelphia, and New York. Italians played a significant role in both unions.

Anzuino Marimpietri, a young tailor from Rome, helped Sidney Hillman establish the ACWA in Chicago. Louis Chiostra, who immigrated to Chicago from Tuscany, helped organize health plans and introduced opera to the union's cultural programs.

Some believed that unions were becoming part of a system that oppressed workers. Among them were Giuseppi Bertelli, a leading Socialist, and Frank Pellegrino, a founding member of the Communist Party of America. In their eyes, the ILGWU simply collaborated with the capitalists.

The story of Angela and Maria Bambace reveals a great deal about the important role Italian women played in the labor movement.

Angela Bambace was part of that southern Italian migration that had gone halfway around the world looking for a home. She and her family first settled in Portchester, New York, and later in East Harlem, where Angela attended school. As teenagers, Maria and Angela traveled to their garment district jobs on the subway. The girls were often accompanied to union meetings by their mother, who carried a rolling pin to protect her daughters from suitors as well as from the thugs hired by owners to beat up striking workers. At the meetings, Angela and Maria listened to Socialist and anarchist orators and became aware of the potential in their lives through cooperative efforts. It was at one of these anarchist meetings (which often were part social and part political) that Maria met "Nino" Capraro (already an ILGWU organizer), who became her husband.

Both sisters helped organize the citywide needleworkers' strike in 1919. Despite the prevailing stereotype of Italian workers, even by some of their own leaders, as either strikebreakers or flaming radicals, in 1919 ten thousand Italian workers were organized in the mainstream needle trades union. Later that year, with the help of Maria, an Italian local was established and given the number 89 by Arturo Giovannitti, in memory of the French Revolution of 1789. Most of the Local 89 organizers were born in Sicily; the more militant, such as John Gelo and Giovanni Sala, were from Grotte and Trapani, respectively—both towns that had a revolutionary heritage from the *Fasci* movement.

Among the first leaders of the needleworkers were the Bambace sisters, who visited the homes of non-strikers and talked to families about the importance of unity, targeting key workers whose absence would cripple production lines. Their ability to speak to workers in their own dialect won confidence. And if all else failed, Angela, the more militant of the two, would say to her sister, pointing to a strikebreaker, "Don't talk to her. Punch her in the nose."

With the support of Nino Capraro, both women began to break away from the constraints of "the old way." Capraro ridiculed the attitude of most men, who wanted to deflect women from political activity and would keep women's hands in "tomato sauce and making gnocchi."

In 1925, when the Communists called for a general strike, Angela joined them in spite of the fact that Luigi Antonini decried "the revolutionary action." By 1934, Local 89 was the largest local in the United States, with forty thousand members. Angela Bambace, with her strong intuitive feel for the times, survived most of the ideological battles to become a leader in the American labor movement.

★ ★ ★

The unions played a large role in bringing the immigrants into American life. In New York City alone, there were 100,000 Italians in various unions: builders, stonemasons, bricklayers, carpenters, excavators, roofers. In some locals the entire membership was Italian. Six bricklayer locals had a total membership of twelve thousand, more than half of whom were Italians. Unions provided interaction with non-Italians, as well as helpful educational programs through self-published Italian newspapers and regular radio broadcasts. Arturo Giovannitti, Vincenzo Cacirca, and Vanni Montana were among the union leaders who participated in these educational broadcasts.

The movement toward a more conservative union movement no doubt reflected the desire of the majority of Italian immigrants simply to make a living in the best way they could in a new world they had yet to understand.

CHAPTER 18

Divertimenti: The Early Period

The first Italian immigrants found their divertimenti close to home, through religious *feste,* vaudeville, theater, puppet shows, picnics, wedding parties, and family games. They held family celebrations, usually on Sundays, to honor engagements (a special macaroni was served for such an occasion, *zitti,* which literally means "engaged"), birthdays, baptisms, christenings, graduations, and visiting relatives. After a sumptuous meal, the women talked among themselves while the men played card games: usually *tresette* and *briscola,* which eventually were supplanted by the American poker, or *pochero* (as it became known among the Italians). During Christmas and New Year's entire families, including teenage children, played for small stakes.

At most of the larger gatherings, there was music—Italian arias and songs from a gramophone or a player piano pumped by one of the children. Some celebrations even featured solo performances by guitar and mandolin players. Among the most-sought-after vocalists were the newly arrived immigrants, partly for reasons of nostalgia, and partly because it was believed that their voices had not yet been contaminated by American air.

EARLY MUSIC AND THEATER

With the exception of Garibaldi, no Italian political leader could arouse the immigrants' visceral attachment to their homeland as fiercely as a celebrated opera singer. Yet live Italian opera was the rich man's pleasure—popular with affluent Americans like the Vanderbilts and the Astors. Until radio came along, the Italians tried to satisfy their appetite for music with free band concerts (sponsored by Italian groups such as the Sons of Italy), the gramophone, and the most American of recently invented instruments, the player piano. These instruments were among the first American status symbols acquired in an immigrant home. The gramophone enabled them to hear the voices of their operatic idols, however imperfect the recordings; the player piano, by the simple effort of pumping its pedals, made it possible for them to hear and to sing along with their favorite opera arias and popular songs.*

The installment plan of the twenties was a factor in the instrument's popularity. But entertainment was not the only incentive for acquiring a player piano; for parents who dreamed of having one or more of their children become concert artists, the same instrument could also serve the purpose of providing piano lessons—something that only the rich had been able to afford in Italy.

On Manhattan's Lower East Side, the religious processions of saints and Madonnas became a springboard for amateur theater clubs, which performed in church basements on Sundays in Italian dialects. These early productions, tailored for uneducated, gregarious audiences, consisted mainly of melodramas and *commedia dell' arte* improvisations of character sketches with which the audience could readily identify. To promote attendance, these amateur theater clubs augmented the theatrical performances with songs and dances. Admission was free.

Partly because of the occasional crudities in presentation, and partly for financial gain, the theater clubs eventually moved their activities to hired halls and cafés, where the producers could share in

---

*It was mainly through the gramophone that Caruso became a hero to the Italian immigrants. Although Caruso lived apart from the Italian community, he never avoided them. On one occasion, a group of Italian miners from Colorado returning to Italy to join in the fighting of 1915 stopped to see him. They offered all the money they could spare to have him sing for them, since they could not afford the scalpers' prices for one of his concerts. Caruso refused their money and told them to return with as many friends as they could gather. He then sang to dozens of workingmen for hours.

the profits derived from drinks and refreshments sold to the audience. A typical evening in one of the Bowery's hired halls included a farce entitled *Nu Muoro che non e Morto (The Corpse That Wasn't a Corpse)*, presented in Neapolitan or Sicilian dialect. There were also comedies such as *Pasca' si a'nu porcu (Pascal, You're a Pig)*, followed by a grand ball in which members of the audience could participate. If there was no ball, the audience could count on being entertained by solo dancers, magicians, guitar and mandolin soloists, vocalists, and even prizefighters and sharpshooting rifle demonstrations.

The success of these amateur ventures encouraged professional actors and directors to stage more serious drama in standard Italian: plays by Shakespeare, Schiller, and Vittorio Alfieri. Because proper Italian was difficult for the majority of the immigrants to understand, attendance was poor. Generally, comedies and melodramatic potboilers, together with a variety theater similar to American vaudeville, proved the most popular with immigrant audiences.

The atmosphere of an old Bowery theater used for Italian performances was captured in the twenties by the novelist Carl Van Vechten:

> The theater is filled with all sorts and conditions of men and women, working men in their shirt sleeves for it is summer, women with black hair parted over their oval olive faces, suckling their babies, or with half-nude infants over their knees. Boys in white coats with baskets of multi-colored pop and various forms of soda water, passing up and down the aisles looking for customers, and you see mother and children, young girls with their young men, grey haired grandmothers, tightly bound in thick black shawls in spite of the heat, sipping the red and pink and yellow pop through long straws or directly from the bottles. In a box a corpulent gentleman fingers his watch chain across his ample paunch.

Audiences became as talkative and gregarious as they might at a wedding feast or picnic. Whether the curtain was up or down, they conversed with one another, shouted greetings upon spotting acquaintances and, when the curtain was up, addressed themselves directly to one or more of the actors on stage. Depending on what was unfolding, the audiences sang, wept, or laughed and hissed the villain with the same intensity they cheered the hero. The management seldom objected. Theater managers were known to keep the house lights on during performances so as not to inhibit conversations in the audience, which at times were louder than the lines being delivered on stage. From the audience often would come a warning to the actor playing the role of the husband that his wife was being unfaithful, or that the villain was about to kill the hero.

Occasionally, the drama was extended outside the theater. One reporter recalled that after an evening performance some members of the audience, angered by the villain's abusive treatment of the innocent family they had just witnessed on stage, gathered at the stage door, determined to beat up the actor who had played the villain. Only the timely arrival of policemen made it possible for the actor to escape unharmed.

Certain aspects of audience reaction to these presentations led one observer to perceive the Italian audiences as a chorus to what happened on and off stage. Giuseppe Cautela, a sophisticated theatergoer, tells of witnessing an offstage scene that might have been written by Luigi Pirandello during the years when the playwright was exploring his obsession with the lack of demarcation between reality and illusion. The scene took place during a play entitled *The Revolution of the Bums,* at the end of the second act, when "a pale young man comes like a ghost before the footlights." Addressing the audience, he explains: "My name Vincenzo Bello appears on the program as the author, but the work you have seen on this stage tonight is not my work." The audience is plainly delighted with the playwright's protest, though the play on stage is not over. After the playwright has withdrawn, the actor playing the lead comes forward with his defense: "I'm sorry that the play being given tonight has failed. I told the author that the work had merit but was not actable. We've done the best we could . . ." But the actor is not allowed to finish. "Yells, hisses, insults, popcorn, apple cores, candy and bottles fly on the stage, and just as a fellow in one of the boxes is about to throw a chair at him, the actor jumps for his life."

For realism in the ordinary sense, the Italian audiences cared little. Some critics were offended by the crude scenery of these stage productions. Writing of the set for a production of *Othello,* one of them fumed: "Desdemona and Emilia could be plainly seen through the aperture of the castle wall where they were quietly waiting for their cues to go on stage." Yet the same critic marveled that the

Italians in the audience remained unperturbed by such imperfections, and finally conceded that "for them the play was everything and they willingly imagined the palaces and battlements by signs and simple settings." Another critic congratulated the Italians for overlooking any defects in the productions. "Quick to respond to emotional situations, they do not need realistic settings and services to make them feel the illusion of the stage."

Apart from a lack of interest in the world of the arts, especially on the part of *prominenti,* whose cultural sights seldom extended beyond banquets and bankbooks, the explanation for the failure of a more sophisticated theater to attract support could be attributed to the fact that in Italy opera, not theater, was the popular art form. The theatrical tradition was secondary to the musical one, as expressed in popular songs and operas. The satirical singer Farfariello ("Little Butterfly") became the idol of the Italian community within a few months after his arrival in New York in 1898. His real name was Eduardo Migliaccio, and he was born in 1880 at Cava dei Terreni, a small town near Naples that was also the birthplace of Enrico Caruso. Migliaccio migrated to the United States at the age of eighteen and worked in a New York garment sweatshop until he was fired for burning a hole in a pair of pants. Bored with ordinary work, he began appearing at a café, the Villa Vittorio Emmanuele, singing popular Neapolitan melodies. One of them, *"A Morte d'e femmene"* ("The Death of Women"), he adopted as his opening song at every performance. His stage identity became associated with the name of the character in the song "Farfariello." But though credited with a pleasant baritone voice, his fame and popularity were based on character sketches, *macchiette,* a familiar aspect of the Italian *commedia dell'arte.* The character he personified with all its peculiarities and innuendoes (sometimes pornographic) was recognized the moment the comedian appeared on stage.

In one character sketch, Farfariello became the typical Italian immigrant with all his eccentricities, foibles, speech patterns, mannerisms, and hand gestures. When the *macchiette coloniale,* or colonial sketches, of Farfariello first appeared on the stage, they took the Italians by storm. "There they were, just as they saw themselves. They laughed themselves sick. And after they got through laughing it made them think."

One of Farfariello's targets was the Italian military clubs and marching bands that were organized in New York by superpatriotic

Italians, who held occasional parades through the streets of Manhattan "with their gold laces dragging under their heels, and carrying their sabres as so many broomsticks on their shoulders." The parades ended soon after Farfariello had castigated them with a sharply pointed *macchietta*. Some of Farfariello's other satires dealt with street cleaners, undertakers, firemen, bankers, policemen, and icemen.

When the stage attendant replaced the placard on the announcement easel with one with the single word FARFARIELLO, there would be thunderous applause—and awakened infants bawled aloud in chorus. Farfariello would appear first in evening clothes, sing his opening *"Femmene"*—and leave. On his return he would be transformed into a French concert-hall singer, with transfigured eyes and a new nose. "His gesture, voice, all his powers, physical and mental, are molded in a new metal," wrote an American critic.

He shrieks his vapid ditty in a raucous falsetto; he flicks his spangled skirt; he winks at the orchestra leader and shakes his buttocks; his bosom has become an enormous jelly. Again he leaves but soon the figure of an Italian patriot appears, a large florid person with heavy hair and moustache. Across his chest, over his shoulder and ending in a sash at his hip, he wears the tricolor of Italy. Farfariello paints the man in action; he is forever marching in parades; he is forever making speeches at banquets; he is forever shouting *Viva L'Italia*.

Next, he might appear as a Spanish dancer, or as one of the characters invented from the immigrants he had lived with: Rosalina, Patsy, Francisco the Groom. Whatever the characters, he always ended with that of the "issaman," the iceman, singing amusing folksongs of Italy.

Farfariello's characters were created from the Italians he saw in America—their behavior in their new environment under new conditions in new occupations. The immigrant he portrayed might be a street vendor, a ragpicker, an organ grinder, a pick and shovel man, and of course, the greenhorn who murdered both the English and the Italian languages. Farfariello was at once hero and clown, exposing the foibles of the more affluent and pretentious people around him and somehow triumphing over them. For the Sicilians in the audience, his satirical characterizations evoked their own Juffa, the legendary character who was the counterpart of Farfariello in their towns and villages.

A Farfariello song that became a favorite described the effect the New World had in undermining the Italian class structure. Titled *"La Sciabola,"* the lyrics toyed with the double meaning Italian Americans gave that word (which in Italian means "saber" but which among Italian Americans with their distortion of English was the word for "shovel").

La Sciabola

The new world is upside down
And the *cafone* here can smile
For the coat of arms had no renown
And calluses are in style.
In Italy the *signore* raises his sabre [*sciabola*]
When his sacred honor's hurt
But here the shovel [*sciabola*] is used in labor
And raises most dirt.

Farfariello's comic genius was also appreciated by Italians in Italy. The New York correspondent for *Il Seccoli di Milano* in Milan wrote:

Farfariello has created with words, music, costume and makeup the most delightful colonial sketches . . . ironic, serious or gay, joyous or grotesque . . . they have all come from the art of this young man of genius. From the little shopkeeper parvenu, decked out in the uniform of a general, the *cafone* who comments on current topics and argues with the American who discredits the far-off fatherland, the simple and stubborn spirit, gaily bizarre, or a little veiled in melancholy comes to us through his art.

Farfariello's popularity became a significant factor in the establishment of San Francisco's Washington Square Theater, where he was invited to perform by its founder. The 1,000-seat auditorium, which was in a remodeled Russian church, was the dominant cultural institution of the Italian community, the only legitimate theater in San Francisco to change its program every day, and twice on Saturday and Sunday. Admission was a dime (later 20 cents). The mainstay of the schedule was opera, but there were also Shakespearean plays and works by Dumas, Goethe, and Jules Verne, as well as melodramas written by the actors themselves. "Highbrow" and "lowbrow" entertainment were mixed in the same program and enjoyed by the same audience. On one occasion *The Barber of Seville* was billed with a championship wrestling match.

Heading the Washington Square Theater was a resourceful actress and impresario, Antoinetta Pisanelli Allesandra, a Neapolitan, who had first performed in New York's professional theaters as a singer, dancer, and actress, achieving such popularity that she went on tour to many cities where there were Italians. It is she who is credited with the discovery of Farfariello as a comic genius and with being instrumental in launching him on his career. By the time he had become the idol of the New York Italians, Allesandra had moved on to San Francisco and was working toward establishing the Washington Square Theater. Farfariello was happy to oblige his old friend when summoned to San Francisco. There he made as deep and lasting an impression as he had in New York. His *macchietti coloniale* were received with such enthusiasm that he was encouraged to take his act on tour in Italy.

Farfariello's great popularity could be attributed to the strong sense of identification his immigrant audience derived from his sketches. By reflecting the immigrant experience, Farfariello highlighted for the immigrants where they had come from and what they were becoming.

Italian American theater prospered through the 1920s as barriers between immigrants of different regions gradually dissolved. Farfariello used his native Neapolitan dialect in his impersonations but also attracted Italians from different regions. The same was true of Giovanni DiRosalia, whose monologues as the character "Norfio" steadily attracted large audiences representing a cross section of the *Mezzogiorno*, even though they were performed in his native Sicilian dialect. The Neapolitan and Sicilian dialects of the comics were generally understood by all Italians from the *Mezzogiorno*. Non-dialect Italian was used in classical dramas, which may have accounted for their failure.

Immigrants who could seldom afford to attend the opera settled for the *Opera dei Puppi*. As in Sicily and Naples, puppet shows were the cheapest and most popular entertainment on the Lower East Side in New York. Their mainstay was the continued battle between the armored puppets representing Christian knights and Saracen war-riors based on episodes from *Orlando Furioso,* the chivalric epic by the sixteenth-century poet Ludovico Ariosto. The most noted practi-tioner of Sicilian puppetry was Agrippino Manteo and his family, who migrated to the United States in 1919, along with fifty puppets, which were advertised as "Papa Manteo's Life-Size Marionettes."

Restrictive immigration laws and the burgeoning film industry wiped out the marionette theater. The only surviving practitioners of the art became the Manteo family. As the other theaters closed, Agrippino Manteo purchased their puppets and, with his sons and daughters assisting him, went on presenting "Papa Manteo's Life-Size Marionettes."

At Agrippino's death he was succeeded by his eldest son, Mike, who kept the puppet theater barely alive by staging performances in schools and churches frequented by Italian Americans. In recent years, a new generation of the Manteo family has continued the tradition by performing in folk festivals and exhibiting their pup-pets in stage sets at museums. Recalling the early days in New York, Mike Manteo stressed that the art of puppetry, so far as he and his Italian audiences were concerned, expressed more than make-believe. "They may be marionettes, but when somebody died and my father and my sister would put on a beautiful scene—with such sadness, my father crying, my sister crying—you could hear the audience sniffle too."

FASCISTS AND ANTI-FASCISTS

The rise of Benito Mussolini's party led to the exodus of the *Fuorus-citi,* as the anti-Fascists were known. The United States became the primary battleground (since all opposition had been suppressed in Italy) both for Italians who honored Mussolini and for those who opposed him. The rise of Mussolini began almost immediately after World War I, when the chief concern of the Italians was pending legislation that would drastically restrict immigration from Eastern and Southern European nations. In 1917, Congress passed a bill restricting immigration over Wilson's veto, and it became the law of the land. An unknown poet expressed the unhappy reaction of some of the immigrants to the new law:

We've dug your million ditches
We've built your endless roads,
We've fetched your wood and water,
And bent beneath your loads.
We've done the lowly labor
Despised by your own breed,
And now you won't admit us
Because we cannot read.

Seven years later, Congress passed the Immigration Act of 1924, which all but slammed the "golden door" and made it clearer than ever that non-Anglo-Saxon peoples like the Italians were not wanted. This was at a time when Adolf Hitler's *Mein Kampf*, with its emphasis on the supremacy of the Aryan race, was attracting disciples. In the conviction that the American people were basically Anglo-Saxon both racially and culturally, and should be protected from the threat of being submerged by "a flood of racially inferior" humans, Congress made certain that the new law favored immigrants from Great Britain and other Northern European nations. "New immigrants"— Slavs, Russians, Poles, Greeks, and Italians—were drastically curtailed. Great Britain, for example, was allowed an annual immigration quota of 65,000 people, whereas the annual quota from Italy, which for many years between the turn of the century and 1914 had sent in excess of 200,000, was now set at less than 6,000.

Contrary to the expectations of Italian political leaders in Rome, who had been encouraging emigration in the belief that with a smaller population, economic and social conditions would improve, there was little improvement. Testifying before a congressional investigating committee in 1920, Constantine Panunzio pointed out that although Italy had lost over 10 million of its population through emigration during a period of forty years, the nation's birthrate had increased even more than it would have under ordinary circumstances.

Fascism arose out of the northern and central regions of Emilia, Tuscany, and the Po Valley. As Dennis Mack Smith points out, the Fascists "obtained their money and brains from Milan, their thugs from Tuscany and their orators and agitators from Romagna" (Romagna being Mussolini's home) ". . . where there was a tradition of armed banditry which went back to time immemorial." As with the *Risorgimento,* it was the regions north of Rome that benefited from Mussolini's grandiose public works projects. The southern population was left to suffer high unemployment under Fascist laws that prohibited emigration.

The Fascists had no political experience, no constituency; they had only raw power. They were responsible to no one. In the smallest towns and villages, clones of *Il Duce* appeared, calling themselves by the ancient Roman titles of *questore* and *podeste*. Job and school admissions now depended on Fascist connections. The Fascist slogan, "Mussolini is always right," stenciled on the walls of southern towns, did little to conceal the poverty fascism forced onto peasant workers. The opposition was brutally suppressed. The great *latifondista* who owned huge tracts of land profited from laws that prevented peasants from emigrating or even moving to the cities. A Fascist mayor could order a peasant to lift his plow (which his mule dragged home at night from the fields) because it disturbed his sleep. Some peasants were so intimidated that they carried the plow themselves when they neared town. Others, however, were not so easily intimidated.

One morning a mayor found a pile of turds on his doorstep. The offender, no doubt an anarchist poet, left this note:

Qua la faccio
qua la lascio
merda al Duce
merda al Fascio

Here I did it
Here I leave it
Shit on *Il Duce*
Shit on his *Fascio*

All the forces of fascism were unleashed to discover the culprit. One Giuseppe Collura was arrested, given a trial before the special tribunal, and sentenced to the prison of San Vito in Agrigento. The Mayor-Duce, in a gesture typical of the petty arrogance of the Fascists, handed the prisoner 10 lire and said, "Buy yourself some tobacco in San Vito." Collura then took the money in his manacled hands and threw it in the mayor's face. This was not the end of it, however. When the prisoner returned to the town after serving his time, he was accused of having committed a murder he could not possibly have committed. Collura was tried and of course the Mayor-Duce came to testify against the prisoner. All that the accused could do from his cage in court was to spit squarely at the mayor as he passed him to take the witness stand. Collura was once again sent to prison. Such justice was typical of what the Fascists called their drive to stamp out criminality.

The Fascists had devised a system of fighting mafia and *cammorra* in the South. Whenever a crime was committed, the local Fascists would pick up an anti-Fascist or anyone against whom they held a grudge, accuse him of the crime, and before a special tribunal quickly sentence him. The method gave the world the impression that fascism effectively fought the mafia, while in truth real crime went unpunished and injustice flourished. A Socialist merchant in the province of Agrigento, who offended one of the strutting mayors addicted to *gallismo* (roosterism), was hounded out of business. His son, Salvatore Greco, known as *Ciniredda* ("Little Ash") emigrated to Virginia, where in time he became a union organizer.

Many of the alleged criminals said to be "swarming" to the United States in the early 1920s were actually victims of Fascist policies. Upon their arrival, these *Fuorusciti* were often shocked to learn of the staunch support for Mussolini among leading politicians, businessmen, and Italians in the land of the free.

Italians in America paid little attention to *Il Duce* during his early years of rule. A few went on record as anti-Fascist, but they were opposed by the many more Americans of all backgrounds who admired fascism—including the Catholic Church, which saw *Il Duce* as a bulwark against atheism and communism.*

Mussolini played on the inferiority feelings of the Italians with

---

*As an ardent Socialist in his youth, Mussolini loudly bragged of his atheism. In Switzerland, where he had gone to avoid military duty, he challenged a minister of religion to a debate, and in the course of it told his audience that if God existed, he would give Him five minutes to "strike me dead." Five histrionic minutes later the audience cheered him wildly. Even after he had turned his back on socialism following his ouster from the Socialist Party for being a "renegade," he continued attacking religion. "We detest from the depths of our souls all Christianity from Jesus to Marx. . . . Today two religions are competing for the domination of the soul and the world, one in Rome and one in Moscow. We [the Fascists] are the heretics of both religions." He also called for the confiscation of all Church property. Yet in his first public speech as prime minister, he invoked God and asked for His help. He also hastily had his two children baptized. Although he never made any other effort to identify himself with the Church, Mussolini consistently stressed its spiritual importance in Italy and cited Catholicism as "the only universal living ideal of ancient Rome." By 1929, he was able to accomplish what no previous prime minister had been able to do since the unification of Italy: the reconciliation of the Roman Catholic Church with the Kingdom of Italy.

campaigns designed to promote national power and pride. Fascist propaganda was steadily disseminated in the largest cities through Italian consuls. With the help of the American press and Italian-language media (including *Il Progresso*), Mussolini created an image as a strong ruler who had rescued his nation from Socialists and Bolsheviks and set it on a course of prosperity and efficiency. Various prominent Italian Americans, including Generoso Pope, the publisher of *Il Progresso*, went to Rome to be knighted by *Il Duce* as *Cavaliere* and *Commendatore*.

Thousands of Italian immigrants, with no real understanding of fascism, were swayed by nostalgia, pride, and a newfound nationalism. In 1935, Fascist sympathizers in the United States asked immigrants to send their wedding rings to Mussolini to help finance the war in Ethiopia.

Anti-Fascists in the United States were a coalition of old Wobblies, anarchists, conservative unionists, and progressive labor leaders such as Tresca, Giovannitti, Ettor, Capraro, and Giuseppe Bertelli, the Florentine Socialist who joined with Luigi Antonini and Vanni Montana of the ILGWU. Among the newly arrived *Fuorusciti* to join the anti-Fascist block were Carmelo Zito, a Calabrian, who started an anti-Fascist paper on the West Coast; Count Carlo Sforza, the former Italian Minister of Foreign Affairs; Giuseppe Modigliani, Socialist deputy and brother to the painter; Gaetano Salvemini, a former member of the Italian Chamber of Deputies; and Don Luigi Sturzo, a Sicilian priest.

Those politically aware Italians who had come to America decades before also played a large role in fighting Fascist influence in America. They ranged along every point on the political arc; most, however, were from the left.

The battle between supporters and opponents of fascism in America began in the Italian-language papers. The Fascists found their voice and support in *Il Progresso* and dozens of other papers such as *L'Italia* and *Il Grido della Stripe (The Cry of Our Race)*. Even such genteel organizations as the Dante Alighieri Society admired Mussolini; after all, it was said that Mussolini whispered Dante's verse as he copulated with visiting women on his famous desk.

Wherever American Black Shirts held demonstrations, the anti-Fascists, often led by Carlo Tresca, appeared to oppose them.

The confrontations took a nasty turn in New York when Fascist Black Shirts raided the offices of Tresca's *Il Martello*, smashing furniture and printing presses. In turn, Tresca and his men stormed meetings of the Fascists, heckling, brawling, swinging baseball bats (no doubt the American answer to the Fascist *manganello* or black-jack).* Over a dozen lives were lost. But it was the Memorial Day killing of two Black Shirts on their way to a Fifth Avenue parade in 1927 that demonstrated the convoluted political relations and violence among anti-Fascists as well as Fascists.

The incident had its roots in 1924, when Mussolini ordered the formation of the Fascist League of America. Its objective was to use the Black Shirts as they were used in Italy, to silence anti-Fascists and establish dominance over the Italian communities in America. On Memorial Day, 1927, two Black Shirts were killed in what appeared to be a brawl with anti-Fascists. Their knife-cut and bullet-riddled bodies were found on 183rd Street; in their hands were the steel-tipped whips the Black Shirts liked to carry. Ten thousand people turned out for their funerals; flowers were strewn in the path of the cortège, and the bodies were later taken to Italy, where they were buried beside other Fascist martyrs. Mussolini demanded revenge not only from Fascists in America but also from the American government.

The New York City Police raided Tresca's offices, destroying furniture and equipment and beating workers, but they uncovered no evidence linking Tresca or his newspaper, *Il Martello,* to the killings. Within a month, however, Donato Carillo and Calogero Greco, two anti-Fascist anarchists, both born in Sicily, were arrested for the murders. Carillo and Greco were followers of the anarchist group led by Galleani, who detested Tresca for including Communists in his campaign against the Fascists.

As for Carlo Tresca, his life ended in January 1943 when he was shot dead by "unknown" persons while walking home along Fifth Avenue and 15th Street. His killers were never found. The attempts to explain his murder are as intricate as the politics. Those who hated the Communists were convinced it was Vittorio Vidali, who committed the murder on orders from Moscow. The anti-Fascists blamed Mussolini, who had sworn to get Tresca. Others said Tresca was

---

*To put an end to Fascist meetings, Tresca and his friends developed a technique which consisted of provoking a brawl in the audience soon after a meeting began, at which point a Tresca aide would go to the telephone and summon the police and fire departments. In the ensuing chaos, members of the audience made a beeline for the exits. Eventually, there were no more Fascist meetings in Manhattan.

killed by gangsters, pointing a finger at Carmine Galante, who was involved in garment industry rackets and with whom Tresca had dealings. Given the circumstantial evidence, it would appear that the hoodlums Galante and Frank Garofalo, with the complicity of Generoso Pope, were responsible for Tresca's murder. But as Dorothy Gallagher points out in her biography of Tresca, it would be best to pronounce all three of them innocent until proven guilty.

Tresca's life and character were best summed up by Giovannitti, who said of him:

"He liked to call himself an Anarchist, and if that term connotes a man who is absolutely free, then he was an Anarchist; but from the point of view of pure doctrine he was all things to all men and in his endless intellectual vagabondage he never really sought any definite anchorage or moorings."

The anti-Fascist movement in the United States brought together Italian intellectuals who had left Italy as political dissidents with American intellectuals who foresaw the dangers inherent in the rise of Mussolini (and Hitler) long before they were understood by most Americans and the American press. Together, by their educational efforts, they sowed the seeds that were to contribute to the mass defection of pro-Mussolini Italian Americans as soon as Mussolini declared war on the United States. The dramatic extent of that defection was documented by the fact that although the Italian immigrant population in 1941 included more than 600,000 Italians who had yet to become American citizens, only 250 were interned by the Department of Justice at the start of the war as "potentially dangerous aliens of enemy nationality." So reassuring was this statistic to the Roosevelt administration that in October 1942, less than a year after Pearl Harbor, a presidential executive order exempted all the non-citizen Italian population (except for the few interned) from the restrictions imposed on other aliens of enemy nationality. More than all the patriotic rhetoric of the Italian press, which had formerly been pro-Fascist, the presidential exemption dramatized the government's confidence in the desire of all generations of Italian Americans to be assimilated into American society.

The anti-Fascist movement in America united those who had left Italy decades before out of economic necessity and those bourgeois, even aristocratic, intellectuals who left as political dissidents in fear of their lives. But in the end, if *Il Duce* gave some comfort to the hurt pride of some Italian Americans, the vast majority could not forget that they had left a land that treated them as dumb animals. Nor could they forget that once, in the name of Italy, the North had brought misery to the South, as now once again the North, this time in the name of Mussolini, sent cruel and senseless orders. If there had been some ardor for *Il Duce,* as soon as he went to war alongside Hitler it quickly evaporated, even more quickly than when Americans began regarding Mussolini as a clown once he declared war on the United States. Then, too, most of those early immigrants were seeing their children become Americans, and the future lay with the young, not with the old.

PART EIGHT

Assimilation

CHAPTER 19

Changing Images of Italian Americans

A civilization cannot simply transplant itself, bag and
baggage. By crossing a frontier, the individual becomes a
foreigner. He "betrays" his own civilization by leaving it
behind.

—FERNAND BRAUDEL, *THE MEDITERRANEAN,* VOL. I.

The inner conflict Italians experienced in becoming Italian Americans, and eventually Americans, was evident in the changing
character and image of the immigrants—as perceived by themselves,
and by the world around them. This conflict was evident also in the
changing roles of women in and out of the family, as well as in the
effects of two world wars.

IRISH CARDINALS—ITALIAN *FESTE*—AND THE WORD OF GOD

"The great mass of the immigrants," writes Silvano M. Tomasi, a
noted Church historian, "brought with them to the United States a

cautious suspicion from their country, a mistrust . . . a total lack of confidence in the institutions of the state and the Church." That "mistrust" was based, in part, on the papacy's opposition to the unification of Italy as well as its support of Mussolini. The longstanding tradition of anticlericalism was especially virulent among males; however, the Church continued to be nourished by women. A few Italian clerics, like Bishop Scalabrini and Mother Cabrini, sought to rectify this situation in the United States by providing whatever assistance they could to the immigrants. But the problem was exacerbated by the dominance of Irish Catholicism, which bore little resemblance to the Catholicism practiced in Italy (particularly in the *Mezzogiorno*). For their part, the Irish priests felt they could not approve of a people who so glorified the Virgin Mary and staged gaudy religious festivals that smacked more of paganism than piety.

Rather than provide the immigrants with Italian priests, the same bishop (Scalabrini) sent Irish priests to Rome for training. This policy had dire consequences for the Church and for the immigrants.

With American roots that dated back to 1830, the Irish had attained power in the Catholic Church that they had little desire to share with new immigrants, especially Italians. As far as the Irish were concerned, the Italians who had sided with Garibaldi, an enemy of the papacy, were sinfully anticlerical.

Although the Irish were more advanced economically and socially than any of the other new immigrants, many were still unskilled laborers who found themselves competing with Italian laborers willing to work for substandard wages. The two peoples seemed to be irreconcilable, especially in the great disparity in their concept and practice of Catholicism. While both groups considered themselves Roman Catholic, the Irish adhered strictly to the Church's official liturgy and doctrine and revered their clergy, whereas the southern Italians showed little respect for the clergy and practiced a folk religion that had changed little since the birth of Christ.

The southern Italian religion was based on awe, fear, and reverence for the supernatural, "a fusion of Christian and pre-Christian elements of animism, polytheism and sorcery along with the sacraments prescribed by the Church." These Italians believed in the power of the evil eye and in spells cast by witches that could kill a person or destroy a crop. To protect themselves against malevolent forces, a peasant family might employ an exorcist when prayers to the local patron saint, the central figure in any southern village, went unheeded.

Only as a last resort did the villagers turn to the clergy for help. Village priests were generally regarded as parasites, demanding money of the poor while being supported by the government. Then, too, the village priest often was badly educated, limited in intelligence, and poor as a church mouse.

Yet for all their anticlerical attitudes, the southern Italians were a deeply religious people. Southern Italian antipathy toward the priesthood was largely fueled by men who seldom attended church except when their presence was required for a baptism, wedding, or funeral. The men who went to church regularly were usually those of advanced age who had begun thinking about the pending confrontation with their maker. Others were generally scornful of all priests, viewing them as both corrupting and corruptible. "If you want to be rich," an adage advised, "become a thief, a policeman, or a priest." An enduring belief in God deterred the men from preventing their wives and children from attending church; however, they did object when their wives developed "too close" an attachment.

Overriding all other criticism of the Italian clergy was the belief that the village priest almost invariably sided with the gentry. The animosity between priests and villagers was such that the village priest rarely followed his parishioners to America.

The initial failure of the American Catholic Church to reach out to the Italian immigrants gave rise to the general impression that this Church was even more indifferent to their needs than the Church in Italy had been.

The great differences between Irish and Italian worship created hostility on both sides. In contrast to the formal Irish Catholic services, the Italian mass was one of intimate and joyous celebration. An Irish friend of Richard Gambino, the historian, told him that his parents were "shocked and aghast" at the Italian women in their church who kissed and caressed statues of religious figures. Father Thomas Hilferty, an Irish priest assigned to an Italian parish in Philadelphia, found the Italian attitude toward religious statues "a startling contrast" to that of his fellow Irish, who regarded the statues as symbols. To the Italian worshippers, they were far more than that: "they would actually get up and talk to the statues," marveled Hilferty. "They would say, 'Anthony, my son's been involved with bad people. You either straighten this situation or I am not going to pray to you.' The Irish never did that."

There was also a difference in how the Italian and Irish worshippers viewed sin. For the Irish, a mortal sin that went unconfessed placed one's soul in jeopardy. The Italians in contrast viewed God as an all-understanding, compassionate, forgiving being.

Although it was the policy of the Catholic Church to receive all immigrant Catholics with open arms (if only to prevent them from being converted to the Protestant faith), the Italians rarely received this welcome. Many of the same factors that hindered their Americanization prevented the immigrants' assimilation into the American Catholic Church. They were also affected by the fact that, unlike the other immigrant groups (such as the Poles, who arrived with their families intact and their village priests in tow), the first Italian immigrants were mainly fathers and sons who came with the expectation of returning to Italy after a few years. Poles and other Slavic Catholics benefited immediately from the network of parishes and parochial schools that not only made the Church a central feature of their community life, but also contributed to their assimilation into American society.

Venomous rhetoric prolonged the hostility between Irish and Italian Catholics, despite the efforts of Bishop Scalabrini and Mother Cabrini. The hostility was especially strong in neighborhoods where Italians had replaced Irish and Germans. Few pastors were equipped to deal with a poor congregation that did not understand English.

One of the most vocal advocates for the Italian Catholics was Reverend Aurelio Palmieri, a scholarly Augustian priest who had lived in the United States for many years. Palmieri held the Catholic Church in America responsible for the immigrants' negative attitudes and for their failure to attend services in large numbers. He was especially critical of the Church's practice of assigning Irish or German priests to congregations that were largely Italian, and of the policy of segregating Italian children in some parochial schools. "Is it any wonder," he wrote, "that our immigrants turn their backs to a church which reserves for them insults and disgust . . . and which sprays in their faces the gall of slander?"

Some churches sat the Italians with the blacks in rear pews. Others told worshippers bluntly that they were not wanted and even denounced them as "Dagoes."

Part of the "Italian Problem" derived from the Church's failure to recognize that far from being an anarchistic people, the great majority of Italian immigrants were of the conservative southern peasantry. It was this conservatism that caused them to resist changing their traditions.

That anticlericalism among Italians existed in America was undeniable. No one was more aware of that than the comparatively few clerics who had, independently of their Italian congregations, joined the great migration to America. All too often they were badly treated by their compatriots, especially by northern Italians, who were far more militant in their anticlericalism than were Italians from the South. Rudolph Vecoli records some typical instances: Priests arriving in Chicopee, Kansas, were greeted by coal miners with a volley of rocks and rotten vegetables; and in Barre, Vermont, stoneworkers drove an Italian priest out of town. These were by no means isolated episodes.

Ironically, it took an edict from Rome, issued by Pope Leo XIII in 1899, to persuade the American Catholic hierarchy to be more responsive to the needs of the various nationality groups under its jurisdiction. No Italians were then admitted into the Irish-dominated hierarchy, but the Church did begin permitting "national" (i.e., ethnic) parishes, and to some extent even assisted in their development. Within the course of a single decade, seventeen Italian churches were established in Buffalo alone.

By the end of World War I there were between five and six hundred Italian parishes in operation, some of which included schools. These parishes gave the immigrants the opportunity to practice their religion, with *feste* and processions, as they had in Italy. The Italian ethnic churches took the position that the interests of democracy were best served when immigrants were permitted to follow their own customs of worship; that the immigrants could achieve Americanization without any Church intervention.

Nonetheless, the Irish hierarchy continued to ensure that priests assigned to national parishes came from northern Italy, since they were likely to be more critical of the "paganistic" Catholicism practiced by their southern Italian brethren.

The Protestant churches were not much more welcoming to the Italians. In their Calvinistic conviction that the poverty of the great mass of immigrants was a sign of unworthiness, the Presbyterians could declare: "With the Slavs and the Italians we are receiving into our nation the Continental idea of Sunday as a day of pleasure and recreation, the idea of socialist government, the idea of community property and the idea of paganism in religion. These ideas are antagonistic to those incorporated in our civilization and free institution, our American ideals being for the most part derived from our Protestant faith."

However, this declaration did not deter the Presbyterians from their willingness "to preach God's word to the new immigrants." Norman Thomas, who developed his Socialist faith while serving as a Presbyterian minister in Harlem, believed that "the Italian needs to be Americanized as a pure Christian." Methodists, Baptists, Episcopalians, and other Protestants soon developed similar plans for the souls and minds of the Italians, who, as they imagined from their difficulties with the Catholic Church, were ripe for conversion to "more American" forms of Christianity. The description in their evangelist literature of the Italians as "Dagoes who drink excessively, live in a state of filth, and use the knife on the slightest provocation . . . with gusty passions both of sex and temper" only increased the zeal of the missionaries, who went forth to do battle with the forces of sin affecting the Italians in the big-city slums, which they termed "cesspools of vice."

Every major Protestant denomination joined the battle for converts, with increasing expenditures of money, time, and energy. Wherever there were Italian settlements, they waged their evangelical mission—under tents, in settlement houses, churches, and missionary centers. Seeing Italian men as indifferent to all religions, they initially focused on the women, who, once converted, would presumably convince their husbands and children to become Protestants.

When evangelism produced too few converts, the Protestants changed their strategy (though not their ambitions), offering gifts of food in exchange for church attendance. Other allurements included child care, nurseries, band concerts, and English-language classes. Children, instructed by their parents, would attend as many as three different denominational services in order to provide the family with enough of the free handouts. When three Protestant missions became suspicious and compared notes, they discovered that 75 percent of the Italians belonged to all three parishes. Constantine Pannuzio, who by 1917 had become a Methodist minister in the Boston area, after observing the activity of a fellow minister, concluded, "The Italian situation in this city [New York] is a big farce."

Some Italians, after dealing with Protestant missionaries, social workers, teachers, and ministers, did become convinced that Protestantism was a surer road than Catholicism to assimilation. But they were relatively few. For all of the Protestant efforts, fewer than 21,000 Italians converted. For most southern Italians, becoming Protestant was seen as betraying one's heritage.

To counteract the proselytizing campaigns of the Protestants, the Catholic Church stepped up its social services. In New York, a branch of the St. Raphael Society—taking its cue from Bishop Scalabrini and Mother Cabrini's activities—established nurseries, evening schools, sewing classes, theater groups, reading rooms, hospitals, orphanages, and a home for new immigrants. "Through such forms of assistance," Vecoli tells us, "the Italian priests sought not only to offset the material inducements offered by the Protestant missions, but also to refute the socialist charge that they were the natural allies of the rich."

By 1918, twenty-six religious orders consisting of missionary priests trained in Italy at Bishop Scalabrini's instigation had succeeded, in various parts of the nation, in establishing Italian parishes with schools staffed by Italian-speaking priests and teachers. Yet for all such valiant efforts, the Italian immigrant population continued in the main to be wary of the American Catholic Church. The hostility of the Irish Catholics toward the Italians had become too flagrant for them to overlook. Only the children and the grandchildren, in their instinctive effort to become assimilated, were willing to join mainstream American Catholicism. Perhaps the most concrete evidence of that is the high rate of intermarriage between Italian and Irish Catholics. However, intermarriage came too late to alleviate the breach between the American Church and the Italian immigrants. Statistics show that at the end of World War I, in 1918, less than one third of the 600,000 Italians in New York City were practicing Catholics. The situation did not improve with time; fifty-five years later, another survey showed that whereas 91 to 100 percent of the Irish attended mass every Sunday, for the Italians the percentage varied from a low of 27 on Sundays to a high of 76 percent on holidays. There were other indications of the Church's failure to exert its influence on Italian Americans, particularly the decreasing birth rate among Italian American women of all generations. By 1965, 68 percent were using some form of birth control not prescribed by the Church. The village priest in the South of Italy who routinely encouraged all men to marry with the admonition, "Are you going to remain a capon all your life?" would have been appalled.

Although the American way was making significant inroads into traditional Italian life, the immigrants continued to remain faithful to their own methods of worshipping God, a situation that persuaded the Irish leaders of the Catholic Church to lock the Italians out of any position of influence. As a result, Italian Catholics were unable to rely on the Church as an institution that could be counted on to act in their behalf; they remained what they had been on arrival—solitary Christians who "faced all other challenges of American life alone."*

Much later, the great changes brought about by Pope John XXIII during his brief reign (1958–63) still did not affect the Italian immigrant population; but undoubtedly they influenced the numerous children of the immigrants, who by the 1960s were moving up the economic ladder, acquiring enough affluence and self-confidence to question the dictates of the more conservative popes who followed. When the Apostolic Delegate to the United States rescinded the right of women to play a role in the communion ceremony, an angry nun, who may well have reflected the outrage of many an Italian American daughter, remarked that "a woman could carry the body of Jesus in her womb for nine months but is not deemed worthy to hold the Eucharist in her hands for even a few minutes during mass."† The great majority of parishioners also reacted to the severe dictates against any form of birth control by no longer attending services.

How the Italian ethnic churches throughout the country reacted to the controversies that stemmed from the reign of Pope John is not known. But there is ample evidence to indicate that during the late forties and early fifties, when great numbers of the American-born children of immigrants were reaching their majority, the Italian ethnic churches around the nation were flourishing, despite the negative attitudes toward them of the leadership in the American Catholic Church.‡

---

*It was not until 1982 that the first Italian American cardinal, Joseph L. Bernadin, the son of an immigrant stonecutter, was appointed by Pope John Paul II, replacing the autocratic Irish American cardinal John Patrick Cody. Bernadin was born in Columbia, South Carolina, the eldest son of parents from Fiera di Primiero in the northern Italian region of Trento. In the language of the Church, he is seen as "diligent, accessible, a seeker of consensus."

†*The New York Times*, October 10, 1982.

‡A candid criticism of the Catholic Church's attitude came with the publication in 1975 of Silvano Tomasi's *Piety and Power*. In the Preface, Tomasi, a highly respected Italian

In his book *The Madonna of 115th Street*, Robert Orsi, a university professor of religious studies who was once an altar boy in a North Bronx Italian parish, described his experiences:

> Our church was a Franciscan one and in all seasons the monks could be seen walking about the Bronx neighborhood in brown sandals and capes. Most of these men were Italian Americans, born in places like Jersey City and Union City, but some came from Italy. . . . These older monks fascinated me. My father told me stories about their special powers and histories; one was said to be an exorcist, another a visionary. They had names like Pacifica and Ludovico, and contact with them was mainly as their altar boy at very early morning Masses. They were rough with me, knuckling me in the head with hard, calloused knuckles, roughly adjusting my surplice, treating me in fact like a beloved but intractable barnyard animal; they were also the ones to go and get me coffee and rolls in the mornings when I served the six o'clock mass. . . .
>
> The nuns who taught us were members of an Italian American order, brought especially to the neighborhood in the late 1940s by an Italian pastor, a smart and experienced man, who had no intention of having his people's children exposed to the prejudices of Irish American nuns. That is not to say that our nuns were without prejudices. They were tough women, rough and determined in their labor of shaping the matters that came into their thick hands.

Also imprinted in Orsi's memory were the funeral services he attended several days a week:

> These were not quiet and dignified affairs. The old Italians in the neighborhood wanted to make sure that Jesus, Mary and the

American historian and a member of the Jesuit Order, characterized the American Catholic Church's administration of immigrant Catholics as a flagrant case of ecclesiastical colonialism "for having distorted the interpretation of American Catholicism by deliberately ignoring the fact that the majority of American Catholics are either immigrants or children and grandchildren of immigrants, whose origins are not Anglo-Saxon. . . . The immigrant groups, which provided the amazing growth and vitality of American Catholicism, created parishes, schools, orphanages, hospitals and other institutions which reflected the native environment and the many cultural traditions . . . of their country of origin. The variety of ethnic congregations within American Catholicism, however, was seen as a threat to its unity, as an anti-American label or as a useless complication."

saints heard what they were thinking and feeling. . . . Through-out the Masses, people moaned and screamed and got up con-stantly to touch and talk to the casket. But the real time of sor-row came at the end of the Mass, as the priest and through him the rest of the world that was not related to the dead person said goodbye. After this, the family would be on their own for a time. Old women threw themselves onto the casket, trying to prevent it from leaving the church; men tore at the ends of their handker-chiefs with their teeth. Then the priest intoned what was really a farewell: "May the angels take you into paradise, may the mar-tyrs welcome you on your way . . ." At this moment, the under-takers, dressed delicately in pinstripes, wearing gray gloves and walking with a stern and detached compassion, would appear from the shadows of the side aisles and move toward the coffin. The priest and the altar boys, at least one of the boys inevitably in tears . . . turned away. Strong hands would grasp the most distraught of the women. The coffin was wheeled out. And I went back to school.

Although the Italian ethnic parishes were generally successful, there were not enough of them to deter the Catholic Church's cam-paign to impose on the children of immigrants a style of worship unlike that of their parents. Feelings of guilt and confusion for no longer accepting their parents' mode of worship were also experi-enced, of course, by the offspring of Italian immigrant parents who were not of the Catholic faith. The writer Barbara Grizzuti Harrison, who divorced herself from the Jehovah's Witness sect of her Italian parents, reflects:

> I think of my gentle father, who has learned painfully to love his maverick daughter, who defends me even when he finds my life incomprehensible. And then I think of a few bitter women, who are not protected, not loved, because in some way they have vio-lated the sacred rules of this large, lusty family composed of good men and bad men, of strong women and selfless women. I think of the strength of Italian women, of strength perverted and strength preserved. And I am painfully confused. I want all of these people to love me, to comprehend me: I want none of them to constrain or confine me. And I know that what I want is impossible.

Time and the American experience were pulling the children of the early immigrants away from the *via vecchia* (the old way) and into a new way of life.

THE CHANGING ROLES OF WOMEN

The images of Italian American women in films and television have for the most part been as misleading as the images of Italian American men as mafia criminals or working-class hulks.

Italian women came to America with a wide variety of experiences and memories that belie the stereotype of the Italian American wife who suffers her lot in silence, only shouting *"Mangia, mangia!"* from time to time. In America she lost her ties with her old community and had difficulty entering the new. She lived in Little Italy, speaking her dialect at work and within the family circle. But for the first time she may have been expected to contribute to the financial as well as the physical well-being of her family.

The new environment was devastating for some women. The cold-water flats in most cities in winter were frightening and bone-chilling. Women who worked at home huddled near gas burners or wood-burning stoves on which were set cauldrons of boiling water to help heat the room. Though warm, the room would remain damp and clammy. All other rooms were without heat, ice cold. Many women, having come from stone-built houses, had a great fear of fires in these tenements built with so much wood. An aging woman still remembered the first words she learned and laughingly repeated: "Fiyah! Fiyah!" Little wonder then if many women—in the congested, cold, fetid tenements of New York—forgot the poverty of Italy and remembered the sunshine, the scenery, and the fresh air instead.

An inability to speak English also isolated these women, especially if they arrived after school age. If they went to work (usually chaperoned by a brother or uncle), it was often for an Italian boss or in places where the workers spoke Italian; thirty or forty years later, some women still spoke no English.

Many women did piecework at home that enabled them to enlist the help of the rest of the family. In Morristown, New Jersey, a mother and daughter working on carpet rags had to work seven to eight hours to earn 50 cents. Putting safety pins onto cards earned

8 to 10 cents per 100 cards—this too earned 50 cents for a day's work. Often the women and children worked throughout the day and well into the night. The average wage of a working woman came to $1.04 a week.

For their part, these first-generation Italian women did not think much of *L'Americana*. To them, the American woman was often seen as flighty. "I can't understand why any Italian girl would want to become American," one eighty-three-year-old woman said, as she flicked her hand beneath her chin. "There is no real respect for her in an American house. In the Italian home a woman is the heart and the soul."

The Italian woman, who had to conform to the strictures of the old society while living in the new, paid the price of seeing her daughters move away into the American world; all she could do in her old age was resign herself with the phrase, "However it ends is good. Whatever you all want to do, do." The clash of cultures created a gulf between first and second generation, mother and daughter. The remarks of a number of second-generation women attest to this.

"The family takes care of the children . . . but it is when the child grows up that they don't know how to handle us," said one, and again, "Children become upset when I'm with my mother because I am treated like a child . . . and I guess I act like a child when I'm around my mother."

"My husband's mother still thinks of him as her son and some-times as the father of her grandchildren . . . but he is not seen as my husband," another testified.

The conflicts sometimes provoked early marriages by second-generation women eager to gain control of their lives and escape the dominance of their families. Many of these rushed marriages re-sulted in alienation and resigned unhappiness. Yet women remained in such marriages out of fear of the community's reaction, for their children, and for economic reasons.

Later generations of women went further. Young women schooled in America resented the control of their fathers. When it came to choosing a husband, they rejected the prospect of marrying a man who might treat his wife like the mother who had pampered him. Some males were aware of this; they too resented the "all pervasive nurturing which was very supportive but often resulted in much too much control."

Then, too, the old way told the young woman that "The husband must be satisfied by his wife, it is her duty. A man has certain needs that a wife must fulfill." It was admitted that sex was sometimes unpleasant, "but if a husband is expected not to wander, his need must be satisfied by his wife. It is a wife's duty."

The bitterness of such "duty" surfaced in one first-generation woman who said, "Men think a cut on the face or a bruise from a fight is so horrible and painful, but I'd like to hear their moans if their bodies swelled up for nine months, then opened up like a bloody cavern to expel a child. That is the real meaning of life . . . pain, motherhood." This from a woman who had had nine children.

While men could pursue a variety of activities, women traditionally were limited primarily to housework and child care. "Therefore, a woman's survival rested on her ability to seduce and hold a husband. In effect, sex became a female's economic way of life; while men worked to live . . . women mated to live."

Certainly the first-generation mother in Little Italy could not help but pass on to the daughter her sense of pragmatism: "A good steady job is enough," "Too much is bad for you," and, "You look after me as I looked after my mother." No use the daughter pointing out that most first-generation women left their mothers in Italy to be taken care of by others. The second-generation daughter was left with her sense of duty to her mother and a sense of duty to herself, which often led (and still leads) to a great sense of turmoil and guilt.

Since one of the strictures of the "old way" was that a daughter must look after her aging parents, the second generation of women, who frequently found this impossible in America, have been left with a sense of guilt over their aging parents. Individual tragedies are played out between aging mothers and their daughters.

One woman wrote this revealing letter to the *Staten Island Advance* on July 16, 1989:

When I was a young woman of 23, I had a dream. I dreamt that I hung my mother out on a clothesline to dry in the wind, as she did with her laundry each and every day. However, in this instance I dreamt she dropped from the clothing and died. This dream was so devastating that I have lived with guilt since that day.

Why would I want to kill my mother? She had always taken

such good care of me and she had always been so concerned with my well-being.

In reality, each time I brought a boyfriend home, my mother knew exactly why he wasn't right for me. She would explain that he was too short, his shirt was not ironed properly, or that his occupation was not good enough for me. When I thought of going to college she said adamantly, high school would be sufficient for a lady. She added, college would take too long, and women did not need higher education.

My mother seemed to know precisely what was best for me. Then why, why did I have this dream which cast a shadow on my conscience all these years?

Now I am married to a not-so-perfect husband and have two not-so-loving children (at least in my mother's estimation). Now, my mother has reached a point in life when she no longer is able to hang her clothes to dry. With time, the wind has also turned the scene around, and now I must hang her clothes to dry. Perhaps, since I care for her so much, I now can understand why the time has come for me to find fault with all her choices. Sadly, my mother has lost the capacity to know when to eat, when to bathe, and when to dress warmly. Unwittingly, I now am in command, and now I know what is best for her. . . .

And from an aging mother:

Now I am eighty. Look at my legs, those swollen veins. And still they hold me up, these legs of mine. I am not complaining because I am old. To become old is according to God's will. But to be old and alone—even dogs have their companions. . . . It's certain that I got things here which in Italy, I never could have gotten. But I had things in Italy which America, still cannot find— yeast, yeast, for the soul.*

In 1950, 77 percent of Italian American women still worked as operators in the needle trades; by 1970, the number had dropped to 25 percent. In the clerical field over the same period, this figure jumped from 8 to almost 40 percent. Few women (2–9%) acquired positions of power or managerial posts. If the percentage of women entering the professions jumped slightly (from 2 to 9%), this could

*Valentine Rossilli Winsey, in *Essays in Honor of Covello*, p. 199.

be attributed to Italian American women entering "the female ghettos of the work force (nursing, social work, and teaching)."*

Films and television habitually still portray Italian women as fertile, overwrought, and preoccupied with cooking pasta. An image of the "professional Italian" has surfaced in such commercially successful films as *Moonstruck* and *Prizzi's Honor,* as well as in tomato sauce commercials. Almost invariably the woman is either fat or sensual and speaks with a marked "Noo Yawk" accent.

When these women brought their children to school for the first time, they were received by an imposing principal. She (or he) would look at the child's birth certificate, which might read, say, "Calogero Chiarelli" and then declare, "We'll call the boy Charlie Carcelli." The children accepted that change for the rest of their lives; and the mothers for their part saw their children take a step away from them.

The effect of such subtle bigotry, in the name of Americanization, on the sons and daughters of those early immigrants needs no sociological data. From the early writers through Pietro Di Donato and down to lesser-known writers, all remind us of the disastrous effects.

Certainly children were cut off from the heritage of their parents—even when well-intentioned schoolteachers recalled Dante, Michelangelo, and Da Vinci. These names meant nothing to the children of southern immigrants. Even among those who in later years discovered Croce, Giovannitti, Verga, and Pirandello for themselves, the effect of the bigotry they had encountered lingered in their personality and character.

It was from these second-generation children that most of those who entered higher learning were to come. But not without confronting numerous difficulties.

The American educational system still lived with the image of Renaissance Italy, ignoring the reality of the new immigrants. The Casa Italiana of Columbia University is a case in point. Ironically, it was immigrants who had raised money to build the Casa Italiana. Francesco Cordasco bitterly remembers: "In my four years on Morningside Heights, the Casa Italian was a foreign presence, inhospitable to, and unconcerned with, the few Italian Americans in Columbia College . . . in a WASP fortress of social class and privilege."

*Mortorella, *The Italian American: Strategies for Coping with Value Conflict.*

This attitude was understandable; between 1876 and 1924 there was no immigrant presence in the American colleges and universities.

Only after World War II did the second generation, with their war experience and service, begin to enter colleges and universities, helped largely by the GI Bill of Rights.

THE WARS ITALIAN AMERICANS FOUGHT

Ernest Renan, the French historian, observes that a nation is forged when a people suffer together. Certainly the effort made in World War I by Italian immigrants, and in World War II by their sons and grandsons, accelerated their assimilation. In World War I, when Italy was an ally of the Americans, about 12 percent of the U.S. Army was made up of Italian immigrants and (to a lesser extent) their American-born sons. Even before the United States entered the war in 1917, a large contingent of immigrants had left the country to do military service in the Italian Army. One hundred of them received Distinguished Service Crosses from the American government, and two immigrants' sons, Private Michael Valente and Private Joseph Mastine, received Congressional Medals of Honor for their outstanding heroism. All foreign-born soldiers who had fought in the U.S. Army without citizenship achieved U.S. citizenship while in the Army.

After the war ended, the War Department pointed out that although the Italians constituted only 4 percent of the nation's population at that time, 10 percent of the men killed were Italian.

Despite this service, a wave of anti-immigration sentiment surfaced after the war, expressed in the popular slogan "America for Americans." Advocates demanded new immigration laws to keep the nation "more American." Madison Grant, author of *The Passing of the Great Race,* which attained some popularity in the 1920s, attacked the new immigrant groups as a weak and inferior people. Grant held that persons from Northern Europe were superior to those from the Mediterranean and Balkan nations, whom he referred to as "human flotsam" who had lowered "the whole tone of American life." Grant and his followers feared that, with the end of World War I, millions of Europeans from Southern and Eastern Europe would emigrate. Immigrants were denounced as radicals with dangerous foreign ideas and blamed for the labor disturbances that were in fact dominated by native-born Americans. In 1919, the Department of Justice arrested and deported hundreds of aliens on the spurious grounds that they were dangerous radicals responsible for a great deal of the subversive activity throughout the nation. The effect of these mass arrests—enacted largely through the office of Attorney General A. Mitchell Palmer, with the approval of Woodrow Wilson—was to make Congress and the public more determined than ever to restrict immigration.

World War II had a much more positive effect on the relationship between Italian Americans and the rest of the nation. A general labor shortage opened up new employment opportunities for the formerly shunned Italian American workers.

In October 1942, ten months after declaring war on Germany, Japan, and Italy, the United States (as we have seen) exempted all 600,000 Italians from the wartime restrictions imposed on all other aliens of enemy nationality. This exemption was made after fewer than 250 Italians residing in the United States had been interned under the Department of Justice's selective internment program established for some 10,000 aliens (German, Japanese, and Italian) who were suspected of being potentially dangerous to the national security. The second assurance that the Italian alien population represented no threat derived from the fact that in February 1942, only two months after Pearl Harbor, 10 percent of the Italian aliens had husbands or sons in the American armed forces, and the number was steadily increasing.*

World War II quickly Americanized the second generation. More than 500,000 (5% of the Italian American population) served in the armed forces.

Since Italy was fighting on the side of the enemy, it became an unspoken policy to send Italian Americans to the Pacific rather than to the European theater. Some, such as Max Corvo, volunteered to fight with the OSS and took part in the invasion of Sicily. At least a dozen won the Congressional Medal of Honor. One recipient was

---

*The selective internment program conducted by the Department of Justice during World War II is not to be confused with the mass internment of the Japanese on the West Coast conducted by the War Department. The Department of Justice, in the person of Attorney General Francis Biddle, was opposed to the mass internment program, but his arguments were ignored. The Alien Enemy Act of 1789, which was upheld by the U.S. Supreme Court at the start of World War II, permitted the internment of any resident alien of enemy nationality in time of war. As commander-in-chief of the armed forces, President Franklin D. Roosevelt had the final word in deciding which internment program would be followed.

Marine Sergeant John Basilone, who for three days battled an entire Japanese regiment in Guadalcanal with no other means than his machine gun. General Douglas MacArthur called him "a one-man army." For a moment, Basilone was a national hero and returned to spark bond drives, only to resume combat in the Pacific, where he was killed during the Marine landings on Iwo Jima. There were other remarkable heroes, among them the Damato brothers, both killed in action; Captain Don Gentile, a war ace who downed thirty enemy planes; and Major A. Martini, who downed twenty-two Nazi planes over the skies of France. "The Italians in America have been through eras in which their ultimate loyalty has been put to the test, and their choice has left no doubt as to their true feelings. The sentiments of the Italian-Americans should now be known to all," concluded one Italian American writer soon after the war.

Hardly anyone noticed that Italian Americans fought in the Korean War and in Vietnam—although one amputee from Brooklyn did show up in the documentary film *Hearts and Minds*.

CHAPTER 20

The Postwar Years—
Organized Crime and
Cultural Anger

I could declare myself an organized crime reporter
tomorrow and just get everybody's books and write stories.
Nobody's going to sue me. It's not like something you might
say about the governor or about the head of U.S. Steel,
where you're going to get sued. You can go on and on; it's
not even new stuff. What you're reading today, you read ten
years ago. Same names. Whether it's true or not true, it's
there. And the outrageous fact is that newspapers don't care
about intelligent articles. They just print it and reprint it.

—THOMAS PUCCIO, U.S. ATTORNEY,
EASTERN DISTRICT, 1980

The Ring," "the rackets," or "the Mob" played a role in assimilating many immigrant groups. That much of the responsibility for
organizing crime groups was laid at the feet of Italian Americans
created a cultural anger among the children of the immigrants, who
saw it as a form of bigotry.

By the early 1930s, Luciano, Costello, and Capone had risen to high positions; all three regarded themselves above all as Americans. Shortly before he went to jail, Al Capone told a reporter: "I've been spending the best years of my life as a public benefactor. I've given people the light pleasures, shown them a good time. And all I get is abuse—the existence of a hunted man—I'm called a killer.

"Well, tell the folks I'm going away now. I guess murder will stop. There won't be any more booze. You won't be able to find a crap game even, let alone a roulette wheel or a faro game. I guess Mike Hughes [Chicago's police chief] won't need his 3000 extra cops, after all."

If such men as Luciano and Capone were Americanized by their criminal associates and experiences, the postwar period eased many others into political-criminal associations in America.

Abe "Kid Twist" Reles, who was the Valachi of his time, is a good example.

Abe Reles, born in Brooklyn in 1907, was the caricature of the hood—short, stocky, and long-armed, with a raging temper. Reles once killed a car wash attendant who was too slow. Before he reached drinking age, he had fourteen murders to his credit. On February 2, 1940, he was arrested for the murder of a Brooklyn gang leader and made an informant's deal with District Attorney William O'Dwyer. Reles described a national organization he called "the Combination" with "troops" directed by head men. These troops "conferred and agreed on certain rules." The names that came up then were: Moe Dalitz of Cleveland and Dandy Phil Kastel of New Orleans; and Lepke Buchalter, who was "authorized to create an enforcement arm for the national syndicate, which would eventually become Murder Inc."

Reles testified against most of these men until 1941, when he jumped or was pushed out of the fifth-floor window of the Half Moon Hotel in Coney Island, where he was under police protection. The death was ruled accidental, and no one asked how Reles could have jumped to his death while being guarded day and night by a platoon of police.

This incident took place during the mayoral elections of 1941, which pitted Fiorello La Guardia against the "gangbuster" William O'Dwyer. When La Guardia brought up the issue of Reles, O'Dwyer promptly accused La Guardia of seeking Communist support. It was only Roosevelt's backing that tipped the mayor's seat to La Guardia.

* * *

Soon after World War II, Carmine De Sapio rose in the ranks of the Democratic Party organization of New York City known as Tammany Hall. By the 1950s, De Sapio, as leader of Tammany Hall, controlled New York City through patronage and his ability to deliver votes. He named judges and administrators, granted construction contracts, and conferred innumerable jobs to the faithful. He worked and was friendly with men who lived on the edge of legality, including Frank Costello, William O'Dwyer, and Longy Zwillman. Soon De Sapio was targeted by a reform movement in New York, despite a number of reforms he had brought about within the Democratic organization. In September 1961, De Sapio was defeated in a primary runoff for district leader in Greenwich Village. When he ran again in 1963, he was defeated by 41 votes by Edward Koch who, as a future mayor of New York (one can say with some Italian irony), was to have his own problems with corruption.

With the demise of De Sapio as a political power came the end of the Tammany Society. In May 1966, one officer of the society remained: "eighty-one-year-old Judge Edward McCullen, Tammany scribe." Tammany's century-long domination of the city, brought about by alliances between politicians and racketeers, was finally over. Their legacy endured, however. In 1983, Virgil Peterson, a former FBI agent turned historian, in his monumental study of the Mob could still write:

> Alliances between political leaders and underworld bosses are still with us. And they are still the very lifeblood of organized crime.
> They are not peculiar to New York City. On the contrary, they prevail wherever organized crime flourishes.

The nation's obsession with the Mafia had been dormant from 1915 to 1945, when various investigations tended to focus on the ties between crime and politics. This changed during the postwar period as congressional investigating committees turned to foreign conspiracies to explain the phenomenon of American organized crime. The dramatic testimony of Joseph M. Valachi finally gave one committee the evidence it wanted.

Valachi was born in New York City in 1903 of immigrant parents from Naples. Like so many of the young who became criminals, he left school when he was a teenager and quickly fell into a life of petty crime. At eighteen he was convicted of carrying a loaded revolver; at twenty he was sent to Sing Sing for burglary; and in 1956 he entered Atlanta Federal Prison on a narcotics charge. In 1962, Valachi killed an inmate he believed to be a hit man. At the trial, psychiatrists found him to be suffering from a "paranoid state" characterized by "delusions of persecution." His family too had a history of mental illness; his brother had spent thirty-two years in a mental institution, and his sisters and grandmother had suffered mental disorders.

After being sentenced to life, Valachi was removed from the Atlanta prison, questioned about organized crime, and in September 1963 taken to testify before the Subcommittee on Investigations headed by Senator John McClellan.

Much of Valachi's testimony was not new. Nonetheless, Robert F. Kennedy referred to Valachi as the first insider in the rackets to break the Code of Silence, although twenty years earlier Abe (Kid Twist) Reles had exposed the workings of Murder Inc.

Valachi's testimony told of a secret nationwide organization he called "La Cosa Nostra," built around families, with a corporate structure and *"consiglieri," "capo regime,"* and "soldiers." This image took hold with the press. The terms "Cosa Nostra" and "Mafia" became interchangeable. The presidential Commission on Law Enforcement concluded:

> The core of organized crime in America . . . consists of twenty-four groups, known as families, which operate as criminal cartels in large cities across the nation. Their membership is exclusively men of Italian descent, they are in frequent communication with each other, and their smooth functioning is ensured by a national board of overseers known as the commission. The name of the organization is Cosa Nostra.

The influence of Valachi's testimony is immeasurable. Virgil Peterson points out that Valachi

> made a remarkable impact on the literature relating to organized crime. In fact, it was Valachi who quite likely coined the name Cosa Nostra, using it to denote the Italian criminal organization. During the years following his revelations, the great majority of published books, articles and news items that have attempted to

describe the structure of organized crime in America clearly reveal a heavy reliance on Valachi. His disclosures have been accepted without much questioning by many official agencies . . . writers have either misinterpreted portions of Valachi's testimony or attributed to him statements he never made at all . . . some of Valachi's testimony was extremely confusing, and inconsistent . . . it would appear he either withheld facts . . . or deliberately lied.

Peterson concluded: "Valachi was a man of limited intelligence. He was attuned only to New York, where he was a low man on the totem pole . . . he was never in a position to provide an accurate blueprint of the structure of organized crime. . . ."

Out of this, nonetheless, came an avalanche of books, headed by Peter Maas's *The Valachi Papers,* described by the *Saturday Review* as "A frightening book . . . it shows how easily a secret criminal organization can become a spreading cancer." *The New York Times* book reviewer termed it "A bloody history of the mafia as lived by one of its members . . . for those who still dismiss the Cosa Nostra as the fanciful creation of ambitous D.A.s . . . there finally emerges the dark outline of a state within a state—a second government." Columbia Pictures and Dino De Laurentiis made a movie called *The Valachi Papers* starring Charles Bronson.

References to the Mafia in the *New York Times* escalated from 2 in 1962, to 67 in 1963, and 359 in 1969 (the year Puzo's *The Godfather* was published). Biographies were quickly put together of Costello, Genovese, and Gambino. There was a rush to imitate Puzo, old adventure stories were reissued as new books with new titles, and some novels changed the names of characters to Italian ones. Noel Clad's *The Savage,* published in 1958, became *The Mafia* in 1970. Ben Appel's *Brain Guy,* first published in 1934, now became *The Enforcer* (advertised as a successor to *The Godfather*). Of the dozens of books that suddenly reappeared or appeared for the first time, all were marketed as "more exciting than *The Godfather.*"

In a symposium held by the magazine *Attenzione* devoted to Italian American affairs, specialists in the field of crime discussed how the government agents handled the information from the Valachi hearing.

Ralph Salerno, an investigator for the Central Intelligence Bureau, the New York City Police Department, and a consultant to the

U.S. Department of Justice, maintained that the Valachi hearings were part of an organized strategy:

> Robert Kennedy, who was the first witness at those hearings, was seeking legislation, and he knew that you cannot expect such recommendations to pass on their merit alone. What you have to do is get support for the legislation you are seeking. You've got to get people to write to their congressman, or call their congressman. You've got to get an editorial comment in the *Times* and other important newspapers. So that the decision to let Valachi come forward was to support the need for the legislation Robert Kennedy was requesting.

Victor Navasky, editor-in-chief of *The Nation,* responded that that was the point.

> The government tried to manage the story down to its last detail, including picking the writer who would tell the story. So they picked Peter Maas, who is you know a solid character and who had his own career as an investigative journalist prior to that time . . . they gave Maas access to Valachi while Valachi was in prison, which is a violation of federal prison policy. No one else was able to do that for many years before or after. All he did was he let Valachi tell his story. The result of it was that what we got was this uni-dimensional story. It may or may not be true, but it was never checked out.

Dwight Smith, Professor of Criminal Justice at Rutgers University and author of *Mafia Mystique,* told the symposium that its conclusions "were based on the assumption that the most important thing about organized crime was that it was an alien conspiracy. That it's something out there which is foreign to our own economy, to our own culture, which has come and done this thing to us."

From a distance, British historians such as Dennis Mack Smith and Christopher Duggan have a more objective and truer picture of the American underworld. In 1986, Duggan concluded:

> Recent studies have tended to underline the fact that there is no firm evidence for a criminal organization: and my own work on the 1920s strongly supports this line. Some kind of transforma-

tion may have occurred since the war; but evidence for this is not convincing. Indeed both the pathology and official diagnosis of the evil appear much the same as a century ago. To my mind, ideas about the mafia are largely subjective and stem from confusion, political calculation and prejudice.

By 1987, Joseph Giordano, writing in the *U.S. News and World Report,* could point out:

The Mafia mystique has reached such levels that art is often mistaken for reality, folklore for fact. At the recent "pizza connection" trial, actors were engaged by the court to read transcripts because the defendants' Sicilian dialect was not understood by the jury. In turn, real gangsters begin to fulfill the television and film stereotypes. U.S. Attorney Rudolph Giuliani noted a distinct difference in the wire taps of Italian American criminals before and after *The Godfather.* Many, Giuliani said, began to sound like characters in the film. On the tapes the theme from the movie can be heard in the background."

And Rudolph Giuliani himself, in *Fra Noi* (a newspaper for Chicago's Italian American community), commented:

If you do a case involving 19 members of the Mafia—Pizza Connection case of the Columbo case of the many cases we've done—it gets a tremendous amount of attention. Front page. If you do a similar case, say a black organized crime group or a Colombian or Israeli or motorcycle gang or Nigerian, all of which we have done cases on in the last year—they get moderate attention. The end result is that it creates a misimpression that the Mafia is the only significant crime group. It isn't true. It's only one of 20 or 25. We should try to find a way to balance the attention given to these groups so we don't continue this misimpression.

Fuel was added to these stereotypes from the 1970s on as Italian American gangsters such as John Gotti and Jerry Angiulo became Mafia superstars.

Gotti was born of Neapolitan parents in the South Bronx when it was still a livable working-class neighborhood. When Gotti was twelve, the family moved to the Brownsville-East New York section of Brooklyn. Gotti went to one of those vocational high schools, where working-class boys were simply dumped; his education came from street gangs such as the Fulton-Rockaway Boys. His hero might have been Marlon Brando in the role of Johnny in *The Wild One*, as he moved up the gang ladder, first as a junior gang member and then a senior. At sixteen Gotti quit school, and his life as a gang member became a full-time occupation.

To many in his neighborhood, it seemed the press and the government persecuted Gotti because he was Italian. In the face of so much crime in the city, it seemed unfair to pick on Gotti. He was acquitted. When he was arrested again on new charges, he became a hero and role model for some of the young, just as the gangsters of the past were role models for Gotti. But, then, in a corrupt city the successful criminal is often applauded by the poor.

In Boston, another gangster was also fitted to the Procrustean bed of Mafia. Jerry Angiulo came out of Boston's North End, where Irish-Italian feuds had festered for years.

In the 1930s, when Angiulo was growing up, the North End was controlled by Irish known as the Gustin Gang. In the Irish-Italian gang wars that raged, the Gustin Gang was ambushed in a shootout and its leaders wiped out. The killings were later attributed to the "Mafia," although the word was not in vogue at the time. The disappearance of the Gustin leaders did not do away with the ethnic variety of criminals in Boston. There were still Irish leaders such as Dan Carrol, and Jewish leaders such as Charles (King) Soloman, whose death was attributed to the Irish hit man James P. "Skeets" Coyne.

Gennaro (whose name was Americanized to Jerry) Angiulo was born of poor southern Italian parents. His life followed the pattern of the immigrant son who left school at an early age and acquired his trade in the streets of America. He learned quickly to have politicians and police on his payroll in the persons of such men as Carl Larson, a state police official, and Herbert Mulloney, the Boston police chief. He, too, was made to fit the image of mafia, although he was divorced in 1963—an unheard-of act for an allegedly family-oriented Mafia Don.

When Robert Kennedy, whose family came out of the environment of the Boston Irish-Italian gang wars, became Attorney General, the number of FBI agents assigned to "mafia" cases rose from 3 to 150. The men who were assigned to the Angiulo case included Dennis Condon and Ed Quinn, both products of Boston's North End.*

In December 1989, the obviously demented Vincent Gigante was prosecuted under the Italian-sounding Racketeer Influenced and Corrupt Organizations (RICO) Act. Reporters around the country wrote of Vincent "the Chin" Gigante, member of the Genovese family, and used such words as "made members" and "Capo Regime," adding quickly, "according to the FBI law enforcement officials." By attributing the language to the FBI, reporters were absolved from any effort to check the facts. "In no other matters," one outraged Italian said, "would they accept government handouts." But then, as Anthony Lewis observed in the *New York Times* of May 11, 1990, "the American press, for all its independence, relies on the official institutions in Washington to legitimize its choice of what is news."

In the meantime the books by Lincoln Steffens, Herbert Asbury, Virgil Peterson, Dwight Smith, and Christopher Duggan, and James Mills's *The Underground Empire—Where Crime and Governments Embrace,* all of which reflect independent research, were ignored, and even today are never consulted by those who accept the government handout, leaving a residue of anger among many Italian Americans.

*O'Neil and Lehr, *The Under Boss.*

CHAPTER 21

The Writers Between Two Cultures: 1890–1960

> This letter is the cry of a soul stranded on the shores of
> darkness looking for light—a light that points out the path
> toward recognition, where I can work and help myself. I am
> not deserting the legions of toil to refuge myself in the
> literary word. No! No! I only want to express the wrath of
> their mistreatment. I seek no refuge. I am a worker, a pick
> and shovel man—what I want is an outlet to express what I
> can say besides work.
>
> —PASCAL D'ANGELO TO CARL VAN DOREN

The novelists in Italy had little to say about the ongoing migration.
The silence of Giovanni Verga and of Luigi Pirandello, who
were so sensitive to the suffering of the people of the South, on the
exodus seems incomprehensible.

Yet Italian writers were aware of America. Verga at age sixteen
wrote a 700-page book on George Washington; and Pirandello, who
was awarded the Nobel Prize for Literature, had visited the United
States twice in the twenties and again in the thirties and was well
aware of the large Italian immigrant population.

Leonardo Sciascia, whose stories and novels have been translated into English, considered it ironic that during the years when

Verga was writing his finest novels, which were hailed as master-pieces of realism, he made no mention of the exodus taking place in Sicily, where he lived and wrote. "Even our realists," said Sciascia, "are lacking in realism." For his part, Sciascia writes of the immi-grants in a tragi-comic tone, as in the short story *La Zia d'America (My American Aunt,)* and in *Il Lungo Viaggio (The Long Voyage)*, in which an "honest" con man promises to take a group from Sicily to *Nugiorrsi* (New Jersey) and *Nuovaiorca* (New York). The group has visions of disembarking in *Brucchlin* (Brooklyn), only to find out as they scatter ashore that they have landed in Sicily.

Of the literature published during the great exodus, only two short stories by Maria Messina of Palermo deal with the theme of emigration. *La Merica* depicts the torment of mothers and wives when the idea of America smites a man in the family "like an illness." Another Messina story centers on the grief of a widowed mother whose only son goes off to America, leaving his motherless child with her.

Not until 1929, when "American fever" had abated, did an Italian novelist attempt to convey the sorrows of emigration. Fran-cesco Perri's prize-winning novel *L'Emigranti* is set in a poor Cala-brian village, where circumstances compel a number of its young men to emigrate to the United States. The book reflects the positive and negative myths in circulation throughout the *Mezzogiorno:* that there was more joy and comfort in America, where men were not merely beasts of burden; but that there was also great loneliness, tuberculosis, injuries while working, and thieving compatriots.

The dramatic warnings implicit in this 1929 novel appeared just as the mass exodus had reached its end. Would *L'Emigranti* have deterred Italians from migrating had it been published during the peak of the exodus? Probably not. Aside from the fact that the great majority of immigrants had too little schooling to read novels, or were illiterate, the image of America was too firmly entrenched in their imaginations as their El Dorado for any warnings against emi-gration to have been taken seriously. In official language, the Italian government had warned prospective immigrants that leaving for America might not solve their problems; but such warnings had little or no effect.

If the immigrants did not read and knew less about the Italian novels, they did bring with them a form of literature in their proverbs, their legends, and in the oral tradition of their *cantastorii* (the village storyteller), who recounted the stories of miracles, of monsters, and of wars between Christians and Islam in the Little Italies of America.

One can hear the voices of those immigrant storytellers in early novelists such as Joe Pagano, especially in *The Golden Wedding,* whose opening lines read: "First, I think I should tell you how my mother and father happened to come to this country. . . . A family, you understand, is not unlike a plant; it has its branches as well as blossoms; it has, above all, its roots."

If they read at all, the early immigrants tended toward the literature of courtly romances and fantasies. Nonetheless, there was a smattering of intellectuals, especially among those involved in radical politics. Sacco and Vanzetti were both avid readers, as was Anthony Capraro, one of the strike leaders in Lawrence, and the Bambace sisters. Then, too, the early novels were more likely to give American readers what they wanted to hear of Italian immigrants than realistic portrayals. An early novelist, Bernardino Ciambelli, who wrote such novels as *I Misteri di Mulberry Street* (1893) and *I Diletti de Bosses* (1895), was a forerunner of our present-day writers about the Mafia. Early novels such as Luigi Ventura's *Peppino* (published in 1913) and Silvio Villa's *Claudio Graziani* found few readers among turn-of-the-century immigrants.

The first bibliography of Italian American writers, compiled by Olga Peragallo in 1949, listed just 59 writers, out of a population of nearly five million: "It was no elite minority that crossed the ocean," wrote Giuseppe Prezzolini, the former head of the Casa Italiana at Columbia University.

At least four of the Italian immigrants who arrived in the early years of the century absorbed enough of the nation's culture to record impressions of the New World that merit inclusion in the pantheon of Italian American literature. Of these, Pascal D'Angelo stands out for his tenacity in transcending his life as a laborer to become a published poet.

D'Angelo (as we saw) came from the Abruzzo region with his father in 1910, when he was sixteen years old. His father left not long afterwards, discouraged by the hardships, but Pascal chose to remain. "Something was keeping me in this wonderful perilous land where I had suffered so much and where I had so much more to suffer. . . . There was a lingering suspicion that somewhere in this vast country an opening existed, that somewhere I would strike the light. I could not remain in the darkness perpetually."

Several years of arduous and dangerous labor on work gangs followed. D'Angelo lived in a boxcar while repairing damaged tracks, carrying wet ties and rails in bitterly cold weather over icy surfaces, often being bullied by tyrannical bosses (some of them Italians), whose frequent threats of firing evoked visions of aimless wandering and dark months of unemployment. At one point D'Angelo badly injured his hand while trying to carry out the commands of a sadistic boss, and was summarily dismissed until he could use it again.

Worn and penniless, D'Angelo taught himself English with the help of a pocket dictionary. As he gradually learned to put words together into sentences, he developed a passion for poetry. In 1919, he quit his job as a laborer and moved to New York to devote all his time to writing poetry. He submitted poems to a number of newspapers and magazines, but none were accepted. Inevitably becoming discouraged, he went back to work, this time in a shipyard, deciding, "there are too many authors, too many poets, novelists, dramatists, too many people honestly yearning to speak their souls, and this commercial world cannot assimilate them all."

D'Angelo tried to resign himself to "the drab, hard life which it seems fate had allotted me," but even after months had passed, he could not shed the dream of a literary career. Again he quit his job. This time his decision was motivated by a poem on the editorial page of "a staid and respectable newspaper," which struck him as "the most blatant and silly trash imaginable." Perseverance, he decided, was what he had lacked; he pinned the bad poem on his door as a reminder that his poems were far superior, and renewed his attempts to get them published. This time he went to an Italian newspaper, thinking he might find some encouragement there "from people of my own blood," but was told that they published only works by well-known writers. When he offered the poems for as few dollars as the newspaper was willing to pay, or "for nothing," he was shown the door.

To save money, he moved to Brooklyn, where he rented a small room that had formerly been a chicken coop and wood shack, with an entrance "through a toilet which served ten families besides unwelcome strangers." The room had no stove and no heat, and on cold days he remained huddled in bed in order to keep warm. With little money left, he could only afford to eat stale bread. During the winter of 1920 his meals consisted of stale bread softened with cold soup and occasionally overripe bananas, if he could get them cheaply enough. Meanwhile, he was going to the public library and writing more poems, and, when he had the strength, paying visits to newspaper offices to deliver the poems and invariably have them rejected.

Toward the end of the year, "as winter grew more severe," his condition became desperate. "My books and papers were molding from the damp. I, too, felt that I was moldering." One day he returned to his room and when he opened the door,

> in the dark I could hear a splashing on the floor as if water were there. The window was open. Snow poured in. The children of the neighborhood had opened it during my absence in order to look at my books and papers. Rain and snow had wet a good half of the bed and quilt. Someone had also tried to warm the pipes in the lavatory and they had burst. Before the water could be turned off enough of it had flowed under my bed to spoil my stale bread and my extra pair of trousers and underwear. . . .
> The stale bread gave such an evil toilet smell that I could not eat it in spite of my hunger. Shivering, sleepy, hungry, tired, I huddled on the dry end of the bed and pressed my face in anguish against the quilt. How long, O God, how long was this going to last. Would I ever get out of this gulf of sorrows?

Still he endured. Toward the end of the year, he submitted three poems to an annual contest in *The Nation*. When after a month there was no reply, "as a sort of despairing gesture" he sent a letter to the editor.

Carl Van Doren, the literary editor, was one of the first major American critics to pay attention to D'Angelo's poetry—and he may have saved D'Angelo's sanity and even his life. In the Introduction to *A Son of Italy*, the autobiography that D'Angelo later wrote at his suggestion, Van Doren recalled "with a vividness of memory which has never been dimmed that in January 1922 I first learned of his existence." At that point he was wondering whether it was really worth any editor's trouble to offer an annual prize for poetry and was, as usual, "growing skeptical and more skeptical over the bales of rhymed and unrhymed mediocrity which I had to handle—so many poems and so few poets"—when he came upon D'Angelo's despairing letter. The writer identified himself as an ignorant "pick and shovel man" who had never studied English. The letter was a poem in itself, describing his travails and hopes. In the final paragraph he pleaded with such intensity of emotion that Van Doren could neither doubt nor ignore his authenticity: "Oh please hear me. I am telling the truth. And yet who knows it? Only I. And who believes me? Let my soul break out of its chrysalis of forced ignorance and fly toward the flower of hope, like a rich butterfly winged with a thousand thoughts of beauty."

Thanks to Van Doren, "the miracle happened" and there was "a new world of hope." D'Angelo found himself known, talked about, and invited to submit his poetry to prestigious literary publications. A number of his poems were soon published and praised. His story became a subject for newspaper articles throughout the nation and abroad. The literary world adopted him as a great curiosity; he was, in his own words, "literally feasted, welcomed and stared at. . . . But more sincere and dearer to my heart were the tributes of my fellow workers who recognized that at least one of them had risen from the ditches and quicksands of toil to speak his heart to the upper world."

When his autobiography *A Son of Italy* was published in 1924, with the Introduction by Van Doren, the reviewer in the *New York Times Book Review* wrote:

> He is one of the few Americanized immigrants whose success has been non-worldly yet decisive. Edward Bok, Jacob Riis, to mention but two of our best national conversions, stand for the practical, solid achievement that constitute mundane success. Pascal D'Angelo is one of that class of men, rare in America, whose success is so spiritual as to be almost entirely devoid of material embellishments.

An innocent and an idealist, D'Angelo did not take advantage of his celebrity status to accept any of the editorial positions offered to him. As Van Doren put it,

> After paying so high a price to be a poet, he was not willing to take his reward in some meaner coin. . . . Some incalculable chance had put the soul of a poet in the body of an Italian boy whose parents could not read or write and who came into no heritage but the family tradition of hopeless labor . . . his career

is one of the most thrilling episodes in American literature. *A Son of Italy* unquestionably belongs with the precious documents of the literature of Pascal D'Angelo's adopted country.

The closing paragraph of Van Doren's Introduction is worth recording for the connection it makes between "the hopeless labor" that many an immigrant endured in the early decades of the century and the aspirations of a common laborer from the Abruzzo region of Italy, the same region that produced Ovid:

No American after watching a gang of brown Italians in a ditch, can help asking himself whether there is not some Pascal D'Angelo among them, perhaps reasoning thus: "Who hears the thuds of the pick and the jingling of the shovel? Only the stern-eyed foreman sees me. When Night comes and we all quit work the thuds of the pick and the jingling of the shovel are heard no more. All my works are lost, lost forever. But if I write a good line of poetry—then when night comes and I cease writing, my work is not lost. My line is still there. It can be read by you today and by another tomorrow. But my pick and shovel works cannot be read either by you today or by anyone else tomorrow."

Is this not the ageless sentiment of the artist who desires to snare some beauty and hold it above the waters of oblivion which drown all things, ugly and beautiful together? Who better than Pascal D'Angelo has snared the beauty of the contrast between a rushing train and an inconspicuous pedestrian—a contrast which must have been near Mr. D'Angelo every day of his life as a laborer?

One poem by D'Angelo reads:

In the dark verdure of summer
The railroad tracks are like the chords of a lyre
gleaming across the dreaming valley,
And the road crosses them like a flash of
lightning.
But the souls of many who speed like music on the
melodious heart-strings of the valley,
Are dim with storms;
And the soul of a farm lad who plods, whistling,

on the lightning road
Is a bright blue sky.

D'Angelo's success, however, was short-lived. Eight years after the publication of *A Son of Italy,* he died destitute, at thirty-eight, in a hospital ward following an appendectomy, and was buried in Brooklyn. Friends and admirers paid for his burial and founded a D'Angelo Society which, for a number of years, awarded a D'Angelo Medal each year for the best poetry submitted by young Americans. D'Angelo's papers have never been gathered into book form, nor is any record of his writings to be found in the standard biographical directories of American writers.

Like Pascal D'Angelo, Constantine Panunzio, author of the autobiographical *Soul of an Immigrant,* was a young teenager when he arrived in the United States. But he was unlike D'Angelo in nearly all other respects. Resourceful and worldly, Panunzio was an encouraging example to subscribers of the melting pot concept. At thirteen, he persuaded his southern Italian parents in his native town of Molfetta in Apulia to permit him to go to sea rather than continue his education. His employment as a cabin boy took him to Boston, where, to escape a sadistic captain, Panunzio deserted ship.

His early experiences were those of constant struggle as he went from one misadventure to another before he became a successful American. But Panunzio finally achieved the happy ending of the classic American success story when he began to meet Americans whose goodness changed his opinion of America. The "success story" led to an educational career, which Panunzio attributed to his association with "the best American people" and his "deep-seated faith in America." Thereafter he became an ardent convert to Americanism and eventually a Protestant minister of the gospel.

In his autobiography, Panunzio criticized the nation's failure to allow immigrants access to "the real life of America." Forgetting that he had previously described his own immigrant experiences as "average," he wrote: "The fact is that mine had been an extraordinary opportunity to come in contact with the best people in America; whereas the vast majority of what are here called 'foreigners' remain pretty much segregated, living very much the same life . . . as they lived in the countries from which they originally came."

Describing an Italian slum area in Boston, Panunzio waxed indignant at the absence of "all the constructive forces of American society" in the Italian community, and asserted that "some of its very worst features seemed to have been systematically poured into the neighborhood to prey upon the life of the people in their all too apparent helplessness. Here within this half mile square were no less than 111 saloons, not because the people wanted them . . . but because the saloons were needed for revenue."

In many ways, *The Soul of an Immigrant* is a direct descendant of Franklin's *Autobiography*. Both works aim to teach the value of self-improvement by example. There is no sense of loss in his story; Panunzio's work bears witness to the exhilaration of a conversion.

If Panunzio stands out as an immigrant who successfully assimilated into the society of his adopted country, Emanuel Carnevali is conspicuous as a bird of passage, the poet who captured the feeling of rootlessness that characterized the lives of the great majority of Italian immigrants. Like Panunzio and D'Angelo, Carnevali arrived in the United States as a young teenager with no knowledge of the English language. Very little worked for him, except the poetry he wrote in his new language, which began appearing in such prestigious literary journals as *Poetry, The Seven Arts,* and *Broom.* Before he was established as a writer his life became a nightmare as he tried to support himself in New York with menial jobs he detested and soon quit. Going hungry at times and moving incessantly from one furnished room to another, he viewed the metropolis as a metaphor for all that was ugly in America: "I walked the streets often in a frenzy of hatred and sang an Italian song sometimes and stopped to cry."

The furnished rooms were especially depressing; with each new job came a new room. "If all the hours I spent in the furnished rooms of America could be strung as beads are strung they would form the notes of one eternal howl that might perhaps at last reach the ear of God." His "howling," which often included his complaint of the impossibility of writing poetry in such a mechanized society, underlined Carnevali's inability to straddle the cultures of his two countries, but also resulted in avant-garde poetry that reflected the mood of American writers in the twenties who were trying to break with traditional writing. Carnevali's strong sense of alienation pervades much of his correspondence. To the philosopher Giovanni Papini in Italy, he wrote: "I don't have anything . . . I don't even have a country anymore. I am the foreigner here. They like me and admire me, but I am a foreigner."

Carnevali remained in the United States only eight years, first in New York, then in Chicago, until he became a victim of *encephalitis lethargica* (sleeping sickness). By then his works had made him an accepted member of the American cultural elite. His friends included Waldo Frank, the novelist, and Harriet Monroe, the editor of *Poetry*, who had rescued him from New York by employing him in Chicago as one of her editorial assistants. Ezra Pound helped to finance his return to Italy, sharing Carnevali's hope that he might be cured there. William Carlos Williams welcomed him into the pantheon of revolutionary poets like himself, although he saw Carnevali as "an obviously lost soul." Sherwood Anderson dedicated his poem "A Dying Poet" to him. And soon after Carnevali returned to Italy, Robert McAlmon, the Paris-based connoisseur of writings by the American avant-garde, such as Gertrude Stein, Hemingway, Kay Boyle, and Pound, published Carnevali's collection of short stories, *A Hurried Man,* which the *Saturday Review of Literature* characterized as "the book of homeless men . . . of the uprooted soul floating in every American city . . . the poor immigrant . . . the adolescent . . . and the non-conformist."

Though he remained an invalid the rest of his life, Carnevali continued writing in English, taking backward glances at his American experience. One of his poems, written as he approached his native land, bespeaks his ambivalent feelings and those of many another immigrant toward both Italy and America. "In America," he wrote,

> . . . everything
> Is bigger, but less majestic . . .
> Italy is a little family:
> America is an orphan
> Independent and arrogant,
> Crazy and sublime,
> Without tradition to guide her,
> Rushing headlong in a mad run which she calls
> Progress.

American cities, he continues, are mechanical; "in their hurry, people forget to love and be kind. Immigrants are hungry not only

for bread but for people, but America you gather the hungry people /
And give them new hungers for the old ones."

Carnevali died in 1944, at the age of forty-seven, not having lived
long enough to see a group of his poems included in a 1957 anthology of leading American poets, *The New Poetry,* edited by Harriet
Monroe and Alice Corbin Henderson. In a biographical note,
Monroe said of him: "His poetry had been, from the first to last, a
powerfully realistic recital of his emotional rebellion against the conditions of his life, and that of the poor in great cities."

Thirty years later, the novelist and poet Kay Boyle, recalling the
impact of Carnevali's writings on the writers of her generation, published a compilation of Carnevali's available work: *The Autobiography
of Emanuel Carnevali.* In her Introduction she wrote that when she
first encountered his poems in the twenties, she was young and "had
no way of knowing that Carnevali's radiant vision, unextinguished
by the misery of his defeat, was already metaphor to the poets of
America." *The Autobiography,* a patchwork of everything by Carnevali she could find, continues to keep his memory alive.

Perhaps best remembered of all the Italian immigrant poets is Arturo
Giovannitti, who, both for his poetry and his close involvement with
the social problems of his fellow immigrants, was generally regarded
as their poet laureate, despite the fact that he published only one
collection of poems, *Arrows in the Gale,* in 1914, when he was thirty
years old.

Like D'Angelo and Panunzio, Giovannitti was a teenager when
he left his native Abruzzo for Canada. For several years he was a
laborer in a railroad work gang, but found time to continue his
education at McGill University. Disillusioned by the harsh treatment
accorded to immigrants by employers, he left Canada to work in the
coal mines of Pennsylvania, only to find that immigrant workers
fared no better there. Their exploitation disturbed him deeply; despite the fact that he came from a well-to-do family of pharmacists
and lawyers, Giovannitti became involved in the Socialist movement.
For a time he was also attracted to Protestantism and went so far as
to acquire a bachelor's degree at a seminary. When he found that his
socialistic views conflicted with the current Protestant ideology, Giovannitti changed the direction of his life, moved to New York, and
continued his political activities while taking courses at Columbia
University.

Giovannitti was the most extrovert of the Italian immigrant poets. Nearly six feet tall, he was given to accentuating his Byronic appearance with flowing cravats and velvet vests. His gift for oratory, coupled with his ability to speak eloquently in both Italian and English, set him apart from other labor leaders. Carlo Tresca resembled him in height and charisma, but only in Italian could Tresca, who spoke English atrociously, compare with Giovannitti as a master orator. Giovannitti became a forceful voice in the IWW and in the radical labor movement.

His poem "The Walker" (see p. 289) was hailed as a masterpiece. Several critics compared it favorably to Oscar Wilde's poem about his own imprisonment, "The Ballad of Reading Gaol." A prominent drama critic, Kenneth McGowan, said of it that the poet "has painted the prison as no man, not even Wilde, has done."

In addition to poetry, Giovannitti wrote several plays in Italian, and numerous articles. All of his writings attest to his passionate crusade for the rights of mankind and against the enslavement of men and women.

Before the children of the immigrants were old enough to write their stories, they were preceded by a small group of Italian-born writers whose novels dramatized problems of assimilation as seen from the immigrants' point of view. One of the first was Giuseppe Cautela, who arrived at the age of sixteen and was immediately apprenticed to a barber shop to learn a trade he was to pursue the rest of his life. Unlike most Italian immigrant barbers with intellectual leanings, whose monologues are the mark of their profession, Cautela did more writing than talking. In addition to producing three novels, only one of which was published, Cautela contributed short stories and articles to H. L. Mencken's newly born iconoclastic magazine, *American Mercury*. His only published novel, *Moon Harvest* (1925), delves into conflicts that develop within a family of immigrants from a somnolent small village in southern Italy, where the villagers enjoy a life of simple pleasures, the most joyous of which is the celebration of the annual moon harvest. Intoxicated by the magical rumors of what America can offer, a young couple and their child allow themselves to be uprooted like "a tree struck by a cyclone," and are deposited on the alien shores of the promised land. The simplicity of their lives comes to an end as the husband gradually assimilates modern attitudes, which lead him to have an affair with an American woman, in conflict with his wife's growing adherence to old traditions and customs. The conflict drives the wife back to their native village, where she mourns and dies.

Three years after the publication of *Moon Harvest*, Louis Forgione, a friend of Pascal D'Angelo whose roots also stemmed from the region of Abruzzo, published *The River Between*. Taking the theme of family relationships one step further than Cautela, the narrative centers on the clashing values of an immigrant father, Demetrio, and his slow-witted son Oreste and Oreste's wife Rose, whose aggressively Americanized ways set her against both her husband and her father-in-law. The plot is weighed down with symbolic developments: Demetrio, once an influential member of the Italian community, slowly goes blind. Rose, unwilling to accept the Old World attitude of her assertive father-in-law, leaves home and takes to the streets. Eventually Demetrio, completely blind and on the verge of madness, does the same and becomes a beggar. In a scene that lends itself readily to opera, Rose encounters the blinded Demetrio and, pitying him, leads him back to Oreste's house, only to find it enveloped in flames. The symbolism is clear enough; but Forgione, unwilling to take a negative view of their situation, attributes a new beginning to all three of his protagonists, in which Rose, the pivotal member of the trio, accepts "the actualities of existence" by rejoining the men, "old traditions and all."

It was in the realm of fiction rather than poetry or autobiography that Italian American writers began to gain a foothold in the literary mainstream, but that was not to happen until the children of the immigrants were old enough to take stock of their bicultural situation. Most of these were children who, rejecting their parents' values, turned to writing about the subject they knew best as a means of trying to assert their individuality while also depicting the Italian American experience.

Many were like George Orwell, who said that writing fiction for him was a way of "getting back" at an unfriendly world that had rejected him during childhood. Other writers have expressed the belief that writing novels, involving as it does so many disparate elements, arises from the compulsion to make order out of chaos.

Some of these reasons undoubtedly fostered the writing of novels about Italian Americans by Italian Americans. Certainly, no future novelist could have felt more rejected or more displeased with reality than a sensitive second-generation Italian American at odds with the bi-cultural role thrust on him. For such future novelists, writing became an act of self-redemption—one that might bring them a more acceptable self-image. For their readers, some of the novels they produced reflect the soul and sociology of a people who were being subjected to blatant stereotyping. The best novels and memoirs provide the reader with insights into the Italian American experience that have often eluded the most scholarly studies on the subject.

Although their authors usually came from working-class homes, where books were seldom seen or welcomed—unless they were schoolbooks—and where parents and relatives spoke broken English or no English at all, the future novelist often had the distinctive advantage of listening to tall stories well into the night. The least educated immigrant was often naturally endowed with a strong gift of narrative that planted the seeds for their offspring's form of storytelling. The future novelist also had the advantage of absorbing inside information about relatives and ancestral culture that was beyond the reach of the outsider.

The clash of cultural values among the first and second generations of Italian Americans can be seen clearly in the works of Garibaldi Lapolla. Although born in Italy, Lapolla was only two years old when he arrived in the United States with his parents. He grew up in Harlem's Little Italy, where he was well aware of his bicultural heritage.

The most successful of Lapolla's novels, *The Grand Gennaro* (1932), has as its central character a ruthless Italian immigrant who claws his way to wealth and power until he is murdered by a former friend and business partner he has cheated. The murderer, ordinarily a gentle soul who symbolizes the gracious quality of Old World personal relationships, warns Gennaro: "The touch of gold in your hands has been too much. We are not used to it. It does queer things to us . . . the good it makes mad, the mean it makes brutal. Give me the money that is mine and you can have the business. You stay here. I'll go back to the old country."

While Lapolla was producing his novels, John Fante, a younger contemporary, was discovered by H. L. Mencken, who in 1932 began publishing his work in *American Mercury*. Soon afterwards Fante's short stories were appearing in other leading magazines, among them *Scribner's, Harper's,* and the *Atlantic Monthly,* on a wide range of themes. The best were written from the viewpoint of an American-born son telling of his encounters with relatives, parochial school nuns, and priests in and away from the confessional booth. (The stories were first collected in 1940 in a volume entitled *Dago Red*.)

In order to persuade the publishers to publish his stories (short-story collections in those years seldom sold enough copies to pay for publication expenses), Fante finally succeeded in completing his first novel, *Wait Until Spring, Bandini* (1938), a partly autobiographical family novel that centers on the father, Arturo Bandini, who was to reappear in two other later novels, *Full of Life* and *The Brotherhood of the Grape*. Arturo Bandini is the archetypal immigrant father: reacting to the assaults on his pride perpetrated by New World situations over which he has no control, he either commits adultery, usually with an "Americana," or becomes deranged.

John Fante casts himself as the sensitive American-born fourteen-year-old son, who is convinced that his family's poverty and ethnicity set him apart from "normal people." Like other sons of immigrants with identity problems, Fante eventually left home, first for San Francisco, and later, in 1943, for Hollywood, where he became a screenwriter. One of the most successful of his screenplays was the adaptation of his 1952 novel *Full of Life*. In a literary career that spanned some forty-five years, Fante maintained an enticing voice whose vibrancy of style and language are distinctly American.

In 1985, two years after Fante's death, a collection, *The Wine of Youth*, which included the most anthologized of his short stories, "Odyssey of a Wop," was published.

One editor wrote of these stories:

From Fante's pages one learns what it means to be an Italian by emotion, an American by conviction. To be called a Wop, to take first communion, to steal a stick of candy, to stand at a child's grave, to bat out a three-base hit, to pummel a boy and kiss a girl. A moment stands out with the beautiful naivete of a daguerreotype, a scene runs by with the concise speed of a news-reel, a whole way of life is set down with a jaunty informality that does not hide the depth of feeling behind it.

In 1939, a year after Fante had published his first novel, Pietro Di Donato rocketed onto the literary scene with *Christ in Concrete*. The largely autobiographical novel begins with a horrifying episode in which Geremio, the father, is caught under a falling structure and suffocates to death as a torrent of wet cement impales him on iron rods. When young Di Donato asks a New York policeman whether there is any news of his father, he is told, "The wop is in the wheelbarrow."

Burdened with the task of supporting his mother and his orphaned siblings, the young narrator becomes a bricklayer; but through his love of reading and association with a Jewish friend, he succeeds in rejecting his relatives' fatalism (particularly their faith in life-after-death rewards). When his devout mother thrusts a crucifix upon him in an effort to comfort her son, who has just seen his godfather (a fellow worker) smashed to death in another job accident, he crushes "the plaster man wooden cross" in her presence. Symbolically, at least, he develops into a revolutionary.

The most powerful of all novels published about Italian Americans, *Christ in Concrete* is written with a Joycean flow of diction and cadence to suggest the sonority of the Italian language, and the unorthodox style sometimes overwhelms the narrative, succeeding in conveying the plight of the immigrants in a society that isolates and exploits them. In one of the most striking passages, Di Donato captures the atmosphere of the Workmen's Compensation Bureau when Annunziata (the mother) and her eldest son attend a hearing on the accident:

> . . . the ghostly army of shabby humans with the seeking faces filed humbly past them in the corridors of the vast prison, where there were numerous chambers, and signs sticking out over the doors that said: "Clinic"—"Disability"—"Men's Toilet"— "Adjustments"—"Death Claims." And they saw the sleek flaccid state employees and heard the correct American voices of Parker, Murdin, Norr, Kagan and other passionless soaped tongues that conquered with grammatic clean cut: "What is your name? Your maiden name? How many children? Where were you born? This way please. Sit here please. Please answer yes or no. Eyetalians insist on hurting themselves when not personally supervised . . . directly his fault . . . substantiate . . . disclaim . . . liability . . . case adjourned." And they saw the winning smiles that made them feel that they had conspired with Geremio to kill himself so that they could present themselves there as objects of pity and then receive American dollars for nothing. The smiles that

smelled of refreshing toothpaste and considered flesh. The smiles that made them feel they were un-Godly and greasy pagan Christians; the smiles that told them they did not belong in the Workmen's Compensation Bureau. . . .

Never before or since has the aggravation of the Italian immigrant been more bluntly expressed by a novelist. *Christ in Concrete,* in essence, was a protest novel—or, as the literary critics of the day preferred to call it, "a proletariat novel"; but, unlike most novels of that genre, it sustains the sound of truth that assures it a place in the annals of ethnic literature.

Christ in Concrete was written when Di Donato was twenty-seven years old and deeply involved with the left-wing movement of the Great Depression years. Despite the novel's success in the literary world and in the marketplace (it became the first novel about Italian Americans to be selected by a major book club), he did not publish a second novel until twenty years later. In *This Woman,* Paulie, the narrator, is no longer the would-be revolutionary but a young man who asserts some of the very same Old World values which in *Christ in Concrete* he would have dismissed as reactionary. Now married to an American of Protestant background, Paulie becomes the stereotypically jealous Italian husband, who cannot bear the fact that he is not the first to have had sex with his wife, though her first husband has been dead for some time. In an act that deranges his wife, he insists on exhuming the corpse in order to desecrate it.

In his third and final novel, *Three Circles of Light,* published in 1960, Di Donato returns to continue the story of *Christ in Concrete*—but this time there is no anger. The narrator, no longer a revolutionary, has accepted the major traditions of southern Italian culture, even to the extent that the mother of the family, the symbol of female endurance, must remain loyal to an unfaithful husband. When it becomes public knowledge that the father has taken on an American mistress, a concerned neighbor, impelled by the importance of keeping the Italian family system intact, warns Geremio's wife that she must do something about the situation, but Annunziata does nothing. When Geremio meets the horrific death described in *Christ in Concrete,* his demise is seen by neighbors as the God-given penalty due him.

With *Three Circles of Light,* an older and more temperate Di Donato affirmed the persistence of ethnic attitudes, despite pressures for complete assimilation, even among the American-born offspring of the immigrants.

In 1940, the success of *Christ in Concrete* encouraged publishers to issue two books of short stories about Italian Americans: *Dago Red,* by John Fante, and *The Paesanos,* by Joe Pagano, who, like Fante, had grown up in Denver, Colorado. Both collections were favorably received, but, like most short-story collections of that era, reached a small audience. Undeterred, three years later Joe Pagano published his first novel, *The Golden Wedding,* which like the stories in *Paesanos* was written in the form of a memoir. Not as lighthearted as *Paesanos,* the novel traces the married life of the Simone family from the time the immigrant parents marry as teenagers and take up life in a western coal-mining camp to their golden wedding anniversary. With an objectivity that reflects the author's keen awareness of how two seemingly incompatible parents manage to cope with a series of unexpected crises, *Golden Wedding,* to a greater degree than any other novel depicting Italian Americans, parallels the experience of the immigrants and their children while also placing particular emphasis on the years of the Great Depression and the rise of fascism in Europe.

Pagano's skill in creating believable characters and maintaining a strong narrative pace won the novel favorable reviews, but again it did not fare well in the bookstores.

Sensing the lack of a sufficient constituency among Italian Americans interested in reading about themselves, Pagano in his next novel, *The Condemned* (1947), tried to reach a wider audience by writing a crime narrative with protagonists bearing non-Italian names. *The New York Times* praised it as "an absorbing examination of the underlying causes of crime . . . executed with the swift sure strokes of a craftsman." When *The Condemned* fared no better commercially, Pagano began utilizing his talents as a storyteller to develop a career as a Hollywood screenwriter.

Although Guido D'Agostini, who was born in an Italian enclave adjoining Greenwich Village, published four novels within twelve years, only his first, *Olives on the Apple Tree,* deals with Italian immigrants. Published in 1940, the title refers to Italian immigrants who in their ambition to be accepted into American society try to be what they are not. In a style that sometimes verges on the didactic, the novel emphasizes that too rapid a transformation from Italian into

American can be damaging. As one reviewer put it, "Like old wine, the process needs aging in order to bring out its best qualities."

D'Agostino's main protagonist is Emilio Gardella, a young physician who, in his eagerness to become a member of the establishment, turns his back on "Wop Roost," the Italian enclave where he was reared. His opposite is the immigrant Marco, who explains as he picks up an olive: "The olive that jumps to the apple tree. The olive that shouts it is an apple. There is the mistake. There is the whole trouble . . . I have said it many times and I will say it many times more."

In his haste to become assimilated, Gardella (who is planning to change his name to Gardell) reveals himself as a rank opportunist, *persona non grata* to his American society friends, who is thrust back into the "Wop Roost" he disdained.

The complex question of determining to what extent American-born offspring should adhere to the customs and values that constitute the immigrants' Old World heritage is examined more subtly by Michael De Capite, the youngest of the second-generation Italian American novelists to publish a first novel in the forties. *Maria,* issued in 1943, underlines the difficulties of an American-born daughter of immigrants who, in her effort to comply with her parents' wishes, marries the Italian they have selected for her. The marriage is a disastrous one; the husband is a failure and finally abandons her and their children. Yet Maria, unable to renounce her parents' Old World attitude that a marriage cannot be broken regardless of the circumstances, never stops trying to persuade him to return. Trapped within this abysmal family situation, which occurs during the worst years of the Depression, the oldest of the sons, Paulie, becomes thoroughly bewildered and resentful, unable to cope with either of the two cultures thrust upon him.

One of the most talented of the Italian American novelists, De Capite followed *Maria* with two other novels: *No Bright Banner,* published a year later, in which Paul becomes the central character and, unlike most second-generation Italian Americans, leaves home to go to college and try to find his own way into the American mainstream. Paul moves from one unsatisfactory job to another as he mingles with intellectuals of various nationalities. In the final chapter, he is about to board a troopship to fight for what he hopes will be a better world. Throughout the novel the warm relationship that develops between Paul and the father who had failed as a husband is well depicted. De Capite's final novel, *The Bennett Place,* which received mixed reviews, makes no mention of Italian Americans.

Among the spate of novels in the 1940s by children of Italian immigrants, two were by a woman—Mari Tomasi, the daughter of Piedmont immigrant parents who settled among the Italian granite workers of Montpelier, Vermont. Tomasi's first novel, *Deep Grow the Roots,* was selected by the *New York Herald-Tribune* and the American Booksellers' Associations as "one of the ten most outstanding first novels of the year 1940." Unlike the works of her Italian American contemporaries, Tomasi's novel has an Italian setting, the Piedmont country of northern Italy which she visited with her father as a child. The story, which deals chiefly with two young lovers striving to cope with Fascist Italy's approaching war in Ethiopia, was interpreted by one American critic as "a clever attempt on Miss Tomasi's part to present even native Italians as innocent victims of Mussolini and in so doing further disassociate Italian Americans from Mussolini's action and Italy's involvement in the war." Other critics gave it mixed reviews. One, responding to the young lovers' efforts to avoid participating in "Mussolini's dream of empire," which result in tragedy, praised the narrative as "one of poignant earthy simplicity and beauty written from tender insight and with exquisite restraint." Another critic, however, chided Tomasi for the novel's relentless lyricism, finding the narrative "drenched in an atmosphere of sunshine and poetic writing."

Tomasi's next and last novel, *Like Lesser Gods,* is the work of a more experienced writer. As a child hampered by an injury in infancy which kept her mostly in a wheelchair the first eight years of her life, she became an early observer of human nature. Her favorite pastime was curling up behind a showcase in her father's fruit store in Barre, Vermont, listening to the conversations between her father and the *paesani* stonecutters who were his chief customers. As a grown-up, after her college education was cut short by the sudden death of her father, she taught country school, worked on the staff of the Montpelier *Evening Argus,* and published her first short stories. During the Great Depression she was employed by the Federal Writers' Project in Vermont and contributed to a nonfiction unpublished manuscript of the Writers' Project, "Men Against Granite." In her spare time, partly inspired by the research she did for the Project manuscript, Tomasi began writing *Like Lesser Gods.*

Although "Granitetown" (in reality Barre, Vermont), the "Largest Granite Center of the World," is the focal point of the novel, its cast of characters centers on a penniless elderly schoolteacher from Italy. Unable to support himself in his native Piedmont, he accepts the invitation of a former student, now the head of a family who works as a stonecutter in Granitetown. "Mr. Tiff," as he is called by the children, who have difficulty pronouncing his actual name, Tiffone, becomes the sagacious counselor for several of the characters in the novel who are burdened with problems. He manages to provide solutions for most of them, but cannot help Pietro Dalli, his former student, who becomes a victim of silicosis.

When Dalli's wife and his doctor warn him that he is killing himself by continuing to work as a stonecutter, Dalli tries to explain: "It is a hard stone. Beautiful, lasting. Always when I carve my name on a memorial, I feel, well, important. I carve my name and say to myself, God creates new life and takes it away but the stonecutters take up where He left off. They make a lasting memory of man's life."

Dalli's wife, Maria, out of fear that her husband's love for his craft will cost him his life, takes matters into her own hands. Under cover of darkness, she seriously damages an almost completed large crucifix which he regards as his finest masterpiece, expecting that the damage will be attributed to her husband's careless use of his chisel and he will be fired. The fact that her act of vandalism has been in vain, that the damage she inflicts is so extensive as to be readily attributable to "the intentional butchering of some malefactor," evokes an operatic denouement that detracts from the novel's generally realistic depiction of Italian immigrant families.

Shortly before Tomasi died in 1964 in her early fifties, she published an essay, "The Italian Story in Vermont," which, though lacking the narrative situations that make her novel absorbing, reveals a mine of information about Italian immigrants in Vermont. If in the novel there is a noticeable lack of reference to the radical movement that flourished there among the Italian immigrants, this last published work tells of what ultimately happened to the movement, though from Tomasi's own perspective as a Catholic conservative. Lacking in her explanation (both in the novel and in the essay) is the role of radical union members in Vermont in applying pressure on employers, which resulted in the adoption of safety measures to prevent silicosis.

CHAPTER 22

Scoring in the Sports World of America

The Italian baseball team of Barre, Vermont—state champions of 1909—still peers out at us from a group photo taken at a time when anarchists and other radicals gathered in that city.

From the very beginning, whether in the back alleys of New York's Lower East Side or in rural areas, the children of the immigrants eagerly took up the games and sports of America.

There had been little time or opportunity for these activities in Italy. Hunting, for example, was reserved for aristocrats. In the old country, athletics were considered a useless activity, like the cultivation of ornamental trees.

For the sons of immigrants in ethnic neighborhoods, sports offered not only cheap entertainment but also a way to defuse the exuberant adolescent brawling that sometimes threatened to explode into ethnic violence. Much of the street violence was channeled into boxing. Promoters emphasized ethnic rivalries in marketing fighters, pitting white against black, Italian against Irish or Jew, until the events seemed to be organized street fights in which champions were chosen from street gangs. In one case, Mike Rossman, whose real name was Depiano, was marketed as "the 'Jewish Bomber' by his promoters since his mother was Jewish."

The diffusion of violence through sports was nowhere more apparent than in St. Louis's "Dago Hill" section, which produced more ball players than any other section of the country. According to Gary Mormino:

> The area was honeycombed with gangs: Kings Highway . . . the creek . . . railroad tracks . . . that was our boundary. . . . Up the Hill we had the Blue Ridge Gang—Irish. The northwest we had the Cheltenham Gang—a mixture of Germans and more or less natives. East of Kings Highway was the Tower Grove Gang, what most of us refer as Hoosiers, people up from small towns . . . then the Dog Town Gang to the east. . . . You go beyond that and you get your ass kicked around so you stayed within your limits.

Soon after World War I, "Dago Hill" in St. Louis was crowded with Italian immigrants, primarily from Lombardy and Sicily, attracted by jobs in the brickyards. They first settled in labor camps, which eventually became the Italian community. They were poor and divided until the coming of Prohibition, when Lombards and Sicilians joined to cater to the community's drinking habits, and in the process brought a measure of prosperity to the Hill. Rather than bring violence, as it did to other Italian communities around the country, in Dago Hill the bootlegging industry paid for many houses, as well as for the building of a new church.

The Catholic Church played an important role in the development of ethnic ball players among the poor. Babe Ruth owed his start to the dedicated work of Brother Matthias Boutier, the Xaverian Brother who directed the sports activity of St. Mary's Industrial School in Baltimore. In Dago Hill, Father Causino, a third-generation Bohemian (Kaceno), who Italianized his name and learned to speak Italian in order to work with the young of his parish, was aware of this gang violence; he did much to direct it into sports. It was the dedicated work of such men that attracted the Italian Americans to the game of baseball.

The first Italian-sounding name to appear in the baseball records was Tony Defate, who played with Detroit in 1917 and left the unenviable batting average of .127. That same year he played with

St. Louis of the American League and batted .143. Not a startling debut.

Eight years before—when the Vermont Italian Baseball Team had won the state championship, Honus Wagner won the National League batting title with an average of .339, and Ty Cobb batted .377 playing for Detroit—the record book was filled with Anglo-Saxon and German names. Babe Ruth, it was said, came from a family where German was still spoken. Then twenty-three-year-old Ping Bodie appeared on the Chicago White Sox team in 1911, the year Ty Cobb and Sam Crawford were the most feared batters, and a young rookie, Shoeless Joe Jackson, hit .408. Ping hit .287.

Few knew that Bodie was of Italian origin, except for the Chicago *paesani* who worshipped him as their first baseball hero. Ping Bodie was born Giuseppe Pezzolo, or Francesco Pezzolo, in San Francisco in 1888. The name "Bodie" allegedly came from the town he lived in, although no such town can be found on the map. The "Ping," of course, came from the sound the ball made as it left his 34-ounce bat. He broke into the major leagues with the Chicago White Sox in 1911, later playing for the Philadelphia A's and the New York Yankees; when Babe Ruth came to the Yankees, Ping roomed with the Babe and followed him in the lineup. As Ruth's career ascended, reporters often asked Ping what it was like to room with the Babe. His stock answer was, "I don't room with the Babe; I room with his bags."

It may have been Ping Bodie who first called Ruth "the Bambino," which started the rumor among the Italian immigrants that Ruth was Italian. The rumor no doubt incited an increased interest in the game, which in a few years would spawn a large number of ball players from Italian communities throughout the country.

By the early 1920s there was a smattering of Italian American players in the major leagues, but it was not until the middle of the decade that the sons of Italian immigrants achieved prominence in both the American and National leagues. One of the first was Tony Lazzeri, who by 1926 was playing with the New York Yankees. Later in the decade Ernie Orsatti batted .306 for the St. Louis Browns.

Many of the early players came up with the Browns, whose policy it was to sign up as many young players as cheaply as possible, sell those that developed to more prosperous teams, and discard the rest. Baseball owners then were not much different from mine owners. Many Italian American ball players came up this way, among them Gus Mancuso, who was to have a long career with the New York Giants, and Joe Cicero of Boston. Many more were among those discarded and returned to the brickyards of St. Louis or the fields of California.

A. Bartlett (an obvious echo of Bartolomeo) Giamatti, former president of the National League and of Yale, would as a boy often listen to Boston Red Sox games in the attic of his home in South Hadley, Massachusetts. Although Giamatti was an ardent Red Sox fan, he kept a score card of his own Italian American All Star team, consisting of Yogi Berra behind the plate; first base, Dolph Camilli; second base, Tony Lazzeri; shortstop, Phil Rizzuto; third base, Frank Crosetti; outfielders, Dom DiMaggio, Joe DiMaggio, Sam Mele, Al "Zeke" Zarilla, and Carl Furillo; pitchers, Vic Raschi and Sal ("The Barber") Maglie.

Giamatti's team spanned the three decades in which the children of the early immigrants began to make their mark in sports, so much so that by the 1930s Dizzy Dean could look around the ball park and say, "There are nothing but Romans on this team." He was being polite. "Dago" was the word more often used, even by Italian Americans themselves. Phil Rizzuto recounts a crucial moment when a coach hollered, "Throw it to the dago, the dago," and the catcher, not knowing which "dago" to throw it to—DiMaggio, Crosetti, or Lazzeri—froze and the runner scored.

In 1926, Anthony Lazzeri came up to the New York Yankees from a minor league team in Salt Lake City. A reserved young man, tall, thin, with high cheekbones, he had never been east of the Rockies. Even as a rookie, he spoke little, in a quiet growl as if angry. That he suffered from epilepsy did not prevent him from playing fourteen seasons at shortstop and batting an impressive .297. He was known as Tony "Push 'em up" (shouted in an Italian-accented American) for his ability to hit at crucial moments.

Francesco Crosetti, better known as Frank (Crow) Crosetti, was born in San Francisco in 1910 and arrived at the Yankees' training camp in 1932 as a quiet, determined rookie. He had no other interest but baseball. As a coach for the New York team from 1932 to 1948, Crosetti helped break in such players as DiMaggio and Phil Rizzuto.

Lazzeri and Crosetti seemed to set the pattern for the other ball players who came from the West, especially Joseph Paul DiMaggio.

The three men had a great deal in common: they did not like to talk much and all liked to dress well, especially DiMaggio, who followed the Italian mother's ideal that her son should be *civile*, civilized. Their ability to sit for hours without saying a word became legendary. During DiMaggio's first season they drove cross country, from San Francisco to Florida, for spring training for two days, without a word being spoken between them. It is said that on the third day Lazzeri turned to DiMaggio and asked, "Do you want to drive?"

"I can't drive," DiMaggio answered, and with that bit of information they drove the rest of the way in silence.

Joseph DiMaggio's family were fishermen who had come to California in 1902 from Isola delle Femmine, about ten miles outside Palermo in Sicily. The DiMaggios had been fishermen there for generations. The large, hardworking family spoke the Sicilian dialect in their San Francisco home; the DiMaggio brothers numbered four: Tom, Vince, Joe, and Dom. Tom, the eldest, was the best ball player in the family, but he chose to remain a fisherman. Papa DiMaggio was a practical man who looked upon the game as *'na stupitagina*. He would have preferred to see his son Joe become a bookkeeper. Once he became aware of his sons' success, however, he said laughingly, "No money in bocce ball. Baseball, that's the game."

The DiMaggio brothers came out of the Italian community, helped by a Mr. Rossi who supported the first team Joe played on. When Joe helped the team win the league championship, he received from Rossi two gold baseballs and two orders of merchandise worth $8 each, as a prize.

Vince played ball around San Francisco before Joe was old enough for the game, but he opened the way for Joe. It was Vince (who ended his days as a Fuller brush salesman in L.A.) who helped Joe to get his start:

> I remember taking Joe over to meet the owner of the San Francisco Seals. I had been playing for them, and I told them about my kid brother. They needed a short-stop, so I got Joe the tryout the last day of the season. Once they saw him they liked him, and my older brother Tom negotiated the contract. It's funny how all this began. Maybe if I had kept my mouth shut, I'd be remembered as the greatest DiMaggio.

If baseball introduced the brothers to America, it also broke family tradition. As Vince remembered in *Where Have You Gone Vince DiMaggio* by Edward Kiersh:

When the folks were alive we were a lot closer. But I guess in the last four years I've seen him two or three times. What can I do, I'm Vince, and he's Joe. He's always had a living style higher than mine, or higher than I cared to live. It's only a shame that we have gone such different ways. That's real sad. Family should stick together.

Vince added, as if recalling the Sicilian proverb, "Who plays alone always wins," "Joe's always been a loner, and he always will be."

Vince's career, although overshadowed by his brother Joe, left behind the memory of "the greatest outfielder" (in the opinion of his brother) and a lifetime batting average of .287.

With the 1930s came a second generation of players: Lew Fonseca and Sal Gelatto, both of Cleveland; Tony Rensa of Detroit; George Puccinelli of the St. Louis Cards; and Tony Cuccinello of Cincinnati. In 1931, Ernie Lombardi played in Brooklyn and became part of the "Brooklyn Bums." He was a big, lumbering man of whom it was said that he often hit triples and barely made it to first. There was Joe Palmisano in Philadelphia, and Carl Furillo.

Carl Furillo was a journeyman player, much like a good worker who holds a shop together. Like so many ball players he came from a working-class family in western Pennsylvania. During his years with the Brooklyn Dodgers (1946–57), Furillo played in the outfield of Ebbetts Field, a small park surrounded by the apartment houses of Flatbush. He was the great outfielder of that time, with a riflelike arm that could throw a strike to home plate from the deepest part of right field. He was also a constant .300 hitter. But it did not come easy. He was often thrown at and beaned several times. And although he did not attack the pitchers, once after learning the source of his troubles he rushed to the dugout, seized the manager, Leo Durocher, and almost killed him in a headlock.

The Dodgers released Furillo in 1957 after he suffered a torn calf muscle. He was left with barely enough money to open a grocery store. When that failed, he went to work as an elevator mechanic and finally returned to western Pennsylvania to work in construction. He was remembered by the Italian American newspaper *Fra Noi* as "a superlative ballplayer and one hell of a man. These guys today couldn't hold his glove. On or off the field."

★ ★ ★

Men now in their sixties and seventies who lived in the Italian en-claves remember the voice of Mel Allen shouting on the radio, "The Yankee Clipper comes to the plate with two men on . . ." They can remember the pride they felt that one of their own became the great "DiMage." In the evenings they would walk to the newsstands be-neath the elevated lines in Brooklyn or the Bronx to buy the night edition of the *Daily News* or *Daily Mirror* to see how "DiMage" or Mancuso or Cuccinello had done that day. And the next weekend they imitated DiMaggio's open stance at the plate or Lazzeri's catlike play at second during sandlot games.

Baseball helped Americanize the parents of the second genera-tion as well. Dominic DiMaggio often would read and explain box scores to his father as they followed the careers of his brothers Joe and Vince.

Phil Rizzuto, whose parents came from Calabria, was brought up in Brooklyn, where his father was a subway conductor. Fiore Rizzuto also was opposed to his son playing ball until he saw the money to be made in it. Thereafter he learned to follow the *la basa' bol*, especially the "World Serious," as many immigrants half-jokingly called it.

Italian American ball players flourished in the postwar period. When DiMaggio faded into the realm of coffee commercials, players such as Vic Raschi, Carl Furillo, Yogi Berra, Phil Rizzuto, and Joe Pepitone came to the fore.

In the Italian American dialect that developed during the early days, *faitature* (a fighter) was the immigrants' word for a prizefighter. It meant one who was a battler, one who could take the blows life handed out, come back for more, and if not triumph, then surely survive. These were important attributes much needed in the early twentieth century.

Whereas the early ball players for the most part came from the West, the boxers came from the East, especially from those cities where there were long-established Italian communities. The out-standing boxers all had that quality of *faitature*. Tony Galento, Jake Lamotta, Rocky Marciano, and Rocky Graziano all helped create the image of Italian Americans as "physical."

Anthony Galento was born in Orange, New Jersey, in 1910 of immigrant parents from the Abruzzo region. Galento left school in the sixth grade to work as an iceman, a trade dominated by his Abruzzese relatives. Even before he turned professional, Galento's face reflected the many bareknuckle brawls he engaged in while earning $25 a week as a bouncer. His teeth had been punched through his lips, leaving jagged scars. Cuts above his eyes healed into raised seams on a face that was fat and puffy before its time. At the height of his career, Galento was 5 feet 9 inches and weighed anywhere from 200 to 240 pounds. His fat, rolling gait earned him the nickname of "Two Ton Tony." Galento's moment of glory came in his fight with Joe Louis in 1939, when in the third round he floored Louis with a left hook. In the next round he took such a beating, however, that the referee stopped the fight. In the end Galento was marketed as the inarticulate brawler who did his roadwork with a cigar in his mouth, and who was pictured eating mounds of spaghetti washed down, not with wine, but with twelve bottles of beer. His famous prefight words were always: "I'll moider the bum."

In the middleweight division, Carmen Basilio held the crown in 1957 after winning the welterweight crown in 1956. Between 1930 and 1933, Tony Canzoneri (a cousin of the novelist Robert Canzoneri) won three different boxing titles: featherweight, junior lightweight, and lightweight.

Rocky Marciano was born Rocco Marchigiano, and grew up around Brockton, Massachusetts, in and around those factory towns in which so much Italian American history is rooted. His maternal grandfather, Luigi Picciuto, was a strong, tall *bracciante* from the village of San Bartolomeo near Naples. Marciano's father, who had come from Chieta, a small Abruzzo fishing town on the Adriatic, was not a big man; thin, not quite 5 feet 7 inches, he weighed less than 150 pounds. He was sound enough, however, to have fought in World War I on the French front around Château-Thierry, where he was wounded. After the war, he worked as a shoemaker. Rocky Marciano's first love had been baseball, but his apparent clumsiness ruled out such a career.

When he turned to boxing, those tenacious peasant characteristics of Grandfather Luigi marked his style of fighting. He often emerged from a fight bloodied and battered but victorious. There was much of the transplanted Italian peasant in Marciano—patience, a capacity to absorb punishment, loyalty to friends and relatives, and the ability to survive and endure.

Marciano battered such fighters as Joe Louis, Ezzard Charles, and Jersey Joe Walcott, and he left the world of boxing a wealthy man who distrusted banks and had squirreled away thousands of dollars, which after his death in a 1969 plane crash never resurfaced.

The same qualities were found in such fighters as Jake Lamotta, and in Rocky Graziano, who was born Thomas Rocco Barbella on the Lower East Side of New York. Street fights led him to reform school and the Army, where he was discharged for hitting an officer. Fortunately, Graziano could channel his anger and energy into prize-fighting. Nowhere more than in his fight with Tony Zale did he show that capacity to take punishment and survive; after Graziano's death in April 1990, the fight was recalled by Ira Berkow in *The New York Times*:

> I was a boy in the summer of 1947. His second fight with Tony Zale for the middleweight championship of the world. . . . The memory of the savagery of that fight is spine-chilling. . . . By the sixth round, Graziano was cut and bleeding badly, sagging on the ropes, his eyes glazed, when suddenly he summoned strength and crashed a right to Zale's jaw. Moments later, Zale was defenseless against Graziano's barrage. The fight was stopped and Graziano's arm was raised as the new champ.

Graziano went on to become a television personality, an amateur painter, and a comedian who played the role of the immigrant who mangles the English language. When asked if he knew of the painter Van Gogh, he answered, "I didn't know the guy, but I liked his pitchers a lot."

By the 1970s, Italian Americans were moving out of the working-class sport of boxing toward managerial positions. Angelo Dundee, born Merena, came up to the rank of trainer in the gyms of South Philadelphia, and then moved on to the Stillman Gym in New York. His greatest satisfaction, after training Muhammad Ali, Dundee said, came in managing such fighters as "Sugar Ray" Leonard in the 1970s and 1980s. In baseball, Tommy Lasorda, whose father came from the same province as Rocky Marciano's father, started as a pitcher in the major leagues. He was kept on as a scout and in time moved up to a managing position with the Dodgers. In 1974, Lasorda returned to his father's birthplace to instruct baseball coaches at the request of the Italian Baseball Federation. He quickly realized that sport was a form of entertainment and as manager of the Los Angeles Dodgers did just that.

Tony La Russa, manager of the Oakland A's, has been called a capitalist-industrialist manager who "returns to baseball's fundamental trade-off the purchase of opportunity by the coin of risk." The old Italian anarchists would have said that sport was truly the opiate of the people.

By the time DiMaggio and Crosetti became famous in baseball, other Italian Americans began to appear on the football fields of America.

At the University of Chicago, the venerable coach Amos Alonzo Stagg had Felix Caruso and Adolphe Toigio on his teams; of Toigio, Stagg said, "He was one of the three immortals."

At Notre Dame with the "fighting Irish," during the years of Knute Rockne, two of the outstanding players were Frank Cardeo and Joe Savoldi. Papa Savoldi was annoyed, however, when his son was referred to as one of the fighting Irish. "Irish," he replied, "they's a-good too, but not-a like the Italians."

In the 1930s and 1940s many still played under anglicized names. Luigi Piccolo coached the Columbia teams for many years under the name of Lou Little, and Giordano Olivieri coached the Yale team as Jordan Oliver.

Although there were many who starred, such as Trippi at Georgia, Macaluso at Colgate, and Bellino at Navy, Italian Americans in football became prominent only with the start of professional ball. And that period soon became the Vince Lombardi era.

Football as we know it was invented by the Ivy League colleges and thus dominated by those who could afford the time and money to let their sons attend college. Not until the 1930s did Italian names begin to appear in the lineups. The Child Labor Law of 1916 had the effect of extending the education of immigrants' children beyond grade school. Needing to accommodate the ensuing influx of students, high school administrators (to relieve the restlessness of children in large classes) imitated private schools by introducing football as well as coaches and larger playing fields, things unheard of before the child labor laws. As a result, football gradually lost its elitist status and grew into a national sport. Whereas the 1915 Yale team consisted entirely of prep school graduates, mainly from Exeter, in 1976 the Yale team had only one player who hailed from a private school. On the Harvard side, the "preppies" did a little better with seven representatives on a squad of seventy-two.

In 1932, Jimmy De Angelis made the Yale team. (This was at a time when members of the team played without the use of substitutes for the full sixty minutes.) Later Felix Caracciolo played for two seasons, starting in 1936. By 1952, Yale had an Italian American coach, Joe Fortunato. And in 1965, Carmen Cozza became Yale's "winningest" coach. No doubt these early players became role models for the scores of Italian American football greats who were to follow, from Hank Lauricella, All American (1951), to Joe Montana, quarterback of the San Francisco Giants.

No one has left a greater mark on professional football than Vincent Lombardi. Born in Brooklyn, he attended St. Francis Preparatory School, where he "majored" in football, basketball, and baseball. Lombardi went on to play football for Fordham University and became one of the seven "Blocks of Granite" that made up the Fordham line in the 1930s. What he lacked in size he made up for in ferocious charges and violent tackles that made him loom much larger than his 172 pounds. Lombardi also developed into an excellent student; after graduation he studied for a law degree while playing for a semi-professional football team—the Brooklyn Eagles.

Lombardi soon stopped playing and took a job as assistant coach at a New Jersey high school, where he also taught physics, algebra, and Latin. Later he held coaching positions at Fordham and West Point, where he perfected such strategies as the T formation. From there he went on to coach the New York Giants, but it was not until he became head coach of the Green Bay Packers that Lombardi came into his own. Before Lombardi's arrival, Green Bay was considered the "Siberia" of professional football. Within a year he had brought a spirit of endurance and determination to the team that reflected his immigrant upbringing. Giving up was prohibited. His battle cry became: "Winning isn't everything, it's the only thing." After his first year in Green Bay, Lombardi was named coach of the year.

The once lowly Packers won five national championships in the sixties. Lombardi left an indelible mark on professional football before dying of cancer in 1970 at the age of fifty-seven.

Joe Paterno of Pennsylvania State University was also a product of American-born parents who raised their children in Brooklyn.

Paterno began his football career playing guard at Brooklyn Prep, despite his weight of just 125 pounds. Among the Irish who dominated the school he became the resident "Wop." In Joe's senior year he captained the team; the only loss was to Vince Lombardi's St. Cecilia team. At Brown University, Paterno played football in his senior year as quarterback, during a season of eight wins and one loss. His brother George played on the same team as a running back and they quickly became known as the "gold dust twins" from Brooklyn. Soon after, to the dismay of his mother, he accepted a job as assistant coach at Penn State University. By 1983, Joe Paterno's standing among active coaches was second only to Barry Switzer of Oklahoma.

By the 1980s, assimilation of Italian Americans into American life was so complete that little attention was paid to ethnic origin. The running back Franco Harris (son of an Afro-American father and an Italian mother) remarked, "I didn't know I was part Italian until I became famous." Likewise, it was only the Italian American newspapers that remembered Dan Marino's Italian origins. Marino came out of those Catholic high schools that produced so many Italian American football players. He was born and raised around Pittsburgh and attended schools there. It was at the University of Pittsburgh that he began his career, and by 1990 he was the star quarterback for the Miami Dolphins.

Joe Montana dominated the professional football world in the 1989–90 season. In a rating based on percentage of touchdown passes per attempt, he topped all quarterbacks going back to 1943, when professional football came into its own, in the number of times he was intercepted, and in average yards gained each time he threw a pass.

He also brought the excitement of the underdog, whom one reporter described as having "the eyes a poker player would kill for . . ." and "a gaze both dispassionate and compelling. The 49ers' quarterback is able to mask his emotions." In 1988, after ten seasons of play, an injured back threatened to end his career. Yet after surgery he came back to play one of his most exciting games against the Dallas Cowboys, in which in a last-minute rally he turned apparent defeat into victory.

By 1990, the boy from the coal fields of Pennsylvania had become if not the Babe Ruth of football, then certainly the Joe DiMaggio.

CHAPTER 23

Hollywood—and Show Business

> . . . I knew that a film is a dichotomy of business and art
> and there's no other way you can figure it. And you have got
> to make both work. You've got to pay attention to both.
>
> If your film loses money, you're not going to make many
> more films. Your films have got to be successful. I know you
> don't think talking of commerce is very important. But don't
> lose sight of the fact that if you don't make money with your
> films you're not going to make many films. You might be
> working in films but if you're going to be filmmakers, you
> must pay attention to the money side, the financial side.
> Write a book, you know, you buy a typewriter and you buy
> some paper and that's it, that's the total expense and the rest
> of it is your time. Making a picture is hundreds of thousands
> of dollars, millions of dollars, tens of millions of dollars
> perhaps, and that's an enormous responsibility.
>
> —FRANK CAPRA

THE YEAR VALENTINO DIED: 1926

Young Italian American males like those who frequented the
dance halls of Second Avenue in New York in the 1920s imitated Rodolfo Guglielmi, who became the idol of many Americans

as Rudolph Valentino. His death marked a transition from Italian to Italian American in the film industry—from the first generation of entertainers to the second generation, from Frank Capra to the early Frank Sinatra.

Valentino's life was the epitome of the immigrant success story. Born in Castellaneta in southern Italy on May 6, 1895, he came to America in 1913, where he worked as a dishwasher, a janitor, and a clerk in an Italian grocery. He was as lonely and homesick as any young immigrant in a New York City "where even the Irish cops were contemptuous of Italians." Valentino learned to ape the manners of the elegant Americans for whom he worked as a gardener. He also frequented those Second Avenue cabarets where many a young Italian immigrant spent his Saturday nights. Legend has it that his tango dancing turned him into an astute gigolo. American men looked upon him as effete, an attitude which contributed to Valentino's dislike of American ways and produced an arrogance in him that was seen as aristocratic haughtiness.

Valentino toured the country as a tango dancer with Bonnie Glass, an established dancer. Glass introduced Valentino to show business and advised him to sign with the William Morris Agency. A tour brought him to Los Angeles, where he was discovered not in the proverbial drugstore but in a bar of the Alexander Hotel at Fifth and Spring Street. The promiscuity of relations in Hollywood was said to have appalled Valentino. Nonetheless, he married the actress Jean Acker on the spur of the moment, only to find himself locked out of their bedroom soon after the wedding ceremony. A new meaning was added to the Italian word *cornuto* (cuckold).

Valentino was rescued by the scriptwriter June Mathis, who suggested him for the role of Julio, a tango-dancing dilettante, in *Four Horsemen of the Apocalypse* (1922). As Julio Desnoyers, Valentino dies on the battlefields of France while the Four Horsemen—War, Conquest, Famine, and Death—in a newly invented film technique, gallop over the scene.

The bloody battles of World War I were still fresh in the minds of audiences, and the senseless death of the vital Julio struck a mournful chord. The film became a great success and Valentino was hailed as a star. C. Blythe Sherwood in *Motion Picture Classic* (June 1920) wrote:

He has . . . the reverence of Dante who would worship; the vitality of Don Juan who would woo; the extravagence of Don Quixote who would exaggerate; the courage of D'Artagnan who would dare; the restraint of Sordell who would court in deed; the desire of D'Annunzio who would achieve; the strength of Vulcan who would excel; and the philosophy of Omar for whom "yesterday is dead and tomorrow never comes."

Two more movies, *The Sheikh* and *Blood and Sand,* followed, and Valentino became a legend.

When he died unexpectedly of peritonitis at the age of thirty-one, his body was brought to the Campbell Funeral Home in New York City, where thousands came to pay their last respects. The funeral became a carnival marked by five Black Shirts who appeared after midnight to place a wreath on Valentino's casket bearing the inscription: FROM BENITO MUSSOLINI. All was dutifully photographed for the morning papers, which provoked a near riot when the Anti-Fascist League came to protest. As it turned out, the Fascist honor guard had been the idea of a press agent, Harry Klemfuss. Although the Fascists were authentic, the flowers were from the funeral home, and it was Klemfuss who had hired the local Fascists and taught them the military movements as they stood guard at Valentino's coffin.

In the same year Valentino died, 1926, Frank Capra made his first film, *The Strong Man,* starring Harry Langdon.

Francesco Capra was born in Bisaquino, Sicily, and brought to California by his parents when he was three years old. His father worked as a fruit picker in the San Fernando Valley, as did he and his six siblings. In 1915, Capra entered the California Institute of Technology in Pasadena with the intention of becoming a chemical engineer. He paid for his education by playing the banjo in the local cabarets, waiting tables, and "wiping engines in the municipal power plant at Pasadena for 25 cents an hour."[*]

Even with a college degree he was unable to find work in 1919; he spent several years hitch-hiking, hopping trains, and sleeping in flophouses. In San Francisco he met an old Shakespearean actor, Walter Montague, who had bought an abandoned gymnasium with the intention of producing "picture poems," images representing the

[*]*The New Yorker,* February 24, 1940.

feelings of poems such as Kipling's "Fultah Fisher's Boarding House." On the strength of the fact that Capra was from Hollywood, Montague hired him to make films. After a year, as Montague's films became more and more "poetic," Capra left to write gags for Mack Sennett and to work as a free-lance director for $1,000 a film. It was the start of one of the most enduring careers in Hollywood.

The films he produced and directed over his long career—*Mr. Deeds Goes to Town, You Can't Take It with You, Mr. Smith Goes to Washington*—were so sentimental that they were dubbed "Capracorn." The Depression-era works were aimed at uplifting the mood of a nation by showing that money wasn't everything, that the rich were an unhappy lot, and that love, affection, and honesty were far more important for a truly good life. There is some irony in the fact that the son of a Sicilian made these most American of films.

Critics in the 1930s felt that Capra's films, particularly *American Madness* (1932), evinced a nostalgia for nineteenth-century simplicity, an era peopled by Horatio Alger and Frank Merriwell that probably never existed—a less complicated, smaller America when the employer knew all his workers and cared for their well-being. Tom Dickson, the banker in *American Madness,* is just that kind of man, who feels that the right security for loans is not "stocks and bonds that zig-zag up and down, not collateral on paper, but character." Dickson fights a merger with the heartless big banks, and when his own bank is brought to the edge of bankruptcy by a depositors' panic, he is saved at the last minute by the goodness of the businessmen he has helped over the years. It may be true that the film represents a yearning for nineteenth-century America. Yet for Capra it was a nostalgia for his own childhood, in the heart of his family, within the Italian community.

He tells this story: When he was a boy, a man arrived fresh from Italy at his parents' home with only the clothes on his back and a few cans of tomato paste. The tomato paste was a marvel. When the family asked what he intended to do with it, he answered, "I like to make it." Capra's father took him to the small Bank of Italy where the banker tasted the sauce, asked the man to make some more, and when he was assured that the man had made the sauce himself, said he would build a plant for him! The banker was Giannini, founder of the bank that would become the Bank of America, who as Capra remembered, "lent money on character." As for the tomato paste maker? "So the guy began to make tomato paste. I forget what the hell happened to him, he could be Del Monte."

If there is a strain of nostalgia for an imaginary, less complicated time of childhood in Capra's films, there is also a dislike, a distrust of those in power that harks back to southern Italy. In *It Happened One Night* (1934), the rich, and particularly Claudette Colbert, are depicted as spoiled, unhappy people leading meaningless lives. Only their contact with "real people"—in the person of Clark Gable—redeems them. "What makes dames like you so dizzy?" Gable asks Colbert, and the phrase sounds naive decades later. As in most of Capra's films, the people win out. Clark Gable gains the heart of the rich girl, to carry her off to a real life among the people of Depression America.

Capra's distrust of those in power showed up in his relations with producers who controlled the purse strings of the industry. As president of the Screen Directors Guild, he forced Joe Schenck, leader of the producers, to recognize the Guild, while establishing minimum salaries and restricting the degree to which a producer could edit his directors' films.

Throughout his film career, Capra believed in the strength of his own modest origins and the opportunities America gave the humble. In a moment of discouragement, after he retired, Capra returned to the home he had lived in as a boy and reflected in his autobiography upon a house that

> had been built by courage: the courage of two middle-aged, penniless, illiterate peasants who had dared travel halfway around the world to meet the unknown fearful challenges of a strange land, a strange people, and strange language. And who slaved like oxen and fought like tigers to feed and clothe their children . . . and one of them became a film director. And became famous. And retired. And now he was belly-aching because he was not needed. . . . I had to return to my roots for a much-needed draught of peasant courage. Out of the refill came . . . a try at saying to the discouraged, the doubting what I had been presuming to say in films: "Friend, you are a divine mingle-mangle of guts and stardust. So hang in there! If doors opened for me, they can open for anyone."

During the 1980s there was a revival of interest in Capra's films. He was enthusiastically received on college campuses by a new generation that no doubt had need of "Capracorn," unaware perhaps of his opposition to authority. Capra himself said: "I rebel against control of any kind. I'm a bad organization man, I like to be my own man and I don't like somebody else to tell me what to do. It was just the natural rebel in me that I couldn't take orders. Also, I felt that I knew more about films than the people who tried to tell me how to make them."

Frank Sinatra and Frank Capra were almost a generation apart in age and pursued different careers—Sinatra as singer and film actor, Capra as director—yet both succeeded in achieving great wealth and adoration, enough to make them feel free to do things "their own way" despite the Hollywood moguls. They were alike in another significant respect. Although Sinatra was born in Hoboken, New Jersey, he, too, had Sicilian parents.

Sinatra, born in 1915, was named Francesco Alberto Sinatra, and grew up in a neighborhood that was known in Hoboken as "Guinea Town"—an epitaph that angered Sinatra, who said, "I'll never forget how it hurt when kids called me a 'dago' when I was a boy." Yet unlike most children of Italian immigrant parents, Sinatra came from a comparatively well-off home; his father's job as a fireman meant security throughout the Depression and his mother's work for local politicians permitted them to live a comfortable life.

An uncle bought him a ukulele, and as a boy he sang beneath street lights on summer nights. As a teenager he sang in the small nightclubs, at church dances and local taverns. It was good training for the singing he was to do later with the big bands of Tommy Dorsey, Jimmy Dorsey, and Benny Goodman. His voice had the vibrance of the early Italian American singer Russ Colombo, who, although he died tragically at an early age, influenced a whole generation of crooners. Colombo's influence on Sinatra is well known. A lesser-known influence is Carlo Butto, who performed on the Italian Radio Hour aired throughout the New York area soon after World War I. The mothers of Sinatra's generation raised their children to the dulcet tones of Butto. Of course, Sinatra added his own genius to the singing.

During his wild days, when Sinatra roamed the casinos of Las Vegas with his friends, who became known as "the Rat Pack," he liked to be called "Ciccu" or "Cicciu"—an American corruption of the Sicilian nickname for Francesco. Some of his more intimate friends would call him "Uncle Frank" or "Lu zi Cicciu." His love for his fellow Italians made him vulnerable to the accusation that he was part of organized crime. This infuriated him. He often said, "If I get together with two other Italians it's called mafia."

Sinatra's singing also captured an American spirit in the jaunty happiness of "It Was Just One of Those Things" and the romanticism of "When Somebody Loves You." Yet there is much that remains Italian in his spirit and resonance. And if Sinatra yearned for Ava Gardner, he also never lost track of his Italian first wife or his family.

Sinatra influenced a whole generation of popular singers, including Dean Martin, Vic Damone, Julius La Rosa, and Tony Martin, who went so far as to pretend he was of Italian origin. Today, Harry Connick, Jr., is the latest to be billed as "the next Sinatra."

In the 1950s, as the country indulged itself in the materialism denied during the Depression and the austerity of the war years, it was easy for young singers to revel in the lilting, rakish style of Frank Sinatra, which seemed to say to hell with tomorrow; we have suffered and endured. Sinatra gave the American public a swagger they felt they had earned.

There were other echoes of Italy in the casual, limp style of Pierino (Perry) Como, who sounded like a weary peasant singing to himself after a hard day's work and in the operatic style of Julius (Giuliano) La Rosa. Antonio Benedetto (Tony Bennett), born in Astoria, Queens, sang of his heart being lost in San Francisco; Vito Farinola (Vic) Damone was considered the "world's greatest singer" by Sinatra. Other famous names come to mind: Annette Funicello, Connie Francis, Bobby Daren, and Sal Mineo.

The year Valentino died, James Francis Durante was singing as part of a jazz trio that included Lou Clayton and Eddie Jackson in the nightclubs and stages of New York City.

Durante was born in 1893 to immigrant parents from Salerno, Italy, and raised on the Lower East Side of New York. His father owned a barber shop that catered to Tammany Hall bigwigs. Durante seemed destined for the barber's trade, but, like so many of the second generation, was drawn to the world of entertainment. He dropped out of school in the seventh grade to play the piano wherever people would pay to hear him play. By the time he was twenty-three, "Ragtime Jimmy" had his own five-piece band. It was the beginning of the Jazz Age.

In New Orleans, Dominic James ("Nick") LaRocca founded the original Dixieland Jazz Band that became famous all over the world. LaRocca was born in New Orleans in 1889, of Sicilian parents. He taught himself to play the cornet, which was twice crushed by his father, who believed the boy's future lay in medicine. As a self-taught musician, LaRocca contributed to improvisational music's new rhythms that later became jazz. Louis Armstrong paid his respect to LaRocca in 1936: "Only four years before I learned to play the trumpet . . . the first great jazz orchestra was formed in New Orleans by a cornet player named Dominic James LaRocca. They called him 'Nick' LaRocca. His orchestra had only five pieces but they were the hottest five pieces that had ever been known before. LaRocca named this band 'The Old Dixieland Jazz Band.' "

Armstrong added:

> . . . he had an instrumentation different from anything before . . .
> an instrumentation that made the old songs sound new. . . .
> They all came to be famous players and the Dixieland Band has
> gone down now in musical history. Some of the great records
> they made, which carried the new jazz music all over the world
> in those days, were: "Tiger Rag" . . . "Ostrich Walk" . . . "Livery Stable Blues" . . . his fame as one of the great pioneers of
> syncopated music will last a long, long time, as long I think, as
> American music lives.*

LaRocca's early bands consisted of Tony Sbarbaro on drums, Eddie Edwards on trombone, Larry Shields on clarinet, and LaRocca on cornet. It was an innovative time. Sbarbaro used cow bells, the rhythm became syncopated, animal sounds were incorporated into the pieces Nick wrote himself: "Livery Stable Blues" and "Tiger Rag." LaRocca would dance and instruct the crowds in the new rhythms—the two-step and the shimmy that gave the dances a lewd reputation. So did the four-letter word used to describe the new music, which was first called "Jass," then evolved to "Jasz," and finally to "Jazz."

*Armstrong, *Swing That Music.*

Jimmy Durante was weaned on Nick LaRocca; like many of the second-generation Italian Americans, he entered show business by playing the music popularized by LaRocca. Durante's career began on Broadway, where his trio played in Ziegfeld's *Show Girl* in 1929. He moved easily from films to stage and then to radio.

In Durante, one could hear the voice of an immigrant mimicking himself—his awkwardness—butchering the English language, the gravelly voice of the street kid mimicking the seriousness of those who thought themselves better than the newcomer. The "shnozze," as he liked to refer to himself, was part of this act. If Americans thought that immigrants were dumb, then Durante would play them dumb. John Barrymore once suggested, "You know, Jimmy, you should play Hamlet." And of course Durante answered, "The hell with those small towns. New York is the only place for me." Durante set the role of the good-natured working-class Italian that would later prosper in, for example, the characters of Tony Banta and Louie DePalma in the television series *Taxi*.

Soon after the death of Valentino, a series of gangster films in the 1930s began the image of Italians as organized crime figures. At first they shared the stage with an Irish gangster in the person of James Cagney. In 1930, Lew Ayres played the first Italian gangster as Louis Recarno, an intellectual hood, in *Doorway to Hell*. The film failed at the box office and with the critics. But that same year Edward G. Robinson immortalized the Italian American gangster in *Little Caesar*, in which he played the role of Rico Bandello. Rico is short, dresses well, and has the accent of the Italian brought up in Brooklyn.

In 1932, Paul Muni, in the role of Tony Camonte in *Scarface* (later reprised by Al Pacino), introduced the good Italian boy, who loved his mother, ate his spaghetti on command, looked after the virtue of his sister, lusted after the blond American girl, and went down in a hail of bullets like a sniveling coward. But then it was *de rigueur* to have the gangster die a coward's death, no matter how glorious and heroic his life had been. Even Cagney, playing an Irish mobster, often went to the chair weeping to show that crime did not pay (the Hayes Office censoring films would not have it otherwise), although it paid handsomely at the box office.

The avalanche of Italian gangster roles portraying second-generation Italian Americans did not come about until after 1945, when the "Mafia" became bankable. The spirit of the old immigrants lingered in the voice of Durante, in the films of Capra, and in the early songs of Sinatra; but the memory of Valentino faded, and the young found a more American voice in the later songs of Sinatra, as well as in the new songs of Frank Zappa, Madonna, or Billy Joel, in the films of Francis Ford Coppola and Martin Scorsese, and in the acting of Robert De Niro and Al Pacino.

PART NINE

Old Wine in New Bottles, 1940–1990

CHAPTER 24

Politics and Business

POSTWAR POLITICS

The prosperity that followed World War II improved the economic status of many Italian Americans. The house they had dreamed of during the Depression and the war, the new car, the festive meals of beefsteak, roasted chicken, and ravioli—all could now be bought.

This rise in status brought Italian Americans into the mainstream of American politics. The Palmer raids of the 1920s, the executions of Sacco and Vanzetti, the Dies Committee of the 1930s, McCarthyism, and the Cold War helped move Italians further toward the center. There were still, however, a few remaining radicals.

Vito Marcantonio, an East Harlem congressman from 1934 to 1948, was one of the last great Italian American radicals. Marcantonio's grandfather had come to America soon after the unification of Italy. Saverio, his father, was born in New York City, whereas his mother, Angelina Dedobitis, was born in Italy. East Harlem during Marcantonio's childhood was poor and predominately Jewish; the area did not see a large influx of Italians until the 1930s. Socialism was in the air. Early on, Marcantonio belonged to the local *Circolo Italiano,* a club dedicated to maintaining Italian culture. It was there that he took part in theater, acting in the plays of Pirandello. On one occasion Pirandello himself sat in the audience.

His father was a hardworking, relatively prosperous carpenter, who permitted Marc to attend high school and New York University, where he earned a law degree. While in school he also worked with immigrants in the social agency Harlem House, where he met his future wife, Miriam Sanders, a social worker.

This union between an Italian American and a New Englander whose ancestry could be traced to seventeenth-century Boston was regarded as tradition-breaking on the part of both, within and outside the Italian American community. Only in future generations would the children of Italian immigrants generally feel free to marry non-Italians.

From the beginning of his political career, when he was first elected to the U.S. Congress in 1934, Marcantonio espoused unpopular causes, introducing bills to abolish the poll tax, arguing against loyalty oaths, and defending immigrants. When conservatives denounced radical labor organizations as traitorous, Marcantonio spoke of capitalist oppression and evoked the martyrs of labor—Sacco and Vanzetti. In many ways he was a transitional character between the outsider radicals of the early days and the later generation who aspired to conform. Although he never joined the Communist Party, Marcantonio often supported Party policy. As president of the New York City chapter of the American Labor Party and as congressman during the time of the Hitler-Stalin Pact, he voted against military expenditures and opposed intervention in European affairs. But soon after the German invasion of the Soviet Union, he pushed for intervention in the European war. If his heart was with the Communist movement, his pragmatic political sense was not.

Since opposition to the Tammany Democrats made Republicans in New York take a more liberal stance than Republicans elsewhere, Marcantonio first ran on the Republican ticket. Yet he broke with the more radical Italian Americans, such as Carlo Tresca, who berated Marcantonio's short-lived stance on the Hitler-Stalin Pact as the practical politician's way of placating "his large fascist-oriented constituency in East Harlem."

When Italian Americans came under attack as enemy aliens soon

after the bombing of Pearl Harbor, Marcantonio gave a powerful
radio address:

> . . . These detractors and maligners of our loyal Italian Ameri-
> cans are, by this most un-American activity, causing disunity in
> our country. . . . In short, it is they who have become a menace
> to America's victory program. The contributions of Americans of
> Italian extraction in blood, toil, and wealth is the devastating an-
> swer to those who seek to discriminate against them . . . we, too,
> true sons of Garibaldi . . . pledge and rededicate our energies
> and our lives for the victory of our arms, for the victory of our
> cause.

At heart Marcantonio was a grass-roots politician, living in a
four-room rent-controlled apartment in East Harlem all his life. He
never took a vacation and was usually to be found in his office
assisting immigrants with red tape, helping others to get on welfare,
or giving legal advice free of charge. In the crucial election of 1948,
when all Soviet actions were deemed hostile to the United States and
Marcantonio was accused of being a Soviet agent, he cried out on the
street corners of East Harlem: "Do you want the 400 or do you want
me, one of the 140,000,000 working Americans? I was born three
blocks from here. I have shared your sorrows and our victories."
That year he was reelected.

Marcantonio never lost the accent or manners of that neighborhood. He dressed sloppily and often forgot to shave until Fiorello La
Guardia, his mentor in many ways, encouraged him to make himself
more presentable. Thereafter Marcantonio became an easily recog-
nizable figure as he walked in the area, greeting friends and listening
to constituents. In his dark suit and fedora hat with its rim turned up
all around, he had the air of an Italian American workingman in his
Sunday best.

During his last years in Congress, Marcantonio fought against
the anti-Communist tide, which he said was a cover for conservatives
to enact their anti-labor laws and build a lucrative military-industrial
complex. This strategy, he pointed out, had invariably been the
practice of the Republicans, who used war heroes and figureheads to
gain power while they pillaged the public coffers. His insistent opposition to the Cold War and his support of civil rights laws made him

a loner. In 1950, Marcantonio was defeated. He died of a heart attack the following year.

Marcantonio's political career was rooted in Italian American radical tradition. Yet it reflected the changing attitudes and aspirations of Italian American communities. He became the down-to-earth politician helping his constituents with their day-to-day problems. Whereas the radicals of the turn of the century were not burdened by foreign policy issues and could concentrate all their efforts on what they considered the evils of capitalism at home, Marcantonio, handicapped by his obvious support of Communist Party politics, fell victim to Stalinism and the Cold War that crippled the American left.

Marcantonio's practice of ardently "voting his conscience," as he often said, not only cost him his seat in Congress but alienated him from the powerful. The hierarchy of the Catholic Church refused to have him buried in consecrated ground, because he "was not reconciled with the Church before his death." Yet he died wearing a religious medallion. In good Italian radical tradition, he abhorred the Church but believed in God. He was buried in Woodlawn Cemetery in the Bronx, not far from the grave of Fiorello La Guardia, after some twenty thousand men and women paid homage as the funeral cortège passed through the streets of his old neighborhood.

In Peter Vincent Cacchione, the first Communist Party member to be elected to public office, there were still strong currents of the immigrants' radical experiences of earlier days. Cacchione was born in 1897, in the small railroad town of Sayre, Pennsylvania, close to the New York border. His parents, Bernardo and Anna Maria, had come from Potenza, Italy, a few years before—Bernardo to work as a shoemaker, while Anna Maria cared for a large house which accommodated relatives and borders. Cacchione grew up in an extended family where early in life he learned the importance of cooperation and unity. He was the first boy from the Italian neighborhood to be graduated from high school, although during those school years he worked part time for the Lehigh Valley Railroad as a trainman and in its repair shop.

Cacchione resumed his job with the railroad after serving in the Army in 1917, and in 1922 as a member of the Brotherhood of Railroad Trainmen he took part in the strikes of the union. Soon after, he began a vagabond life of looking for work throughout the

American West. In Nevada he accumulated enough money to start a construction company, but it failed and he was forced once again to go looking for work as a laborer. He walked at night, to avoid the heat of day. At times he crowded into boxcars with others looking for work, only to be dumped in areas out of town. None of the townspeople wanted unemployed men among them. These were echoes of harsher times when workers were beaten and shot in the Telluride and Coeur d'Alene mines of a few decades before.

By 1932, Cacchione was thirty-five years old and penniless when he arrived in New York City to live in the flophouses around the Bowery. His experience with the railroad unions helped him organize the unemployed and tenants who were threatened with eviction in those Depression days. This experience prompted him to take the lead in organizing a contingent of veterans to march on Washington, demanding a bonus for their wartime service:

"I remember the bonus march of 1932. I remember that the U.S. Army was called out to tear-gas, bayonet and shoot World War veterans in Washington. I remember that first night when the cavalry came to Anacostia Flats and drove out 20,000 vets and their families. . . . two babies were trampled to death by the horses. A woman's leg was laid open from knee to ankle. A boy's arm was shattered. I saw two men killed."

Cacchione recalled that when newspapermen asked the police chief for a statement on these events, the chief answered, "I told General Douglas MacArthur there are women and children among them, and General MacArthur said, 'I know it.' "

When Cacchione returned from the Bonus March to join the Communist Party, his hometown paper, the *Evening Times,* sported the headline: PETE CACCHIONE HIGH AMONG BIG CITY REDS.

In Brooklyn he settled in working-class neighborhoods—first Red Hook and then Bensonhurst—where he married Dorothy Rosenfeld in 1937, the same year he first ran for the City Council. After several defeats, Cacchione was elected in 1941 and again in 1943 and 1945. Cacchione focused his issues close to home: jobs, relief, and welfare for the unemployed. He was also known as the defender of the Soviet Union. Like Marcantonio, Cacchione was defeated at the outset of McCarthyism and died shortly thereafter.

The most practical of Italian American men in politics was Fiorello La Guardia (also known as the Little Flower), who was born in New

York City's Little Italy in 1882. La Guardia started off with advantages few other immigrant children had. His father was an accomplished musician, who had first come to America in 1878 as an arranger and accompanist to the soprano Adelina Patti. Later, as a bandmaster in the U.S. Army, Achille La Guardia took his family to Arizona, where young Fiorello grew up. He traveled widely with his parents. As a young adult he lived in Greenwich Village, where he mingled with the radicals and Bohemians of the times, many of whom were Italian-born. Among his acquaintances were August Bellanca, the labor leader; Antonio Calitri, the poet and a former Catholic priest; Onorio Ruotolo, a Renaissance man, poet, painter, and editor; and Arturo Giovannitti, the radical labor organizer and poet.

La Guardia's first political venture was to run for a seat in the House of Representatives in 1914 and lose. Two years later, he waged a vigorous campaign against the Tammany machine. He resigned from the House in 1917 to join the U.S. Air Force on the Austrian-Italian front, first as a lieutenant, then captain, finally rising to the rank of major. His war experience—in which he mingled with diplomats and soldiers—brought him a good press, especially his lunch with the poet-soldier D'Annunzio, who remarked: "The people don't understand your Italian but they pretend they do. They don't understand mine either, but they ask what I'm trying to say."

In 1921 La Guardia tried to win the Republican nomination for the New York mayoral office, despite the advice of a Republican political boss, Sam Koenig, who warned him that New York wasn't yet ready for an Italian American mayor. He lost by a large margin. During the campaign, the press derided him as "the Little Garibaldi" with such persistence that he failed to carry any of the boroughs, including his own. He returned to the House of Representatives in 1923 and remained there for the next ten years. As a congressman, he fought for numerous reforms. One of them, the Norris-La Guardia Act, prevented injunctions in labor disputes. In 1933 he came back to New York and, backed by Samuel Seabury, a former judge who became the nemesis of the Tammany machine, ran for the office of mayor. This time he won. He would hold the office for three consecutive terms, and become famous as an aggressive reformer, who not only fought successfully against local political corruption but also established slum-clearing projects, as well as programs for beautifying the city.

In 1945, La Guardia declined to run for the office of mayor and in that year he became director of the United Nations Relief and Rehabilitation Administration. He died in 1947, and was mourned by millions for his courage, honesty, and energy, among them Eleanor Roosevelt, who once told an acquaintance that La Guardia was one of the few Republicans she could ever vote for.

With the disappearance of such men as Marcantonio, Cacchione, and La Guardia, Italian American politicians took a distinctive turn to the right. The career of John Vincent Volpe is a case in point.

Volpe, born in 1908, grew up in an immigrant home where his father maintained strict discipline. Though he had hoped to attend MIT, the failure of his father's business made it necessary for Volpe to take a job as a plasterer at age fifteen. By 1933 he had founded his own company, which was a thriving concern when World War II began. Soon after the nation entered the war, he gave up his prosperous civilian life to join the Navy, and trained construction units known as Sea Bees. When the war ended, he left the Navy with the rank of lieutenant commander and returned to head the Volpe Construction Company, building hospitals, schools, and military installations. His work brought him into the world of Republican politics, and in 1957 President Eisenhower appointed him head of the Federal Highway Administration.

In 1961, Volpe ran for the office of governor of Massachusetts, becoming the first Italian American to achieve the office of state governor. Later, he was appointed Secretary of Transportation by President Nixon, despite Nixon's voiced belief that all Italians were crooks.

More recently, a myriad of Italian American politicians all over the country have shown a tendency to move toward the political right. They range from such conservatives as Frank Rizzo, the hard-nosed former mayor of Philadelphia*; to John J. Marchi, bastion of conservatism in the New York State legislature, from Staten Island; to U.S. Senator Denis DiConcini (D) from Arizona and Senator Peter V. Domenici (R) of Colorado; to the more mainstream politicians such as Alfonse M. D'Amato (R) of New York, Governor Mario Cuomo of New York, and Geraldine Ferraro, the first Ameri-

---

*Frank Rizzo died in 1991 while campaigning in the primaries for his return to the mayor's office, this time on the Republican ticket.

can woman to be nominated for the office of Vice President. Ella
Grasso was the first American woman to achieve the office of state
governor (Connecticut) in her own right. John Pastore of Rhode
Island was the first Italian American to be elected to the U.S. Senate.
A few men, such as New Jersey Congressman Peter Rodino, played
an important part in uncovering Nixon's role in the Watergate scandal. Among the myriad of Italian Americans in the judiciary, one of
the most influential was Judge John J. Sirica, who in large measure
was responsible for Richard Nixon's political demise. In the last
years of the Reagan administration, the appointment of Antonin
Scalia to the Supreme Court by Ronald Reagan underscored the
movement of Italian Americans to the right.

In 1930–36, 26 percent of all Italian American voters voted
Republican. By 1942–46, the figure stood at 44 percent. "At this
point," wrote Vincent Tortora in *The Nation* in June 1953,

> . . . the Democrats were no longer able to take the Italian Ameri-
> can vote for granted. . . . During this period [1942–46] solidly
> Italian American wards of Brooklyn, Manhattan, and Pittsburgh
> that had gone Democratic four to one in the 1930's on the aver-
> age evenly divided their vote between the two parties. Several
> wards in Philadelphia that had been overwhelmingly Democratic
> ten years earlier now gave 60 or 65% majorities to the Republi-
> cans.

Tortora noted that the reasons for the swing among Italian
Americans to the Republican Party were complex. Many of those
who were born in Italy felt that the abominable economic conditions
in postwar Italy were the Democrats' fault. They felt, too, that the
McCarran/Walter Bill (both were Democrats) discriminated against
Italian immigrants. So they voted Republican.

The upward mobility soon after the war meant that many Italian
Americans now left the Democratic Party to the poorer ethnic
groups—the blacks and the Puerto Ricans. Still others voted Republican out of resentment toward the Irish, who dominated the Democratic Party. Tortora concluded: " . . . as the Italian American started
on his upward social and economic climb, his dependence on the
ward politician diminished. He became a thinking individual. He
began to vote as he pleased."

Increasingly, Italian American politicians had to contend with the image of Mafia imbedded in the minds of the American public. Geraldine Ferraro is a good example.

Ferraro, after serving in Congress, was the first woman and the first Italian American to run on a national ticket, as the vice-presidential Democratic candidate in 1984. She immediately felt the stigma of Mafia attached to her name as newspapers around the country, including the Philadelphia *Inquirer,* the *New York Post,* and the *Wall Street Journal,* insinuated that the Ferraro family was connected with organized crime. That Ferraro had helped form the National Organization of Italian American Women, that she had been an effective congresswoman for years, that there was no evidence for the accusation, was all overlooked. Ferraro, angered, said: "Because I am Italian, I or my family is suspected of being gangsters." What angered her even more was that the Italian community, intimidated by the accusation, was silent. "And I must say," Ferraro went on, "that while we were heavily involved in a grueling presidential race, many of the leaders in our [Italian American] community . . . seemed ready to remain silent and let others shape events."

Ferraro was not the only victim of the Mafia label. Joseph Alioto, once mayor of San Francisco, was forced out of politics by the same accusation.

ENTREPRENEURS

As early as 1890, Italian immigrants were developing businesses that led to enormous enterprises. From small merchants and importers who peddled a few barrels of wine or some rounds of cheese, cans of tomatoes, or the gallons of olive oil (so dear to the early immigrants, who thought butter was a strange mixture to put on bread or cook with), these early merchants saw their enterprises develop into well-organized and firmly established corporations.

In 1911, Alberto Pecorini could write: "Four-fifths of all trade between Italy and the United States, which amounts to $100,000,000 per year, passes through New York, and the greater part of it is controlled by Italians, from the importation of raw silk to that of lemons, olive oil and macaroni."

If some Italian bankers were still rapacious *banchisti* sitting in their storefront offices, swindling fellow immigrants while pretending to serve them, more stable banks were beginning to appear. By

1910, the Italian government opened branches of the Bank of Naples in the United States to facilitate the transfer of funds to relatives in Italy. Italian businessmen established their own Italian American Trust Company, which by 1911 had deposits of $2 million. Out of these early financial houses came several notable Italian American businessmen, including Andrea Sbarboro, the well-known builder of wineries and cooperatives in California. There were also lesser-known entrepreneurs who rose among the men of commerce to become executives in American industries.

One example is Amedeo Obici, who came to the United States when he was a boy of twelve in 1889 with his parents from Aderzo, in the provence of Tresviso. By the time he was forty, Obici was a millionaire who had given the United States one of its most enduring symbols of enterprise—the cocky peanut in a top hat, leaning jauntily on a cane, that still adorns every jar of Planters nuts. His fortune was based on the lowly nickel.

Obici began his career as a fruit peddler, who learned that Americans were more willing to spend 20 nickels than a dollar. The item that would be bought for a nickel, he discovered (if it were roasted and packaged), was the peanut. By 1931 he was head of one of the great corporations of the United States, with factories in Suffolk, Virginia, Wilkes Barre, Pennsylvania, San Francisco, and Toronto; over two thousand employees; and $7 million in capital.

The enterprise started with a $4.50 roaster and stand, over which he posted the sign: OBICI, THE PEANUT SPECIALIST. In each package of nuts he put a coupon bearing a letter of the alphabet. Any purchaser who collected coupons that spelled out the name OBICI was awarded a watch. In two years he had awarded twenty-thousand watches. Obici experimented with various roasts, and salted the peanuts; he also made and sold candy bars. With the help of M. M. Peruzzi, his sales manager, he founded the Planters Peanut Company of Wilkes Barre, Pennsylvania. When landlords, seeing his business flourishing, raised his rents, Obici went into the real estate business and was soon buying his own buildings. He purchased farmlands in Virginia and grew his own peanuts. Before long, he owned and controlled every aspect of his enterprise—from factories to clean the peanuts to tracts of timber to produce his own packaging, and even mills to process the timber. He also produced his own tin to package nuts in cans. By the 1930s Obici was the peanut king of America, if not the world (to this day peanuts are called *noccioline Americani* in Italy).

Vincent Riggio did not enter the world of American business independently, but via the competitive rungs of the corporate ladder.

Riggio was born in 1877 in Nicosia, Sicily, one of five children who came with the family when he was six years old to settle in Manhattan's Lower East Side. He too started in the Horatio Alger tradition, running errands for local merchants. Although Riggio had a poor formal education, he had a great deal of ambition. In 1905, Riggio began a career in the tobacco industry as a salesman for Pall Mall cigarettes. His methods were so simple as to seem nowadays the height of naivete. When his first efforts at selling failed, he spent nights preparing and memorizing a sales pitch. The next time he went out selling, it resulted in twenty-four orders. When Butler & Butler, Inc. became the American Tobacco Company in 1907, he was named division manager. In Buffalo, New York, he managed to upgrade Lucky Strikes from the poorest-selling cigarette of the nation to the most popular brand.

Riggio rose to become vice-president and then president. He lived with his wife, the former Antoinette Gallo, on a 112-acre estate in Chappaqua, New York, where he raised cows, pigs, and sheep, and sold them to local restauranteurs.

Henry Viscardi, Jr., born in New York in 1912 of southern Italian parents, had a more altruistic career. At Viscardi's birth, as he described in his autobiography, "What should have been legs were half formed deformities, stumps, like somebody's unfinished statue." He spent his childhood in hospitals, but once fitted with special shoes, in spite of his dwarflike stature, his arms almost touching the ground, he devoted all his intelligence and energy to graduating from high school, taking courses at Fordham University, and coaching a basketball team. He also found time to read law at the offices of a law firm. All this proved too much for Viscardi's frail body, and he dropped out of Fordham. Nonetheless he went on to found an electronics firm called "Abilities," which chiefly employed disabled persons—amputees and those crippled by disease.

Later, Viscardi founded JOB (Just One Break), a government agency dedicated to finding work for the disabled. He toured the country defending the rights of the disabled to work, not in special workshops, but in mainstream industry. Toward the end of his life

Viscardi was honored by Eleanor Roosevelt and awarded honorary doctorate degrees from the Fordham University, Hofstra University, Clarkson University, Long Island University, and Sung Kyun Kwau University in Seoul.

One of the most well known Italian American businessmen of our time is Lido (Lee) Anthony Iacocca, long-time president of Chrysler Corporation.

Nicola, Iacocca's father, who had a great influence on him, came from San Marco, about 25 miles northeast of Naples in the province of Campania. Nicola immigrated as a frightened boy of twelve in 1902 to Garrett, Pennsylvania, where for just one day he worked in the coal mines. "He liked to say," Iacocca writes in his autobiography, that "it was the only day in his life that he ever worked for anybody else." The father who left the world of working-class Italian immigrants to enter the world of entrepreneurs, was key to Iacocca's future.

While Lido (eventually Americanized to Lee) was growing up, his father was acquiring various properties: first a modest restaurant, the Orpheum Wiener House, then several movie houses and a rental car agency. Young Iacocca began learning about marketing from his father. "The kids who came down to the Saturday matinees used to get more excited about his special offers than about the movies. People still talk about the day he announced that the ten kids with the dirtiest faces would be admitted free. . . ." writes Iacocca.

When the Depression came, Nicola Iacocca lost all of his businesses except for the Wiener House restaurant. During that period his mother went to work in a silk mill while her son had his first encounter with bigotry: in his innocence, he assumed at first that "Dago" and "Wop" were place names and went to look for them on a map of Europe.

Iacocca's close relationship with his father sustained him as he earned a bachelor of science degree in industrial engineering at Lehigh University. Then began the long climb up the corporate ladder.

Sales Americanized Iacocca. His first mentor at Ford, Charlie Beacham, whom Iacocca affectionately called "my tor-mentor," taught him the rudiments of salesmanship in America and how to get along in the South. First he told Iacocca to slow down his speech and "tell them you have a funny first name—Iacocca—and that your family name is Lee." Beacham, a southerner who was the regional manager for the East Coast, was "the kind of guy you'd charge up the hill for," Iacocca said.

When Robert S. McNamara advanced in the company's hierarchy, Iacocca moved with him to Dearborn and the world of high executives. There his work involved producing and marketing the Ford Mustang, which sold almost a half million units. The rest was to be corporate politics until 1970, when Iacocca was named president of the Ford Motor Company. When difficulties arose between Henry Ford II and Iacocca, Iacocca discovered that as an Italian American he would always be considered an outsider. Ford insinuated that Iacocca was in with the Mafia. In 1975, Iacocca wrote that Ford was convinced "I was in the mafia. . . . I guess *The Godfather* was enough to persuade him that all Italians were linked to organized crime."

Iacocca learned much from the men he admired (his father, Charlie Beacham, and finally Robert S. McNamara), and this produced a relationship somewhat like that between the teacher who needs a good student and the student who is ready for a good teacher.

The story of Iacocca's dismissal from Ford became well known, as did his work thereafter for Chrysler. His image as a president of Chrysler and as an astute salesman who saved a great American corporation has woven his name into the fabric of American immigrant history.

CHAPTER 25

Hollywood—The Later Period

THROUGH A SCREEN DARKLY

One must look closely into the world of the Italian American filmmakers to find an awareness of their heritage. (There are few Hollywood films about Sacco and Vanzetti. If they were made at all, they were usually left to others. The Italian director Giuliano Montaldo made one in 1971. *Give Us This Day,* based on *Christ in Concrete,* was made in England by Edward Dmytryk in 1949.) Francis Ford Coppola, Martin Scorsese, Brian de Palma, and Michael Cimino are a world apart from the early immigrants. But today, in order to recoup the enormous production and marketing costs of a commercial film, huge audiences are needed and films must cater to what are believed to be the fantasies of the mainstream.

Francis Ford Coppola did not come from a working-class family. His grandparents were from the region around Naples and from Tunis, where many southern Italians had settled. His father, Carmine Coppola, was a concert flutist, who played with Toscanini's NBC Symphony Orchestra and with the "Ford Sunday Evening Hour Radio Show," which explains young Francis's middle name—Ford. His mother, Italia Pennino, was born in Brooklyn, and acted in films. Francis was born in 1939 in Detroit, was brought up in Queens, and attended schools on music scholarships. In high school he was fascinated by Sergei Eisenstein and decided on a career in film.

Coppola went on to study filmmaking at UCLA, where the academic and intellectual climate suited him well. He attributed his temperament to a bout with polio as a boy, which taught him to be alone. As he said, "The popular kid doesn't sit around thinking about who he is or how he feels. But the kid who is ugly, sick, miserable or schlumpy sits around heart-broken and thinks."

After apprenticing as a screenwriter and general handyman with Roger Corman, Coppola directed his first commercial film in 1962, at the age of twenty-three. *Dementia 13* is a horror film. The film was made—manufactured, really—in a curious and innovative way.

Corman had paid Boris Karloff to shoot two days' worth of film on leftover sets, with no other notion but to have a few yards of Karloff on the shelves. "My job," Coppola recalls, "was to figure out what to do with two days' worth of shooting." If the experience taught Coppola to treat film as so much carpeting, it did pave the way to the job he craved—directing.

Coppola's second film, *You're a Big Boy Now,* told the story of a Candidelike character whose mother, Mrs. Chanticleer, would keep him innocent forever. The film brought him to the attention of the public and the Hollywood powerbrokers, and he was offered the job of scripting the story of General Patton.

Coppola believed Patton to be "nuts"; to make him a hero would not only "be laughed at" but would prove what his peers at UCLA said of him, that he had sold out. If, however, he condemned Patton, the film would not be made. In the land of compromise, Coppola compromised. He solved the problem by wrapping the "nutty" general in an enormous American flag and in essence telling his audience that in war "we need a man like that."

The film was a success. The critics admired it for "the finest battle featuring mechanized weaponry ever put on the screen." And one is left with the image that in war, as in Hollywood, victory is not everything, it is the only thing. Coppola was now ready to make *The Godfather.*

Coppola had not liked the novel and hesitated taking on the job of directing it. But the producers were persistent, and over the phone sweetened their offer. Coppola turned to his colleague, George

Lucas, and asked, "Should I make this gangster picture?"

"Francis," Lucas replied, "we need the money."

From the start Italian American organizations denounced the book and the proposed film as a denigrating image of Italian Americans. While the film was being made with a script by Coppola and Puzo, the project was harassed by confrontations with the Italian-American Civil Rights League. A deal was made: The League would stop creating problems for the project if the filmmakers deleted all references to the Mafia and the Cosa Nostra. Based on a novel that had become one of the biggest bestsellers in American publishing history, the film's omission of the Mafia would fool no one. Yet Coppola felt inclined to assert that *The Godfather* was not really about the Mafia, that it could just as well be about the Kennedys or the Rothschilds, about a dynasty which demands personal allegiance to a family that transcends even one's obligation to one's country."*

Once Coppola had convinced himself that he was not making a gangster movie but rather a family saga, he went on to create a powerful myth of the Mafia, for which the American public had been prepared by the television exploits of the Kefauver Committee and the Puzo novel. As in the Patton story, he found a way of making despicable characters like Don Vito Corleone almost endearing. And therein may lie the explanation for the film's enormous success, both with critics and the public. During the early months of its long run *The Godfather* was grossing more than $1 million a day. The following year, 1972, the Academy of Motion Picture Arts and Sciences honored it with Oscars for best picture, best actor, and best screenplay based on material from another medium.

With skills that could wreak cynical mischief with the art of mythmaking, Coppola and Puzo were able to make sympathetic characters out of vicious criminals. The explanation for this feat may lie in an observation of Robert K. Johnson, a biographer of Coppola, to the effect that the film avoids basic truths. Actually, except for Michael Corleone's Anglo-Saxon wife, none of the characters in the narrative is burdened with any sense of virtue. As one critic put it, "After all the murders and vendettas, Puzo had not illuminated any aspects of the human condition."

Sympathy for the characters is achieved through distortion of reality. Although Don Corleone is presented as someone who would

---

New York magazine, August 23, 1971.

never double-cross anyone, the history of the Mob wars that began in the 1930s plainly indicates that mobsters, and especially their godfathers, repeatedly double-crossed one another. And although Don Corleone is depicted as being opposed to drug dealing, genuine mobsters have no such qualms. If the Don is to be judged in terms of the real world, his refusal to enter the drug trade is not based on ethical grounds but rather on the reality that it would create problems with his political friends, difficulties that would be bad for business.

Don Corleone is presented as a good family man with all the clichéd qualities of the Italian American Papa. He is a loving father and grandfather, he shops for fruit, he looks gentle, he wears rumpled clothes. He's no Scarface, in the Paul Muni tradition, no Al Capone, nor a Giancana who shared a mistress with John Kennedy. Coppola's Godfather kills and maims only to protect his loved ones, and in the name of family values. In an era when the American family was being torn apart by divorce and mobility, the image of a man who would do anything for his extended family was cheered by the American public. In a time, too, when heroes were needed, the *mafiosi* were presented as the only loyal and courageous men.

Rizzi, who marries the daughter of Don Corleone, is killed for wimpish actions unbecoming a "family" member. The non-Italian who marries the widowed daughter is also a weak fop who can't handle his wife in the manner in which Sicilian women apparently are accustomed to being treated in the cliché world. The United States senator Gerry has no morals at all. This image of a corrupt Senator led Coppola to further rationalize his making the film by asserting that "The Mafia is a metaphor for this country."

One would have to look hard to find this metaphor in the few remarks made by Michael Corleone as he walks with his New England beauty in the person of Diane Keaton. The metaphor quickly evaporates. But we do have the persistent presence of Michael, whose American education and heroic service as an officer during World War II have little effect on this Don's son. It is Sicilian genes that matter, and he is doomed to take over his father's position. Michael's return to Sicily and his association with *mafiosi* there give further credence to the notion that organized crime was brought to America from Sicily. One is left with the feeling that Coppola's comment that mafia is a metaphor of corrupt America is less applicable to America than it is to his and Puzo's compromise with their own principles and aspirations.

Joseph Caruso, at a symposium of the American Italian Historical Association, put it more bluntly: "Puzo pushed a myth, which is destroying the image of the Italian American in the United States." The anger of many Italian Americans was best expressed by Giovanni Sinicropi when he wrote: "Unfortunately Puzo and Coppola are not looking for truth but for certainty. And certainty is another divinity which has its recognized tabernacle in the bookshelves."

Life began to imitate fiction. Italian American high school students in New York organized "families" to extort money from their classmates; they had only to imitate the style and manners of *The Godfather* to intimidate their victims.

The Godfather catered to established familial clichés as well. The women in the film are secondary, usually bouncing squalling babies on their hips as they cook. Shut out of male affairs, they are sequestered or protected by their brothers.

The physical details are grittily true, and this adds to the credibility of the film: the mother's clothes and hairstyle make her look as if she has stepped out of the thousands of photographs sent back to Italy by immigrant daughters. The furniture is Italian American Baroque. The actors, from the mother to Al Pacino, have the gestures and accents they grew up with in Brooklyn and the Bronx. In this sense *The Godfather* is the first authentic Italian American film, far different from such earlier attempts as the original *Scarface* or the film that recorded the life of Rocky Graziano in 1956, *Somebody Up There Likes Me*.

Coppola's enormous success, both financial and critical, made it possible for him to satisfy his need "to be a solo guy." He went on to make *Apocalypse Now* (1979), his hallucinatory view of the Vietnam War, in which the script tried to combine the black vision of Conrad's *Heart of Darkness* with the symbolism he admired so much in Eisenstein. Captain Willard (played by Martin Sheen), an American officer, is handed the task of hunting down a fellow officer, one of the best and brightest, who has gone insane and, in the process, has created an empire and an army of his own deep in the jungles of Vietnam. Marlon Brando, who had been the mafia Don in *The Godfather*, now became the American officer driven insane by an insane war.

Captain Willard's odyssey begins as a general tells him that the mission, for reasons of state, must "never exist," and warns him that "out there with those natives there's a temptation to play God." On his journey, Willard meets up with a general of helicopter infantry who is a caricature of the General Patton Coppola wanted to create, but did not, in *Patton.* This general wears an old cavalry hat, sports a pearl-handled gun, and goes in to destroy a peaceful village "where the surfing is good" with Wagnerian music blasting from the loud-speakers mounted on his helicopters.

The deeper one moves into the heart of the jungle, the stranger are the events (a tiger leaps out at a man who is looking for mangoes), and the more insane the faces drifting by the camera's eye, until it seems as if Coppola is passing in review the ghosts of all past intrud-ers upon Indochina: the Japanese, the French, and the bewildered Americans. At the heart of the insane world we find Colonel Kurtz, an intellectual warrior who reads *The Golden Bough* and T. S. Eliot, and whose madness foreshadows the madness of Pol Pot and the Khmer Rouge. At the end of this extraordinary film, Kurtz is slaugh-tered at the same time and in the same way as an ox is slaughtered by the native people. All that is needed now is for Captain Willard to call for an air strike of B-52 bombers—and the screen is filled with an apocalyptic firestorm. While there is no trace of political ideology in Coppola, no echo of Carlo Tresca or Giovannitti in this or any of his other films, *Apocalypse Now* is a powerful indictment of war.

With success, Coppola became a Hollywood entrepreneur in his own right. He bought a studio of his own and went on to make films in his own manner that would "explore what we are as a people a nation and a world."

One of his more successful projects was of modest size—*The Conversation* (1974), a psychological horror story about a bugging expert who himself is being bugged and who goes mad trying to discover who is watching and listening to him.

In *Attenzione,* the film critic John Mariani attributes Coppola's fascination with the subject of bugging to his Italian American back-ground, "where everyone is constantly reporting each other's mis-deeds and honor is constantly assailed by unfounded rumor and gossip." Aptly enough, the paranoid bugging expert in the film is a Catholic. Its opening sequences include a scene inside a confessional booth. Commenting on this, Coppola said: "I thought confession was one of the earliest forms of invasion of privacy—earliest forms of surveillance—that I could think of. Confession, at first, was some-thing I thought related to the central theme. The fact that he went to confession made him a Catholic. The whole Catholic sense of guilt is related also. But that just evolved. I didn't do it deliberately."

In 1974 he declared: "I was raised to be successful and rich. . . . I do not really wear well being famous or successful. . . . I don't know the real answer, I just want honestly to follow my inclinations." He had become wholly American. Today, there seems to be little of Italy or the Italian American experience left in his work.

After a series of box-office and critical failures—*One from the Heart, Rumble Fish, Tucker*—Coppola, in need of money, returned to the gangster theme. In 1990 he directed *Godfather III*, which brought Michael Corleone back to Sicily, where he dies an old, defeated, and lonely man.

If the Catholicism of his Italian American background had little influence on Coppola's Hollywood career, the same could not be said of Martin Scorsese, who was born in the heart of Manhattan's Little Italy in 1942.

No one has captured the suppressed rage and anger of the immigrant like Scorsese. Much in his films reflects life in Manhattan's Little Italy. Raised a devout Roman Catholic, Scorsese abandoned his study for the priesthood after he heard a priest endorse the war in Vietnam as "a holy cause."

Although he came from working-class immigrant parents, Scorsese, like Coppola and Brian De Palma, entered the academic world. He studied filmmaking at New York University not far from the Little Italy where he was reared.

In 1968, while on the teaching staff of New York University's film department, he wrote and directed his first professional film, *Who's That Knocking at My Door?*, which centers on a young Italian who struggles to reconcile the rigid Catholic mores implanted in him by the Irish priesthood with the turbulence of a Little Italy far removed from middle-class America. In 1973 he made *Mean Streets* with the actor Robert De Niro, who was also brought up in Little Italy. *Mean Streets* is the story of Charlie, a young, ambitious third-generation Italian American trying to make it in the streets of New York. He moves among the petty hoods who con visiting teens out of $20 and use the money for movies. They brawl with opposing gangs, more for image than for profit. Charlie's hero is a *mafioso* who speaks perfect Italian. But it is Johnny Boy, played by Robert De Niro, who exposes the insanity provoked in the outsider who yearns to break into respectable society. Johnny Boy puts dynamite in mailboxes and refuses to pay a loan shark, going so far as to insult him in public. From the rooftops of tenements he shoots at open windows for fun.

Charlie, played by Harvey Keitel, has the burden of protecting Johnny Boy from himself and the forces around him. The *mafioso* insists that Charlie get rid of Johnny Boy, as if to get rid of all the insanity provoked by life in the streets of Little Italy. But Charlie is burdened with Johnny Boy as part of his Catholic upbringing. Pursued by the avenging loan shark, they flee to Brooklyn (of all places), seeking a safe haven. The avenger follows them, and from the back seat, Martin Scorsese (playing the hit man himself) shoots Johnny Boy and Charlie, whose car runs off the road, uprooting a fire hydrant. As the water shoots up into the night, we are left with a scene of horror.

What is one to make of this in the flow of the Italian American experience? Who is Scorsese shooting as he pulls the trigger? The rage of Johnny Boy is that of the children of the immigrants who felt caught in a dead-end situation from which there was no viable access into mainstream America (except for the few). The accents of Johnny Boy are the accents the second-generation De Niro and Scorsese grew up with. Scorsese chose De Niro because "he was perfect for the part, because he knows the life. *Mean Streets* is all about that; and that's what Bob used to do—hang around."

Rage permeates a number of Scorsese's films and De Niro's characters. Immigrant workingmen of past generations could certainly understand the character of Travis Bickle, played by De Niro in Scorsese's *Taxi Driver* (1980). De Niro exudes enough suppressed rage to kill a presidential candidate or a pimp—it doesn't matter which. There is simply a necessity to kill.

One theme dominates many of Scorsese's films, from *Mean Streets,* through *Raging Bull,* to the later *Last Temptation of Christ:* redemption of sin through suffering and sacrifice.

In *Mean Streets,* Charlie sacrifices his ambition, and his life, to comfort and protect the violent Johnny Boy, who by his actions demands to be hurt. In *Raging Bull,* Jake Lamotta is portrayed as a masochist who loves being hit. In one scene he demands that his brother hit him "harder harder harder." In *The Last Temptation of Christ,* we are almost embarrassed when Christ cries out: "I want to be crucified. I want to be crucified."

In *Goodfellas* (1990), Scorsese returns once again to the mean streets of his youth. This time, however, he draws closer to the Mafia clichés the public has become accustomed to: the Italian gangster who loves to cook (fat sausages, veal cutlets), the boring violence that does "little to illuminate the human condition." Such violence covers an anger within Scorsese that he has not yet learned to understand. As Pauline Kael wrote in *The New Yorker*, "But this picture [*Goodfellas*] doesn't have the juice and richness that come with major performances. It has no arc, and doesn't climax; it just comes to a stop."

Michael Cimino also came to film from the academic world. Born in New York City in 1943, he was raised at a time when affluence permitted many middle-class Italian Americans to leave Brooklyn, the Bronx, or what was rapidly becoming the inner city for the suburbs of Staten Island, Westchester, or Long Island. He grew up on Long Island and went to Yale, where he graduated with a degree in theater. In New York he worked making television commercials and was soon writing and directing his own commercials. He began work in Hollywood in 1973, collaborating with John Milius.

While Coppola and De Palma began their Hollywood careers by making their own horror films, Cimino's career opened with *Magnum Force* (1973), starring Clint Eastwood, the second in the series of films that gave the world "Dirty Harry." From *Magnum Force* he went on to make *Thunderbolt and Lightfoot*.

It was *The Deer Hunter*, however, that brought him to the attention of the film world in 1978, when he won an Academy Award at the age of thirty-five.

Cimino's scenes of the Russian roulette game forced upon young soldiers not so much by the enemy as by the war itself capture the randomness of death in battle. The tension built with each pull of the trigger as the player points the gun barrel to his temple is too much for most audiences. These scenes were criticized for being "unrealistic." Yet how else to suggest the choice of who lives and who dies in combat? It is the dramatization of the eternal soldier's proverb, "When a bullet has your name on it, it's time to go."

Cimino's success with *The Deer Hunter* gave him the opportunity to make *Heaven's Gate* (1980), in which he attempted to depict the price immigrants paid in coming to America. It did not succeed, although in the eyes of most critics it was the grandest failure in the history of motion pictures.

The film is interminable. Cimino lingers over scenes for no apparent reason; the pace is slow and could be cut by an hour. When *Heaven's Gate* appeared in 1980 it was almost four hours long, as if a committee were unable to decide what should be cut and what added. But the critics' derision now seems as heavy-handed as Cimino's camerawork. Good or bad, the film is a document of the anger of an immigrant's son against the men who humiliated the generation of his grandparents.

Cimino's next film was *The Year of the Dragon*. Then, in collaboration with Puzo, he made *The Sicilian*, which was so inept as both book and film that after a brief showing in New York it disappeared into the world of videocassettes. The promising career of a filmmaker with an instinctive social conscience appears to have come to an end.

The further one gets from the world of the early immigrants, the less socially aware the filmmakers seem to become—until one ends up with the work of Michael Sylvester Stallone.

Stallone bankrolled the rage and violence of the immigrants in such films as *Rocky I* and *II* and, of course, the *Rambo* series. Following the success of *Rocky*, Stallone attempted to make films closer to his ethnic experience. In 1978, he starred as an idealistic labor leader in *F.I.S.T.* (Federation of Interstate Truckers). It was a flop. Stallone tried again with *Paradise Alley*, the story of two immigrant brothers on the Lower East Side. This, too, was disaster. He then returned to the successful theme of rage and revenge with *Rocky—Rocky II* in 1979 and *Rocky III* in 1982, until he reached the ultimate in revenge fantasy in *Rambo*.

If Puzo, Coppola, and Scorsese with his *Goodfellas* contributed to the image of the Italian American *mafioso*, Stallone added to the caricature of the Italian American who is all brawn and no brain, as Stallone was once characterized by his father.

THE ACTORS

By the 1950s, the acting scene was dominated by those actors born and raised in New York City, most of whom came from working-class parents.

Henry Armetta, the roly-poly Sicilian-born actor who made over three hundred films, usually played the Italian-accented comic. He died in 1945; with him died one stereotype of Italians as portrayed in Hollywood films. His death marked the beginning of a period of apprenticeship for many second-generation Italian American actors who made striking contributions to the film industry. The first to become successful came from outside the New York City area. Don Ameche, for example, came from Kenosha, Wisconsin, where his parents owned a tavern and could afford to send young Ameche to the University of Wisconsin, where he became interested in theater. His voice—much like his brother's, who was Jack Armstrong the "all-American Boy" on radio—opened up a career that included hundreds of Hollywood films.

Richard Conte came from Jersey City and after playing in hundreds of films ended his career in Coppola's *The Godfather* as a *mafioso*. His most memorable film was *A Walk in the Sun* (1946), in which he played an Italian American GI fighting in Italy.

Anthony Papaleo, born in 1928, took his mother's maiden name, Franciosa. He was born in East Harlem, and his career began when in a chance encounter at the YWCA he was asked to audition for a part in Noël Coward's *Brief Encounter*. As he said, he saw acting as a way out of a life he did not like. "I didn't want to be Italian. I was under the impression that all Italians were gangsters or gamblers or racketeers."* His acting education, like that of many who followed, began with a four-year scholarship to the New School for Social Research. Then came years of traveling with stock companies around the country. He returned to New York to enroll in the Actors Studio. The success that followed his Broadway career finally brought him to Hollywood.

James Coca, the comic actor, was also born in Manhattan of working-class parents who wanted their son to become a shoemaker like his father. He began his acting career in children's theater, acting and managing productions.

Biago Anthony Gazzara—better known as Ben Gazzara—was born in Manhattan of parents who had come from Cianciana, a sulphur-mining town in Sicily. He, too, came from working-class people, who lived on 29th and Second Avenue—part of the Italian emigration that was moving out of the Lower East Side to the upper parts of Manhattan. He was influenced by the New School for Social Research, which did much to help his speech, marked by the fact that

*Pageant, November 1958.

he spoke Sicilian before he ever spoke English. His success on Broadway led to a long career in films and television.

Contrary to the immigrant tradition that children should go to work as soon as they were employable, Annemarie Italiano's mother scraped together enough money to send her to the American Academy of Dramatic Arts. Annemarie went on to become Anne Bancroft.

The image created by Hollywood, radio, and newspapers over the years of brutish, physical males who often abuse their wives continued to foster anger in some Italian Americans. As one critic put it, "Coppola, and Scorsese with his *Goodfellas* are still in the Step and Fetchit era. . . ."

CHAPTER 26

The Writers: 1960–1990

Quannu unu e pinsiunatu
campa 'mpintu a lu ciatu
When you're living on a pension
you are always out of breath.

—ITALIAN PROVERB, TRANSLATED BY GAETANO CIPOLLA

STORMING THE STRONGHOLD

In a 1974 study of American literature dealing with the Italian American experience, *The Italian American Novel: A Document of the Interaction of Two Cultures,* Rose Basile Green notes that during the decade 1960–70 "the Italian-American novel made a great leap into the stronghold of American letters." As in the two previous decades, these are largely novels of recall, based in varying degrees on the authors' own experiences as the offspring of immigrant parents. Although the protagonists are either Italians or their American-born children, the best of the novels achieve a universality that transcends Italian American specifics. Among the notable writers of that decade are Joseph Papaleo, Rocco Fumento, Michael De Capite, Lucas Longo, Robert Canzoneri, and Mario Puzo.

With the exception of Puzo's *The Fortunate Pilgrim* (which benefited from the publication of *The Godfather* three years later), all of these novelists' work, though favorably reviewed, quickly went out of print and was soon forgotten.

Puzo's novel would have suffered the same fate had it not been for the sensational sales record of *The Godfather*. When first published in 1964, *The Fortunate Pilgrim* received enthusiastic reviews, one of them in the *New York Times,* which called it a "small classic." It also evoked much praise from other writers. Joseph Heller said: "No one I know can create a city scene with more vivid accuracy, and there is not a character in this novel of New York City Italians who does not give me the feeling that I had met him in life." Despite the accolades, it failed in the bookstores and netted Puzo just $3,000, even less than his first novel, *The Dark Arena.* Taking into account the money he owed to relatives, finance companies, banks, and assorted bookmakers, Puzo admitted that after believing in art all of his forty-five years, it was "time to grow up and sell out as Lenny Bruce once advised." Acting on the hint by an editor that *The Fortunate Pilgrim* would have made money if it had "a little more of the Mafia stuff," his next book was *The Godfather.*

The most autobiographical of his novels, *The Fortunate Pilgrim,* according to Puzo, was intended to express his childhood dread of "growing up to be like the adults around me." Into the years of his adolescence he was contemptuous of adults and looked down at them for their willingness to settle for very little in life. "And so," he writes, "with my father gone, my mother the family chief, I, like all the children in the ghettos of America, became locked in a bitter struggle with the adults responsible for me. It was inevitable that my mother and I became enemies." One of Puzo's complaints was that his mother's highest ambition for him was to become a railroad clerk.

Puzo, however, matured into an adult with a sense of perspective and compassion. He was still bitter about his Italian relatives when he began writing *The Fortunate Pilgrim,* and had every intention of portraying himself as "the sensitive, misunderstood hero, much put upon by his parent and family"; but to his astonishment, his mother soon took over the novel and became its heroine. Moreover, the Italians of his youth whom he had regarded with contempt "turned out to be heroes." What struck Puzo most, in retrospect, was their courage. "How," he asks, "did they ever get the balls to get married, have kids, go out to earn a living in a strange land, with no skills, not even knowing the language? . . . Heroes all around me. I never saw them. But how could I?"

If this admission smacks of sentimentality, there is almost a complete lack of it in *The Fortunate Pilgrim.*

The central character is Lucia Santa, a tough-minded, indomitable matriarch who, through force of circumstances, is burdened with the responsibility of raising six children. Puzo has explained that Lucia Santa bears a close resemblance to his own mother who, at the age of eighty-two, was "positively indignant that death dares approach her." Like Puzo's mother, Lucia Santa comes from an impoverished and illiterate family from the hills around Naples. So poor are they that when she reaches the age of seventeen, she is informed by her father that because there is no money and many debts she cannot hope for a dowry—sentencing her, in effect, to spinsterhood for the rest of her life. In a spirit of rebellion, Lucia marries by proxy an immigrant in America whom she can barely remember as a childhood playmate. By traveling 3,000 miles to a strange country and a strange people, she follows the example set by the American pioneers, even though, as Puzo says, "they never walked an American plain. Actually, the immigrants moved in a sadder wilderness, where the language was also strange, where their children became members of a different race. It was a price that had to be paid."

The price that Lucia Santa has to pay would have defeated a less courageous woman. Besides her two unfortunate marriages, there is the task of dealing with the disparate temperaments of her six children, who are exposed to the turbulence and pitfalls of an Italian American enclave on Tenth Avenue. Their activities constitute the main thrust of the narrative as Lucia Santa's Old World standards come into conflict with the standards of the New World of her children. Puzo's artistry interweaves their actions with those of Lucia Santa against the background of a Little Italy during the hard times of the Depression, justifying Puzo's own contention that *The Fortunate Pilgrim* is the best of his novels.

One novel of the sixties that impressed the critics but failed in the marketplace is Rocco Fumento's *Tree of Dark Reflection.* Narrated in the first person by the central character, Danny Faustino, it delves deeply into the psychological forces unleashed in a father who, driven by a profound sense of guilt to hate and fear those he loves, virtually destroys the life of his family. At the heart of the problem is Catholicism's powerful grip on the psyche of the immigrants and their progeny.

The central drama evolves around Danny's attempts to resolve the fragmentation of his self, which veers between the extremes of his mother's passivity and religiosity and his father's brutish sensuality and scorn for the sacred. Despite the novel's theological nuances, which are partly introduced through Danny's relationship with a Jewish immigrant's daughter, the author's synthesis of guilt and behavior promotes a relentless sense of truth and drama which, according to the critic Frank Rosengarten, rivals in intensity William Styron's *Lie Down in Darkness*—another novel of a doomed family. Both novels, Rosengarten suggests, approach "the intensity of conflict achieved in another literary sphere, that of the drama by such playwrights as Eugene O'Neill and Tennessee Williams." Thanks to the veracity of novelists like Fumento, the popular stereotype of the warm, loving, fun-filled Italian family projected in films like *Moonstruck* takes on the aspect of a bad cartoon.

Finally, there is a group of second-generation writers who at one time or another returned to Italy and because of this have felt the pull of their parents' homeland more than others. A noteworthy example is Nat Scammacca, poet and co-founder in Sicily of the Anti-Group of poets, felt the pull of that homeland so strongly that after serving in the U.S. Army Air Force, he returned to Sicily to stay.

Scammacca was born in Brooklyn, where his parents spoke Sicilian in whispers, "so that their children would not learn the idiom." Yet the family returned to Sicily several times. During World War II, Scammacca as a commissioned officer served as a pilot over the Himalayas in the India-Burma-China theater. After the war, he stayed long enough in the United States to earn a B.A. from Long Island University and a master's from New York University, and then decided to go to Sicily to make it his homeland. There he spent over thirty years writing and organizing poets' happenings and conferences in the Mediterranean. In 1989 he returned to the United States for a farewell tour. He gave readings of his works in Chicago, was interviewed by Studs Terkel, and returned to his home in Trapani with his Sicilian wife, Nina.

The poets and novelists of this early period, from D'Angelo to Puzo, still bear witness to what it meant to live between two cultures.

While Mario Puzo's *The Godfather* was outselling all other American novels in 1969, the American Italian Historical Association was devoting its second annual conference to the subject of the "Literary Value and Social Significance of the Italian American Novel." Established the year before with the objective of "illuminating all aspects of the experience of those millions of Americans whose origins lie in the vast stream of Italian immigration," the association consisted mainly of scholars.

At the outset there was concern that too few books about the Italian American experience were being accorded the degree of critical attention and wide distribution a novel requires to survive beyond its first printing. The American literary establishment was partly responsible, probably because too few of its members were even aware of what Italian American novelists were publishing. Also responsible, according to Rudolph J. Vecoli, president and keynote speaker of the conference, was the fact that most of the Italian immigrants came from a premodern society, where a large percentage were either illiterate or had too little learning to have made book reading part of their life. Their fondness for narrative, Vecoli explained, was expressed not through the written word but by centuries of lively storytelling. Even among family members who could read English, their reading was usually confined to newspapers. Perhaps more than any other nationality, Italians looked upon reading as a luxury not to be indulged in if there was something else to do. During an era when few of the children of the immigrants went to college, the attitude of their parents toward books could not help but have a negative influence. A librarian working in an immigrant neighborhood told Vecoli that in some households schoolchildren were actually told that too much reading was bad for their mental health.

Contemplating the relatively small shelf of Italian American novels—small in relationship to the huge Italian immigration of the first two decades of the century—Vecoli also blamed the Americanization campaign pursued in the public schools, which had a de-ethnicizing influence on the young.

Not surprisingly, not everyone attending the conference acknowledged the value of reading good fiction. Leonard Moss, an anthropologist known for his extensive work in southern Italy, reminded the scholars of the importance of fiction:

> As one who considers himself a social scientist who attempts to understand a society, its culture, its values, its traditions, its beliefs, I would suggest that the scholar who ignores the creative

writer does so at his own peril. The creative writer is heart and guts of his culture: yes, even the disturbed writer, the psychotic writer, the alienated writer; the disturbed writer is disturbed within a context of social values which must be understood in order to understand the culture in which man is operating.

In the 1970s an increasing number of Italian Americans, particularly of the third and fourth generations, pursued intellectual concerns. At a time when ethnicity was becoming widely valued, the offspring of immigrants found it nurturing to rediscover their ethnic background. Some of this neo-*Italianita* was expressed in such works as Lou D'Angelo's *What the Ancients Said* or Joseph Papaleo's *All the Comforts* and *Out of Place*. Other writers utilized Italian American characters while concentrating on themes not explicitly linked to the Italian American experience: Eugene Mirabelli's *No Resting Place* and Tony Ardizzone's *In the Name of the Father,* whose chief protagonist, the son of a Jewish father he never knew, is named Tonto Schwartz.

Pietro Di Donato, whose *Christ in Concrete* (1939), unlike the novels of most of his contemporaries, continues to command critical attention, in 1978 referred to the novelists of his generation as "the Tony Macaroni writers" and declared them to be "shot," finished. Addressing "this new breed of writers," he predicted they would be in the forefront of a "renaissance" as "aristocrats of the soul," adding: "Our time is now. I see it because you are no longer *figli di muratori* (children of construction workers); you go to school and you are children with brains."

Di Donato either did not know or forgot that a number of his own contemporaries, such as Bernard de Voto, Hamilton Basso, and Paul Gallico, though second-generation "children with brains," had consciously or subconsciously avoided the subject matter of Italian Americans, or else had deliberately anglicized their names, as in the case of the acclaimed biographer of Renaissance personalities, Frances Winwar. "If you love and care for what Italians are and have done in America for America, you must say good-bye to them," Winwar said to Joseph Tusiani, the Italian American poet, who like herself was Italian-born. The poet whose work is acclaimed for his insights into the immigrant experience reports that to conceal his perplexity on hearing this advice, he asked Winwar "half facetiously and half impertinently" why she had changed her name. She replied because her publisher said that her name, "Vinciguerra," would not fit on the spine of the little volume. Tusiani also learned that her advice to say "good-bye to" Italians was based on her fear that if she were to remain within the Italian American community, she would not "see its life on a larger scale."

The ability of the younger Italian American writers to see America "on a larger scale" engendered a growing body of literature by poets, playwrights, literary critics, novelists, and short-story writers. The playwrights were in the minority.

The single Italian American playwright to occupy the limelight for any extended length of time was Albert Innaurato, whose full-length comedy *Gemini* attracted Broadway audiences for several years. Adding to his fame, though not to his bank account, was a one-act tragedy, *The Transfiguration of Benno Blimpie*. Both are written in an Italian American idiom, expressing the tensions between the Italian American and WASP worlds. Whereas *Gemini* uses comedy to develop the playwright's theme of acculturation, the more experimental *Benno Blimpie* employs powerful images to accentuate the fatal isolation of Benno, who commits suicide by stuffing himself with food.

Another playwright who deals with universal themes in an Italian American idiom is Joseph Pintauro, an ex-priest, poet, and novelist. *Cacciatore,* his best-known work, consists of three one-act plays emphasizing themes of separation and rejection. The characters include two brothers, a husband and wife "locked in a terrible tightness," and an elderly bachelor remembering past rejection. The *New York Times* commended the playwright's talent for pungent and idiomatic dialogue, to which an Italian American critic, Carol Bonomo Ahearn, added that Pintauro's ability to write dialogue rested in "his skillful capturing of the exact cadence of Italian American speech."

Two of the more successful Italian American poets, Gregory Corso and Lawrence Ferlinghetti, came out of the Beat generation in the sixties; only Ferlinghetti identified himself in his poetry as an Italian American. Ferlinghetti was born to immigrant parents, and changed his name to Lawrence Ferling in the interests of Americanization. In 1954, he reclaimed his original family name and moved to San Francisco. There he founded the famous City Lights Bookstore, which carried and also published books written in the anarchist, civil-libertarian, and anti-authoritarian tradition. City Lights became the publisher of *Howl*, Allen Ginsberg's first and best-known book of poetry.

Ferlinghetti, however, concentrated on his own writing, chiefly poetry distinguished by its earthy language and an abiding concern for social and political problems. His collections of poems, including *A Coney Island of the Mind* and *Pictures of the Gone World*, evoke his heritage. Speaking of the Italians in San Francisco's North End, Ferlinghetti wrote:

> For years the old Italians have been dying
> all over America
> For years the old Italians in faded felt hats
> have been sunning themselves and dying
> You have seen them on the benches
> In the park in Washington Square
> The old Italians in their black high button shoes
> The old men in their old felt fedoras
> with stained hatbands
> have been dying and dying
> day by day . . .

The Boston-born son of Italian immigrants, John Ciardi published some forty books of poetry and criticism, and translated all of Dante. He also served as poetry editor and contributor to the *Saturday Review* for sixteen years. He was a perennial figure on the lecture circuit from the time he withdrew from the academic world as a professor to become a full-time writer and lecturer. As a weekly commentator on the origin of words, his wit and erudition reached millions of listeners on National Public Radio until the last few months of his life. Only a few of his poems, which deal chiefly with his parents, suggest his Italian ancestry. One of them, about his mother's *Mezzogiorno* birthplace near Avellino, was much appreciated by her *paesani;* in an elaborate ceremony attended by Ciardi and his family—with fireworks and a parade led by a band— the poem was set into a plaque of Carrara marble and placed in the village town hall.

"A writer doesn't choose what he will write about," Ciardi told an interviewer in 1987, "he writes what comes; at least that is what a poet does." When asked about his identity as an Italian American, he responded: "I'm in-between, in a way. When I'm in Italy, I get along for a while and suddenly someone will say, 'You're not really Italian!' . . . I tell them: *Sono un Italiano diracinto*. I'm an uprooted Italian. I was born in the North End of Boston but we moved out when I was a baby." Questioned about anti-Italian attitudes he might have encountered, Ciardi replied that as a youngster he occasionally heard people express such feelings. He recalled that while riding along in his $70 jalopy during his high school days, he picked up a man who needed a lift and "who gave me a lot of stuff like: 'You goddam Italians coming over here and getting all the cars while native Americans like myself don't have one.' What could I say?"

Ciardi's anger was stirred up by the memory of a note Robert Lowell sent him after Ciardi had published a poem in *Atlantic Monthly* about Italy and Mussolini. "It was a bit of satire on Italian *orgoglio* and all those chin-thrusting plaster images of Mussolini— and about an Italian background. In the note Lowell said that it was the best Italian-American poem he had ever seen. And I thought, Does that son of a bitch think he is more American than I am? (laughs) Where did he think I was brought up. . . . Had it been a Yankee name, he would have thought 'Ah, a scholar who knows Italy.' . . . I can't grant for a minute that Lowell is any more American than I am. I was brought up here and had Yankee school teachers. I have lived in this country and have been abroad now and then. I was in the American army and out of it, thank God. And I'm an American man of letters. There's no hyphenation in that."

Ciardi died in 1986. He wrote his own epitaph:

Here lie Ciardi's pearly bones
In their ripe organic mess
Jungle blown, his chromosomes
Breed to a new address.

Not all of the immigrants' offspring who became poets were as much at ease in America as Ciardi. But the most gifted of them were able to transcend the specifics of the Italian American experience through the more subjective and symbolic language of their craft. For poets deeply imbued with the experience of trying to straddle two cultures, such as Lewis Turco and Frank Polite, poetry became the vehicle by which they could transmit the loneliness of their alien-ation with impunity, without denying or betraying their Italian con-nection. Like Ciardi, both Turco and Polite, speaking the universal language of good poetry, found acceptance in such nonethnic national periodicals as *The New Yorker, Harper's Poetry,* and the *Saturday Review.* Some of their poems may have dealt with their fathers, but they are fathers that could be recognized by readers of any nationality.

In a letter and a long unfinished poem, "The Mirror," Polite expressed in universal language the anger he felt as he viewed the image of Italian Americans as projected by the media. The letter bluntly deplored "the images presented through the American-Wasp media which represent Italians and other Mediterranean types as gangsters, clowns, or other exotics. . . . On TV today Italians still sell wine or stand around a pot of spaghetti sauce exclaiming 'Mama Mia!', or you get Godfathers and punch-drunk boxers. . . . Not images I could identify with and so the *split,* the alienation, and the *long way* around to become whole again." A few lines from "The Mirror" express "the split" in the language of poetry:

He was, and he was not
one of them
by anyone's stretch of imagination
except his own,
and so

year after year after year
he split down
the middle

of a mirror

until his eyes
were half his, and half
a child

who turned away from him, and rode
with the heroes
and stayed
a child.

Lewis Turco, one of the most prolific of the Italian American poets, gradually distanced himself from his past as he journeyed toward the mainstream. By the time he was in his thirties, in 1973, when he published the collection *Pocoangelini: A Fantography,* Italianate poems constituted only a third of the contents. They were a group of so-called "Sketches," which A. R. Ammons characterized as "an autobiography of biographies," and which prompted the Italian American critic Felix Stefanili to write, "We have a poet who is direct, clear-seeing, musical and quite real. Poems like Guido the Ice House Man, Ercole the Butcher and Mrs Martino the Candy Store Lady speak to the human condition with grace, always a strong point with Turco, and warmth."

This warmth and grace are delightfully evident in "An Immigrant Ballad for My Father":

My father came from Sicily
(O sing a roundelay with me)
With cheeses in his pockets and
A crust of black bread in his hand.
He jumped ashore without a coat,
Without a friend or enemy,
Till Jesus nailed him by the throat.

My father came to Boston town
(O tongue a catch and toss one down)
By day he plied a cobbler's awl,
By night he loitered on the mall.
He swigged his wine, he struck his note,
He wound the town up good and brown,
Till Jesus caught him by the throat.

He heard of Hell, he knew of sin
(O pluck that wicked mandolin)
But they were for the gentle folk,
The cattle broken to the yoke.
He didn't need a cross to tote:
His eyes were flame, his ears were tin,
Till Jesus nabbed him by the throat.

He met a Yankee girl one day
(O cry a merry roundelay)
Who wouldn't do as she was bid,
But only what the good folk did.
She showed him how the church bells peal
Upon the narrow straitaway,
And Jesus nipped him on the heel.

My father heard a sermon said
(O bite the bottle till it's dead)
He quit his job and went to school
And memorized the Golden Rule
He drained his crock and sold his keg,
He swept the cobwebs from his head,
And Jesus hugged him by the leg.

The girl was pleased: she'd saved a soul
(O light a stogie with a coal)
No longer need she be so wary:
Daddy went to seminary
To find how warm a Yankee grows
When she achieves her fondest goal.
And Jesus bit him on the nose.

At last he had a frock to wear
(O hum a hymn and lip a prayer).
He hoisted Bible, sailed to search
for sheep to shear and for a church.
He asked the girl to share his life,
His choir-stall and shirt of hair,
For Jesus bid him take a wife.

My father holds a pulpit still
(O I have had enough to swill)
His eye is tame, his hair is grey,
He can't recall a roundelay.
But he can preach and he can quote
A verse or scripture, as you will,
Since Jesus grabbed him by the throat.

The humor here is strikingly reminiscent of Robert Canzoneri's novel *A Highly Ramified Tree* (1976). Canzoneri's father was also a Sicilian immigrant who married, in his case not a Yankee but a southern woman, and he too became a minister in the Baptist Church.

By 1990, after publishing his twelfth collection of poems, there is little or no evidence of the Italian experience in Turco other than the spelling of his surname. His recent collection of poetry, *The Shifting Web* (1990), which contains new as well as selected poems from his past, is a far cry from the earlier poems about Italian

Americans. One critic wrote of it: "Dominated by images of snow, shadow, dust and decay, *Web* ignores urban life and human traffic . . . Yet it is deeply philosophical."

The pessimism often found in second-generation Italian American writers is not as prevalent in the poetry and novels of the generations that follow, whose perception of the immigrant experience is based chiefly on hearsay. Yet, subconsciously at least, there is a sense of loss and longing. As Babette Ingleheart puts it, the price the offspring of the immigrants had to pay was a cultural vacuum that could not be filled by any amount of success in the American mainstream.

One of the third-generation novelists acutely aware that America had substituted very little for whatever cultural tradition it took away from the immigrants and their children is Tina DeRosa, whose Chicago childhood was spent in a closely knit Italian immigrant enclave. Shortly before her first novel was published, she posed several questions which constituted a poignant conundrum for educated ethnic Americans like herself:

> What happens to a person who is raised in a passionate, furious, comic and tragic emotional climate, where the ghost of one's grandmother is as real as the food on one's plate . . . ? What happens to a person who is raised in this environment, and then finds herself in a world where the highest emotional charge comes with the falling of the Dow Jones average, or yet another rise in the price of gold?

Replying to her own questions, DeRosa says that such a person often winds up alienated from both worlds—the one in which she grew up and the one she has been forced to choose. Alienation came from her parents' insistence that she become educated. But education changed everything. Her relatives and her father began to regard her differently. She no longer had their approval, nor did she have the approval of the world they had thrust her into. "I belonged nowhere," she wrote. "That is the price you pay for growing up in one culture and entering another."*

DeRosa's *Paper Fish,* her first novel, has the ring of poetry as it tells the story of a young girl growing up in one of Chicago's largest

*DeRosa, "An Italian American Woman Speaks Out," *Attenzione,* 2, 1980.

Italian enclaves shortly before its demise. In an interview, DeRosa spoke of her role as an Italian American writer: "Our grandparents and parents were bound to survival; we, on the other hand, have become freer to use our own talents and to rescue the talents of those who came before us. Because we have passed through more time, we have a perspective that gives us the ability to look back and to judge their experiences as treasures that we cannot throw out."

Increasingly the "new breed" of Italian American novelists began to include women, among them Helen Barolini, a third-generation Italian American who had been publishing short stories and articles in literary periodicals. Her first novel, *Umbertina* (1979), explores on an epic scale the lives of three women of the same family, each of whom is caught in the tangle of Old and New World values. The oldest is Umbertina, who as an illiterate goat girl from the hills of Calabria immigrates to New York in the late nineteenth century. The narrative first takes her to an East Side slum populated by a half million Italians who have no police protection. Her resourcefulness stands her in good stead as she finds a way of escaping with her family to a congenial small town in upstate New York where, thanks to Umbertina's leadership, the family thrives.

Umbertina's indomitable personality becomes the touchstone for the arduous identity quest of the two other women in the novel, her granddaughter and great-granddaughter.

The last section focuses on the great-granddaughter, Tina, who never knew Umbertina but is profoundly influenced by the stories she hears of her strength of mind and purpose. Tina's identity problem is compounded by the traditional views of her native Italian father, which conflict with the love she has for a young American of her generation whose New England family is thoroughly Anglo-Saxon. In resolving the conflict, she is impelled to make a distinction between her American and Italian heritages.

Written with engaging sensitivity and verve, *Umbertina,* the first Italian American novel to intertwine American and Italian characters in both countries, became a major contribution to ethnic literature. Six years later, Barolini published *The Dream Book* (1985), an anthology of writings by fifty-six Italian American women, including Anne Paolucci, Mary Gordon, and Barbara Grizzuti Harrison. "Being Italian American, being female, and being a writer is being thrice an outsider," Barolini writes in her preface, "and why this is so is partly in the history and social background of the Italian women who came to this country, partly in the literary mold of the country itself." The title is taken from a manual brought to a Colorado mining town at the beginning of the century by an Italian immigrant family and used frequently by neighboring Italian women as "a Baedeker of their dreams" with which they tried to understand the foreign world around them.

A surprising number of writers represented in the anthology have published at least one book. One of the most versatile is Anne Paolucci, whose contribution here is four poems, but whose work also includes books of literary criticism (one of them a study of Pirandello), historical plays, essays, and short stories. Concurrently with the publication of *The Dream Book* Paolucci published a collection of short stories dealing with Italian Americans, *Sepia Tones,* of which the *New York Times* said: "If more Italian American writers do not speak up soon, much of their experience in the 20th century will go unrecorded. Anne Attura Paolucci's slim volume helps dispel the silence. By the end of the book, the author has invoked the world of an ingrown community where family pride cautions, 'Keep your eyes shut and say nothing . . . dust always settles.' "

Apparently, the *Times* reviewer was unaware of the body of fictional work by Italian American writers who are anything but silent. Several of those virtually forgotten writers are represented in *The Dream Book,* some with short fiction or memoirs, others with excerpts from their published novels, such as Antonia Pola's *Who Can Buy the Stars?* (1957); Julia Saverese's *The Weak and the Strong* (1952); Diana Cavallo's *A Bridge of Leaves* (1961); Marion Benasutti's *No Steady Job for Papa* (1966); Octavia Capuzzi Waldo Locke's *A Cup of the Sun* (1961); and Nancy Maniscalco's *Lesser Sins* (1979).

The better-known writers in the anthology are those whose work is currently in view; among them is Barbara Grizzuti Harrison, who is known more for her nonfiction than for her 1984 novel, *Foreign Bodies*. A third-generation Italian American, brought up in Bensonhurst, Brooklyn, Harrison in 1978 wrote *Visions of Glory: A History and a Memory of Jehovah's Witnesses,* which poignantly described her experiences in joining and later breaking with the Jehovah's Witnesses. The book ends with a conversation she had with her father:

"Explain to me why God sent the bears to rip the children who mocked Elijah."

"I can't."

"When you were nine years old, you knew all the answers. And the answers separated us. It's different now."

Everything is different now.

Another extract in the anthology highlights an important book-length autobiography, *Rosa: The Life of an Italian Immigrant,* a classic of ethnic literature. The book is based on the story told by Rosa Cassettari to Marie Hall Etts, a Chicago social worker who encountered Rosa in the settlement house where she was employed on the cleaning staff.

Barolini takes issue with those who would idealize the Italian American woman's place in the home, arguing that "True, she was the center of life of the whole ethnic group; true she must be useful to her family, for her value is based on practical usefulness; but it is less true to women than to men . . . that this ideal of *serieta*—or seriousness—was the be-all and end-all of a woman's life." To bolster her argument, Barolini quotes from Rosa's oral autobiography: "I have it like heaven now," says the widowed Rosa Cassettari at the end of her life: "no man to scold me and make me do this and stop me to do that. . . . I have it like heaven—I'm my own boss. The peace I've got now it pays me for all the trouble I had in my life." Barolini adds: "Even unlearned and unlettered women like Rosa had a sense of there being something more to their lives than family service."

The Dream Book includes a number of other writers whose stories document Barolini's contention that the

> strong hallmark of the Italian American family is changing because the young people are leaving home to go to college . . . as they follow the pattern of Italian American achievement, they are often subjected to the mobility and rootlessness of corporate American life. . . . The professors and other professional apologists of the Italian family had better listen to the women and to their literature of the voices of women writers who are telling it as it is. Home life was never as solid and satisfying as the men said it was; it was what it was for historic and social reasons that are now surpassed.

Nearly half of the anthology's contributors are poets; all of them have previously published work in magazines, anthologies, or collections of their own. More than half have had far more education than their parents. Some of them, though acknowledging their heritage in their poems, have non-Italian names—either because of marriage or because their original surnames were too difficult for non-Italians to pronounce. Possibly the most arresting example of name changing is that of Kathy Telesco, who became Kathy Freeperson to reflect her rebirth as a feminist. One of the familiar names among the poets is that of Diane di Prima, who had already published twenty-five collections of poetry and prose in pamphlet or book form. Barolini describes her as "the most important poet of the counterculture which grew out of the 1960s." A 1971 collection of her poems published by City Lights Books, *Revolutionary Letters,* opens with a poem entitled "April Fool Birthday Poem for Grandpa," which pays homage to the "anarchist wisdom" of her grandfather for "talking love, talking revolution, which is love, spelled backwards."

Perhaps the most celebrated author of Italian American background is Daniela Gioseffi, thanks to a profusion of national performances, readings, interviews, and publications in which she has participated. In addition to writing poetry, she is a novelist (*The Great American Belly Dance* was published in 1977), playwright, teacher, musician, actress, and dance performer. A collection of her poems, *Eggs in the Lake,* appeared in 1979.

One poem by Gioseffi—possibly the most outspoken in the collection—is entitled "Bicentennial Anti-Poem for Italian-American Women." It is preceded by a quotation:

"You are one of only two or three Italian-American women poets in this country," said the professor. "You are a pioneer. There are fewer of you than Black women poets."

The lines about her grandmother end with

I remember Grandma, her olive face
wrinkled with resignation,
content just to survive
after giving birth to twenty children,
without orgasmic pleasures or anesthesia. . . .

I remember
Grandma

got out of bed
in the middle of the night
to fetch *her husband* a glass of water
the day she died,
her body wearied
from giving and giving and giving
food and birth.

The Dream Book does more than accomplish Barolini's aim "to encourage the emergence of Italian American women from their traditional silence and subordination, and to give expression to the special insights born of their special experience." She highlights the various obstacles that have deterred all writers of the Italian American experience, male and female, from being accepted by the nation's literary establishment. "It is not that Italian Americans have not written work of value," she points out.

It is that the dominant culture, working under its own rules and models, within a tight network of insiders—editors, agents, reviewers, critics—is not eager to recognize and include in its lists that which does not reflect its own style, taste and sense of what is worthwhile. Italian American novelists are not generically "second rate"; they handle different material and handle it with the newness and perhaps rawness—but also passion—of the just-born and self-made writer. Literature is not only in the great and practiced writer. It is also in the new voices which add to the store of human experience; in the voices which, by enriching and extending the national literary achievement, become a permanent value.

By the 1980s and 1990s Italian American writers tended to be better educated, and were generally more sophisticated in style than those published in earlier decades; their works became less autobiographical and less explicitly Italian.

For some of these novelists, the urge to express their Italian heritage came only in middle age. George Cuomo, whose paternal grandparents came from Italy, had been writing mainstream novels and short stories since the early sixties. Not until the early eighties, at age fifty-two, did he publish *Family Honor,* which traces the life of

Vinny Sirola in a family of Italian and German immigrants. Sirola is a passionate labor leader, who appeals to men of various national backgrounds, as his father had done before him—a subject that has been largely ignored by Italian American novelists.

Another novelist who dealt belatedly with her Italian American experience was Josephine Gattuso Hendin, daughter of a Sicilian immigrant father and a Neapolitan mother who grew up in the Little Italy of the borough of Queens. In a daring step, Hendin left her family at the age of sixteen and enrolled in New York's City University. She went on to be graduated with a *magna cum lauda* degree and to acquire a doctoral degree. "I must have had the feeling on some inarticulate, subconscious level that it was impossible to achieve anything within the context of the family, which is why I left," she told an interviewer. "At commencement my mother looked at me and said, 'Well, I'm glad you got an education. But who will marry you now?'"

Hendin married the following year and launched her teaching career at Yale, eventually becoming a full professor of American literature at New York University. Her first book, published in 1970, was a critical study, *The World Around Flannery O'Connor*. Eight years later she published *Vulnerable People,* an examination of American fiction since the end of World War II.

Hendin's identification with her Italian ancestry, though late in occurring, inspired her to write a novel about a father-daughter conflict. *The Right Thing to Do,* published in 1988, was greeted with accolades. "In terms of style and structure," wrote the editor of *Voices in Italian Americana,* "it represents a real coming of age of the Italian American experience in American literature. It is important in that it represents a rare look at the old-new world crisis in the light of a father-daughter relationship."

Hendin says: "I think my sense of *Italianita* is rooted in my vision of the abiding moral concerns of Italian life. . . . I think Italians place a heavy emphasis on fulfilling their obligations, keeping their word, behaving properly towards others in a modern sense of Virgil's sense of pietas. In my novel both the father and daughter are each trying to do what they believe is right as they see it. . . . The trouble is that what is right in America in the 1980's may be more complicated than either thought."

Perhaps the least heralded of all the Italian American works published in the eighties is a memoir by a writer who as a four-year-old in an American orphanage operated by nuns was adopted by a childless, illiterate, and impoverished Sicilian immigrant couple living in a small Ohio town. Published in 1986 by a small press that was unable to provide enough distribution and promotion to attract many readers, Joseph Napoli's *A Dying Cadence: Memories of a Sicilian Childhood* is virtually unknown. The subtitle is somewhat misleading, since the setting is an Ohio town. Yet it is a true title, since the author's childhood was spent among Sicilians who lived for the most part in circumstances only slightly better than those they left behind. The Sicilian Napoli knew as his father was a tough, unforgiving parent, who beat him often. Yet Napoli continued to love him even after he reached adulthood. While serving as a U.S. intelligence officer in Italy during World War II, Napoli could not resist the urge to visit his parents' native village in Sicily. Few memoirs have ever been written with as much sensitivity, wisdom, and wit. Rudolph Vecoli described *A Dying Cadence* as "one of the most vivid, evocative accounts of a childhood in an immigrant family I have ever read. Joseph Napoli is indeed a skillful writer. While he does not disguise the grim aspects of working class immigrant life, the account is relieved by humor and affection." Napoli, a septuagenarian when he published his memoir, has yet to be discovered by the literary world.

The Italian American writers who rose to prominence during the 1980s, either as novelists, poets, or critics—for example, George Viscusi, Felix Stefanile, Frank Lentricchia, and Fred L. Gardaphe—were chiefly third generation. Tony Ardizzone published his first novel, *In the Name of the Father,* in the seventies but won recognition in the next decade as one of the more promising writers of his generation. In his second novel, *Heart of the Order,* the main character is Danilo Bacigalupo, the Chicago-born son of Italian immigrants, who cannot escape his boyhood memory of having batted a line drive that fatally injured a playmate. In his guilt-ridden state of mind, Bacigalupo, who grows up to be a minor league baseball star, literally enters the realm of surrealism when he adopts as his own persona that of the playmate he has "murdered." This duality has the effect of Americanizing the novel. "By marrying the story of an Italian American to America's favorite pastime, baseball," writes the Italian American critic Fred L. Gardaphe, "Ardizzone transcended the realistic, parochial world of Little Italies and established a work that speaks to all of America."

Heart of the Order was awarded the 1987 Virginia Prize for Fiction for "its narrative voice, which is full of wisdom and good humor." That same year Ardizzone published his first book of short stories, *The Evening News,* which won the Flannery O'Connor Award for Short Fiction. By and large the stories in the collection deal with hyphenated Americans, mostly of Italian origin, who, as one reviewer put it, were raised in "close-packed ethnic neighborhoods, and educated by nuns in paraochial schools."

Within a few months after the publication of Ardizzone's *Heart of the Order,* Jay Parini published his second novel, *The Patch Boys,* and Kenny Marotta his first, *A Piece of Earth.* All three writers were grandsons of Italian immigrants. All three wrote their novels while earning a livelihood as English professors at prestigious campuses. And all three chose to set their novels in the time period of their immigrant forebears.

The only one of the novels that sold well enough to go into a second printing was Parini's *The Patch Boys,* partly because of favorable reviews which occasionally compared it to *Huckleberry Finn,* and partly because Parini had already drawn attention in the book world with an earlier novel, *The Love Run,* and two volumes of poetry, *Singing in Time* and *Anthracite Country* (a title that refers to the Pennsylvania coal-mining area which is the setting of *The Patch Boys* and Parini's birthplace).

Sammy di Cantini, the hero-narrator of Parini's novel, at the age of fifteen in the summer of 1925 is nearing the end of his childhood. Sammy's best friend is Will Denks, an orphan, who lives in a dilapidated shack near the river. There is also a Becky Thatcher–like girl with whom Sammy is in love. The core of the narrative, however, centers on Sammy's relationship to his Italian American family, particularly to his oldest brother, Vincenzo, a potential major league pitcher who, after their father has been killed in a mine accident, becomes instead a union organizer for the surviving miners. In recounting Sammy's experiences during the eventful summer of 1925, Parini produced a novel that is a shrewd and poetic admixture of American and Italian elements.

Until the last two decades of the present century, Italian American literature occupied a special but isolated niche in American culture which, with few exceptions, was removed from the mainstream of the nation's literature. Negative stereotyping has resulted in two contradictory images. On the one hand, Italian Americans were seen as a people generally given to crime and violence. All too often, crime movies involving an Italian killer have presented him as something of a robot, one who kills simply because he is an Italian. Almost invariably some form of pathology is attributed to the American villain to explain his motivation for killing; the same is seldom true of the Italian killer. The audience is left with the impression that, although in all other respects he may be a model and even lovable father, killing people is something he does instinctively.

On the other hand, on the screen and on television we see the image of a simplistic, one-dimensional people, given to what Joseph Papaleo, a student of Italian stereotyping, describes as "excessive and unsuitable emotions." Such emotions, he explains, denote a lack of control, an expenditure of unnecessary energy amounting to a case of inefficiency, "a grave sin in American society."

The impact of nearly a century of negative stereotyping of Italians may well have deterred Americans (including those of Italian ancestry) from reading novels dealing with Italian Americans—unless they were crime novels, which attract for their entertainment value.

Fortunately, this phenomenon has abated as young writers emerge in a new society that increasingly equates cultural pluralism with democracy; for these writers, an Italian past is bound to be a source of literary strength.

Looking ahead, Fred L. Gardaphe notes: "We can expect that as long as there is an Italy, as long as there is a memory flavored with Italianita there will be the American writer of Italian descent whose contribution to American letters adds new dimensions to what it means to be American. It remains to be seen, however, if Italian Americans will drink from this rich foundation of work to nourish a distinct Italian American identity."

Within this optimism, however, lies a residue of anger—a cultural anger that still runs through the writing of the children of the immigrants.

The anger of Italian Americans appeared in January 1980 in a short story, "Tony," by Joseph Papaleo, published in *Attenzione*. During an imagined conversation with a variety of "Tonys," Papaleo presents the various images of Italian Americans: There is Tony the butcher, Tony the barber, Tony the bookie, the hairdresser, the tailor, and Tony the politician and Tony the crooner. They all admit to being the "smiling wop" in order to be liked. The waiter plays the "smiling wop" in order to buy his house in Massapequa and to put his kids through college. The baker plays the "smiling wop" for security in his neighborhood. Tony the crooner admits that "everybody likes the Italian image. It's happy-go-lucky. So I act happy-go-lucky. And I had couple of gold records. My albums still sell fast and steady. . . ."

It is Tony the politician who explodes in anger:

> Did I do everything to please to give them my smile so that they would say I was a good boy? It was either that or be branded . . . Commie or idiot. I found out, my friends, that we are . . . all of us prisoners of the crooner, the barber, the butcher and the rest. There is nothing wrong with that except the way *they* create it and stuff it down our throats. Then we have done what they wanted. We use stupidity for safety when we meet them. And if the stereotype is gone, then why are we still the most self-hating buried bastards in the entire world? I can spot one of us all the time—in the handshake. After two minutes' conversation. And I'm sick of you. But I'm just like you. I am. I don't even change my name to rid myself of the disgusting image that carries around rags in the personality until it sees itself as the ragpicker. . . . (I thought) I might have had a cabinet post years ago when I was deserving, more deserving than the mob of swine I saw march through the statehouse for twenty years, calling me Tony right away until I had to avoid them and their latest mafia joke and turn into myself and my painting. I found out right away that we were a group not permitted our normal rage.*

Joseph V. Scelsa, director of the Italian American Calandra Institute, recently pointed out in the *New York Times,* May 1, 1990, that "there is a white underclass in New York beyond Italians, and New York City needs to address that segment. . . . There is the perception that Italian American youths are not going to be given the same opportunities as those in affirmative-action categories. It creates anger. Unfortunately black men become a symbol of the special treatment."

One man who returned to Bensonhurst, where he was brought up, captured the anger and uneasiness of Italian Americans in this

---

*Attenzione, January 1980.

letter to the *New York Times* in 1991, soon after the shooting of Yusuf K. Hawkins:

In Bensonhurst in the 1930s when Italians began moving into that neighborhood, 18th Avenue between Bath Avenue and 86th Street, there was a black community just behind St. Finbar's Church where on Sundays I could see the Blacks sitting in the back pews. In P.S. 200 from the third to sixth grade I sat with Willie Miles a black boy with whom I shared lunch and played ball in the school yard. But once out of school I never saw him. When we graduated from our "rabbit avance" class (our Brooklyn way of saying Rapid Advance), I went on to a Junior High beyond 86th Street and Willie disappeared. Where he went I never knew until I was advised to go to Straubenmuller High School, a vocational school where I, supposedly, was to study textiles in preparation to becoming a cutter in the garment industry. I was sent to the 28th Street Annex and there I didn't meet Willie Miles, but half the class was black. The teachers, for the most part left us alone and read newspapers while we talked and smoked in the back. I spent most of my time with a Black classmate from Harlem. I read Thomas Wolfe's *You Can't Go Home Again* held beneath my desk, he talked to me angrily about Langston Hughes. He looked like a young James Baldwin and was twice as angry. I remember his anger but not his name. The last time I saw him we ate sandwiches and talked about the evils of nicotine while we sat on the steps of the annex watching the 6th Avenue El being torn down. We understood that we were not really wanted in class and I spent most of the days at the Burlesque Houses, the old Eltinge, watching Margie Hart lower her G string to give us a peek at her russet pubic hairs. My black friend never came to the burlesque with me. I never asked why and he never asked to come. I never knew if my James Baldwin-like friend ever graduated. In any case he disappeared also when I transferred to the 18th Street main building. And as I climbed that academic ladder blacks became fewer and fewer until in the graduating class of 532 there were only ten.

My last social event with blacks was a punch ball game between our Lincoln Bulldogs and a Black team from 18th Avenue. We played on our home block, Bay 25th Street. I don't remember who won. All I remember was that they hit grounders the first four innings and surprised us in the 5th by hitting nothing but long fly balls. We probably lost. I remember too that out of those teams came gangs that often fought in the streets. One Halloween one such gang, a horde of white guys from another neighborhood, many carrying silk stockings filled with hardened cement, came roaring down the street looking for a fight. We ran and hid in the cellars until they passed.

Army life was all white as was college after the war.

After an absence of 30 years I returned to Bensonhurst, soon after the Yusuf Hawkins killing. The houses looked tired. On the steps in front of the apartment house named The Providence, were worn spots in the shape of tractor seats, on a street where generations of Italian and Jewish immigrants raised their children, in a time filled with common angers, when the area elected Peter Cacchione, a Communist, to the City Council.

People were sullen, angry and frightened and would not talk about Blacks. Those who did, resented that the working class was being asked to bear the brunt and stress of bringing equality to Blacks. Competition for Civil Service jobs, construction jobs was exacerbating the conflict; jobs were going to Blacks, they said, and this angered the young.

It was then that one young construction worker who had dropped out of college complained: "I see blacks on T.V. They're all well dressed living in fine houses, using Milk of Magnesia. Cosby is a nice guy living someplace in Scarsdale. I hear that rap music all over the place. What do I get about Italians? Some slob eating spaghetti, or being stupid like Tony Danza or a shrimp of a . . . like Danny DiVito or some hood putting three shots in somebody's head. College, yeah I went . . . the blacks were getting all the honorary this and honorary that just because they were black. . . . Why the hell should I stay in college, I'm among my own here. And some white woman gets raped and beaten the . . . out of her and the . . . blacks go stomp rolling in court and get freed. Around here some blacks come looking for trouble and they tell us we're racists, my . . . . Did anybody parade around Central Park where that woman was raped. . . . ? . . . no. They parade around here, don't they? Nobody gives a shit about us. But Us."

As I walked up to the 18th Ave. station I remembered a doctor in Vermont who was enraged by Anna Quindlen's column in the *New York Times,* enraged enough to write to the editor:

"Racism in Bensonhurst is not the product of the Italian half of the residents' hyphen. It is the American half. America that is crime-ridden, drug-infested, and unsafe for families and property. Similarly, the violence is American, not Italian. In any given year there are as many homicides in Manhattan borough as there are in the entire Italian peninsula, Sicily and Sardinia combined. Ms. Quindlen's attack on some of America's most patriotic, hardworking, and family-committed citizens is shameful. It strains the traditional forebearance of a proud and accomplished people. . . . We and you cannot tolerate it."

I took the B.M.T back to the city, and as I looked at the worried faces around me I wondered what had become of my James Baldwin-like classmate's anger and of Willie Miles.

The letter was never printed.

THE ARTISTS

As has been the case with Italian American writers, only a few of the numerous Italian American artists who have made noteworthy contributions to American art are remembered. Even Constantino Brumidi, the "Michaelanglo of the nation's capitol," has been virtually forgotten. Not quite forgotten is the first of the Italian immigrants to acquire the status of a major American painter—Joseph Stella, who arrived in New York from a mountain village near Naples in 1896 at the age of nineteen. He first gained public attention with his drawings of immigrants arriving at Ellis Island and of workers in coal mines and steel plants published in national magazines. But it was in Europe, among the Futurists and Cubists of France and Italy, that he found a sense of direction that would break with standard art traditions. "Stagnation," he wrote at the time, "is death. A true art cannot live on the crumbs of the past." Returning to New York after a three-year absence, while still in the throes of Futurism, he painted *Battle of the Lights, Coney Island,* which art critics hailed as "the last word in modernism." The painting implanted in Stella an obsession with the idea of representing New York as a mold of modern civilization, and in the early twenties resulted in a composite panel of five large paintings titled *The Voice of the City of New York Interpreted.* The most reknowned of them, titled *The Bridge,* was actually the Brooklyn Bridge, which he admired as an engineering epic in steel, and depicted as "a precise network of cables and arches as seen at night."

The five paintings won Stella recognition as one of the foremost painters of the twenties, but his fame and fortune were cut short by the anxieties of the Great Depression and declining health. When he died in 1946, he had lived long enough to see his major work acquired by the Newark Museum of Art for permanent exhibition, but not long enough to be assured that his contribution to American art would be credited as a pioneering influence in establishing New York as the international center of the modern art world.

Outstanding in the field of sculpture was Beniamino Bufano, who belonged to the generation that followed Stella's. He arrived with his immigrant parents at the age of five. After studying the art of sculpture in New York and the art of glazing in China, he developed into one of the first Italian-born American sculptors to win recognition as a nontraditionalist. An ardent pacifist, he shocked the nation during World War I by cutting off one of his fingers and sending it to President Wilson as "my contribution to the peace effort." One of three sculptures he created for the city of San Francisco is fashioned in the form of a projectile titled *Peace* to assert his observation that "modern war involves the bombing of women and children; not the peace interpreted by the conventional motif of olive branches and doves." Another is a statue of Sun Yat-sen, the Chinese statesman Bufano had much admired during his travels in China. His most famous work, which was commissioned by the city of San Francisco in 1937, is a monumental statue of Saint Francis of Assisi; five feet taller than the Statue of Liberty, it dominates a large section of the city's landscape.

In the next generation Mark di Suvero won international recognition as a nontraditionalist sculptor given to work with large, heavy materials. He was born in China in 1933 of an Italian father who represented the Italian government as a business agent and a mother of Italian and French ancestry. The family moved to California in 1941, where as a college student di Suvero combined the study of sculpture with that of philosophy. His first New York show in 1960 included several large-scale works, prompting one critic to predict that "from now on nothing will be the same." As a conscientious objector to war, he refused to continue exhibiting his work in the United States while the war in Vietnam was in progress, and moved to Venice. While residing there his work was exhibited in France,

Germany, and the Netherlands. His first major American show came in 1975, when New York's Whitney Museum staged a history-making exhibition which, in addition to fifty large works on display inside the museum, also included a number of huge works scattered in open spaces throughout the city, among them two-ton objects. One of his later works was even more monumental, weighing thirty-five tons.

Di Suvero's creations, along with the brilliant painting-sculpture of his younger contemporary Frank Stella (no relation to Joseph Stella), are hardly typical of the numerous Italian American painters and sculptors who through the generations have made their mark in the American art world with more conventional styles. Their impact on American art has been a collective one distinguished mainly by the variety of and quality of their works. Their names and credentials abound in all editions of *Who's Who in American Art*. A name that will be missing from the older editions of that directory is that of Ralph Fasanella, the self-taught primitive painter who was not discovered until 1972, when he was fifty-seven years old. Born in Greenwich Village in 1914 of immigrant parents, his father was an iceman, his mother a buttonhole maker. He dropped out of school at the age of fourteen, and as a youth fought against Fascism in Spain with the Abraham Lincoln Brigade; he also became involved with the American Labor Party and worked as a labor organizer as well as a manual laborer. He began teaching himself the art of painting toward the end of World War II while supporting his family by pumping gas over a period of nearly thirty years. During that time no gallery or museum would accept his work. "My paintings smell of oil and garlic and salami and some people just don't smell anything." All that began to change when the discovery of Fasanella was proclaimed in a cover story in *New York* magazine, which cited him as "the best primitive painter since Grandma Moses," an opinion eventually born out by the widespread critical acclaim his work has evoked throughout the nation and Europe. Baseball, politics, and labor struggles are among the favorite subjects that Fasanella had dealt with throughout the evolution of his unorthodox career.

Italian American art has also encompassed artists who could apply their skills to the field of design. Prominent among them was Nicola D'Ascenzo, whose creations included stained and leaded glass windows as well as mosaics. Samples of his work are to be found in the windows of the Washington Memorial Chapel at Valley

Forge, the Folger Shakespeare Library in Washington, D.C., and the Cathedral of St. John the Divine in New York City.

Frank Gasparro is another example of an artist who was able to utilize his talents as a sculptor in the art of engraving designs on many of the coins that have been handled daily by millions of Americans. A freelance sculptor in the twenties, Gasparro was on the payroll of the WPA Federal Art Project during the thirties. After its demise in the early forties, he was employed as an assistant engraver by the United States Mint in Philadelphia, a position he held until 1965, when he was appointed chief engraver of the Mint by President Johnson. In that lifelong appointment he functioned until his retirement in 1981. During his tenure his engravings appeared on such coins as the Lincoln Memorial penny, the Eisenhower dollar and the Susan B. Anthony dollar; they were also on the inaugural medals for six presidents of the United States as well as on a series of medals to honor famous personages, ranging from Queen Elizabeth and John Wayne to Winston Churchill and George Washington.

All in all, in every American field of endeavor that requires artists, from the time the Republic was founded Italian Americans have left their imprint.

CHAPTER 27

At Home and Uneasy in America

Italian Americans have made great economic strides since 1910, when they were the lowest-paid workers—making an average weekly wage of $10.50 while the American worker averaged $14.37 (except for blacks, who averaged $10.66). Yet even this was a great improvement for many who came almost penniless and from towns and villages where they earned far less.

In 1985, the sociologist Richard Alba wrote that "The third and fourth generations, those born after World War II, and those of mixed background have either caught up or are about to do so. The changes have been spectacular especially in the realm of education, where the Mezzogiorno ethos would have seemed to doom Italians to inferiority for generations."*

Like most groups who have been Americanized, the later generations have all but given up the customs and traditions of their grandparents and parents. In addition, changes affecting the modern American family have also affected the Italian American family.

*Alba, *Italian Americans into the Twilight of Ethnicity.*

Italian Americans are marrying later and divorcing more. Intermarriage has increased, as has the absence of marriage—the third and fourth generation are, like their American peers, living together before marriage (much to the horror of the older generations). Intermarriage between the children of Italians and Irish has virtually ended the old hostility between the two groups.

Madonna, the all-American material girl who has captured the attention of everybody in the past decade, reflects this fourth-generation break with the past. Her Italian grandmother would hardly recognize Madonna Louise Veronica Ciccone, of whom *Vanity Fair* (April 1990) wrote: "Madonna is more than a celebrity, she is that perfect hybrid that personifies the decadently greedy, selfish sexual decade that spawned her—a corporation in the form of flesh." The grandmother would also throw up her hands in despair to see Madonna, bare-breasted, wearing a derby hat, prancing around on top of a bar in the film *Truth or Dare*.

For the children of immigrants, the greatest challenges have been the unresolved problems of identity resulting from being Italian at home and American elsewhere, the inability (and sometimes unwillingness) of parents to provide their offspring with any more education than that required by law, and a general sense of inferiority, provoked in part by anti-Italian prejudice resulting from the media's exploitative love affair with "the Mafia" and its various synonyms.

Psychologically, at least, the immigrants were better off than their children. They had no identity problem, nor were they afflicted with feelings of inferiority—no more so than they had experienced in their native land in dealing with the *galantuomini* (gentry). With an Old World pragmatism grounded in centuries of foreign domination, they could adjust to the difficulties of living among foreigners with foreign customs; hence the general lack of outrage. They failed to understand the dilemmas of their American-born children, who were constantly being pulled in two directions: by their parents, and by their teachers and classmates. The grandchildren (and subsequent generations), while not indifferent to the negative stereotypes about Italian Americans, have had a far easier time than their immediate elders. In increasing numbers they have acquired college degrees and professional status. Unlike earlier generations, they can appreciate the culture of the immigrants without any sense of conflict; in fact, often with curiosity and pride. Some have reclaimed their original family names. Yet, though grateful for their heritage, these modern

Italian Americans have had no difficulty discarding Old World notions that strike them as narrow. By the third generation, both sexes were attending college and for the most part were permitted to choose whatever course of studies appealed to them.

These changes have not taken place without consequence. Their price is illustrated in the history of Roseto, Pennsylvania, a small village that took its name from Roseto, Valforte, in southern Italy. The arrival of the Italians there in 1882, earlier than in most areas of the United States, evoked the hostility of Welsh, Dutch, and German groups in neighboring villages. Yet by 1912, Roseto (under the leadership of an Italian-born priest) had incorporated as an exclusively Italian American community governed by its own elected *paesani*. Considerable economic growth ensued, accompanied by a decline in the hostile attitudes of neighboring communities. In 1962, Roseto received nationwide attention when the results of a seven-year study revealed "a picture of healthy, prosperous, long lived and remarkable cohesive community with . . . a low rate of coronary disease among the living, despite the fact that the conventional coronary risk factors were found to be as prevalent in Roseto as in the two neighborhood control communities included in the study." The study attributed this phenomenon to traditional values brought from Italy. The family, rather than the individual, had continued to be the primary unit of society. According to the report:

> The community was their base of operations and each inhabitant felt a responsibility for its welfare and quality . . . the elderly were not only cherished but, instead of being retired from the family and community responsibilities, they were promoted to the "supreme court." Although the Rosetans experienced many of the same problems and personal conflicts as those in nearby villages, their philosophy of cohesion, with power support from family and neighbor made it possible for them to counteract stresses.

Twenty-five years later, the same team of researchers found that owing to sweeping social changes, the Rosetans had gradually lost their immunity to heart problems. Among other striking social changes was the collapse of the village taboo—ostentation. No longer were children taught that any display of wealth or superiority over a neighbor would bring misfortune. Expensive automobiles began appearing on the streets of Roseto, and families who had lived in small houses close to neighbors were moving to the suburbs and ranch houses. Intermarriage became popular, and even the tradition of naming infants after their grandparents was dropped. Parents were installed in nursing homes. The individual, not the family, was now the basic unit.

The same factors that led to the decline of the immigrant culture in Roseto were at work throughout most of the Little Italies in the nation.

As the generations moved into the mainstream, the Italian-language press in the United States has shrunk to a few weekly newspapers, most of them in English, a small number in Italian and English. Once almost every city and town with an Italian community from the East to the West had its Italian newspaper. Most papers at the height of immigration reported news from Italy and the Italian communities around the country, and defended the good name of Italian Americans. In 1908 *La Tribuna Italiana,* in Chicago, encouraged its readers to oppose restrictions on immigration. As early as 1914, *L'Italia* ran an editorial protesting movies that portrayed Italians in an offensive manner. During the 1920s and 1930s many of these papers promoted fascism and Mussolini. There were also, of course, anarchist and Socialist newspapers. But by 1990 most had disappeared, except for such papers (mostly weeklies) as the *Italian American Digest* of New Orleans and *Fra Noi* in Chicago. Recently, attempts have been made to publish national magazines with an appeal to the general public, such as *Attenzione* (which went under in 1987) in New York City and *Il Caffè* in San Francisco (which is still publishing).

In its heyday, the Italian American press was exceeded only by the German and the Jewish press in its variety and scope. The most successful of all the Italian-language newspapers by far was founded in 1880 by a former *padrone* from Tuscany, Carlo Barsotti. Launched as a four-page weekly, of which two pages consisted of advertisements, *Il Progresso Italo Americano* was the first to profit from the massive Italian immigration. Barsotti was less interested in promoting the interests of the Italian immigrants than he was in making a profit. Unscrupulous advertisers placed advertisements for medicines that purported to cure almost any disease. The circulation of *Il Progresso* grew rapidly (to 127,000 by 1920), and in 1921 Barsotti sold the newspaper to Generoso Pope.

Pope was an immigrant who had arrived in 1904 and made a fortune in the sand, gravel, and construction business. The popularity of *Il Progresso* enabled him to rise in the political ranks of the New York Democrats. By the 1930s, his influence extended to the White House. Pope was also highly regarded in Fascist Italy. However, he was among the first to denounce Italian fascism when it became apparent that Mussolini's ambitions for Italy were no more acceptable to Italian Americans than were those of Adolf Hitler.

After Pope's death in 1971, his son Fortune managed to keep the newspaper alive until 1980.

Brooklyn has *Arba Sicula (Sicilian Dawn, a Journal of Sicilian Folklore and Literature),* published both in Sicilian dialect and in English. This journal, which first started in Brooklyn's Bensonhurst section at the Church of St. Finbar, now is published with the cooperation of St. John's University in Queens. Under the auspices of Purdue University, a new literary and cultural review, *Voices in Italian Americana,* or *VIA,* has supplemented *Italian Americana,* which stopped publishing in 1986 but was resurrected in 1990 at the University of Rhode Island.

In the big cities, those few enclaves that are still recognizably Italian (such as parts of Greenwich Village in New York, the North End in Boston, and South Philadelphia) have tended to become tourist attractions, known for their restaurants, outdoor food markets, and religious festivals. Yet in some of these same enclaves vestiges of the past can still be found that belie their surface vibrancy. Some young Italian Americans, for lack of education, are still locked in a self-imposed ghetto atmosphere. Their resistance to education was documented in a 1990 study which revealed that one out of every five Italian American students in New York City does not complete high school. With a dropout rate of 21 percent, Italian Americans ranked third highest, behind blacks and Hispanics. Joseph V. Scelsa, as we saw earlier, has referred to a developing educational underclass. And this despite the great increase in college-educated Italian Americans from the third generation on.

★ ★ ★

By 1990, Italian Americans were scattered throughout the United States. The old areas—the Atlantic seaboard, Chicago, New Orleans, San Francisco—still held about 56 percent of the population. Arizona, southern California, Florida, and the Northwest have seen an increase of Italian Americans, but these new areas have not become Italian neighborhoods.

Elected members of the U.S. Congress reflect this scattering. There have been (and are) several Italian American governors, among them Ella T. Grasso of Connecticut, John Volpe of Massachusetts, James Florio of New Jersey, and Mario Cuomo of New York, each one the first Italian American to achieve that office.

Of all the Italian Americans to campaign for high political office, Cuomo was the first to use the concept of family to political advantage. The family, with its implication of communal strength and of obligation to the whole, became the highlight of his first campaign for the office of governor. "It is a notion that owes less to the arguments of political philosophers than to my own experience," Cuomo wrote in his published diary of that campaign.

Cuomo's heritage and upbringing is rooted in the Italian American experience as the story of the great migration comes to an end. Cuomo was born and raised in Queens, New York. He grew up speaking the Neapolitan dialect and hardly knew English until he started school. He won scholarships to St. John's Prep, where he was not only a good student but also excelled in sports. He was a good enough ball player to be signed by the Pittsburgh Pirates in 1951. His career as a baseball player, however, was cut short when he was beaned by a fastball.

He too felt the sting of prejudice, when as a young lawyer he was advised to change his name to something that did not end in a vowel. These early experiences colored a political career in which Cuomo has fought for education programs, increased benefits in Medicaid for the poor and Medicare for the aged, and increased Social Security benefits. His battle cry in the nineties has been a strong one. "Given the country's commitment to the savings and loan bailout, it's a disgrace to say we can't afford National Health Insurance. It's a disgrace, it's an abomination to say we can't help the homeless."★ Yet his insistence, in good peasant logic, that some services must be

★*The Atlantic,* December 1990.

cut and taxes must be raised has cost him some popularity.

Nonetheless, in the last decade of the twentieth century, Mario Cuomo has often been identified as the Democrats' best chance of winning the presidency of the United States, if not in 1992, perhaps in 1996.

Epilogue

A t the fifth centennial anniversary of the discovery of the New World, Italian Americans seem to be more at ease in America, although it is difficult to find a voice common to them all.

Time has split those who came before World War I in two. One part has remained behind in the written record of newspapers, commission reports, articles in monthlies, and scholarly journals. The second part has moved on in time to settle in the memories of the men and women who lived through the experience. The first, curiously enough, reflects a more depressing, despairing America. The second, after speaking to those Italians who live scattered through the country and who seem like so many survivors now, shows a happier, tougher, more contented America. They often quote the old proverb, *"Il tempo e un gentiluomo e perdona tutto"* (Time is a gentleman and forgives us everything).

Italians who arrived during the great migration were not all of one piece, nor did they become so as time, circumstances, and the new environment have nurtured them into Italian Americans. Robert Canzoneri was raised in Mississippi, by a Sicilian father turned Baptist minister. He became a sophisticated writer and professor, while a cousin, Anthony Canzoneri, nurtured in the onion-farming region of northern New York State, became a punishment-absorbing prizefighter.

With the passage of the Immigration Act of 1965, which permitted relatives of U.S. citizens to enter the country, there was a new flow of emigration from Italy. Between 1965 and 1973, the number of immigrants wavered at around 25,000 a year. By 1974 there was a steady decline, until 1986, when less than 5,000 entered. The late 1980s saw the greatest number of immigrants to the United States since World War II—but this time the smallest number were from Italy.

The decline can be attributed to Italy's economic prosperity, which by the mid-seventies provided opportunities and jobs at home. During the 1980s, rather than providing emigrants to other countries, Italy was attracting immigrants from Central Europe and North and Central Africa. By 1990 Italy had an immigration problem of its own, and the government contemplated using the armed forces to prevent clandestine immigration that was taxing its social services, creating unemployment problems, and causing racial tensions.

The great Italian migration to the New World begun in 1880 has come to an end, not because of U.S. legislation but of its own volition. With the absence of Italian-born people to maintain the Italian language and customs, the Old World aspects of the culture by the 1990s are fading and the survival of that culture in the United States, most observers feel, is less likely. Time, new experiences, and a new environment are changing the offspring of the early immigrants.

According to the census of 1980, of the 12 million citizens who declared themselves Italian American, just over 6 million claimed both parents as being of Italian origin; 5 million said that only one parent was of Italian origin. Intermarriages were changing Italian families. Gone, as for the rest of Americans, was the family with ten or twelve children. Birth rates declined to the "typical" American family of 1.5 children. By the third generation, divorce (although lowest among Italian Americans) was prevalent, more so among those of one-parent ancestry.

Although Italian Americans made great strides in many fields, 1975 left the statistics which tell us that the professoriate was still 75 percent of British or Northern European origin, almost the same as it was in 1900. In 1989, at a state university college in New York where 25 percent of the student body was of Italian American origin, only 2 percent of the professoriate was so.

The increase in Italian American college students did not bring a corresponding increase in Italian American professors. With the rise of state universities in the 1960s, for example, there was a rise in the number of third-generation students attending college, mostly from working-class families. Yet the number of Italian American professors did not increase proportionately, a situation that could be attributed to various factors—among them, affirmative action criteria, which tend to exclude Italian Americans, and the shrinking market for academic appointments.

Perhaps these statistics bear witness to the facts of assimilation; nonetheless, assimilation for the bulk of the second and third generations found Italian Americans in proletarian or lower-middle-class jobs and positions—nursing, elementary school teachers, high school teachers in ghetto areas, and football coaches in Staten Island or Chicago. As Vecoli pointed out in 1989, "The schools did fail generations of immigrant youth because of their middle-class bias; immigrant kids were tracked into industrial arts . . . and from there into the factories."

Italian Americans will survive as an ethnic group well into the twenty-first century. It is disconcerting to such observers as Joseph Scelsa, however, who see Italian Americans being divided into two groups: those who are entering the professions (about 20%) and those who are poorly educated and falling into unskilled jobs. "Italian Americans," he writes, "will have replicated the two-class system of the late 19th century Southern Italy."

Much has been gained in economic well-being, in opportunities for greater possibilities, greater horizons. John Ciardi's father was a shoemaker, Joe DiMaggio's father was a fisherman, Mario Cuomo's parents were grocers.

Yet there is also a yearning for the home left behind—and more so for the second generation, whether it be the home of childhood or the land their parents left.

All immigrants, from the first English Puritans to the latest arrivals, have felt this yearning—a sense of loss (even guilt) and of anxiety at tearing up home roots. For this reason the word "home" has a special meaning in America.

There is no word for "home" in Italian. There is *casa* (house), *fucolaro* (hearth), but no word for home (as if they had no need for it) as in English. In American English the yearning for home looms large: in American literature the theme of home and search for home is persistent, from Mark Twain's *Huck Finn* through Melville's *Moby Dick* to Thomas Wolfe's *Look Homeward, Angel* and *You Can't Go Home Again.* American songs like *Home, Home on the Range, Old Folks at Home,* and *Me and Bobby Magee* along with Protestant hymns are peppered with the word. Baseball, that most American of games, has as its object to reach home safely as often as possible.

The Native American James Yellowbank, looking back at Columbus, reminds us that Columbus called the native people he encountered "a people of God" and added: "We are individuals, bound together by the universe, by the Earth, by commonalities such as language, environment and heredity. We must live as individuals and appreciate differences."*

At the five hundredth anniversary of Columbus's voyage, we can look back at those adventurers and explorers who came from Italy in the service of others—at the musicians, painters, and artisans in the eighteenth and nineteenth century, and at the great wave of immigrants of the late nineteenth and early twentieth centuries that followed, all of whom in the end were looking for a place as safe as home.

Italian Americans as individuals "bound together by commonalities of language, environment and heredity" have found their American home, with all the conflicts inherent in most families.

*Fra Noi, September 1991.

Bibliography

GENERAL WORKS

Abba, Giuseppe Cesare. *The Diary of One of Garibaldi's Thousand*. London and New York: Oxford University Press, 1962.

Abbot, Edith. *The Tenements of Chicago, 1908–1935*. Chicago: University of Chicago Press, 1936.

Abbott, Grace. *The Immigrant and the Community*. New York: Century, 1917.

———. *Immigration Problems in Massachusetts; Report of the Commission on Immigration*. Boston: Wright & Potter, 1914.

Abruzzi, G. G. *Leonardo Sciascia e la Sicilia*. Rome: Bulzoni, 1974.

Acton, Harold. *The Bourbons of Naples (1734–1825)*. London: Methuen, 1956.

———. *The Last Bourbons of Naples (1825–1861)*. London: Methuen, 1961.

Adamic, Louis. *Dynamite, The Story of Class Violence in America*. Gloucester, Mass.: Peter Smith, 1960.

———. *A Nation of Nations*. New York: Harper, 1944.

Adams, Graham, Jr. *Age of Industrial Violence 1910–15*. New York: Columbia University Press, 1966.

Addams, Jane. *Democracy and Social Ethics*. New York: Macmillan, 1920.

———. *The Second Twenty Years at Hull House: 1909–1929*. New York: Macmillan, 1930.

———. *The Spirit of Youth and the City Streets*. New York: Macmillan, 1909.

———. *Twenty Years at Hull House*. New York: New American Library, 1961.

Age of Industrial Violence: The Activities and Findings of the U.S. Commission on Industrial Relations. New York: Columbia University Press, 1966.

Agliano, Sebastiano. *Questa Sicilia*. Venice: Corbo e Fiore, 1982.

Ahmed, Aziz. *Islamic Surveys*. Edinburgh: Edinburgh University Press, 1975.

Alba, Richard. *Italian Americans into the Twilight of Ethnicity*. Englewood Cliffs, N.J.: Prentice-Hall, 1985.

Albini, J. *The American Mafia*. New York: 1971.

Aleandri, Emelise. "The Origins of Italian-American Theatre in New York City During the 19th Century, 1871–1900." Master's thesis, New York: Hunter College, 1980.

Alessi, Biaji. *Naro: Guide Storica e Artistica; Edizion: Centro Culturale "L. Pirandello."* Agrigento-Palermo: Centro Culturale, 1976.

Allport, Gordon. *The Nature of Prejudice*. New York: Doubleday Anchor, 1958.

Allswang, J.M. *The Political Behavior of Chicago's Ethnic Groups*. New York: Arno Press.

Amari, M. *Storia dei Musulmani di Sicilia*. Catania: Prampolini, 1935.

Amato, Joseph. *Mirrors of Ourselves*. Minnesota: Marshall, Amati Venti, 1880.

American Italian Historical Association. An Inquiry into Organized Crime. October 1970.

Amfitheatrof, Erik. *The Children of Columbus*. Boston: Little Brown, 1973.

Andreozzi, John. *Guide to the Records of Sons of Italy of America*. Immigration History Research Center, University of Minnesota, 1989.

Antonini, Luigi. *Dynamic Democracy*. New York: Eloquent Press, 1944.

Angle, Paul. *Bloody Williamson; A Chapter in American Lawlessness*. New York: Knopf, 1952.

Areleo, Joseph. *The Grand Street Collector*. New York: Walker, 1970.

Arlacchi, Pino. *Mafia Business*. London: Verso, 1983.

Armstrong, Louis. *Swing That Music*. London, N.Y.: Longmans Breen, 1936.

Asbury, Herbert. *Assimilation of the Italian Immigrant (The Italian American Experience)*. New York: The Free Press, 1958.

———. *The French Quarter*. New York: Knopf, 1936.

———. *The Gangs of New York*. Garden City: Knopf, 1927.

———. *Gem of the Prairie; An Informal History of the Chicago Underworld*. New York: Century, 1917.

Ayres, Leonard P. *Laggards in Our Schools. A Study of Retardation and Elimination in City School Systems*. New York: Russell Sage Foundation, 1909.

Bach, Steven. *Final Cut*. New York: New American Library, 1985.

Balancio, P., and D. Fusaro. "The Italian American Clan." In *American Italian Historical Association* 13, Annual Conference, 1980.

Banfield, Edward. *The Moral Basis of a Backward Society*. New York: The Free Press, 1958.

Barolini, Helen, ed. *The Dream Book, An Anthology of Writings by Italian American Women*. New York: Schocken Books, 1985.

———. *Festa: Recollections of New York*. Harcourt Brace. 1988.

Barrese, Orazio. *I Complici, Gli anni dell'Antimafia*. Milan: Feltrinelli, 1973.

Barth, Frederik. *Ethnic Groups and Boundaries*. Boston: Little, Brown, 1969.

Barzini, Luigi. *From Caesar to the Mafia*. New York: The Library Press, 1971.

———. *The Italians*. New York: Bantam Books, 1965.

———. *O America: When You and I Were Young*. New York: Harper & Row, 1977.

Battaglia, G. G. *La Rivoluzione Sociale Siciliana*. Palermo: David Malato, 1970.

Battistella, Graziano, ed. *Italian Americans in the '80s*. New York: Center for Migration Studies, 1989.

Baur, John. *Joseph Stella*. New York: Praeger, 1971.

Bayor, R.H. *Neighbors in Conflict—The Irish, Germans, Jews, and Italians of New York City, 1929–1941*. Baltimore: Johns Hopkins University Press, 1978.

Bazan, Ernesto. *Il Passato Perpetuo: Fotografie de Ernesto Bazan con due saggi da Robert Viscusi e Jerre Mangione*. Palermo: Edizione Novecento, 1985.

Belfiglio, Cavaliere. *Italian Experience in Texas*. Austin: Eakin Press, 1983.

Bell, D. *The End of Ideology*. New York, 1960.

Bell, R. M. *Fate and Honor, Family and Village*. Chicago: University of Chicago Press, 1979.

Belmonte, Thomas. *The Broken Fountain*. New York: New York College University Press, 1979.

Benton, Barbara. *Ellis Island: A Pictorial History*. New York: Facts on File, 1985.

Bergman, Frank, ed. *Upstate Literature: Essays in Memory of Thomas F. O'Donnell*. Syracuse, New York: Syracuse University Press, 1985.

Bernardo, Stephanie. *The Ethnic Almanac*. Garden City: Doubleday, 1981.

Berstein, I. *Turbulent Years: A History of the American Worker 1933–1941*. Boston: Houghton Mifflin, 1969.

Bezza, B., ed. *Gli Italiani Fuori d'Italia*. Milan: Franco Angeli, 1983.

Biagi, Ernest. *Italian Name-Places in the United States*. Philadelphia: 1970.

———. *The Italians of Phil elphia*. New York: Carleton Press, 1967.

———. *The Purple Aster: A History of the Order of the Sons of Italy in America*. Veritas Press, 1961.

———. *Vol. II, The Italians of Philadelphia and Delaware County*.

Bianco, Carla. *The Two Rosetos*. Bloomington: Indiana University Press, 1974.

Billington, R. A. *America's Frontier Heritage*. New York: Holt, Rinehart, 1966.

Bliss, Michael. *Brian De Palma*. Metuchen, N.J.: The Scarecrow Press, 1983.

Block, Alan. *East Side*. Cardiff, Wales: University of Cardiff Press, 1980.

Blok, Anton. *The Mafia of a Sicilian Village*. New York: Harper & Row, 1975.

Bodnar, John. *The Ethnic Experience in Pennsylvania*. Lewisburg, Penn.: Bucknell University Press, 1973.

———. *Life of Their Own: Blacks, Italians and Poles in Pittsburgh*. Pittsburgh: University of Pittsburgh, 1982.

———. *Workers' Word, Kinship Community, and Protest in an Industrial Society, 1900–1940*. Baltimore: Johns Hopkins University Press, 1982.

Boehlhower, William. *Immigrant Autobiography in the U.S.: Four Versions of the Italian American Self*. Verona, Italy: Essedue Edizioni, 1982.

Bohme, Frederick G. *A History of Italians in New Mexico*. New York: Arno Press, 1975.

Bonanno, Joseph, with Sergio Lalli. *A Man of Honor*. New York: Simon & Schuster, 1983.

Boody, Bertha M. *A Psychological Study of Immigrant Children at Ellis Island*. Baltimore: Williams and Wilkins, 1926.

Borghi, Armando. *Mussolini: Red and Black*. New York: Freie Arbeiter Stimme, 1938.

Bove, Susan Barber. *The Early Italian Immigrants in Seneca Falls, New York (1884–1930)*. Canandaigua, N.Y.: W. F. Humphrey Press, 1983.

Boysen, Sue. *Some Historical Highlights of the History of Pittsburgh.* California: 1964.

Brace, Charles L. *The Dangerous Class of New York.* New York: 1872.

Brancati, Vitaliano. *Bell'Antonio.* Translated by Stanley Hochman. New York: Ungar, 1978.

Brancato, Francesco. *La Mafia.* Cosenza: Pellegrini, 1986.

Brandenburg, Broughton. *Imported Americans.* New York: Frederick Stokes, 1903.

Braudel, Fernand. *Capitalism and Material Life 1400–1800.* Translated by Miriam Kochan. New York: Harper & Row, 1973.

———. *The Mediterranean.* 2 vols. New York: Harper & Row, 1972.

Breckinridge, S. P. *New Home for Old.* New York: Harper, 1921.

Breslin, Jimmy. *The Gang That Couldn't Shoot Straight.* New York: Viking, 1969.

Briani, Vittoria. *Italian Immigrants Abroad: A Bibliography on the Italian Experience Outside Italy in Europe, The Americas, Australia, and Africa.* Detroit, Mich.: Blaine Ethridge, 1979.

Briggs, John. *An Italian Passage: Immigrants to Three American Cities, 1880–1930.* New Haven: Yale University Press, 1978.

Brody, David, ed. *The American Labor Movement.* New York: Harper & Row, 1971.

Brown, J., W. Roucek, and S. Slabey, eds. *Our Racial and National Minorities: Their History, Contributions, and Present Problems.* New York: Prentice-Hall, 1937.

Brown, Kenny L. *The Italians in Oklahoma.* Norman, Ok.: University of Oklahoma Press, 1980.

Browning, Frank, and John Gerassi. *The American Way of Crime.* New York: G.P. Putnam's Sons, 1980.

Brownstone, David M., et al. *Island of Hope, Island of Tears.* New York: Rawson, Wade, 1979.

Bruhn, John G., and Stewart Wolf. *The Roseto Story: An Anatomy of Health.* Norman, Ok.: Oklahoma University Press, 1979.

Budish, J. M., and B. Soule. *The New Unionism in the Clothing Industry.* New York: Harcourt, Brace and Howe, 1920.

Burattini, Roberto. *Italians and Italo Americans in Ver.* Barre, Ver.: 1931.

Busk, R. H. *The Folk Songs of Italy.* London: Swan, Sonnensschein, Lowrey and Co, 1887.

Butcher, Philip. *The Ethnic Image in Modern American Literature. 1900–1950.* 2 vols. Washington, D.C.: Howard University Press, 1984.

Butta, Giuseppe. *Un Viaggio Da Boccadifalco A Gaeta: Memorie della revoluzione dal 1860 al 1861.* Milan: Bompiani, 1985.

Cahn, William. *Lawrence 1912: The Bread & Roses Strike.* New York: The Pilgrim Press, 1954.

Caico, L. *Sicilian Ways and Days.* New York: Appleton, 1910.

Callow, Alex, ed. *The City Boss in America.* New York: Oxford University Press, 1976.

———. *The Tweed Ring.* London: Oxford University Press, 1965.

Calvino, John. *The Selected Letters of John Ciardi.* Edited by E. M. Cifelli. Fayetteville, Ark.: University of Arkansas Press, 1991.

Cammett, John, ed. *The Italian American Novel. Proceedings of the Second Annual Conference AIHA.* New York, October 1969.

Candida, Renato. *Questa Mafia.* Caltinisetta: Salvatore Sciascia, 1956.

Cantor and Laurie. *Class, Sex and the Woman Worker.* Westport, Conn.: Greenwood Press, 1977.

Canziani, E. *Through the Apennines and the Lands of the Abruzzi*. Boston: Houghton Mifflin, 1928.

Capitini, Aldo. *Anti fascismo Tra I Giovani*. Trapani: Celebes, 1966.

———. *Religione Aperta*. Pisa: Ugo Guanda, 1955.

Cappon, Paul. *Conflict entre les Neo-Canadiens et les francophones de Montreal*. Quebec: Les Presses de l'Université Laval, 1974.

Capra, Frank. *The Name Above the Title*. New York: Bantam, 1972.

Capuzzi, Octavia. *A Cup of the Sun*. New York: Harcourt, Brace and World, 1961.

Caracciolo, Alberto. *L'Inchiesta Agraria Jacini*. Torino: Giulio Einaudi, 1958.

Carlson, Peter. *Roughneck, The Life & Times of Big Bill Haywood*. New York: W. W. Norton, 1983.

Carnevali, Emanuel. *The Autobiography of Emanuel Carnevali*. Compiled by Kay Boyle. New York: Horizon Press, 1987.

Caroli, Betty. *Italian Repatriation from the United States, 1900–1914*. New York: Center for Migration Studies, 1973.

Caruso, Bruno. *Sicilia*. Palermo: S. F. Flaccovia, 1974.

Caso, A. *Mass Media vs. the Italian Americans*. Boston: Branden Press, 1980.

Caso, Vincent A. *The One Hundredth Anniversary of the Arrival of Giuseppe Garibaldi in New York in Exile from 1850 to 1853*. New York: New American Publishing, 1950.

Casso, Evans J. *Staying in Step: A Continuing Italian Renaissance*. New Orleans: Quariga Press, 1984.

Cateura, Linda B. *Growing Up Italian*. New York: William Morrow, 1987.

Cautela, Giuseppe. "The Italian Theater in New York." *American Mercury* 12 no. 45 (Sept. 1927), 106–112.

Cavaioli, Frank J., and Salvatore J. LaGumina. *The Peripheral Americans*. Malabar, Fl.: Robert E. Krieger, 1984.

Cerase, F. *L'Emigrazione Di Ritorno*. Rome: University di Roma, 1971.

Chandler, Bernard S., and Julius A. Molinaro, eds. *The Culture of Italy: Mediaeval to Modern*. Toronto: Griffin House, 1979.

Chandler, Billy Jaynes. *King of the Mountain: The Life and Death of Giuliano the Bandit*. Dekalb, Ill.: Northern Illinois University Press, 1988.

Chapin, Robert C. *The Standard of Living Among Workingmen's Families in N.Y. City*. New York: Russell Sage Foundation, 1909.

Chapman, Charlotte. *Milocca—A Sicilian Village*. Cambridge: Schenkman, 1971.

Chetwood, John. *Immigration Fallacies*. Boston: Arena Publishing Co., 1896.

Chesnais, J.C. *Histoire de la Violence Lafont*. Paris: Robert Laffont, 1981.

Child, Irving. *Italian or American? The Second Generation in Conflict*. New Haven, Conn.: Yale University Press, 1943.

Churchill, Charles W. *The Italians in Newark*. New York: Arno Press, 1975.

Ciardi, John. *The Selected Letters of John Ciardi*. Edited by E. M. Cifelli. Fayetteville, Ark.: University of Arkansas Press, 1991.

Cinel, Dino. *From Italy to San Francisco, the Immigrant Experience*. Palo Alto: Stanford University Press, 1982.

Ciuffoletti, Zeffiro. *L'Emigratione Nella Storia D'Italiani, 1868–1975*. Florence: Vallecchi, 1978.

Claghorn, Kate H. *The Immigrant's Day in Court*. New York: Harper, 1923.

Clark, Ramsey. *Crime in America*. New York: Simon & Schuster, 1970.

Clivio, Gianrenzo P. *The Development of the Italian Language and its Dialects in The Culture of Italy*. Toronto: Griffin House, 1979.

Cocchiara, Giuseppe. *Storia del Folklore in Italia*. Palermo: Sellerio Editorie, 1981.

Cohen, David S., ed. *America the Dream of My Life: Selections from the Federal Writers' Project's N.J. Ethnic Survey*. New Brunswick: Rutgers University Press, 1990.

Cohen, Mickey. *In My Own Words*. Englewood Cliffs, N.J.: Prentice Hall, 1975.

Cohen, Stanley. *A. Mitchell Palmer: Politician*. New York: Columbia University Press, 1963.

Colajanni, N. *I non Desiderabili*. Rome: 1909.

———. *La Criminalita Degli Italiani Negli. Stati Uniti*, 1909.

Colburn, D. R., and G. E. Pozzetta, eds. *America and the New Ethnicity*. Port Washington, N.Y.: Kennikat Press, 1979.

Cole, D. B. *Immigrant City*. Chapel Hill, N.C.: University of North Carolina Press, 1963.

Colombo, Furio M. "Immigrant Women in Industry." Ph.D. diss., New York University, 1979.

Commons, John R. *Races and Immigrants in America*. New York: Macmillan, 1920.

Connable, A., and E. Silberfarb. *Tigers of Tammany: Nine Men Who Ran New York*. New York: Holt, Rinehart and Winston, 1967.

Connell, Evan S. *Son of the Morning Star*. San Francisco: North Point Press, 1984.

Consolo, Vincenzo. *Le Sourire*. Paris: Bernard Grasset, 1980.

Cont, Gaetano. *Dieci Anni in America; Impressioni e Ricordi*. Palermo: G. Spinnato, 1903.

Cordasco, Francesco. *The Italian American Experience*. New York: Arno Press, 1975.

———. *Italian Mass Emigration: A Bibliographical Guide to the Bolletino Dell Emigrazione, 1902–1927*. Totowa, N.J.: Rowman & Littlefield, 1980.

———. *The Italians: Social Backgrounds of an American Group*. Clifton, N.J.: A. M. Kelly, 1974.

———. *Italians in the City: Health and Related Social Needs*. New York: Arno Press, 1975.

———. *Italians in the U.S.—A Repository of Rare Tracts and Miscellanea*. New York: Arno Press, 1975.

———. *Protestant Evangelism Among Italians in America*. New York: Arno Press, 1975.

———. *La Societa Italiana di Fronte alle Prime Migrazioni di Massa*. New York: Arno Press, 1975.

Cordasco, Francesco, and E. Bucchioni. *Immigrant Children In American Schools*. New York: Arno Press, 1976.

Cornelisen, Ann. *Torregreca*. Boston: Little Brown, 1969.

———. *Women in the Shadows*. Boston: Little Brown, 1976.

Correnti, S. *Leggende di Sicilia*. Milan: Longaneri, 1975.

Corsi, Edward. *In the Shadow of Liberty*. New York: Arno Press, 1969.

Coulter, Charles W. *The Italians in Cleveland*. Cleveland, Oh.: Cleveland Americanization Committee, 1919.

Covello, Leonard, with Guido D'Agostino. *The Heart Is the Teacher*. New York: McGraw-Hill, 1958.

Crawford, Francis M. *The Rulers of the South*. London: Macmillan, 1900.

Cresci, Paolo, and Giuseppe Guidobaldi, eds. *Partono i Bastamenti*. Milan: Arnoldo Mondadori Editore, 1980.

Cressey, Donald. *Theft of the Nation*. New York: Harper & Row, 1969.

Crispano, James A. *The Assimilation of Ethnic Groups: The Italian Case*. Staten Island, N.Y.: Center for Migration Studies, 1980.

Croce, Benedetto. *A History of Italy, 1871–1915*. Oxford: Clarendon Press, 1929.

———. *History of the Kingdom of Naples*. Chicago: University of Chicago Press, 1970.

———. *History as the Story of Liberty*. Translated by Sylvia Sprigge. New York: W. W. Norton, 1941.

Cronin, Constance. *The Sting of Change*. Chicago: University of Chicago Press, 1970.

Cuomo, Mario. *Diaries of Mario M. Cuomo*. New York: Random House, 1984.

Curran, Thomas J. *Xenophobia and Immigration, 1820–1930*. Boston: Twayne Publishers, 1975.

D'Amico, Joseph T. *Italian Farmers of Canastota*. Ph.D. diss., Syracuse University, 1939.

Da Bisticci, Vespasiano. *Renaissance Princes, Popes & Prelates*. New York: Harper & Row, 1963.

Dana, Julian. *A. P. Giannini, Giant in the West*. New York: Prentice-Hall, 1947.

D'Angelo, Pascal. *Son of Italy*. New York: John Day Co., 1924.

Daniel, Pete. *The Shadow of Slavery: Peonage in the South 1901–1969*. Chicago: University of Illinois Press, 1972.

Daniels, John. *America via the Neighborhood*. Reprint. Patterson Smith, 1971.

Da Ponte, Lorenzo. *Memoirs of Lorenzo Da Ponte*. Translated by Elizabeth Abbott. Philadelphia: J. B. Lippincott, 1929.

Daughen, Joseph R., and Peter Binzen. *The Cop Who Would Be King: The Honorable Frank Rizzo*. Boston: Little Brown, 1977.

Davis, A. F. *Spearheads for Reform: 1890–1914*. New York: Oxford University Press, 1957.

Davis, J. *Land and Family in Pisticci*. London: Athlone Press, 1973.

Davis, Michael Jr. *Immigrant Health and the Community*. New York: Harper, 1921.

DeBosis, Laura. *The Story of My Death*. New York: Oxford University Press, 1933.

DeConde, Alexander. *Half Bitter, Half Sweet*. New York: Charles Scribner's Sons, 1971.

DeDonato, D., ed. *I Fasci Siciliani*. Bari: DeDonato, 1976.

Deforest, Robert W., ed. *The Tenement House Problem*. 2 vols. New York: Macmillan, 1903.

De Grazia, Victoria. *The Culture of Consent*. Cambridge: Cambridge University Press, 1981.

Del Carria, Renza. *Proletari Senza Revoluzione: Storia delle Classe Subalterne dal 1860 al 1950*. 2 vols. Milan: Edizione Oriente, 1970.

Della Chiesa, Nando. *Delitto Imperfetto*. Milan: Mondadori, 1984.

Della Femina, Jerry, and Charles Sopkin. *An Italian Grows in Brooklyn*. Boston: Little Brown, 1978.

DeLeon, Solon, ed. *The American Labor Who's Who*. New York: Hanford Press, 1925.

DeMarco, William M. *Ethnics and Enclaves, Boston's Italian North End*. Ann Arbor: University of Michigan Press, 1980.

DeMaris, Ovid. *Judith Exner: My Story*. New York: Grove Press, 1977.

————. *The Last Mafioso*. New York: Bantam Books, 1981.

DeMichele, Michael D. *The Italian Experience in America: A Pictorial History*. Scranton, Penn.: Ethnic Studies Program, University of Scranton, 1982.

DeRoberto, Frederico. *The Viceroys*. New York: Harcourt, Brace and World, 1959.

DeRosa, Tina. *Bishop John Baptist Scalbrini, Father to the Immigrants*. Oak Park, Ill.: Father of St. Charles-Scalabrinians, 1987.

D'Este, Carlo. *Bitter Victory: The Battles for Sicily, 1943*. New York: Dutton, 1988.

DeStafano, Francesco. *Storia Della Sicilia Dall' XI Al XIX Secolo*. Rome: Laterza, 1977.

Devereaux, G. *From Anxiety to Method*. Paris: Moutou, 1967.

Devos, George, and Lola Romanucci-Ross. *Ethnic Identity, Cultural Continuities and Change*. Palo Alto, California: Wenner-Gren Foundation for Anthropological Research, 1975.

Di Bartolomeo, Albert. *The Vespers Tapes*. New York: Walker & Co., 1991.

Dickenson, Joan Younger. *The Role of the Immigrant Women in the U.S. Labor Force, 1890–1910*. New York: Arno Press, 1980.

Dickerson, Robert E. *The Population Problem of Southern Italy: An Essay in Social Geography*. Syracuse, N.Y.: Syracuse University Press, 1955.

Di Dommenica, Angelo. *Protestant Witness of a New American: Mission of a Lifetime*. Philadelphia: Judson Press, 1956.

Diggins, John. *Mussolini and Fascism*. Princeton, N.J.: Princeton University Press, 1972.

Dinnerstein, Leonard, and David M. Reimers. *Ethnic Americans: A History of Immigration and Assimilation*. New York: Dodd, Mead, 1975.

Dipietro, Robert J., and I. Ifkovic, eds. *Ethnic Perspectives in American Literature*. New York: Modern Language Association of America, 1983.

Di Prima, Diane. *Revolutionary Letters*. San Francisco: City Lights Books, 1971.

Di Scala, Spencer. *Dilemmas of Italian Socialism. The Politics of Filippo Turati*. Amherst, Mass.: University of Massachusetts Press, 1980.

Di Stasi, Lawrence. *Dream Streets: The Big Book of Italian American Culture*. New York: Harper & Row, 1989.

————. *Mal Occhio*. San Francisco: North Point Press, 1981.

Divine, Robert A. *American Immigration Policy, 1924–1952*. New Haven: Yale University Press, 1957.

Dolci, Danilo. *Banditi a Partinico*. Bari: Laterza, 1956.

————. *Il Dio della Zecche*. Milan: Mondadori, 1976.

————. *Enquete à Palerme (traduit de l'Italien par Maria Brandon Albini)*. Paris: Réné-Julliard, 1967.

————. *Outlaws*. New York: Orion Press, 1961.

————. *Sicilian Lives*. New York: Pantheon, 1981.

————. *Spreco*. Torino: Ginandi, 1960.

————. *To Feed the Hungry*. London: McGibbon & Kee, 1959.

Donofrio, Beverly. *Riding in Cars with Boys*. New York: William Morrow, 1990.

Dore, Grazia. *La Democrazia Italiana e L'Emigrazione in America*. Morcelliano, 1964.

Douglas, Norman. *Old Calabria*. London: Martin Secker, 1923.

Dubinsky, David and A.H. Raskin. *David Dubinsky: A Life with Labor*. New York: Simon and Schuster, 1977.

Dubofsky, Melvyn. *"Big Bill" Haywood*. New York: St. Martin's Press, 1987.

————. *Industrialism and the American Worker, 1865–1920*. Arlington Heights, Ill.: AHM, 1975.

————. *We Shall Be All: A History of the I.W.W.* Chicago: Quadrangle Books, 1969.

————. *When Workers Organize: New York City in the Progressive Era*. Amherst, Mass.: University of Massachusetts Press, 1968.

Duggan, Christopher. *Fascism and the Mafia*. New Haven: Yale University Press, 1989.

Dumas, Alexander. *On Board the Emma: Adventures with Garibaldi's "Thousand" in Italy*. New York: D. Appleton, 1929.

Dundes, Alan, ed. *The Evil Eye: A Folklore Casebook*. New York: Garland, 1981.

Ehrlich, Richard L., ed. *Immigrants in Industrial America—1850–1920*. Richmond, Va.: University Press of Virginia, 1977.

Ehrmann, H.B. *The Untried Case*. New York: The Vanguard Press, 1960.

Eisenberg, Dennis, Uri Dan, and Eli Landau. *Meyer Lansky*. New York: Paddington Press, 1979.

Elliott, Jean Leonard, ed. *Immigrant Groups*. Scarborough: Prentice-Hall of Canada, 1971.

Erickson, Charlotte. *American Industry and the European Immigrant, 1860–1885*. Cambridge, Mass.: Harvard University Press, 1957.

Ets, Marie Hall. *Rosa: The Life of an Italian Immigrant*. St. Paul, Minn.: University of Minnesota Press, 1970.

Evans, Jean. *Three Men: An Experience in the Biography of Emotion*. New York: Alfred Knopf, 1954.

Fairchild, Henry Pratt. *Immigration: A World Movement and Its American Struggle*. New York: Macmillan, 1917.

Fante, John. *Selected Letters 1932–1981*. Edited by Seamus Cooney. Santa Rosa, Calif.: Black Sparrow Press, 1991.

Fava, Giuseppe. *Gente di Rispetto*. Milan: Bompiani, 1975.

Feldstein, Stanley, and Laurence Costello, eds. *The Ordeal of Assimilation*. Garden City: Anchor Books, 1974.

Felt, Jeremy P. *Hostages of Fortune: Child Labor Reform in New York State*. Syracuse, N.Y.: Syracuse University Press, 1965.

Femminella, Francis, ed. *AIHA Proceedings, Power and Class*. New York, 1971.

Fenton, Edwin. *Immigrants and Unions, A Case Study: Italians and American Labor, 1870–1920*. New York: Arno Press, 1975.

Ferber, Nat. *A New American: From the Life Story of Salvatore A. Cotillo, Supreme Court Justice, State of New York*. New York: Farrar and Rinehart, 1938.

Fermi, Laura. *Atoms in the Family: My Life with Enrico Fermi*. Chicago: University of Chicago Press, 1954.

————. *Illustrious Immigrants: The Intellectual Migration from Europe 1930–1941*. Chicago: University of Chicago Press, 1971.

Fernandez, Dominique. *Mer Méditerranée*. Paris: Editions Bernard Grasset, 1965.

Fernando Armesto, Felipe. *Columbus and the Conquest of the Impossible*. New York: Saturday Review Press, 1974.

Ferrari, Robert. *Days Pleasant and Unpleasant in the Order of the Sons of Italy in America*. Clifton, N.J.: Augustus M. Kelly, 1974.

Ferri, Enrico. *Criminal Sociology*. New York: D. Appleton, 1900.

Ferroni, Charles. *The Italians in Chicago: A Study in Assimilation*. New York: Arno Press, 1980.

Fiaschetti, Michael. *You Gotta Be Rough.* Garden City, N.Y.: Darin, 1930.

Filipuzzi, Angelo. *Il Dibattito Sul Emigrazione.* Florence: Felice LeMonier, 1976.

Fine, Sidney, ed. *Recent America.* New York: MacMillan, 1962.

Fink, Gary, ed. *Biographical Dictionary of American Labor Leaders.* Norwalk Conn.: Greenwood Press, 1974.

Finley, M. I. *Ancient Sicily: To the Arab Conquest.* New York: Viking Press, 1968.

Finley, M.I., Dennis Mack Smith, and Christopher Duggan. *History of Sicily.* New York: Viking Press, 1986.

Fiori, Giuseppe. *Antonio Gramsci: Life of a Revolutionary.* New York: E. P. Dutton, 1971.

Fischer, Claude. *The Urban Experience.* New York: Harcourt, Brace, Jovanovich, 1976.

Fisk, Henry A. "The Fishermen of San Francisco Bay." In *Proceedings of the National Conference of Charities and Connection of the Thirty-Second Annual Session held in the City of Portland, Oregon, July 15–21, 1905,* edited by Alexander Johnson. San Francisco: 1905.

Fleischman, Harry. *Norman Thomas, a Biography.* New York: W. W. Norton, 1969.

Flynn, Elizabeth Gurley. *The Rebel Girl.* New York: International Publishers, 1955.

Foerster, Robert E. *The Italian Emigration of Our Times.* Cambridge: Harvard University Press, 1919.

Foner, Philip S. *The A.F.L. in the Progressive Era 1910–1915.* New York: International Publishers, 1980.

———. *History of the Labor Movement in the United States.* Vol. 2. New York: International Publishers, 1955.

———. *History of the Labor Movement in the United States,* Vol. 4, *Italian Militants.* New York: International Publishers, 1973.

Fraenkel, O.K. *The Sacco-Vanzetti Case.* New York: Alfred A. Knopf, 1931.

Fraley, Oscar. *The Last of the Untouchables.* New York: Popular Library, 1962.

Franchette, Leopold, and Sidney Sonnino. *Inchiesta in Sicilia.* Florence: Vallecchi, 1974.

Frankfurter, Marion D., and Gardner Jackson, eds. *The Letters of Sacco and Vanzetti.* New York: E. P. Dutton, 1960.

Fraser, James George. *The Golden Bough: A Study in Magic and Religion.* New York: Macmillan, 1948.

Freeman, E. A. *Historical Essays.* London: Macmillan, 1892.

———. *History of Sicily.* 3 vols. London: Oxford University Press, 1891.

———. *The Story of Sicily.* New York: G. P. Putnam's Sons, 1892.

Fried, Marc. *The World of the Urban Working Press.* Cambridge, Mass.: Harvard University Press, 1973.

Frischauer, Paul. *Garibaldi: The Man and The Nation.* London: Ivor Nicholson and Watson, 1935.

Fromm, Erich. *The Anatomy of Human Destructiveness.* New York: Holt, Rinehart and Winston, 1973.

Fronsini, Vittorio, Francesco Renda, and Leonardo Sciascia. *La Mafia.* Bologna: Massamiliano Boni, 1970.

Gabaccia, Donna. *From Sicily to Elizabeth Street.* Albany: State University of New York Press, 1984.

Gabree, John. *Gangsters from Little Caesar to the Godfather.* New York: Galahad Books, 1973.

Gabriel, Richard A. *Ethnic Attitudes and Political Behavior in City and Suburbs: The Irish and Italians of Rhode Island.* New York: Arno Press, 1980.

———. *The Ethnic Factor in The Urban Polity.* New York: MSS Information Corporation, 1973.

Gage, Nicholas. *The Mafia Is Not an Equal Opportunity Employer.* New York: McGraw-Hill, 1971.

Gaja, Filippo. *L'esercito della Lupara.* Milan: Arca, 1962.

Gallagher, Dorothy. *All the Right Enemies: The Life and Murder of Carlo Tresca.* New Brunswick, N.J.: Rutgers University Press, 1988.

Gallo, Fortune T. *Lucky Rooster.* New York: Exposition Press, 1964.

Gallo, Max. *La Mafia.* Paris: Seghers, 1971.

Gallo, Patrick. *Ethnic Alienation: The Italian-Americans.* New Jersey: Cranbury, N.J.: Fairleigh Dickinson University Press, 1974.

———. *Old Bread, New Wine: A Portrait of the Italian Americans.* Chicago: Nelson, Hall, 1981.

———. *The Urban Experience of Italian Americans.* Staten Island, N.Y.: American Italian Historical Association, 1975.

Galluzzo, Lucio Tommaso Buscetta. *L'uomo Che Tradi'se Stesso.* Aosta: Musumeci Editore, 1984.

Gambino, R. *Blood of My Blood.* New York: Anchor Books, 1975.

Gans, Herbert. *The Urban Villagers: Group and Class in the Life of Italian-Americans.* New York: The Free Press, 1982.

Gardaphe, Fred, ed. *Italian-American Ways: Recipes and Traditions.* New York: Harper & Row, 1989.

Garibaldi, Clelia. *Mio Padre.* Rome: Vallechi Editore, 1948.

Garibaldi, Giuseppe. *Life of Garibaldi.* London: Ernest Benn Limited, 1931.

———. *The Memoirs of Garibaldi.* Edited by Alexandre Dumas, George Sand, and Victor Hugo. London: Ernest Benn Limited, 1931.

Garrett, Charles. *The La Guardia Years.* New Brunswick, N.J.: Rutgers University Press, 1961.

Gatti-Casazza, Giulio. *Memoires of Opera.* New York: Charles Scribner, 1941.

Gelli, Iacopo. *Banditi, Briganti, Brigantesse Nell '800.* Florence: Bemprad, 1931.

Gerson, Simon W. *Pete, The Story of Peter V. Cacchione, New York's First Communist Councilman.* New York: International Publishers, 1976.

Giacosa, Giuseppe. *Novelle e Paesi Valdostani.* Milan: Attilio Barion, 1923.

Giamatti, A. Bartlett. *Take Time for Paradise.* New York: Summit Books, 1989.

Giancana, Antoinette, and T. C. Renner. *Mafia Princess.* New York: Avon Books, 1985.

Ginger, Ray. *The Bending Cross, a Biography of Eugene V. Debs.* New Brunswick, N.J.: Rutgers University Press, 1949.

Ginzberg, Eli, and H. Berman. *The American Worker in the Twentieth Century.* New York: The Free Press of Glencoe, 1963.

Giordano, Joseph, ed. *The Italian-American Catalog.* Garden City, N.Y.: Doubleday, 1986.

Gioseffi, Daniela. *On Prejudice,* New York: Anchor Doubleday, 1993.

Giudice, Gaspare. *Pirandello, A Biography.* New York: Oxford University Press, 1975.

Glanz, Rudolfl. *Jew and Italian.* New York: Shulsinger Brothers, 1970.

Glatzer, Richard, and John Raeburn, eds. *Frank Capra, the Man and His Films.* Ann Arbor, Mich.: University of Michigan Press, 1975.

Glazer, Nathan, and Daniel Moynihan. *Beyond the Melting Pot*. Cambridge: MIT Press, 1964.

———. *Ethnicity*. Cambridge: Harvard University Press, 1975.

Gleason, Philip, ed. *Contemporary Catholicism in the U.S.* Notre Dame, Ind.: University of Notre Dame Press, 1969.

Glueck, Eleanor T. *The Community Use of Schools*. Baltimore, Md.: Williams and Wilkins, 1927.

Goethe, Johann Wolfgang von. *The Autobiography of Goethe: Truth and Poetry: From My Own Life. The Concluding Books. Also Letters from Switzerland and Travels in Italy*. Translated by the Rev. A.J.W. Morrison. London: George Bell & Sons, 1874.

Goldstein, Sidney. *The Norristown Study*. Philadelphia: University of Pennsylvania Press, 1961.

Gordon, Milton. *Assimilation in American Life*. New York: Oxford University Press, 1964.

Gosch, Martin, and Richard Hammer. *The Last Testament of Lucky Luciano*. Boston: Little Brown, 1974.

Gossett, Thomas F. *Race: The History of an Idea in America*. New York: Schocken Books, 1963.

Granzotto, Gianni. *Christopher Columbus: The Dream and the Obsession*. Translated by Stephen Sartarelli. Garden City, N.Y.: Doubleday, 1985.

Gray, J. Glenn. *The Warriors: Reflections on Men in Battle*. New York: Harper Torch Books, 1967.

Greeley, Andrew M. *Ethnicity in the U.S.* New York: John Wiley and Sons, 1974.

———. *An Ugly Little Secret*. New York: Sheed Andres and McMeel, 1977.

Green, Colin, ed. *Divided Society*. New York: Basic Books, 1974.

Green, Rose Basile. *The Italian-American Novel*. Rutherford, N.J.: Fairleigh Dickinson University Press, 1974.

Green, Victor R. *The Slavic Community on Strike: Immigrant Labor in the Pa. Anthracite*. Notre Dame, Ind.: University of Notre Dame Press, 1968.

Guenther, Anthony L., ed. *Criminal Behavior and Social Systems: Contributions of American Sociology*. Chicago: Rand McNally, 1971.

Gumina, D. P. *The Italians in San Francisco, 1850–1930*. New York: Center for Migration Studies, 1978.

Gutman, Herbert G. *Work, Culture and Society in Industrializing America*. New York: Vintage Books, 1977.

Guttuso, R. *Catalogo della Monstra antologica dell'opera di Renato Guttoso, Palazzo del Normanni* [A catalog of the works of Renato Guttoso], Febbraio 14 Marzo 1971, Testi di Leonardo Sciascia, Franco Russoli, Franco Grasso. Palermo: Assemblea Regionale Siciliana.

Guttuso, Renato. *Mestiere di Pittore*. Bari: De Donato, 1972.

Halberstam, David. *Summer of '49*. New York: William Morrow, 1989.

Hammer, Richard. *Playboy's Illustrated History of Organized Crime*. Chicago, Ill.: Playboy Press, 1973, 1974.

Handlin, Oscar. *Immigration as a Factor in American History*. Englewood, N.J.: Prentice-Hall, 1959.

———. *A Pictorial History of Immigration*. New York: Crown, 1972.

———. *The Uprooted*. Boston: Little Brown, 1951.

———. *The Uprooted* (second edition, enlarged).

Hansen, P. *The Immigrant in American History.* Cambridge, Mass.: Harvard University Press, 1942.

Hare, Augustus. *Cities of Southern Italy and Sicily.* New York: Routledge & Sons, 1947.

Harney, R., and V. Scarpaci, eds. *Little Italies in North America.* MHSO.

Harris, H. S. *The Social Philosophy of Giovanni Gentile.* Urbana: University of Illinois Press, 1966.

Hartmann, E. G. *The Movement to Americanize the Immigrant.* New York: Columbia University Press, 1948.

Harvard Encyclopedia of American Ethnic Groups. Cambridge, Mass.: Harvard University Press, 1980.

Haslam, Gerald W. *Forgotten Pages in American Literature.* Boston: Houghton Mifflin, 1970.

Haywood, William D. *The Autobiography of William D. Haywood.* New York: International Publishers, 1929.

Heaps, Willard A. *The Story of Ellis Island.* New York: The Seabury Press, 1967.

Heckscher, J., and P. Robinson. *When La Guardia was Mayor.* New York: W. W. Norton, 1978.

Hershkowitz, Leo. *Tweed's New York.* Garden City, N.Y.: Anchor Books, 1978.

Hibbert, Christopher. *Garibaldi and His Enemies.* Longmans, N.Y.: Green, 1965.

Higgins, Jack. *Luciano.* London: Collins, 1981.

Higham, J. *Strangers in the Land.* New Brunswick, N.J.: Rutgers University Press, 1959.

Hilton, David. *Brigandage in South Italy.* Vol. 2. London: Samson Low, Son and Marston, 1864.

Hitti, Philip. *History of the Arabs.* London: Macmillan, 1956.

Hobsbawm, E. J. *Primitive Rebels.* New York: W. W. Norton, 1959.

Hoffa, James. *Hoffa, The Real Story.* New York: Stein and Day, 1975.

Hollon, W. E. *Frontier Violence.* New York: Oxford University Press, 1974.

Holt, Hamilton, ed. *The Life Stories of Undistinguished Americans as Told by Themselves.* New York: James Pott, 1906.

Horowitz, Irving, ed. *The Anarchists.* New York: Dell, 1964.

Hosay, Philip M. *The Challenge of Urban Poverty: Charity Reformers in N.Y.C., 1835–1890.* New York: Arno Press, 1890.

Hostetter, Richard. *The Italian Socialist Movement I: Origins (1860–1882).* New York: Van Nostrand, 1958.

Hourwich, Issac A. *Immigration and Labor: The Economic Aspects of European Immigration to the United States.* New York: B. W. Huebach, Inc., 1912.

Howells, W. D. *Venetian Life.* New York: Hurd & Houghton, 1866.

Hughes, Stuart. *The United States and Italy.* Cambridge, Mass.: Harvard University Press, 1979.

Hutchinson, E. P. *Immigrants and their Children: 1850–.* New York: Wiley, 1952.

Hymes, Dell, ed. *Reinventing Anthropology.* New York: Pantheon Books, 1972.

Ianni, F.A. *Black Mafia: Ethnic Succession in Organized Crime.* New York: 1974.

Ianni, Francis, with Elizabeth Reuss-Ianni. *A Family Business: Kinship and Social Control in Organized Crime.* New York: Russell Sage Foundation, 1972.

Ianni, Francis, and Elizabeth Reuss-Ianni, eds. *The Crime Society.* New York: New American Library, 1976.

International Migration Review (journal). Staten Island, N.Y.: Center for Migration

Studies. Vol. 4, Fall 1969, #10 (Immigration in Canada); Vol. 8, Spring 1974, #25; Vol. 8, Summer 1974, #26 (Policy and Research on Migration Canada & World Perspectives).

Iorizzo, Luciano, ed. *An Inquiry Into Organized Crime.* Staten Island, N.Y.: The Italian American Historical Association, 1970.

————. *Italian Immigration and the Impact of the Padrone System.* New York: Arno Press, 1980.

Iorizzo, Luciano, and Salvatore Mondello. *The Italian Americans.* New York: Twayne Publishers, 1971.

Italian Americana (journal). Vol. 1, No. 1, Autumn 1974; Vol. 1, No. 2, Spring 1975; Vol. 2, No. 1, Autumn 1975; Vol. 2, No. 2, Spring 1976; Vol. 3, No. 2, Spring–Summer 1977; Vol. 4, No. 1, Fall–Winter 1978.

Jackson, Brian. *The Black Flag—The Strange Case of Nicola Sacco and Bartolomeo Vanzetti.* Boston: Routledge and Kegan, 1981.

Jackson, Giovanna. *Leonardo Sciascia: 1956–1976.* Ravenna: Longo Editore, 1981.

Jackson, Joy J. *New Orleans in the Gilded Age: Politics and Urban Progress, 1880–1896.* Baton Rouge, La: Louisiana State University Press, 1969.

Jaffe, Irma. *Joseph Stella.* Cambridge, Mass.: Harvard University Press, 1970.

Jaffe, Julien. *Crusade Against Radicalism: New York During the Red Scare, 1914–1924.* Port Washington, N.Y.: Kennikat Press, 1972.

Jay, Michael C., and A.C. Watts, eds. *Literature and the Urban Experience.* New Brunswick, N.J.: Rutgers University Press, 1981.

Jensen, Vernon H. *Heritage of Conflict: Labor Relations in the Nonferrous Metals Industry up to 1930.* New York: Greenwood Press, 1968.

Johnson, Ben, ed. *Stories of Modern Italy from Verga, Svevo and Pirandello to the Present.* New York: Random House (Modern Library edition), 1960.

Johnson, Robert K. *Francis Ford Coppola.* Boston: Twayne Publishers, 1977.

Jones, P., and M.G. Holli, eds. *Ethnic Chicago.* Grand Rapids, Mich.: William B. Eerdmans, 1981.

Jones, Thomas Jesse. *The Sociology of a New York City Block.* New York: Columbia University Press, 1904.

Juliani, Richard, ed. *The Family and Community Life of Italian Americans.* Staten Island, N.Y.: The Italian American Historical Association, 1983.

Kalish, Richard A., and D. K. Reynolds. *Death and Ethnicity: Psychocultural Study.* Los Angeles: University of Southern California Press, 1976.

Kaplan, Justin. *Lincoln Steffens, a Biography.* New York: Simon & Schuster, 1974.

Karp, Abraham J. *Golden Door to America.* Penguin Books, 1977.

Katz, Leonard. *Uncle Frank.* New York: Drake Publishers, 1973.

Kefauver, Estes. *Crime in America.* New York: Doubleday, 1951.

Kelly, Kitty. *His Way.* New York: Bantam Books, 1986.

Kessner, Thomas. *The Golden Door: Italian and Jewish Immigrant Mobility in New York City 1880–1915.* New York: Oxford University Press, 1917.

Kiersh, Edward. *Where Have You Gone Vince DiMaggio.* New York: Bantam Books, 1983.

King, Bolton. *Italy Today.* James Nisbet Ltd., 1904.

Klein, J. "Ethnotherapy with Jews." *International Journal of Mental Health,* Fall 1976, 79–85.

Kobler, John. *Ardent Spirits.* New York: G. P. Putnam's Sons, 1973.

————. *Capone.* Greenwich, Conn.: Fawcett, 1971.

Kornbluh, Joyce L., ed. *Rebel Voices: An I.W.W. Anthology*. Ann Arbor: University of Michigan Press, 1964.

Krase, Jerome, and R. Egelman. *The Melting Pot and Beyond: Italian Americans in the Year 2000*.

Kraut, Alan. *The Huddled Masses*. Arlington Heights, Ill.: Harlan Davidson, 1982.

Krickus, Richard. *Pursuing the American Dream: White Ethnics and the New Populism*. Bloomington: Indiana University Press, 1976.

Kubly, Herbert. *Easter in Sicily*. New York: Simon & Schuster, 1956.

LaGuardia, Fiorello. *The Making of an Insurgent*. Philadelphia: Lippincott, 1948.

La Gumina, Salvatore John. *From Steerage to Suburb: Long Island Italians*. New York: Center for Migration Studies, 1988.

———. *The Immigrants Speak: Italian Americans Tell Their Story*. New York: Center for Immigration Studies, 1979.

———. *Vito Marcantonio, The People's Politician*. Dubuque, Ia.: Kendall Hunt Publication Co., 1969.

———. *Wop. A Documentary History of Anti Italian Discrimination in the U.S.* San Francisco: Straight Arrow Books, 1973.

LaMar, E. *Philadelphia Clothing Workers*. New York: Amalgamated Clothing Workers of America, 1940.

Landesco, John. *Organized Crime in Chicago* (Part III of the Illinois Crime Survey). Chicago: University of Chicago Press, 1929.

Landis, Paul Henry. *Three Iron Mining Towns*. New York: Arno Press, 1970.

Lang, Peter. *Studies on Italy 1943–1975: Select Bibliography of American and British Materials in Political Science, Economics, Sociology and Anthropology*. Torino: Fondazione Giovanni Agnelli, 1977.

La Sorsa, Saverio. *Usi costumi e Feste Del Popolo Pugliese*. Bari: F. Casini and Figlio, 1925.

La Sorte, Michael. *La Merica*. Philadelphia: Temple University Press, 1985.

Leiter, Robert C. *The Musicians and Petrillo*. New York: Bookman Associates, 1953.

Leonard, Henry B. *The Open Gates: The Protest Against the Movement to Restrict European Immigration, 1896–1924*. New York: Arno Press, 1980.

Leprohon, Pierre. *The Italian Cinema*. London: Secker & Warburg, 1966.

Levi, Carlo. *Christ Stopped at Eboli*. New York: Farrar, Strauss & Co., 1947.

———. *Words Are Stones*. London: Victor Gollancz, 1959.

Levine, Louis. *The Women's Garment Workers*. New York: B. W. Huebasch, 1924.

Levy, M., and M. Kramer. *The Ethnic Factor: How America's Minorities Decide Elections*. New York: Simon & Schuster, 1973.

Lewis, Alfred Henry. *The Apaches of New York*. London: Dillingham, 1912.

Lewis, Norman. *The Honored Society*. New York: Putnam's, 1964.

———. *Naples '44*. New York: Pantheon Books, 1978.

———. *The Sicilian Specialist*. London: Collins, 1975.

Linkh, Richard M. *American Catholicism and European Immigrants (1900–1924)*. New York: Center for Migration Studies, 1975.

Lopreato, Joseph. *Italian Americans*. New York: B. F. Buck, 1905.

———. *Peasants No More*. California: Chandler Press, 1967.

Lord, Eliot. *The Italian in America*. New York: B. F. Buck, 1905.

Loschiano, Giuseppe. *100 Anni di Mafia*. Rome: Vito Bianco, 1962.

Lowe, Alfonso. *The Barrier and the Bridge*. New York: W. W. Norton, 1972.

Lubell, S. *The Future of American Politics*. New York: Harper & Row, 1965.

Lucino, Marcello. *Verita sulla Nascita del Fascismo*. Bologna: Edizione Calderini, 1973.

Lussana, Filippo. *Lettere di Illetterati*. Rome: 1913.

Lynd, Alice, and L. Staughton, eds. *Rank and File—Personal Histories by Working Class Organizers*. Boston: Beacon Press, 1973.

Maas, Peter. *The Valachi Papers*. New York: Bantam, 1968.

MacLean, Don. *Pictorial History of the Mafia*. New York: Galahad Books, 1974.

Mafai, S. Essere. *Donna in Sicilia*. Rome: Editori Riuniti, 1976.

Maffesoli, Michal. *L'Ombre de Dionyson*. Paris: Meridiens, 1982.

Maisel, Albert Q. *They All Chose America*. New York: Thomas Nelson, 1957.

Mangano, Antonio. *Sons of Italy: A Social and Religious Study of Italian Americans*. New York: Russell and Russell, 1917.

Mangione, Jerre. *America is Also Italian*. New York: Putnam's, 1965.

———. *The Dream and the Deal: The Federal Writers' Project 1935–1943*. Boston: Little Brown, 1972.

———. *An Ethnic at Large*. New York: G.P. Putnam's Sons, 1978.

———. *Mount Allegro*. Boston: Houghton Mifflin, 1943.

———. *Mussolini's March on Rome*. New York: Franklin Watts, 1975.

———. *A Passion for Sicilians*. New York: William Morrow & Co., 1968.

———. *Reunion in Sicily*. New York: Columbia University Press, 1984.

———. *The World Around Danilo Dolci*. New York: Harper & Row, 1968.

Mann, Arthur. *La Guardia, A Fighter Against his Times*. Philadelphia: Lippincott, 1959.

Marcantonio, Vito. *I Vote My Conscience*. New York: The Vito Marcantonio Memorial, 1956.

Marchione, Margherita, ed. *Philip Mazzei: Jefferson's "Zealous Whig."* New York: American Institute of Italian Studies, 1975.

Marden, Charles F. *Minorities in American Society*. New York: American Book, 1952.

Margariti, Antonio. *America! America!* Milan: Galzerano Editore, 1979.

Mariano, John H. *The Italian Contribution to American Democracy*. New York: Arno Press, 1975.

———. *The Italian Immigrant and Our Courts*. Boston: 1925.

———. *The Second Generation of Italians in New York*. Boston: Christopher Publishing House, 1921.

Marino, Giuseppe. *L'opposizione Mafiosa*. Palermo: Flaccovio, 1964.

Marino, S.S. *Costumi e usanze dei Contadini di Sicilia*. Palermo: Audo, 1968.

Martellone, Anna Maria, ed. *La "questione" dell'immigrazione negli Stati Uniti*. Bologna: Il Mulino, 1980.

Masini, P. C. *Storia degli Anarchici Italiani da Bakunin a Malatesta Pizzoli*. Milan: Bompiani, 1969.

Massara, Giuseppe. *Viaggiatori Italiani in America 1860–1970*. Rome: Edizioni di Storia e Letteratura, 1976.

Masson, Georgina. *Frederick II of Hohenstaufen—A Life*. London: Secker & Warburg, 1957.

Mathias, Elizabeth, and R. Raspa. *Italian Folktales in America*. Detroit: Wayne State University Press, 1985.

Matulich, Loretta. *A Cross Disciplinary Study of the European Immigrants, 1870–1925*. New York: Arno Press, 1980.

Maxwell, Gavin. *The Ten Pains of Death*. London: Longmans, Green & Co., 1959.

Mazzei, Philip. *My Life and Wanderings.* Translated by S. Eugene Scalia, edited by Margerite Marchione. Morristown, N.J.: American Institute of Italian Studies, 1980.

McGoldrick, Pearce, and J. Giordano. *Ethnicity and Family Therapy.* New York: Guilford Press, 1982.

McGovern, R., and P. Guttridge. *The Great Coalfield War.* Boston: Houghton Mifflin, 1972.

McKay, Keith. *Robert DeNiro, The Hero Behind the Masks.* New York: St. Martin's Press, 1986.

Mckelvey, Blake. *Rochester: An Emerging Metropolis, 1925–1961.* Rochester, N.Y.: Christopher Press, 1961.

———. *Rochester the Flower City. 1855–1890.* Cambridge, Mass.: Harvard University Press, 1949.

———. *Rochester, The Quest for Quality.* Cambridge, Mass.: Harvard University Press, 1956.

McPharlen, Paul. *The Puppet Theater in America.* Boston: Plays, Inc., 1969.

Mele, Frank. *Polpetto.* New York: Crown, 1973.

Mencken, H. L. *The American Language.* New York: Knopf, 1937.

Messana, E. N. *Racalmuto nella Storia della Sicilia.* Canicatti: 1969.

Miller, Randall M. *Ethnic Images in American Film and Television.* Philadelphia: Balch Institute, 1978.

Miller, J., and P. Marszik, eds. *Immigrants and Religion in Urban America.* Philadelphia: Temple University Press, 1977.

Mills, James. *The Underground Empire.* New York: Dell, 1986.

Mingarelli, G. *Gli Italiani di Montreal.* Montreal: Centro Italiano, 1980.

Moens, W. J. C. *English Travelers and Italian Brigands.* New York: Harper and Brothers, 1866.

Moldea, Dan. *Dark Victory—Ronald Reagan, MCA and the Mob.* New York: Viking Penguin, 1986.

———. *The Hoffa Wars.* New York: Charter Books, 1978.

Molfese, Franco. *Storia del Brigantaggio Dopa L'unita.* Milan: Feltrinelli, 1964.

Mondello, Salvatore. *The Italian Immigrant in Urban America, 1880–1920, As reported in the Contemporary Periodical Press.* New York: Arno Press, 1980.

Montana, Vanni B. *Amarostico Testimonianze Euro-Americane.* Livorno: University Bastogi, 1975.

Montgomery, Robert. *Sacco-Vanzetti—The Murder and the Myth.* Belmont: Western Island, 1960.

Moquin, Wayne, ed. *The American Way of Crime.* New York: Praeger, 1976.

———. *A Documentary History of the Italian Americans.* New York: Praeger, 1974.

Mormino, Gary Ross. "The Playing Fields of St. Louis: Italian Immigrants and Sports, 1925–1941." *Journal of Sports History,* 1949, 72–85.

Mormino, Gary Ross, and George Pozzetta. *Immigrants on the Hill: Italian Americans in St. Louis, 1882–1982.* Champaign, Ill.: University of Illinois Press, 1986.

———. *The Immigration World of Ybor City: Italians and their Latin Neighbors in Tampa, 1885–1985.* Champaign, Ill.: University of Illinois Press, 1986.

Morreale, Ben. *Down and Out in Academia.* New York: Pitman, 1972.

Morris, Richard, ed. *Labor and Management.* New York: Arno Press, 1973.

Morrison, Samuel. *Admiral of the Ocean Sea*. Boston: Little Brown, 1942.

Moscow, Warren. *The Last of the Big-Time Bosses: The Life and Times of Carmine DeSapio*. New York: Stein and Day, 1971.

Moses, Robert. *La Guardia, A Salute and a Memoir*. New York: Simon & Schuster, 1967.

Muraskin, W. "The Moral Basis of a Backward Sociologist." *American Journal of Sociology* 74, no. 6 (May 1974).

Murphy, Edmond. *Henry De Tonty: Fur Trader of the Mississippi*. Baltimore: John Hopkins University Press, 1941.

Murray, Robert K. *Red Scare: A Study of National Hysteria, 1919–1920*. New York: McGraw-Hill, 1955.

Musmanno, Michael A. *The Story of the Italians in America*. Garden City, N.Y.: Doubleday and Co., 1965.

Mustain, G., and J. Capeci. *Mob Star. The Story of John Gotti*. New York: Dell, 1989.

Nam, Charles B. *Nationality Groups and Social Stratification*. New York: Arno Press, 1980.

Namias, June. *First Generation*. Boston: Beacon Press, 1978.

Nash, Jay Robert. *Bloodletters and Badmen*. New York: Evan & Co., 1973.

Nash, Michael. *Conflict and Accommodation: Coal Miners, Steel Workers, and Socialism, 1890–1920*. Westport, Conn.: Greenwood Press, 1962.

Nelli, Humbert. *Italians in Chicago 1880–1930: A Study in Ethnic Mobility*. New York: Oxford University Press, 1973.

———. *Proceedings of the 9th American Italian Historical Association*, 1976.

———. AIHA proceedings 1976. *The United States and Italy: the First Two Hundred Years*.

———. *The Business of Crime*. New York: Oxford University Press, 1976.

———. *From Immigrants to Ethnics: the Italian Americans*. New York: Oxford University Press, 1983.

Nettlau, M. *Histoire de L'Anarchie*. Paris: Editions du Cercle, 1971.

New York State Assembly. *Third Report of the Factory Investigating Commission, 3 Vols*. Albany: J.B. Lupns Co., 1924.

Nicolosi, Pietro. *50 Anni di Cronaca Siciliana 1900–1950*. Palermo: S.F. Flaccovio, 1975.

Niell, Gary, and Carl Stone. *The Italian Americans*. Harrisburg, Penn.: Stackpole Books, 1976.

Nitti, Francesco. *Opere di Francesco Saverio Nitti. Scritti Sulla Qestione Meridionale, Vol. 1*. Rome: Editori Laterza, 1958.

Norwich, John J. *The Kingdom in the Sun*. New York: Harper & Row, 1970.

Occhipinti, Maria. *Una Donna di Ragusa*. Milan: Feltrinelli, 1957.

Odencrantz, L. C. *Italian Women in Industry*. New York: Russell Sage Foundation, 1919.

O'Grady, J. P., ed. *The Immigrants' Influence on Wilson's Peace Politics*. Lexington, Ky.: University of Kentucky Press: 1967.

O'Neil, William L., ed. *Insights and Parallels: Problems and Issues of American Social History*. Minneapolis, Minn.: Burgess Publishers, 1973.

O'Neil, G., and D. Lehr. *The Underboss*. New York: St. Martin's Press 1989.

Orsi, Robert A. *The Madonna of 115th Street: Faith and Community in Italian Harlem, 1880–1950*. New Haven, Conn.: Yale University Press, 1988.

Pacifici, Sergio. *A Guide to Contemporary Italian Literature.* Cleveland: World Publishing, 1962.

Palazzeschi, Aldo. *Roma.* Chicago: Henry Regnery, 1960.

Palmer, R. *The Age of Democratic Revolution.* Princeton: Princeton University Press, 1959.

Pane, Remigio U. *AIHA Proceedings: Italian Americans in the Professions.* 1979. Staten Island, N.Y.: American Italian Historical Association.

Pane e Lavoro. *The Italian American Working Class.* Proceedings of the 11th Annual Conference of the American Italian Historical Association, October 1978.

Panella, Vincent. *The Other Side: Growing up Italian in America.* Garden City, N.Y.: Doubleday, 1979.

Panetta, George. *We Ride a White Donkey.* New York: Harcourt, Brace, 1944.

Pantaleone, Michele. *The Mafia and Politics.* London: Chatto and Windus, 1966.

Pannunzio, Constantine M. *The Deportation Cases of 1919–1920.* New York: Commission on the Church and Social Service, 1921.

———. *Immigration Crossroads.* New York: Macmillan, 1927.

Paolucci, Ann. *Pirandello's Theater: The Recovery of the Modern State for Dramatic Art.* Carbondale, Ill.: South Illinois University Press, 1974.

———. *Problems in National Literary Identity and Writers as a Critic.* Bergenfield, N.J.: Griffon House, 1980.

Parenti, Michael J. *Ethnic and Political Attitudes.* New York: Arno Press, 1975.

———. *Power and the Powerless.* New York: St. Martin's Press, 1978.

Park, Robert E. *The Immigrant Press and Its Control.* Westport, Conn.: Greenwood Press, 1970.

Parmet, Robert D. *Labor and Immigration in Industrial America.* Boston: Twayne, 1981.

Parrillo, V. N. *Strangers to These Shores: Race and Ethnic Relations in the U.S.* Boston: Houghton Mifflin, 1980.

Paterno, Joe. *Football My Way.* New York: Collins Books, 1971.

Patri, Angelo. *A Schoolmaster of the Great City.* New York: Macmillan, 1923.

Pave, Remegio, ed. *Italian Americans in the Professions.* Staten Island: Italian American Historical Association, 1983.

Pellegrini, Angelo. *American Dream.* San Francisco: North Point Press, 1986.

———. *Americans by Choice.* New York: Macmillan, 1956.

———. *Immigrants Return.* New York: Macmillan, 1951.

Peragallo, Olga. *Italian American Authors and Their Contribution to American Literature.* New York: S. F. Vanni, 1949.

Perilli, Giovanni. *Colorado and the Italians in Colorado.* Denver: Smith Brooks, 1922.

Peroni, Peter A. II. *The Burg: An Italian American Community at Bay in Trenton (N.J.)* Washington, D.C.: University Press of America, 1976.

Perretta, Armando. *Take a Number.* New York: William Morrow, 1957.

Perri, Francesco. *Emigranti.* Milan: Mondadori, 1929.

Petacco, Arrigo. *L'Anarchico Che Venne Dall' America.* Verona: Mondadori, 1974.

———. *Joe Petrosino.* New York: Macmillan, 1972.

Peterson, Virgil. *The Mob.* Ottawa, Ill.: Green Hill, 1983.

Pierce, Bessie Louise. *A History of Chicago.* New York: Knopf, 1957.

Pileggi, Nicholas. *Wiseguy.* New York: Pocket Books, 1985.

Pilla, Eugenio. *Giacomo Cusmano*. Palermo: Boccone del Povero, 1978.

Pirandello, Ann Paolucci, ed. *Review of National Literatures*. New York: Griffon House Publications, 1987.

Pirenne, Jacques. *Civilisations Antiques*. Paris: Editions Albin Michel, 1951.

Pirro, Ugo. *A Thousand Betrayals*. New York: Trident Press, 1961.

Pisani, Lawrence Frank. *The Italian in America: A Social Study and History*. New York: Exposition Press, 1967.

Piston, J., and R. Woodley. *Donnie Brasco*. New York: New American Library, 1987.

Pitkin, Thomas. *Keepers of the Gate*. New York: New York University Press, 1975.

Pitre, Giuseppe. *Bibliografia Delle Tradizioni Popolari D'Italia*. New York: Burt Franklin Reprints, 1974.

———. *Sicilian Folk Medicine*. Translated by P.H. Williams. Lawrence, Kans.: Coronado Press, 1971.

———. *Usi e Costume, Credenze e Pregiudizi dei Popolo Siciliano*. 2 vols. Rome: Casa Editore del Libro Italiano, 1885.

Post, Louis F. *The Deportation Delirium of the 1920s*. Chicago: Charles H. Kerr, 1923.

Pozzetta, George, ed. *Pane e Lavoro*. New York: American Italian Historical Association, 1978.

———. *Pane e Lavoro: The Italian American Working Class*. Toronto: The Multicultural History Society of Ontario, 1980.

Preston, William Jr. *Aliens and Dissenters: Federal Suppression of Radicals, 1903–1933*. Cambridge, Mass.: Harvard University Press.

Preziosi, Giovanni. *Gl'Italiani negli Stati Uniti del Nord*. Milan: Liberia Editrice Milanese, 1909.

Procacci, Giuliano. *History of the Italian People*. New York: Pelican Books, 1973.

Quasimodo, Salvatore. *The Poet and the Politician*. Carbondale: Southern Illinois University Press, 1964.

Radin, Paul. *The Italians of San Francisco. Their Adjustment & Acculturation*. Abstract from the SERA Project Z-F2-98. July, 1935.

Raffaele, Joseph. *The Mafia Principle*. Washington, D.C.: University Press of America, 1979.

Raggucci, Antoinette Therese. *Generational Continuity and Change in Concepts of Health, Curing Practices, and Ritual Expressions of the Women of an Italian-American Enclave*. Ann Arbor, Mich.: University Microfilms, 1979.

Ramirez, Bruno. *When Workers Fight: The Politics of Industrial Relations in the Progressive Era, 1898–1916*. Westport, Conn.: Greenwood Press, 1978.

Ravera, Camilla. *Breve Storia del Movimento Femminile in Italia*. Rome: Riuniti, 1981.

Reely, Mary K. *Selected Articles on Immigration*. New York: H. W. Wilson Co., 1917.

Register of Graduates and Former Cadets of the United States Military Academy (Cullum Memorial edition–1970 [1802–1970]). West Point, N.Y.: The West Point Alumni Foundation, 1970.

Reichert, William O. *Partisans of Freedom, A Study in American Anarchism*. Bowling Green, Oh.: Bowling Green University Press, 1976.

Reid, Ed. *The Grim Reapers*. New York: Bantam, 1969.

———. *Mafia*. New York: Random House, 1952.

———. *Mickey Cohen, Mobster*. New York: Pinnacle Books, 1973.

———. *The Mistress and the Mafia*. New York: Bantam, 1972.

Reid, Ed, and Ovid DeMaris. *The Green Felt Jungle*. New York: Trident Press, 1963.

Reismann, Janos, and Carlo Levi. *Eternal Italy*. New York: Viking, 1960.

Renda, Francesco. *I Fasci Siciliani, 1892–94*. Torino: Einuadi, 1977.

———. *Il Movimento Contadino in Sicilia*. Bari: DeDonato, 1976.

———. *Risorgimento e Classi Popolari in Sicilia 1820–21*. Milan: Fetrinelli, 1968.

Renshaw, Patrick. *The Wobblies*. New York: Doubleday, 1967.

Report of the Royal Commission on Bilingualism and Biculturalism, Book IV: The Cultural Contribution of the Other Ethnic Groups. Ottawa: Queen's Printer, Oct. 23, 1969.

Rexroth, Kenneth. *An Autobiographical Novel*. Santa Barbara, Ca.: Ross-Erikson, 1978.

Reyneri, Emilio. *La Catena Migratoria*. Bologna: Il Mulino, 1979.

Reynolds, G. M. *Machine Politics in New Orleans, 1897–1926*. New York: Columbia University Press, 1936.

Ridley, Jasper. *Garibaldi*. New York: Viking, 1974.

Riesman, David. *The Lonely Crowd*. New Haven, Conn.: Yale University Press, 1932.

Riis, J. *Battle with the Slum*. New York: Scribner's, 1902.

———. *Children of the Tenements*. New York: Macmillan, 1903.

———. *How the Other Half Lives*. New York: Scribner's, 1890.

Rizzardi, Alfredo, ed. *Italy and Italians in America: Proceedings of the Seventh National Convention of the Associazione Italiana di Studi Nord-Americani held at the University of Catania*. Padova, Italy: Piovan Editore Abano Terme, 1985.

Roberts, Peter. *The New Immigration: A Study of the Industrial and Social Life of Southeastern Europeans in America*. New York: Arno Press, 1970.

Roediger, Dave, and Franklin Rosemont, eds. *Haymarket Scrapbook*. Chicago: Charles H. Kerr, 1986.

Rogers, D. T. *Work Ethic: 1850–1920*. Chicago: University of Chicago Press, 1978.

Rolland, Romaine. *Empodocle D'Agrigente*. Paris: Sablier, 1931.

Rolle, Andrew. *The American Italians: Their History and Culture*. Belmont, Ca.: Wadsworth Publishing, 1972.

———. *The Immigrant Upraised*. Norman: University of Oklahoma Press, 1960.

———. *The Italian Americans—Troubled Roots*. New York: The Free Press, 1980.

Rosado, Anna. *Serrati Nell' Emigrazione 1899–1911*. Rome: Riuniti, 1972.

Rose, A. L. *Storyville New Orleans*. University of Alabama Press, 1974.

Rose, Peter L. *Mainstream & Margins*. New Brunswick, N.J.: Transaction Books, 1983.

Roselli, Bruno. *Vigo: A Forgotten Builder of the American Republic*. Boston: Stratford, 1933.

Rosoli, Gianfausto. *Un Secolo di Emigrazione Italiana*. Rome: Centro Studi Emigrazione, 1978.

Rosselli, John. *Lord William Bentinck and the British Occupation of Sicily 1811–1814*. London: Cambridge University Press, 1956.

Rossi, Adolfo. *An Italian in America*. Milan: Casa Editrice La Cisaplina, 1899.

Rovere, Richard. *Howe and Hummel*. New York: Farrar & Strauss, 1947.

Rubenstein, Annette T. *Vito Marcantonio—Debates, Speeches, Writings 1935–1950*. Clifton, N.J.: Augustus Kelley, 1973.

Russell, Francis. *Sacco & Vanzetti.* New York: Harper & Row, 1986.

———. *Tragedy in Dedham.* New York: McGraw-Hill, 1962.

Sabetti, Filippo. *Political Authority in a Sicilian Village.* New Brunswick, N.J.: Rutgers University Press, 1984.

Saladino, Salvatore. *Italy from Unification to 1919.* New York: Thomas Crowell, 1970.

Salerno, Ralph. *The Crime Confederation.* New York: Doubleday, 1969.

Salomone, A. William. *Italy from the Risorgimento to Fascism.* Garden City, N.Y.: Doubleday, 1970.

———. *Italy in the Giolittian Era: Italian Democracy in the Making.* Philadelphia: University of Pennsylvania Press, 1945.

Salomone, M. S. *Customs and Habits of Sicilian Peasants.* East Brunswick, N.J.: Fairleigh Dickinson University Press, 1981.

Salvatore, Nick. *Eugene J. Debs, Citizen & Socialist.* Urbana: University of Illinois Press, 1982.

Salvemini, Gaetano. *Italian Fascist Activities in the United States.* New York: Center for Migration Studies, 1977.

———. *Mazzini.* Stanford, Ca.: Stanford University Press, 1957.

———. *Under the Ax of Fascism.* New York: Howard Fertig, 1969.

Sanders, J. W. *The Education of an Urban Minority: Catholics in Chicago 1833–1965.* New York: Oxford University Press, 1977.

Sandler, G. *The Neighborhood. The Story of Baltimore's Little Italy.* Baltimore: Bodine and Associates, 1974.

Sartorio, Enrico. *Social and Religious Life of Italian Americans.* Clifton, N.J.: Kelly, 1918, 1974.

Satriani, R. L, ed. *Credenze Populari Calabresi.* Napoli: Fratelli de Simone, 1951.

Saveth, E. N. *American Historians and European Immigrants, 1875–1925.* New York: Columbia University Press, 1948.

Scammacca, Nat. *Bye Bye America: Memories of a Sicilian American.* Trapani: Editrice Antigruppo Siciliano and Cross Cultural Communications, 1986.

———. *Siklano L'Americano.* Trapani: Cross Cultural Communications, 1989.

Scarne, John. *The Mafia Conspiracy.* North Bergen, N.J.: Scarne Enterprises, 1976.

Scarpaci, Jean. *Italian Immigration in Louisiana's Sugar Parishes, 1880–1910.* New York: Arno Press, 1980.

Scarpaci, V. *A Portrait of the Italians in America.* New York: Scribner's, 1982.

Scaturo, Ignazio. *Storia di Sicilia.* 4 vols. Rome: Raggio, 1950.

Schachter, Gustav. *The Italian South: Economic Development in Mediterranean Europe.* New York: Random House, 1965.

Schaffer, Alan. *Vito Marcantonio, Radical in Congress.* Syracuse: Syracuse University Press, 1966.

Scherini, Rose Doris. *The Italian American Community of San Francisco: A Descriptive Study.* Berkeley, Ca.: University of California Press, 1976.

Schiavo, G. E. *Italian-American History: The Italian Contribution to the Catholic Church in America.* New York: Arno Press, 1975.

———. *Italians in Chicago.* New York: Arno Press, 1975.

———. *The Truth About the Mafia and Organized Crime in America.* New York, 1962.

Schiro, George. *Americans by Choice: History of Italians in Utica.* New York: Arno Press, 1975.

Schoener, Allen. *The Italian Americans*. New York: Macmillan, 1987.

Schulman, Irving. *Valentino*. New York: Trident Press, 1967.

Sciacca, Tony. *Luciano*. New York: Pinnacle, 1975.

Scichilone, G. *Documenti Sulle Condizioni della Sicilia*. Rome: Edizioni Dell' Ateneo, 1952.

Scotellaro, Rocco. *Contadini del Sud*. Bari: Laterza, 1955.

Seller, Maxine. *Ethnic Theater in the U.S.* Westport, Conn.: Greenwood Press, 1971.

———. ed. *Immigrant Women*. Philadelphia: Temple University Press, 1981.

Sennett, Richard. *The Hidden Injuries of Class*. New York: Vintage Books, 1973.

Servadio, Gaia. *Angelo La Barbera: The Profile of a Mafia Boss*. New York: Stein & Day, 1975.

———. *Mafioso*. Briarcliff Manor, N.Y.: Stein & Day, 1976.

Seton-Watson, Christopher. *Italy from Liberalism to Fascism*. London: Methuen, 1967.

Sforza, Carlo. *Italy and Italians*. New York: Dutton, 1948.

Shaw, Arnold. *Sinatra*. New York: Holt, Rinehart, 1969.

Silberman, Charles. *Criminal Violence, Criminal Justice*. New York: Random House, 1978.

Silone, Ignazio. *The School for Dictators*. Translated by William Weaver. New York: Atheneum, 1963.

———. *Silone in The God that Failed*. New York: Bantam Books, 1952.

Silverman, S. "Agricultural Organization . . . Amoral Familism Reconsidered." *American Anthropologist* 70 (Feb. 1970), pp. 1–20.

Sladen, Douglas. *In Sicily*. 2 vols. London: Sands & Co., 1901.

Slotkin, R. *Regeneration Through Violence*. Middletown, Conn.: Wesleyan University Press, 1973.

Smith, Dennis Mack. *Garibaldi: A Great Life in Brief*. New York: Knopf, 1956.

———. *A History of Sicily*. 2 vols. London: Chatto & Windus, 1968.

———. *Italy, a Modern History*. Ann Arbor: University of Michigan Press, 1959.

Smith, Dwight. *The Mafia Mystique*. New York: Basic Books, 1975.

Smith, William C. *Americans in the Making: The Natural History of the Assimilation of Immigrants*. New York: Appleton Century, 1939.

Sollors, Werner. *Beyond Ethnicity: Consent and Dissent in American Culture*. New York: Oxford University Press, 1986.

Sondern, F. Jr. *Brotherhood of Evil: The Mafia*. New York: Farrar, Straus & Cudahy, 1959.

Sori, E. *L'Emmigrazion Italiana Dall' Unita alla Seconda Guerra Mondiale*. Mulino: Societa editrice Il 1975.

Sorrentino, Anthony. *Organizing Against Crime*. New York: Human Sciences Publications, 1977.

Sowell, T. *Ethnic America: A History*. New York: Basic Books, 1981.

———. *Markets and Minorities*. New York: Basic Books, 1981.

Spada, A. V. *The Italians in Canada*. Montreal: Italo-Canadian Ethnic and Historical Research Center, 1969.

Spengler, Paul A. *Yankee, Swedish and Italian Acculturation and Economic Mobility in Jamestown, New York*. New York: Arno Press, 1980.

Speranza, Gino. *Race or Nation: A Conflict of Divided Loyalties*. Indianapolis: Bobbs Merrill, 1923.

———. *Speranza Papers*. New York Public Library.

Spinazzola, Vittorio. *Cinema e Pubblico: Lo Spettacolo Filmico in Italia 1945–1965*. Milan: Bompiani, 1974.

Spradley, James, and David McCurdy. *Conformity and Conflict*. Boston: Little Brown, 1971.

Steffens, Lincoln. *The Autobiography of Lincoln Steffens*. New York: Harcourt, Brace, 1931.

———. *The Shame of the Cities*. New York: McClure, Phillips & Co., 1904.

Stein, L., ed. *Out of the Sweatshop—The Struggle for Industrial Democracy*. New York: Quadrangle, 1962.

———. *The Triangle Fire*. Philadelphia: Lippincott, 1961.

Stein, Maurice, Arthur Vidich, and David Manning White. *Identity and Anxiety*. Glencoe, Ill.: The Free Press of Glencoe, 1960.

Stienberg, S. *The Ethnic Myth: Race, Ethnicity and Class in America*. New York: Atheneum, 1981.

Stiener, E. A. *From Alien to Citizen*. New York: Fleming Revell, 1914.

———. *On the Trail of the Immigrant*. New York: Fleming Revell, 1906.

Stella, Antonio. *Some Aspects of Italian Immigration to the United States (The Italian American Experience)*. New York: Arno Press, 1975.

Stolarik, Mark, and Murray Friedman, eds. *Making It in America: The Role of Ethnicity in Business Enterprise, Education and Work Choices*. Lewisburg, Penn.: Bucknell University Press, 1986.

———. *The Other Ports of Entry to the U.S.* Philadelphia: Balch Institute Press, 1988.

Stolberg, B. *Tailor's Progress*. New York: Doubleday, Doran, 1938.

Suggs, George G., Jr. *Colorado's War on Militant Unionism*. Detroit: Wayne State University Press, 1972.

Swain, Joseph. *The Ancient World*. 2 vols. New York: Harper & Brothers, 1950.

Sweet, May M. *The Italian Immigrant in His Reading*. Chicago: American Library Association, 1925.

Talese, Gay. *Honor Thy Father*. New York: Nelson, Foster & Scott, 1971.

———. *Unto The Sons*. New York: Knopf, 1992.

Tamburri, Giordano, and L. Gardaphe, eds. *From the Margin: Writings in Italian Americana*. West Lafayette, Ind.: Purdue University Press, 1991.

Tarizzo, D. *L'Anarchia*. Milan: Mondadori, 1976.

Taylor, Philip. *The Distant Magnet*. New York: Harper & Row, 1971.

Tentler, Leslie W. *Wage-Earning Women, 1900–1930*. New York: Oxford University Press, 1979.

Teresa, Vincent. *My Life in the Mafia*. Garden City, N.Y.: Doubleday, 1973.

Thayer, W. R. *The Life and Times of Cavour*. 2 vols. Boston: Houghton Mifflin Co., 1911.

Thomas, W. I. *Old World Traits Transplanted in Americanization Studies*. Reprint. Montclair, N.J.: Patterson Smith, 1971.

Thompson, Bryan. *Cultural Ties as Determinants of Immigrant Settlement in Worcester, Mass. 1875–1922*. New York: Arno Press, 1980.

Thompson, Frank. *Schooling of the Immigrant*. New York: Harper, 1920.

Thompson, W. I. *At the Edge of History*. Harper Colophon Books, 1972.

Tommasi, Lydio. *Italian Americans; A New Perspective in Italian Immigration and Ethnicity*. Staten Island, N.Y. Center for Migration Studies, 1985.

Thrasher, Frederic M. *The Gang: A Study of 1,313 Gangs in Chicago*. Chicago: University of Chicago Press, 1927.

Toffler, Alvin. *Future Shock.* New York: Bantam Books, 1971.

Tomasi, S. M. *Perspectives in Italian Immigration & Ethnicity.* New York: Center for Migration Studies, 1977.

———. *Images: A Pictorial History of Italian Americans.* New York: Center for Migration Studies, 1981.

———. *The Italian in America.* New York: Center for Migration Studies, 1972.

———. *Piety and Power.* New York: Center for Migration Studies, 1975.

Tomasi, S. M., ed. *The Religious Experience of Italian Americans.* American Italian Historical Association proceedings, November 1973.

Tomasi, S. M., and M. H. Engel. *The Italian Experience in the United States.* Staten Island, N.Y.: Center for Migration Studies, 1970.

Tosches, Nick. *Power on Earth.* New York: Arbor House, 1986.

Trease, Geoffrey. *The Italian Story.* New York: Vanguard Press, 1963.

Trevelyan, George. *Garibaldi and the Thousand (May 1860).* New York: Longmans, Green and Co., 1948.

———. *Garibaldi and the Making of Italy, June–November 1860.* New York: Thomas Nelson and Sons Ltd., 1920.

Trevelyan, Raleigh. *Princes Under the Volcano.* New York: William Morrow, 1973.

Tricarico, Donald. *The Italians of Greenwich Village.* New York: Center for Immigration Studies, 1984.

Tripp, Edward. *The Meridian Handbook of Classical Mythology.* New York: Meridian, 1970.

Trolander, J.A. *Settlement Houses and the Great Depression.* Detroit: Wayne State University Press, 1975.

Troppea, J., and L. Miller. eds. *Support and Struggle: Italians and Italian Americans in a Comparative Perspective.* New York: AIHA, 1986.

Trout, Charles. *Boston, the Great Depression and the New Deal.* New York: Oxford University Press, 1977.

Tugwell, Rexford G. *The Art of Politics as Practiced By: F.D.R., Luis Munoz Martin and Fiorello La Guardia.* Garden City, N.Y.: Doubleday, 1958.

Tyler, Gus, ed., *Organized Crime in America.* Ann Arbor: University of Michigan Press, 1962.

Ucello, Antonio. *Carcere e Mafia Nei Canti Popolari Siciliani.* Bari, Italy: DeDonato, 1974.

Unrau, Harlan. *Statue of Liberty National Monument. Vol. I, II, III.* Washington, D.C.: U.S. Government Printing Office, 1984.

U.S. Senate. *Reports of the Immigration Commission,* 1911.

U.S. Dept. of State. *Papers Relating to the Foreign Relations of the U.S.* Washington, D.C.: U.S. Government Printing Office, 1895–1913.

———. *Reports of Diplomatic and Consular Officers Concerning Emigration from Europe,* 1889.

Vailland, Roger. *The Law.* New York: Knopf, 1958.

Valletta, Clement I. *A Study of Americanization in Carneta. Italian American Identity Through Three Generations.* New York: Arno Press, 1975.

Vann'anto. *Indovinelli Popolari Siciliani.* Caltanissetta: Edizioni Salvatore Sciascia, 1954.

Varbero, Richard A. *Urbanization and Acculturation: South Philadelphia's Italians.* Philadelphia: Temple University Press, 1975.

————. *Chicago's Italians Prior to World War I: A Study of Their Social and Economic Adjustment*. Madison: University or Wisconsin, 1972.

————. *E Tel Gli Italiani Negli Stati Uniti*. Florence: Instituto di Studi Americani Universita degli Studi di Firenzi, 1969.

Vecoli, Rudolph J., ed. *Italian American Radicalism. Old World Origins and New World Developments*. American Italian Historical Association proceedings, June 1972.

————. *The People of New Jersey*. Princeton, N.J.: D. Van Nostrand, 1965.

————, ed. *Italian Immigrants in Rural and Small Town America*. New York: American Italian Historical Association, 1987.

Velikonja, J. *Italians in the U.S.* Carbondale, Ill.: University of Southern Illinois Press, 1963.

Ventresca, Francesco. *Personal Reminiscences*. Chicago: Empire-Stone Press, 1951.

Vergara, Joe. *Love and Pasta: The Story of an Italian Immigrant and the American Family He Raised*. New York: Harper & Row, 1968.

Veronesi, Gene P. *Italian Americans and Their Communities of Cleveland*. Cleveland: Cleveland State University Press, 1978.

Villari, Luigi. *Italian Life in Town and Country*. New York: Putnam, 1902.

————. *Gli Stati Uniti d'America e L'Emigrazione Italiana (The Italian American Experience)*. New York: Arno Press, 1975.

Villari, Rosario. *Il Sud Nella Storia D'Italia*. Bari: Laterza, 1961.

Villano, Anthony. *Brick Agent*. New York: Quadrangle, 1977.

Visconti, Luchino. *La Terra Trema Senso*. New York: Orion Press, 1970.

Vittorini, Domenico. *Drama of Luigi Pirandello*. New York: Dover, 1957.

Vizzini, Sal. *Vizzini*. New York: Arbor House, 1972.

Voigt, David Quentin. *American Baseball. Vol. I. From Gentlemen's Sport to the Commissioner System*. Norman, Ok.: University of Oklahoma Press, 1966.

Voigt, David Quentin. *American Baseball. Vol. II. From the Commissioner to the Continental Expansion*. Norman, Ok.: University of Oklahoma Press, 1970.

Voigt, David Quentin. *American Baseball. Vol. III. From Postwar Expansion to the Electronic Age*. University Park, Penn.: Pennsylvania State University Press, 1983.

Wald, Lillian. *The House on Henry Street*. New York: Henry Holt, 1915.

Walsh, George. *Public Enemies*. New York: W.W. Norton & Co., 1980.

Washington, Booker T. *The Man Farthest Down: A Record of Observation and Study in Europe*. New York: Doubleday, Page and Co., 1915.

Ward, David. *Cities and Immigrants*. New York: Oxford University Press, 1971.

Ware, Caroline F. *Greenwich Village, 1920–1930*. New York: Octogan Books, 1977.

Weisz, H. R. *Irish-American and Italian-American Educational Views and Activities, 1870–1900: A Comparison*. New York: Arno Press, 1976.

Weis, Bernard J., ed. *American Education and the European Immigrant, 1840–1940*. Urbana: University of Illinois Press, 1982.

Weyl, Walter. "Italy's Exhausting Emigration." *Review of Reviews*, February 9, 1909, 2–7.

Wheeler, Thomas, ed. *The Immigrant Experience*. New York: The Dial Press, 1971.

Whyte, William Foote. *Street Corner Society*. Chicago: University of Chicago Press, 1943.

Willet, Mabel Hurd. *The Employment of Women in the Clothing Industry*. New York: AMS Press, 1968.

Wilson, E. *Sinatra*. New York: Macmillan, 1976.

Wilson, S. P. *Chicago and Its Cesspools of Infamy*. Chicago: N.P., 1910.

Wittke, Carl. *We Who Built America: The Saga of the Immigrant*. New York: Prentice-Hall, 1939.

Wolfe, G., and J. Dimona. *Frank Costello*. New York: William Morrow, 1974.

Woods, Robert, ed. *Americans in Process*. Boston: Houghton Mifflin Co., 1902.

WPA Federal Writers Project. *California*. New York: Hastings House, 1939.

———. *Connecticut: A Guide to Its Lore and People*. Boston: Houghton Mifflin, 1938.

———. *Copper Camp Stories of the World's Greatest Mining Town, Butte, Montana*. New York: Hastings House, 1943.

———. *Delaware: A Guide to the First State*. New York: Viking Press, 1938.

———. *Illinois*. Chicago: McClurg, 1939.

———. *The Italian Theater in San Francisco*. San Francisco: 1939.

———. *The Italians of New York*. New York: Random House, 1939.

———. *The Italians of Omaha*. New York: Arno Press, 1975.

———. *Louisiana*. New York: Hastings House, 1941.

———. *Maryland*. New York: Oxford University Press, 1940.

———. *Massachusetts*. Boston: Houghton Mifflin, 1937.

———. *Michigan*. New York: Oxford University Press, 1941.

———. *New Jersey*. Viking Press, 1939.

———. *New Orleans City Guide*. Boston: Houghton Mifflin, 1938.

———. *New York*. Oxford University Press, 1940.

———. *New York City*. Random House, 1939.

———. *New York Panorama*. New York: Random House, 1939.

———. *Pennsylvania*. New York: Oxford University Press, 1940.

———. *Philadelphia*. Philadelphia: William Penn Association, 1937.

———. *Rhode Island*. Boston: Houghton Mifflin, 1937.

———. *San Francisco: The Bay and Its Cities*. New York: Hastings House, 1940.

———. *Washington*. Portland, Oreg.: Binford and Mort, 1941.

Yans-McLaughlin, Virginia. *Family and Community—Italian Immigrants in Buffalo, 1880–1930*. Ithaca, N.Y.: Cornell University Press, 1971.

Yellen, S. *American Labor Struggles 1877–1934*. New York: Arno Press, 1969.

Yellowitz, Irwin. *The Position of the Worker in American Society, 1865–1896*. Englewood Cliffs, N.J.: Prentice-Hall, 1969.

Zeiger, Henry. *The Jersey Mob*. New York: Signet, 1975.

———. *Sam the Plumber*. New York: Signet, 1970.

Ziegler, Benjamin Nunn. *Immigration: An American Dilemma*. Boston: D. C. Heath, 1953.

Zorbaugh, Harvey Warren. *The Gold Coast and the Slum: A Sociological Study of Chicago's Near North Side*. Chicago: University of Chicago Press, 1929.

NOVELS, SHORT STORIES, PLAYS, AND POETRY

Alexander, Alfred, ed. *Stories of Sicily*. New York: Schocken Books, 1975.

Ardizzone, Tony. *The Evening News*. Athens, Ga: University of Georgia Press, 1986.

———. *Heart of the Order*. New York: Henry Holt, 1987.

———. *In the Name of the Father*. Garden City, N.Y.: Doubleday, 1978.

Barolini, Helen. *Umbertina*. New York: Seaview, 1979.

Bonaviri, Giuseppe. *Il Fume di Pietra*. Torino: Einaudi, 1964.

———. *Il Sarto Della Stradalunga*. Torino: Einaudi, 1954.

Calitri, Charles. *Rickey*. New York: Charles Scribner's Sons, 1952.

———. *Strike Heaven in the Face*. New York: Crown, 1958.

———. *Father*. New York: Crown, 1962.

Canzoneri, Robert. *Barbed Wire and Other Stories*. New York: Dial, 1970.

———. *A Highly Ramified Tree*. New York: Viking Press, 1971.

———. *I Do So Politely*. Boston: Houghton Mifflin, 1965.

———. *Men With Little Hammers*. New York: Dial Press, 1969.

Caruso, Joseph. *The Priest*. New York: Macmillan, 1965.

Ciambelli, Bernardino. *I Misteri di Mulberry*. New York: Frugone & Ballietto, 1893.

Ciardi, J. *Selected Poems*. Fayetteville, Ark.: University of Arkansas Press, 1984.

Cuomo, George. *Family Honor*. Garden City: Doubleday, 1983.

D'Agostino, Guido. *Olives on the Apple Tree*. New York: Doubleday, Doran & Company, 1940.

D'Ambrosio, Richard. *No Language But a Cry*. New York: Doubleday, 1970.

D'Angelo, Lou. *What the Ancients Said*. New York: Doubleday, 1970.

D'Annunzio, Gabriele. *The Dead City*. Rendered into English by Prof. G. Mantellini. Chicago: Laird & Lee, 1902.

———. *Terra Vergine*. Milan: Souzogno, 1904.

De Capite, Michael. *Maria*. New York: John Day, 1943.

———. *No Bright Banner*. New York: John Day, 1944.

DeRosa, Tina. *Paper Fish*. Chicago: The Wine Press, 1980.

Di Donato, Pietro. *Christ in Concrete*. Indianapolis: Bobbs-Merrill, 1934.

———. *This Woman*. New York: Ballantine Books, 1959.

———. *Three Circles of Light*. New York: Ballantine, 1960.

Fante, John. *Ask the Dust*. Santa Barbara: Black Sparrow Press, 1980.

———. *Dago Red*. New York: Viking, 1940.

———. *Full of Life*. Boston: Little Brown, 1952.

———. *Wait Until Spring Bandini*. New York: Stockpole Sons, 1938.

Ferlinghetti, Lawrence. *A Coney Island of the Mind*. New York: New Directions, 1958.

———. *Landscapes of Living and Dying*. New York: New Directions. 1979.

Fratti, Mario. *Our Family, Toys (Two One-act Plays)*. Whitestone, N.Y.: Griffon House Publications, 1986.

Fumento, Rocco. *Devil by the Tail*. New York: Knopf, 1954.

———. *Tree of Dark Reflection*. New York: Knopf, 1962.

Gambino, R. *Bread and Roses*. New York: Avon Books, 1982.

———. *Vendetta*. New York: Doubleday, 1977.

Gioseffi, Daniela. *Eggs in the Lake*. New York: Boa Editions, 1979.

———. *The Great American Belly*. New York: Doubleday, 1993.

Giovannitti, Arturo. *Collected Poems of Arturo Giovannitti*. Salem, N.H.: Ayer Company Publishers, 1975.

Iannuzi, John. *Sicilian Defense*. New York: Signet, 1973.

Innaurato, A. *Bizarre Behavior*. New York: Avon Books, 1980.

Lampedusa, Giuseppe. *The Leopard*. New York: Pantheon, 1960.

———. *Two Stories and a Memory*. New York: Pantheon, 1962.

Lapolla, Garibaldi. *The Fire in the Flesh*. New York: Vanguard Press, 1931.

———. *The Grand Gennaro*. New York: Vanguard Press, 1932.

———. *Miss Rolins in Love*. New York: Vanguard Press, 1932.

Malaparte, Curzio. *The Skin*. New York: Avon, 1952.

Mangione, Jerre. *Night Search*. New York: Crown, 1965.

———. *Ricerce nella notte*. Palermo: Sellerio, 1987.

———. *The Ship and the Flame*. New York: A. A. Wayne, 1948.

Mays, Lucinda. *The Other Shore*. New York: Atheneum, 1979.

Meltzer, Milton. *Bread and Roses: The Struggle in American Labor, 1865–1915*. New York: Knopf, 1965.

Mirabelli, Eugene. *The Burning Air*. Boston: Houghton Mifflin, 1959.

———. *No Resting Place*. New York: Viking Press, 1972.

———. *The Way in*. New York: Viking Press, 1968.

Monroe, Harriet, and Corbino Henderson, eds. *The New Poetry: An Anthology of 20th Century Verse in English*. New York: Macmillan, 1937.

Morreale, Ben. *A Few Virtuous Men*. Montreal: Tundra, 1973.

———. *Monday, Tuesday, Never Come Sunday*. Montreal: Tundra, 1977.

———. *The Seventh Saracen*. New York: Coward McCann, 1958.

Napoli, Joseph. *A Dying Cadence: Memories of a Sicilian Childhood*. West Bethesda, Md.: Marna Press, 1986.

Pagano, Joe. *The Condemned*. New York: Prentice-Hall, 1947.

———. *The Golden Wedding*. New York: Random House, 1943.

———. *The Paesanos*. Boston: Little Brown, 1940.

Panetta, George. *The Sea Beach Express*. New York: Harper & Row, 1966.

Panunzio, Constantine. *The Soul of an Immigrant*. New York: Macmillan, 1921.

Paolucci, Ann. *Cipango! A One-Act Play in Three Scenes about Columbus*. Whitestone, N.Y.: Griffon House, 1985.

———. *Eight Short Stories*. Whitestone, N.Y.: Griffon House, 1977.

———. *Riding the Mast Where It Swings*. Bergenfield, N.J.: Griffon House, 1980.

———. *Sepia Tones*. Whitestone, N.Y.: Griffon House, 1985.

Papaleo, Joseph. *All the Comforts*. Boston: Little Brown, 1967.

———. *Out of Place*. Boston: Little Brown, 1970.

———. *Picasso at 91 Poems*. Harriman, N.Y.: Seaport Press, 1987.

Parini, Jay. *The Patch Boys*. New York: Henry Holt, 1986.

Pei, Mario. *The Sparrows of Paris*. New York: Philosophical Library, 1958.

———. *Swords of Anjou*. New York: John Day, 1953.

Pellegrini, Angelo. *Atti Unici; La Giara; L'Imbecile; Lumie di Sicilia*. Milan: Mondadori Editorie, 1942.

———. *L'Aube Nait de la Nuit* (traduit de l'Italien par Jacquelin Herselin). Paris: Editions de la Paix, 1949.

Pirandello, Luigi. *Feu Mathias Pascal*. Paris: Rombaldi, 1969.

———. *I Vecchi e I Giovani*. Milan: Mondadore, 1975.

———. *Les Trois pensées de la petite bossue* (traduit de l'Italien par Jacquelin Herselin). Paris: Editions du Pré-aux-Clercs, 1947.

———. *Liola: Cosi e (Se Vi Pare)*. Milan: Arnoldo Mandadori, 1957.

———. *Naked Masks: Five Plays*. Edited by Eric Bentley. New York: E. P. Dutton & Co., 1958.

———. *Quand j'etais fou. . . .* , Vol. 2 (Traduit de l'Italien par Jacquelin Herselin). Paris: Les Editions Mondiales, 1950.

———. *Saggi a cura di Manlio LoVecchio Musti*. Milan: Arnaldo Mondadori Editore, 1939.

Puzo, Mario. *The Dark Arena*. New York: Fawcett, 1955.

————. *Fools Die.* New York: New American Library, 1978.

————. *The Fortunate Pilgrim.* New York: Lancer Books, 1964.

————. *The Godfather.* New York: G.P. Putnam's Sons, 1969.

————. *The Godfather Papers and Other Confessions.* Greenwich, Conn.: Fawcett, 1973.

————. *Inside Las Vegas.* New York: Charter Books, 1976.

————. *The Sicilian.* New York: Linden Press, 1984.

Scammacca, Nat. *Schammachanat.* Trapani, Italy: Coop. Anti-Gruppo, 1985.

Sciascia, Leonardo. *La Corda Pazza.* Torino: Einaudi, 1970.

————. *The Day of the Owl.* Boston: David Godine, 1964.

————. *Gli zii di Sicilia.* Torino: Einaudi, 1958.

————. *Il Mare Colore del Vino.* Torino: Coralli, 1973.

————. *Il Teatro della Memoria.* Torino: Einaudi, 1981.

————. *Mafia Vendetta.* Translated from the Italian by A. Colquhoun and A. Oliver. New York: Knopf, 1964.

————. *A Man's Blessing.* New York: Harper & Row, 1968.

————. *La Parrocchie di Regalpetra.* Bari: Laterza, 1956.

————. *Pirandello e la Sicilia.* Rome: Scascia, 1961.

————. *Salt in the Wound. Followed by The Death of the Inquisitor.* Translated by Judith Green. New York: The Orion Press, 1969.

————. *La Sicile Comme Metaphore.* Paris: Stock, 1979.

Stiener, Edward. *From Alien to Citizen.* London: Flemming Revell and Co., 1916.

Tomasi, Mari. *Deep Grow the Roots.* Philadelphia: Lippincott, 1940.

————. *Like Lesser Gods.* Milwaukee: Bruce, 1949.

Tusiani, Joseph. *Gente Mia and Other Poems.* Stone Park, Ill.: Italian Cultural Center, 1978.

————. *The House by the Medlar Tree.* New York: Signet, 1964.

Verga, Giovanni. *I Malvanoglia.* Verona: Mondadori, 1952.

————. *Maestro Don Gesualdo.* Verona: Mondadori, 1952.

————. *Maestro Don Gesualdo.* Translated by D. H. Lawrence. New York: Grove Press, 1955.

————. *Little Novels of Sicily.* Translated by D. H. Lawrence. New York: Grove Press, 1953.

————. *The She Wolf.* Berkeley: University of California Press, 1958.

————. *Tutte Le Novelle.* Milan: Mondadori, 1940.

Vittorini, Elio. *Conversazione in Sicilia.* Milan: Bompiani, 1962.

————. *Diario in Pubblico.* Torino: Bompiani, 1976.

————. *Erica e i Suoi Fratelli.* Milan: Bompiano, 1956.

————. *In Sicily.* New York: New Directions, 1949.

————. *Le Donne di Messina.* Milan: Bompiani, 1949.

————. *Uomini e no.* Milan: Bompiani, 1945.

————. *A Vittorini Omnibus.* New York: New Directions, 1960.

————. *Women of Messina.* New York: New Directions, 1973.

Vivante, Arturo. *A Goodly Babe.* Boston: Little Brown, 1959.

————. *Doctor Giovanni.* Boston: Little Brown, 1959.

————. *Run to the Waterfall.* New York: Scribners, 1965.

PROCEEDINGS OF THE AMERICAN ITALIAN HISTORICAL ASSOCIATION

The Family and Community Life of Italian Americans. Edited by Richard N. Juliani. 1983.

The Interaction of Italians and Irish in the United States. Edited by Francis X. Femminella. 1985.

The Interaction of Italians and Jews in America. Edited by Jean A. Scarpaci. 1976.

The Italian American Novel. Edited by John M. Cammett. 1969.

Italian Americans in the Professions. Edited by Remigio U. Pane. 1983.

Italian American Radicalism: Old World Origins and New World Developments. Edited by Rudolph Vecoli. 1973.

Italian Americans: The Search for Usable Past. Edited by Richard N. Juliani and Philip V. Cannistraro. 1989.

The Italian Americans Through the Generations. The First One Hundred Years. Edited by Rocco Caporale. 1986.

Italian American Women in North America. Edited by Betty Boyd Caroli, Robert Harney, and Lydio Tomasi. 1977.

Italian Immigrants in Rural and Small Town America. Edited by Rudolph J. Vecoli. 1972.

The Melting Pot and Beyond: Italian Americans in the Year 2000. Edited by Jerome Krase and William Egleman. 1987

Pane e Lavoro: The Italian American Working Class. Edited by George E. Possetta. 1980.

Power and Class: Italian American Experience Today. Edited by Frank Femminella. 1971.

The Religious Experience of Italian Americans. Edited by Silvano M. Tomasi. 1974.

The Urban Experience of Italian Americans. Edited by Pat Gallo. 1975.

CONGRESSIONAL DOCUMENTS

Senate Documents, 61st Congress, 2nd Session, Vol. 76.

NEWSPAPERS

The Daily Picayune, New Orleans, Louisiana.
Fra Noi, Chicago.
Giornale di Sicilia.
Italian-American Digest, New Orleans, Louisiana.
The Mascot. New Orleans, Louisiana.
The New York Times, June 18, 1892.
Notizie Dall'Italia, Fondazione Giovanni Agnelli.
OSIA News, Worcester, Massachusetts.
Il Progresso, New York.
La Repubblica, Rome, Italy.
La Tribuna del Popolo, Detroit, Michigan.

JOURNALS

Arba Sicula, Brooklyn, New York.
Ambassador, National Italian American Foundation.
Attenzione, New York.
Il Caffè, International Journal of the Italian American Experience, San Francisco.
Columbus: Countdown 1992.
Italian Americana, SUNY Buffalo, New York.
Malgrado Tutto, Periodico Cittadino Di Commento e Cultura, Racalmuto, Sicilia.
Nuovi Quaderni del Meridone.
I Siciliani, Giuseppe Fava, ed., Palermo, 1984.
Via (Voices in Italian Americana). Purdue University.

Index